Constitutional Change in the United Kingdom

The years since New Labour came to power in 1997 have seen changes on an unprecedented scale in Britain's constitutional arrangements. The reforms have been widespread and far-reaching in their implications: devolution to Scotland, Wales and Northern Ireland; reform of the House of Lords; the Human Rights Act 1998; and significant changes in the rules of the political game.

This book is one of the first to examine all the changes collectively and in detail, to place each in its historical context, and to analyse both the problems and the solutions, with pointers to further reform in future. It is comprehensive in its coverage, and clearly written. It should be an ideal resource for undergraduate students of British politics and constitutional law who seek to make sense of this dynamic and complex subject.

Nigel Forman was the Member of Parliament for Carshalton and Wallington between 1976 and 1997. During that time he was also a Parliamentary Private Secretary at the Foreign and Commonwealth Office and the Treasury, as well as a Minister at the Department for Education. He has taught at several universities and is a visiting lecturer at the Civil Service College. His other publications include *Mastering British Politics* with N.D.J. Baldwin (Macmillan, 1985; fourth edition 1999).

Constitutional Change in the United Kingdom

F.N. Forman

The Constitution Unit

London and New York

First published 2002
by Routledge
11 New Fetter Lane, London EC4P 4EE

Simultaneously published in the USA and Canada
by Routledge
29 West 35th Street, New York, NY 10001

Routledge is an imprint of the Taylor & Francis Group

© 2002 F.N. Forman

Typeset in Century Old Style by Keystroke,
Jacaranda Lodge, Wolverhampton
Printed and bound in Great Britain by St Edmundsbury
Press, Bury St Edmunds, Suffolk

British Library Cataloguing in Publication Data
A catalogue record for this book is available from the
British Library

Library of Congress Cataloguing in Publication Data
A catalog record for this book has been requested

ISBN 0–415–23035–7 (hbk)
ISBN 0–415–23036–5 (pbk)

To the memory of my mother

Contents

Illustrations

Figures

Boxes

Preface

This is a comprehensive account of constitutional change in the United Kingdom. Because such change has often taken place over a very long period of time, the book does not focus exclusively on what has happened since Labour came to power in May 1997, but reaches back, where appropriate, to explain the historical background to the significant reforms pursued by successive Blair Administrations. It also uses a broad definition of what is involved in constitutional change for the very good reason that in the United Kingdom, to a greater extent than elsewhere, almost all significant political reforms can have constitutional consequences.

New Labour came to power in May 1997 on the basis of a Manifesto in which it declared:

> our system of government is centralised, inefficient and bureaucratic. Our citizens cannot assert their basic rights in our own courts. ... There is unquestionably a national crisis of confidence in our political system to which Labour will respond in a measured and sensible way.

Four or five years later we are in a better position to judge the significance of these words and the extent to which the Labour Government has met the expectations which it raised.

Certainly the scope of constitutional reform under Labour has been wide-ranging; but in the eyes of some people it has been essentially cautious, pragmatic and occasionally incoherent in its implementation. This has left campaigners for constitutional reform, such as those in Charter 88, in the Liberal Democrats and in the academic community, disappointed with Tony Blair's apparent unwillingness to exploit huge Labour majorities in two successive Parliaments in order to transform the constitutional context within which our system of government operates. In particular, there has been disappointment in these quarters at the lack of substantial progress towards radical reform of the House of Commons, full British participation in Economic and Monetary Union in Europe, and the introduction of proportional representation as the basis for elections to the Westminster Parliament. Yet it remains possible that these outstanding goals will be achieved during the remainder of Labour's period in office and the author of this work is in no doubt that future historians will acknowledge the enduring significance of the constitutional reforms introduced by successive Blair Administrations.

The attentive reader will quickly appreciate that there are several important themes running through the agenda of constitutional change in this country, although the Lord Chancellor, Lord Irvine of Lairg, was content to say that 'principled pragmatism' is the unifying thread which has run through the whole of Labour's programme. In the author's opinion, one theme has undoubtedly been the political determination of Ministers to honour the legacy of the late John Smith, who was a genuine believer in the value of comprehensive constitutional reform, mainly by implementing a devolution strategy which so far has contained the political threat to the Labour Party from buoyant nationalism in Scotland and Wales.

A second theme has been the need to restore hygiene and respectability to our political system, something which was identified by Tony Blair and his senior colleagues in Opposition as an urgent priority for a New Labour Government after years of Tory sleaze. This has been largely a matter of making a virtue of necessity by tightening up the rules of what had become a manifestly sleazy political game, moving from a culture of official secrecy towards freedom of information, adjusting the methods of democratic decision making in an attempt to make elections cleaner and more attractive to the general public, and searching for many new ways for politicians to relate to the people they represent in what is nowadays a notably spontaneous and unpredictable political culture.

Traditionally, such a 'soft' discussion would probably not have been included in a book of this kind – certainly not one written by a constitutional lawyer or a political scientist. Yet there is compelling evidence that a combination of changing social attitudes and dynamic technological advances has affected not only our ways of conducting politics but also the rules of the political game and hence the constitutional arrangements within which those active in the policy community have to operate.

A third theme has been 'modernisation', which is the elastic term used by Tony Blair and his New Labour colleagues to present, explain and justify all manner of reforms, whether governmental, institutional or legal. Thus there have been ambitious attempts to modernise both central and local government by changing the pattern of goals and incentives for civil servants and local councillors alike. It is a nice irony, however, that in spite of the decentralisation implicit in the Government's policy of devolution, the policy of modernisation has entailed the further concentration of power within central Government and in the structures of government overall at the expense of the more traditional power centres in Whitehall Departments and regional or local authorities.

Modernisation is a term which has been applied by successive Blair Administrations to the presentational adjustments that have been made to the functioning of the Monarchy, the compositional adjustments to the membership of the House of Lords and the procedural adjustments to the working of the House of Commons designed to make the Lower House more professional and effective in processing Government business.

In the legal sphere, which has been the expanding bailiwick of the Lord Chancellor, there has been much use of the 'm' word to describe the Government's reforms. Yet it would be more accurate to say that the traditional institutions and practices of the law have been transformed by Lord Irvine's reforming zeal, aided and abetted by learned reports from Lord Woolf, Lord Justice Auld and Sir Andrew Leggatt. Indeed, it is already clear that this area of the Government's reform agenda is likely to have far-reaching consequences, especially if it leads to genuine democratisation of the judiciary and the whole legal profession over a period of time.

A fourth theme has been the steady, almost remorseless, Europeanisation of our constitutional arrangements which has manifested itself in some obvious and some less obvious ways. For example, since our entry into the European Communities in 1973, we have been drawn ever more deeply into adopting European legal norms, such as the doctrines of positive rights, purposive legal interpretation, proportionality in jurisprudence and direct effect in Community law. Since the 1998 Human Rights Act came into force in October 2000, we have laid ourselves open to the possibility that British courts, inspired by what might once have been described as alien legal doctrines, will increasingly feel able to look Parliament in the eye and so begin to cast doubt upon the much vaunted principle of Parliamentary supremacy.

As a significant sub-plot in the European play, we have seen the steady growth of regulation at arm's length by quasi-judicial (sometimes supranational) authorities rather than by elected Ministers accountable to national Parliaments; we have seen a growing tendency to pool national sovereignties and so create a justiciable body of superior constitutional law via cumulative international agreements enshrined in further European treaties; and we have witnessed a gathering crisis of democratic legitimacy in all our representative institutions which has encouraged more frequent recourse to referenda to resolve big constitutional issues in which the interests of national Parliaments are at stake.

These have been among the really important themes of constitutional change since Labour came to power in May 1997 and indeed over a longer period as well. They have brought into play the law of unintended consequences which has been exemplified in several interesting ways. For example, the drive for Celtic devolution has thrown a spotlight on various awkward aspects of the English question, such as the need (but not yet an overwhelming demand) for new governmental structures in England at the regional and municipal levels; and on various equally awkward aspects of the Union question, such as the need for a financial rebalancing between the four constituent 'nations' of the United Kingdom, regardless of what structural changes may or may not be made to the pattern of local government in England.

Another example of unintended consequences might well be the fact that those who want further reform of the Upper House have discovered that their goal makes little sense – and is probably unsustainable in the long run – unless they also tackle the more fundamental need for parallel reform of the Lower House and maybe the Monarchy as well for good measure. This realisation serves to emphasise the reality that in a political system without the fixed points and political anchors of a codified constitution, it is effectively impossible to make a single discrete change in our constitutional arrangements. Sooner or later this generation of constitutional reformers will need to present a coherent and synoptic view of everything which they have been trying to do. Otherwise their ambitious reforms will not be sufficiently understood or appreciated by the people whom they seek to serve.

Looking to the future, there are at least three large constitutional uncertainties which could challenge many of our current assumptions. The first is whether or not the Government, Parliament and people of this country will finally resolve to abolish the pound and adopt the euro, thus rendering much more likely the eventual submersion of the United Kingdom into the political depths of the European Union. The second is whether or not the same triumvirate of forces will ever resolve to abandon first-past-the-post elections to the Westminster Parliament and adopt instead some version of proportional representation. The third is a categorical question: whether the United Kingdom is likely to remain the most satisfactory political and constitutional structure within which to strive for the timeless goals of peace, prosperity and public welfare; or whether we shall need to think more globally and act more locally in the twenty-first century.

Whatever the answers to these questions may be, I must now record my debts of gratitude to all those who have assisted me in different ways with the production of this book. I begin by thanking Professor Robert Hazell of the Constitution Unit at University College London, whose suggestion it was that I should write this book and who kindly brought his editorial skills to bear upon the text, and his Assistant, Lucinda Maer, for her help in editing much of the text. I must also thank Mark Kavanagh and Heidi Bagtazo, Craig Fowlie, Jenny Lovel and Iain Hunt of Routledge, and Rosamund Howe, the copy editor, for all their help and support throughout the two years and more that were involved in the writing and publication of this book.

A number of friends whose judgement I respect have been kind enough to read and comment upon parts of the text: Dr Nicholas Baldwin, Professor Vernon Bogdanor, Oonagh Gay, Christopher Jary, Professor George Jones, Peter Riddell, Dr Frank Vibert, Dr Tony Wright MP and Sir George Young Bt MP. Others have kindly supplied me with useful material: Dr Tony Barker, Caroline Bell, Rebecca Blackwood, Richard Cornes, Jeremy Croft, Katherine Fisher, Avis Furness, Gabrielle Garton Grimwood, Dylan Griffiths, Timothy Holmes, Mary Morgan, Dr Roger Mortimore, Kirsty Nichol, Meg Russell, Bryan Wells and Professor Bob Worcester. Any value which there may be in this volume owes a great deal to all these people. Any errors of fact or dubious opinions are my own responsibility.

The book has been described as 'a mono-text' – a mixture of monograph and textbook. Although this is an inelegant description, it captures something of the hybrid quality of the subject and indeed of the author's claims to be able to write about it. My main hope is that the reader will find the narrative and the argument clear and convincing and will be encouraged to embark upon further exploration of what I have found to be a dynamic and fascinating subject.

London

December 2001

F.N. Forman

Part I

THE LEGACY OF HISTORY

Chapter 1

Historical background

From the century of revolution

There has always been both change and continuity in the constitutional arrangements of the United Kingdom. Since the election of the Labour Government in May 1997, we have been living through a period of accelerated change, but this is not unprecedented in historical terms. It was during the seventeenth century – 'the century of revolution' in the words of Christopher Hill – that many of the basic principles, rules and conventions of our constitution were gradually established, notably the ending of the Divine Right of Kings and in its place the emergence of constitutional Monarchy and the principle of Parliamentary supremacy.[1]

Three things essentially distinguished the English revolution of the seventeenth century from its analogues in other countries: its pioneering characteristics, its provisionality and its influentially long-lasting consequences. It offered the first modern example of an internally generated transformation of an established constitutional and political order. It took the best part of a century to accomplish and did not leave behind any lasting forms of pathological politics, such as organised political terror or brutal military dictatorship. Its legacy has been seen in the constitutional attitudes and institutional arrangements not only in this country but also in the United States and in many members of the Commonwealth.

Most of the constitutional changes which took place in England between 1603 and 1714 were unintended, unplanned – at any rate when they were initially embarked upon. Charles I provoked the men of the Long Parliament to oppose his rule by seemingly attacking their faith, their liberty and their property. The King went to Parliament to arrest his opposition and soon after the Civil War began. However, subsequent events were to show that those opposed to the Stuart monarchy were not themselves united. The revolutionary camp was divided into those, such as Levellers in the rank and file of the army, who advocated a contractual theory of government according to which 'every man that is to live under a government ought first by his own consent to put himself under that government', and

a group of senior officers who put the case for a restricted franchise based upon 'those persons in whom all land lies and those in corporations in whom all trading lies'.[2] In the former quotation we can see signs of the desire and argument for further democratisation which lasted until the mid-twentieth century; in the latter we can see the outlines of the constitutional settlement which was reached with the restored Stuart monarchy in 1660.

It is commonly asserted that this country has never had a codified constitution assembled at one particular time into a single consolidated document. Yet attempts have been made to do just this, including the Instrument of Government written by Major-General Lambert and his fellow Major-Generals in 1654. However, the package of proposals, which included a powerful Executive on which senior army officers would have had a decisive and permanent majority, proved unacceptable to the landed gentry and the urban merchants who were so amply represented in the House of Commons.

Charles II and his court-in-exile were eventually able to return to England in 1660 after the King had agreed to the Declaration of Breda which offered an indemnity to those who had opposed Charles I, a settlement of disputes about the sale of royalist lands, and liberty of conscience to reassure the various religious tendencies and sects – all underpinned by the promise to refer all disputed questions to 'a free Parliament by which, upon the word of a King, we will be advised'. The years from 1640 to 1660 in England therefore amounted to a great upheaval but not a Great Revolution. They produced some significant instalments towards the eventual settlement of constitutional accounts in 1688–89, but also left some unfinished constitutional business which had to be resolved during the reigns of William and Mary (1689–1702) and Queen Anne (1702–14).

The period from 1660 to 1689 saw the further consolidation of Parliamentary power at the expense of the Monarchy and it was only in the failure to put successive (Catholic) Exclusion Bills on the Statute Book between 1679 and 1681 that the Protestant propertied classes were significantly balked by Stuart cunning and the passage of events. In many important respects Parliament got its way during the reign of Charles II – at any rate up to 1681 when the King dispensed with Parliament altogether and chose to rely for his revenue on financial support from Louis XIV. Successive statutes consolidated the power of Parliament and served to reduce the chances of Stuart recidivism. For example, the 1664 Triennial Act ensured that Parliament would meet at least every three years (in fact it met every year until 1681); the 1673 Test Act ensured that all civil and military office holders were Anglicans in their religion; and the 1679 Habeas Corpus Act outlawed the tyrannical practice of imprisonment without trial.

The brief and turbulent reign of James II from 1685 to 1688 was yet another eruption of political and constitutional instability in what had already been a very bumpy progress towards relatively stable constitutional Monarchy and Parliamentary government. When the King sought to turn the clock back by returning to personal rule and openly favouring Roman Catholicism, Parliamentary leaders once again decided that it would be expedient to sound out a potential alternative Monarch for the country – in this case the Dutch Prince William of Orange who was married to Mary, the daughter of James II – to see whether they were prepared to take up the reins of constitutional Monarchy in England on Parliamentary terms. In the event a pragmatic agreement was reached with William and Mary in February 1688 and later spelled out in statutory form in what came to be known as the Bill of Rights in October 1689.

The *Bill of Rights* makes interesting reading for anyone who wishes to understand why the Stuarts were by then irredeemably beyond the pale for nearly all the English ruling class and what were the 'civil rights' to which leading Parliamentarians attached overriding importance. The first part consisted of a twelve-point indictment of what the former King James II had done 'to subvert and extirpate the Protestant religion and the laws and liberties of this kingdom'. The second part was a straightforward declaration of the illegality of seven different practices associated with the Stuart Kings, ranging from the suspension of laws and the levying of money via prerogative powers to the raising or keeping of a standing army in time of peace; coupled with a list of six different fundamental rights for Members of Parliament or the people whom they sought to represent, ranging from the right of Protestants to bear arms in their own defence and the rights of free elections and free speech for Members of Parliament to the right of Parliament to be summoned frequently and to be beyond impeachment or challenge in any court or 'place out of Parliament'. In other words, the members laid claim more comprehensively than ever before to the notion of *Parliamentary supremacy*, which has remained ever since a fundamental principle of the British constitution.

The third part of the document expressed 'an entire confidence' that their intended Monarch, the Prince of Orange, would 'preserve them from the violation of their rights which they have here asserted and from all other attempts upon their religion, rights and liberties'. In return, they were prepared to offer the crown to William and Mary jointly for the duration of their separate lives and thereafter to any direct heirs of Princess Mary and, failing that, to her younger sister Princess Anne of Denmark and any of her direct heirs and, failing that, to the 'heirs of the body of the said Prince of Orange'. Quite apart from the deliberate detail in this Royal succession planning, the constitutionally significant point was that this was a *contractual arrangement* between Parliament and the proposed Monarchy, and one in which there was little doubt as to which party was intended to dominate.

Beyond this the members of the Convention Parliament in 1689 wanted to leave as little as possible to chance, so in later parts of the document they went on to draw up new oaths to be sworn by all civil and military office holders, firstly of allegiance to the new Monarchs and secondly of anathema towards Papists in particular and all foreign pretenders to the throne in general. Indeed, there were some memorable passages in which they declared that the rights and liberties upon which they insisted were 'the true, ancient and indubitable rights and liberties of the people of this kingdom', which should be 'firmly and strictly holden and observed . . . in all times to come'; and other passages in which it was made crystal clear that any Catholic or person marrying a Catholic should be debarred from the throne, successors to the throne should swear a Coronation oath to uphold the Church of England, and in the ghastly event of a Papist seizing the throne, 'the people of these realms shall be and are hereby absolved of their allegiance' to such a Sovereign.

The Bill of Rights was thus the coping stone of the structure of constitutional Monarchy which had been painfully constructed piece by piece over the preceding years since the execution of the King in 1649. This metaphor implies that it needed the support of other Parliamentary statutes to buttress its durable properties and such buttresses were built during the following years until the succession of George I in 1714.[3]

Via a long era of consolidation

If constitutional change brought about by frequent political upheavals was a hallmark of the seventeenth century in England, constitutional continuity and consolidation were dominant characteristics of the British Isles in the eighteenth century and into the early decades of the nineteenth century. This long period of constitutional stability at home had as its counterpart the development of a volatile and combative policy abroad – a growing tendency which contributed to no fewer than seven wars against France between the Glorious Revolution in 1689 and the final defeat of Napoleon Bonaparte at the battle of Waterloo in 1815.

It is important to emphasise the *singularity* of Britain's political and constitutional experience during the eighteenth century as a Protestant, island polity governed with 'an ill-defined dualism between a Crown theoretically supreme in matters of administration and policy and a Parliament sovereign in matters of legislation and finance'.[4] This constitutional dualism, which in formal terms embraced only a small manipulated electorate and an even smaller ruling class, was sustained by success in war, imperial aggrandisement and trade expansion; all of which contributed to a successful and peculiarly British form of nationhood. Or as Linda Colley put it so well, 'being a patriot was a way of claiming the right to participate in British

political life, and ultimately a means of demanding a much broader access to citizenship'.[5]

The period from 1714 to 1782 in Great Britain was described by Sir David Lindsay Keir as an 'Augustan age of wealth, success, self-confidence and enlightenment' in which 'the problems of organizing society and government which had vexed previous ages seemed, under the direction of a capable and energetic aristocracy, to have been triumphantly solved'.[6] The constitutional arrangements of that time were admired by enlightened Frenchmen, such as Voltaire and Montesquieu, and celebrated by legal apologists such as Blackstone in his *Commentaries*. The checks and balances between Monarch, Lords and Commons were widely regarded as the secret of British constitutional stability and were usefully supported by constitutional conventions amounting even to political consensus, especially once the Jacobite threat from the Stuart 'Young Pretender' to the throne had been dispatched in 1745. Aristocratic 'influence' and 'interest' were the order of the day and were applied equally by parson and squire in their respective spheres of church and state. The management of the political process on this elitist basis was so effective that His Majesty's Government did not lose a single General Election from 1714 to 1782 (with the possible exception of Walpole's defeat in 1741) and this way of doing things was not seriously challenged until the overthrow of Lord North's Administration in 1782 in the wake of the loss of the American colonies.

The eighteenth century was a golden age for those who controlled pre-democratic local government in that the gentry and merchants who dominated local politics and society in their role as Justices of the Peace were answerable in their interpretation of statute and common law essentially only to the courts. The power of central government remained relatively weak (except in relation to foreign policy and military adventures abroad) and the first two Hanoverian Kings were prepared to entrust the management of national politics to their largely Whig Ministers who controlled Parliament through their placemen. However, it remained 'His Majesty's Government' in more than formal terms, since George III actually presided at Cabinet meetings as late as 1779 and 1781. The convention that there should be a 'Prime Minister' had emerged during the long political ascendancy of Sir Robert Walpole (1721–42), although his power and that of his successors in the office depended upon both their ability to retain the personal favour of the Monarch and their effectiveness in leading and managing Parliament.

The lasting influence of the post-1689 constitutional settlement was nowhere more visible than in the respect which successive Whig Administrations after 1714 paid to the conventions of the constitution. With the single exception of the 1737 Act which required that all stage plays should be licensed by the Lord Chamberlain, none of the statutes which buttressed the 1688–89 settlement was repealed or amended during the first half of the eighteenth century. It was plain that Sir Robert Walpole and his colleagues understood very well what to leave alone and had no appetite for stirring up any constitutional controversy. The system continued to work well in the interests of the political class for most of the eighteenth century. It was cemented and underpinned by Crown patronage for the 'insiders' and the very restricted (and often corrupt) franchise which controlled and limited 'new entrants' into the political market. Indeed, the fruits of the system had been made more attractive by the *1715 Septennial Act*, which extended the life of Parliaments to seven years and which was to remain on the Statute Book until the 1911 Parliament Act; and by the fact that the House of Commons insisted upon retaining the right to self-regulation by adjudicating upon any disputed election results and banning any reports of its own proceedings. In short, Parliament, as a gentlemen's club for members of the ruling class, held constitutional sway virtually unchallenged by either the Monarch from above or the people from below for the best part of a hundred years.

However, at the very time when the methods of eighteenth-century politics might have seemed most entrenched, the members of the ruling class began to fall out among themselves and popular discontent with the system began to grow. Under George III the so-called Rockingham Whigs found themselves excluded from office when Lord North

became Prime Minister in 1770 and they came to resent the way in which the system of political preference and patronage was used against them. At the same time popular pressures for reform had built up in London and elsewhere, notably following the 1768 Middlesex Election when the radical John Wilkes was elected three times by the electorate but expelled three times by the unreformed House of Commons for having successfully challenged the political Establishment on the issue of seditious libel. The result was that the newly formed 'Society of Supporters of the Bill of Rights' called for the implementation of radical political reform, including a wider and more democratic franchise, the exclusion of placemen from Parliament, the subordination of MPs to the wishes of their constituents, and the introduction of annual Parliaments.

The origins of the constitutional changes which were made in the nineteenth century can be found in the first stirrings of rebellion and revolt during the second half of the eighteenth century. Successive Tory Administrations led by Lord North from 1770 to 1782 conducted what was essentially a rearguard action against opposition on two flanks from the excluded Rockingham Whigs and from the populist radicals. Even the Pitts, father and son, recognised the expediency of some electoral reform to create a wider and more publicly acceptable franchise. In 1770 Chatham (Pitt the Elder) put forward a proposal that there should be a third member for each County; and in 1782 Pitt the Younger proposed a Bill to buy out 50 rotten boroughs, redistribute the 100 seats thus made available to the counties and the newly expanding urban areas, and enlarge the limited electorate to include those who held their property by copyhold. In the event, none of these proposals was passed into law because George III was hostile, all Cabinets were divided on the issue, and the unreformed House of Commons was not surprisingly unpersuaded.

Constitutional reform of some kind might have come sooner than 1832 if it had not been for the cautious and even reactionary attitudes which characterised successive Administrations and virtually the whole political class during the long war against revolutionary France from 1793 to

1815. With the very existence of the nation in peril and an imminent threat of invasion by Napoleon's army, it is not altogether surprising that pressures for constitutional reform made no headway. Indeed, the political imperatives of the time were all in the other direction, towards greater central Government power. However, once the dangers of war and invasion were past, even the reactionary Tory Administrations led by Lord Liverpool (1812–27) were unable to prevent a significant recrudescence of popular pressures for political reform.[7]

The experience of war against revolutionary France, combined with the political influence of such radicals as Thomas Paine, engendered growing pressure for constitutional reform both inside and outside Parliament during the first few decades of the nineteenth century. The campaign was led by the opposition Whigs, such as Earl Grey, Lord John Russell and Sir Francis Burdett, and given intellectual substance by the Utilitarians led by Jeremy Bentham who in 1817 published his own plan for Parliamentary reform.[8] Gradually, at least the progressive section of the political class came to the conclusion that the pressures for reform should not be resisted, but rather should be embraced with timely concessions.

Through a century of democratisation

It can legitimately be maintained that the century and more which followed the first Reform Act of 1832 was characterised in the United Kingdom by a gradual process of *democratisation* culminating for the purposes of this account in Labour's landslide victory at the 1945 General Election. The big constitutional story for most of those years was the gradual extension of the franchise which by 1928 had given the right to vote in Parliamentary elections to all British men and women over the age of 21 (with the exception of lunatics, felons and peers of the realm), and which brought in its wake increased power for the political parties seeking to appeal for the support of an increasingly large electorate.

It was significant at the outset that the *1832 Reform Act* was described in its preamble as 'an Act to amend the representation of the people' – no longer referring to 'interests' or 'communities', as would have been the way in the eighteenth century. Yet the Act represented both change and continuity in British constitutional arrangements. The drive for change came in the shape of a redistribution of seats in the House of Commons from the smaller 'rotten' Boroughs to the rapidly growing new urban areas and, to a lesser extent, to the Counties as well. This had the effect of more fully enfranchising the urban and moneyed sections of the growing middle class, especially in London, the Midlands and the industrialising North, to the extent that 141 seats were forfeited by the smaller moribund Boroughs. Of the seats in the Commons thus liberated, 65 were used to enfranchise vibrant new urban centres and 65 to increase County representation. Change was also brought about through a new voting qualification for £10 occupiers which enfranchised the urban middle class and so increased the electorate by roughly half or about 217,000 people, sufficient for the urban electorate to become a numerical majority of the total new electorate. To put it symbolically, we could say that Old Sarum, Wendover and Castle Rising had to give way to Manchester, Birmingham and Leeds.

The power of continuity, on the other hand, was reflected in the cardinal fact that the 1832 Act upheld the traditional English connection between property and political power, but based it upon a broader and more inclusive definition of property. The overall effect of the changes made by the Act should also not be exaggerated for two other reasons: firstly, the qualified electorate was only increased from 3 per cent to 5 per cent of the total adult population; and secondly, actual membership of the House of Commons continued to be subject to property qualifications – a conservative safeguard which was not removed until 1858. Sir David Lindsay Keir was right to remind his readers that 'what the landed interest consented to in 1832 was . . . not a surrender, but a partnership in power' (with the new urban middle class).[9]

Taking a longer, historical view of the 1832 Reform Act and its constitutional consequences, it gave impetus to a number of very significant developments which were gradually established throughout the rest of the nineteenth century. It diminished the powers of patronage and nomination exercised by the Crown and its allies. It brought to an end the triangular equilibrium between Monarch, Lords and Commons derived from the constitutional settlement of the 1688–89 Glorious Revolution, but which had gradually begun to shift in favour of the Commons. It enhanced the power and purpose of the Prime Minister and Cabinet and helped to create a situation in which both were increasingly dependent upon shifting majorities in the House of Commons rather than upon the personal favour and support of the Monarch. It helped to provoke the development of recognisably modern political parties which began to organise systematically in the constituencies as well as at Westminster. Above all, it stimulated further public demand for electoral reform which for a century concentrated mainly on completing the adult franchise in successive Representation of the People Acts, but which also entailed other initiatives of political modernisation that had long-lasting effects upon the British constitution and British society.

A second important theme which runs through the century of democratisation is the growing significance of *constitutional conventions* in British political arrangements. We see this exemplified in the office and practice of the Prime Minister, but more vitally in the way in which it took at least 30 years of political experience for it to be definitively established that an Administration has to resign *en bloc* if it has been defeated at a General Election, and cannot simply cling onto office until it loses a vote of confidence in the House of Commons. Whereas it may have sounded threatening and even somewhat heretical in 1839 when Peel argued that it was 'at variance with the spirit of the constitution for a Ministry to continue in office without the confidence of the House' (implying, if not explicitly stating, that this meant the confidence of the electorate who had returned the Members to Parliament), by 1868 when Disraeli's Administration immediately resigned in the wake of defeat in the General Election in that year, it could be

argued (on the basis of convention) that ultimate sovereignty had come to reside with the people and not their elected representatives.

Throughout the nineteenth century another driving force of constitutional change in the United Kingdom was *organised and vociferous public opinion* as articulated by all those who sought to mobilise or exploit the legitimate grievances felt by the excluded majority of the British public, and most notably those who campaigned for a wider franchise and more direct forms of democracy. Perhaps the two best-known examples of this characteristic tendency of the nineteenth and early twentieth centuries were the Chartist movement which was so prominent in the 1830s and 1840s and the Suffragette movement which had some dramatic political influence during the years leading up to the First World War. The effectiveness of directly mobilising public opinion (and large public demonstrations) to put pressure on Parliament to bring in reforms had also been vividly demonstrated earlier in the nineteenth century when Wilberforce's anti-slavery movement was triumphantly successful in persuading Parliament to outlaw the barbaric and previously lucrative slave trade; and by Peel's anti-Corn Law League which put such pressure on Parliament in the 1830s and 1840s that in 1846 the Corn Laws were finally repealed.

It is interesting to summarise *the Chartist programme of 1838* and to remind ourselves of how long it subsequently took to put it into practice. The abolition of property qualifications for membership of the House of Commons was effected in 1858; the secret ballot at Parliamentary elections was achieved in the *1872 Ballot Act*; the payment of salaries to MPs was first introduced on a modest scale in 1911; complete adult suffrage for men was achieved in the *1918 Representation of the People Act*; and more equal electoral districts became one of the criteria in the *1944 Redistribution of Seats Act* which established the Independent Boundary Commissions to adjudicate on issues of electoral geography. Only the call for annual Parliaments (in other words, the obligation to hold a General Election every year) has not yet been adopted as a constitutional rule in the United Kingdom.

Just as the 1832 Reform Act had been preceded by enlightened Whig initiatives in Parliament and popular pressures outside, so a similar sequence of events gave rise to the *1867 Representation of the People Act*. However, what was unusual on this occasion was that it was the Tories under the leadership of Benjamin Disraeli who 'dished the Whigs' by introducing and passing this landmark measure of franchise reform during their brief term of office in 1867–68. The 1867 Act was a sign of political realism on the part of Disraeli, who had come to appreciate that such reform was inevitable and would have to be taken further as the century progressed and that there might be considerable political advantage to be gained by whichever party was instrumental in extending the franchise in this way. As things turned out, Disraeli's enlightened self-interest was completely vindicated in both constitutional and political terms. Constitutionally, the Act marked another important step in the long march towards real democratisation of the British political system; politically, it doubled the size of the urban electorate and in the process gave new political muscle to the artisan 'upper' working class, which enabled the Tories to broaden their political appeal and thus to share power by turns with Gladstone's Liberals for the rest of the century.

Once again it is salutary to enter a few words of caution about the extent to which the *1867 Representation of the People Act* and the subsequent reform legislation of 1884 and 1885 dramatically changed the electoral and constitutional landscape: the truth is that in each case only incremental improvements were made. The 1867 Act, which only increased the electorate to 13 per cent of the adult population, still left the newly expanding urban areas and the north of the country relatively under-represented, since the larger towns could return only 34 of the 334 borough MPs and two-thirds of all the constituencies represented in Parliament were located south of a line from the Wash to the Severn. Equally, although the *1884 Representation of the People Act* extended the householder franchise to the counties, the electorate was only increased to 25 per cent of the adult population and a considerable number of electoral anomalies remained in both urban and rural parts of the country, while the *1885 Redistribution of Seats Act*, which effectively made the single-member constituency the norm, nevertheless left untouched several quaint anomalies (such as plural voting for university graduates and the enduring 'business vote' available to employers at their place of work) that had to be addressed in subsequent legislation of 1918, 1928 and 1948.

The process of gradual democratisation in the United Kingdom in the nineteenth and early twentieth centuries was not simply the result of a pragmatic political elite making timely tactical concessions to the growing force of mass public opinion. It also stemmed from the rational analysis of many principled reformers who set out to *modernise* British politics and public administration in order to rid the government of their country of the taint of patronage and other anachronistic practices. The drive for administrative reform, which had begun with the arguments of Jeremy Bentham and the Utilitarians in the first few decades of the century, bore its first fruit with the abolition of the old Exchequer Office in 1834 and the creation of the unified office of Paymaster-General in 1836. Gradually, the problems posed by an inefficient and potentially still corrupt civil service financed from a bewildering variety of sources (including the Civil List, the Consolidated Fund and direct levies or fees) were addressed by Parliament and in 1849 for the first time the Civil Estimates as a whole were laid before Parliament.

By mid-century most of the Departments of central Government had begun to recruit via systems of examination or initial probationary periods. Yet there was obviously still room for improvement, so William Gladstone (then Liberal Chancellor of the Exchequer) asked Sir Stafford Northcote (a Liberal politician) and Sir Charles Trevelyan (a civil servant) to consider the outstanding issues and make suitable recommendations. In 1854 their report was published and accepted by Mr Gladstone on behalf of the Government. As a result the Civil Service Commission was set up in 1855 to take a systematic grip on the methods of recruitment to the various Departments and to eliminate any lingering traces of patronage or corruption. It took a while to change the administrative culture in all Departments, but the goal was largely achieved by 1870 when an Order in Council was passed which sought to make universal throughout the public administration the practices of recruitment on merit and open competition by written examination at the outset of every civil servant's career.

During the same period between the first and second Reform Acts the sphere of local government was also subjected to a degree of modernisation. The *1834 Poor Law Amendment Act* grouped parishes into unions to administer poor relief through salaried officials answerable to a new Poor Law Board. The *1835 Municipal Corporations Act* extensively reformed the administration of Boroughs by sweeping away the old oligarchies and replacing them with local Councils elected by ratepayers. The new Councils were given statutory authority to legislate through by-laws, to appoint town clerks and borough treasurers, and to exercise administrative powers over police, finance and property matters – all subject to Treasury control over loans and the sale of assets. The shelf life of this reform was truly striking in that the committee system which it established in local government lasted in its essentials until the Local Government Act 2000 that provided for elected Mayors or, as an alternative, a Cabinet system for leading local Councillors. Subsequently, the *1888 Local Government Act* established elected County Councils for the first time in new administrative Counties to which almost all of the powers traditionally exercised by Justices of the Peace were transferred, except for the licensing of public houses and police matters. A few years later in 1894 Urban and Rural District Councils were created from the old sanitary districts and given consolidated powers over highways and (in rural districts) over poor relief. Thus by the end of the nineteenth century patterns of 'modernised' government had been established both at the national and at the various local levels and these were to last in their essentials until the end of the Second World War and, in the case of local government, somewhat longer.

Throughout the nineteenth century two other slow and gradual trends were at work in the United Kingdom which had marked effects upon our evolving constitutional arrangements. The first was *the reform of Parliament itself* which could in many ways be regarded as the institutional counterpart of the successive extensions of the franchise from 1832 to 1948. This process really began a few years *before* the Great Reform Act when the *1829 Catholic Emancipation Act* finally permitted the participation of Catholics in Parliament and in judicial and corporate offices of state (but not the ancient and hybrid office of Lord Chancellor). It continued with a series of procedural changes in the way that Parliament conducted its business, which had the cumulative effect of making both Houses more efficient at processing legislation and the Commons more open and accountable to the growing electorate. The main milestones along this road were the 1835 decision to print Parliamentary Questions, the 1839 decision no longer to debate public petitions, the 1840 decision to publish Parliamentary papers (e.g. Select Committee reports), the 1849 decision to dispense with debate on the First Reading of Bills, and the 1855 decision to provide support from public funds for the publication of *Hansard*. Even more central to the task of modernising the House of Commons was the initiative taken by the Select Committee on Public Moneys in 1856 which later gave rise to the *1866 Exchequer and Audit Departments Act* that created the newly combined office of Comptroller and Auditor General. This change was designed to make it certain that all categories of public expenditure were first approved by Parliament and that, with the aid of the Select Committee on Public Accounts created by Mr Gladstone in 1861, MPs were able to satisfy themselves retrospectively that public funds were actually spent on the purposes for which they had been appropriated by Parliament.

There were some significant procedural reforms in the 1880s, prompted by the obstruction caused by Charles Parnell and his Irish Nationalist colleagues in their sustained opposition to the 1881 Coercion Bill and their subsequent efforts through filibusters and similar techniques to highlight their displeasure at the defeat of two successive

Irish Home Rule Bills. The most important of these procedural reforms was the Standing Order approved by the House of Commons in 1887 which had the effect of allowing any Member of the House (subject to the Speaker's veto) to move a closure forthwith to legislation which was being unreasonably delayed and to move a so-called 'guillotine' motion which in similar circumstances would allow undiscussed clauses in Bills to be carried without debate and Bills to be timetabled in a guillotine motion put by a member of the Government. This reforming drive, which was intended to make it easier for the majority in the House of Commons to get its way when faced with implacable opposition from obstructionist minorities, continued well into the next century, notably until the 1911 and 1949 Parliament Acts.

The second gradual but significant trend during the century of democratisation was to be seen in all the various *changes in the social context of British politics*. This was determined very largely by great events, such as the two world wars and the economic depression in between, but also by the changing political response to such developments which, in many cases, made certain constitutional changes effectively inevitable. Social change can be either a cause or a consequence of constitutional change and sometimes both. In the case of the eighteenth and early nineteenth centuries in Great Britain, technological advances – such as James Watt's invention of the steam engine in 1769 or the pioneering development of the railways by George and Robert Stephenson in the 1830s and 1840s – brought significant economic and social changes in their wake which in turn encouraged the political changes associated with the drive towards greater democracy.

The most obvious consequence of industrialisation was that the population of England grew from just under 9 million in 1801, of whom more than three-quarters lived in rural areas, to just under 18 million in 1851, of whom under half lived in rural areas, to just over 35 million in 1901, of whom less than a quarter lived in rural areas.[10] This growth of population and the accompanying shift of population from the countryside to the new industrial towns were by far the most significant

determinants of franchise reform and indeed of the long sequence of social and administrative reform until the outbreak of the First World War.[11]

It could be argued that interventionist legislation was necessitated by the dramatic changes in the economic and social composition of the nation. In 1801 there had been only fifteen towns in England with a population over 20,000, whereas by 1891 there were 63, including Leeds, Manchester, Sheffield and Birmingham. Such mighty social changes were bound to affect the balance of power between the two Houses of Parliament, the relationship between MPs and their constituents, the focus of legislation and the prevailing view of the nation state.

The politicians realised that they had to organise their efforts more systematically if they were to improve their chances of gaining and retaining power by appealing to an ever wider electorate. Recognisably modern political parties began to form, at least in embryo, quite early during the century of democratisation. The Conservatives were first into the field with the formation of the Carlton Club in 1832, the introduction of an approved list of Parliamentary candidates in 1852 and the establishment of the National Union of Conservative Associations in 1868. The Radicals (later the Liberals) were not far behind with the establishment of a national Registration Office in 1835, the Birmingham Association in 1868 under the dynamic leadership of Joseph Chamberlain, and the National Liberal Federation in 1887.

Nor were the political interests of organised labour neglected at this time, although the essential difference was that for the whole of the nineteenth century the political objectives of this growing and increasingly influential section of the population were pursued by the trade unions *outside* Parliament by exerting sustained pressure upon elected representatives inside Parliament. The Trades Union Congress held its first annual meeting in 1868 and the member unions were soon successful in persuading Parliament to pass legislation in 1871 (under a Liberal Administration) and in 1875 (under a Conservative Administration) which ensured that trade union action in restraint of trade was no longer illegal, the internal affairs of trade unions were free from external interference, and trade union breaches of contract and peaceful picketing 'in contemplation or furtherance of a trade dispute' were declared lawful. If it had not been for the notorious Taff Vale judgement of 1901 which subsequently threatened the legal immunity of trade unions, the Independent Labour Party founded in 1893 and the Labour Representation Committee formed in 1900 might not have decided to join battle with the employers and the judges as active participants within Parliament but rather to continue operating as a successful pressure group outside it. Thus by the end of the nineteenth century all the main economic and social interests in the land – including an increasingly committed vanguard of women who were active in the Suffragette movement – sought to be politically effective (i.e. directly represented) *within* Britain's evolving Parliamentary democracy rather than continue as mere passengers or spectators who might or might not feel grateful for what was done for them.

A second area in which the political responses to social change were of fundamental long-term significance was that of *the gradual spread of property rights* among an ever larger proportion of the population – a process which was gradually ratified in successive Acts of Parliament as the progressive element in the political class at any rate came to recognise arguments based upon democratic principle and social justice. In 1860 England was the richest country in the world with a per capita income 50 per cent higher than France's and almost three times that of Germany.[12] Yet during the same period of British dominance, wealth and power were still very unequally held and this persistent inequality naturally detracted from the degree of real democratisation that could be achieved.[13]

To bring women in particular within the pale of the nineteenth-century constitution it was necessary for Parliament to recognise that they should be allowed to own property in their own right rather than continue themselves to be regarded as but one form of property which was owned or disposed of by their fathers and husbands. This change was vital because of the enduring constitutional link between property and political power, and it was largely achieved in the *1870 and 1882 Married Women's Property Acts* which altered not only the law of the land but also the way in which women's *political* rights were perceived by the then all-male political class. Of course, these developments in statutory law were not sufficient in and of themselves to give women political rights equal to those of men. It required several other significant pressures – notably from courageous suffragettes – to bring about even qualified female suffrage in 1918 and for the first woman to take her seat in the House of Commons in 1919.

Notwithstanding the slow progress made towards democratisation, the electoral system in the United Kingdom was still characterised by complexity, anomalies and democratic injustice. There were two large, inter-connected issues to be resolved: *firstly*, the width and overall scope of the franchise (i.e. how far and how fast to include those *without* property of their own who remained essentially 'second-class citizens'); and *secondly*, the distribution of voting power within and between country and town, old and new areas of settlement and population. On the first point, while the 1884 Representation of the People Act had extended the householder franchise to the Counties and so nearly tripled the size of the electorate from 900,000 to 2,500,000, it failed to tackle plural voting, votes based upon ancient rights, or women's suffrage, all of which had been advocated unsuccessfully by Joseph Chamberlain and the Radicals. On the second point, the 1885 Redistribution of Seats Act was more ruthless towards conservative interests in that the disenfranchisement of 142 seats meant that most counties and boroughs were divided into single-member constituencies with an average of 54,000 inhabitants in each; this broadly brought to an end the long-established political dominance of the South over the North and of the landed interest over everyone else. Thus although territorial justice preceded social justice in the process of electoral reform, the strategic thrust was in a democratic direction.

The constitutional crisis of 1909–11 qualifies as one of the defining episodes in the history of

Parliament and in the constitutional history of the United Kingdom – comparable perhaps in significance with the Glorious Revolution of 1688–89 and the upheaval which led to the first great Reform Act of 1832. Two inconclusive General Elections in 1910 and the express willingness of the new King George V to create (if necessary) over 400 new Liberal peers were required to persuade the in-built majority of hereditary Tory peers to give way to the settled will of the Liberal majority in the House of Commons.

The 1911 Parliament Act, which was the statutory fruit of the crisis, established once and for all the Parliamentary supremacy of the Commons by severely curbing the constitutional powers of the Lords and to some extent balancing that change with a reduction in the maximum lawful duration of a Parliament from seven to five years, thus repealing the long-standing Septennial Act of 1715. However, in spite of a declaration of intent in the Preamble to reconstruct the Upper House on an elected basis, the Act did nothing to alter its composition. It effectively ended all power or influence for the House of Lords over Money Bills by confining the Parliamentary consideration of such legislation to the Commons and giving the Speaker exclusive power to certify which Bills were or were not Money Bills. Thus the Lords were formally deprived of a fiscal power which had fallen into disuse since their last-gasp opposition to the repeal of paper duties in 1860 (a stance which was effectively rendered pointless by the decision of the Commons to bundle together all Money Bills into one consolidated Budget which would be beyond challenge by the Upper House). With regard to all other Bills, the 1911 Act provided that if a Bill was passed by the Commons in the same form in three successive sessions of Parliament, then it should get the Royal Assent without the need for further approval by the Lords, provided that at least two years had elapsed between its Second Reading in the first session and its Third Reading in the third session. The Act effectively reduced the delaying power of the Lords from nearly seven years to two years, a significant redressing of the relationship between the two Houses which subsequently had to be invoked only twice during the period from its passage until the outbreak of the Second World War.[14]

The right of the House of Lords to appeal to the electorate at a subsequent General Election against what it might consider to be the constitutional unwisdom of a measure passed by the House of Commons was not entirely removed by the 1911 Act, but was only used very infrequently and with diminishing conviction throughout the rest of the twentieth century. All in all, the verdict of history seems to have been that the 1911 Act was a decisive constitutional change. It did, however, also have the longer-term effect of putting the severely truncated powers of the Upper House on a clear statutory basis which arguably endowed it with more legitimacy than it would have had if it had continued to function simply on the basis of constitutional conventions and established custom and practice.

Whereas the trajectories of both Parliamentary and franchise reform for the rest of the century of democratisation became somewhat predictable and could be regarded as mopping-up operations after the titanic constitutional clashes of the years before, the trajectory of social change still had the capacity to create important political and constitutional effects. Let us consider a few examples. The effects of total military and civilian mobilisation in 1916 and thereafter were enormously far reaching and were personified in the collapse of the Asquith Administration and the arrival of Lloyd George as a prototypical twentieth-century war leader. The volunteer army, which had been 164,000 strong in August 1914, grew to a remarkable peak of more than 5 million men under arms following the introduction of conscription in 1916. Essential industries, such as munitions, railways, shipping and food, were taken under complete Government control in what eventually amounted to a command economy.

In such dramatically transformed economic and social circumstances it would have been simply extraordinary if, when the country emerged exhausted but victorious from what was until that time the greatest war in human history, its political and constitutional arrangements had remained unchanged. In so many ways the end of the war was a time when debts of all kinds had to be paid and old scores had to be settled. Consequently, although the Liberal Lloyd George along with his Conservative supporters were swept back into power in the so-called 'khaki election' of 1918, the Liberal Party was fatally split and the young Labour Party made a significant gain from 29 to 57 Parliamentary seats, arriving in the first peacetime Parliament strongly committed to its own 1918 Socialist constitution.

In the same year the *1918 Representation of the People Act* was passed, emphasising that the egalitarian experience of the trenches and the full participation of women in the heroic war effort simply *had* to be recognised in terms of a wider and more democratic franchise. Specifically, this meant that complete adult manhood suffrage was finally achieved without qualification (whether of property or education) and qualified female suffrage was introduced for women aged 30 and over who in their own right or through their husbands occupied premises or land with an annual rental value of £5 or more. This extended the vote to more than 8 million women, thus contributing to a larger electorate of 21 million people or three-quarters of the total adult population.

Ten years later the *1928 Representation of the People Act* completed the job as far as women were concerned in that it extended the vote to those adults aged 21 and over who were resident or who occupied premises with an annual value of £10 or more or who were married to such people. The legislation was cast in these seemingly convoluted terms because at that time private rented housing constituted about 60 per cent of all housing tenure (compared with less than 10 per cent today) and owner occupation was nothing like so widespread as it is now. This Act had the effect of enfranchising nearly everyone aged 21 and over, and produced an even larger electorate which accounted for 99 per cent of the entire adult population.

In spite of this further step in the direction of completely democratic voting rights, there were still a few residual wrinkles which had not been ironed out: business votes were still available (but exercisable only in respect of one set of business premises) and university graduates still had two votes each (in recognition of their supposedly superior intelligence). These and other small anomalies, such as the last remaining dual-Member constituencies, were finally abolished in the *1948 Representation of the People Act*.

We can now see how, slowly but surely, British constitutional arrangements were democratised and modernised during what we have called the century of democratisation. Some of the impetus came from enlightened political leaders, especially Whigs and Liberals in the nineteenth century; some came in response to great public campaigns and popular pressures, such as the Chartists or the Suffragettes; but perhaps the greatest part, whether in the nineteenth or the twentieth century, was attributable to the great engines of economic and social change which had varied and often unpredictable effects upon the constitution and the body politic.

A period of consensus, then confrontation

In British eyes the Second World War, both at home and overseas, provided a vindication of the nation state and all its works. By extension, it also endorsed our own particular form of Parliamentary democracy as it had developed until that time. Virtually no one who held any real influence in the politics of post-war Britain seriously questioned our national institutions or the ways in which they were supposed to operate. It was almost as if the constitutional rules of the game had been sanctified by the heroism of the glorious dead and the stoicism of millions on the Home Front. Although the incoming Labour Government's policies and priorities were very different from those of the pre-war Governments dominated by the Conservatives, all parties accepted (even venerated) the constitutional framework which had been inherited from the past and no politician of any significance propounded the case for fundamental constitutional change. Indeed, so confident and almost complacent were the members of the British political elite during the first two decades after the war that some of them spent much of their time seeking to export what was called 'the Westminster model' of government to the British colonies as each of them moved towards independence.

Following the 1945 General Election, the Labour Party was swept into power with an overwhelming Commons majority of 144 seats and a clear mandate for the introduction of the Socialist measures which had been bundled rather surreptitiously into the party's Manifesto for 1945. The political priority for the Labour Government was to *use* the power that had been given to it by the electorate rather than to spend time reforming the rules of the game.

In so far as the Attlee Administration turned its attention to procedural and institutional matters, it immediately acted to make the House of Commons even more 'efficient' at processing and passing government legislation. In response to a rather cautious report from the Select Committee on Procedure in 1945, it used its large majority in the House to impose further restrictions upon the conduct of Budget debates, to increase the number of Standing Committees for detailed consideration of legislation, and to apply the 'guillotine' to proceedings in Committee 'upstairs' as well as on the floor of the House. It also effectively eliminated Private Members' Bills by starving them of Parliamentary time on the grounds that all the available time was needed for putting through its great programme of economic and social reforms. The overall effects of this new instrumental approach towards Parliamentary proceedings were greatly to strengthen the dominance of the Executive over the Legislature, to create an efficient Parliamentary machine for speedily turning the victorious party's electoral mandate into the law of the land, and to reduce to virtually zero the Parliamentary impact of individual backbench Members of Parliament.

When towards the end of the 1945–50 Parliament a little legislative time seemed to be available for constitutional measures, the Labour Government turned its attention to the connected tasks of tidying up the remaining anomalies in the franchise and redistributing constituency electorates, with the intention of producing votes of more equal value in different parts of the country. The former task was achieved by the *1948 Representation of the People Act* which abolished the university and business franchises, together with the remaining dual-Member constituencies. The latter task was achieved by the *1949 Redistribution of Seats Act*. It was not to be until the end of the next period of Labour Government from 1964 to 1970 that a further step would be taken in the *1969 Representation of the People Act* to lower the minimum voting age from 21 to 18 years in line with the general cult of youth which characterised the late 1960s.

In the late 1940s it seemed inherently unlikely that much Parliamentary time would be spent on constitutional measures. However, a more self-confident Opposition emerged in the House of Lords against Labour's proposed nationalisation of the iron and steel industries. This Conservative opposition was seen by the Labour Cabinet to be in defiance of the spirit, if not the letter, of the so-called 'Salisbury convention' which held that the Lords should not challenge at Second Reading any measure which had been foreshadowed in the 1945 Labour Manifesto. This opposition greatly irritated senior Ministers and led them to use their huge majority in the Commons to push through the *1949 Parliament Act* which reduced the power of the Lords still further by cutting the delaying power of the Upper House from two years to one year.

Only a few minor measures disturbed the calm surface of the constitutional status quo during the 1950s and early 1960s. The *1958 Life Peerages Act* made possible the creation of Life Peers (i.e. peerages which cannot be inherited) and the measure included the creation of peerages for women in their own right. The *1963 Peerage Act* enabled hereditary peers to renounce their titles, while in no way impinging upon the rights of their heirs and successors, in order to make themselves eligible for election to the House of Commons, and enabled female hereditary peers to sit in the House of Lords. Neither of these changes affected the right of hereditary peers to sit in the House of Lords, but their longer-term significance was probably greater than at first appeared because Life Peers have since made a real and growing contribution to the work of the Upper House and some hereditary peers who renounced their titles – e.g. Alec Douglas-Home and Tony Benn – played a distinguished and influential part in the Lower House.

By the end of the 1960s the sap of constitutional reform was beginning to rise again in the British body politic – particularly as the then Labour Government under the leadership of Harold Wilson searched rather desperately for measures of institutional reform to tame the trade unions and modernise the structures of government, including the two Houses of Parliament. In the House of Commons, there were some rather desultory and inconsequential attempts at procedural reform, such as morning sittings and the establishment of a new structure of Select Committees, both of which were later modified or reversed.

There was also a hapless attempt to reform the House of Lords via the *1968 Parliament (No. 2) Bill* which sought to make both a reduction in the total number of peers and an attack on the hereditary principle. The Bill secured a comfortable majority on Second Reading in the House of Commons, but subsequently in Committee on the floor of the House it suffered a slow death by a thousand cuts at the hands of Michael Foot and Enoch Powell, a unique combination of House of Commons tradi-tionalists from Left and Right respectively, who argued that any significant reform of the Second Chamber was likely to strengthen it at the expense of the Lower House. In the face of such determined and time-consuming opposition from both ends of the political spectrum, the Wilson Administration concluded that discretion was the better part of valour and abandoned the Bill, thus leaving the House of Lords unreformed in terms of its com-position and its functions.

Harold Wilson, who had been a prominent civil servant during the Second World War, established a Royal Commission under Lord Fulton to consider the future of the civil service and another under Lord Redcliffe-Maud to consider the future of local government. The 'new managerialism' was the spirit of the times and fashionable opinion tended to favour a 'corporate' approach to the reform of government, whether at central or local level.

The Fulton Report was published in 1968 and its main institutional consequences were the establish-ment of a new Civil Service Department and a new Civil Service College to proselytise for the new way of doing things. The Redcliffe-Maud Report was published in 1969, but was not acted upon until 1972 under a Conservative Government. These relatively long lead-times did not make much difference to the policies which emerged, since the new managerialism appealed at least as much to the Heath Administration from 1970 to 1974 as it had done to the Wilson Administrations from 1964 to 1970.

This bi-partisan consensus was reflected in the 1970 White Paper on the reorganisation of central Government, which it fell to the new Conservative Government to introduce. The emphasis was very much upon the desirability of importing (American) business methods and ideas into the sphere of British Government and of strengthening the so-called 'central' departments of government in relation to the territorial or functional fiefdoms, such as the Home Office and the Scottish Office or the Department of Health and Social Security and the Ministry of Defence. Since Edward Heath, who had also been a civil servant at an earlier stage in his career, was very keen on the application of rational business methods to the process of govern-ment, he took the first opportunity to establish two new 'super-departments' (Trade and Industry, and the Environment) which absorbed a number of smaller departments – again in the name of greater efficiency (but perhaps less accountability) in central Government.

The other great constitutional theme which ran like an ominous thread through British politics in the 1960s and early 1970s was that of the United Kingdom's relations with the European Community. Both main parties since the time of Harold Macmillan in 1960 came to the conclusion, when in office, that since this country had been unable to prevent the Continental Six from forming a Common Market around a powerful Franco-German axis, it would be wiser for the United Kingdom to seek to join the great European adven-ture after all and so reap the apparent economic benefits of membership. Thus the Macmillan Administration applied for British membership of the Common Market in 1961, but had its application vetoed by the French President,

General de Gaulle, in January 1963. The second Wilson Administration applied again for British membership in 1967, but was spun along by the French without result until the resignation of de Gaulle in 1969. Finally, in 1971, the Heath Administration was successful in persuading de Gaulle's successor, President Pompidou, that the United Kingdom had become sufficiently 'European' to be allowed into the European Community on 1st January 1973.

Successive British Governments of both main parties managed to convince themselves that joining six of the other Western European nations at that stage in their journey towards 'an ever closer union of European peoples' could be presented to the British public as part of a great 'modernisation' project – a sort of secular determinism to match the ideology of Marxism-Leninism which had been imposed upon the nations of Eastern Europe by the Red Army ever since the end of the Second World War. Perhaps one of the explanations for this conviction was that *American* influence had consistently been exercised in favour of Western European unity ever since the beginning of the Cold War in 1947 and this weighed heavily with successive British Governments which had tended to pride themselves upon their 'special relationship' with their counterparts in Washington.

One of the consequences of this approach to UK entry into the European Community in 1973 was that the leading members of the British political elite were not clear, arguably not even honest, with the British public about the full political and constitutional implications of embarking down the European road. If they had been, the story of this country's constitutional development since the 1970s might have been very different, because the British Parliament and people might not have agreed to participate in the great adventure which has since become the European Union.

To summarise the story so far in relation to the period since 1945 in the United Kingdom, its principal hallmarks are broad consensus on the political structures, the policies to be followed and the 'rules of the political game'. The country was governed by a comfortable political duopoly of the two main parties which typically attracted together more than 90 per cent of the votes cast at most General Elections. When Governments changed, they changed within fairly narrow policy parameters and there was virtually no significant disagreement on constitutional questions or the rules of political competition. Above all, the so-called mandate theory of government was accepted by both main parties and Parliament became much less of a vehicle for political representation and much more of a machine for ratifying the decisions and processing the legislation of the Government of the day.

In defence of the decisions actually made during this period, it can be said that the *performance* (i.e. economic and social ouputs) of the political system was respectable and attractive to the British public, even if it did not look so good in comparison with our counterparts on the Continent. There was not much criticism of, and still less overt resistance to, the *constitutional processes* of government, firstly because of the materialist success just mentioned, but secondly because the party mandates, when put into effect, were broadly in tune with the contemporary public mood and did not seriously threaten the interests of those who were excluded from power but still commanded a modicum of public sympathy and support. Perhaps it is not surprising that for many British people alive at the time this was seen as something of a golden age, notwithstanding our slow national decline relative to other European nations.

The years 1973 and 1974 really constituted something of a watershed in post-war British political history. Political consensus was severely disrupted by the events of those years, notably the international oil crisis which saw the world price of crude oil increase by nearly five times in the twelve months following the Yom Kippur War in October 1973 and the domestic confrontation between the Heath Administration and the National Union of Mineworkers during the first months of 1974 which precipitated the February 1974 General Election. The sage political talk was all about the alleged ungovernability of the United Kingdom.

The initial political reaction to these events was surprisingly muted in that following the February 1974 General Election the Labour Party under

Harold Wilson found itself returned to office with a tiny majority in the House of Commons, while the Conservative Opposition under Edward Heath was shellshocked and licking the wounds inflicted upon it not only by the trade unions and the Labour Party but also by the resurgent Liberals who had gained 19 per cent of the votes cast. Nevertheless the seeds had been sown for some fundamental rethinking not only by the Conservative Party about the nature and reasons for its shock defeat, but also by the Left wing of the Labour movement (both inside and outside the House of Commons) which had been effectively radicalised by the exhilarating experience of 'class warfare' in action. The net effect of these developments was that British politics began to polarise on sharply divided Left–Right lines.

Over the following fifteen years or so, this produced a revival of hard-edged economic and political ideology in both the main parties. The Labour Party lost the 1979 General Election following the shambles caused by the so-called 'Winter of Discontent' when the radicals in the trade unions once again struck against a Government-imposed incomes policy. Then a succession of Conservative Administrations under Margaret Thatcher became more radically free market in their approach as their confidence grew. This in turn contributed to the radicalisation and fragmentation of the Labour Party, with some members staying loyal to mainstream Labour policy, some promoting the Alternative Economic Strategy of the Hard Left, and the so-called 'Gang of Four' (Roy Jenkins, David Owen, Shirley Williams and Bill Rodgers) leading a group which broke away from the Labour Party and created a new Social Democrat Party which then formed an alliance with the Liberals for the 1983 General Election. Thus political polarisation and party fragmentation came to characterise British politics in the 1980s. Neither main party was immune from this virus, since even the Conservatives (with their tradition of party loyalty) suffered damaging splits between the so-called Wets and Dries (old-style and new-style Conservatives respectively) and later between the Europhiles and the Eurosceptics on the vexed issue of the extent of Britain's involvement in the process of European integration.

The mandate theory of government thrived as never before under Margaret Thatcher's leadership in the 1980s. This meant that the governing party claimed the right to impose all sorts of radical and unpopular policies upon the country (such as water privatisation or the poll tax) by dint of the fact that it had attracted about two-fifths of the votes cast or one-third of those qualified to vote at the previous General Election. It was argued by Left-inclining academic critics at the time that Thatcherite Conservatism had attained a 'political hegemony' in the United Kingdom to such an extent that all opposition within the Conservative Party was reduced to political impotence and a modernising faction within the Labour Party was persuaded by the facts of political life to adjust Labour's policies and image in a neo-Thatcherite direction.

The Conservative political hegemony at Westminster gave fresh impetus to the campaigns for devolution for Scotland and Wales as part of a much wider campaign for comprehensive constitutional reform. Under both Margaret Thatcher and John Major Conservatism was seen by its critics in local government and the peripheral parts of the United Kingdom as excessively English, centralist and Whitehall-dominated. These perceptions contributed strongly to a revived interest in 'constitutional' solutions to the problems caused by hegemonic one-party rule from Whitehall and Westminster.

In moving from a period of consensus to one of confrontation over a number of years, British politics also moved into a period of constitutional change and innovation. Some of the main lines of constitutional change, such as the strategic decision in 1971–72 to apply for membership of the European Communities and hence subject this country to the jurisdiction of European law, attracted all-party support and became a matter of dispute at least as much within parties as between them. However, it did mean that from 1st January 1973 onwards politicians in the United Kingdom had to face three new legal and constitutional problems.

Firstly, legal provision for UK membership of the European Communities (as the European Union was then called) had to be effected by passing an

Act of Parliament – the *1972 European Communities Act* – and not simply by constitutional amendment, as in Ireland. Thus the legal means of providing for permanent membership of the European Communities was the distinctly impermanent mechanism of an Act of Parliament which, by its very nature, could be amended or repealed at any time.

Secondly, the British attitude towards international law has always been essentially dualist, which means that national and international law are regarded as quite distinct, and international treaties cannot take legal effect in the United Kingdom without the essential enabling mechanism of an Act of Parliament. By contrast, in other European countries with codified constitutions, such as France or Germany, international treaties signed by their Ministers take precedence over national law and are automatically embodied within their national jurisprudence.[15]

Thirdly, the encroachment of European law directly challenges and appears to contradict the hallowed British constitutional principle of Parliamentary supremacy. In theory, this peculiarity of the British constitution means that Parliamentary supremacy and the primacy of European law in the areas of activity covered by the European treaties are fundamentally incompatible. In practice, the circle was squared by the rather casuistic doctrine contained in Section 2 (1) of the *1972 European Communities Act* which held that Parliament evidently *intended* that all other Acts of Parliament, whether before or after that Act, *should* be subordinate to European law in those areas of jurisdiction covered by the European treaties and open to interpretation by the European Court.

These constitutional problems might not have loomed so large in the course of subsequent British politics if it had not been for the simple fact that the final destiny of the European Union was gradually revealed to be the creation of a European state based upon a growing number of constituent 'nations' increasingly subject to the jurisdiction of a single European law. It was this essential prospect which was described in such vivid metaphor by Lord Denning as Master of the Rolls in 1979 when he referred to the threat from 'the flowing tide of

Community law' and warned that 'we have to learn to become amphibious if we wish to keep our heads above water'.[16] In other words, as long as successive British Governments and Parliaments have taken the view that British membership of the European Union is beneficial on balance to the interests of this country, the United Kingdom has been increasingly woven into the fabric of European law and has gradually lost much of its legal autonomy.

Throughout the 1980s and early 1990s Britain's membership of the European Community came to pose increasingly acute political and constitutional dilemmas. Margaret Thatcher had entered 10 Downing Street in 1979 determined to secure a substantial rebate for Britain's disproportionate contribution to the European Community Budget and by 1981, after two years of persistent negotiations and aided by the more diplomatic Lord Carrington as Foreign Secretary, this British goal was largely achieved. Yet scarcely was she able to relax before the European Community entered one of its periods of dynamic development under the guidance of the new President of the Commission, Jacques Delors. In no time at all the member states had agreed to establish a Single European Market by 1992, a momentous step involving further pooling of national sovereignty which, in the case of the United Kingdom, was incorporated into our domestic law via the *1986 Single European Act*. Although Margaret Thatcher would later claim that she was misled by her ministerial colleagues about the far-reaching consequences of this step, history already shows that it constituted the single biggest leap forward in European integration since the Six agreed to establish the European Coal and Steel Community in 1950. It meant the introduction of much more (albeit qualified) majority voting on all the policy issues connected with the creation of the Single Market and its implications for British national sovereignty were fundamental. Above all, it demonstrated a basic incompatibility between alleged national autonomy in economic decision making and free market economics at a European level.

The political and constitutional implications of the 1992 Treaty of Maastricht were probably even more far-reaching than those of the 1986 Single European Act. However, John Major and his Cabinet colleagues managed to negotiate an 'opt-out' from the Treaty clauses dealing with Economic and Monetary Union and an agreement to differ on the so-called Social Chapter of the Treaty. This meant that those clauses would not apply to the United Kingdom until it made a conscious decision to join. Thus in terms of the pooling of national sovereignty, this Treaty was not *immediately* as significant for the United Kingdom as the Single European Act, although in the longer run it is likely to have more far-reaching political and constitutional implications.

In 1997 the New Labour Government lifted the British reserve on participation in measures under the Social Chapter and adopted a *seemingly* more positive line on the desirability of British participation in Economic and Monetary Union. It will, however, be a momentous step to abolish the Pound and adopt the Euro as our currency in the United Kingdom and it is certain that Mr Blair and Mr Brown will not embark upon a referendum campaign to secure the endorsement of the British people for such a policy departure unless they feel confident of winning public support. Of all the big political decisions facing the British Government, Parliament and people over the coming years, those concerning the extent of Britain's participation in the next phases of European integration are likely to have the most significant constitutional implications.

It was as true of the Conservative Governments of the 1980s as it had been of Labour Governments in the 1960s and 1970s that some of their most important political projects had far-reaching constitutional effects, even if in the former case the leading Ministers of the period would never have admitted to having explicit objectives for constitutional reform. For example, Margaret Thatcher and her closest colleagues felt threatened by the most powerful public sector trade unions and by what the Conservative-supporting tabloids described as the 'loony Left' in local government and indeed within the Labour movement as a whole. One of their strategic objectives was therefore to emasculate these competing power centres

and they set out quite deliberately to do this with a three-pronged assault.

The first prong was represented by successive phases of legislation to curb the economic and political power of trade unions, notably the main legal immunities which they had enjoyed for about 80 years and which, when exercised in the public sector, had been able almost to bring the country to its knees.

The second prong was represented by the systematic legislative assault upon the powers and autonomy of local government. It has been calculated that at least 150 Acts of Parliament were put onto the Statute Book in the years between 1979 and 1997 which in one way or another were designed to diminsh or had the effect of diminishing the powers of local authorities.[17] The limiting case of this policy was the *1985 Local Government Act* which abolished the Greater London Council and six other Metropolitan County Councils essentially because their Labour leaders (notably Ken Livingstone at the GLC) used their local mandates directly to challenge the policies and priorities of the Conservative central Government.

The third prong was represented by legislation which cumulatively privatised at least two-thirds of the state industrial sector that the Conservatives had inherited from Labour in 1979. The overt aim was to reduce the size of the state and all its works, but the covert aim (at least initially) was to secure massive financial windfalls for the Exchequer and, to a lesser extent, for those who bought discounted shares in the newly privatised undertakings or exercised their rights as tenants to buy their Council accommodation at discounted prices. Along with this deliberate shrinking of the state went a programme of civil service reform that had as one of its most prominent features a steady reduction in the total number of civil servants, from more than 700,000 in 1979 to fewer than 500,000 in 1997.

Regardless of the merits or the demerits of these policies, the fact is that such powerful political drives provoked countervailing reactions from other parts of the political spectrum, including dissidents in the Conservative Party itself. After a while all these various critiques of Thatcherism tended to coalesce around one fundamental argument, namely that the Conservatives had proved to be excessive centralisers who sought to eliminate all opposition which lay in their path and who ignored the traditional checks and balances which had largely depended upon constitutional *conventions* rather than entrenched constitutional law. So thinking people turned their attention towards lobbying for fundamental constitutional reforms in the hope of making it much more difficult, if not impossible, for such things to happen in future.

One manifestation of this reaction was *Charter 88*, the multi-party and non-party campaign for thoroughgoing constitutional reform which began to attract extensive intellectual and political support in the late 1980s. It put forward a ten-point programme which called, among other things, for a new Bill of Rights, a truly independent and reformed judiciary, and proportional representation for elections to Parliament at Westminster. Subsequently, in 1995, the independent *Constitution Unit* was formed by Robert Hazell, a former Home Office official, and it has since provided a wide range of expert analysis and advice, focusing in an impartial way upon the problems arising in the implementation of constitutional change.

The fact of a Government which was simultaneously English, Conservative and London-based, and which had been in power at Westminster for a decade, was quite enough to convince even some doubtful Scottish and Welsh people that there was a powerful case for devolution. The Conservative Party, which tended to come a miserable fourth in most Scottish and Welsh elections and opinion polls, steadfastly refused to shift from its pro-Unionist position in defence of the United Kingdom. This Conservative attitude, on which John Major laid considerable stress during the 1992 General Election campaign, undoubtedly acted as a recruiting officer for the cause of devolution in the early 1990s.

Only in grappling with the age-old controversies in Northern Ireland did the Conservative Administrations led by Margaret Thatcher and John Major make conscious efforts to promote political and constitutional reform. In 1985 Margaret Thatcher was persuaded by her Cabinet colleagues and by the US Administration to conclude the *Anglo-Irish Agreement* which sought to enlist Dublin's co-operation in efforts to isolate the men of violence in the North in return for giving the Government south of the border more of a legitimate say in what was to become 'the peace process'. In December 1993 the two Prime Ministers, John Major and Albert Reynolds, signed the *Downing Street Declaration* which led to exploratory peace talks on Northern Ireland between officials in London and Dublin and between each of the Governments and representatives of the two traditions in Northern Ireland. These delicate negotiations bore fruit the following year with the announcement by the Provisional IRA of a ceasefire in August 1994, to be followed by further talks about talks at official level. Notwithstanding some further difficulties and terrorist outrages along the way, further progress was made which eventually paved the way for the *Belfast Agreement* on Good Friday in April 1998. This enabled the New Labour Government in London to join the Fianna Fail Government in Dublin and all the parties in Northern Ireland (with the exception of the Democratic Unionists) in creating a precarious peace for the troubled Province. Once this was blessed with weighty public support in referenda north and south of the border, the foundations were laid for elections to a new Northern Ireland Assembly and the creation of a power-sharing Executive in June 1998.

Perhaps one other area of constitutional initiative during the years of the Major Administration should be mentioned in this section: the compelling need which the Prime Minister felt to establish Committees of Inquiry (more than 60 in all during his time at 10 Downing Street), especially when he was faced with having to deal with various forms of scandal or sleaze associated with Conservative Ministers and MPs. The most publicised examples were the *Scott Inquiry* which was set up in 1992 and which reported in 1996, having examined in great detail all the events of the Matrix-Churchill Affair concerning the sale of defence-related equipment to Iraq in breach of a United Nations embargo and UK Government guidelines; and the *Nolan Inquiry* into Standards in Public Life which was established in October 1994 as a permanent body and which submitted its first Report in May 1995, making recommendations on how to deal with aberrant political behaviour, such as MPs taking cash for asking Parliamentary Questions and other forms of corruption mainly associated with Conservative MPs and Ministers.

The constitutional significance of these developments was really twofold. *Firstly*, the political and media conclusions drawn from these tawdry and disreputable events were that Parliament in general and individual MPs in particular could no longer be trusted to regulate themselves as they had done for centuries past. *Secondly*, the institutional mechanisms and procedures recommended to deal with any recurrence of such problems provided further examples of the ways in which an allegedly supreme Parliament was losing power to commissioners, judges and other extra-Parliamentary decision makers in an increasingly unrestrained society. In these circumstances our traditional constitutional arrangements were becoming increasingly ineffective and even irrelevant and would need to be reformed by the first Government that had the courage and Parliamentary authority to do so.

With New Labour into a new Britain

By the time the Labour Party was swept into power following its landslide General Election victory in May 1997, it had persuaded the British people that it had become a safe alternative to the terminally discredited Conservatives. Tony Blair had insisted upon keeping Labour's policy commitments to a minimum in order not to frighten 'middle England' in the way that the party had done under Michael Foot in 1983 and, to a lesser extent, under Neil Kinnock in 1987 and 1992.

The idea of *modernisation* had been a key theme for New Labour in Opposition and it seemed logical to Tony Blair and his closest advisers to present modernisation in government as a natural development of the earlier modernisation of the Labour Party which had begun under Neil Kinnock and continued under John Smith. For New Labour, the idea of modernisation was to be applied to the way

in which the country was governed as much as to the policies which would be pursued in office. Indeed, Tony Blair had made this clear in his 1996 John Smith Memorial Lecture when he said: 'I do not regard changing the way we are governed as an afterthought, a detailed fragment of our programme – I regard it as an essential part of the new Britain, of us becoming a young confident country again'.[18]

With such fine declaratory statements ringing in their ears, politicians, academics and media commentators should not have been surprised when the New Labour Government embarked upon an ambitious programme of constitutional legislation in the first session of the Parliament. Twelve constitutional Bills were introduced in that time and all but the European Parliamentary Elections Bill became the law of the land during the first long session of Parliament. See *Box 1* for a list of Labour's main consitutional measures, 1997–2001.

The most significant items were the *1998 Scotland Act*, the *1998 Government of Wales Act* and the *1998 Northern Ireland Act*, which provided the statutory basis for devolution to each of those parts of the United Kingdom. We should also mention in this category the *1998 European Communities (Amendment) Act* which served to build the 1997 Amsterdam Treaty into UK domestic law, the *1998 Bank of England Act* which gave operational (but not policy) independence to the Bank of England in the conduct of British monetary policy, and the *1998 Human Rights Act* which made the 1951 European Convention on Human Rights justiciable in British courts with effect from October 2000.

The legislative items of a more technical nature were the *1997 Referendums (Scotland and Wales) Act* which authorised devolution referenda to be held in each of those parts of the United Kingdom (on this occasion *before* rather than after the Westminster Parliament dealt with the legislation), the *1998 Northern Ireland (Elections) Act* which provided for elections to the proposed Northern Ireland Assembly, and the *1998 Regional Development Agencies Act* which provided for the establishment of these executive bodies in each of the eight planning regions of England outside

Box 1 Labour's main constitutional measures, 1997–2001

- Referendums (Scotland and Wales) Act 1997
- Scotland Act 1998
- Government of Wales Act 1998
- European Communities Amendment Act 1998
- Bank of England Act 1998
- Human Rights Act 1998
- Northern Ireland (Elections) Act 1998
- Regional Development Agencies Act 1998
- Greater London Authority Referendum Act 1998
- Registration of Political Parties Act 1998
- European Parliament Elections Act 1998
- Freedom of Information Act 2000
- Local Government Act 2000
- Political Parties, Elections and Referendums Act 2000

to constitutional reform.[19] He began by pointing out that during Labour's long years in Opposition a number of constitutional problems had been clearly identified. Among these were a national Government that was over-centralised, a structure of local government in need of reform, excessive official secrecy, a lack of clarity about individual rights and deficient means of enforcing them, the House of Commons in need of modernisation and the House of Lords anachronistically dominated by an in-built Conservative majority based upon hereditary peers, a nation that was sidelined in Europe when it should have benefited from decisive and committed leadership in that context, and what he described rather apocalyptically as 'a national crisis of confidence in the political system'. Against that background the measures which were being introduced had two things in common: *firstly*, they were the product of long-standing dissatisfaction with constitutional practice in relation to particular issues which in some cases dated back more than a century (e.g. the need to remove the hereditary peers from the House of Lords); *secondly*, they were essentially incremental and constituted logical developments of earlier reforms under previous Governments of both parties.

The Government's overall aim in its constitutional reform programme was 'to develop a maturer democracy with different centres of power, where individuals enjoy greater rights and where government is carried out closer to the people'. The unifying theme of all the measures was *principled pragmatism* based upon a belief that what matters is what works and that there was no point in seeking to impose uniformity for uniformity's sake. Such problems needed to be tackled across a broad front and no single blueprint for change would suffice. In order to achieve its constitutional reform objectives, the Government also needed to achieve a number of supporting objectives: *institutional change* to both Houses of Parliament and to the system of government itself; *changes in the law* to establish a clear framework of rights and ensure greater openness and transparency in the activities of government; *adjustments to the electoral systems* 'to ensure that the central democratic act [voting] occurred on a basis reflecting a consensus of what

London (Scotland, Wales and Northern Ireland having had the benefit of such Development Agencies for many years). Other items in this category were the *1998 Greater London Authority Referendum Act* which provided for a referendum to be held to establish whether or not Londoners wanted to have a democratic contest for an elected Mayor, the *1998 Registration of Political Parties Act* which for the first time made the political parties in the United Kingdom subject to statutory regulation and formally recognised in public law, and the *1998 European Parliamentary Elections Act* which, after much wrangling between the Commons and the Lords, introduced a proportional voting system on the basis of closed regional lists for European Parliament elections.

This large corpus of reform introduced in the first session of the Parliament prompted Lord Irvine, the Lord Chancellor, to take an opportunity provided by the Constitution Unit in December 1998 to set out the Government's general approach is fair'; and *changes in political and administrative culture* notably by moving from 'a bureaucratic, centralised and closed system to one permeated by a culture of rights, openness and accountability'.

Throughout his long speech Lord Irvine adopted a surprisingly defensive tone as if he were constantly expecting the Government to be attacked by academics, pressure groups and the media for the incoherence of its constitutional reform policy. In an attempt to put the essence of his argument in a single sentence, he said: 'our objective is to put in place an integrated programme of measures to decentralise power in the United Kingdom, and to enhance the rights of individuals within a more open society'. At least this statement provides a few benchmarks by which it should be possible to judge the effects of Labour's constitutional reforms at the end of two or three Parliaments.

In a different but complementary speech in 1999 the then Home Secretary, Jack Straw, sought to put his mark on the same territory and chose a rather different emphasis from that of the Lord Chancellor.[20] He maintained that the principal aim of the policy was to create a new constitutional relationship between the citizen and the state, and to change the social culture to one in which rights were balanced with responsibilities. Mr Straw particularly commended the *1998 Human Rights Act* and the Freedom of Information Bill which his Department was then responsible for piloting onto the Statute Book. He also argued that the Government's devolution policy, its reforms of local government and its modernisation of electoral arrangements were all intended to revitalise British democracy.

General reflections

The history of constitutional change in the United Kingdom can be traced through the evolution of *sovereignty* over a long period from Elizabeth I to Elizabeth II. The *Concise Oxford Dictionary* (tenth edition) defines sovereignty as 'supreme power or authority', a laconic definition which underlines what a difficult concept it can be to pin down. If it is equated principally with supremacy (constitu-tional, legal and political) within a single state or political entity, we can see how it resided with the *personal* sovereignty of the Monarch in the time of Elizabeth I and the first two Stuart Kings, but passed to the *representative* sovereignty of both Houses of Parliament at the time of the Glorious Revolution and later to the *democratic* sovereignty of the people from about 1945 onwards.

It is something of an irony that only a few years after the British people finally began to assert their unchallenged sovereignty, successive Governments with the (often reluctant) support of Parliament began to give away, or at least to pool, some of our national sovereignty to supra-national institutions such as NATO and the European Community. This tendency has continued apace in the modern world, for example with Britain's membership of the World Trade Organisation and the Government's support for the idea of creating an International Criminal Court – not to mention the many undeclared concessions of national sovereignty to multi-national companies, media conglomerates and financial institutions.

In theory, these concessions of sovereignty have never been accepted as final or irreversible by many politicians and constitutional theorists in the United Kingdom, because of the tenacious doctrine of Parliamentary supremacy and the democratic theory that no representatives of the people have a right to alienate national sovereignty which ultimately belongs to the people. Even when a Parliamentary decision of great significance, such as the decision to enter the European Community in the early 1970s, is subsequently ratified in a national referendum, British constitutional theory holds that the electorate is perfectly entitled to overturn one of its own previous decisions, just as Parliament need not feel bound by the decisions, however final in intent, of its predecessors. In other words, when it is argued that Parliamentary supremacy remains intact in the United Kingdom, what this really means is that it is impossible to take away from the people the ultimate right to govern themselves, since in the end MPs are no more and no less than temporary representatives of the people.

In practice, there have been four main phases in the long historical build-up to the recent constitutional changes in the United Kingdom. First, there was government by *divine right* under the Tudors and early Stuarts. Then this was transformed during the century of revolution into *constitutional Monarchy* which, in formal terms, remains an accurate description of the United Kingdom to this day. Then we evolved into government by *Parliamentary supremacy*, which really came to mean the supremacy of the Government of the day supported by a working majority in the Commons. Today we live in *a dynamic mixed polity* in which sovereignty is shared between a considerable number of more or less legitimate stakeholders: Parliament and the general public, the media and the markets, bureaucrats and pressure groups, sub-national and supra-national institutions, financiers and judges, and even some of those in non-governmental organisations who exert temporarily decisive influence or force at any rate in relation to single issues.

The contemporary reality is that the United Kingdom is constitutionally only one example (but an important and influential one) of the species of *nation state* of which there are now about 190 belonging to the United Nations. It exists in a precarious and ever changing balance with other nation states and supra-national and sub-national institutions, all competing for the available opportunities in the world. Its current constitutional arrangements, which have been considerably influenced by history, exist to rationalise, order and control an unsettled political situation. Consequently, they need to be dynamic, flexible, responsive to internal developments and open to influence from the outside world. It seems that they satisfy the first three criteria quite well, but there remain some doubts about the fourth because of the insularity and complacency which still characterise many of our national instincts and traditions.

Questions for discussion

1 To what extent are current constitutional arrangements in the United Kingdom a legacy of the past?

2 'A twenty-first-century society with nineteenth-century institutions'. Discuss this interpretation of the United Kingdom today.

3 The idea of national sovereignty can be traced back at least to Tudor times in this country. How meaningful is it in our contemporary world?

Notes

1 See Christopher Hill, *The Century of Revolution, 1603–1714*, Nelson, Edinburgh, 1961.

2 *Ibid*; p. 131. It should be noted that Gerrard Winstanley, speaking for the Diggers at this time, put forward the much more radical idea that the franchise should not be confined to 'free men', but extended to all adults – including landless labourers, servants and women. Such political discourse was way ahead of its time and foreshadowed the doctrine of communism which was to be developed by Marx and Engels in the nineteenth century.

3 The main statutes in this category were: the *1689 Toleration Act* which allowed religious dissenters freedom of worship but denied them the right to public office or a seat in Parliament; the *1694 Triennial Act* which required that Parliament be summoned by the Monarch at least every three years; the *1694 Bank of England Act* which meant that both the Government and the people could borrow at lower interest rates than before and which made it attractive for the emerging capitalist class to lend money to the Government on profitable terms; the *1701 Act of Settlement* which ordained that in the event of Queen Anne having no heirs, the Crown would pass to the House of Hanover, specifically the descendants of James II's daughter Elizabeth and her husband, the Elector Palatine; and the *1707 Act of Union* which (along with a parallel Act of the Scottish Parliament) constitutionally united Scotland with England under a single Parliament of Great Britain.

4 D.L. Keir, *The Constitutional History of Modern Britain, 1485–1951*, 5th edn, Black, London, 1953; p. 289.

5 Linda Colley, *Britons – Forging the Nation, 1707–1837*; Pimlico, London, 1994; p. 5.

6 D.L. Keir, *op. cit.*; p. 292.

7 One measure of this was the fact that between 1798–1800 and 1826–31 the number of Petitions to Parliament increased twentyfold – see Cecil Emden, *The People and the Constitution*; 2nd edn, Clarendon Press, Oxford, 1956; p. 77.

8 Jeremy Bentham had first turned his mind to

Parliamentary reform in 1809 when he published his *Catechism*, which insisted upon probity, intellectual aptitude and active talent as the necessary qualifications for Members of Parliament. In 1817 he published his *Plan for Parliamentary Reform* and in 1819 a draft *Radical Reform Bill*. In the latter, he stated the four key principles which should govern a reformed Parliament: 'secret, universal, equal and annual suffrage'. Typically for the time, his second principle excluded from the franchise women, children, lunatics and criminals in prison. See J.R.M. Butler, *Passing of the Great Reform Bill*; Longmans Green, London, 1914; pp. 29–30.

9 D.L. Keir, *op. cit.*; p. 404.
10 See Asa Briggs, *A Social History of England*; 2nd edn, Penguin, London, 1987; p. 288.
11 The catalogue of great 'improving' Acts of Parliament included: the 1834 Poor Law Amendment Act, the 1835 Municipal Corporations Act, the Factory Acts of 1833, 1847 and 1901, the Public Health Acts of 1848 and 1869, the Education Acts of 1870 and 1902, the 1908 Pensions Act, the 1909 Finance Act and the 1911 National Insurance Act.
12 A. Briggs, *op. cit.*; p. 271.
13 According to a Domesday Survey of 1873, four-fifths of English land was held by only 7,000 people, with peers prominently represented among this number.
14 The two occasions between 1911 and 1939 on which the Parliament Act 1911 had to be invoked were to secure the passage through Parliament of the 1914 Irish Home Rule Act and the 1914 Welsh Disestablishment Act, both of which statutes were not put into effect until after the First World War.
15 This theoretical difference between the United Kingdom and its European partners has diminished in practice over the years. For example, President Mitterrand decided to submit the 1992 Maastricht Treaty for the approval of the French people in a national referendum (and very nearly lost it), while in Germany the same treaty had to secure a favourable opinion from the Federal Constitutional Court before it could be ratified by both Houses of the German Parliament.

16 See *Shields v. E. Coombes (Holdings) Ltd* (1979) 1 All ER 456, 461–2.
17 F.N. Forman and N.D.J. Baldwin, *Mastering British Politics*; 4th edn, Macmillan, Basingstoke, 1999; p. 423.
18 Quoted in V. Bogdanor, *Power and the People*; Victor Gollancz, London, 1997; p. 14.
19 See the first annual Constitution Unit lecture given by the Lord Chancellor, Lord Irvine, at Church House, Westminster on 8th December 1998.
20 See the second annual Constitution Unit lecture given by the Home Secretary, Jack Straw, at Church House, Westminster, on 27th October 1999.

Further reading

Vernon Bogdanor, *Power and the People*; Gollancz, London, 1997.
Asa Briggs, *A Social History of England*; Penguin, London, 1987.
J.R.M. Butler, *The Passing of the Great Reform Bill*; Longmans, London, 1914.
Linda Colley, *Britons – Forging the Nation, 1707–1837*; Pimlico, London, 1994.
Cecil Emden, *The People and the Constitution*; Clarendon Press, Oxford, 1956.
Christopher Hibbert, *The English – a Social History, 1066–1945*; Guild Publishing, London, 1987.
Christopher Hill, *The Century of Revolution, 1603–1714*; Nelson, Edinburgh, 1961.
Nevil Johnson, *In Search of the Constitution*; Methuen, London, 1980.
David Lindsay Keir, *The Constitutional History of Modern Britain, 1485–1951*; Black, London, 1953.
Andrew Marr, *Ruling Britannia: the Failure and Future of British Democracy*; Michael Joseph, London, 1995.
Ferdinand Mount, *The British Constitution Now*; Mandarin, London, 1993.

Part II

ISSUES OF IDENTITY AND TERRITORY

Chapter 2

Nationalism and devolution

The historical influence of nationalism

The origins of the United Kingdom as a multi-national polity can be traced back at least to the battle of Bosworth Field in 1485 when Henry Tudor (a Welsh warlord) defeated King Richard III and seized the throne of England which was to be retained for over a century by his Tudor dynasty. At the behest of his son, Henry VIII, the English Parliament endorsed royal authority over the whole of Wales in an Act of 1536 which laid down the general terms of the Union between England and Wales, and which provided for Wales to send Members to Parliament at Westminster for the first time since the days of Edward II. This paved the way for a subsequent Act in 1543 which provided in some detail for the political assimilation of Wales into the Union with England and divided the principality into twelve Counties.

If England and Wales were originally united by Acts of Parliament which ratified previous military action, England and Scotland were united by dynastic union in 1603 following the death of Queen Elizabeth I when James VI of Scotland (the son of Mary Queen of Scots) succeeded to the throne as James I of England, thereby creating another dimension of the United Kingdom. This dynastic Union did not immediately produce a unitary state, not least because both James I and his son Charles I ruled autocratically without Parliament for long periods of their reigns. Indeed, from the very beginning of the United Kingdom to this day the Scots have retained their own legal system, their own church and their distinctive intellectual traditions; so it is hard to argue that either in 1603 or in 1688–89, when the Westminster Parliament offered the throne which had been deserted by James II to William of Orange and his wife Princess Mary, did the United Kingdom become a single British nation. As Linda Colley has so persuasively argued, the British nation was forged over a much longer period of time between the *1707 Acts of Union* which linked England, Wales and Scotland under one Parliament at Westminster and the beginning of the Victorian age in 1837.[1]

The historical relationship between Ireland and England (and later between Ireland and the rest of the United Kingdom) has been troubled and contradictory from the very beginning to the present day. The first systematic attempts to subjugate the Irish were made by the French-speaking Normans in the twelfth century under the reign of Henry II. Gradually over the centuries which followed, a hierarchy of feudal obligations to the English Monarchy was created and consolidated in Ireland, although the actual extent of effective English authority was usually confined to a relatively small geographical area around Dublin known as 'the Pale'. It was not until 1541, when Henry VIII had himself proclaimed 'King of this land of Ireland as united, annexed and knit forever to the Imperial Crown of the realm of England', and not until the end of his reign a few years later when the Fitzpatricks and other Irish warlords finally submitted to English sovereignty, that English power and administration ultimately controlled from London could be said to have been established in Ireland.[2]

Even ruthless Tudor rule of Ireland was always more precarious and ambiguous than its equivalent in Wales, and such a project was never really attempted by the English in Scotland. Violent conflict between the uncompromising Tudors and the chaotic Gaelic chieftains of Ireland was endemic for many years, even though the latter were encouraged to surrender title of their lands to the English Monarch prior to being granted a lease to occupy and work their lands. Failing this 'peaceful' kind of settlement, the Tudors, the Stuarts and Oliver Cromwell were all in the habit of suppressing Irish rebellions and then confiscating rebel lands. Such land could not just be left unattended, so in the sixteenth and seventeenth centuries it was extensively and repeatedly 'planted' by English and Scottish settlers who were invariably militant Protestants or Presbyterians. Yet even on the huge estates which had been confiscated from the Catholic Irish, the Protestant planters remained an embattled and often paranoid minority in a largely Catholic country.

In the English mind there has been an easy and long-standing confusion between the separate concepts of 'kingdom', 'state' and 'nation', such that many people have found it hard to pinpoint unambiguously those occasions on which the United Kingdom became a state and the state itself became a self-conscious nation. What we can say with a reasonable degree of certainty with regard to the post-medieval, modern period is that the Monarchy of England became the United Kingdom of England and Wales by an Act of Union in 1536 under Henry VIII, the United Kingdom of England, Wales and Scotland by Acts of Union in 1707 under Queen Anne, and the United Kingdom of England, Wales, Scotland and Ireland by an Act of Union in 1800 in the reign of George III. *The unitary state* later known as the United Kingdom was recognisably in existence in Tudor times, notably by the reign of Elizabeth I when the House of Commons came into its own by providing essential support for the Queen's government through its willingness to raise money for the state, as long as the Monarch and her Ministers took heed of the interests and views of the representatives of the people. However, a sense of *British nationhood* took much longer to emerge, since it had to be forged on the anvil of successive wars against Spain, Holland and France and successive imperial conquests which became truly impressive in the eighteenth century – all symbolically reinforced by widespread and heartfelt commitment to constitutional Monarchy, Parliamentary supremacy and, to a diminishing extent, the established Anglican Church.

Perhaps it should not be thought surprising that political nationalism first made itself felt as an influence within the United Kingdom in the various parts of the Celtic fringe as an understandable reaction to perceived English arrogance and political domination of the British Isles. English nationalism, on the other hand, was forged only partly in opposition to the other nations and peoples of the British Isles, but mainly in often lengthy and repeated wars against rival powers on the Continent of Europe – originally against France for control of disputed territory on the European mainland during the fourteenth and fifteenth centuries, and later against Spain and Holland for control of trade routes and the high seas in the sixteenth and seventeenth centuries. The sense of nationalism felt by the various non-English minorities in the United Kingdom became a matter of self-conscious identity, which was sometimes *passive* in that it provided a self-ascriptive answer to questions about who these different peoples thought they were; and sometimes *active* in that it motivated some of them to join nationalist political movements and, in extreme cases, clandestine groups which used terrorist methods and believed in direct action to support their nationalist causes. Whether active or passive, such nationalisms could legitimately be considered as something more than 'local patriotisms' and were often inspired by the noble motives of charismatic individuals who wanted to free their nations from perceived English domination and oppression.

With this historical background in mind, it is possible to discern an important common theme in the way that the English (the dominant partner in all 'international' relations within the UK) approached each of the three historic occasions on which it seemed expedient and desirable to the rulers in London to conclude an Act of Union with one of the other nations within the United Kingdom. The common theme was undoubtedly the imperative of guaranteeing *English security* in times of war against France and active hostility towards the threat of continental Catholicism. In this sense, it can be said that France has done more than any other single nation to provoke a specifically *British national interest*, which led the English at decisive moments in their history to show real magnanimity towards their national neighbours in the British Isles and which led their weaker partners to conclude that they had more to gain than to lose from the Union with England. Thus with the *1536 and 1543 Acts of Union with Wales* Henry VIII and the English Parliament essentially decided to secure England's rear at a time when the country was at war with France and at odds with the Papacy over the English Reformation. In the case of the *1707 Acts of Union with Scotland*, the British Parliament essentially decided that it was vital to secure England's northern flank at a time when the nation was once again at war with France – on this occasion with the Catholic despotism of Louis XIV. In the case of the *1800*

Act of Union with Ireland, Pitt the Younger and the British Parliament resolved to secure Great Britain's western flank against the real threat of a French invasion launched from Irish soil.

Differing political responses at Westminster

The long but intermittent process of achieving complete political integration throughout the United Kingdom over the course of at least 500 years was driven more by a sense of strategic necessity and political expediency than by constitutional principle or ideological conviction. It might, therefore, be argued that today the English (principally) and the other nationals who inhabit the British Isles need not stand in the way of the gradual disintegration of the United Kingdom into its main component parts now that such a process of reverse engineering seems unlikely to pose any significant threats to the people's security or well-being. Yet it is clear that this is not, by and large, the view held by the political class at Westminster or by their clienteles in the various UK-wide political organisations. Indeed, it is obvious that over the last 40 years or so senior Labour (and Liberal) politicians have felt threatened in their Celtic strongholds by the rise of political nationalism in Scotland and Wales, while senior Conservative (and Unionist) politicians have strongly opposed all the nationalist political forces which seemed to threaten the proud achievement of a politically integrated United Kingdom.

While identifying non-English nationalism as a fairly constant and ostensibly growing threat to the integrity of the United Kingdom, it is important to stress that it has not been the same phenomenon in all three cases. In Ireland there was always majority support for the cause of Irish nationalism (except in Northern Ireland from 1921), whereas in Scotland and Wales nationalist parties have never gathered more than 30 per cent of the votes cast at a General Election (the level of support achieved by the SNP in October 1974). Moreover, the long campaign for Irish independence was punctuated by violence and terrorism, whereas with a few notable but minor exceptions Scottish and Welsh

nationalists have always used lawful, democratic methods to advance their cause. For their part, the three main political parties, when in Government at UK level, have responded to the various forms of Celtic nationalism in very different ways, and we should note in passing that neither the Labour Party nor the Conservative Party has been monolithic or undivided in its responses to these challenges over the years. Reviewed historically over a period of more than a century, the Liberal Administrations of Gladstone in the late nineteenth century and Asquith in the early twentieth century favoured the policy of devolution (or Home Rule, as it was then called) and sought to apply it particularly to the pathological case of relations between Ireland and the rest of the UK; subsequent Labour Administrations under Harold Wilson and James Callaghan in the 1960s and 1970s and under Tony Blair since 1997 have favoured the same broad policy, although primarily in response to nationalist aspirations in Scotland and Wales.

Mainstream Conservative policy, on the other hand, has been based upon repeated English assertions of the value and integrity of the United Kingdom and the perils of even suggesting any policy of concessions to the nationalists in the non-English parts of the UK on the grounds that this would disadvantage English MPs and their constituents (the so-called West Lothian Question) and eventually lead to the disintegration of the United Kingdom which has been so painfully and laboriously constructed over many centuries with a mixture of brutality, guile and sacrifice. Indeed, in the eyes of many MPs in the modern Conservative Party, the dangers of devolution are writ even larger when seen alongside the perceived threat from the supra-national institutions of the European Union in Brussels, Luxembourg and Strasbourg to the well-being and perhaps even survival of British political institutions – notably their own power base, Parliament at Westminster.[3]

Just as measures of devolution have not been seen as a sustainable or safe solution to the problems of non-English nationalism by some members of the political class at Westminster in both the two largest parties, so they have been exploited by the smaller parties (with the exception of the various factions of Ulster Unionists) as a staging-post on the way either to a federal future for the UK (a Liberal goal) or to various forms of national independence for Scotland and Wales, and possibly eventual national reunification for Ireland. There is therefore an obvious ambiguity about the devolution policy which means that it can be susceptible to at least two contrasting interpretations which have been put forward with equal vehemence from time to time both within and between the parties at Westminster and in the country at large. Indeed, there is also a third view which holds that devolution, when fully implemented, will not make much difference to the constituent parts of the UK or to the polity as a whole; but this view is coming to seem increasingly untenable as the empirical evidence accumulates of the dynamic political consequences of embarking upon this road in the first place.

One of the most authoritative and concise definitions of devolution as it has been introduced in the United Kingdom was provided by Vernon Bogdanor, who defined it as 'the transfer to a subordinate elected body, on a geographical basis, of functions at present exercised by Ministers and Parliament'.[4] This makes it clear that devolution in the British context has some rather precise and carefully calculated characteristics which have been designed by Ministers and officials in London to achieve only limited political objectives. Yet before we go on to consider in more detail what these characteristics and objectives are in relation to each of the distinctive nations within the UK, we need to stand back a bit and review the main strategic options which have been in the minds of English and non-English political decision makers alike when addressing the phenomenon of nationalism in the UK – seeing it either as an opportunity or as a problem, depending upon their political priorities at the time.

Options for the various nationalities

The options available for *non-English nationals* in the United Kingdom have been broadly four over a long period of time. Firstly, they could accept the *evolved multi-national integration* which grew out of centuries of gradual assimilation of the Welsh, the Scots and the Irish into the British political system and British political culture. Essentially, this entailed having direct representation in Parliament at Westminster and thus sharing on equal terms with the peoples of all the other parts of the UK the legal rights and duties of British subjects. It also entailed learning to use the English language, being free to integrate fully into the larger British economy and society, and in many cases fighting and dying for the English cause in wars against 'foreigners'.

Secondly, they could exert pressure upon successive UK Governments and Parliaments in attempts to persuade them to introduce *administrative or legislative devolution* to Ireland, Scotland and Wales (or Home Rule as it was called in the nineteenth and early twentieth centuries). In the 1880s, when Irish Nationalists held more than four-fifths of all the Irish seats at Westminster, this entailed the use of Parliamentary filibusters and other obstructionist tactics in order to dramatise the growing popular dissatisfaction in Ireland with the inability of Gladstone's Administrations and the unwillingness of Conservative and Unionist Administrations to deliver Irish self-government for Irish affairs. In the 1960s and 1970s, when the Welsh and Scottish Nationalist parties revived as political forces and began to win occasional Parliamentary by-elections, it entailed raising the profile of nationalism in each of those parts of the UK and thus making political life increasingly difficult for the Labour and Liberal parties, both of which enjoyed disproportionate political strength in Scotland and Wales. In the 1980s, when the forces of English Thatcherite Conservatism were politically dominant at Westminster and most people in the outlying parts of the United Kingdom (including the far north and west of England) felt excluded and ignored, it entailed banding together with all other like-minded parties and with non-partisan interests to campaign for an overall programme of constitutional reform in which the policy of devolution occupied a prominent place.

Thirdly, they could campaign for *a confederal or federal structure* to be imposed upon the United Kingdom by Act of Parliament, presumably with the endorsement of a majority of the people in a UK referendum. This line of argument has been associated for a long time with the Liberal Party which itself is organised on federal lines. It also represented one of the main planks in the platform of overall constitutional reform put forward by Charter 88 in the late 1980s and early 1990s. Indeed, since the Treaty of Amsterdam in 1997 there has been gathering intellectual force behind the argument that the interests of good governance would be well served by the development of a federal United Kingdom within a federal European Union. It is worth noting that the key novelty (and difficulty) in adopting this option would be that it would probably require the dismantlement of England into eight or nine political regions, each with its own legislative or administrative autonomy. There have even been some who are relaxed about the idea of an 'international federation' of England, Scotland and Wales, although Northern Ireland has always seemed to merit separate constitutional treatment from the rest of the United Kingdom. While the English as a whole have never been persuaded of the need for federalism in their own country, the non-English have realised that this would complicate and delay their chances of achieving devolution or eventually independence for their own particular parts of the United Kingdom.

Fourthly, they could campaign and agitate for *sovereign independence* for Scotland, Wales and Northern Ireland respectively, although in the last case the suspicion must remain that this would produce a sub-optimal political entity, much less satisfactory than the inherited option of devolving power to the one remaining part of Ireland still under British sovereignty. In twenty-first-century political conditions, the main attraction of sovereign independence for all ardent non-English nationalists is that they can now present it more reassuringly than before as Scottish or Welsh or Northern Irish independence *within the European Union* – i.e. as potential member states comparable in population with Luxembourg, Ireland, Finland

or Denmark. It may, however, be said that the desirability of this option is rather doubtful, because there are already a large number of small states in the world and it is by no means clear that gratuitously adding to their number would improve the governance of the European Union (or indeed the United Nations) whose procedures are already overloaded with having to meet the political expectations of the smaller member states.

Broadly, there have been only four main options available for *English nationals* in the United Kingdom over many years. The first, which may seem to some observers to be increasingly untenable in the modern world, is the almost heroic option of clinging tenaciously to the idea of *Parliamentary supremacy within a unitary state* and enforcing it rigorously with all the legal and constitutional weaponry at the disposal of Whitehall and Westminster. Some might say that this was the habitual approach of Margaret Thatcher during her years as Prime Minister and, with the notable exceptions of the *1985 Anglo-Irish Agreement* and the *1986 Single European Act*, it could be presented as a fair description of her attitude and practice towards any institutions or popular movements which mounted a serious challenge to her belief that British (read English) Parliamentary sovereignty was inalienable. Incredibly, however, Margaret Thatcher later maintained in her *Memoirs* that she had been misled by her Ministerial colleagues about the full implications of these measures. In the case of Ireland, she affected to believe that the 1985 Agreement was simply a way of enhancing cross-border cooperation against IRA terrorism. In the case of Europe, she appears to have been so seduced by the liberalising economic agenda of the Single Market programme that she forbore from raising objections to the necessary increases in qualified majority voting which had the effect of reducing the autonomy of each of the member states in the sectors of economic activity covered by the Single European Act.

What these two examples underline is the fact that untrammelled nationalism may be asserted but cannot be made completely effective for any nation, large or small, in the modern world. This is because the global media and global markets can exert formidable countervailing power, while the huge trans-national companies and interest groups can wield more economic clout than all but the largest and most powerful nation states. Moreover, this binding of Leviathan is equally manifest in the likely inability of any UK Government, now or in the future, to reverse the growth of non-English nationalisms – indeed, the harder that Whitehall and Westminster might try to do such a thing, the more likely it would be that their actions would merely act as recruiting officers for whichever nationalist cause was seen to be under the English cosh. The only response from the authorities in London which is likely to be effective is to kill with kindness the forces of non-English nationalism and even that strategy is unlikely to be able to compete with the political effects of rising nationalist expectations which will probably outrun what is deliverable at any time.

The second option is gracefully *to accept devolution* to Scotland, Wales and Northern Ireland as accomplished facts and to begin developing new laws and conventions capable of keeping the driving forces within reasonable bounds, so that even in the fullness of time there emerges no serious threat to the very integrity of the United Kingdom. This option is a counsel of realism for English (Tory) politicians, since it is firmly based upon an intelligent recognition of the 'political impossibility' of reversing the constitutional changes introduced by the 1998 Westminster legislation. It would only be if the policy of devolution were to become a massive disappointment *in practice* for the Scots, the Welsh or the Northern Irish that an opportunity might arise for a future Government in London to claw back the powers already devolved to Edinburgh, Cardiff and Belfast. Even then it might be that the general conclusions drawn from the perceived 'failure' of devolution were that the policy had been too cautious and timid rather than too reckless and bold. In such circumstances the political pressures might be for a push towards some form of federalism in the UK or even formal independence for one or more of the constituent nations rather than any return to the arrangements which applied before devolution.

The third option is to make deliberate moves towards either *confederal or federal arrangements* for the entire United Kingdom including, of course, England, which has long seemed like the 'cuckoo in the nest', apparently determined to marginalise (or even kill) all the other smaller and weaker chicks. To make such far-reaching changes work, it would probably be necessary to break England up into perhaps eight or nine regional political and administrative units each with its own Executive and structure of democratic representation in the form of directly or indirectly elected regional Assemblies. A regionalised United Kingdom of this kind would be compatible with the present devolved arrangements for Scotland, Wales and (query) Northern Ireland; but it would certainly leave the national Government in Whitehall with much less to do and the national Parliament at Westminster with much less to do if these powers were genuinely dispersed to future regional 'states' in England.[5]

The fourth option for the English people and their elected representatives in Parliament at Westminster may one day be to acquiesce in the achievement of *sovereign national independence* by Scotland, Wales and (query) Northern Ireland, thus implicitly tolerating the disintegration of the United Kingdom. This is probably regarded as the dooms-day scenario by virtually all members of our national political class who now pursue their political vocation in Whitehall and Westminster. Yet they should acknowledge that a very large number of ordinary people in all parts of the UK – especially in England where tax-payers contribute disproportionately to transfer payments which favour Scotland and Northern Ireland (but not Wales) at the expense of even the poorer parts of England – might be quite content to negotiate a formal divorce from such 'partners' if it meant that there was no longer any housekeeping or alimony to be paid.[6] Indeed, it is likely that if this radical scenario ever came to pass, the current drive towards more pronounced regional identities within England – whether focused upon an emergent city-state like Birmingham or the revival of a traditional pole of allegiance such as Cornwall – would seem less compelling, especially if the achievement of greater financial self-reliance and a constant process of economic competition with their counterparts were also involved. Moreover, a unitary England of about 50 million people would be well able to defend its national interests and hold its own as a major player within the European Union, whereas each of the regional entities in a Balkanised England would fare much less well, lacking both the territorial coherence and political clout of an independent Scotland, Wales or even Northern Ireland.

The main point of this section has been to emphasise that without the spur of nationalism in the non-English parts of the United Kingdom, successive UK Governments in both the nineteenth and the twentieth centuries would almost certainly *not* have sought to legislate for devolution or Home Rule. This is essentially because the long-term trend towards the construction of a unitary UK state, based upon predominant English power, can be traced back at least to the Tudor era and has remained the constitutional orthodoxy until very recent times. The current commitment to devolution as one way of ordering relations within a multi-national United Kingdom may have been motivated more by political expediency than by constitutional conviction. Yet it is very likely to outlast New Labour's period in office, and by the time there is a change of Government at Westminster, new constitutional habits and relationships will have been formed which will be politically very difficult to unravel.

General reflections

It has become a commonplace to observe that the present Labour Government, and indeed some previous Labour and Liberal Governments, have been prepared to bring forward schemes of asymmetrical devolution which have not treated all parts of the United Kingdom equally. In former times there have been several examples of willingness at the highest political levels in London to tolerate such asymmetries and discrepancies in the structure of the United Kingdom. These have included Gladstone's determination to introduce

Home Rule for Ireland in 1885–86. They include Lloyd George's willingness to acquiesce in the determination of Edward Carson and James Craig in 1912–14 and again in 1918–22 to ensure the exclusion of the six Unionist-dominated counties in Northern Ireland from the political deal which he concluded with Arthur Griffith and Michael Collins in order to end the conflict between the United Kingdom and the Irish Republicans and so help to bring into existence a territorially and constitutionally incomplete independence for the other 26 counties of Ireland. They include the two attempts by the Callaghan Administration in 1977 and 1979 to introduce first a combined scheme of devolution to Scotland and Wales and then two separate schemes – legislative devolution for Scotland and administrative devolution for Wales.

Of course, all those attempts are now history, but the story of devolution within the United Kingdom seems to conjure up an almost endless procession of ghosts at the feast. When the first Blair Administration came into office following an electoral landslide in 1997, it was determined not to repeat the mistakes of its predecessors in respect of devolution and so it injected some astute new ingredients into the policy mix in order to improve its chances of dealing successfully with the various issues of identity and territory raised by the needs and wishes of the distinctly different parts of the United Kingdom that aspired to a greater degree of political autonomy. Yet the fundamental asymmetries remained in relation to each 'national community' seeking devolution.

Firstly, let us recall the asymmetrical *purposes* of devolution. In the case of *Northern Ireland*, once partition had become an established fact, it was essentially a matter of appeasing Irish Nationalist aspirations without so alienating the 'loyalist' Unionist majority that the latter carried out their repeated threats to take the law into their own hands. In the case of *Scotland*, it was a matter of heading off the Nationalist political threat to Labour's political dominance north of the border without inflicting damage upon sometimes resentful elements in the regions of England. In the case of *Wales*, it was a matter of making the fewest concessions to nationalist sentiment which Labour could get away with, while taking steps to ensure that the Labour Party in Wales was not irreparably split by the policy.

Secondly, there have been asymmetrical *processes* for taking forward devolution in the various parts of the United Kingdom. In *Northern Ireland*, where previous British Governments had tried nearly every conceivable variant of devolution, the first Blair Administration (with strong backing from the United States) opted for the active promotion of power sharing and aimed for parity of esteem between the two communities, all intelligently buttressed by a framework of international agreements which turned the Dublin Government into a full partner in the 'peace process'. In *Scotland* the Labour Government has strongly promoted a scheme of classic devolution which has already restored to that ancient and proud part of the United Kingdom an autonomous Parliament with extensive legislative powers and an option to exercise very limited fiscal powers. In *Wales* the process could briefly be described as slipstreaming Scotland, but in a rather half-hearted way with a form of administrative devolution initially not much more impressive than the powers of primary local authorities in England.

Thirdly, there have already been asymmetrical *outcomes* to the processes of devolution in the different parts of the United Kingdom, although after only a few years it would be unwise to draw any definitive conclusions. In the case of *Northern Ireland* most objective observers would probably agree that the Nationalists have had the better of the peace process and that the greater part of public opinion in the world at large seems to sympathise with the goal of peaceful reunification between the six counties and the rest of Ireland, if that can be achieved with the explicit consent of the Northern Ireland people in a referendum. At the same time there must be a good deal of public sympathy with David Trimble and the pro-agreement sections of the Ulster Unionist community who have had to wait a long time for the IRA to put even some of their weaponry 'beyond use', as required by the terms of the 1998 Belfast Agreement.[7]

In *Scotland* the prospects for permanent success in the devolution policy seem to be much better and for the foreseeable future it looks as though the current devolution settlement will endure, at least until there is another Conservative Government in London or a Scottish Nationalist Party Government in Edinburgh. As long as the United Kingdom continues to do without a codified constitution, there can be no absolute entrenchment of the devolution settlement. In these circumstances it would be perfectly possible for the SNP to win majority power in the Scottish Parliament at a future Scottish election and then use its electoral momentum to persuade the Government in London to hold another Scottish referendum not on devolution but on the question of Scotland's independence. Technically, this would not be permitted without legislation to amend the 1998 Scotland Act, but in political reality it could happen if the Scottish people were sufficiently determined and the English people remained as relaxed about the prospect of Scottish independence as they appear to be today.

In *Wales* executive devolution has produced another unstable settlement, but one which may last because the people of Wales still seem to be divided north and south, east and west on the merits of devolution. Furthermore, Plaid Cymru managed to make no net gains in Parliamentary seats at the 2001 General Election even though it campaigned particularly hard for Welsh nationalism in the industrial areas of south and east Wales where traditionally its support has always been rather weak.

On a visit to the Welsh Assembly in October 2001, Tony Blair took the opportunity to remind those present and the public at large that devolution to Wales has been 'just one part of a much wider programme of constitutional reform designed to move us away from a centralised Britain to a more democratic, decentralised and plural state' and that the policy 'fits within a broader framework, rebalancing power between citizen and Government and modernising Britain's constitution'.[8] It was salutary that the Prime Minister should have sought to remind us of the more idealistic justification for this and other aspects of the Government's programme of constitutional reform, since during Labour's second term of office doubts have come to be expressed about Labour's apparent unwilling-ness to accept the substance of devolution as well as the facade.[9]

Of course, there may come a time when our national political leaders and the general public come to the conclusion that the United Kingdom has outlived its usefulness; but that time has definitely not yet arrived. Unless and until it does, we can reasonably assume that all the political and other interests which have sought to protect and foster the United Kingdom will continue to see a successful policy of devolution as preferable to the leading alternatives for dealing with the issues of identity and territory in what is already a multi-national and multi-cultural polity. For the time being, the most tenable conclusion may be that the leaders of the various levels of government in all parts of the United Kingdom (possibly with the singular exception of Northern Ireland) remain comfortable with the fact that the processes of devolution have begun to change this country from a highly cohesive and unitary state towards a multi-national and quasi-federal union of states without yet stirring up such mutual animosity that our underlying unity is put at risk.

Questions for discussion

1   To what extent is historical nationalism a complete explanation for the drive towards devolution in any one part of the United Kingdom where there is now devolved government?

2   Has a British identity always been little more than a mask for English interests?

3   Is it inevitable that devolution in the United Kingdom should be asymmetrical or is there a case for coherent federalism as a constitutional structure for a multi-national United Kingdom?

Notes

1   See Linda Colley, *Britons – Forging the Nation 1707–1837*; Pimlico, London, 1994.

2   Quoted in Robert Kee, *The Green Flag*; Weidenfeld & Nicolson, London, 1972; p. 11.

3   Since 1997 the leadership of the Conservative Party has come to terms with the realities of devolution in Scotland and Wales. For example, it put up candidates and secured proportional list seats in both Assemblies following the 1999 elections.

4   Vernon Bogdanor, *Devolution in the United Kingdom*; Oxford University Press, Oxford, 1999; p. 2.

5   See Mark Sandford and Paul McQuail, *Unexplored Territory – Elected Regional Assemblies in England*; Constitution Unit, London, July 2001.

6   Opinion poll evidence collected by MORI in August 1997 suggested that the English have had a broadly supportive attitude towards Scottish devolution, with 59 per cent supporting it (compared with 60 per cent in Wales and 60 per cent in Scotland). When asked whether voters in England should have an opportunity to vote on the proposals for setting up a Scottish Parliament and a Welsh Assembly, 46 per cent of the English respondents said Yes (compared with 31 per cent in Wales and 19 per cent in Scotland), which did not really suggest English apathy on the subject, but did suggest that the Scots at least have tended to regard devolution as very much their own affair.

7   At the time of writing it seemed that David Trimble and his colleagues in the Ulster Unionists had finally lost patience with the lack of real progress on arms decommissioning by the terrorists and that the leaders of Sinn Fein were unable to deliver these aspects of the Belfast Agreement. Consequently, after two suspensions of the Agreement in 2001, the Northern Ireland Secretary, John Reid, reluctantly decided to reintroduce Direct Rule after David Trimble had withdrawn his party from the Assembly in protest at the IRA prevarications. However, in October 2001 the situation improved when the IRA eventually agreed to put some of its weaponry beyond use and the independent decommissioning body under General John de Chastelain endorsed this action. This paved the way for David Trimble to resubmit himself for the post of First Minister of the Northern Ireland Executive (notwithstanding the decision of two backbench members of his party not to support his candidature) and this particular crisis was finally overcome when two members of the non-sectarian Alliance Party temporarily re-designated themselves as 'Unionists' in order to fulfil the complicated requirements of the 1998 Belfast Agreement.

8   See Tony Blair's speech to the Welsh Assembly in Cardiff, 30th October 2001.

9   See Kevin Brown, 'The stony road of devolution', *Financial Times*, 11th November 2001.

Further reading

Anthony H. Birch, *Political Integration and Disintegration in the British Isles*; Allen & Unwin, London, 1977.

Vernon Bogdanor, *Devolution in the United Kingdom*; Oxford University Press, Oxford, 1999.

Linda Colley, *Britons – Forging the Nation – 1707–1837*; Pimlico, London, 1994.

Norman Davies, *The Isles: a History*; Macmillan, London, 1999.

Christopher Hibbert, *The English – a Social History, 1066–1945*; Guild Publishing, London, 1987.

Miroslav Hroch, *Social Preconditions of National Revival in Europe*; Columbia University Press, New York, 1985.

Robert Kee, *The Green Flag*; Weidenfeld & Nicolson, London, 1972.

M. Sandford and P. McQuail, *Unexplored Territory – Elected Regional Assemblies in England*; Constitution Unit, London, July 2001.

Anthony D. Smith, *National Identity*; Penguin, London, 1991.

Chapter 3

The Irish question

The pursuit of a nationalist dream

Ireland may have been the last of the non-English parts of the United Kingdom to become constitutionally united with the other nations in the British Isles when the Irish House of Commons voted by a majority of 46 for the Act of Union in 1800, but it was also the first to struggle for the modification or overthrow of this status, whether by the limited mechanism of Home Rule or the unlimited mechanism of national independence. The reasons for this apparent paradox are very evident and were clearly exposed during the course of Irish history.

To begin with, it must be said that Ireland was for centuries treated as if it were an English colony rather than a proud and equal part of the United Kingdom. This was evident in the severity with which every Irish rebellion was put down from the time when Cromwell's army suppressed the armed resistance of the Catholic Irish in 1652 to the time when the British army backed by the Irish gentry suppressed the rebellion led by Wolfe Tone from 1794 to 1798. In between those two flashpoints of colonial oppression were long years of exploitation and neglect of the ordinary Irish people.

The loss of the American colonies in 1776 was undoubtedly a wake-up call to the British ruling class which from then on was better disposed towards the idea of making some timely concessions to emergent Irish nationalism. This somewhat altered the balance of power between Britain and Ireland, so that when the Irish Volunteers were formed in 1778 to take the place of British troops dispatched from Ireland to fight against the Americans in their War of Independence, the political climate in Ireland soon became sufficiently conducive under the moderate leadership of Henry Grattan to persuade the Irish Parliament in Dublin to vote unanimously in 1782 for an Irish Declaration of Independence. Only two years previously this Declaration had been defeated in the same assembly by the use of patronage on behalf of the British Government.

The institutional result of these developments was the establishment of what historians came to call 'Grattan's Parliament' which lasted from 1782

to 1801. This marked at least a tacit acceptance by politicians at Westminster of a right to self-government for the Irish people, albeit involving an oath of allegiance to the British Crown.[1] Grattan himself explained the situation in these terms: 'connected by freedom as well as by allegiance, the two nations – Great Britain and Ireland – form a constitutional confederacy as well as an Empire'; and went on to portray the people of Ireland as 'standing or falling with the British nation'.[2]

Towards the end of the eighteenth century great events initiated outside Ireland and strategic necessity in England combined to give the wheel of Irish history new forward momentum. The French Revolution, which broke out in 1789, led quite quickly to the outbreak of war between revolutionary France and Tory Great Britain in 1793. These events, in their turn, had a galvanising effect upon the more radical elements of the local (Protestant) ruling class in Ireland both north and south. The immediate political result was that Wolfe Tone and others established the Society of United Irishmen in Belfast in October 1791 and in Dublin in November 1791 with the intention of uniting Ireland north and south, Protestant and Catholic, in a single nationalist cause. At the outset the United Irishmen were quite moderate reformers who sought immediate recognition for the dignity, independence and self-respect of the Irish nation in the establishment of an allegedly free Irish Parliament to determine Irish affairs, but ultimately in a rather misty vision of complete national independence.

This sort of nationalist challenge could perhaps have been tolerated, and probably managed, by the British rulers of Ireland in Dublin Castle (and by the landowning Protestant gentry and Catholic hierarchy who between them did much of the dirty work for the Imperial British power in Ireland at the time) if it had been confined to the original objectives of the United Irishmen. But revolutionary events in France developed a dynamic of their own which within two years had inspired the United Irishmen to call for universal male adult suffrage and annual Parliaments in Ireland, and which, with the outbreak of war between Britain and France in the same year, led the British

Government to take both tender and tough steps to deal with what it had come to regard as a subversive and increasingly dangerous nationalist movement. So at the behest of the British Government the Irish Parliament passed the 1793 Catholic Relief Act, which gave the vote to Catholic 40-shilling freeholders but left Catholics still debarred from holding public office in Ireland; three years later the Westminster Parliament passed the draconian Insurrection Act and suspended Habeas Corpus in order to deal ruthlessly with what it saw as treasonable rebellion in Ireland. The United Irishmen, once proscribed and driven underground, responded with a commitment to 'a republican government and separation from England'. They also joined forces all over Ireland with the clandestine Catholic movement, the Defenders, and began to make serious overtures to revolutionary France for assistance in their nationalist struggle against Great Britain.

From the end of 1796 the French Revolutionary Directorate agreed to give military assistance to the embattled Irish nationalists and dispatched to Ireland a French expeditionary force of 14,000 troops in 43 warships which, however, failed to put its men ashore when it reached Bantry Bay in early 1797 because the prevailing winds made this impossible. At the same time the Irish insurgents were riven with sectarian strife between the Protestant north and the Catholic south as the newly formed Orangemen (the successors of the Peep o'Day Boys) began to indulge in a late-eighteenth-century version of ethnic cleansing of Catholics in Ulster and as the Defenders retaliated in kind. However, the mass of ordinary Irish people in the countryside were more concerned simply to survive and, if possible, get redress for their long-established grievances over lack of personal security and the iniquities of the land tenure system. Thus, although the Irish nationalists attempted one more abortive rebellion in County Wexford in 1798 and the French military attempted two more invasions of Ireland in support of the half-hearted Irish insurrection in the same year, British intelligence and coercive measures easily got the better of them and this whole seven-year episode in the long history of Irish nationalism ended in

predictable humiliation and heroic failure when Wolfe Tone was captured, tried for treason and, while awaiting execution, committed suicide in a Dublin jail.

The political mood in Ireland was one of bitter resignation on the part of the down-trodden Catholic masses and self-interested calculation on the part of the property-owning classes, whether Protestant or Catholic. In such circumstances, during a truce in the long war against revolutionary France, it made good sense for Pitt and the British Government to seek to engineer a new settlement with Ireland based upon legislative Union and projected Catholic emancipation. This also came to make sense, albeit for contrasting reasons, to both Protestant Unionists and Catholic Nationalists: the former allowed themselves to be bought by the patronage which Cornwallis the Viceroy and Castlereagh the Chief Secretary organised in 1799 and 1800 to ensure the passage of the necessary legislation through the Irish Parliament; the latter were persuaded that they would have more to gain than to lose from legislative Union with Britain. The Act of Union was one answer to the strategic concerns of the British Government about the vulnerability of mainland Britain to the threats of insurrection in and invasion from Ireland. Yet it never really provided a solution to the problems of the Irish people, because callous exploitation and culpable neglect remained among the defining characteristics of British attitudes towards Ireland.

Notwithstanding the grandiloquent language of the Younger Pitt when commending the Act of Union to the British House of Commons, successive British Governments and Parliaments from 1800 to 1921 were inconsistent and often downright hostile towards legitimate Irish expectations and claims upon the Union. Pitt had spoken movingly of

> the voluntary association of two great countries, which seek their common benefit in one Empire, in which each will retain its proportionate weight and importance, under the security of equal laws, reciprocal affection and inseparable interests, and in which each will acquire a strength that will render it invincible.[3]

Yet Grattan was right to dissociate himself and his party from this prospectus at the time; and subsequent events merely emphasised how little natural justice or even fair recognition the Irish people could really expect from most of the British political class at any time between the Act of Union and Partition.

Three enduring Irish problems

Throughout the history of Ireland's relationship initially with England and later with Great Britain, there have been three great enduring problems: land tenure, religious discrimination, and how to find a generally acceptable political structure for Irish nationality. None of these problems was really addressed in good time by the British ruling class during the whole period before Partition and the last remains unresolved to this day.

For centuries *the system of land tenure* in Ireland had given no reliable rights to the millions who worked and lived off the land (as distinct from the gentry, both Protestant and Catholic, who owned it), and the problem was compounded by the general absence of other means of making a living for the mass of the people – apart from industrial jobs for the Protestant working class in Ulster and the ultimate expedient of emigration for those who were left with no alternative in the south. Throughout the nineteenth century, and indeed well into the twentieth, property rights were a shibboleth of the British 'constitution' and nowhere more so than in Ireland where for long years (between periods of acute crisis) what was out of sight was out of mind.

Typically, there could be as many as seven different layers of tenancy for agricultural land, ranging from the freehold owner of a large estate down to the meanest tenant (serf) farming perhaps a mere 5 acres who had to sell all his cash crops to pay the excessive rent and was therefore reliant upon potatoes to feed his wife and numerous children. The human results of this primitive and precarious economic system were all too frequently abject poverty, disease, communal brutality and periodic starvation. For example, it has been estimated that the Great Famine of 1845–48 killed one-eighth of the Irish population and forced a further 1 million wretches to emigrate, mainly to the United States. Numerous official investigations were undertaken and reports subsequently written, but the prevailing ideology of *laissez-faire* in the mid-nineteenth century effectively prevented British Ministers from taking substantial action either to head off or to alleviate the tragedies. Such alleviation as there was came from the Catholic church and various philanthropic charities.

It required the sustained pressure of grassroots agitation by tenant farmers in Ireland acting upon the liberal and reforming conscience of William Gladstone once he became Prime Minister in 1868, together with subsequently effective political campaigning by the National Land League formed under Charles Parnell in 1879, to bring about the successive waves of Westminster legislation which by the time of Partition in 1921 finally rectified the scandal of Irish land tenure. The *1870 Land Act* had marked a modest beginning by requiring landlords who sought to evict tenants for any reason other than non-payment of rent to pay financial compensation to the tenants for the improvements they had made to their holdings during their tenure; but this still left landlords with the loophole of raising rents to a level which, while not 'exorbitant' (prohibited under the Act), was high enough to trigger failure to pay the rent by their tenants and so open the way for the landlords to repossess. Naturally, the Act did not satisfy the vast mass of tenants who simply wanted legal freedom from eviction.

The *1881 Land Act*, which was Gladstone's second legislative response to the problem, marked a big step in the right direction by granting tenants security of tenure provided the rents were paid, according tenants the right to sell their interest in the land and the value of their improvements to others, and decreeing that rent levels would be adjudicated by specially created Land Courts. However, it failed to meet the core demand of Irish tenant farmers which was for a system of strictly controlled rents and a guarantee of no eviction as long as such 'fair rents' were paid. It took the *1886 Land Purchase Act* and subsequent, more ambitious versions of the same legislation in 1903 and 1909 to enable the vast majority of Irish tenant farmers to achieve their final goal of *outright land ownership*, thanks to successive developments of the phased purchase schemes under which by 1921 no fewer than 400,000 of the 470,000 land holdings in Ireland had been bought by tenant farmers.[4]

Religious discrimination against Catholics was for a very long time one of the defining characteristics of English (and Scottish) attitudes towards the Irish. Pitt the Younger had tried to combine a Bill on Catholic Emancipation with the Act of Union with Ireland in 1800, but failed because George III and a good part of the Cabinet would not tolerate it. The idea was taken up again with great energy in 1823 when Daniel O'Connell founded the Catholic Association for the purpose of adopting 'all such legal and constitutional measures as may be most useful to obtain Catholic Emancipation'.[5] In the years which followed, O'Connell's campaign made remarkably impressive headway, first with the election of an Emancipation candidate at Waterford in 1826 and later when O'Connell himself stood as a 'Man of the People' candidate in an election at County Clare and was triumphantly elected to Parliament in 1828. So impressive were the obvious organisation and discipline of O'Connell's supporters that even Robert Peel (then Home Secretary) and the redoubtable Duke of Wellington agreed that the game was up and in early 1829 swiftly introduced a Catholic Emancipation Bill which became the law of the land later that year. Before the Act, O'Connell had been elected but as a Catholic had been debarred from taking his seat. After the Act, he was re-elected unopposed and returned in triumph to take his seat at Westminster. Thus O'Connell's insistence upon lawful, disciplined political pressure had made possible a famous victory for Irish nationalism which, at any rate for Parliamentary campaigners, was to set a pattern for the nationalist movement during the rest of the nineteenth century.

The logical corollary of Catholic emancipation was Protestant disestablishment. By legislating to disestablish the Protestant church in Ireland, Gladstone's Liberal majority challenged that part of the 1800 Act of Union which had declared that a united Protestant church was an indissoluble foundation for the United Kingdom, even though five-sixths of Ireland's population were Catholic and

had strongly resented paying tithes to the minority church of the Protestant Ascendancy.

While the 1869 Irish Disestablishment Act was a significant measure *against* religious discrimination by the politically and economically dominant minority in Ireland, the sectarian pressures in subsequent political developments – especially in Ulster – had the opposite effect, entrenching Protestant commitment to the Union at all costs and gradually distancing Protestant radicals from their earlier association with the cause of Irish nationalism. Leading Protestants, such as Charles Parnell, played very prominent parts in the long campaign for Home Rule and some, such as Sir Roger Casement, took part in the military preparations for the 1916 Easter Uprising. However, the long historical trend in the north of Ireland to parade a militant Protestant Unionism, and in the south – especially after the promulgation of the 1937 Irish constitution – to bolster an insecure national identity with five Articles defining nationalist and religious 'rights', only served to make the partition of Ireland all the more entrenched and to confirm the Protestants of Ulster in their belief that the institutions of a united Ireland would be republican and oppressively Catholic.[6]

The greatest and most enduring problem which has beset British–Irish relations has been *how to accommodate Irish nationalism* within or (for most of the twentieth century) alongside the United Kingdom. As we have already noted, when the Act of Union between Great Britain and Ireland was concluded in 1800, William Pitt the Younger spelled out with the starkest clarity what would be, in effect, the preconditions for a successful union; but when his famous declaration is deconstructed, we can see that his preconditions were unfulfilled in every particular. Is it any wonder that a growing proportion of Irish patriots in succeeding generations gradually came round to the idea that only republican national independence would satisfy the vast majority of the Irish people?

William Pitt's first assumption in 1800 was that the Union was a *voluntary* association of two great countries; yet it is an undeniable historical fact that the members of 'Grattan's Parliament' effectively allowed themselves to be bought and bribed into the Union, so any notion of popular consent for this momentous step was completely fanciful. Secondly, Pitt had declared that the Union should be for the two countries' *common benefit* in one Empire, yet there were few signs during the subsequent century of any benefits from it for the Irish, except possibly for the landowning class in the south and the new industrial working class in and around Belfast. His third condition was that there should be '*proportionate* weight and importance' for the Irish and British elements in the United Kingdom and, in an ironic sense, it could be said that this was exactly how things turned out in that the dominant partner (Great Britain) exerted greater power and influence (balanced by frequent indifference), proportionate to its power and influence in the United Kingdom, while Ireland, as the weaker partner in the political arrangement, suffered all the frustrations of its marginal, quasi-colonial status. His fourth stipulation was that the two countries should have the 'security of *equal laws*', a statement which might seem to have been farcical if it had not been so tragically far removed from the truth for the whole of the nineteenth century. One has only to consider the exclusion of Catholics from public office until 1829, the scandal of Irish land tenure until its rectification was finally completed by legislation in the early 1900s, and the frequent resort by the British authorities to coercive and draconian measures whenever they were stirred by threats of Irish insurrection to see the strength of this interpretation.

Pitt's final rhetorical flourish in the House of Commons in 1800 had been to speak of '*reciprocal affection*' and '*inseparable interests*' between the two partners in the Union – yet another claim which, in the light of history, should really be understood as hollow at best and hypocritical at worst. Whereas the British authorities had callously allowed a million Irish people to die in the Great Famine of the 1840s, during the first two years alone of the First World War more than 80,000 Irishmen volunteered for the British army; about 27,000 of them were Ulster Volunteers and about the same number National Volunteers from the rest of the country.[7] For anyone reflecting dispassionately upon the history of British–Irish relations, it is shocking to weigh up the terrible imbalance between what the Irish were prepared to do for Britain and what the British were prepared to do to Ireland.

Daniel O'Connell was the first great Irish leader who concluded that the 1800 Act of Union had been the equivalent of an unjust treaty, but he remained outwardly loyal to the British monarchy to his dying day. The Catholic Association, which he had founded in 1823, achieved the great success of the 1829 Catholic Emancipation Act by the simple expedient of overawing the unreformed British Parliament with the power of a well-organised mass movement. However, his subsequent campaign to bring about the repeal of the Act of Union by a combination of Parliamentary initiatives at Westminster and extra-Parliamentary popular pressure in Ireland came to nothing. This was essentially because British Unionists during the first half of the nineteenth century, whether Whig or Tory and later Liberal or Conservative, were convinced that O'Connell's half-way house would be fatal to the United Kingdom. What is more, they did not have to depend politically upon O'Connell and his 'Repealers' for their continuance in office at Westminster. With the slogan 'a real Union or no Union', O'Connell argued for an Ireland which would be a distinct country with its own independent legislature, but formally subject to the British monarchy and prepared to support the *external* causes of the British Empire. Prophetically he forecast that, if the Union remained as it was, the consequences would be fatal for the United Kingdom and eventually lead to complete Irish separation. These arguments held no attractions for Sir Robert Peel and the Conservatives, who argued that the repeal of the Act of Union would lead to the disintegration of the British Empire and the reduction of Great Britain to a fourth-rate power in Europe and the world.

Having failed to persuade successive British Governments of the merits of repealing the Act of Union by using political arguments and Parliamentary manoeuvring, O'Connell founded the *National Repeal Association* in 1841 as a mass organisation to exert extra-Parliamentary pressure upon Westminster in the same way that his Catholic

Association had done for the cause of Catholic emancipation nearly two decades before. The campaign, which climaxed in 1843 with huge open-air meetings in Ireland attracting audiences of 500,000 and more on some notable occasions, failed to overawe or persuade the British authorities who, on the contrary, went as far in the following year as to secure the conviction for conspiracy of O'Connell and six other leaders of the movement – a court judgement which, when later overturned by the Law Lords, led to O'Connell's dramatic release and return in triumph to Ireland where he was hailed as the national 'Liberator'.

As so often in Irish history, a great historical moment proved to be largely inconsequential and nugatory in its effects and in this case all the patriotic fervour of 1843 and 1844 was doused by the outbreak in 1845 of lethal potato blight which led to the Great Irish Famine during the years to 1848. Such acts of God (or nature) were generally considered beyond the reach of official Government intervention in those times of extreme *laissez-faire* and the main response of Peel's Administration in London was to introduce another Coercion Bill to deal with the rural unrest and violence caused by the dreadful suffering and to imprison Smith O'Brien, one of the leaders of the so-called Young Ireland movement which had been formed in 1842 by Thomas Davis and some other young Dublin radicals. So it could be said that, when O'Connell died a broken and dispirited man in Lyons in 1847, virtually no significant political progress had been made towards the goals of moderate, Irish nationalism and the mass of the Irish people found themselves deep in a human tragedy which seemed hopeless even by the standards of Irish history.

Revolutionary events in Paris and in other European capitals in 1848 had some galvanising effect upon the Irish nationalists left behind by O'Connell, especially the members of the newly created *Irish League*. Smith O'Brien and a handful of other romantics launched a futile uprising that year, only to be captured, convicted of treason and then deported to Tasmania. The events of the 1840s crystallised the central dilemma for all Irish nationalists in the mid-nineteenth century and for many years to come. As Robert Kee put it, 'to work obliquely towards nationality was the only way of making it a reality; yet, by thus appealing primarily to other interests and other loyalties (e.g. land reform and the Catholic faith), the goal of nationality itself became secondary'.[8] Furthermore, when confronted with a British ruling class which was by turns ruthlessly coercive and callously indifferent to the mass of the Irish people, all varieties of Irish nationalist – whether Parliamentary reformers or proponents of direct action – were largely powerless to secure timely and effective changes in Ireland's status within the United Kingdom which might have been to the mutual benefit of the Irish and British peoples.

The combined effects of the Great Irish Famine and the huge wave of Irish emigration to the United States which followed were both to strengthen the influence of the Irish diaspora upon the development of Irish nationalism and to make the political goals of the movement more revolutionary and radical. It was in these circumstances that a new secret society, the Fenians, was established by James Stephens in south-west Ireland in 1857 and another, the Irish Republican Brotherhood, was established in Dublin in 1858. The Fenians had been radicalised by their bitter experience of famine, disease and poverty, while their ideas had been coloured by the Irish-American vision of a free, independent and republican Ireland.

Because the Fenians who operated in Ireland were directly in touch with the poorer elements in Irish rural society, their programme contained at least one realistic and vital objective, namely to agitate and terrorise in favour of land reform in Ireland. By 1867 they were ready to launch, with Irish-American backing, a terrorist operation in England to precede a guerrilla war in Ireland which was intended to provoke American intervention against Britain. Yet it all went terribly wrong when their plans to seize guns and ammunition from Chester Castle were revealed by a Fenian informer in the pay of the British intelligence service, and later when an attempt by William Allen, Philip Larkin and Michael O'Brien to rescue two of their co-conspirators (Captain Kelly and Captain Deasy) from a police van in Manchester resulted in the death of an English police sergeant. Their subsequent capture and conviction for murder led swiftly to their execution and elevation to Irish martyr status. Needless to say, the planned uprising in Ireland became a fiasco when most of the conspirators were captured and a few were killed.

These events served to emphasise once again that no sacrifice in Irish nationalist history – however futile or tragic – was ever allowed to pass uncelebrated; and every failure was treasured in the polemical tradition of Irish nationalism as one more step on the way to the goal of a united and independent Ireland. In this case the Fenians and the Irish Republican Brotherhood can be regarded as the progenitors of Sinn Fein and the Irish Republican Army, the twin radical forces in Irish politics which in the early decades of the twentieth century were to overtake the more moderate proponents of Irish Home Rule and then, in 1921, achieve national independence for all but six counties in Ulster.

Without the influence of this turbulent and tragic period in Irish history during the middle decades of the nineteenth century, it is unlikely that William Gladstone would have said on entering office as Prime Minister in 1868 that his mission was 'to pacify Ireland' – by which he meant, of course, to find a peaceful solution to the age-old Irish problem which would be acceptable to Britain and Ireland. He started out by assuming that he could achieve the goals of his Irish policy by disestablishing the Irish Protestant church and by legislating to improve tenants' rights within Irish land tenure. Yet when he had achieved the former and made a cautious start on the latter, he was faced by a newly unified Home Rule movement in Ireland which from its first conference in Dublin in 1873 agitated for a separate Parliament for Ireland (matching equivalent institutions for Wales and Scotland), but subordinate to the Imperial Parliament at Westminster.

The long struggle for Home Rule

Disraeli and the Conservatives held office from 1874 to 1880 and by the time that Gladstone

returned to office to form his second Administration in 1880 *Charles Parnell* had become the leader of the Irish Home Rule party. As such he was head of a disciplined Parliamentary contingent of Irish Nationalist politicians who had learned how to use all the techniques of Parliamentary obstruction to delay legislation of which they disapproved and to highlight the causes of Irish nationalism, whether land reform or more equitable arrangements for the *self-government* of Ireland within the United Kingdom. Certainly by the early 1880s Charles Parnell and the Irish National League had become a political force to be reckoned with, since there were now effective structures of constituency organisation in Ireland to support the claims and the activities of the Irish National Party at Westminster. Quite apart from occasional terrorist outrages, such as the murder of Lord Frederick Cavendish at Phoenix Park in 1881 by extremists of the Irish Republican Brotherhood, the future government of Ireland had become the central issue of British politics thanks to the brilliance of Charles Parnell and the energy and unity of his colleagues.

The immediate result of this wave of public sentiment in Ireland was that Parnell's Irish Home Rulers won 85 of the 103 Irish seats at the 1885 General Election, including 17 of the 33 seats in Ulster. The further consequence was that Gladstone decided to introduce his first Home Rule Bill for Ireland in 1886. At Westminster Parnell declared that he was content with the legislation and regarded it as an adequate response to Irish nationalist demands at the time, yet a year or so earlier in a memorable speech at Cork on 21st January 1885 he had declared that 'no man has a right to fix the boundary of the march of a nation; no man has a right to say to his country: thus far shalt thou go and no further'. Just when it seemed possible that there could be a timely legislative solution to the constitutional problem of how best to govern Ireland within the United Kingdom, a dual disaster struck Gladstone and his recently re-elected Administration. *Firstly*, the Home Rule Bill was defeated in the House of Commons by the defection of Right-wing Liberal Unionists under Lord Hartington and radical Liberal Unionists under Joseph Chamberlain, who combined with the Tories to defeat the measure. *Secondly*, this development prompted Chamberlain and the other 'Liberal Unionists' to join the Tories, thus paving the way for a Conservative and Unionist victory at the General Election in 1886 and a period of unsympathetic Conservative Administration until 1892.

There is little doubt that the formula of *Irish self-government for Irish affairs* – with an Irish Executive responsible to an Irish Legislature in turn subordinate to the UK Parliament at Westminster for all Imperial affairs and with all the Irish people continuing to recognise the formal sovereignty of the British monarchy – would have satisfied the preponderance of Irish opinion in the 1880s and might have created political structures which would have stood the test of time. On the other hand, it is undeniable that the *1886 Irish Home Rule Bill* had some fatal flaws and internal contradictions in English eyes which meant that it was vulnerable to attack from two opposite directions. Joseph Chamberlain and the 'Liberal Unionists' drew attention to the danger that the Irish would not for long be satisfied with a constitutional compromise under which they would continue to be taxed and have their foreign and commercial policy determined by the UK Parliament and yet would be deprived under the Bill of their representation at Westminster. Sooner or later this would lead to Irish demands either to be free of all policy and impositions determined by the Imperial Parliament or to have their Parliamentary representation at Westminster restored so that they could have at least some say in legislation which directly affected them. Equally, they themselves were not willing to countenance any political concessions to Irish nationalism which would have the effect of undermining the British Empire and the political integrity of the United Kingdom.

In the end the most tricky constitutional issue in 1886 was how to deal with any proposal by a British Chancellor of the Exchequer to raise, amend or repeal any tax then levied in Ireland by the authority of Parliament at Westminster or to impose an entirely new tax which, under the reserve Imperial powers of Westminster, would have to be levied in Ireland as much as in any other part of the United Kingdom. Gladstone's ingenious solution to this acute problem was to let the 103 Irish members return to Westminster to speak and to vote on such occasions and, indeed, on any proposed amendment to the Home Rule constitutional settlement. With the wisdom of hindsight, we can now see that this clever 'in and out' solution was likely to be unacceptable to the preponderance of British MPs and almost certainly unworkable as well. It was probably a blessing that it never had to be put into practice.

One general issue was thrown into sharp relief by Gladstone's Home Rule Bill of 1886 and was to dog devolution schemes for any part of the United Kingdom. This was the need to choose between a scheme which gave to a devolved part of the country the *double* advantage of excluding others elsewhere in the UK from any say in its self-government *and* still participating/interfering in the local government of other parts of the country by dint of its continuing membership of the UK Parliament; and a scheme which consciously deprived the self-governing territory (nation) of full rights of representation in the UK Parliament, even though the Imperial connection via a common allegiance to the British Crown and a common duty to pay British taxes and (perhaps) to serve in the British armed forces were to be maintained.

At various times Gladstone and his Liberal successors sought to deal with this fundamental problem of Home Rule or devolution by tweaking the variable of Parliamentary representation at Westminster – for example, by excluding Irish MPs, allowing them to participate only on certain issues, or reducing the number of their representatives to below that to which they would otherwise have been entitled as a non-devolved part of the UK. Yet even such intellectual acrobatics could not evade the need to face up to the fundamental inconsistency at the heart of all such policy in the United Kingdom from 1886 to the present day: namely, the logical impossibility of sustaining over any length of time a hybrid policy which both preserves and departs from the political integrity of the United Kingdom.

When Gladstone took his next opportunity to introduce a *second Home Rule Bill in 1893*, similar

Irish nationalist disappointment was engendered when it was passed in the House of Commons but thrown out by the Tory-dominated House of Lords. Gladstone adjusted his approach somewhat by providing for 80 Irish MPs to retain their seats at Westminster after Home Rule in an obvious attempt to meet the argument that if Ireland were to remain within the United Kingdom and the Empire, then it should be directly represented in the Imperial Parliament. Unlike the 1886 Bill, the Upper House in a bi-cameral Irish Legislature was to consist of 48 members elected under a restrictive property franchise designed to protect minority Protestant interests, while the Lower House was to consist of 103 members elected from the usual constituencies by the limited electorate of that time. The idea was that each House in the Legislature should be empowered to veto the decisions of the other (the notion of concurrent powers). In the event, the Protestant Unionists were completely unpersuaded that their position would be adequately safeguarded by a Legislative Council with a franchise based upon a property qualification as low as £20 annual rateable value (which would let in many Catholic Irish tenant farmers), and their Tory allies in the House of Lords were unpersuaded that the Bill would be anything other than the thin end of a wedge which would lead inexorably to Irish separation.

As with the first Home Rule Bill in 1886, there was still a good deal of uncertainty and ambiguity about the extent to which the proposals in the 1893 Bill would have been regarded as a final settlement of the Irish question by all the various elements in Irish nationalism. Michael Davitt, the Irish Nationalist MP for Cork North East, described the Bill as 'an honourable and lasting compact between the people of Ireland and Great Britain'; but the new leader of the rump of nine Parnellites, John Redmond, said in his speech on Second Reading that he did not expect the Bill, if passed, to be 'absolutely final or immutable', and in his speech on Third Reading he roundly declared that 'no man in his senses can any longer regard it as a full, final or satisfactory settlement of the Irish National Question'.[9] The hinge of the whole constitutional argument and the real sticking point for Irish

Nationalists and Unionists alike was the doctrine and practice of Parliamentary supremacy for the 'Imperial' Parliament at Westminster. This *might* have been acceptable to flexible and moderate Nationalists such as Michael Davitt and John Dillon; but it was not acceptable to more ambivalent figures such as Parnell and Redmond, and it had long been unthinkable for successive generations of real Irish nationalists. On the other side of the argument, the principle of Parliamentary supremacy for Westminster throughout the United Kingdom, and at that time the British Empire as well, was the ark of the covenant for all Unionists, all British imperialists and some leading authorities on the British constitution such as A.V. Dicey.

It was always difficult or impossible to reconcile these two incompatible positions in the repeated arguments about the British constitution down the centuries. Either it was accepted that Parliament at Westminster had complete political and legislative supremacy throughout its acknowledged area of jurisdiction or it was not. If it was, there could be no legitimate challenge to its position from any part of the United Kingdom or indeed the Empire and Commonwealth; if it was not, the honest response of those who disagreed had to be rebellion and a continuing struggle for national independence.

The confusion – we might even say schizophrenia – in the minds of the Irish people towards the British and all their works at the end of the nineteenth and the beginning of the twentieth centuries was exemplified by the fact that there was an Irish Nationalist Brigade which fought alongside the Boer rebels *against* the British colonial power in South Africa and a number of famous Irish regiments which fought *for* the British army against the Boers. This uncertain split was reproduced during the First World War a decade or so later when in 1916 thousands of Irishmen were fighting and dying *for* the British Empire on the Western Front, while at the same time a few hundred Irish Republican rebels were in the process of preparing and launching the Easter Uprising *against* British rule in Ireland.

Against this background, Arthur Griffith, then an obscure young compositor but later a journalist and agitator of some talent, took steps in 1900 to found an organisation called *Cumann na Gaedheal* (later to become *Fine Gael*) which attracted members from various nationalist societies and drew some of its inspiration from the experience of active support for the Boers through the Irish Transvaal Committee. Griffith and his colleagues went on to found *Sinn Fein* (Ourselves Alone) in 1905 as a new party explicitly open to any Irish patriot pledged to restore Ireland to 'her former position of sovereign independence'; they made use of a newspaper then called the *United Irishman* to propagate their doctrine. In their pressure for an indigenous Irish Parliament of Three Hundred (evoking the memory of Grattan's Parliament of 300 MPs before the 1800 Act of Union) they were variously influenced by the example of the withdrawal of the Hungarian deputies from the Austro-Hungarian Imperial Parliament in 1861; the widely supported moves for an Irish cultural revival in art, music and poetry; and the military experience of Boer guerrilla warfare against the British in South Africa. This may have been a heady brew, but at that time both Cumann na Gaedheal and Sinn Fein were tiny uninfluential minorities within the Irish nationalist movement which was still dominated by Redmond and his Westminster Parliamentary colleagues.

When the Liberals were swept back to power with a landslide victory at the 1906 General Election, they certainly did not need any help or support from the Irish Nationalists whose leverage over the British political situation was commensurately reduced. The Liberals had assured the British public in the election campaign that they would not grant Home Rule to Ireland without further reference to the electorate at a subsequent General Election. In these circumstances the Bill introduced by the new Liberal Administration in 1907 was a very modest measure of administrative devolution which would have involved moving some administrative powers from Westminster to what was described as an Irish Council of 106 members in Dublin, 82 of whom would have been elected and the remainder nominated by the British Government. Such a Council would have had no law-making or tax-raising powers, but would have been able to take administrative control of eight of the 45

areas of policy affecting Ireland – such as education, public works, agriculture, etc. Arthur Griffith described the Bill as an insult to the Irish and called once again for the withdrawal from Westminster of the entire contingent of Irish MPs. This made it politically impossible for John Redmond and his Irish Nationalist colleagues to commend it in Parliament and not long after that the Liberal Government decided to drop it for lack of any real Irish support.

The Irish question was relegated to the second division of constitutional issues in British politics for a few years while the Liberal Administration proceeded to confront successive challenges to its electoral mandate from the Tory peers in an unreconstructed House of Lords. After the Lords' rejection of Lloyd George's radical Budget of 1909, the constitutional issue really came to a head and the Liberals went to the country twice in one year (1910) in their attempts to secure decisive public support for their determination to cut the recalcitrant, Tory-dominated House of Lords down to size. In this they were only partially successful since in neither of the two 1910 elections did they achieve anything like overwhelming public support for their position and the second General Election in that year produced a 'hung Parliament' with the Liberals and Conservatives exactly tied on 272 seats each. This gave a new opportunity to the Irish Nationalists with 82 seats and the infant Labour Party with 42 seats to exert effective political pressure. The former soon extracted a promise from an unenthusiastic Asquith that he would introduce another Home Rule Bill for Ireland once the constitutional challenge from the House of Lords had been dealt with by the passage of the 1911 Parliament Act. In these circumstances Arthur Griffith and his colleagues in Sinn Fein played no direct part in Westminster politics and were willing to hold back for a while to allow John Redmond and his colleagues the time and space to promote Home Rule for Ireland by Parliamentary means.

By the time that the Asquith Administration eventually introduced *the third Irish Home Rule Bill* in April 1912, the opposition to such a measure from the Conservatives in Great Britain and the Protestant Unionists in Ulster had assumed new and potentially alarming proportions. This fraught situation stemmed from the establishment of the Ulster Unionist Council in 1905 and its creation of an armaments fund in 1910, as well as the emergence of new and uncompromising leadership from Sir Edward Carson, a Liberal Unionist lawyer from Dublin, and his deputy James Craig, an Ulster Unionist from Belfast who had been a British army officer in the Boer War. It was also exacerbated by the growing Unionist tendencies within the Conservative Party when Andrew Bonar Law, an uncompromising Ulster Scot, succeeded Arthur Balfour as Leader of the Opposition. With mass demonstrations and quasi-military drilling becoming more frequent occurrences in Ulster, where the conventions of the British constitution were not fully accepted, the Conservatives and the Unionists were able to exert much greater pressure than the increasingly ineffectual Irish Nationalists under Redmond. Consequently, the question which came to be posed more and more often in London was not whether Ireland as a whole should be given Home Rule, but whether the Unionists in Ulster should be forced out of the United Kingdom into a nationalist and republican political structure for Ireland against which, it was believed, they would take up arms.

Ultimately, it mattered not what safeguards and assurances were built into the legislation for the benefit of the Ulster Protestants and Unionists – such as the overriding supremacy of the Westminster Parliament, the check of a nominated Irish Upper House and the deliberate over-representation of Ulster in the Irish Lower House, as well as concurrent powers for the two Houses in the event of disputes between them – as long as the situation persisted in which they were so easily convinced that there would be no secure half-way house between Union and separation. Even though the Conservatives and Unionists had a widely recognised fall-back position in the partition of Ireland and the exclusion from Home Rule of six of Ulster's nine counties, their threats to defy the law of the land (with military force if necessary) if the Bill reached the Statute Book without special provision being made for the exclusion of Ulster were always given more credence by Asquith's Administration than any threats ever made by Redmond and the Nationalists.

Even before the 1912 Irish Home Rule Bill got its Second Reading for the second time in March 1914 under the provisions of the 1911 Parliament Act, the issue had become a matter of pretty one-sided power politics. The Ulster Volunteer Force formed in January 1913 soon had 50,000 men under military training; towards the end of 1913 George V was instrumental in arranging secret meetings between Asquith and Bonar Law in an attempt to broker a compromise on Ireland; and Asquith privately told Redmond that he feared large-scale resignations of British officers should he have to order the army to suppress a Unionist insurrection in Ulster. Ideals of good government or a genuine search for ways to accommodate several proud nations within one United Kingdom were by this time very far from the minds of any of the key players in the game – unlike the more principled attitude which had characterised Gladstone's approach to the Irish problem a generation before. The Liberal Government and its Nationalist allies were at sixes and sevens on the issue, with Asquith hoping he could get away with no more than administrative devolution for Ulster within a framework of all-Irish legislative Home Rule, Lloyd George and Churchill arguing in Cabinet for at least the temporary exclusion of six of Ulster's nine counties, and Redmond feebly arguing for uniform Home Rule for the whole of Ireland.

At this critical stage in Irish history it is clear that at least temporary victory went to the resolute Unionist minority rather than to the irresolute and relatively ineffectual leaders of the Nationalist majority. In essence, although the third Irish Home Rule Bill eventually found its way onto the Statute Book in September 1914, a month or so after the outbreak of the First World War, it was a pyrrhic victory for Redmond and the Parliamentary Nationalists and a cautionary tale for Arthur Griffith, Patrick Pearse and the small band of extra-Parliamentary Nationalists who in June 1915 saw Asquith bring Bonar Law and Carson into the War Cabinet and thus seriously lengthen the odds against the temporarily suspended Home Rule legislation ever being put into effect in its intended form.

As the conflict on the Western Front got fiercer at the end of 1915 and as the prospect of conscription to replace those who had been killed or wounded became more urgent, the Irish National Party passed a resolution against such a policy being applied to Irishmen, while the mere threat of conscription acted as a recruiting sergeant in Ireland for the Sinn Fein volunteers. In the event, when the Westminster Parliament finally passed the Conscription Act in January 1916, the British Government had enough sense not to apply it to Ireland for fear of igniting rebellious passions. Meanwhile the clandestine Executive of the Irish Republican Brotherhood had formed a Military Council to plan an armed uprising against British rule. For many months Sir Roger Casement had been in secret talks with the Germans in an attempt to secure their assistance with weaponry and materiel for an Irish rebellion.

The Irish Uprising, which began on Easter Monday 1916 with the unexpected capture of the General Post Office in Dublin by a few hundred Irish volunteers led by Patrick Pearse, James Connolly and Joseph Plunkett, took nearly everyone by surprise. The idea of such a rebellion had been strongly resisted a few months earlier by Eoin MacNeill, the head of the Irish Volunteers, who had argued with his colleagues that the only possible basis for successful revolutionary action was deep and widespread popular discontent and that this did not exist at that time in Ireland. It took less than a week for the British military forces stationed in Dublin to achieve the suppression and surrender of the rebels, although the preponderance of the casualties in the fighting was on the Government side.

The various mini-rebellions in other parts of Ireland were put down pretty swiftly by the military and the police. The penalties of martial law were imposed rapidly and ruthlessly on the rebels, with the result that fifteen of the ringleaders were summarily tried and shot within a few weeks of the fateful uprising – while many others, such as Eamonn de Valera (then an American citizen) and William Cosgrave, had their death sentences commuted. In this respect the events of Easter 1916 symbolised the unerring proclivity of Irish nationalists for heroic gestures which were doomed to failure. On the other hand, the brutal way in which the British army put down the rebellion served to convert the initiative of an eccentric and unpopular minority into an heroic nationalist cause which then began to attract wide support in most of Ireland.

By 1916 the war against Germany was going very badly for the Allies and Asquith was leading a Grand Coalition with the Conservatives. In so far as the Prime Minister was able to devote time to the Irish problem, he was obviously keen to placate the Ulster Unionists and their Tory friends. He could safely discount the political claims of Redmond and the Parliamentary Irish Nationalists, but he was faced with the political imperative of placating Irish-American opinion in the hope of drawing a reluctant United States into the First World War on the Allied side. It was in this spirit that he handed to Lloyd George the poisoned chalice of seeking yet another 'permanent solution' to the Irish problem – in other words, finding how to reconcile the insistence of Carson and his Unionist friends upon the *permanent* exclusion from Home Rule of all the nine counties of Ulster with the protestations of Redmond that the very least he and his increasingly demoralised Nationalist colleagues could possibly accept was the *temporary* exclusion of the four most Protestant counties of Ulster. In the event Lloyd George gave matching and contradictory undertakings to each of his interlocutors in a policy of classic duplicity.

When Lloyd George succeeded Asquith as Prime Minister and head of the Coalition Government in December 1916, he had brokered a Parliamentary compromise on Ulster which the Cabinet had approved as a permanent solution to the Irish problem. This was that only *six* counties in Ulster would be excluded from the scope of the Home Rule settlement, but their exclusion would be of *indefinite* duration. The first point was a concession by Carson and the second a further concession by Redmond. In social and community terms, the compromise meant entrusting the fate of some Protestant Unionists to Catholic nationalist control in the counties of Donegal, Cavan and Monaghan, while entrusting the fate of some

Catholic nationalists to Protestant Unionist control in the counties of Fermanagh and Tyrone.

By the time the Americans entered the war in 1917, all Irish nationalists had become pretty despondent about their chances of achieving anything like their historic objectives and for the time being they were prepared to put their faith in the prospect of the International Peace Conference which President Wilson planned to hold when the war was finally won. Irish nationalist aspirations, which before the war had been attracted by the example of Austria-Hungary as a possible model for the British–Irish relationship, now looked to the examples of Canada or Australia as semi-independent dominions within the British Commonwealth. On the other hand, the pragmatic and unprincipled Lloyd George was quite prepared to ratify whatever he could get the warring parties in Ireland to agree upon between themselves – assuming that any agreement was ever likely to be possible.

To this end he organised an all-party Convention (boycotted by Sinn Fein) which opened in Dublin in July 1917, the month in which De Valera was triumphantly returned to the Westminster Parliament as Sinn Fein MP for East Clare, having been previously released under amnesty from an English prison where he had been serving a long sentence for his part in the Easter Uprising. De Valera had stood for election quite simply as the candidate who favoured a united Republic of Ireland, no more and no less, and on that simple platform he had roundly defeated Redmond's Irish National candidate. It was not surprising that the Convention got precisely nowhere and eventually collapsed in April 1918, since it was essentially a dispute between an intransigent Ulster Unionist Party and an increasingly ineffectual Irish National Party, while the only party truly capable of delivering worthwhile nationalist consent to a settlement (Sinn Fein) was excluded from the proceedings by its own choice.

The wheel of Irish history began to turn quickly once again during the final year of the First World War. In March 1918 John Redmond died in London after a short illness. In April 1918 the War Cabinet eventually decided to extend conscription to Ireland in a last-ditch attempt to replace some of the British casualties suffered when the Germans had launched their final offensive on the Western Front the previous month. This not only boosted Irish support for Sinn Fein but also provoked condemnation by the Catholic hierarchy in Ireland. In May 1918 the new British Viceroy, Field Marshal Lord French, declared that a German plot had been discovered in Ireland and this led the British authorities to arrest Arthur Griffith, Eamonn De Valera and 71 other leading figures in Sinn Fein, thereby increasing the party's popularity with the Irish people. Thus, when a General Election was held in December 1918 on the new, much wider franchise, the ever-patient Irish National Party was reduced from 68 to six seats (of which four were in Ulster thanks to an electoral pact with Sinn Fein in the Province), whereas Sinn Fein (of whose candidates 25 were returned unopposed and 48 were in jail during the campaign) won 73 seats and effectively became the voice of Irish nationalism; meanwhile the Ulster Unionists disappointed their supporters by gaining a majority of the popular vote in only four of Ulster's nine counties.

Robert Kee has argued that in the immediate aftermath of the First World War, the majority preference in Ireland as a whole was for Irish Home Rule with dominion status within the British Commonwealth; the Ulster exclusion problem could have been addressed by making a nationalist appeal on behalf of the whole of Ireland at the Versailles Peace Conference; and there was no widespread public support for any campaign to win sovereign independence for Ireland by force of arms or terrorism.[10] Yet this assessment of the situation in 1918 highlights the confusion and wishful thinking which characterised public attitudes to the Irish question at that time. *Firstly*, neither Home Rule for Ireland within the United Kingdom nor dominion status within the British Commonwealth was acceptable to an influential minority within Sinn Fein and the Irish Republican movement. *Secondly*, the leading participants at the 1919 Versailles Peace Conference were unwilling and unable to resolve the Irish problem, essentially because the British Government, representing one of the three victorious powers, was not going to be told what to do about this internal matter by the representatives of other nations. *Thirdly*, the paucity of public support for the Irish Republican hard-liners was never likely to deter such fanatics from what Charles Townshend has called their 'demonstration politics, the armed propaganda of a self-selected vanguard which claimed the power to interpret the [Irish] general will'.[11]

The history of the first few years after the First World War revealed a very great deal about the reasons why first Home Rule and then dominion status within the British Commonwealth failed to settle the Irish question. The concessions made to Irish nationalism by Lloyd George's post-war Coalition Administration were consistently too little and too late to satisfy Sinn Fein and the Irish Republicans, but simultaneously far too much to be acceptable to James Craig and the Ulster Unionists. Devolution, or Home Rule for all of Ireland within the United Kingdom, was no longer persuasive either to Irish Republicans or to Ulster Unionists once the Easter Uprising had taken place in 1916 and Sinn Fein had comprehensively replaced the Irish National Party as the voice of Irish nationalism at the 1918 General Election. Dominion status within the British Commonwealth may have been a British assumption or conceit which underpinned the Anglo-Irish Treaty in 1921; but it was never seen as an acceptable final settlement of the Irish question by Irish Republicans, whether pro-Treaty pragmatists like Griffith and Collins or anti-Treaty purists like De Valera; and in any case the Ulster Unionists and their Tory supporters had succeeded in bullying successive Liberal Administrations before the war and persuading Coalition Administrations during and after the war into accepting the exclusion of six counties in Ulster from any legislative arrangements for Irish Home Rule, albeit supposedly on a provisional basis.

The elected representatives of the Irish people at the first meeting of the *Dáil Éireann* (Irish Parliament) held in Dublin in January 1919 pledged themselves to accept nothing less than complete separation from Great Britain and issued a so-called Irish Declaration of Independence inspired by Patrick Pearse's Declaration at Easter 1916. Furthermore, many prominent members of the Dáil (such as Cathal Brugha and Michael Collins)

served in dual capacities both as members of the newly formed Irish Provisional Government and as Directors of Operations in the clandestine Irish Volunteers and Irish Republican Brotherhood. They regarded themselves as at war with the British, and from January 1919 to July 1921 they conducted a dual strategy of democratic initiatives and armed struggle against the British authorities in Ireland – principally against the officers of the Royal Irish Constabulary.

It could equally be said that the British Government under Lloyd George was pursuing a dual strategy towards Irish nationalism. On the one hand, it was engaged in the traditional British policy of coercion when it suppressed the Dáil in August 1919, proscribed *Sinn Fein* in November 1919, and deployed the notorious Black and Tans and Auxiliaries in January 1920 in those parts of Ireland which had become increasingly ungovernable; on the other hand, it brought forward in December 1919 new legislative proposals for Home Rule in Ireland which were to become the *1920 Government of Ireland Act* by the end of the following year. These were the first British Government proposals for the future governance of Ireland to take realistic account of Unionist determination to secure exclusion from Home Rule for the six most Protestant and Unionist counties in Ulster.

The proposals provided for six of the nine counties in Ulster and the twenty-six counties in the rest of Ireland to have their own devolved Assemblies (one at Stormont and one in Dublin) which would be constitutionally subordinate to the Imperial Parliament at Westminster. In practice, the most important difference was that whereas Craig reluctantly accepted devolution for Ulster as 'a final settlement' for the six counties, Collins and the other nationalist leaders rejected any institutions with a status subordinate to Westminster and continued the struggle for national independence free from allegiance to the British Crown and semi-colonial status in the British Empire. Nominal obeisance was paid in the legislation to the idea of maintaining a united Ireland by providing for the establishment of a Council of Ireland with 40 members drawn equally from each Irish Assembly which would be given the legal power, without further reference to Parliament at Westminster, to fuse the two Irish Assemblies into a single national Parliament – a pretence which Lloyd George must have known was an empty gesture and a dead letter in the light of Ulster Unionist determination to remain part of the United Kingdom at all costs.

The shape of things to come in the vexed relationship between Irish nationalism and British Unionism was clearly visible in some of the seminal events of this time. For example, the first feelers towards confidential talks between Lloyd George and Arthur Griffith in December 1920 were vitiated by the former's insistence that the Irish Republicans should surrender some of their arms before any talks could begin. When Lloyd George later went public on the idea in April 1921 by telling the House of Commons of the British Government's willingness to talk to 'representatives of the Irish people', he attached two key provisos: (1) there should be no coercion of Ulster (a virtual impossibility since 1912); and (2) the strategic unity of the Empire should be safeguarded (code for continuing Irish allegiance to the British Crown and Irish recognition of the ultimate supremacy of the Westminster Parliament).

The first proviso was soon to be resolved by the institutionalisation of partition when George V officially opened the devolved Parliament at Stormont in May 1921. The second proviso proved to be a major ambiguity and stumbling block both in the tortuous negotiations which produced the Anglo-Irish Treaty of December 1921 and in the subsequent slippery relations between the Irish Free State and the United Kingdom. When the British and Irish delegations finally signed the *1921 Anglo-Irish Treaty*, Lloyd George and his colleagues implicitly acknowledged that they no longer had the stomach to pursue a policy of 'colonial oppression' in Ireland and that the Irish representatives should be given the substance (if not all the forms) of national independence, at any rate in 26 of the 32 counties. They also recognised the ultimate failure of Home Rule or devolution as the basis of a durable political settlement for the bulk of Ireland. Equally, Michael Collins and his pragmatic colleagues who signed the Treaty in December 1921 implicitly

recognised the reality of Ulster Unionist power in six counties of Northern Ireland and hence their failure to achieve their goal of all-Ireland nationalism. Yet as Michael Collins later argued in the ratification debate in the Dáil, the Treaty at least gave Irish nationalists the possibility of achieving complete freedom from British rule (at some indeterminate point in the future); so there was still some hope of fulfilling the old Irish dream of Tone, O'Connell and Parnell.

On the whole, the Treaty signified for both sides a triumph of realism over fantasy and of war-weariness over muscular militarism. There was joint recognition of the political realities of partition, symbolised by the results of the May 1921 elections to the two Irish Assemblies in Belfast and Dublin.[12] There was joint recognition that the Ulster Unionists and their Conservative allies at Westminster would insist upon retaining the organic connection between Northern Ireland and the rest of the United Kingdom and that they might well seek to exploit the mechanisms of devolution for their own sectarian ends. There was joint recognition that the Irish Republicans would negotiate (and fight) for as much real independence as they could secure at that time, while keeping open the option of manoeuvring and fighting for more if opportunities should arise in the future. There was joint recognition that the British Government and people were losing the will to use force indefinitely in order to prevent the Irish Republicans from fulfilling their nationalist dream, at any rate outside the six counties where the forces of Ulster Unionism could be counted upon to prevent it.

The successive attempts by Gladstone, Asquith and Lloyd George in the late nineteenth and early twentieth centuries to devolve executive and legislative powers to Ireland within the United Kingdom or latterly within the British Empire and Commonwealth can be seen, *retrospectively*, to have been doomed to failure. This was essentially because policy makers in London had to try to reconcile the irreconcilable: the fundamental incompatibility of the *Nationalist* tendency, whose goal (at any rate by 1921) was clearly an independent republican Ireland and who considered themselves Irish first and last, and the *Unionist* tendency concentrated in the north-east of Ulster (but still extant as an abandoned minority in the south of Ireland) whose goal was the preservation at all costs of the Union with the rest of the United Kingdom and who considered themselves British first and Irish only after that. All the varieties of Home Rule or devolution that were proposed for Ireland over the period from 1886 to 1921 suffered from the fatal flaw of appearing to militant Nationalists to be an unsatisfactory half-way house on the road to republican independence and of being anathema to militant Unionists (and their strident allies in the British Parliament who were concerned above all to preserve the integrity of the British Empire) who felt threatened with expulsion from their own country and domination by intolerable Catholic and Nationalist rule from Dublin.

It could perhaps be advanced as a plea in mitigation on behalf of three great Liberal Prime Ministers of the United Kingdom that each of them had to contend with two fatal difficulties in wrestling with the Irish problem. *Firstly*, the Parliamentary leaders of Irish nationalism were consistently inconsistent (and arguably downright dishonest) in the conflicting signals they gave about the acceptability of Home Rule as a final settlement of the Irish question. *Secondly*, from the very beginning of the search for a viable solution to the Irish problem there was never the basis of all-party agreement or even governing party unity that would have been essential to the success of any measure of constitutional change of the significance of Home Rule for Ireland. Such measures of devolution for Ireland as were introduced by Liberal Administrations (in 1886, 1893, 1907, 1912 and 1920) were, with the exception of Gladstone's first Home Rule Bill, brought forward without much genuine conviction and largely in a spirit of political expediency or, latterly, weariness and desperation. Indeed, the absence of a positive political consensus at Westminster *in favour* of devolution for Ireland, which nevertheless threatened something akin to mutiny in some units of the British army in 1914, arguably helped to precipitate the nationalist Easter Uprising in 1916 and contributed to the so-called

war for Irish independence from January 1919 to July 1921.

Partition and devolution to Stormont

The history of Northern Ireland from 1921 to 1972 provides a rare, possibly unique, example in democratic societies of a form of devolution which, although originally *imposed* upon an unwilling people, was almost immediately exploited by the majority community in the Province for its own sectarian purposes. It will be recalled that Carson and Craig (with the militant backing of the Ulster Volunteers and strong support from certain elements of the officer class in the British army) had successfully bullied and intimidated the Asquith Administration in 1912–14 into granting the option of exclusion from all-Ireland Home Rule to at least six of the nine counties of Ulster (Antrim, Armagh, Down, Derry, Tyrone and Fermanagh). With the passage of the *1920 Government of Ireland Act* this option became a reality in that under the legislation the newly formed devolved Government of Northern Ireland was given one month's grace following ratification of the Anglo-Irish Treaty by the Westminster Parliament (effected by the 1922 Irish Agreement Act) within which to opt out of the so-called Irish Free State and go its own way on the basis of both executive and legislative devolution within the United Kingdom.

The most salient consequence of this chain of events was that whereas the leaders of the new Irish Free State had negotiated and fought for nearly complete independence from the United Kingdom based upon a rather ambiguous dominion status within the British Commonwealth, the leaders of the newly devolved Administration in Northern Ireland had reluctantly accepted a provisional settlement for the six counties which, under the terms of the Anglo-Irish Treaty of 1921, could theoretically be modified by a tripartite Boundary Commission (consisting of representatives from Whitehall, Dublin and Belfast) but which in practice was regarded as permanent by the Ulster Unionists and arguably by the British

Government as well. Vernon Bogdanor was right to observe that

> the decision to establish a Parliament [at Stormont] for the six counties was therefore not based on any considered view of good government in Ireland, but was rather the by-product of an attempt by the British Government to extricate itself completely from Irish affairs.[13]

From the very outset of devolution to Stormont three key questions were posed which could only be definitively answered by the passage of events over a period of time. The first was whether the partition of Ireland agreed in the 1921 Anglo-Irish Treaty and institutionally reinforced by the terms of the 1920 Government of Ireland Act would be provisional or permanent. The second was whether devolved power in Northern Ireland would be exercised on a basis of power sharing between the communities in the Province or of power holding by the dominant Protestant and Unionist interest. The third was whether the governance of Ireland would be a matter of sustained British interest or of renewed British indifference, at least as long as there were no crises to force the Irish question back to the top of the political agenda in Westminster and Whitehall.

As to whether partition would be provisional or permanent, it was obvious from the impassioned speeches made during the ratification debate in the Dáil in December 1921 and January 1922 that no Irish nationalist (whether pragmatist or purist) was then prepared to write off the future possibility of Irish reunification. Arthur Griffith commended the Treaty which he had helped to negotiate by claiming that it was 'honourable to Ireland' and safeguarded vital national interests. Michael Collins argued that it gave the new Irish Free State 'the freedom to achieve ultimate freedom', almost certainly a reference to the final goal of Irish republican independence on an all-Ireland basis. Kevin O'Higgins (later a leading member of the first Fine Gael Government) described the Treaty as 'a basis for peaceful political evolution', which implied a willingness to negotiate but not to fight for all-Ireland unity. Eamonn de Valera adopted a rejectionist position on the grounds that 'we are signing our names to a promise we cannot

keep' and his sticking point was his refusal to countenance any oath of allegiance to the British Crown. However, in his notorious Document No. 2 he seemed prepared to accept the provisions on partition. At the end of the day none of the leading Nationalists in the Dáil, whether pragmatists or purists, was prepared to sacrifice the achievement of virtual Irish independence in 26 counties for the distant possibility of complete Irish independence in 32 counties.

As far as the British Government was concerned, it was necessary to distinguish between what was said formally for the record and the confidential assurances that were given by Lloyd George to Sir James Craig, the leader of the Ulster Unionists, and to senior members of the Coalition Government such as Winston Churchill. The formal position of the British Government was clearly set out in the official summary of the *1920 Government of Ireland Act* which stated:

> although at the beginning there are to be two Parliaments and two Governments in Ireland, the Act contemplates and affords every facility for Union between North and South, and empowers the two Parliaments by mutual agreement and joint action to terminate partition and to set up one Parliament and one Government for the whole of Ireland.[14]

The informal position was conveyed in secret correspondence between Lloyd George and Sir James Craig to the effect that the Ulster Unionists would not be coerced by the British Government out of the United Kingdom and into a union with the rest of Ireland – an undertaking which had first been given in a similarly covert way by Asquith to Carson during the period immediately before the First World War. So although the British Government appeared ambivalent about partition, it took no active steps to bring the division of Ireland to an end.

The Ulster Unionist position on partition was adamantly opposed to any further concessions to the Irish Nationalists, whether located south or north of the inner-Irish border. As Sir James Craig wrote in a letter to Lloyd George which was quoted in the Northern Ireland House of Commons, 'much against our wish but in the interests of peace we accepted this [the 1920 Government of Ireland

Act] as a *final settlement* of the long outstanding difficulty with which Great Britain has been confronted.'[15] In other words, he was saying with all the force at his command that he and the people he represented would much rather *not* have been starting from where they were, but given that they were where they were, they were determined to see that the political arrangements which had been imposed upon them were vigorously defended and, by implication, exploited for any advantages which might flow to their embattled community.

Thus the constitutional Monarchy in the United Kingdom was replicated in miniature in Northern Ireland with a Governor-General and two Houses of Parliament: a devolved House of Commons of 52 members elected by proportional representation (a feeble concession to power sharing with northern Nationalists) and a Senate of 26 members, two of whom were *ex officio* and the other 24 elected by the Lower House according to proportional principles. The Governor-General was the nominal head of the Government in Northern Ireland, but he acted on the advice of the Prime Minister and six other members of the Northern Ireland Cabinet, and these Ministers were in their turn responsible to both Houses of the Northern Ireland Parliament. Stormont (as it became known in political shorthand) was supposed to legislate for 'the peace, order and good government' of Northern Ireland, while the Imperial Parliament at Westminster retained two categories of powers: 'excepted powers' in relation to peace and war, foreign policy, etc.; and 'reserved powers' in relation to UK taxation, land purchase, etc. The organic connection between Stormont and the mother country was retained by giving Northern Ireland the right to send a reduced contingent of thirteen MPs to Westminster who were elected by first-past-the-post (like all other Westminster MPs) and were able to speak and vote on 'Imperial matters' which affected Northern Ireland as much as other parts of the United Kingdom.

There was a third category of statutory provisions in the 1920 Act which concerned matters entrusted to the competence of the so-called *Council of Ireland*. This provided the machinery to terminate partition without further reference to the Imperial Parliament at Westminster. It was supposed to consist of a President nominated by the Governor-General and 40 representatives drawn equally from Stormont and the Dáil. In the event this path-finding body never met and so the vain idea of north–south reconciliation without any further interference from London was still-born. Indeed, if it had ever met and tried to operate effectively, it would almost certainly have been hopelessly deadlocked because the exact parity of representation would have given each side a veto over the other.

The ideal of power sharing between the two embattled communities in Northern Ireland flickered briefly into life when, as a result of the first elections to Stormont in 1921 (under proportional representation), the Unionists won 40 seats, the Nationalists six seats and Sinn Fein six seats – which gave the minority community at least some representation in every part of Northern Ireland except Belfast city. However, old habits of abstention and rejectionism would not die and the members of both the nationalist parties refused to take their seats in what they considered was an illegitimate Parliament. Thus all 24 indirectly elected members of the Senate were chosen by Protestant Unionists, and Northern Ireland politics began to polarise fatally and obsessively on either side of the Unionist–Nationalist divide. The situation was made worse in February 1922 when there was an outbreak of vicious inter-communal violence with the Catholics/Nationalists getting the worst of the exchanges. These developments in their turn gave Sir James Craig and his Unionist colleagues an excuse (if they needed one) to introduce draconian measures of law and order which further alienated the minority community and confirmed them in their attitude of suspicion and hatred towards the Protestant/Unionist majority. Undoubtedly, the Nationalist minority in the north would have much preferred rule from Dublin to any arrangements made under the 1920 Government of Ireland Act; but one suspects that even in 1921–22 they would have preferred continued rule from London to rule from Stormont in any shape or form.

The vain hope of power sharing in Northern Ireland was kept alive principally by the fact that the 1920 Act had outlawed any change in the electoral system for Stormont for at least the first three years of its operation. However, the same dispensation did not apply at local council level and proportional representation for local elections was abolished in 1922. This encouraged the Ulster Unionists to continue with their notorious gerrymandering of local district and constituency boundaries which had already enabled them in the previous year to increase Belfast's representation at Stormont from four to sixteen seats, of which only one was won by a Nationalist. At the second Stormont election held in 1925 (still under proportional representation), when only 40 of the 52 seats were contested, the Official Unionists won 22 seats, the Independent Unionists five seats, the Nationalists nine seats, the Republicans one seat and the Labour Party three seats. This result represented another very comfortable victory for the Unionists in a miniature political system that was fast becoming rigid and corrupt, and in which the political alienation of the minority community was rapidly becoming pathological.

By the next Stormont election in 1929, the ruling Unionists had changed the electoral system to first-past-the-post. This had the desired effect (from their sectarian point of view) of ensuring the entrenchment of bi-polar politics in the six counties, with the polarisation based upon the Unionist versus Nationalist divide and upon some carefully drawn constituency boundaries which guaranteed a Unionist victory nearly everywhere every time. Sure enough, when the election was held, it was even more of a foregone conclusion than the previous two elections, with 22 out of 48 seats uncontested (the remaining four university seats were still elected by proportional representation) and with members for the 26 contested seats elected as follows: Unionist eighteen, Independent Unionist two, Nationalist five and Labour one. At the following Stormont election in 1933 no fewer than 33 of the seats were uncontested (70 per cent of the total) and 'democracy' in Northern Ireland had become a tragic farce.

The conclusive answer to our second question about power sharing or power holding in Northern Ireland during the entire period of devolved

government from 1921 to 1972 must be that the arrangements put in place by the British and then ruthlessly exploited by the Ulster Unionists for at least half a century thereafter were a travesty of democracy. They produced prolonged and sterile political polarisation between Unionism and Nationalism, voter apathy leading to alienation especially of the minority community, and renewed temptations to replace the ballot box with other, often more violent means of effecting political change.

As to the question of whether the governance of Ireland would be a matter of sustained British interest or of renewed British indifference, the answer really depended upon the attitude with which Lloyd George's Coalition Administration and subsequent British Governments approached the anomaly of a divided Ireland in the twentieth century. It was also influenced no doubt by the priorities of British public opinion and the extent to which developments originating in Northern Ireland were capable of disrupting the flow of larger events affecting the United Kingdom. If previous experience over several centuries was anything to go by, the likelihood was that the British people and their Government would be generally indifferent to events and conditions in Ireland, whether north or south, unless of course some vital British national interests seemed to be involved.

It was paradoxical, to say the least, that while the *1920 Government of Ireland Act* ringingly declared the absolute supremacy of the Westminster Parliament 'over all persons, matters and things in Northern Ireland and every part thereof', successive British Governments paid remarkably little attention to events in the Province – and indeed events in Ireland as a whole – once it became clear that vital British interests were unlikely to be threatened either by Unionist institutionalisation of sectarian advantage in the north or by internecine strife and civil war between the Nationalist factions in the south. Even though the financial arrangements between the United Kingdom and Northern Ireland were seriously unbalanced, in that Westminster authorised about four-fifths of Northern Ireland revenue and Stormont authorised about four-fifths of Northern

Ireland expenditure, British politicians of all parties seemed quite relaxed about the situation – as they were in relation to the residual financial obligations of the Irish Free State which were written off by the British Government in 1925.

One can speculate about why it was that Westminster did not apparently object when Stormont passed the *1922 Civil Authorities Act* which provided the Northern Ireland Minister of Home Affairs with draconian emergency powers – such as detention without trial, rights of search and entry for the Royal Ulster Constabulary, and punishments of flogging and hanging for various firearms and explosives offences – and why it was that Stormont was permitted to pass the *1926 Emergency Powers Act* and then use it against trade unions in the Province. Perhaps it was because the use of draconian powers by the properly constituted authorities was merely the latest instance in a long tradition of coercive government in Ireland and in the year of the General Strike on the mainland of Britain coercive legislation against trade unions did not seem out of place to members of the ruling class, whether in London or Belfast. For whatever reasons, there appeared to be a well-founded consensus by which politicians at Westminster and at Stormont agreed that they would not invade each other's jurisdiction. Even though provision had been made in the 1920 Government of Ireland Act for any disputes over legislative competence between Stormont and Westminster to be submitted to the Judicial Committee of the Privy Council for final adjudication, in the first sixteen years of Northern Ireland's existence as a subordinate jurisdiction only two contested cases were brought before the courts.

When it had become crystal clear from the sustained Ulster Unionist boycott of the proposed Council of Ireland that such a mechanism of north–south reconciliation was going to make absolutely no headway and when any ideas of adjusting the inner-Irish border had been finally abandoned in 1925, the Westminster Parliament seemed perfectly content in 1926 to abolish this body which had never been convened. Equally, when in 1938 de Valera at the head of the *Fianna Fail* Government in Dublin strongly sought the return to Eire of the two naval bases in Bantry Bay and at Queenstown near Cork which the British had retained under the 1921 Anglo-Irish Treaty, the Chamberlain Government in London apparently saw no problem in acceding to the Irish request. All in all, one is drawn to the conclusion that, compared with the great events of the inter-war period which preoccupied the rest of the United Kingdom – e.g. the General Strike, the Great Depression, the Statute of Westminster and the ominous rise of Fascist dictatorships in Germany and Italy – developments in Ireland, whether north or south, must have seemed rather parochial and unimportant in London, if they made any impact at all.

Whatever may have been the *reasons* for British indifference towards Ireland during the period of Stormont rule, the *effect* was certainly to allow the Unionist authorities in Northern Ireland to exercise a degree of political autonomy virtually as great as that for which the Nationalists had fought so hard and spilled so much blood in the Irish Free State. For many years the authorities in London seemed to find it both convenient and congenial (1) to insist upon the constitutional convention that Westminster should not interfere with, still less overrule, the powers that had been transferred to Stormont under the 1920 Act; and (2) to acquiesce in a political situation in which the statutory safeguards that had been built into the 1920 Act to protect the Catholic and Nationalist minority in the north were not invoked or made effective. It is sobering to note the force of Vernon Bogdanor's observation that 'on no occasion until 1969 did Westminster legislate for Northern Ireland within the sphere of transferred matters against the wishes of the Northern Ireland Government'.[16]

Once again we can see how the history of British–Irish relations endlessly repeats itself, since callous and complacent indifference among the British political class at Westminster was as evident during the period of Stormont rule as it had been in earlier centuries when Ireland as a whole had been by turns neglected, exploited, coerced and ignored. Specifically, successive British Governments, both Labour and Conservative, showed themselves unwilling to take a proper interest in

Northern Ireland or to use Westminster's much vaunted legislative supremacy until they were forced, perhaps shamed, into doing so in the late 1960s by the protests of the civil rights movement in Northern Ireland against the policies of the Stormont Government. Hence from 1968 onwards the Wilson Administration in London urgently pressed a serious and belated reform programme upon the Stormont Administration led by Captain O'Neill; and a Downing Street Declaration in August 1969 sought to insist upon equal rights and full protection of the (British) law for the citizens of Ulster as much as for the citizens of other parts of the United Kingdom.

It is thus perfectly justifiable to indict successive British Governments and Parliaments at Westminster for not having acted more purposefully and sooner to rectify the accumulated abuses which were associated with Unionist rule in Ulster. It was a disgrace that Westminster 'was able to bring its supremacy into play only under pathological conditions when the normal working of devolution had been disrupted by sectarian protest'.[17] The fact that the actual relationship between Northern Ireland and the rest of the United Kingdom during the whole period of Stormont rule had many *quasi-federal* characteristics is not a matter for which anyone can take any credit, since it was far removed from what was *originally intended* and provided none of the constitutional safeguards which are normally associated with a genuinely federal constitution in which the powers and functions of the various levels of government are properly codified and independently monitored by a supreme court. When in the early 1970s the political practices of Stormont rule in Northern Ireland were finally recognised as being beyond redemption – largely as a result of the civil rights disturbances and the refusal of Brian Faulkner, the Northern Ireland Prime Minister, to cede control of security in the Province to London – the Heath Administration decided to abolish the Stormont Parliament and institute a period of direct rule from London.

Direct rule from Westminster

The prorogation of the Stormont Parliament in 1972, its abolition in 1973 and replacement with direct rule from London amounted to a traumatic experience for the Ulster Unionists who had been running their own show in Northern Ireland for more than 50 years with relatively little interference from London, except on financial matters. With a newly created Northern Ireland Office headed by a Secretary of State in the British Cabinet, the politicians and people of Northern Ireland had to get used to something akin to client status, mitigated only by the fact that for most Ulster Unionists direct rule from London seemed preferable to being 'sold into the slavery' of Papist rule from Dublin.

With the Stormont Parliament abolished, the number of Northern Ireland MPs at Westminster was gradually increased over the following years from twelve to eighteen and a Grand Committee for Northern Ireland was created in the House of Commons to scrutinise the draft Orders in Council in which form most of the direct rule legislation for the Province was considered by Parliament at Westminster. Procedures for controlling and supervising the Northern Ireland Office relied upon the traditional mechanisms of Parliamentary questions and debates, but in 1994 they were supplemented by the establishment of a Northern Ireland Select Committee. The safeguard for the Unionist majority against the possibility of involuntary reunification with the rest of Ireland, which under the terms of the *1949 Ireland Act* would have required the consent of the Stormont Parliament, was replaced by the guarantee contained in Section 1 of the *1973 Northern Ireland Constitution Act* which provided that neither Northern Ireland nor any part of it would cease to be a part of the United Kingdom 'without the consent of the majority of the people of Northern Ireland voting in a poll'. Provision was made for such a poll to be held at intervals of not less than ten years; but when the first poll was held in March 1973, the authority of the result (99 per cent in favour of Northern Ireland remaining part of the UK) was reduced by the low turnout of 58 per cent caused by the Nationalist parties in the Province advising their supporters to boycott it.

Whereas the Nationalist community in Northern Ireland had had a range of legitimate grievances against the dominant Ulster Unionists when they had ruled the Province from Stormont, the changes of 1972–74 inevitably redirected their grievances towards the quasi-colonial characteristics of direct rule, while most of the Ulster Unionists felt themselves to be little more than spectators of their own political process. The recourse to direct rule, which was always regarded as a temporary expedient by successive Governments in London, perhaps came to be seen as the preferred second-best option for the government of Northern Ireland by all communities and interests in the Province, but that did not mean that anyone (other than successive Ministers in the Northern Ireland Office) was really prepared to speak up for it. Admittedly, some of the Ulster Unionist MPs at Westminster (especially Enoch Powell who sat for South Down) saw it as a significant step towards the reintegration of the six counties into the UK. Yet on the other side of the political divide in Northern Irish representation at Westminster, Social Democratic and Labour MPs, such as Gerry Fitt and John Hume, voiced the grievances of all non-Unionist people in Northern Ireland who felt themselves marginalised and politically dispossessed by London's take-over of Northern Ireland politics. The most dangerous consequence of the move to direct rule, however, was that the previous iniquities and injustices of Unionist-dominated devolved politics had been replaced neither by strengthened local government nor by truly accountable public administration in the Northern Ireland Office, but by something of a political vacuum which the Catholic Irish Republican Army (IRA) and their Protestant counterparts in the Ulster Volunteer Force (UVF) were keen to fill.

Quite apart from the very real danger in the late 1970s and early 1980s that the men of violence on both sides of the sectarian divide in the Province would come to dominate and even obliterate the democratic political process, cogent constitutional criticisms could be made of the administrative and legislative arrangements for Northern Ireland under direct rule. *Firstly*, the arrangements for legislation on Northern Ireland were deeply un-satisfactory in that the prevalence of Orders in Council (which could not be as thoroughly scrutinised at Westminster as primary legislation) meant that there were lower standards of Parliamentary control for the Province than there were for the rest of the United Kingdom. *Secondly*, there was no way in which local government could adequately close the democratic deficit in Northern Ireland, both because most local functions were performed by non-elected Boards answerable to Ministers in the Northern Ireland Office and because Stormont had previously steamrollered what little local government there had been in the Province before 1972. Notwithstanding these very real problems, the 'temporary' expedient of direct rule lasted from 1972 to 1997, while successive British Governments strove mightily to see off the terrorist threats to public security in the Province (and sometimes on the mainland of Britain too) *and* to find a durable basis for the so-called 'peace process' which was designed to reconcile the two communities in Northern Ireland within a wider international framework.

Three separate attempts were made in the 1970s and 1980s to introduce various forms of devolution for Northern Ireland on a modified basis. The first, which was introduced under the terms of the 1973 Northern Ireland Constitution Act, involved *the creation of an Assembly* with 78 members elected by single transferable vote and the creation of a broadly based Executive including representatives of both the Unionist and the Nationalist communities in Northern Ireland. The main powers to be transferred to the Executive and the Assembly were in the areas of health and social services, education, housing, agriculture and the environment, since Westminster was to retain responsibility (at least initially) for law and order, anti-terrorist measures and anything to do with the electoral franchise. Elections to the new Assembly took place in June 1973 and a power-sharing Executive consisting of members of both communities was formed in January 1974. What came to be known as a North–South 'Irish dimension' to the arrangements was embodied in the creation of a *Council of Ireland* with limited, cross-border executive functions and made up of seven Ministers from the newly formed

Northern Ireland Executive and seven from the Government of the Republic of Ireland. This reflected the growing consensus in London that the influence of Dublin needed to be brought more into play in an attempt to reassure the minority Catholic community in the north and to encourage greater cross-border cooperation in dealing with Provisional IRA threats to the security of the Province.

Once again, an initiative for devolution in Ireland was vitiated by the Ulster Unionists who on this occasion objected vehemently to the cession of sovereignty implied by the proposal for a Council of Ireland in which certain cross-border responsibilities of Northern Ireland and the Irish Republic would have been exercised in common with representatives from the South. It seemed that any initiative of this kind, however mild, which was designed to engender greater North–South cooperation in Ireland was always going to be regarded by the Ulster Unionists as the thin end of the wedge which might lead one day to Irish reunification. In this paranoid atmosphere Brian Faulkner, the Unionist leader who had been willing to embark upon such an experiment in intra-Irish cooperation, felt it necessary to resign from the Ulster Unionist Party, although he continued as leader of the Executive in a personal capacity.

The position of any other Unionists who might have been willing to entertain the prospect of even limited power-sharing with Irish Nationalists was further weakened when candidates backed by the so-called United Ulster Unionist Coalition managed to win eleven of the twelve Northern Ireland seats at Westminster at the General Election which was prematurely and disastrously called by Edward Heath for the end of February 1974. However, the *coup de grâce* was administered by the Ulster Workers Council, supported by various loyalist paramilitaries and other die-hard Unionist elements, who in May 1974 staged a general strike in Northern Ireland. This finally precipitated Brian Faulkner's resignation as leader of the Executive and the prorogation of the Assembly, effectively rendering it impossible for this particular experiment in devolution to continue.

The General Election of February 1974 had surprisingly been won by the Labour Party and the new Government soon persuaded Parliament to pass the 1974 Northern Ireland Act which dissolved the Assembly and restored direct rule to the Province. The legislation also paved the way for a second, rather unconvincing attempt to explore a new route to devolution via *a Northern Ireland Convention* elected by single transferable vote, but this failed to make any real progress by agreement between the two communities in Northern Ireland and was in its turn subsequently dissolved in 1976. For the balance of its term in office until 1979, the Labour Government abandoned attempts to conciliate the Nationalists and their supporters in the Dublin Government, but instead pursued a tough counter-terrorist policy under the codename 'Operation Motorman', designed to make life increasingly difficult for the Provisional IRA. The opportunity for renewed devolution seemed to have passed.

The third attempt at devolution during the period of direct rule in Northern Ireland was launched by the Thatcher Administration under the 1982 Northern Ireland Act, not long after the British Government had successfully faced down Bobby Sands and other Provisional IRA prisoners who had gone on long hunger-strikes in the Maze Prison. It provided for yet another *Northern Ireland Assembly* elected by single transferable vote in order to ensure fairly balanced representation for both communities. The devolved functions were to be more limited than those of the equivalent Assembly proposed in the early 1970s and greater emphasis was placed upon the scrutiny of legislative proposals put forward by the Northern Ireland Office. Allowance was made for the future possibility of so-called 'rolling devolution' of further functions to the Assembly if at least 70 per cent of the members agreed to the proposals or if the Secretary of State deemed that they were acceptable to both communities in Northern Ireland. On the whole, this meant that the Assembly members themselves retained control of the pace and direction of devolution and it was certainly envisaged that a genuinely power-sharing Executive acceptable to both communities would have to be formed before the Westminster

Parliament would give its authority by Order in Council for the process to proceed.

On this occasion the project fell foul of the SDLP and other Nationalists in the North who decided to abstain from participation in the Assembly because they considered the plans gave insufficient weight to the so-called Irish dimension; doubtless they also felt somewhat captured and outnumbered in an Assembly dominated by various categories of Unionists. This made it impossible to maintain that the arrangements had attracted real support from both communities and consequently the Assembly had to be dissolved in June 1986 after having promised much and absorbed a good deal of British Ministerial energy, but ultimately having failed to achieve its power-sharing objectives.

Internationalising the peace process

After all the failures and disappointments for those in Britain (and the United States) who genuinely wanted to see progress made towards overcoming the intractable Northern Irish problems, officials and Ministers in the British Foreign Office under Sir Geoffrey Howe and in the Northern Ireland Office under firstly Jim Prior and then Tom King began to realise that the log-jam could only be broken if the Governments in London and Dublin cooperated more constructively to develop political institutions within which legitimate representatives of both communities in Northern Ireland could agree to take shared responsibility for the fate of the six counties. From the very inception of this period it dawned upon Ministers and their advisers in both capitals that each would have to try to 'deliver' its client community to the inter-communal negotiating table, and that if they were to have any serious chance of achieving this, they would have to use all the leverage and patience of which they were capable – and have recourse to increasingly helpful pressure from the Americans upon both communities in Northern Ireland as well. Thus it was that efforts to resolve the residual 'Irish problem' were gradually transformed into an internationalised 'peace process'; and a centuries-old domestic political problem for the British and the Irish evolved during the 1980s and 1990s into a much wider challenge for the international community in which there were many more stake-holders than simply the Unionist and Nationalist communities of Northern Ireland.

The shift towards an internationalised peace process had begun rather tentatively in 1981 when the British and Irish Governments had agreed to undertake a series of joint inter-governmental studies of the Northern Ireland problem. For a time this quiet work at official level was eclipsed by the proceedings of the so-called New Ireland Forum, a conference of the main Irish nationalist parties (excluding Sinn Fein) from both north and south of the border which was established in Dublin in 1983. However, when this conference reported in 1984, its proposals were really too partial to be politically acceptable to other parties at the time since they focused upon only three options: a reunited Ireland, a federal Ireland, and a Northern Ireland governed by the joint authority of London and Dublin.

Accordingly, the Thatcher Administration in London and the Haughey Administration in Dublin persevered with their own joint search for a more suitable inter-governmental framework and eventually arrived at the *Anglo-Irish Agreement of 1985*. This took the form of an international treaty and was to provide the overall framework within which the peace process for Northern Ireland took place for many years thereafter. It established four main principles: firstly, any change in the constitutional status of Northern Ireland would require the consent of a majority of the people of Northern Ireland, but with the added implication that the British Government would facilitate the reunification of Ireland in the event of this condition being satisfied; secondly, an inter-governmental conference, jointly chaired by British and Irish Ministers with a permanent secretariat in Belfast, should be established to seek agreement upon practical measures to benefit both communities in Northern Ireland; thirdly, agreement would be required upon the goal of administrative devolution in Northern Ireland, again on the understanding that this achieved the cooperation of both communities; and fourthly, cross-border coopera-tion on security matters between London and Dublin should continue and be enhanced.

Over the following years the British and Irish Governments were keen to maintain the momen-tum of the peace process and especially to create an inter-governmental framework and a political atmosphere in which Sinn Fein and the IRA might initiate a ceasefire in their terrorist campaign against the security forces in Northern Ireland and sometimes on the mainland of Britain as well. Thus the so-called *Downing Street Declaration of December 1993* jointly issued by the two Prime Ministers, John Major and Albert Reynolds, put the emphasis upon the possibility of Irish reunification with the concurrent consent of the Irish people north and south of the border, and was under-pinned by both a British Government reassurance that it had 'no selfish strategic or economic interest in Northern Ireland' and by an Irish Government reassurance that 'the democratic right of self-determination by the people of Ireland as a whole must be exercised subject to the agreement and consent of a majority of the people of Northern Ireland'.[18]

It seems that gradually this process of political signalling to the leaders of the paramilitary groups – whether in the IRA or the UVF – began to pay off, since in the autumn of 1994 both sides announced a ceasefire in their terrorist operations. This in turn helped to create further momentum for the peace process, which was soon reflected in the publica-tion by the British and Irish Governments of so-called *Joint Framework Documents* in February 1995. These documents stressed the desire of both Governments to achieve the greatest pos-sible measure of democratic self-government in Northern Ireland within a framework of external guarantees for both communities. As far as the first aspect was concerned, this was to be achieved by setting up a proportionally elected Assembly to oversee the administration of the various functional departments of the Northern Ireland Office, and to exercise legislative powers on devolved matters subject to the safeguards of weighted majorities and blocking mechanisms on the most contro-versial issues. The overall intention was that such

institutions should work by consensus between the two communities, with the extra external safeguard of continuing constitutional guarantees from the British and Irish Governments against discrimi-natory executive or legislative action by the devolved authorities in Northern Ireland.

The North–South strand of the peace process contained in the Joint Framework Documents relied upon the creation of a new north–south body composed of the political heads of the various departmental committees in the Northern Ireland Assembly and their political counterparts from the Irish Government in Dublin. Such a body was to have powers of an indeterminate nature over a range of policy matters to be agreed, but almost certainly focusing executive powers upon all-Ireland issues such as transport networks, indus-trial development, tourism and the administration of cross-border projects supported by the European Union. North–South harmonisation of policy was envisaged for such matters as agriculture and fisheries, energy, education, health and social services; and it was further suggested that there might be a Parliamentary tier to oversee such new administrative structures.

The East–West strand of the peace process envisaged the further development of the arrange-ments originally put forward in the 1985 Anglo-Irish Agreement, but enshrined in a new inter-governmental treaty. The Anglo-Irish Inter-Governmental Conference would continue to exercise a consultative role on all matters not devolved to the Northern Ireland institutions and to supervise and guide the development of the new institutions subject to the continuing sovereignty of the British and Irish Parliaments over their respective jurisdictions.

The constitutional agenda had also to be addressed in the Joint Framework Documents, because the legacy of history was still not finally resolved to the satisfaction of all parties. Essen-tially, this meant that Articles 2 and 3 of the Irish constitution and Section 75 of the 1920 Government of Ireland Act needed to be changed to reflect full acceptance by both sides of self-determination for the people of Northern Ireland by withdrawing any territorial claim by the Irish Republic to the six counties, while at the same time keeping alive the possibility of the reunification of Ireland by mutual consent of the people north and south of the border. It was also suggested that a common charter or covenant should be adopted by the elected representatives of the people in both parts of Ireland to strengthen the protection of human rights for people of all communities and traditions throughout the island of Ireland.

By this stage it was already apparent that success in resolving the Northern Ireland problem required simultaneous action on a number of different political levels and different political dimensions. It required institutions and processes for inter-communal reconciliation between the two communities *within Northern Ireland*; it required confidence-building solutions for so-called north–south relations *between the legitimate politial authorities in Belfast and Dublin*; it required a continuing relationship of mutual trust and support *between London and Dublin* in order to buttress the other arrangements with suitable external guarantees; and it required changes or amendments to the *constitutional arrangements of both the United Kingdom and the Irish Republic* in order to overcome some of the remaining legacies of history. It might even be added that the best efforts of moderates in both communities in Northern Ireland and of patient diplomacy in London and Dublin were not sufficient to clinch the eventual achievement and full implementation of the Belfast Agreement of Good Friday 1998, since this also required the helpful intervention and encouragement of the Clinton Administration in Washington and the patient good offices of Senator George Mitchell in his role as external mediator in the peace process.

Power sharing and the Belfast Agreement

The constitutional position of Northern Ireland, for which the New Labour Government in London inherited responsibility in May 1997, had certain unique and perverse characteristics which were the product of Irish history. Firstly, while Northern Ireland has been clearly subject to *UK constitutional jurisdiction* since the 1920 Government of Ireland Act and, before that, the 1800 Act of Union, its fate has been strongly influenced by the *Irish nationalist aspiration*, which was explicitly expressed in Articles 1 and 2 of the 1937 Eire constitution, to assert a right of self-determination for the Irish nation and thus to lay claim (at least formally) to the whole territory of Ireland including the six counties of Northern Ireland. Secondly, while the determination of the Protestant and Unionist majority in the North to remain within the United Kingdom has been recognised by successive British Governments and Parliaments at least since the partition of Ireland in 1920–22; this has appeared to thwart the wishes of the Catholic and Nationalist minority in the North and (arguably) of a sympathetic majority in the South to achieve their long-standing, historic goal of a united republican Ireland. The consequence of these two conflicting realities is that the 'Northern Ireland problem' involves trying to reconcile two sets of apparently irreconcilable aspirations held respectively by the 50 per cent of Northern Irish people who vote for some variety of Unionism and the 40 per cent who vote for some variety of nationalism, with the remaining 10 per cent voting for the non-sectarian Alliance Party.

When in Opposition, the Labour Party's approach to these seemingly intractable problems had been to favour the peaceful reunification of Ireland by popular consent both north and south of the inner-Irish border, as exemplified by a resolution to that effect at the 1991 Labour Party Conference. Yet when New Labour came to power with a landslide victory in May 1997, the *context* of its policy towards Northern Ireland was decisively different from that of its Conservative predecessor in two vital respects: firstly, it was committed to applying the principles of differentiated devolution throughout the United Kingdom; and secondly, it was committed to introducing legislation incorporating the provisions of the European Convention on Human Rights into the body of UK law – this was subsequently achieved in the 1998 Human Rights Act. Thus although there was considerable continuity of policy towards Northern Ireland between the pre-1997 Conservative Government and the post-1997 Labour Government, it could be argued that there were also new opportunities for resolving the Northern Irish problem – opportunities which Tony Blair seized with both hands and which eventually bore fruit in the Good Friday Agreement signed in Belfast in an atmosphere of exhaustion and euphoria on 10th April 1998.

The momentum of progress in the peace process was satisfactorily maintained in that in May 1998 the Agreement was strongly endorsed in parallel referenda north and south of the border (71 per cent in favour in Northern Ireland and over 90 per cent in favour in the Irish Republic). In June 1998 elections on a basis of proportional representation were held for the newly established Northern Ireland Assembly and effective power sharing between democratic representatives of the Unionist and Nationalist communities was begun.

It is fair to say that the Belfast Agreement broke fresh ground in Northern Ireland in a number of important ways. Firstly, it recognised the vital importance of power sharing between the two communities and made provision for this principle to be reflected in many of the institutional arrangements proposed both for government and for representation in the new Assembly. For example, the Chief Minister for Northern Ireland, the Unionist leader David Trimble, was balanced by the SDLP Deputy Leader, Seamus Mallon, in the role of Deputy First Minister. The Ministers in charge of each of the departments of devolved government were appointed in proportion to the party strengths, which meant that Unionists and Nationalists each enjoyed their fair share of executive power – including Sinn Fein, the political wing of the IRA, which was allocated two Ministerial posts provided it (like all the other parties) agreed to abandon its support for violence in favour of peaceful democratic methods of persuading the public. See *Box 2* for the key points in the 1998 Belfast Agreement.

Indeed, the principles of strict proportionality and bi-communal support were taken further by the provisions in the Agreement which require that certain particularly sensitive decisions, such as the establishment of new cross-border bodies, attract the support either of a majority of the members of each main community in the Assembly or of a weighted majority of 60 per cent of all the members of the Assembly including at least 40 per cent support from each main community. As for the new Northern Ireland Assembly itself, this involved the election of 108 members on the basis of single transferable votes in order to ensure a high degree of proportionality in the representation of each main community. The Agreement also provided for the establishment of Assembly committees to oversee the activities of each department of devolved government in Northern Ireland and for the chairmen and deputy chairmen of the committees to be appointed in proportion to the strength of the parties in the Assembly. In short, simple majoritarianism was effectively ended in the governance of Northern Ireland.

These devolved structures and complex power-sharing arrangements were designed to fulfil what was described as *Strand 1* of the Agreement which dealt with the internal government of Northern Ireland. However, as befits a policy of devolution rather than anything more autonomous, key decisions relating to law and order, defence, external relations, taxation and social security were among the powers retained by the UK Government and Parliament in London and any political or constitutional disputes between the UK and devolved institutions would be settled in the final analysis by the Judicial Committee of the Privy Council. It was also decided, as in Scotland and Wales, to retain a Secretary of State for Northern Ireland at the head of a slimmed down Northern Ireland Office to deal with the limited range of matters which were not within the allocated competence of the devolved institutions.

In view of the background of human rights abuses perpetrated over many decades by the Unionist majority upon the Nationalist minority in Northern Ireland, it was considered essential by both the British and Irish Governments that the Good Friday Agreement should include additional safeguards which reflected 'the principles of mutual respect for the identity and ethos of both communities and parity of esteem'.[19] Thus it was agreed that, as well as applying the European Convention

Box 2 Key points in the 1998 Belfast Agreement

- The principle of power sharing is at the heart of the Agreement, with Ministers in the devolved Executive appointed in numbers related to the party strengths revealed at the Assembly elections.
- Particularly sensitive decisions require specially weighted majorities to ensure that each main community was manifestly committed to them.
- Membership of the Assembly is based upon 108 members elected by single transferable vote to ensure a high degree of proportionality in the popular representation.
- Chairmen and Deputy Chairmen of the oversight committees were to be appointed in proportion to the strength of the parties in the Assembly.
- Decisions on defence, law and order, external relations, taxation and social security are reserved to the UK Government and Parliament at Westminster.
- The Northern Ireland Office with a Secretary of State and junior Ministers was retained to deal with matters not allocated to the devolved institutions and to handle periodic political crises in the Northern Ireland parties.
- Extra safeguards for human rights in the form of a Northern Ireland Bill of Rights, a Human Rights Commission and an Equality Commission were introduced to reinforce 'mutual respect for the identity and ethos of both communities and parity of esteem'.
- A North–South Ministerial Council was established with equal representation from each Administration in Belfast and Dublin to implement agreed cross-border initiatives.
- An 'East–West' Inter-Governmental Conference was established between London and Dublin to deal with non-devolved issues, such as security and policing.
- A Council of the Isles was established including representatives from all parts of the British Isles which could discuss matters of common interest.
- Agreement was reached to reform and rename the Royal Ulster Constabulary along the lines suggested in the Patten Report.
- Agreement was reached that all parties in the peace process would use their 'best endeavours' to persuade the paramilitaries to begin decommissioning their weapons under the supervision of an independent decommissioning body.
- Agreement was reached that in the event of such paramilitary decommissioning the British Government would consider at least partial demilitarisation of the Province.

on Human Rights to Northern Ireland (through the aegis of the 1998 Human Rights Act), there should be a separate Northern Ireland Bill of Rights to be enforced by a Northern Ireland Human Rights Commission, and an Equality Commission with a broader remit to monitor the achievement of such rights for all the inhabitants of Northern Ireland. To the untutored outside observer, these extra safeguards might seem like institutional and legal overkill, but any dispassionate reflection upon the tragedies and scandals of Irish history should

quickly dispel such a thought. Indeed, as part of this human rights package, the Dublin Government also undertook to strengthen the constitutional protection of human rights within its own jurisdiction with the ultimate aim of achieving equivalent levels of protection for its current (and possibly future) citizenry, in view of the theoretical possibility that one day Northern Ireland could be reunited with the Irish Republic by consent and, in that eventuality, what would then be a Protestant and Unionist minority in the entire island of Ireland would deserve as much protection from any abuses emanating from the Catholic majority as the Catholic and Nationalist minority in Northern Ireland deserve today.

Strand 2 of the Agreement dealing with North–South relations within Ireland has repeatedly proved to be both difficult and controversial for both main communities within Northern Ireland, but especially for paranoid Unionists. Once again, the patient negotiators had to square circles and reconcile irreconcilables, since nationalists have long wanted north–south bodies with executive powers as a tangible move towards real unification, while Unionists have been prepared to countenance such developments only if they amounted to no more than inter-governmental cooperation between two separate and distinct jurisdictions. In fact, the words of the Agreement sought to make it clear that any such cross-border arrangements would require the consent of both sides north and south of the border and thus uphold the clear distinction between Northern Ireland and the Irish Republic and implicitly the right of either to veto anything proposed under this heading. In the event it was agreed that there should be a North–South Ministerial Council, with equal representation from the Administrations in Belfast and Dublin, to agree upon cross-border initiatives which might be implemented either separately in each jurisdiction or jointly by common implementation bodies. Areas of activity which seemed to lend themselves to a cautious application of this approach included tourism, agriculture and fisheries, transport and industrial development.

Strand 3 of the Agreement provided for new 'East–West' institutions within which London and Dublin could continuously cooperate on the Northern Ireland question. Specifically, a new Inter-Governmental Conference was established to take responsibility for matters which would not be devolved to the authorities in Northern Ireland, e.g. security and police matters. Furthermore, it was agreed that there would be a new over-arching body called the Council of the Isles which would assemble representatives from all the constituent parts of the British Isles (including the Isle of Man and the Channel Islands) together with represen-

tatives of the British and Irish Governments to discuss and possibly act upon matters of common interest, such as transport links, environmental protection, etc. Once again, a layer of institutional superstructure was created in order to give further reassurance to Protestant Unionists in Northern Ireland who still had strong reservations about the 'North–South' institutions proposed under Strand 2 which they saw as weakening their integral connection with the rest of the United Kingdom.

As Kevin Boyle and Tom Hadden have pointed out in their excellent analysis of these issues, the Belfast Agreement differed from earlier ideas worked out in the Joint Framework Documents in four respects.[20] *Firstly*, a new Council of the Isles was created to balance the new 'North–South' institutions. *Secondly*, the human rights of all Northern Ireland citizens (and by extension all Irish citizens) were buttressed by the creation of new Human Rights and Equality Commissions in Northern Ireland. *Thirdly*, a bold decision was made to go for dual rather than triple leadership of the Northern Ireland Executive, thus focusing the responsibilities of the new arrangements upon the leaders of what were then the two main political parties in the province (the official Unionists and the SDLP). *Fourthly*, it was decided to forgo explicit powers of direct intervention for the London and Dublin Governments on the grounds that this omission might encourage the Northern Ireland parties to pull their own chestnuts out of the fire. On the other hand, the fact remained that no Government in London or Dublin would actually stand idly by if things went disastrously wrong in Northern Ireland.

Indeed, it has been obvious during the period since the signing of the Belfast Agreement on Good Friday in April 1998 that both Governments in London and Dublin have had to take a continuing and close interest in all political developments in Northern Ireland and to intervene quite forcefully from time to time in order to shore up the fragile peace process. For example, as Northern Ireland Secretary, Peter Mandelson had to suspend the operation of the Northern Ireland Assembly in February 2000 when Sinn Fein/IRA failed to meet the arbitrarily imposed deadline for arms decommissioning set by the Ulster Unionist Council at an extraordinary meeting in December 1999. This bold Ministerial decision may well have contributed to the ground-breaking IRA statement in May 2000 that it was prepared to put at least some of its arms and other war-making materials 'beyond use' and to do so subject to inspection and verification by an independent body on arms decommissioning headed by the Canadian General John de Chastelain.

Since May 2000, however, progress on decommissioning has been so minimal that in protest David Trimble resigned as First Minister at the beginning of July 2001 and the British and Irish Governments felt obliged to come forward with further joint proposals for breaking the deadlock which were put to the pro-Agreement Northern Ireland parties in August 2001. Yet this initiative was of no avail, since both the Unionists and the Nationalists appeared to be split on whether or not to go forward with the Belfast Agreement in the absence of anything like complete satisfaction for either side about the way in which the other was honouring (or failing to honour) it. David Trimble was under mounting pressure from the hard-liners in his own party (not to speak of those in the Democratic Unionist Party who had rejected the Agreement from the outset) to precipitate the collapse of the Executive and the Assembly because the IRA had not actually *delivered* any visible arms decommissioning. Gerry Adams and his colleagues in Sinn Fein seemed to find it impossible to persuade the paramilitaries on the I.R.A. Council to make the visible and symbolic *act* of decommissioning even a token amount of their weaponry at the behest of the Unionist Party before there had been any significant demilitarisation of the Province by the British armed forces.

In these circumstances of deadlock over a typically symbolic issue, the Northern Ireland Secretary, John Reid, decided to suspend the Northern Ireland Assembly and its Executive for 60 days from the middle of August 2001 and shortly after that the IRA announced that it was withdrawing its previous offer to put (some of) its arms 'beyond use'. If there is no tangible progress towards bridging this symbolic divide on arms decommissioning, it seems likely that the Government will have to bring back direct rule from Westminster and another valiant and painstaking attempt at power sharing in Northern Ireland will have foundered upon the rocks of sectarian dogma on both sides.[21]

General reflections

Even after so many years of trouble and strife, there are some vital, unresolved issues for Northern Ireland, many of which do not derive from problems generated in Northern Ireland. Perhaps the most notable of these is the cardinal and continuing importance of the principle that any major constitutional change which would have a significant effect upon the status of Northern Ireland should be subject to the consent of the people of Northern Ireland. *Firstly*, this means that the Protestant and Unionist community in Northern Ireland should not be forced by any decision of a London Government and the Westminster Parliament out of the United Kingdom and into the Irish Republic, because such an act of British Parliamentary supremacy (as provided for in Section 75 of the 1920 Government of Ireland Act) would nowadays be constitutionally unacceptable – just as it was politically intolerable to all Unionists in Lloyd George's time. Indeed, it is arguable that the Judicial Committee of the Privy Council would not (should not) uphold such a move, if it were ever attempted, on the grounds that it would be contrary to the spirit of constitutional entrenchment in the 1800 Act of Union with Ireland.

Secondly, it means that the Protestant and Unionist community of Northern Ireland should not be moved into the jurisdiction of the Irish Republic as a result of a simple majority vote in a future Northern Ireland referendum in the event of the Catholic and Nationalist population eventually becoming larger than theirs. This danger is more real than the first, not only because the Catholic birth rate in Northern Ireland exceeds its Protestant equivalent, but also because the latest changes in the Irish constitution which flow from the Belfast

Agreement still pose a predatory threat to the integrity of the Unionist connection between Northern Ireland and the rest of the United Kingdom. The new Article 2 of the Irish constitution refers to 'the entitlement and birthright of every person born in the island of Ireland . . . to be part of the Irish nation'; and Article 3 refers to 'the firm will of the Irish nation . . . to unite all the people who share the territory of the island of Ireland', although it does go on to recognise that 'a united Ireland shall be brought about only by peaceful means with the consent of a majority of the people, democratically expressed, in both jurisdictions in the island'.

What these two unresolved constitutional issues clearly suggest is that there are continuing grounds for Unionist suspicion and even paranoia towards the 'peace process' in Northern Ireland and that in these circumstances Northern Ireland may need to have its own constitution and to have it entrenched somehow against all present and future threats to either of its communities which may emanate from politicians in London and Dublin or from the nationalist and republican aspirations of men of violence in the IRA. Whether it is politically realistic to imagine that this sort of entrenchment can ever be achieved is more dubious. It may be only in the framework of an emerging constitution for the whole of the European Union that it will be possible for the current majority community in Northern Ireland to achieve what it might regard as watertight constitutional guarantees and for the current minority to accept the possibility of indefinitely deferred gratification of its long-standing nationalist aspirations.

It is a historical understatement to say that Ireland has had a chequered and often tragic history since it was first conquered and colonised by its British neighbours. Full integration with the rest of the United Kingdom was attempted in the 1800 Act of Union and was not really called into question in Great Britain at any rate until Gladstone's first Home Rule Bill in 1886. Varying degrees of devolution for the whole of Ireland were attempted from 1886 to the 1920 Government of Ireland Act. Partition accompanied by devolution imposed upon six counties in Ulster was attempted from 1922 until 1972, when Stormont was eventually suspended.

Direct rule by the British Government under Westminster legislation was attempted from 1972 to 1997. Devolution and power sharing with international guarantees have been attempted since the 1998 Belfast Agreement. It remains to be seen whether this hopeful formula will survive or whether the Government in London will have to fall back upon direct rule should the parties to the conflict be unable to implement important aspects of the Agreement.

Questions for discussion

1   Could the history of Anglo-Irish and later British–Irish relations over the centuries have turned out differently and if so what might have been the constitutional implications?

2   Why has direct rule from Westminster tended to be everyone's second-best solution for the Northern Ireland problem?

3   Analyse the strengths and weaknesses of power sharing under the aegis of the 1998 Belfast Agreement.

Notes

1   In 1783 the Westminster Parliament was prevailed upon by the newly self-confident Irish MPs to pass the so-called Renunciation Act which had the effect of repealing both the 1719 Declaratory Act, which had affirmed Westminster's right to legislate for Ireland, and that part of Poyning's Law which had obliged the Irish Parliament to submit its legislation to the Westminster Parliament for prior approval.
2   Robert Kee, *The Green Flag*; Weidenfeld & Nicolson, London, 1972; p. 33.
3   Quoted in *ibid*; p. 159.
4   *Ibid*; pp. 356–7, 373, 378–82.
5   *Ibid*; p. 182.
6   R.F. Foster, *Modern Ireland, 1600–'1972*; Allen Lane, London, 1988; pp. 543–5.
7   Figures given in R. Kee; *op. cit.*; p. 525.
8   *Ibid*; p. 292.
9   Quoted in *ibid*; pp. 415–16.
10   *Ibid*; p. 624.
11   Quoted in R.F. Foster: *op. cit.*; p. 487.
12   At the May 1921 elections, 40 Unionists and twelve

Nationalists were elected to the Stormont Parliament in Belfast, while 124 Nationalists (Sinn Fein) and four Unionists (Members for Trinity College, Dublin) were elected to the *Dáil* in Dublin.

13 V. Bogdanor, *Devolution in the United Kingdom*; Oxford University Press, Oxford, 1999; p. 65.

14 Quoted in Nicholas Mansergh, *The Government of Northern Ireland, a Study in Devolution*; Allen & Unwin, London, 1936; p. 110.

15 *Ibid*; p. 112.

16 V. Bogdanor, *op. cit.*; p. 75.

17 *Ibid*; p. 80.

18 Quoted by K. Boyle and T. Hadden in R. Blackburn and R. Plant (eds), *Constitutional Reform*; Longman, London, 1999; p. 296.

19 *Ibid*; p. 288.

20 *Ibid*; pp. 297–8.

21 Subsequently, in October 2001, the IRA High Command felt constrained by the wave of American revulsion against all forms of terrorism, in the wake of the outrageous attacks on 11th September 2001 on the World Trade Center in New York and the Pentagon in Washington, DC, to make an offer of at least partial decommissioning of terrorist weaponry. This was validated by General de Chastelain and the members of the independent decommissioning body and paved the way for David Trimble to put himself forward once again for the position of First Minister of the Northern Ireland Executive, an act which was endorsed by the devolved Northern Ireland Assembly only after two Alliance Party members voted for it in the temporary guise of Unionist members.

Further reading

Vernon Bogdanor, *Devolution in the United Kingdom*; Oxford University Press, Oxford, 1999.

R.F. Foster, *Modern Ireland, 1600–1972*; Allen Lane, London, 1998.

Robert Hazell (ed.) *The State and the Nations: the First Year of Devolution in the United Kingdom*; Imprint Academic, London, 2000.

Robert Kee, *The Green Flag*; Weidenfeld & Nicolson, London, 1972.

Nicholas Mansergh, *The Government of Northern Ireland, a Study in Devolution*; Allen & Unwin, London, 1936.

R. Wilford and R. Wilson, *A Democratic design? The Political Style of the Northern Ireland Assembly*; Constitution Unit, London, 2001.

website for the Northern Ireland Assembly: www.ni-assembly.gov.uk

The issue of Scotland

A nation all along

Scotland was a proud and separate nation long before it became part of the United Kingdom with England in 1603 and long before it became part of the unitary state of Great Britain following the Acts of Union in 1707. It had not been conquered by the Romans or the Normans and had never been subjugated by the English, at any rate north of the Scottish Lowlands. Admittedly, Scotland had frequently had to fight and scheme to preserve its often tenuous independence, invariably with the aid of the 'auld alliance' with France which dated back to 1295 and common Franco-Scottish resistance to the formidable English military power of Edward I.

When Edward I had himself proclaimed Overlord of Scotland in 1305 and drew up something resembling a constitutional settlement for English government of the defeated Scottish kingdom, he established a Council which was half English and half Scottish in its composition, but which recognised distinctive Scottish traditions by permitting the retention of separate legal and administrative systems in Scotland. This pattern of two nations under one crown (and later within one state) foreshadowed the sort of constitutional relationship between England and Scotland which was to be reflected in subsequent arrangements binding the two countries together in the seventeenth century and thereafter. In the words of the eminent historian Sir Reginald Coupland, Edward I and all subsequent rulers of England (and later of the United Kingdom) learned that 'Britain could not be united without the recognition of a separate Scottish nationhood'.[1]

In the sixteenth century the degree of Scottish independence from England was crucially dependent upon Scottish rulers enlisting the support of France through the establishment of repeated dynastic connections. England and Scotland were eventually brought together dynastically in 1603 and constitutionally in 1707 by 'a transcendent common cause . . . the protection of national freedom and the Protestant faith from the ascendancy of the Catholic monarchies of continental Europe'.[2]

In the mid-seventeenth century it proved impossible for Scotland, having been dynastically united with England, to stand aside from the English Civil War. Indeed, in some respects the Scottish Covenanters were ahead of the game in 1638 when they rebelled against the 'Papist' regime of Archbishop Laud and their Central Assembly unilaterally abolished episcopacy in Scotland. Whereas in England the Civil War was essentially a struggle to uphold the rights of Parliament against the tyranny of the Stuart kings and the perceived Papist threat to established religion, in Scotland it was essentially the resistance of the Kirk to the Papist inclinations of the Stuart monarchy.

Having won the English Civil War and then executed Charles I in 1649, Oliver Cromwell and his fellow Parliamentarians did not feel completely secure from Scottish threats to their new republican dispensation, but equally they had no real desire to impose a draconian settlement upon Scotland by force of arms. So after a Cromwellian army had defeated the Scottish Presbyterians at the battle of Dunbar in 1650, both the secular and the religious settlements imposed upon Scotland were moderate and reasonable. During Cromwell's Protectorate the 1654 Ordinance which determined the government of Scotland provided for 30 Scottish MPs in a unicameral Parliament at Westminster, ensured that Scotland paid its fair share of taxes towards the common revenue of the country, and guaranteed completely free trade between England and Scotland on equal terms. Furthermore, the independent status of Scottish law and the Scottish church was not seriously challenged, so to all intents and purposes Scotland fared better under Cromwell than it had done for many years under the first two Stuart kings.

Different considerations had come to dominate the political relationship between Scotland and England by the time that the *Acts of Union* were concluded in 1707. *Firstly*, Britain had been at war with Louis XIV's France since 1702 and this made it strategically imperative in English eyes to secure the country's northern flank against possible invasion, or at any rate subversion, launched from Scottish soil. One way or another, Scotland had to be constitutionally bound more closely to England in order to ensure England's security at a time when Catholic France was the dominant European power and a very serious threat to the British nation. *Secondly*, as far as Scottish interests were concerned, it is worth noting that the Scottish political class did not sell Scotland cheaply or quickly into the constitutional framework of English government, since the negotiations between the two sides lasted on and off for five years from 1702 to 1707. The deal finally negotiated between London and Edinburgh was not without considerable advantages and attractions for the people of Scotland: the Scottish Kirk preserved its independence from the Church of England; Scottish law was kept distinct from English law; Scottish national dignity was preserved by requiring the explicit consent of the Scottish Parliament to the Acts of Union; and, most influential of all the factors in the deal, there was the considerable lure of completely free trade with the much larger English market at a time when Scottish industrial and commercial interests had been seriously disadvantaged by the previous economic arrangements.

The 1707 Acts of Union constituted not so much an 'unequal treaty' as measures of expediency by the English and Scottish political elites who each had their own different reasons at the time for reaching agreement upon the deal. Public opinion on both sides of the border was unpersuaded of the merits of Union and it is interesting to note that the business managers in the Westminster Parliament allowed no amendments to the Bill when it was under consideration in both Houses for fear of upsetting and unravelling the delicate deal which had been reached between the two national Parliaments. On the Scottish side, the key factor which made everything possible was that the Kirk leaders were eventually satisfied about their future rights and independence; without this the Bill would not have received the approval of the Scottish Parliament. Because the legislation was essentially a matter of 'two sovereign states merging their separate sovereignties into one', it was only possible on the basis of voluntary agreement and mutual consent.[3] Thus the Acts of Union passed by the English and Scottish Parliaments had sufficient legitimacy to provide a constitutional foundation for the political entity which came to be known as the United Kingdom.

Even though many energetic and ambitious Scots did pretty well out of the union with the rest of the United Kingdom during the eighteenth and nineteenth centuries, and allowing for the fact that Scots played a prominent part in building the British Empire in many parts of the world, they had some legitimate *political* grievances towards the English ruling class in London which began to be expressed in the mid-nineteenth century. When W.E. Aytoun took the initiative of forming a non-party *National Association for the Vindication of Scottish Rights* in 1853, the manifesto of the new organisation contained no explicit criticism of the Union but it did deplore what it regarded as English neglect of Scottish political interests. It called for the restoration of the office of Secretary of State for Scotland which had been abolished in 1746; and for an increase in Scottish Parliamentary representation at Westminster in proportion with that of Ireland and Wales. Such political pressure to increase Scottish representation at Westminster did not have any discernible effect upon British politics until 1863 when the number of Scottish MPs was raised from 53 to 60 in a House of 658 members and again in 1885 when the number of Scottish members was raised to 72 in a House of 670 MPs.

The idea of Scottish devolution had little impact upon the Westminster agenda until the early years of the twentieth century. For decades the Liberals had given priority to the Irish question, although a Scottish Secretary of State with a seat in Cabinet was created in 1886. Moreover, the Scottish Liberals were themselves divided, with some wanting Scottish self-government and some opposing the idea that Glasgow should be governed from Edinburgh. Meanwhile the Conservatives remained resolutely Unionist and under their Administrations Scottish devolution was effectively off the agenda.

Following the Liberal landslide victory at the 1906 General Election, a Scottish Grand Committee was established at Westminster in 1907 and the policy of devolution became part of the Scottish Liberal platform in 1908. By 1912, when the Asquith Administration introduced the third Liberal Home Rule Bill for Ireland, it was explicitly presented as the first instalment of a wider policy of 'Home

Rule all round' which might encompass Scotland and Wales in due course. For the Conservatives, Arthur Balfour made it clear that this would be unacceptable and unworkable because England would be much too large *vis-à-vis* the other three nations of the United Kingdom and if this problem of disparity were to be solved by breaking England up into more manageable regions governed by 'glorified County Councils', then that would be unacceptable to him and his party. There is no evidence that propitiating aspirations for Scottish self-government figured seriously in the minds of any of the leading politicians at Westminster at that time.

However, it is well to heed Christopher Harvie's words on the Scottish dimension of the case for devolution in the late 1970s:

> no understanding of the forces making for a re-negotiation of the Union is possible which omits the historical factors which have kept the Union in being not as the absorption of one nation by another but as an unique balance of assimilation and autonomy.[4]

It was the pursuit of this balance which had allowed A.V. Dicey and R.S. Rait to argue in good faith in 1920 that it was possible to be a sincere Scottish nationalist (small n) and an advocate of the Union at the same time.[5] On the other hand, this attitude was not shared by the members of the Scottish Home Rule Association which emerged in 1918 from a period of political hibernation during the First World War. Nor was it shared by the likes of C.M. Grieve (aka Hugh MacDiarmid) when in 1927 he published his Scottish Nationalist (big N) manifesto entitled *Albyn or Scotland and the Future* on behalf of the growing band of more romantic Scottish nationalists.

This small upsurge of nationalist sentiment in Scotland had led some Labour MPs in particular to introduce Home Rule Bills for Scotland from time to time in the Westminster Parliament (the first in 1922); but, more significantly, it also led to the formation of the *National Party of Scotland* in June 1928 by two refugees from the Independent Labour Party, Roland Muirhead and John MacCormick. In its early days this fledgling political party could not easily make up its mind where it stood on the dominating economic and social issues of the time

(jobs, free trade or protectionism, and the right degree of economic redistribution), so it lacked coherence and credibility in the minds of many of its potential supporters in Scotland. This left a gap in the political market for the formation of the *Scottish Party* in 1931, which was a more Right-leaning group drawing upon the ranks of Liberals and Unionists in Scotland. It soon became clear that each party was far too small to make any significant impact upon the political process on its own, so the two parties wisely merged in 1934 to become the *Scottish National Party* with a programme based upon the goal of Home Rule for Scotland. Two years later, in 1936, the cultural dimension of Scottish nationalism was given a significant boost by the formation of the *Saltire Society* in Edinburgh, although there was really no Scottish equivalent of the *Eisteddfod* movement in Wales since at that time only 2 per cent of the Scottish population could speak Gaelic.

For the entire period between the two world wars there seemed to be little understanding and even less sympathy for the cause of Scottish nationalism at the decision-making levels of British politics. This was because all senior figures in the Conservative-dominated Governments of that time were preoccupied (like their Labour counterparts) with the big economic and social questions and with the looming threat of war. For example, Stanley Baldwin was almost contemptuous of nationalist aspirations when he observed in 1932 that 'there is no evidence that the creation of small units [e.g. a quasi-independent Scotland] makes for the prosperity of the world'.[6] In saying this he may well have been influenced by the emergence of a range of small and essentially unviable nation states on the Continent of Europe in response to the ideology of national self-determination which had been idealistically fostered by President Wilson of the United States at the time of the Versailles Peace Conference and which became the dominant ethos of the ill-fated League of Nations. The most that any British Government was prepared to concede to Scottish sensibilities at that time was a favourable response to the 1937 Gilmour Report which recommended the transfer of Scottish administration from Whitehall to St Andrew's

House in Edinburgh, a bureaucratic move which was achieved in 1939.

Against this unsympathetic political background and in the absence of any popular groundswell for more autonomy in Scotland, it is not surprising that the small Scottish Nationalist movement began to fragment, with Douglas Young leading a radical group which began campaigning against Scottish conscription into the British armed forces in 1940–41 and John MacCormick (who was more of a Home Ruler) leading a break-away from the party in 1942 (after he had been defeated at the party's annual Conference) and establishing a more moderate *Scottish Union* which was later known as the *Scottish Convention*. Thus the Scottish nationalist movement split once again between fundamentalists and realists – the former increasingly tempted by forms of direct action against the English connection, and the latter increasingly open to the idea of multi-party and non-party cooperation to campaign for new political structures in which the Scottish national identity and interests could be recognised.

Nevertheless, the Second World War was also a massive engine of change in the United Kingdom, especially on the home front for the duration of Winston Churchill's Coalition Government from 1940 to 1945. As far as Scotland was concerned, these new opportunities were personified in Thomas Johnston, the Labour MP for West Stirlingshire, who became Secretary of State for Scotland in February 1941 and proceeded for the rest of the war very effectively to promote the well-being of Scotland and the cause of devolution on every possible occasion. In this way Scottish nationalism was maintained within the Union and the Scottish people came to benefit from a semi-privileged status which brought them more than their fair share of economic and social benefits as compared with other parts of the UK which were equally poor and equally disadvantaged.

For at least 20 years after the war it is fair to say that the cause of Scottish nationalism, and hence any felt need to respond to it in Government circles, languished under Administrations of both major parties. Desultory attempts were made by enthusiasts and sympathisers to rekindle the flame, as

when in 1947 a so-called Scottish Convention was held in Glasgow which attracted the support of a wide range of Scottish institutions and interests and which unanimously passed a resolution in favour of Home Rule for Scotland. This led directly to a similar public meeting the following year in Edinburgh which drafted a so-called *Scottish Covenant* which was agreed at a third 'Scottish Assembly' in 1949 and attracted the signatures of about 2 million Scots. The essential objective of the campaign was to increase the pressure for the establishment of a Scottish Parliament with legislative powers on the lines of the Northern Ireland Parliament at Stormont. It elicited no response, positive or otherwise, from the Westminster Parliament; but it did manage to attract the transient support of Winston Churchill and some other leading figures in the Conservative Opposition, such as Walter Elliot and Peter Thorneycroft, who had apparently convinced themselves that Scotland should not be forced into a Socialist future by a Labour majority in a largely English House of Commons.

At the same time the Liberal Party committed itself once again to the policy of 'Home Rule all round' and hence, by implication, to devolution for Scotland. Yet many others came to regard this position as rather self-serving and parochial, since by the early 1950s the Liberals had been pushed back to the Celtic fringes of the United Kingdom by the political success of the two major parties – neither of which was really drawn towards a policy of devolution for Scotland or Wales. In these circumstances the Scottish nationalist movement also lost coherence and serious political focus. Indeed, it really degenerated into what was described by Christopher Harvie as 'emotional nationalism' with eccentric splinter groups under the leadership of John MacCormick and others indulging in various stunts, such as stealing the Stone of Scone from Westminster Abbey in December 1950 or blowing up Royal Mail pillar boxes in the early 1950s, which largely discredited the cause of Scottish nationalism.

Whereas the Scottish National Party (SNP) contested five seats in Scotland and lost its deposit in four at the 1959 General Election, by the early

1960s it was polling more strongly at by-elections (e.g. at West Lothian in 1962 when William Wolfe came second to Tam Dalyell) and by the mid-1960s it was performing better than the Liberals in Scotland and seriously threatening Labour dominance, at any rate at by-elections. The most dramatic breakthrough for the SNP came in November 1967 when Winnie Ewing defeated a lacklustre Labour candidate at the Hamilton by-election and by the following year the SNP had the largest membership of any party in Scotland and the largest proportion of the votes at local government elections. At that time such by-election victories represented more of a protest against the Government in office in London than a positive endorsement of Scottish nationalism.

Paradoxically, it was the Conservatives (and Unionists) rather than the Labour Party which began to respond by taking the idea of devolution more seriously, and Edward Heath as Leader of the Opposition was the first major party leader to come out in its favour when he proposed a directly elected Scottish Assembly at the Scottish Conservative Conference in Perth in 1968. He then established a Constitutional Committee under Sir Alec Douglas-Home, the former Tory leader and Prime Minister, to explore how it might be possible to satisfy the desire of the Scottish people to have a greater say in the conduct of their own affairs while at the same time preserving the supremacy of the Westminster Parliament throughout the United Kingdom. Sir Alec's committee reported in March 1970 just three months before the General Election of that year. It recommended the establishment of a directly elected Scottish Convention (located in Scotland) to consider and vote upon the Second Reading, Committee and Report stages of all Westminster legislation which had been certified by the Speaker as exclusively pertaining to Scotland; thus only the Third Reading in the Commons and all stages in the Lords would be taken at Westminster.

Even though the recommendations of the Douglas-Home Committee were accepted by the Conservative leadership and incorporated into its 1970 General Election Manifesto, it is notable that the Heath Administration from 1970 to 1974 never legislated to establish a devolved Scottish Assembly. The reasons for this were both obvious and veiled. The obvious reasons were that the Heath Administration chose to respond in 1971 to the 1969 report of the Wheatley Commission on local government reform in Scotland *before* proceeding with any measures for Scottish devolution – a reasonable decision in so far as the Wheatley recommendations for seven large Regional Councils and 49 District Councils were in danger of simply gathering dust if not acted upon fairly early in the new Parliament; and that it chose to await the report of the Crowther/Kilbrandon Commission on the constitution which had been established by the Labour Government in 1969 but which did not finally report until October 1973. By this time the Heath Administration was deeply and urgently preoccupied with the Yom Kippur War in the Middle East and the ensuing world energy crisis and, as it turned out, within only five months of its own demise at the February 1974 General Election. In such fraught political circumstances it was no wonder that the cause of Scottish devolution had to take a back seat to other much more pressing political issues.

The veiled reasons were that the Conservatives were never wholly serious about their commitments to Scottish devolution; even advocates of the policy within the party were disinclined to go as far and as fast in that direction as the satisfaction of nationalist sentiment in Scotland would have required; and in any case (as subsequent events were to show) the party was fundamentally divided upon the wisdom or necessity of the policy and had a long history of strong commitment to the competing *Unionist* cause in Scotland as in other parts of the United Kingdom. Indeed, the entire duration of Conservative Party commitment to Scottish devolution lasted a mere nine years from Edward Heath's ringing declaration in its favour at the 1968 Scottish Conservative Conference in Perth to Francis Pym's quiet burial of the policy in May 1977 when as the Opposition spokesman on devolution he announced that the party's commitment to a directly elected Scottish Assembly had become 'inoperative'.

In party political terms, it had long been the Labour Party which felt most threatened by any resurgence of Scottish nationalism, which explains much, if not all, of Labour policy on the issue from the 1967 Hamilton by-election to the 1997 General Election. However, the SNP threat was never of a completely constant intensity and successive Labour leaders, whether in Government or in Opposition, had different ways of handling the threat. For example, *Harold Wilson* specialised in prevarication and used the device of Royal Commissions very effectively for the purpose. *James Callaghan*, who was certainly not a Scottish nationalist and who sat for a Cardiff seat in Parliament, had less room for manoeuvre on the issue, especially after he found it necessary to enter a pact with the Liberals in 1977 in order to keep his Administration precariously in office until its defeat in the House of Commons in March 1979 (occasioned by the issue of devolution).

Michael Foot, who had been the Cabinet Minister in charge of the ill-fated devolution policy of the 1974–79 Labour Government, was too much of a natural UK Socialist to be particularly credible north of the border as a genuine sympathiser with Scottish nationalism. *Neil Kinnock*, who had been a fierce opponent of devolution in the 1970s and who also sat for a Welsh seat, reluctantly changed his position to support devolution at the 1987 and 1992 General Elections, but his belated conversion never really carried conviction in Scotland. *John Smith*, as the first Scottish leader of the Labour Party for many years who also sat for a Scottish seat, broke the mould by advocating Scottish devolution from conviction more than for political convenience (although both motives were undoubtedly present in his canny mind). Most recently, *Tony Blair*, who inherited the weight of all this Labour Party history of various challenges from and responses to Scottish nationalism, has never appeared to pursue the policy from personal conviction but rather as the payment of a personal debt of honour to John Smith and an interesting experiment in New Labour coalition politics which may have the additional benefit of containing the long-term threat from the SNP to Labour's premier position in Scotland.

One satisfactory explanation for the wide variety of Labour leadership responses to the nationalist threat in Scotland is that the fortunes of the SNP waxed and waned with remarkable volatility for many years after 1967. To begin with, the SNP severely disappointed its supporters at the 1970 General Election when the party polled only 11 per cent of the total vote and Winnie Ewing lost her seat at Hamilton. A few years later the party seemed to be back on the road to success with Margo MacDonald's victory at the 1973 Glasgow Govan by-election which reflected Scottish protest against London Conservative rule, but was also a sharp reminder to Labour (which had previously held the seat) that it was in danger of losing its credibility in Scotland as the main party of opposition to the Conservatives. As British politics became more multi-party in the mid-1970s, the SNP's fortunes began to revive and the party began to surpass the Liberals as the main focus of protest north of the border for all those who felt increasingly dissatisfied with the two main parties. At the February 1974 General Election it won six seats and at the October 1974 General Election it won ten seats, but none of the extra seats came at the expense of the Labour Party, probably because at the last minute the latter had included in its Manifesto a commitment to create a legislative Assembly for Scotland.

As the years went by, circumstances not directly connected with the ups and downs of party political fortunes in Scotland also became more favourable to the prospects of the SNP and Scottish nationalism. Most significantly, after the first commercially viable oil field under the North Sea had been discovered in 1969 in the Norwegian sector at Ekofisk, in 1970 BP discovered a large viable oil field in the British sector at Forties, 120 miles north-east of Aberdeen. These potentially cornucopian discoveries were soon replicated elsewhere on the British continental shelf and began to hold out to the Scottish people in particular the prospect of previously undreamed-of wealth to which the SNP soon laid claim on behalf of the Scottish people in a well-organised campaign proclaiming the arrival of 'Scotland's Oil' for the benefit of the Scottish people. These developments soon transformed the SNP case for greater Scottish autonomy (and eventually perhaps independence) into one in which the party affected to believe that the Scottish people had a legitimate moral claim to the windfall of North Sea oil revenues which belonged to them by right rather than on supplication to the Westminster Parliament. Such claims did not, however, sway English decision makers in London.

The second external development which turned out to serve the interests of the Scottish nationalist cause was the entry of the United Kingdom into the European Community in January 1973 and, especially, the two to one majority vote in the 1975 European referendum in favour of the United Kingdom remaining in the European Community as a full member. Notwithstanding the fact that the SNP had campaigned for a No vote on the grounds that the rest of the United Kingdom had no right to decide Scotland's future in this way, it swiftly switched to a pro-European position after the referendum campaign was over and began to advocate the apparently beguiling prospect of an independent Scotland within a European Community which was increasingly prepared to recognise and reward the aspirations of its smaller member states. The clear implication of this intelligent policy switch was that under an SNP Government in an independent Scotland the Scottish people would be able to have their cake and eat it in that they would have all the pride and *kudos* of independent national status without any of the disadvantages which might be imposed upon them by the remainder of the United Kingdom in the event that Scotland's interests were not legally and constitutionally protected by membership of a Community whose treaty provisions were binding upon all member states alike.

Thus by the time the prospect of devolution for Scotland was firmly back on the British political agenda in the mid-1970s, the Labour Party had moved from strong opposition to the idea to unenthusiastic support, based upon party political calculation and (after 1977) the *force majeure* of coalition politics at Westminster; the Conservative Party had briefly flirted with the idea only to return under Margaret Thatcher's leadership to its visceral

Unionism; the Liberal Party had remained largely consistent in favour of devolution for Scotland and indeed similar arrangements for the rest of the United Kingdom as well; and the Scottish National Party had raised its game from campaigning for devolution within the United Kingdom to campaigning for independent nationhood within the larger constitutional framework of the European Community. Such were the dynamics of volatile four-party politics in Scotland.

Devolution on the political agenda

The initial response of Harold Wilson's precarious Labour Administration in the wake of the February 1974 General Election to the nationalist threat in Scotland (and to a lesser extent in Wales) was to promise discussions on the Kilbrandon Commission Report and to 'bring forward proposals for consideration', although very soon after Mr Wilson was promising a White Paper and a Bill. When the White Paper on Democracy and Devolution in Scotland and Wales was published in September 1974, only decisions of principle were taken by the Government. The most important were that Scotland and Wales would be dealt with together in one large piece of legislation; Scotland would get a directly elected Assembly with legislative powers whereas its Welsh counterpart would get only executive powers; the Assemblies would be elected in first-past-the-post elections and financed by block grants approved by the Westminster Parliament; the Scottish and Welsh Offices with their Ministers of Cabinet rank would remain and the number of Scottish and Welsh MPs at Westminster would not be altered; and finally any idea of devolution in England would be postponed for further consideration.

These decisions, which had been the result of only sketchy consideration in Whitehall and in Cabinet, nevertheless formed the framework of what turned out to be ill-fated attempts to introduce devolution for Scotland and Wales in the 1974–79 Parliament. Controversial as they were, they would have been difficult to push through a House of Commons with a larger and more reliable

Government majority after October 1974, let alone a House in which, after March 1977, the Government had to rely for its survival upon a precarious Lib-Lab Pact and upon the parochial indifference to Westminster politics of some Northern Ireland MPs. It was therefore not surprising when the Government was defeated in February 1977 on a guillotine motion whose passage had seemed necessary if its devolution legislation were not to die a death of a thousand cuts at the hands of the cross-party opposition to the policy which included Eric Heffer, Neil Kinnock and more than 40 Labour MPs. In these seemingly hopeless political circumstances, when the SNP enjoyed 36 per cent support in the Scottish opinion polls and the Conservatives were growing in popularity in England, the Labour Government was desperate to avoid being forced to go to the country and only the Liberals, with their steady commitment to devolution and their hunger for even a junior partnership in Government, offered James Callaghan (by then Prime Minister) and his colleagues a way out of their political *cul de sac* and the remote possibility of being able to make progress again with the project of devolution.

With the Lib-Lab Pact in operation from March 1977, the Callaghan Administration was able to resurrect the devolution policy and have another try at getting legislation through Parliament to establish differing assemblies in Scotland and Wales. The Liberals attempted, but failed, to provide for the assemblies to be elected by proportional representation and endowed with revenue-raising powers. Essentially, these were two demands which many Labour backbenchers would not wear and in any case senior Ministers knew that the Liberal leadership could be faced down, having so recently gained its limited partnership in Government. The second time around the guts of the devolution legislation remained the same, except that on this occasion senior Ministers conceded that since the forms of devolution for Scotland and Wales were different, they should be provided for in different Bills. The two constitutional Bills achieved their Second Readings on consecutive days in November 1977 and the Government business managers succeeded in securing guillotine motions for each of them immediately afterwards.

However, during the passage of the legislation a Conservative amendment, originally tabled by the Earl of Ferrers in the House of Lords, was eventually carried in the House of Commons by one vote at the second time of asking and against the Government's wishes. This became Section 66 of the 1978 Scotland Act which required that if any Commons vote on a devolved matter were only passed thanks to the votes of Scottish MPs at Westminster, an Order could be laid before the House of Commons requiring a second vote to be taken on the matter two weeks later. This was intended to discourage Scottish MPs from participating in the second vote and so deal with the important constitutional anomaly produced by differential or asymmetrical devolution whereby Scottish MPs could vote on strictly English, Welsh or Northern Irish matters at Westminster, but English, Welsh and Northern Irish MPs were debarred from voting on matters which had been devolved to the Scottish Assembly. This tricky issue of unequal representation, which had first given rise to concern in the debates on Gladstone's Irish Home Rule Bill in 1885–86, came to be known in the late 1970s as the *West Lothian Question*, since it was Tam Dalyell, the Labour MP for that constituency, who raised it time after time with Ministers during the committee stages of the legislation in 1977 and 1978. There was no completely satisfactory answer to it then and there is none today, although in practice it does not seem to have proved as irksome as it appeared to be in theory before the devolution legislation came into operation.

Another amendment, which was put down by the Labour backbench rebel George Cunningham, turned out to be the move which eventually did for the cause of devolution to Scotland and Wales in the 1970s. It required 40 per cent of the registered electorate in each of those parts of the United Kingdom to vote *for* devolution in the advisory referenda which followed the passage of the legislation. If this level of public support were not achieved, then an Order in Council would have to be laid before Parliament to repeal the primary legislation and the devolution policy would not come into effect.

The referenda on devolution to Scotland and Wales were held in accordance with the legislation on 1st March 1979 and, as might have been expected in view of the height of the electoral hurdles, the result in Scotland was an insufficiently conclusive victory for the policy, while the result in Wales was a humiliating defeat. *In Scotland*, on a turn-out of 63 per cent, 52 per cent of those voting said Yes and 48 per cent of those voting said No. In other words, of those entitled to vote, about 33 per cent approved the policy while about 31 per cent disapproved – hardly a massive vote of confidence for a cause which had taken up a disproportionate amount of Parliamentary time and brought bitter disappointment to nationalist voters in Scotland. *In Wales*, on a turn-out of 59 per cent, 20 per cent of those voting said Yes and 80 per cent said No; in other words, not many more than one in ten of Welsh voters actually approved of the policy.

In the light of these rebuffs at the hands of the very people whom devolution was intended to please, the policy was discredited (at least at the time) and the Labour Government was mortally wounded. In disgust the SNP immediately tabled a motion of no confidence, although it was not until the Conservative Party (the official Opposition) did likewise that a debate on a motion of confidence was held and the Government was finally defeated by a majority of one vote. The political consequence was the 1979 General Election in which the Conservatives under Margaret Thatcher were victorious in the United Kingdom as a whole, although in Scotland they only managed to win half as many seats as Labour, gaining 31 per cent of the Scottish votes compared with 42 per cent for Labour and 17 per cent for the SNP. The legislative consequence, as far as the policy of devolution was concerned, was that the incoming Conservative Government ensured the early repeal of the 1978 Scotland and Wales Acts and devolution was off the political agenda at Westminster for as long as the Conservatives remained in power.

Devolution as an Opposition cause

In politics no cause is ever completely dead and buried; and the cause of devolution in Scotland was no exception to this axiom. On 1st March 1980, the first anniversary of the devolution referenda, an all-party campaign for a Scottish Assembly was established in Scotland. Needless to say, it got precisely nowhere in its subsequent efforts to persuade the Thatcher Administration to reconsider its contemptuous opposition to what was regarded by the Conservatives in London as potentially another unwelcome layer of government in Scotland, although the goal of devolution continued to appeal to a small minority of Scottish Conservatives who were powerless at that time to do anything about it.

Successive Conservative Administrations in the 1980s were able to govern the United Kingdom with the support of little more than two-fifths of the UK voters at General Elections and indeed with a smaller and declining share of voters in Scotland.[7] This did not seem to cause any real concern to Margaret Thatcher and her senior colleagues who led some of the most centralising Administrations since the time of Henry VIII. They tended to regard, and dismiss, Scotland as a basket case where the public sector was still incorrigibly powerful and the dependency culture of the 1960s and 1970s still deeply ingrained. In 1989 these insensitive English attitudes were vividly portrayed in the Government's decision to introduce the deeply unpopular poll tax in Scotland a year before it was introduced in England and Wales, thus treating the Scots as a kind of living laboratory for increasingly offensive social policies. Unsurprisingly, this created huge resentment in Scotland and presented the SNP, and to a lesser extent the Scottish Labour and Liberal parties, with a further opportunity to rally any undecided opinion to the nationalist and devolutionist cause.

During the long years of Conservative hegemony at Westminster when the Opposition was divided and ineffective, an intellectual critique began to be developed in certain universities against the centralising tendencies of the Conservative Government in many facets of its policy. The diagnosis was one of excessive centralisation of decision making in London and marginalisation of the interests of all regional or national communities outside London and the South-East. The prescription was one of ambitious constitutional reform on a very wide front, notably including strong advocacy of the decentralisation and devolution of power from Whitehall and Westminster to Scotland, Wales and the English regions, virtually all of which were under the political control of Opposition politicians by the end of the Conservative period in office at Westminster. In London this movement of intellectual opinion led to the foundation in 1988 of Charter 88 – a pressure group designed to deploy all the arguments for fundamental constitutional reform in the United Kingdom, including some measures of decentralisation in order to bring government nearer to the people and enhance public accountability.

In Scotland the initiative was taken when the Campaign for a Scottish Assembly appointed a Constitutional Steering Committee which produced what was called a Claim of Right for Scotland and called for the establishment of a *Scottish Constitutional Convention* which would draw up agreed proposals for the reform of Scottish government. The Convention came into being the following year, 1989, declaring at the outset that sovereignty in Scotland resided with the Scottish people rather than the United Kingdom Parliament at Westminster. To begin with, there was some ambiguity about whether this implied the re-creation of an independent Scotland with its own Government and Parliament or whether it implied the more modest objective of creating a devolved Government and Assembly for Scotland *within* the United Kingdom. However, as soon as it became clear that the controlling Labour and Liberal interests in the Convention supported the latter rather than the former, the SNP refused to participate – as did the Conservatives in Scotland for entirely different Unionist reasons.

The Convention produced two reports which effectively sought to demonstrate how a new scheme of devolution could be implemented for Scotland; the most notable difference from the proposals put forward by the Labour Government in 1974 was that the proposed Scottish Assembly or Parliament should be elected by the additional member variant of proportional representation.[8] This change reflected a willingness to compromise among all those who participated in the Convention and set a standard for a new kind of coalition politics which was to catch on among all those who shared the overall objective. Indeed, it was remarkable how closely the legislation, which was later to become the *Scotland Act 1998*, followed the autochthonous blueprint put forward by the broad spectrum of Scottish opinion represented at the Scottish Constitutional Convention. For example, during the passage of the Bill in 1997–98, amendments were refused by Ministers and their supporters on the grounds that they would be inconsistent with the Convention proposals – a sign of the importance which the Government attached to maintaining multi-party support for the legislation.

Many in the Convention wanted to propose that a Scottish Parliament should have revenue-raising powers, but the Labour leadership in London (acting via the instrument of its well-disciplined Scottish colleagues) effectively vetoed this idea for fear that it would damage Labour's prospects at a future UK General Election. In this context, it is worth recalling that the Labour Party had three different leaders during the period of the Convention's existence (1989–97): Neil Kinnock until 1992, John Smith until 1994 and Tony Blair from 1994. Of all these, Tony Blair was the most ruthless and self-disciplined in trying to ensure that nothing promoted by his Scottish colleagues within the context of the campaign for devolution would damage Labour's chances of winning the 1997 General Election. It was for this overriding reason that he insisted upon two further refinements to the pro-devolution policy of a future Labour Government: firstly, that the referenda to be held on devolution in Scotland and Wales should be held *before* the primary legislation was introduced in the Westminster Parliament; and secondly, that in a *differential approach* to devolution in Scotland and Wales the Scottish people should be asked two separate questions in their referendum: whether they wanted a devolved Parliament in Edinburgh *and* whether they agreed that the Parliament should have tax-varying powers – i.e. the ability to raise or lower income tax in Scotland by up to 3 pence in the pound.

Delivering devolution in Scotland

When the New Labour Government under the leadership of Tony Blair was elected with a landslide majority of 177 in May 1997, it was far better placed to deliver its policies on devolution than any previous Administration with a positive commitment to devolution in its programme. This was because it had telegraphed its intentions in the party Manifesto; it was not dependent upon any alliance with another party or parties to get the legislation through Parliament; and it had spiked the guns of any potential opponents of devolution in its own ranks by giving the 1996 commitment that it would only proceed with the policy if the people of Scotland and Wales gave their prior approval in separate referenda in Scotland and Wales respectively.

The referenda were duly held in September 1997 and the degree of public endorsement for the policy was persuasive in Scotland where on a turn-out of 60 per cent, 74 per cent voted for a Scottish Parliament and 64 per cent voted for giving it tax-varying powers – the equivalent of 45 per cent and 38 per cent of those registered to vote in each case.

The legislation which became the *1998 Scotland Act* passed smoothly through both Houses of Parliament at Westminster because it was widely perceived to have the necessary democratic legitimacy, although there was obviously no complete political consensus in its favour even in Scotland. The Conservatives opposed it on Unionist grounds, but hinted that they would work with the new reality once the Scottish Parliament had been established. The SNP did not vote against the legislation, but made it very clear that they saw devolution as an inferior and temporary substitute for an independent Scotland within the European Union. Labour Ministers, such as Donald Dewar, then Secretary of State for Scotland, argued very strongly that a Scottish Executive responsible to a Scottish Parliament with wide-ranging legislative and tax-varying powers would meet the needs and aspirations of the Scottish people for a high degree of self-government, but within the framework of the United Kingdom and leaving to Parliament at Westminster not only a long list of reserved functions but also (in principle) the supreme right to legislate on matters devolved to the Scottish Parliament. See *Box 3* for the key points in the Scotland Act 1998.

The legislation provided for a Scottish Parliament of 129 members directly elected by means of the additional member system of proportional representation, as used in Germany. When the first elections took place in May 1999, 73 Members of the Scottish Parliament (MSPs) were elected from 73 single-member constituencies and the balance of 56 MSPs were elected proportionally from party lists, seven from each of the eight regional constituencies used for elections to the European Parliament. It was ironic that this mixed electoral system enabled the Scottish Conservatives to secure some list-based representation in a devolved institution which they had opposed at a time when they had failed to win any Scottish seats in first-past-the-post elections to the Westminster Parliament in May 1997. The Scottish Parliament was elected for a fixed four-year term and it could only be dissolved in exceptional circumstances if this were supported by a two-thirds majority of the Parliament as a whole or if it were unable to nominate a First Minister within 28 days of its election.

The legislation also provided for there to be a Scottish Executive led by a First Minister chosen from among the elected MSPs, who would be formally appointed by the Queen following election by the Parliament. As is well known, Donald Dewar, the leader of the Labour Party in Scotland and the former Secretary of State for Scotland, 1997–99, was chosen as Scotland's First Minister; but because Scottish Labour emerged from the May 1999 election as only the largest party in the Parliament but without an overall majority, it agreed with the Scottish Liberal Democrats to form a Coalition Government and James Wallace, the leader of that party, accordingly became Deputy First Minister of the new Scottish Administration. The various Ministerial positions in the Scottish Government were then divided up proportionally between the Labour and Liberal Democrat parties according to their strengths in the Scottish

Box 3 Key points in the Scotland Act 1998

- Establishment of a Scottish Parliament of 129 members (MSPs) – 73 elected by first-past-the-post for individual constituencies and 56 elected proportionally from party lists for each of eight regional constituencies – all elected for a fixed four-year term with high hurdles against dissolution at any other time
- A Scottish Executive led by a First Minister chosen from among the MSPs and then formally submitted by the Presiding Officer to the Queen for formal appointment
- Extensive powers of primary legislation for the Scottish Parliament in areas of policy such as education, housing, health, local transport, law and order
- Limited fiscal power for the Scottish Parliament confined to the possibility of varying the British rate of income tax by up to 3p in the pound in either direction
- A long list of reserved powers for Parliament at Westminster, including defence, foreign affairs, European Union issues, social security, broadcasting and the constitutional settlement
- A wide range of procedural and judicial restraints upon what the Scottish Parliament may do and how far it may go in testing the limits of its statutory competences, including the possibility of British judicial review of Scottish legislation
- A web of administrative constraints upon the Scottish Executive and the Scottish Parliament based upon the Memorandum of Understanding and Supplementary Agreements between the British Government and the devolved Administrations
- The ultimate right for the Westminster Parliament to legislate upon or alter any element of the Scottish devolution settlement, matched by the understanding that this would not normally happen except with the agreement of the devolved Parliament in Edinburgh

Parliament. Thus began a new era of genuine inter-party coalition government in a significant part of the United Kingdom.

Distinctive characteristics of Scottish devolution

The most distinctive characteristics of Scottish devolution under the *1998 Scotland Act* are the real restrictions, both theoretical and practical, upon the scope for Scottish politicians seeking to stretch the devolution settlement too far in the direction of national autonomy and independence for Scotland. It is therefore worth itemising one by one the important safeguards and restrictions which were built into the primary legislation.

Firstly, Section 28(7) of the Act makes it clear that the granting of legislative powers to the Scottish Parliament does not affect the supremacy of the Westminster Parliament which continues to hold the power to make laws for Scotland as well as all other parts of the United Kingdom. *Secondly*, Section 35(1)(b) of the Act prohibits the passage of any legislation in the Scottish Parliament which would have the effect of putting the Westminster Parliament in contravention of any of its international obligations (e.g. European law or World Trade Organisation agreements) or which would be deemed harmful to the interests of the United Kingdom as a whole.

Thirdly, the explicit fiscal powers of the Scottish Parliament are limited by the Act to the possibility of varying the standard rate of income tax to be applied in Scotland by a maximum of 3 pence either above or below the rate set by the British Chancellor of the Exchequer in the UK Budget. However, this restriction does not affect the freedom of the Scottish Parliament, the bulk of whose public expenditure is funded by an annual block grant from the British Treasury, to adjust or withhold elements of the revenue support grant for Scottish local authorities and to adjust or abolish the council tax and the uniform business rate in Scotland for its own political purposes. These possibilities might provide hidden revenue-raising powers for a future Scottish Government.

Fourthly, although Schedule 5 of the Act lists the powers reserved to the Westminster Parliament rather than the powers and functions devolved to the Scottish Parliament, the latter institution is still severely constrained by the comprehensive nature of the long list of nineteen different items specified as reserved functions. Apart from the obvious ones such as defence, foreign affairs and all dealings with the European Union which one would expect to find in any such list, there are a wide range of other powers which, if used by London in an energetic way, could very effectively bind any would-be Scottish Leviathan which might try to emerge in Edinburgh. For example, the following are among the matters which are off-limits to the Scottish Parliament according to Schedule 5 of the Act: the Crown, the constitution and the Union itself; the civil service; nearly all aspects of economic, monetary and fiscal policy; immigration and nationality; national security and emergency powers; import and export controls; telecommunications and energy policy; infrastructural aspects of transport policy; nearly all social security policy; employment and health and safety issues; and broadcasting policy.

Fifthly, there are a whole raft of procedural and judicial restraints upon what the Scottish Parliament may do and how far it may go without getting itself *ultra vires* or putting the Monarch (who has a direct constitutional relationship with Parliament both in Edinburgh and in London) in an embarrassing or impossible constitutional position. For example, the Presiding Officer or Speaker of the Scottish Parliament must be satisfied that any proposed Scottish legislation is within its powers according to the terms of the primary legislation; equally he has to allow a four-week delay between the completion of the Edinburgh legislative process and submission of a Scottish Bill for Royal Assent, during which the law officers of the Scottish

Government may refer the complete measure or part of it to the Judicial Committee of the Privy Council for a definitive ruling as to whether it is within or outwith the legislative competence of the Scottish Parliament.

There is also the possibility of judicial review by the courts of any Scottish legislation even after Royal Assent has been received, with judicial determination of the validity of such legislation extending in some cases all the way up to final determination by the Judicial Committee of the Privy Council, which comprises five judges of whom two are likely to be Scottish. Ultimately, under Section 35 of the Act the Secretary of State for Scotland may issue an Order in Council, subject to the negative resolution procedure in both Houses of the Westminster Parliament, which prohibits the Presiding Officer of the Scottish Parliament from submitting a Scottish Bill for Royal Assent if he believes it would be inconsistent with British international obligations or harmful to the interests of the United Kingdom as a whole. In these rather extreme circumstances – which, it is hoped, can be avoided by timely use of inter-governmental mechanisms such as the Joint Ministerial Committee comprising Ministers from London and Edinburgh – the purpose and effect of the safeguards would be to ensure that the Monarch was not offered conflicting advice by two different Governments.

All the safeguards already mentioned, which were designed to ensure that the new devolved jurisdiction in Scotland does not extend beyond the limits that the British Government and Parliament deem proper for a subordinate Government and Parliament in the United Kingdom, are really expressions of the controls which can be imposed by legislative, procedural and judicial means. Yet it is well known that this has never been the preferred approach to dealing with such problems in the long-established British political culture. Members of all Governments down the years have infinitely preferred to develop conciliatory customs and practices – constitutional conventions, if you like – to resolve such problems by trying to prevent them from assuming threatening proportions in the first place.

In the case of the devolution strategies for both Scotland and Wales, the real solutions to such potentially difficult constitutional problems were to be found in the *Memorandum of Understanding and Supplementary Agreements* between the British, Scottish and Welsh Administrations which were published in October 1999.[9] The introduction to the Memorandum made it very clear at the outset that the document was 'a statement of political intent and should not be interpreted as a binding agreement'. It did not create any 'legal obligations between the parties' and was 'intended to be binding in honour only'. Equally, it was made clear that any subsequent concordats concluded between the different Administrations 'are not intended to be legally binding, but to serve as working documents'.[10] Timely communication and consultation between the various Administrations on matters of mutual interest was identified as one of the purposes of the exercise, although the authors were careful to add that the document did not create any statutory or legal right to be consulted in either direction. The Memorandum urged a common methodology to ensure the collection of valid UK statistics to inform policy making in all parts of the country and assumed continuing confidentiality in all dealings between the different Administrations.

By far the most robust passages in the Memorandum were those dealing with 'Parliamentary Business'. These baldly asserted that 'the United Kingdom Parliament retains authority to legislate on any issue, whether devolved or not', although the UK Government would 'proceed in accordance with the convention that the U.K. Parliament would not normally legislate with regard to devolved matters except with the agreement of the devolved legislature'.[11] Equally, the document declared that while it was for the Westminster Parliament to decide what use to make of its 'absolute right to debate, enquire into or make representations about devolved matters', the UK Government would

    encourage the U.K. Parliament to bear in mind the primary responsibility of devolved legislatures and administrations in these fields [devolved matters] and to recognise that it is a consequence of Parliament's decision to devolve certain matters that Parliament

itself will in future be more restricted in its field of operation.[12]

The corollary point was made in the very next paragraph which observed that 'the devolved legislatures will be entitled to *debate* [my italics] non-devolved matters, but the devolved Executives will encourage each devolved legislature to bear in mind the responsibility of the U.K. Parliament in these matters'.[13]

The rest of the Memorandum dealt rather more mildly with the inter-governmental relations which would be necessary to enable all parts of the United Kingdom to cooperate successfully in promoting the British position in European Union affairs and international relations generally and to implement the binding legal obligations which flowed from such external commitments. It sketched out the importance in this process of the *Joint Ministerial Committee* (JMC), which would typically be composed of representatives of all four 'national' Administrations in the United Kingdom (including Ministers from the power-sharing Northern Ireland Executive) and the *JMC Secretariat* which would have both administrative and dispute-resolving roles. The Memorandum made it clear that there would be a joint review of these administrative arrangements at least annually to see that they were working satisfactorily for all involved; and stressed that it regarded the powers of intervention for the Secretaries of State and for the Scottish and Welsh Law Officers as 'very much a matter of last resort', since all involved should 'aim to resolve any difficulties through discussion so as to avoid any action or omission by a devolved administration having an adverse impact on non-devolved matters'.[14]

Since the publication of the Memorandum of Understanding, together with its five Supplementary Agreements (on the Joint Ministerial Committee, coordination of European Union issues, financial assistance to industry, international relations, and official statistics), the Cabinet Office has been at pains to explain to anyone visiting its website that there are now three tiers of proactive guidelines and arrangements designed to head off difficulties before they become too intractable and to set out how the Administrations (in the different parts of the UK and at the different levels of governance) 'intend dealing with one another on issues of common concern, prior consultation and exchange of information'.[15] From this guidance it is clear that the top tier is the Memorandum itself and the Supplementary Agreements, the second tier is made up of bilateral Concordats between individual UK departments and their counterparts in Scotland and Wales, and the third tier consists of a series of Devolution Guidance Notes which will gradually be published for the benefit of civil servants and others in the devolved administrations and the UK Government.

It should be evident from this cat's cradle of mutually reinforcing measures that the chances of the process of devolution spiralling out of control over the years have been kept to the minimum by all the bureaucratic and other devices which Whitehall is so adept at imposing on any develop-ments which seem to threaten the smooth running of (British) government in this country. Never-theless, the devolution process – especially in Scotland where there is such a well-established sense of nationhood – will always represent a rather unstable balance between the nationalist forces for change and the Unionist habits and assumptions of nearly three centuries. Contemporary political dynamics, including growing influences from the rest of the European Union and the general spirit of the times which seems to favour relatively small and cohesive political units in an increasingly global economic and political environment, seem likely to shift the balance in Scotland more in a nationalist than a Unionist direction.

General reflections

Having decided before it came to power in 1997 that it would adopt an asymmetrical approach to devolution in the various parts of the United Kingdom, the newly elected Labour Government in London needed to make it clear that the distinctive characteristics of Scottish devolution would provide an option superior to Unionism on the one hand and federalism or separatism on the other.

It was fairly easy to see how devolution would be superior to Unionism for the Scots if it brought a degree of executive and legislative autonomy for Scotland which far surpassed anything which might have been achieved under the traditional Unionist dispensation. For example, it has enabled the Scottish Parliament to decide under Liberal Democrat and SNP pressure to release university students in Scotland from the obligation each to contribute £1,000 every year towards the costs of their tuition, something which had been imposed by law upon students at universities in the rest of the United Kingdom. This local variation of a UK-wide policy was very embarrassing for the Labour Government in London and to a lesser extent for the Scottish Labour Administration in Edinburgh, but it was attractive to public opinion in Scotland and it was legally possible under the terms of the 1998 Scotland Act. Furthermore, in this and other instances the Labour Party had known for many years that Unionist solutions to problems of this kind were no longer sufficient to satisfy the real expectations of the Scottish people or to protect the Labour Party in Scotland from suffering electorally at the hands of the Scottish Nationalists.

It is perhaps not so easy to see an absolutely clear-cut distinction in the United Kingdom between devolution and federalism. This is essentially the argument that over a number of years devolution will prove to be a slippery slope rather than a defensible constitutional position which can be held indefinitely. Some have even warned of the dangers of Scottish separatism, yet this tendency has received very little support at General Elections, essentially because the vast majority of Scottish people continue to derive more material benefit from being in the United Kingdom than they would from being outside it.

Advocates of the new dispensation in Scotland, however, seek to draw a favourable comparison between devolution and federalism. They point out that the latter concept is still not well understood or appreciated by the mass of the British people, especially the vast majority who live in England where there is no decisive groundswell of opinion in favour of creating perhaps eight or nine English regions to balance greater autonomy for Scotland,

Wales and Northern Ireland. Beyond the ranks of Liberal Democrat Party activists and a small minority of true believers in the principles of federalism, there is no significant live tradition or widespread public sympathy for the introduction of a fully codified constitution with all its institutional implications for Parliament and the courts. Yet this would be a necessary precondition for a decisive move to a federal structure for the United Kingdom within which Scotland would be one of the constituent units. Moreover, there is little or no evidence to suggest that Scottish Nationalists would favour a political future for Scotland as part of a federal United Kingdom any more than most of them are now satisfied with what they regard as the half-way house of devolution.

In short, although devolution for Scotland is a constitutional hybrid, like many other constitutional hybrids in the British tradition, it can be confidently defended and sustained for a long period of time. Of course, no wise politician or political commentator would ever say that a given constitutional settlement will last for ever, because there is always a dynamic in these things which in an open and free society makes any constitutional arrangements susceptible to change, depending upon how objective circumstances and subjective perceptions alter over time. It is equally clear that the supporters of devolution in the Scottish Labour and Liberal Democrat parties fervently believe (and hope) that the policy will prove popular and hence sustainable in the longer term, since if it does not, it will be an open invitation for the SNP to intensify its campaign to 'finish the job' by moving Scotland decisively towards independence.

Technically and legally speaking, the Scottish Parliament with an SNP majority after a future election would not have the right to alter the constitutional status of Scotland, still less the constitutional arrangements for the United Kingdom. Yet in real political terms the late Donald Dewar, James Wallace and the other Scottish party leaders have known that they would have to take full account of the strength of Scottish opinion if a future Scottish referendum held at the behest of a new SNP Government for Scotland resulted in a majority of the Scottish people voting for Scottish independen-

dence. This would amount in practice to a clear decision for Scottish secession from the United Kingdom, an option analogous to the right which has already been made available to the people of Northern Ireland under the 1973 Northern Ireland (Constitution) Act. It is also worth adding that while the uncodified British constitution does not explicitly recognise such a right of secession for any part of the UK, the flexible principle of Parliamentary supremacy, combined with political expediency and weariness on the part of English public opinion, might one day lead the key decision makers in London to react to such an SNP move by simply saying 'good luck and good riddance' to Scotland.

Questions for discussion

1   Is legislative devolution for Scotland a sustainable response to the dynamic relationship between Scotland and the rest of the United Kingdom?

2   How credible is the SNP aspiration for an independent Scotland within the European Union?

3   What constitutional problems are likely to emerge in the relations between the UK government and Parliament on the one hand and the devolved institutions in Scotland on the other?

Notes

1   R. Coupland, *Welsh and Scottish Nationalism, a Study*; Collins, London, 1954; p. 71.
2   *Ibid*; p. 81.
3   *Ibid*; p. 112.
4   C. Harvie, *Scotland and Nationalism*; Allen & Unwin, London, 1977; p. 16.
5   See A.V. Dicey and R.S. Rait, *Thoughts on the Union between England and Scotland*; Macmillan, London, 1920.
6   Quoted in R. Coupland, *op. cit.*; p. 401.
7   In 1979 the Conservative share of the vote in Scotland was 31 per cent, in 1983 28 per cent and

in 1987 24 per cent. Under John Major's leadership it recovered slightly to 26 per cent in 1992.

8 The 1990 report was entitled *Towards Scotland's Parliament* and the 1995 report was entitled *Scotland's Parliament, Scotland's Right*.

9 This was published as a White Paper, *Memorandum of Understanding and Supplementary Agreements between the United Kingdom Government, Scottish Ministers and the Cabinet of the National Assembly for Wales*, Cm 4444, and presented to Parliament by the Lord Chancellor in October 1999.

10 *Ibid*; paras 2 and 3.

11 *Ibid*; para 13.

12 *Ibid*; para 14. This passage was reminiscent of the arguments used by Ministers in 1972 in favour of key clauses in the *1972 European Communities Act* which maintained that European law would thenceforth take priority over national law in the areas of policy covered by the European treaties, because it was tacitly assumed that such an outcome was intended by Parliament at Westminster when it passed the legislation. In other words, in all cases where Parliament gives away some of its supreme power in the United Kingdom, it must be assumed to have intended the consequences of its own actions.

13 *Ibid*; para 15.

14 *Ibid*; para 26.

15 See www.cabinet-office.gov.uk/constitution/2000/devolution.

Further reading

Vernon Bogdanor, *Devolution in the United Kingdom*; Oxford University Press, Oxford, 1999.

Reginald Coupland, *Welsh and Scottish Nationalism, a Study*; Collins, London, 1954.

A.V. Dicey and R.S. Rait, *Thoughts on the Union between England and Scotland*; Macmillan, London, 1920.

Christopher Harvie, *Scotland and Nationalism*; Allen & Unwin, London, 1977.

Robert Hazell (ed.) *The State and the Nations: the First Year of Devolution in the United Kingdom*; Imprint Academic, London, 2000.

Jo E. Murkens, *Scotland's Place in Europe*; Constitution Unit, London, 2001.

Brian Taylor, *The Scottish Parliament*; Polygon, Edinburgh, 1999.

website for Labour's devolution policy: www.cabinet-office.gov.uk/constitution/devolution

website for the Scottish Parliament: www.Scottish.parliament.uk

Chapter 5

The meaning of Wales

Always more than a cultural identity

Wales was always more than a cultural identity within the British Isles and for considerable periods in the mists of time it assumed, or had imposed upon it, many of the characteristics of a nation. For example, under Hywel the Good (920–50) there was some real codification of customary Welsh law and under Gruffydd ap Llywelyn (in 1055) a semblance of national unity was briefly imposed upon the warring tribes of Wales. The Romans had never tried to conquer Wales and centuries later the Norman and Angevin Kings of England never succeeded in conquering all of it.

The most successful conqueror was Edward I, who built majestic English castles at Conway, Caernarvon and Harlech and who by 1284 managed to impose a military settlement on virtually the whole of Wales, but one which left considerable leeway for continuing cultural and religious freedom for the Welsh. The Statute of Wales in 1284 created six Welsh shires west of the Marches and these came to form the territory of Edward I's son who was named as the first English Prince of Wales in 1301. The Principality contained towns with royal charters and was subjected to English criminal law. So robust and enduring was the English annexation of Wales at this time that in 1322 and again in 1326 Edward II summoned Welsh representatives to attend the English Parliament at Westminster. The dynastic and political integration of England and Wales was carried forward by English kings during the first half of the fourteenth century and was symbolised by the ceremony at Westminster in 1343 installing Edward III's son, the Black Prince, as the Prince of Wales. The parallel military integration was necessitated by the English need for Welsh military forces, notably Welsh longbowmen, in battles against the French and the Scots. For example, it has been estimated that in 1346 one-third of the English army at the battle of Crécy against the French consisted of Welsh archers and pikemen.

On the principle that 'the enemy of my enemy is my friend' the French were inclined from time to time in the late Middle Ages to ally with any disaffected Welsh (or Scottish or Irish) rebel leaders who threatened English dominance of the British Isles. This was the case with the rebellion led by Owen Glyn Dwr in 1400–10 which entangled the armies of Henry IV in a long and difficult campaign against Welsh rebels who were fighting on home territory with the support of the people and, after 1404, with the benefit of an alliance with Charles VI of France. As well as combining with the small French expeditionary force which landed at Milford Haven in 1405, Owen was able to make common cause with the Yorkist noblemen Mortimer in the south and Northumberland in the north who were then in arms against the Lancastrian King of England for their own self-serving reasons. For a while Owen made sufficient headway against Henry IV to be able to summon two 'national Parliaments' at Machynlleth in 1404 and Harlech in 1405, and to be taken seriously when he recognised the ultra-montane Papacy in Avignon. Yet from 1408 when he lost his stronghold at Aberystwyth and 1409 when a similar fate befell him at Harlech, Owen began to lose ground and authority to Henry and was eventually forced to take refuge in the Welsh mountains where he later died, a hunted and enfeebled figure, in 1416.

The English responded harshly with a policy of systematic subjugation of any rebellion. Fourteen coercive Acts of Parliament were passed during the period 1400 to 1402 alone and this statutory onslaught was backed by the military power of an English army of occupation. The lesson for the Welsh seemed to be that they would always pay a high price for rebelling against English rule; it was possibly better for them to extract such advantages as they could from the sustained English policy of assimilation. This more compliant approach became somewhat easier for patriotic Welshmen to adopt when Henry Tudor, a Welshman and a Lancastrian, defeated the Yorkist King Richard III at Bosworth Field in 1485 and in consequence became King Henry VII of England. In gratitude to those of his fellow countrymen who had helped him win the crown by force of arms, Henry VII deliberately set out to restore some historic freedoms and opportunities to his 'own people' and it was noticeable for many years that the influential positions at his court were well populated with upwardly mobile Welshmen.

The political assimilation of Wales with England really dates from two Acts of Parliament in 1536 and 1543 during the reign of Henry VIII. From that time onwards Wales was governed under the same laws and constitutional arrangements as England and sent Members of Parliament to Westminster for the first time since the reign of Edward II. The English–Welsh border was altered as part of Henry VIII's reforms of local government, so that Shrewsbury, Hereford and Monmouth, for example, became administratively part of England even though at the time they were more Welsh-speaking than English-speaking. Culturally, the Welsh language and Welsh literature remained distinct, but in the constitutional sphere only the system of local Welsh justice was left unchanged by the reforms of the Tudor period. As Sir Reginald Coupland observed of the Westminster Statutes governing Wales in the 1530s and 1540s, 'political assimilation could go no further: as a separate body politic Wales had virtually ceased to exist'.[1]

The Anglicisation of large parts of Wales, especially the industrial south and east, proceeded apace in the eighteenth and nineteenth centuries. The process of political assimilation, which had derived from the determination of the Tudor kings in the sixteenth century, was subsequently put beyond doubt in a Westminster Statute of 1746 which declared that 'in all cases where the Kingdom of England, or that part of Great Britain called England, hath been or shall be mentioned in any Act of Parliament, the same has been and shall from henceforth be deemed and taken to comprehend and include the Dominion of Wales'.[2]

Over several centuries the Welsh people were socialised and assimilated into the United Kingdom and sinews were created which bound Wales and England ever more closely together. For example, the geographical proximity of Wales to many of the largest population centres in the English Midlands, the expanding network of physical communications (roads, canals and railways), the migration of English labour into Wales to work in the new Welsh industries (principally coal, iron and steel)

which were established by English capitalists, the deepening integration between Welsh and English families through intermarriage and the spread of the English language into Wales (especially the industrial valleys in the south), the integrating influence of British political parties and notably the Liberals who became particularly strong in Wales in the late nineteenth century: all of these influences served to draw the two peoples together into one society and one polity. Yet conversely the two peoples were kept culturally distinct, at any rate in the north and west of Wales, by the continuing influence of the Welsh language and Celtic culture at *Eisteddfodau* and other such celebrations; and by the strong tradition of religious non-conformity and dissent, which manifested itself principally in the long campaign for the disestablishment of the Church of Wales and its institutional separation from the Church of England that was eventually achieved in 1920.

The flame of an earlier and much older Welsh nationalism was never completely snuffed out and the embers were to some extent fanned into life by the desire of some in Wales to emulate Thomas Davis and the Young Ireland movement in the 1840s or Isaac Butt and the moderate Irish Nationalists in the 1870s. In view of the integration of Wales into the structures of British politics, it would also be unrealistic to dismiss the influence upon Welsh political opinion of Gladstone's Home Rule policy as declared, for example, in a great speech which he gave to a vast public meeting in Swansea in 1887 soon after the defeat of the first Home Rule Bill for Ireland. Yet Home Rule for Wales was not seen as a political imperative by the English ruling class in the second half of the nineteenth or the first half of the twentieth century, or even as an expedient concession to nationalism as was the case with Home Rule for Ireland.

By 1885, when the Gladstonian Liberal Party won 30 out of 34 Parliamentary seats in Wales, the Principality might have become one nation politically; but it was balkanised culturally and socially with the increasingly industrial and Anglophone south (and areas of the north-east) ever more integrated into the British economy and polity, while the rural west and north of the country remained much more distinctively Welsh in its language, culture and aspirations. In the absence of an avowedly Welsh nationalist political party, half-hearted nationalist aspirations were articulated by Welsh Liberals or not at all. The pioneering nationalist movement, *Cymru Fydd* (Wales of the Future), which had been established in 1866 in partial imitation of *Young Ireland*, had essentially cultural rather than political objectives and campaigned above all to safeguard the Welsh language and Welsh culture from English contamination. This was a worthy cause, but it was not likely to change the pattern of governance in Wales.

The political agenda of the dominant Welsh Liberals throughout the period until the First World War was much more concerned with social and cultural issues than with any idea of Welsh self-government, still less Welsh political independence. The most insistent political demand was for the disestablishment and disendowment of the Anglican Church in Wales which attracted the allegiance of no more than one-fifth of the population. This cause became part of official Liberal policy in 1887, led to the introduction of Bills at Westminster in 1893 and on several occasions between 1906 and 1914, and was finally implemented by Lloyd George's Coalition Administration in 1920.

There was, however, a brief period in the 1890s when it seemed possible that the causes of Welsh nationalism and Welsh Liberalism might merge and *Cymru Fydd* might capture the Welsh Liberal Federation. This situation came to a head in the mid-1890s under the influence of two compelling young personalities – Tom Ellis, who was first elected as Liberal MP for Merioneth in 1886, and David Lloyd George, who was first elected as Liberal MP for Caernarfon Boroughs in 1890 – each of whom decided to play the nationalist card when the Liberals were divided by rivalry between Rosebery and Harcourt following the retirement of Gladstone.

It seems to be the general view of Welsh historians that whereas Tom Ellis was passionate and sincere in his espousal of Welsh nationalism, which he had imbibed as a keen young student at the newly established University College in Aberystwyth, David Lloyd George was giving an early manifestation of the self-serving opportunism which was to characterise the whole of his long political career. Whatever their personal motives, they were instrumental in persuading the North Wales Liberal Federation to merge with Cymru Fydd in April 1895, but unsuccessful thereafter in persuading the South Wales Liberal Federation to follow suit. This was largely because of the opposition to such a move led by D.A. Thomas, the formidable coal owner and Liberal MP for Merthyr Tydfil from 1888 to 1910, who mobilised the interests of south Wales businessmen against the whole idea. This episode provides more evidence of the cleavage between the industrial heartland of south Wales where people of all classes tended to identify with their counterparts in England and most of the rest of Wales where nationalist identity, traditions and aspirations tended to be much stronger.

For the vast majority of Welsh people during the nineteenth and twentieth centuries, the reality of their British interests outweighed any tendency to indulge their nationalist aspirations. These found outlets and expression not so much in any campaign for autonomy or self-government as in their cultural traditions, religious affiliations and (declining) familiarity with the Welsh language. Undoubtedly, an emerging national consciousness was boosted during these years by the commitment to various strains of Welsh non-conformity, the teaching of distinguished scholars and intellectuals such as John Morris-Jones and Owen Edwards, the influence of journals such as *Y Geninen*, and the powerful symbolism of the *Eisteddfodau* which were occasionally attended by Gladstone and regularly attended by Lloyd George.

The economic, social and political realities of life in Wales underlined the increasing strength and importance of British interests for all but the most esoteric Welsh people, and the weakness or complete absence of many of the attributes normally associated with effective nation building. For example, the Welsh economy both in industry and in agriculture was heavily dependent upon British capital and British or British-controlled markets; the Welsh elite had to look mainly to

English ladders of opportunity if its members were to better themselves and fulfil their personal ambitions; most roads, railways and shipping communications connected with England or other British centres of population and it remained difficult to move goods or people easily north or south in Wales; there was a dearth of distinctively Welsh social and political leadership for any nationalist movement (unlike in Ireland or Scotland) and an absence of any distinctive national institutions; even the separate system of local Welsh justice had been abolished in 1830. In short, the notorious entry in the *Encyclopaedia Britannica* which said simply 'For Wales see England' could not entirely be dismissed as a bad English joke.

In these circumstances the nationalist movement in Wales – if such it could be called – was always metaphorically in the minor key when compared with the major key of the British (English) connection. This is exemplified by the fact that the first branch of the *Cymru Fydd League* was established in London in 1886 and the second in Liverpool in 1887. It was not until 1891 that the first branch in Wales was established at Barry. A genuinely national organisation for Cymru Fydd was established in 1894 at Llandrindod Wells and a new magazine, *Young Wales*, in 1895; yet by 1896 the South Wales Liberal Federation under the leadership of D.A. Thomas had rejected a merger with the Cymru Fydd League, which, however, had already merged quite willingly with the North Wales Liberal Federation under the leadership of Tom Ellis, the first President of the League which had been formed in London.

It is worth recalling the main demands of the Cymru Fydd Manifesto in 1888: the establishment of an elected Welsh Assembly with a Welsh Executive responsible for Welsh affairs both to the Welsh Assembly and to the Westminster Parliament, while the people of Wales were to continue to be represented by their full complement of Westminster MPs. Such a programme had little influence upon the political process at Westminster and we have already noted how in Wales it fell foul of the north–south split within the Welsh Liberal Federation. It was a set-back when Tom Ellis was persuaded to join the Liberal Whips Office in the

House of Commons in 1892 and an even greater blow when he died in 1899 at the early age of 39, while the more general prospects of real influence for the cause were obviously not improved by the two spells of Conservative Administration in London from 1886 to 1892 and from 1896 to 1906. However, the real weakness of the League was essentially structural in that it was too dependent upon an alliance or merger with the Welsh Liberals and hence vulnerable to the differing interests (almost split personality) of Liberal activists in north and south Wales respectively. During its short and ineffective life, the League was no more than 'an artificial construct of packed committees and pliant newspaper editors, not a genuinely popular movement for Home Rule'.[3] It could therefore hold out little or no real prospect of shaping the political future of Wales.

With a Liberal Government back in power after 1906 supported by a massive majority at Westminster, there ought to have been an opportunity to make real Parliamentary progress towards the goals of Welsh nationalism. Further efforts were made by Welsh Liberals under the leadership of E.T. John, the MP for East Denbighshire, to promote a Government of Wales Bill in March 1914, but to no avail because Welsh Home Rule was not regarded by the rest of Parliament as a priority and most Welsh public opinion seemed content with its dual Welsh–British identity. Welsh nationalist political opinion seemed much more determined to secure the passage of the Welsh Church Bill, which reached the Statute Book in 1914 at the third time of asking (having been rejected twice by the House of Lords) and which eventually led to the disestablishment and disendowment of the Anglican Church in Wales over a 30-year period from 1920 onwards.

Integration with England and its discontents

In the early years of the twentieth century the prospects for Welsh nationalism did not seem good. Quite the contrary, the Welsh economy became year by year more integrated with the rest of the United Kingdom and the British Empire; Welsh society was gradually losing some of its distinctive characteristics as non-conformity in religion began to lose some of its coherence and as the Welsh language began to lose its earlier appeal, especially to the young in the most Anglicised parts of the Principality; and Welsh politics became increasingly integrated with British politics during the first two or three decades of the century as the Labour Party came to supplant the Liberals as the real 'party of Wales'.

The bitter industrial struggles in the south Wales coal industry between 1910 and 1912 became a cockpit – at Tonypandy in the Rhondda and elsewhere – for the wider class struggle which was to characterise industrial relations in highly unionised industries throughout Great Britain for decades to come. It was only with the advent of the First World War that the class struggle went into abeyance and then it was superseded in Wales not by a drive for national rebellion against the English and the United Kingdom (as in the case of Sinn Fein and the Irish nationalists) but rather by a mass rallying to the British colours in all-out war against the Germans. Indeed, 280,000 Welshmen served in the British armed forces during the war; this figure, representing about 14 per cent of the adult population, constituted a higher proportion than in England or Scotland. Admittedly, towards the end of the war, when the full horror of the futile carnage on the Western Front had impressed itself upon many people, popular support for the cause became more flaky, especially among radical Left-wingers and pacifists who had opposed the introduction of conscription in 1916 and who were attracted by the Communist idealism of the Russian Revolution in 1917. Yet on the whole the experience of total war, in Wales as in other parts of the United Kingdom, had the effect of uniting rather than dividing the great mass of British people and in the economic and political spheres it served to integrate Wales and the Welsh people even more closely into the United Kingdom.

The other important point to note about the consequences for Wales of the First World War is that the exigencies of the situation in 1916 had precipitated a fatal split in the Liberal Party when

Lloyd George supplanted Asquith as war leader and promptly formed a Coalition Administration with the Conservatives – a split from which the Liberal Party never really recovered. These events had the effect after the war of creating a golden opportunity for the fledgling Labour Party throughout Great Britain and a new political space for the formation of *Plaid Cymru* (the Party of Wales) in 1925. In a sense the legacy of the formerly dominant Liberals in Wales was partitioned: the progressive and radical element was inherited by the young Labour Party, while the nationalist and Celtic element was offered to anyone with the insight and drive to exploit it.

Throughout the inter-war years, the main difficulty for proto-nationalists in Wales was that unfolding economic and political circumstances – i.e. the temporary boom from 1919 to 1922 followed by the recession and then the slump during the rest of the 1920s and the early 1930s – were not in any way conducive to popularising a nationalist appeal which was essentially intellectual and cultural in character and hence far removed from the immediate daily concerns of the mass of the Welsh people who found themselves suffering levels of unemployment and hardship virtually unparalleled in any other part of the United Kingdom at that time. The ineffectual E.T. John (who by that time had joined the Labour Party) played some part in the ill-fated 1920 Speaker's Conference on Devolution and then proceeded to launch a so-called Celtic Congress on a pan-Celtic basis which came to absolutely nothing. Desultory efforts were also made by various Westminster backbenchers to promote the cause of Welsh devolution – e.g. the 1922 Government of Wales Bill introduced by Sir Robert Thomas, the Liberal MP for Wrexham, which was talked out on First Reading – but none of them amounted to anything significant. Equally, no headway was made with projects for *administrative* devolution within the bureaucracy of central Government, because the governing elite in London thought it was perfectly sensible and efficient to administer Wales from England and to divide it into two (north and south) for most administrative purposes.[4]

In this period of political drought for nationalism

in Wales (as in Scotland), the Welsh nationalist political party, *Plaid Cymru*, was formed at a small meeting in a temperance hotel during the *Eisteddfod* in Pwllheli in August 1925. It had six founder members of whom the most distinguished were Saunders Lewis, an expatriate Welsh writer from Liverpool, and Ambrose Bebb, who had been a university lecturer in France. In so far as it also had some organisational progenitors, these were the Welsh Home Rule Army (*Byddin Ymreolwyr Cymru*) which had been founded in Caernarfon in 1924 and the Welsh Movement (*Y Mudiad Cymreig*), a militant pressure group for the Welsh language which had been in existence a little longer. The founders were united by their non-conformist and pacifist traditions and by a rather ethereal commitment to the organic reintegration of Wales into the continental European mainstream where it had belonged before the time of Henry VIII and the Protestant Reformation. Initially, the young party did not commit itself to self-government for Wales, but rather to the objectives of making Welsh the only official language in the country, obligatory for Welsh business and government, and the sole medium of instruction at all levels of education. In short, it was 'more a pressure group on behalf of the language than an organised political party'.[5]

It is important to realise that the emergence of Plaid Cymru from apparently humble beginnings should be understood in the context of a wider and at that time already well-established campaign to preserve Welsh language and culture. During the early years of its existence *political* objectives of a conventional kind were by no means paramount in the minds of its members. Most Welsh nationalists put the preservation of the Welsh language and culture before political self-government. Indeed, the party followed in the wake of the Welsh League of Youth (*Yr Urdd*) which had been founded by Ifan ab Owen Edwards in 1922 with an explicit emphasis upon fostering a *non-political* national consciousness in Wales. Whereas it was not until 1939 that Plaid Cymru was able to claim even 2,000 members, *Yr Urdd* had claimed as many as 50,000 members in 1934. Furthermore, the great majority of those living in Wales could not speak Welsh, so

it seemed natural to most Welsh nationalists to tackle the linguistic and cultural deficit first.

In 1929 the party participated in a General Election for the first time when the Reverend Lewis Valentine, one of the six founder members, contested the Caernarvonshire seat and got 609 votes or about 1 per cent of the poll. In the 1931 General Election the party fought two seats, with Professor Daniel getting 2 per cent in Caernarvonshire and Saunders Lewis getting a much more impressive 18 per cent of the small educated electorate who actually voted in the University of Wales seat. By 1932 the party had begun to elaborate a more recognisable political programme, since in that year it committed itself to the goal of self-government for Wales on a dominion basis within the British Empire (on the model codified in the 1931 Statute of Westminster) and to a Welsh seat at the League of Nations. However, all the while it continued to give the greatest prominence to measures to preserve and advance the Welsh language and culture. Grandiloquent and even risible as the political aspects of this programme may have seemed, the party must have been doing something right because in 1934 it managed to chalk up its first victory when it won a local Council seat in Merioneth.

Indeed, it might have been able to make some further progress in local elections and even at Parliamentary by-elections during the period of gradual economic recovery in Wales and the rest of Britain in the middle and late 1930s if it had not been for the apparently reckless decision by Saunders Lewis, Lewis Valentine and D.J. Williams (three of the six founder members of the party) to confess to deliberate arson at the premises of an RAF bombing range in Pen-y-Berth near Penrhos in Caernarvonshire in September 1936. In order to dramatise their allegedly non-violent Welsh language campaign, they refused to give their evidence in English when they were tried at the Old Bailey and hence were sent to prison for nine months in Wormwood Scrubs for contempt of court. This extravagant and challenging gesture definitely raised the profile of Plaid Cymru in Wales and in England, but it is very doubtful whether it was effective in persuading most law-abiding

Welsh people to subscribe to their cause and it was certainly not a way of endearing them to the English.

During the Second World War the leaders of Plaid Cymru were not particularly sympathetic to the British cause and consequently they failed to attract much popular support at a time of British solidarity and patriotism. Their attitude towards the war could be described as one of lofty, intellectual disdain for what Professor Daniel, by then president of the party, described as 'a clash of rival imperialisms from which Wales, like the other small nations of Europe, has nothing to gain but everything to lose'.[6] By striking such poses the leaders of Plaid Cymru demonstrated that they were out of touch with the feelings of the mass of the people in Wales as in the rest of the United Kingdom; and it clearly did their political cause no good in real tests of public opinion, such as the by-election for the University of Wales seat in January 1943, when the patriotic Professor W.J. Gruffydd for the Liberals easily defeated Saunders Lewis for Plaid Cymru by 52 per cent to 22 per cent of the vote. What is more, the war necessarily entailed complete mobilisation of British society throughout the United Kingdom and this implied even deeper integration between Wales and England.

Another fundamental factor which bound Wales ever more closely to the rest of the United Kingdom and which served completely to integrate Welsh politics with British politics during the second and third quarters of the twentieth century was the remarkable political ascendancy established by the Labour Party in Wales from about 1922 onwards. In that year's General Election Labour won 41 per cent of the vote in Wales and the comparable figures at all subsequent General Elections until 1966 were all higher (reaching 44 per cent even in 1931 when Labour's fortunes at Westminster were at their lowest), on some occasions (notably 1945 and 1950) at the hegemonic level of 58 per cent. What this means is that for about 50 years from the early 1920s to the late 1960s the Labour Party came to embody the complete integration of Welsh and British politics and in the process effectively suffocated Welsh nationalism and Plaid Cymru. During this long period Wales produced some of the most prominent figures in the Labour movement – such as Aneurin Bevan, first elected for Ebbw Vale in 1929, and James Griffiths, first elected for Llanelli in 1936 – few of whom evinced much sympathy with Welsh nationalist objectives. James Griffiths, who was later to become the first Secretary of State for Wales in 1964, was really the most prominent exception proving the rule. On the whole the Welsh Labour 'Taffya' shared the prejudices of Aneurin Bevan who, in a debate in the House of Commons in 1946, described the idea of devolution as 'not Socialism . . . [but] escapism'.[7]

Throughout this period the Labour Party believed in aggregated solutions to the deep-seated problems of poverty and unemployment which beset Wales and many other disadvantaged parts of the United Kingdom. They regarded local nationalism in any part of the United Kingdom as a tiresome irrelevance and harmful distraction from the main purposes of nationalising the commanding heights of the British economy and raising the material standards of ordinary working people in all parts of the country. Devolution was pushed off the agenda by the paramount need to tackle the economic problems of the era.

In so far as Labour Ministers in Churchill's wartime Coalition Government were prepared to make any concessions to Welsh nationalist feelings, these could be categorised under the heading of tokenism. For example, an all-day debate on Welsh affairs was held for the first time in the House of Commons on 17th October 1944. Megan Lloyd George (by that time a Labour MP) spoke first and was later supported by James Griffiths and S.O. Davies, but resolutely opposed in scornful tones by Aneurin Bevan. Prior to that, from 1942 to 1944, there had been a Welsh Advisory Panel on Post-War Reconstruction in which James Griffiths had played a prominent part, but once again this did not really amount to anything very much.

When the post-war Labour Government was swept into power in a landslide election victory in 1945, none of its leading figures (again with the single exception of James Griffiths) seemed remotely interested in addressing the Welsh nationalist agenda. This was principally because they had a much bigger and more important agenda covering the whole of the United Kingdom and the future of the British Empire and Commonwealth, but to a limited degree it also reflected the fact that at the General Election Plaid Cymru had only contested eight seats in Wales and had lost its deposit in seven of them. Clement Attlee, Labour's laconic Prime Minister, regarded the idea of creating a Welsh Office (one of the limited nationalist objectives at the time) as 'an unnecessary duplication' of Whitehall. Herbert Morrison, the great Labour machine politician from London, dismissed the idea of Welsh devolution as unnecessary and inappropriate; and firmly argued in a paper to his Cabinet colleagues in January 1946 that 'the proper remedy for Wales, as for Scotland, is to ensure that they both form part of a single economic plan for the whole country and are not thrown back on their own sectional resources'.[8]

Only gradually and reluctantly did Labour Ministers begin to pay somewhat more heed to the gently growing demands from some Welsh Labour MPs – such as George Thomas and Goronwy Roberts – for more explicit recognition of Welsh nationalist aspirations. Thus it was that in 1948 the rather feeble idea of establishing an *Advisory Council for Wales* (made up of local Councillors and representatives of both sides of Welsh industry and commerce) was mooted as a compromise proposal which might satisfy both James Griffiths and his opponents on this issue, Nye Bevan and Herbert Morrison. It was duly accepted by the relevant Cabinet committee and endorsed by an unenthusiastic Cabinet. The Council was supposed to discuss and advise upon economic and cultural issues affecting Wales. Yet it was never taken seriously and was eventually abolished by a subsequent Labour Government in 1966.

If the post-war Labour Government showed itself to be dismissive towards Welsh nationalist goals and aspirations, the Welsh nationalist movement was commensurately cautious and uninspired. In 1949 a 'Parliament for Wales' campaign was launched on an all-party basis under the auspices of *Undeb Cymru Fydd*, the Welsh language pressure group whose secretary was T.I. Ellis, the son of the charismatic Tom Ellis. The president of the

campaign was Lady Megan Lloyd George and Plaid Cymru was represented on the ruling committee by the young Gwynfor Evans. For as long as Labour remained in office, the campaign achieved very little.

Under subsequent Conservative Administrations, however, Welsh nationalist campaigns seemed to achieve somewhat more with a number of Private Member's Bills and Parliamentary Petitions in favour of some degree of self-government for Wales. In 1951 the incoming Conservative Administration agreed to establish a 'Ministry for Welsh Affairs', although this turned out to be nothing more than a department within the Home Office. Subsequently, the Welsh parcel was passed around Whitehall from one department to another and from one junior minister to another until it became a liability rather than an asset both for Wales and for the British Government. When Henry Brooke held the portfolio in 1957 in his capacity as Minister for Housing and Local Government, he alienated much Welsh opinion by approving the inundation of the Tryweryn Valley in Merionethshire to create a new reservoir to provide Welsh water for the mainly English citizens of Liverpool. This became a *cause célèbre* in Welsh politics and the source of several Welsh grievances which were grist to the mill of Plaid Cymru.

The faltering revival of Welsh nationalism

By the early 1960s Welsh nationalism was at a pretty low point and the secular decline in the Welsh language had largely dashed the hopes of all Welsh nationalists. In 1951 only 28 per cent of the Welsh people could speak Welsh and by 1971 the figure had fallen to 20 per cent, with an even lower proportion of Welsh speakers in Welsh schools. It was obviously a case of now or never for the revival of Welsh national consciousness, since if the militant activists proved unable to arrest the decline in the Welsh language, they would soon have to kiss goodbye to a distinctive Welsh culture and any hopes they might still have had for Welsh self-government.

It was in these ostensibly unpropitious circumstances that Saunders Lewis emerged from semi-retirement to give a new lead to the Welsh nationalist movement. In a memorable lecture on BBC radio on 13th February 1962 entitled 'Tynged yr Iaith' ('The fate of the language') he made an impassioned plea for a more militant effort to defend the Welsh language and to extend its use throughout all spheres for which government, central or local, had any responsibility. His main argument was that the revival of the Welsh language was more urgent and important than progress down the road to self-government. What is more, he told his radio audience, 'success is only possible through revolutionary methods' – something which was soon to inspire his younger and more radical followers on university campuses and elsewhere to launch an energetic campaign of mass demonstrations, sit-ins, traffic blocking, vandalism of TV masts and road signs and, in a few cases, the bombing of Government buildings and threats of assassination against senior Government Ministers.[9]

The organisational consequences of this dramatic initiative were the formation of a new Welsh Language Society (*Cymdeithas yr Iaith Gymraeg*) at the Plaid Cymru summer school at Pontardulais in 1962 and the subsequent establishment of a newspaper for the Society, *Tafod y Ddraig*. The political consequences of the enthusiastic and sustained campaign which ensued throughout Wales over the following years included Harold Wilson's appointment of James Griffiths as the first Secretary of State for Wales in 1964 leading a new Welsh Office in Cardiff and London which took over responsibility for the extensive administrative functions of the British Government in Wales and sought to coordinate in the Welsh interest policies conceived elsewhere, notably in relation to economic and employment issues. A more dramatic political consequence of the revived national consciousness in Wales, at a time when the Wilson Administration was experiencing a period of mid-term unpopularity, was Gwynfor Evans's victory for Plaid Cymru in the Camarthen by-election in July 1966 – a nationalist triumph which produced the first Plaid Cymru MP at Westminster.

This victory for Plaid Cymru was followed in subsequent years by near misses at other by-elections in Rhondda West in March 1967 and Caerphilly in July 1968 when previously impregnable Labour majorities were reduced to much narrower margins of a few thousand votes.

Notwithstanding the fact that the Labour Government had achieved a very comfortable majority of 90 in the Commons at the 1966 General Election, Harold Wilson and his colleagues were becoming increasingly aware of, and responsive to, the nationalist threats to the governing party's position in both Wales and Scotland. As far as Wales was concerned, this led Cledwyn Hughes as Secretary of State for Wales in 1966 to put to his Cabinet colleagues a proposal for a *Welsh Regional Council* with powers over secondary legislation for Wales as an effective 'national' upper tier of local government once unitary local authorities were successfully established beneath it. In the event this idea was a bridge too far for many of his Cabinet colleagues and successful resistance to it was led by Willie Ross, the 'Unionist' Secretary of State for Scotland, and James Callaghan, then Home Secretary and an Englishman who occupied a Cardiff seat; the anti-devolution diehards on the Labour backbenches, such as Ness Edwards and Leo Abse, provided another reason for the Whips to advise against it. The upshot was that the Cabinet agreed upon a diluted compromise and created a Welsh Regional Council which (like its Conservative-inspired predecessor) became simply a nominated advisory body.

More gratifying for Saunders Lewis and his enthusiastic young followers in the Welsh Language Society was their success in persuading the Labour Government to introduce and Parliament at Westminster to pass the *1967 Welsh Language Act* which for the first time secured parity between the Welsh and English languages for all official purposes in Wales. Thus all official documents came to be produced in both languages, as did all road signs and all other symbols of official communication between the public authorities and the Welsh people. Initially, this irritated the monoglot anglophone majority in Wales and there was intermittent talk of an anglophone backlash. Yet the most significant consequences of the Statute were to be seen in Welsh schools and later in Welsh TV broadcasting which by 1982 finally had a dedicated Welsh-speaking channel.

From October 1964 until June 1970 and again from February 1974 to March 1976 Harold Wilson led four Labour Administrations. He was notoriously sensitive to political pressures, especially within his own party, and had a predilection for tinkering with the machinery of government. As a former civil servant and before that an academic who had been drawn into Churchill's war-time Administration as an expert statistician, he was particularly fond of Royal Commissions – a traditional British device for putting off, obscuring or at least defusing tricky political issues. It was not surprising, therefore, that in 1969 he appointed a Royal Commission under Geoffrey Crowther of *The Economist* to examine all aspects of the constitution in the United Kingdom, paying particular attention to the nationalist threats in Scotland and Wales, and to make recommendations as to how such threats should be addressed.

In spite of the fact that the tide of elite political opinion in the United Kingdom seemed to be moving in favour of Welsh nationalism at this time, it was notable that even as a 'protest party' Plaid Cymru did not do particularly well either in the local Council elections of April 1970 or in the General Election of June 1970 when for the first time it contested all 36 Welsh constituencies, but won no seats and actually suffered the dispiriting defeat of Gwynfor Evans in Camarthen. With a Conservative Government in office under the leadership of Edward Heath, no one in Wales held out much hope of securing devolution, still less self-government for Wales. For one thing there were only seven Conservative MPs in Wales and the party at grassroots level was too weak to put much effective pressure upon London to make concessions to Welsh priorities. It was therefore Labour rather than the Tories who seemed to have most to lose from any Welsh nationalist revival and in that context Labour did well to win back Merthyr Tydfil in a by-election in April 1972 following the death of the Independent MP, S.O. Davies, who had been well disposed towards Welsh devolution.

When the Royal Commission on the Constitution eventually reported in October 1973 under the chairmanship of Lord Kilbrandon (Geoffrey Crowther having previously died in harness), it seemed that Wales had been pulled along in the slipstream of Scotland rather than having been capable of making its own compelling case for greater self-government. The Commission, which was deeply divided upon the most appropriate structures for the governance of the United Kingdom, was at least able to agree (in a bare majority of its members) that Scotland and Wales should each have a legislative Assembly with its own budget, tax-raising powers and responsibility for a wide range of public administration functions affecting its territory and people. The principle of Parliamentary supremacy should be preserved, but in relation to Scotland and Wales Westminster should use its overriding constitutional powers only in exceptional circumstances. A few months later, in February 1974, the Conservatives narrowly lost the General Election which Mr Heath had called prematurely in an atmosphere of industrial and political crisis, so nothing was done about the recommendations of the Kilbrandon Report until the electoral dust had settled and a new Labour Government was in office.

New political opportunities seemed to dawn for both the Welsh and the Scottish nationalists after February 1974 essentially because the United Kingdom moved from bi-polar to multi-polar politics. In England a significant protest vote of nearly one-fifth of those voting supported the Liberals at the February and October General Elections in 1974, while the Scottish Nationalists collected 30 per cent of the vote in Scotland and Plaid Cymru collected 11 per cent of the vote in Wales in October 1974. What these figures portended was growing public dissatisfaction with both the major parties and a tendency, which became increasingly significant from the mid-1970s to the late 1980s, for multi-party politics to take hold of the electorate. In Wales Plaid Cymru sought to attract disaffected Labour voters, but it usually had more success in scooping up disenchanted former Liberals and a scattering of Tories in the rural areas of Wales.

When Plaid Cymru succeeded in winning two seats (Caernarfon and Merioneth) at the February 1974 General Election and three seats (the same two plus Carmarthen for Gwynfor Evans) in October 1974, the Labour Government, newly and precariously elected with a majority in single figures, somewhat reluctantly announced its support for devolution in Wales 'as an essential antidote to national pressure for separatism, a half-way house which would nullify the threat of independence, while offering a genuine advance towards local self-government and participatory democracy'.[10] These nationalist pressures meant that Harold Wilson's fourth Administration, which was elected in October 1974, came into office committed to legislate for Scottish and Welsh devolution in one single Bill. This policy was fore-shadowed in a White Paper of November 1975, but not approved at Second Reading in the Commons until December 1976, about nine months after James Callaghan had succeeded Harold Wilson as Leader of the Labour Party and Prime Minister.

In adopting a pro-devolution policy, the Labour Cabinet was mindful of the fact that the committee stage of such a constitutional measure would have to be taken on the floor of the House where it would be wide open to tactics of delay and obstruction by its opponents, many of whom were to be found on its own backbenches. It therefore tried to shelter devolution for Wales under the legislative wing, as it were, of the more popular devolution for Scotland. However, the tactic did not work, since Leo Abse (Labour MP for Pontypool and a dedicated opponent of devolution) succeeded in tabling an amendment to the Bill which would have made its implementation subject to public approval in separate referenda in Scotland and Wales. On 10th February 1977 ministers acknowledged this argument and accepted the Abse amendment as the only way of getting the legislation through the Commons. However, when ministers later tried to regain some control of the legislation with a guillotine motion to timetable Parliamentary debate on the Bill, they failed and the Government motion was defeated by 312 to 283 on 22nd February 1977.

At this stage things looked very bleak for the Labour Government in London. Because of by-election defeats it had lost its slim majority in the House of Commons; it was trailing behind the Scottish Nationalist Party according to opinion polls in Scotland; and it was in danger of being defeated on a vote of confidence unless it could come to some arrangement with the Liberals who were themselves trailing the Conservatives in the opinion polls in England. Thus both the Labour and the Liberal parties were ready for a marriage of convenience (or at least a temporary affair) and the symbol of the relationship was the so-called *Lib-Lab Pact* concluded in March 1977. Essentially, the deal was that in return for giving their support to the Government in the voting lobbies, the Liberals would become (very) junior partners in the process of government with rights to be consulted by their Labour ministerial counterparts; the Labour Government would thus secure some vital extra voting support for its legislative programme in Parliament. The deal included legislation on devolution for Scotland and Wales, which would otherwise have been impossible to get onto the Statute Book, but it stopped short of meeting Liberal demands for legislative assemblies with tax-raising powers, elected by proportional representation.

The main effect of the Lib-Lab Pact upon the devolution legislation, when it was brought before Parliament a second time later that year, was that it was split into two distinct Bills in order to facilitate what Michael Foot, the Leader of the House, described as 'the separate consideration of what are dissimilar proposals'.[11] This time the passage of the legislation promised to be easier and the Government business managers were heartened when the Scotland and Wales Bills were given consecutive Second Readings in the Commons on 14th and 15th November 1977 and successfully guillotined immediately afterwards. It was right to say that the Bills were dissimilar, since whereas Scotland was offered a directly elected Assembly with primary legislative powers over devolved matters, Wales was offered only a devolved institution with secondary legislative powers and executive oversight of the various departments and public bodies which constituted the public administration of the principality.

During the Committee Stage of the Scotland Bill some anti-devolution Labour backbenchers led by George Cunningham, the expatriate Scottish MP for Islington South, were successful in securing the approval of the House of Commons for an amendment which stipulated that unless 40 per cent or more of the registered electorate in Scotland supported the policy in a referendum, the proposed constitutional changes would be null and void. An identical amendment was carried for the Wales Bill and later embodied in the Wales Act 1979. This became the undoing of the devolution policy both in Scotland and in Wales when the two separate referenda were eventually held on 1st March 1979 and both the Scottish and the Welsh electorate declined to support the policy in large enough numbers to bring the legislation into effect.

The Cunningham amendment led to a greater humiliation for Labour advocates of devolution in Wales than for their counterparts in Scotland in that the referendum result in Wales was four to one against the policy with little more than 10 per cent of the registered electorate voting in its favour, whereas there was actually a small majority for the policy in Scotland, although the number of those in favour failed to surpass the threshold of 40 per cent of the registered electorate laid down in the legislation. It must equally have been a source of joy and vindication for the persistent Labour critics of the policy, who had included Neil Kinnock, Leo Abse, Donald Anderson and a number of other prominent Welsh MPs. Yet it was undeniable that in 1979 the Welsh nationalist goal of greater self-government for Wales had suffered its most serious set-back since the failure of Cymru Fydd in 1896.

In the aftermath of the referendum debacle, the political situation was little short of disastrous for everyone except the Tories and the minority in the Labour Party who had opposed devolution. The policy had been decisively rejected by the Welsh people; the Labour Party was demoralised and divided by the experience of 'the winter of discontent' and its subsequent defeat at the polls; the Liberals were marginalised and somewhat discredited by the failure of the Lib-Lab Pact; and the members of Plaid Cymru and other Welsh nationalist groups may well have felt rejected by

their own people. Only the Tories had something to celebrate, but even they had experienced what was essentially an *English* election victory and not all their senior figures in Scotland and Wales were convinced that Margaret Thatcher's instinctive Unionism and visceral opposition to all forms of devolution would do the party any good west of Offa's Dyke and north of Gretna Green.

There had been some validity in the view expressed by the Labour Minister Lord Crowther-Hunt just before the ill-fated 1979 referendum that the policy of devolution for Wales was 'a dog's breakfast', since in thematic terms it was neither one thing nor the other. It did not recognise Welsh nationality by giving the people of Wales a proper subordinate Parliament, but at the same time it disconcerted anglophone Wales and disappointed Welsh-speaking Wales in almost equal measure. It seemed not to recognise the most important characteristics which set Welsh nationalism apart from Scottish nationalism, and it obstinately insisted on lumping the two phenomena together. Essentially, the policy makers in London had failed to take proper account of the historical fact that 'a Welsh community had survived and flourished despite the absence of a Welsh state' and that in these circumstances what was needed was an effective way of buttressing Welsh community life rather than an unconvincing and pale copy of a blueprint designed to assuage Scottish nationalist ambitions.[12]

For the next eighteen years, with successive Conservative Administrations in charge of the United Kingdom and two very different Prime Ministers who had strong Unionist instincts in common, the cause of Welsh nationalism languished and made little or no impact upon the wider political scene. While Nicholas Edwards was Secretary of State for Wales (1979–87), the Principality was quite successful at getting more than its *pro rata* share of inward investment and Treasury support, and in 1982 a dedicated Welsh TV channel finally started broadcasting from Cardiff. Yet as far as the institutions of government were concerned, the previous Conservative Administration (1970–74) had created a two-tier structure of local government in Wales (as in

FOR OVERHEAD

Scotland) which weakened the case for yet another tier of 'sub-national' government in the form of a Welsh Assembly. Moreover, one of the dominant themes of Margaret Thatcher's three consecutive Administrations was the deliberate emasculation of local government – and indeed many other intermediate institutions – in order to pass power *down* to the people at more grassroots levels, whether in schools, hospitals or housing estates. To achieve these policy goals, successive Conservative Administrations had legislated on numerous occasions to take more centralised powers for themselves, so that they could force local authorities at all levels to toe the political line. On those occasions when even this approach did not work, Conservative Ministers were prepared to abolish certain tiers of local government altogether – for example the Greater London Council and the other Metropolitan Authorities in 1985. In such a Jacobin political climate there was obviously no realistic chance of ever persuading the powers that be in Whitehall and Westminster that devolution to Wales (or Scotland) was either desirable in principle or politically expedient.

Of course, Plaid Cymru and other nationalists did not simply fold their tents and slink away during the long period of Tory rule under first Margaret Thatcher and then John Major. They continued to campaign as well as they could for their traditional objectives and, indeed, the experience of Thatcherism in particular may well have put some iron into their souls and enhanced their resolve to attain their goals one day when the political climate became more favourable. In Wales it took a long time for this to happen and it was not really until the late 1980s that the Labour Party began to show a serious interest in devolution once again. The turning point in Opposition Labour attitudes towards devolution was probably in 1992 when John Smith became Leader of the party in succession to Neil Kinnock who, it will be remembered, had been one of the leading Welsh opponents of devolution in the 1970s and consequently was never really credible as a proponent of the policy in later years when he and his advisers judged this to be an expedient line for Labour to take.

Once again it was Scottish nationalism which set the pace and Welsh nationalism seemed to follow in its slipstream. The result was that first John Smith and then Tony Blair committed the Labour Party to introduce distinct schemes of devolution for Scotland and Wales, schemes which in each case were more adventurous than the equivalent proposals which had been unsuccessful in the 1970s. Specifically and most importantly for Wales, Tony Blair made it clear in a speech in June 1996 that on the next occasion referenda to establish whether or not the people of Scotland and Wales approved Labour's new devolution policy would be held *before* rather than after the necessary legislation to provide for it. This turned out to be a shrewd way of ensuring against any repeat of the backbench rebellion against the legislation which had done such harm both to the Labour Party and to the cause of devolution in the late 1970s.

Devolution: not an event but a process

The *1998 Government of Wales Act* provided for a form of devolution for Wales which was significantly different from the Scottish model as set out in the *1998 Scotland Act*. As introduced in the primary legislation, devolution for Wales was something of a constitutional hybrid giving to the Welsh Assembly some second-order legislative powers but making the definition and scope of those powers at any given time subject to decisions taken by United Kingdom Ministers and the United Kingdom Parliament. Pessimists might well argue that the Welsh model of devolution has enabled Whitehall and Westminster to give the *appearance* of devolving effective power to the elected Welsh Assembly and its Executive, but ensured that it will still be possible for London to exercise remote control over decisions supposedly made by the people's elected representatives in Cardiff. Optimists tend to agree with Ron Davies's well-known observation that devolution for Wales will prove to be 'not an event, but a process'.[13] See *Box 4* for key points in the Government of Wales Act 1998.

Box 4 Key points in the Government of Wales Act 1998

- A hybrid model of devolution providing executive devolution for Wales with limited powers of secondary legislation available to the Welsh Assembly
- Establishment of a Welsh Assembly of 60 members – 40 of whom elected by first-past-the-post in single-member constituencies and 20 elected from each of five regional constituencies by the additional member variant of proportional representation on pre-determined party lists
- Assembly elected for a fixed four-year term with no possibility of earlier dissolution
- The Assembly to elect a First Minister who would be able to choose his own 'Cabinet' from the party or parties forming and supporting the devolved Administration
- The Welsh Office and the Secretary of State for Wales retained, mainly on the ground that the power of primary legislation for Wales remained at Westminster
- No tax-varying powers for the Welsh Assembly
- The possibility of transferring additional executive powers to the Assembly by Order in Council in the Westminster Parliament, subject to the affirmative resolution procedure
- The possibility of developing a meaningful distinction between policy and administration for Wales, with the former contained in primary legislation passed at Westminster and the latter contained in Statutory Instruments passed by the Welsh Assembly
- Powers for the Assembly to transfer to itself the responsibility for Welsh Health Authorities and other Quangos and to establish an advisory Partnership Council with Welsh local authorities

The essence of the matter is that the primary legislation provided for a Welsh Assembly of 60 members, 40 of whom were to be elected by first-past-the-post in single-member constituencies, while the other 20 were to be elected (four from each of the five Euro-constituencies in Wales) by the additional member variant of proportional representation, by which the political parties determine the order of batting on the party lists, and the voters, by casting their second votes, determine how many (if any) of the list seats are won by each party. The Assembly was to be elected for a fixed four-year term with no possibility of earlier dissolution in certain circumstances, as is theoretically possible in Scotland. Under the Government of Wales Act no provision was made for the future reduction of Welsh representation at Westminster (as is the case under Section 86 of the Scotland Act), presumably because all powers of primary legislation for Wales were to remain in Westminster's hands. A further reflection of this unwillingness to let go of Welsh affairs is that the office of Secretary of State for Wales was not abolished (any more than its Scottish equivalent) and in spite of the retention of primary legislative powers at Westminster it was hard to see that there would be a meaningful role for a Cabinet Minister deprived of most executive functions and much of the budget by the Welsh Assembly.

The Assembly was, however, given powers to pass secondary legislation in areas of government activity affecting Wales identified by the Secretary of State, but in principle no powers of primary legislation which could turn it into a respectable national Parliament. Under Sections 27 and 28 of the Act the Assembly was given powers to transfer to itself responsibility for Health Authorities and other Welsh quangos. It was also given statutory duties to sustain and promote local government in Wales and to establish an advisory Partnership Council comprising members of the Assembly and members of Welsh local authorities. Unlike Scotland, it was not given tax-varying powers, although by manipulating the level and the distribution of block grants for Welsh local authorities it could exercise some significant fiscal power on the spending side of the public accounts which could have significant implications for the incidence of taxation throughout the United Kingdom.

As regards the executive functions of the Assembly, Section 56 of the Act required the Assembly to elect a First Secretary (an embryonic Prime Minister) and to establish an Executive Committee somewhat on the model of the Leader's Committee in British local authorities. However, the dynamics of Welsh nationalism were never likely to tolerate such arrangements for very long and, sure enough, the original Bill was amended in committee at Westminster to allow the First Secretary to appoint his own 'Ministerial' colleagues for the various responsibilities transferred to the Assembly.

This important amendment was moved by Ron Davies, then Secretary of State for Wales and the man in line to become the original First Secretary when the Assembly was established. Sadly for him, he never fulfilled this particular ambition, because he found it necessary to resign his Cabinet post in London and thus abandon his hopes for leadership in Wales following a series of inadequately explained 'events' on Clapham Common in 1998. This created a political vacuum at the top of the planned Assembly into which Tony Blair insisted upon parachuting the hapless Alun Michael, a perfectly likeable but politically unsuitable candidate for the post of First Secretary who was then a junior Minister at the Home Office. After some arm-twisting within the Labour group, which was the largest single party in the new Assembly, Alun Michael was elected as First Secretary. This was not a politically advisable or sustainable move by Labour Party managers and from the outset it effectively blighted the new First Secretary's authority in Wales, not least because he had to lead what amounted to a 'minority Administration' and he could all too easily be dismissed as 'Mr Blair's poodle'. In due course he and his Executive lost a vote of confidence in the Assembly and had to resign. Shortly afterwards new leadership elections were held and he was replaced as First Secretary by Rhodri Morgan, who has proved to be a more authentic and popular figure in Wales and who leads a coalition Executive with the Liberal Democrats which contains a majority of women Ministers.

There were always some essential flaws inherent in the hybrid model of devolution that has been imposed upon the people of Wales by a Labour Government, some of whose members have had severe reservations about both the need and the desirability of implementing the policy. In a country where, even at the second time of asking in the referendum on 18th September 1997, the majority in favour of devolution was less than 1 per cent in a turn-out of just over 50 per cent, one of the biggest flaws has been that the policy could be vitiated if Labour Ministers persisted in trying to have their cake and eat it by simultaneously devolving and retaining Westminster powers via a model of devolution which, in the words of Vernon Bogdanor, 'involves dividing powers which have hitherto been united and creating a new layer of government to administer a portion of them'.[14]

Distinctive characteristics of Welsh devolution

In many ways devolution for Wales is a more subtle and problematic phenomenon than devolution for Scotland (although not devolution and power sharing for Northern Ireland) and this makes its distinctive characteristics particularly interesting for students of British constitutional arrangements. The main reasons for this seem to be that the policy of devolution for Wales did not spring either from persuasive intellectual conviction or from compelling political expediency, which were the two prime movers within the Labour Party on each occasion that its leaders put forward devolution proposals for Scotland. In so far as political paternity for Welsh devolution can be clearly established, it has to be attributed to periodic, passionate surges from Plaid Cymru aided and abetted by a section of the Welsh Labour Party which was prepared to act as midwife for the institutional response to nationalist aspirations in Wales. It is perhaps for these reasons, among others, that the model of devolution enshrined in the *1998 Government of Wales Act* may produce the worst of both worlds (represented by complete integration or full-hearted legislative devolution) rather than the best of both worlds which is an epithet that one could charitably attach to the model of devolution enshrined in the *1998 Scotland Act*.

To summarise, we can say that devolution for Wales has the following distinctive characteristics. *Firstly*, it is executive devolution only in the sense that it allocates to the Welsh Assembly no primary legislative powers which it can exercise off its own bat – other than in two exceptional cases (of which more below). *Secondly*, it provides no scope for the Assembly freely to expand the range of powers which have been allocated to it, since Parliament at Westminster was careful to keep both lock and key on that possibility. Essentially, under Section 22 of the governing statute the existing powers of a given British Minister can be transferred to the Assembly by Order in Council, subject to the Affirmative Resolution procedure at Westminster; alternatively or in addition, any piece of new primary legislation passed at Westminster which affects Wales may include within it provisions for the transfer of further powers to the Assembly on a case by case and Bill by Bill basis. *Thirdly*, it provides the Welsh Assembly with no tax-varying powers, although there will be some scope perhaps for the Assembly to influence the distribution of public expenditure in Wales by withholding, altering or granting to Welsh local authorities various proportions of the block grant from central Government or the proceeds of certain locally raised taxes, e.g. the council tax.

Fourthly, it seeks to draw a clearer distinction between policy and administration (manifested legally in the distinctions between primary and secondary legislation) than was customary for most of the twentieth century. This seems likely over time to drive the UK Parliament either towards producing more 'framework legislation' for Wales on the Continental model which will leave space for the Welsh Assembly to interpret and vary the implementation in Wales via its control of Statutory Instruments, or to break the habit of centuries by legislating only for England, rather than for England and Wales together as has been customary

for so long. In other words, what was really involved in the *1998 Government of Wales Act* was less a *transfer* or alienation of executive powers (and some limited legislative powers) from United Kingdom institutions to Welsh institutions and more a *partition* of powers between two levels of government.

Fifthly, the original Act provided for a relatively small Assembly of only 60 members with a lower ratio of proportional list members to ordinary constituency members than is the case in the Scottish Parliament.[15] Over time this may have two undesirable effects: it may make the new cooperative or coalition politics which characterise the representative institutions created by devolution marginally more difficult to conduct in Wales than in Scotland, and it will almost certainly make it more difficult to find enough members with enough time to participate in all the various committees which are postulated for the work of the Assembly.

The complete dependence of the Welsh Assembly and people upon Government in Whitehall and Parliament at Westminster for any future move from executive to legislative devolution for Wales is perhaps the most defining characteristic of all. This reality can best be explained by the following political factors. The predominantly Labour MPs who sit for Welsh seats in the Westminster Parliament have long been divided upon the issue of devolution and so the most cautious of the two groups essentially held the whip hand when the policy was drawn up and put through Parliament. Furthermore, the Labour MPs who sit for Scottish seats have been keen to defend their comparative advantage over their Welsh colleagues and would probably resist any future Welsh attempt to depart from this 'lock and key' approach to devolution for fear of destabilising the devolution settlement for Scotland and thus giving the SNP another opportunity to fan the flames of nationalism north of the border. The unusually large number of English Labour MPs elected in 1997 and 2001 have not wished to see Labour's boat rocked, as it might be if scope were given to their Welsh colleagues to increase the powers of the Welsh Assembly, especially if this were seen to be at the expense of their own constituents in the various regions of

England. Since so much of the shape and dynamics of devolution for Wales since 1997 has been driven by *Labour Party considerations*, it is idle to spend any time examining the very different motivations of the other parties. Devolution for Wales (as for Scotland) has been shaped, if not entirely driven, by what leading Labour politicians have deemed to be politically desirable or expedient at any time.

In short, it seems that Welsh devolution has been taken forward by the Labour Government on more of a local government model of governance than a 'national' one. The reasons for this are essentially economic, social and political and are rooted in the history of Anglo-Welsh relations. Put simply, the scheme of devolution implemented in Wales reflects above all the identity of interest between Wales and England and the degree of deeply rooted integration and assimilation between people on both sides of the Anglo-Welsh border. It is right and proper in a democratic society that political arrangements should broadly reflect economic and social realities, and it is in this sense that we have identified somewhat distinctive characteristics of devolution in Wales and Scotland respectively. Yet with each year that passes, it becomes more difficult to conceive of the present scheme of devolution for Wales being reversed or even changed in a direction adverse to Welsh national interests by a Government and Parliament of the United Kingdom.

General reflections

Now that the Welsh people have the opportunity of benefiting from at least a substantial degree of executive devolution, it is important to understand what are the preconditions for the system working satisfactorily in future. The first essential is likely to be that the primary Westminster legislation governing England and Wales, and the attitude of UK Ministers towards their colleagues or perhaps adversaries in the Welsh Executive, should be both looser and less prescriptive than in the past, in order to allow the Welsh Assembly and its political leadership to have a greater and more influential political role in the government of Wales.

This will not be easy to achieve because old British habits die hard and because there are few precedents for Westminster determining political issues which affect only Wales rather than England and Wales or the United Kingdom as a whole. The Welsh Disestablishment Act in 1914 did not really come into this category, because it had considerable consequences for the Anglican Church in England and elsewhere. However, the 1967 and 1993 Welsh Language Acts, as well as the bi-partisan decision in London to provide for a dedicated Welsh TV channel in 1982, probably did come into this category which is clearly so small that the exceptions have usually proved the rule. Moreover, it would be regarded as anomalous and insulting by a broad swathe of Welsh opinion if Parliament at Westminster continued to exercise its legislative supremacy over Wales in this way now that the Principality has its own elected Assembly and political Executive. Such behaviour by the political masters in London would almost certainly act as a recruiting officer for Plaid Cymru and the Welsh nationalist cause, so in its own interests any Government in London would be unwise to carry on in such a way.

The second essential for the smooth working of Welsh devolution in future is likely to be the deliberate development of some new constitutional conventions governing the evolving relationships between Cathays Park and Whitehall, Cardiff Bay and Westminster, and – for good measure – between both citadels of Welsh 'national' government and the various components of Welsh local government. These conventions may take the form of concordats or supplementary agreements – as were sketched out in the October 1999 *Memorandum of Understanding* between the UK Government and (in this case) the Cabinet of the Welsh Assembly – and this is likely to require cooperative ways of working between all the politicians and officials involved. This would be very much the 'British way' of doing things and ought to grow naturally in our political culture.

Yet at the same time we are moving, however tentatively, into a new constitutional era in the British Isles and more widely in the European Union in which divisions of governmental functions, legislative powers and 'national' jurisdictions are increasingly determined in codified constitutional arrangements and arbitrated by established processes of judicial review or by recourse to supreme constitutional courts – whether on the model of the Federal Constitutional Court in Germany or the more reticent Judicial Committee of the Privy Council in the United Kingdom. We can therefore expect a body of case law governing these institutional relationships to grow up over the years and in consequence British politics will never be quite the same as before.

In trying to forecast how things will develop in Wales, we should pay careful attention to Section 31 of the *1998 Government of Wales Act* which places a statutory obligation upon the Secretary of State for Wales to consult the Welsh Assembly in advance on the UK Government's programme (whether involving administrative decisions or legislative proposals) affecting Wales, but only 'as appears to him to be appropriate'. Like other aspects of British custom and practice, this appears to provide real opportunities for a cooperative partnership between responsible politicians and officials in London and Cardiff. On the other hand, in different political circumstances – e.g. with a Conservative Government in Whitehall and a Labour–Liberal Democrat Coalition in Cardiff – it might encourage some political figures who operated at the UK level to ignore Welsh concerns or to stymie the ambitions of politicians who have staked their future upon the Welsh Assembly.

These contrasting possibilities did not escape the notice of the Ministers and officials who were involved in drafting the Government's 1999 *Memorandum of Understanding on Devolution*. In this they sought to explain that the Joint Ministerial Committee (and the JMC Secretariat which serves it), comprising relevant Ministers from the UK Government, the Scottish Administration, the Welsh Executive and the Northern Ireland Executive, would be there to conduct business and sort out any 'international' problems between the various Governments within the United Kingdom through what it was careful to describe as 'normal administrative channels'.[16] Equally, it is obviously hoped and intended by the second Blair Administration

that habits of timely cooperation will develop between the Welsh Assembly at Cardiff Bay and the UK Parliament at Westminster. Inter-Parliamentary cooperation of this kind could prove more difficult to achieve than inter-governmental cooperation – certainly if the mutual suspicion and rivalry between the Westminster Parliament and the European Parliament is anything to go by. Yet any problems with this degree of novelty and sensitivity are not likely to be solved in a flash. Before long the interests of the Labour–Liberal Democrat Coalition led by Rhodri Morgan in Cardiff and those of the re-elected Labour Government in London may begin to diverge. This could create new political opportunities for the Welsh Assembly and play into the hands of the Plaid Cymru at future elections.

Questions for discussion

1   Was Ron Davies right to describe devolution for Wales as 'not an event but a process'?

2   How justifiable is it for Wales to have a weaker form of devolution than Scotland and is such a differentiation between two sets of devolved institutions sustainable in the long run?

3   Rehearse the arguments for full integration between Wales and England in all but cultural matters.

Notes

1   R. Coupland, *Welsh and Scottish Nationalism, a Study*; Collins, London, 1954; p. 48.
2   Quoted in *ibid*; p. 55.
3   K.O. Morgan, *Rebirth of a Nation: Wales 1880–1980*; Clarendon Press, Oxford, 1981; p. 118.
4   The only notable exceptions to this general rule were the decision of the National Government under Ramsay Macdonald in 1931 to grant more powers to the Welsh Board of Health and the decision of the BBC in 1937 to launch the Welsh Home Service.
5   K.O. Morgan, *op. cit.*; p. 207.
6   Quoted in *ibid.*; p. 257.
7   Quoted in V. Bogdanor, *Devolution in the United Kingdom*; Open University Press, Oxford, 1999; p. 152.

8   Quoted in K.O. Morgan, *op. cit.*; p. 377.

9   An example would be the assassination threat issued by the so-called Free Wales Army against Cledwyn Hughes, Secretary of State for Wales, at the *Eisteddfod* in Aberavon in 1966.

10   K.O. Morgan, *op. cit.*; p. 398.

11   *Hansard*, 26th July 1977, Vol. 936, Col. 313.

12   *Ibid*; p. 419.

13   *Hansard*, 8th December 1997, Vol. 302, Col. 677.

14   V. Bogdanor, *op. cit.*; p. 257.

15   The comparable ratios are 40:60 in Wales and 43:57 in Scotland.

16   *Memorandum of Understanding on Devolution*; Cm 4444; London, 1999; para 24.

Further reading

Vernon Bogdanor, *Devolution in the United Kingdom*; Oxford University Press, Oxford, 1999.

Reginald Coupland, *Welsh and Scottish Nationalism, a Study*; Collins, London, 1954.

Ron Davies, *Devolution, a Process not an Event*; Institute of Welsh Affairs, Cardiff, 1999.

Robert Hazell (ed.) *The State and the Nations: the First Year of Devolution in the U.K.*; Imprint Academic, London, 2000.

K.O. Morgan, *Rebirth of a Nation: Wales 1880–1980*; Clarendon Press, Oxford, 1981.

Rhodri Morgan, *Variable Geometry U.K.*; Institute of Welsh Affairs, Cardiff, 2000.

John Osmond (ed.) *A Parliament for Wales*; Gomer Press, Llandysul, 1995.

website for Labour's devolution policy: www.cabinet-office.gov.uk/constitution/2000/devolution

website for the Welsh Assembly: www.wales.gov.uk

Chapter 6

The English question

The ancient sense of England

Whenever constitutional change on the basis of identity or territory has been mooted or achieved, the elusive English question has usually been left unresolved. Indeed for centuries people of both a poetical and a practical disposition in England have had an ancient sense of England, but until recently have not recognised that there is 'an English question' in constitutional terms.

Up to and including Tudor times the largest political issues were to do with the protection of the English realm from internal rebellion and external attack. This meant that on the whole England's fate was dependent upon how its rulers and people dealt with threats from France, Spain or disaffected elements within the British Isles. Following the assimilation of Wales, which was codified in English statutes of 1536 and 1543, England and Wales effectively became a single polity. Thereafter for a period of nearly 400 years English history was played out on an ever larger stage and the idea of England gradually metamorphosed into the concepts of Britain and the British Empire. The main landmarks along the way were the Acts of Union with Scotland in 1707, the Act of Union with Ireland in 1800 and, more generally, the various phases in the expansion of the British Empire across the globe – an Empire on which the sun never set and which probably reached its zenith at the end of the Second World War in 1945.

Throughout this long period of English aggrandisement, the idea of England was increasingly masked by the concept of 'Great Britain', and once the state had become a constitutional Monarchy in 1688–89 it became customary to refer to it as the 'United Kingdom' – the ruling polity at the heart of an imperial system of government. One of the most significant aspects of these developments was that the *English* identity, more than any other, became subsumed in the larger and vaguer identities of Britain and the British Empire, and indeed only very recently has it begun to re-emerge from the misty nostalgia of British history. This was partly because Britain and everything British were divested of much of their accumulated content and meaning for the English by the loss of the Empire

abroad and the erosion of *imperium* within the British Isles when the greater part of Ireland seized its independence in 1918–22 and, much more recently, when Scotland and Wales became semi-detached from England through the process of devolution.

One result of all this is that we can now see more clearly than we did that the word 'British' has always been more of an adjective than a collective noun – unlike, for example, the word 'American' when it is used in the well-known Presidential phrase, 'my fellow Americans'. The English are rediscovering the simple but important truth that their most evocative and meaningful identity (both subjectively and objectively) is as English men and women. Yet if we are to get to grips with the elusive idea of England, we need to explore the following prior issues: what does it mean to be English and what constitutional arrangements do the English now require to fulfil their destiny in the twenty-first century?

In a recent book on the subject Jeremy Paxman pointed out that 'the English have not spent a great deal of time defining themselves because they have not needed to'.[1] This may be one of the reasons why it is difficult to pin down what it means to be English. One way to be English is to have English parentage – to have at least one parent who is recognisably English. Thus in my own case, although I was born in India, both my parents were English and all four of my grandparents were English. For the purposes of legal nationality this meant that I was British, just as someone of Indian ethnicity at least one of whose parents had unqualified British nationality would be legally British – but not, of course, English *and* British in the way that I am.

Another definition of being English is to be born in England, although once again most members of the non-English ethnic minorities who are born in England are likely to regard themselves, and to be regarded by others, as British rather than English in much the same way that the Scottish, the Welsh and the Northern Irish tend to regard themselves as British rather than English, even if they were born in England. Thus under British nationality law the fact that you were born in

England confers British legal nationality upon you, but not necessarily English identity. The same paradox applies to those who have English as their mother tongue and grow up in a home in which English is the first language and go to school where the language of instruction is English. These circumstantial characteristics usually (but not invariably) go with having at least one English-speaking parent, yet this still does not make everyone in this category feel English or be seen as English by other people. Equally, residence in England (for however long) is not a sufficient definition of being English, although once again it may bring in its wake the legal entitlement to British nationality. For example, a talented artist or scientist from overseas, or indeed from another part of the United Kingdom, may take up residence in England, but that fact alone will not necessarily turn such a person into an English man or woman, either in his or her own eyes or in the eyes of other British people.

What we can see here in these various facets of the problem is that there are important distinctions between English identity and British nationality, and, moreover, that there is no such thing as English nationality in the legal sense of being a subject or a citizen of England. While it is equally true that there is no *legal* nationality that people can claim in Northern Ireland, Scotland or Wales which is confined to each of those parts of the United Kingdom, the position of the Irish, Scottish and Welsh people, who live within those parts of the United Kingdom as British subjects and citizens, is that all of them can legitimately describe them-selves as having identities and nationalities which are Irish, Scottish and Welsh respectively. The subtle difference between the predicament of the English and that of others in the United Kingdom is probably best explained by the fact that whereas there is now no English state, in the wake of devolution we can discern the embryonic outlines of a Scottish state and even a Welsh state to match the sense of nationhood in Scotland and Wales respectively, while in the special case of Ireland there is another state (the Irish Republic) which stands ready to grant its legal nationality to the people of Northern Ireland if a majority of the

people in the six counties ever vote in a referendum to accept it.

If we look further and deeper into what it means to be English, however, we soon discover that the idea of England is also a state of mind and that *feeling English* is at least as important to the English as being English, whether in genetic, territorial or legal terms. This then becomes relevant to our exploration of the elusive English question, because it affects the ways in which the English respond to their social and constitutional arrangements. For example, one of the simplest, and perhaps crudest, tests of feeling English was Norman Tebbit's so-called 'cricket test', which was intended to ascertain someone's real identity (and hence degree of commitment to this country) by asking whether he supported England or some other national side in international cricket matches. Thus those who live and work in England, but who support the cricket team of the West Indies or Pakistan, cannot – in Lord Tebbit's eyes – be said to be real English men and women. Equally provocative and fatuous criteria for testing English identity might include worship in the Church of England, subscription to *This England* magazine, or membership of the St George's Society. Disagreeable and politically incorrect as it may be to consider these aspects of the subject, they can all be said to have a bearing on the subjective question of how deeply people *feel* themselves to be English and therefore to determine their identity at least as much as other more objective factors.

It is also worth mentioning the mental and cultural manifestations of English identity, since, as Jeremy Paxman perceptively observed in his book, 'it is not the country in which the English actually live, but the place they *imagine* they are living in' which has long been one of the most important influences upon English identity.[2] This draws attention to the fact that there are certain powerful images, beliefs and ideals shared by most English people, which – for better or worse – have helped to make us what we are today. For example, the archetypal (and largely phoney) image of an essentially rural England was vividly conveyed by Stanley Baldwin in a famous and much-quoted passage of his speech to the Royal Society of

St George on 6th May 1924 when he spoke warmly and evocatively of the sights, sounds and smells of the English countryside: 'the tinkle of the hammer on the anvil in the country smithy, the corncrake on a dewy morning, the sound of the scythe against a whetstone, and the sight of a plough team coming over the brow of a hill'.[3] Equally, the guiding English beliefs, which in many cases have come down to us from the Glorious Revolution in 1688–89, are usually exemplified in our commit-ment to the liberties of the subject, the rights of property, and the maintenance of the Protestant religion – the last precariously embodied nowadays in the attenuated form of the Church of England. As for the English ideals which still attract the allegiance of many English people, we could mention the English commitment to fair play, to common civility and to decent reticence in social relations, and – in the political sphere – to the traditional model of Parliamentary government under a constitutional Monarchy.

If we attempt to draw out some of the most powerful unifying themes from the rich and diverse body of English literature, it is not too difficult to highlight the literary myths and ideas which have done so much to influence the English view of their country and of themselves. One obvious theme derives from the essential geography and typical climate of the British Isles in that the English see themselves as an island people mercifully cut off from foreign entanglements and protected by the English Channel and the Atlantic weather from foreign invasion on at least three critical occasions in their history. Related to this is their accurate perception of England as a 'green and pleasant land' thanks to its relatively high level of rainfall and temperate climate in all four seasons of the year. This characteristic of our native land was always particularly alluring for the thousands of English men and women who went overseas to populate and govern the British Empire, but longed to return to the trees, streams and green fields of England whether on leave or to retire. Another connected theme has been represented in the essentially bucolic image of the English countryside which was evoked musically in some of Handel's ora-torio's, in the literary canon by Thomas Hardy's

Wessex novels and in landscape painting by the works of John Constable.

For several centuries from the Hundred Years War against the French, through the English Reformation imposed upon the country by Henry VIII, right down to the First World War when so many died fighting for God, King and Country, another important theme has been muscular Christianity based upon the idea that England (and later Britain) is blessed by God and that, for some indeed, God is in all likelihood an Englishman. Such magnificent and powerful delusions (which have had counterparts in other nations and faiths during the course of world history) have been institutionally reinforced in the English case by the established Church of England, but have also been powerfully evoked by other sects and denominations such as the Puritans in Cromwell's New Model Army or the religious revivalists in John Wesley's Methodists or General Booth's Salvation Army.

In social relations – later rendered almost pathological by our English obsession with class distinctions – the English have been burdened for many centuries with the essentially feudal legacy of a vision of the well-ordered society in which everyone has his station and everyone knows his place. This archaic notion has been challenged and probably defeated by the spread of democracy and democratic assumptions in the nineteenth and twentieth centuries, but it undoubtedly still exists in the sub-conscious English mind at some rather deep (and shameful?) level and it is still reinforced from time to time, for example, by residual feelings of deference towards the Monarchy.

The notion of England, and London in particular, as 'the hub of Empire' runs deep in the conscious-ness of many English and British people – including the growing minority of 'new British' who have come from Empire and Commonwealth countries to settle in these islands since the 1950s. For centuries these connections have provided a common frame of reference and a body of shared experience for people of all classes, colours and creeds in these islands, but especially in England where our society has become most multi-cultural. One need only evoke a few lines from Rupert

Brooke's poem 'The soldier' written in 1914 to be reminded of the literary and spiritual basis of this imperial theme which has tended to link far-flung parts of the globe with the mother country: 'if I should die, think only this of me; that there's some corner of a foreign field that is forever England'.

Finally, in this catalogue of unifying themes which seem to have emerged from English literature and from English national mythology, there is the ideal of quiet, almost casual, English heroism of great men in our past; for example, Sir Francis Drake completing his game of bowls on Plymouth Hoe before leaving port to lead the Royal Navy in battle against the Spanish Armada, or Captain Oates sacrificing his life for his comrades on Scott's last expedition to the South Pole and saying quietly as he walked out of the tent into the Antarctic blizzard: 'I am just going outside and I may be a little while'.

In politics a long line of great English figures from the past have been able to embody or articulate what it means to be English and to be devoted to the English cause. If we are super-selective, we can confine our choice to a very few. There was *Queen Elizabeth I* who, in a rousing speech to her troops arrayed at Tilbury at the time of the Spanish Armada in 1588, declared: 'I know I have the body of a weak and feeble woman, but I have the heart and stomach of a king, and of a king of England too.' There was *Oliver Cromwell* in the seventeenth century, whose pithy opinions included the comment that 'a few honest men are better than numbers'. In the eighteenth century there was *John Wilkes* who for a time became the personification of English liberties and whose English qualities could be appreciated 'as an argument for change and as an affirmation of existing [English] identity'.[4] In the early nineteenth century there was also *Admiral Horatio Nelson* who famously sent a message to the British fleet at the battle of Trafalgar in 1805 that 'England expects every man will do his duty' and whose death in battle established a model of English heroism which was celebrated in a magnificent state funeral and commemorated for years to come by the erection of Nelson's column in Trafalgar Square.

Later in the nineteenth century there was *Sir Robert Peel* who was instrumental in creating the Conservative Party, founding the Metropolitan Police and championing free trade by abolishing the Corn Laws; *John Bright* who declared England to be 'the mother of Parliaments' and who believed in what are sometimes described as the 'little Englander' goals of 'peace, retrenchment and reform'; and *Queen Victoria*, perhaps best known to the British people for having given her name to an age, a culture and a set of well-documented social attitudes, but who was also capable of some memorably dry observations, such as her admonition to A.J. Balfour at one of the lowest points of the Boer War that 'we are not interested in the possibilities of defeat'.

In the twentieth century political references to England and Englishness were less common, because many people in these islands identified more with Britain and Britishness. For example, *Sir Winston Churchill*, who in his great war-time broadcasts personified this country's indomitable will to resist the might of Hitler's Germany, famously declared during a speech at the Mansion House in November 1942 that he had 'not become the King's First Minister in order to preside over the liquidation of the British Empire'; *Clement Attlee*, a notoriously laconic Englishman, who was nevertheless one of the three or four greatest British Prime Ministers of the twentieth century; and *Margaret Thatcher* whose iron will in the 1980s helped to transform attitudes in the British economy, but who may well be best remembered for her saying (invariably taken out of context) that 'there is no such thing as society'.

Such a list excludes great figures such as Wellington (an Irishman), Gladstone (a Scot), Disraeli (a Jew of Italian extraction), Lloyd George (a Welshman) and even Tony Blair (a Scot with a public school accent). Just as England has tended to dominate the United Kingdom throughout the entire period of its constitutional existence, so a considerable number of formidable Scottish, Welsh and Irish people have succeeded over the centuries in rising to the very top of British society and politics. Indeed, this willingness to serve a common British cause may be one of the reasons why the United Kingdom has held together for so long as a multi-national state in spite of the high levels of pluralism and diversity which have characterised British politics and society.

Whereas our ideas of what is 'British' have changed a good deal over the years, particularly since the decline of the British Empire in the decades after the Second World War and during our slow and somewhat reluctant moves towards closer integration with our partners in the European Union, typical ideas of England have changed little and still seem based upon a determined but largely unproductive nostalgia for certain glorious periods in the past – notably our 'finest hour' in the Second World War when Britain stood alone and defiant against Hitler's Germany and the virtues and solidarities of *English* society seemed to be vindicated.

The elusive idea of England and the rather clearer notions of Englishness can easily become an endless source of enquiry and entertainment. It is an area of psychological exploration which is never likely to be completely mapped and there may always be difficulties in disentangling what is English from what is British. If we accept that the two adjectives *can* be synonymous, it is worth heeding the advice of Ann Dummett who wrote that 'Britishness is partly a matter of culture, values and national character; but perhaps the most obvious feature of Britishness is to be suspicious of any attempt to lay down what our culture, values and character are or should be'.[5] On the other hand, Roger Scruton surely had a point when he observed that 'England furnished us with an ideal, and the English people acquired some of the gentleness, amiability and civilised manners which that ideal prescribed'.[6]

A need for new governmental structures

Turning to the instrumental question of what new governmental structures, if any, the English now need if they are to respond satisfactorily to the dynamics of devolution, it is possible to make some brief and schematic comments which can provide a framework for the rest of this chapter. The traditional answer to the question has tended to be 'none', because the English feel confident and secure in the knowledge that they constitute 85 per cent of the population and an even higher proportion of the political and economic power in the United Kingdom. However, such a macro-analysis may be rather complacent in the post-devolution framework for two significant reasons: *firstly*, the Scots, Welsh and Northern Irish now have in various institutional forms a much more formidable array of powers and instruments with which to attract inward investment, create jobs and generally raise the profile of their particular parts of the United Kingdom – e.g. devolved assemblies, development agencies and highly focused international networks which draw upon their respective diasporas; *secondly*, there are wide disparities of wealth and poverty, power and weakness between the various regions of England and notably between so-called 'hot spots' and 'black spots' *within* particular regions, all of which means that the understandable confidence of the affluent parts of London and the south-east is not necessarily shared under present conditions by those who live and work in the most disadvantaged localities elsewhere in the United Kingdom.

The Institute for Fiscal Studies has compared GDP per capita and per capita tax receipts in each of the eight English regions alongside Scotland and Wales. This research has revealed that Wales is the poorest 'region' on both these indicators, but that Scotland comes third to London and the south-east (in first place) and East Anglia (in second place) in GDP per capita and fifth in per capita tax receipts.[7] If one then measures the regional disparities in public expenditure per head as revealed in a recent Comprehensive Spending Review, one discovers that such expenditure is 15 per cent above the UK average in Wales, 18 per cent above in Scotland and 34 per cent above in Northern Ireland.[8] It may be that English public and political opinion is relaxed about these disparities and that the English people (regardless of their personal circumstances) are in such an altruistic frame of mind that they will not stir themselves in response to any regional or local campaigns in England to redress these imbalances. Yet as such issues are subjected to greater transparency (e.g. as a consequence of the Freedom of Information Act 2000) and as regional movements, such as the Campaign for a Northern Assembly, gather momentum, traditional attitudes will probably change and the various regions of England – together with established interests in local government – will almost certainly exert effective pressure upon central Government to alter the present imbalance of political and institutional power in the United Kingdom to bring it more into line with the economic and social realities.

It seems there are four main options for altering the present pattern of governance in England beneath the quasi-federal UK level. *Firstly*, there is always the option of continuing with the present pattern which can best be described as asymmetric devolution. *Secondly*, there is the option of moving cautiously towards institutional recognition of a re-emergent 'English state' either by creating a separate English Parliament (perhaps in Birmingham or York, to differentiate it by location from the UK Parliament at Westminster) or by modifying the membership and procedures of Parliament at Westminster to achieve what was William Hague's stated goal of 'English votes on English laws'. This option would carry high political risk, since it might have the effect of promoting or ratifying a real English state which could spell the end of the United Kingdom. See *Box 5* for a summary of possible alternative governmental structures for England.

Thirdly, there is the option of deliberately deconstructing England into eight Regions (or more accurately nine, if London is regarded as a separate region) – alongside the three other regions or nations of Scotland, Wales and Northern Ireland – within the constitutional framework of a quasi-federal United Kingdom. We can already see from the regional initiatives taken during Labour's first term of office that there are weak and strong versions of this regional option for England. The weak version would be to build upon the eight new Regional Development Agencies created in April 1999 which are supposed to be in some way accountable to a matching number of Regional Chambers composed of nominated members from elected local authorities (no more than 70 per cent of the total) and from institutions representing the other stakeholders in the regions, such as

Box 5 Possible alternative governmental structures for England

- Continuing with the present approach of asymmetric devolution both within the United Kingdom as a whole and within England whereby different regions choose to follow various routes towards new forms of sub-national governance

- Moving towards the creation of an English state with either a separate English Government and Parliament or modified procedures at Westminster to allow only 'English votes on English laws'

- Deliberately deconstructing England into eight or nine Regions broadly to match the 'nations' of Scotland, Wales and Northern Ireland within a constitutional framework of a quasi-federal United Kingdom. This would probably imply directly elected regional government and elected territorial representation for each Region in a reformed Second Chamber at Westminster alongside elected representatives from Scotland, Wales and Northern Ireland

- Deliberately splitting England into 30 to 40 City Regions of sub-national government which would have the effect of merging each of the conurbations with its rural hinterland within a constitutional framework of a quasi-federal United Kingdom. This would also imply directly elected regional government and elected territorial representation for each City Region in a reformed Second Chamber at Westminster alongside elected representatives from Scotland, Wales and Northern Ireland businesses, trade unions, educational institutions and voluntary bodies.[9]

The strong version of English regionalism would be to legislate for the creation of eight or nine directly elected Regional Assemblies with devolved powers over designated areas of public administration in each region. This structure would respond to the wishes of those who signed the so-called Declaration of the North in 1997 and who have been playing an active part in the Campaign for the English Regions. However, the Labour Government has made it clear that before this strong version of the regional option could materialise, a number of prior conditions would have to be satisfied: there would have to be a unitary structure of local government in the regions concerned (with the creation of regional government contingent upon another round of local government reorganisation in those areas where the Counties are still strong); Parliament would have to give its approval for the creation of such Regions in primary legislation; the National Audit Office would have to confirm that the institutional upheaval involved no additional public expenditure overall (a demanding Treasury condition which might eventually be waived); and the people of each Region wishing to travel this road would have to give their majority approval in specific regional referenda. These are rigorous preconditions which, in the absence of effective and sustained campaigns in all the regions in favour of such a constitutional change, are likely to pose significant obstacles to the realisation of this option. Furthermore, this idea – which has often been called 'rolling devolution' – might well create a rather messy institutional outcome, since people in the various regions of England have differing degrees of interest in or enthusiasm for real regional government and some may continue to oppose it – e.g. in Cornwall where people do not readily identify with the rest of the south-west region, or in Kent and Norfolk where the County Councils are self-confident and relatively powerful compared to the rest.

Fourthly comes what is probably the most radical option of splitting England into perhaps 30 to 40 City Regions, somewhat reminiscent of the pattern established in Germany in the Holy Roman Empire or in Italy at the time of the Renaissance. At first blush this idea might appear to be romantic nonsense, but on closer inspection of the realities of the modern world it may not seem outlandish. The reasons for this view are complex. They are based upon the established political facts that England's urban areas account for 90 per cent of its population, 91 per cent of its economic output and 89 per cent of its jobs.[10] A second argument would be that in London (and later perhaps in Birmingham, Liverpool, Manchester, Leeds, Sheffield and Newcastle) the model of a large conurbation run by a directly elected Mayor who is accountable to a directly elected Assembly has got off to a reasonably credible start following the elections in May 2000, although there are cities like Nottingham, Bradford and Wolverhampton which are apparently not so keen on the idea. A third argument would be that such forms of governance have already achieved considerable success and little apparent grief in city states around the developed world from Hong Kong to Hamburg and from Singapore to Washington, DC and so could perhaps be tried in England.

The record in other countries shows manifest advantages in the new global economy in being an effective niche player, and the most go-ahead city states are well qualified to reap the global advantages of this approach. Indeed a vision of a Europe of city states (reminiscent perhaps of the Holy Roman Empire) is competing for popular support with a Europe of the regions. Greater London can now be regarded almost as a distinct economic and social entity, responsible as it is for about one-fifth of our GNP. Add to these factors the emerging political reality that some leading Labour politicians (e.g. Peter Kilfoyle in Liverpool) have resigned from Ministerial office 'in order to spend more time with their cities' and you can begin to make a fairly persuasive case showing how this particular form of sub-national government *could* work in England. The main problems on the other side of the argument are that this form of governance, if it became generalised beyond what is arguably the special case of London, would be seen as particularly threatening by the Shire Counties and by the political coalitions in favour of orthodox regional government, and that there seems to be no settled agreement in Whitehall and Westminster (especially between Tony Blair and John Prescott) upon the relative merits of the mayoral as opposed to the regional model of local government in England. Until the Government publishes its promised White Paper on regional government in England and legislation is subsequently put before Parliament, it will remain unclear how the various levels of sub-national government in England are to be reformed in the light of devolution elsewhere in the United Kingdom.

English votes on English laws

One idea for the future governance of England which, in the opinion of the constitutional expert Robert Hazell, 'can be quickly dismissed' is to legislate at Westminster for the creation of an English Parliament.[11] Alternatively, there is a variant of this option which aims to achieve 'English votes on English laws' by reforming the structures and procedures at Westminster to turn a part of the United Kingdom Parliament into an English Parliament.[12]

On the face of things, there is a neat symmetry of political causation in the connections between nationalism, devolution and a new English Parliament. Just as the policy of devolution can be considered as the Labour response to nationalist threats to its political position in Scotland and Wales (leaving to one side for the moment the special circumstances surrounding devolution in Northern Ireland), so the ideas of recreating an English Parliament – remembering that there was one before 1536 – or introducing Parliamentary reforms which have only English MPs voting on English laws have been Conservative responses to the perceived unfairness to England of asymmetrical devolution in the United Kingdom.

The idea of recreating an English Parliament as a counterpart to devolution for Scotland and Wales (and Northern Ireland) was first raised in modern times, only to be summarily dismissed, by the Callaghan Administration in the mid-1970s. This was done in a consultative document entitled *The English Dimension* which was published in December 1976 at a time when devolution was a live political issue at Westminster.[13]

The authors of the document in the office of the Lord President of the Council (then Michael Foot with John Smith as his deputy) wasted little time or space in rehearsing arguments *for* an English assembly, but devoted a considerable number of paragraphs to arguing against it. They warned that it would destabilise power relationships within the United Kingdom by making England too strong and independent *vis-à-vis* the other components of the country; it would challenge the traditional legal doctrine of the supremacy of Parliament; it would create a powerful rival for the United Kingdom Government and Parliament (especially if the new representative body for England had its own English executive answerable to it) and leave the UK institutions with too little to do; it would mean that the people of England were over-governed with too many layers of government; it would be economically and socially divisive in a country in which people have broadly common expectations of government based upon a well-developed sense of common rights and entitlements; it would make it less likely that the English would be willing to continue subsidising the other 'nations' in the poorer parts of the United Kingdom; it would entail a move towards a *de facto* federal system of government in the United Kingdom; and it might well unleash the undesirable forces of atavistic English nationalism.

Against the background of these indictments, it was perhaps not altogether surprising that this section of the document concluded with the firm statement that 'the establishment of an English Assembly would carry grave risks for the continuing political and economic unity of the United Kingdom, the preservation of which the Government has regarded as a firm principle which should govern any proposals for devolution'.[14]

About 20 years later, once it became clear from the results of the Scottish and Welsh referenda in 1997 that devolution was virtually certain to go ahead in those two parts of the United Kingdom, English voices began to be raised in support of the idea of similar devolution for England by establishing an English Parliament with executive and legislative powers. At Westminster senior Conservatives in both Houses, such as Lord Baker (a former Education Secretary and Party Chairman) and David Davis (a former Foreign Office Minister and at the time of writing Chairman of the Conservative Party in Opposition), have put forward proposals for the establishment of an English Parliament.

In the country at large an *English Parliament Movement* was established which sought to lobby hard at relevant public meetings, and campaigned prominently under the emblem of the red and white cross of St George. The movement's main objectives are stated in the following terms: 'to establish an honest and democratic Parliament for England . . . excluding the 130 M.P.s that do not represent the people of England', 'to stop the planned fragmentation of England into regions', and 'to create a more structured balance within the Union, giving all countries a fair and democratic political solution'. Many sophisticated people were inclined to dismiss such a campaign and tended to conflate it with the distasteful English nationalism associated with football hooligans and thugs from the Essex marshes. Yet its real appeal lay in a sentimental evocation of English history and it attracted its largest support from middle-class people in the Home Counties who resented the ways in which the British Government seemed to have caved in to the demands of nationalists in Scotland, Wales and Northern Ireland whom they considered to be over-indulged in any case.

The Conservative Party, traditionally Unionist under both Margaret Thatcher and John Major, needed to find a suitable response to Labour's policy on devolution. As William Hague plaintively enquired, 'what happens to the defenders of the [Unionist] status quo when the status quo itself disappears?'[15] He found his response a year later when, in a speech to the Centre for Policy Studies, he asserted his party's 'commitment to making the Scottish Parliament a success for Scotland and a success for the whole United Kingdom' – with a similar assurance about the Welsh Assembly – and went on to argue that 'we have to become

advocates of constitutional change ourselves'.[16] He argued that England was the real loser from 'Labour's chaotic approach to the constitution' and highlighted what he regarded as the two principal unfairnesses of the policy of devolution in practice: that the English are under-represented in Parliament (compared to the Scots and the Welsh) and that English MPs do not have an exclusive say over legislation which affects only England. He was prepared to make a similar point in support of the Welsh over primary legislation affecting England and Wales. For good measure he added that a future Conservative Government would abolish the English Regional Development Agencies and redistribute their functions to other layers of local government.

To those who favoured the creation of an English Parliament, such as Lord Baker, he politely said: 'although I understand the force of the argument . . . I am as yet unpersuaded'. This position then led him to advocate the problematic and controversial idea of 'English votes on English laws'. Under this proposal there would be no English Executive, no separate English Parliament and not even any 'English days' in the Westminster Parliamentary calendar as, in effect, there have been whenever debates are held on English local government. Instead he sketched out a new set of Parliamentary procedures whereby the Speaker would certify certain Bills which affected only England as eligible for exclusively English scrutiny by English MPs at all stages of the legislative process in the House of Commons and the same approach would be applied to exclusively English Statutory Instruments. Since a great deal of primary legislation at Westminster affects England and Wales together (but not Scotland or Northern Ireland), the new procedure would include Welsh MPs for Bills relating to England and Wales.

A Labour Government with a working majority in the Commons on a UK basis may have this majority thanks to the number of non-English Labour MPs. Under Mr Hague's plan only English (and Welsh) MPs would have the right to approve, amend or reject Bills affecting only England (or England and Wales). Such power would belong to the majority party in England (and Wales).

However, when Mr Hague put forward his proposal, the Blair Administration commanded a majority of English MPs, as well as a larger majority of UK MPs, so at that time it would have made no practical difference to the government of England. Yet Mr Hague's policy implied that a majority of the English MPs elected to the Westminster Parliament should be able to insist that their wishes were met by Ministers in the UK Government and, as a corollary, that no UK Government which relied upon Scottish and Welsh MPs for its working majority in the Commons should be able to impose its legislative will upon England without the consent of a majority of the English MPs. Such a formula was based on the need to secure the *concurrent consent* of a UK majority *and* an English majority of MPs in the Westminster Parliament on all purely English legislation.

This Conservative idea, which was encapsulated in the slogan 'English votes on English laws', was strongly criticised by Tony Blair at a conference of regional newspaper editors in March 2000.[17] In a powerful and interesting speech on 'Britishness', the Prime Minister pointed out that the Conservative leader's proposal would have the effect of creating two classes of Westminster MPs, with Scottish MPs at a disadvantage compared with their English (and Welsh) counterparts, and might even influence the make-up of the Executive which would have to reflect the possibility of defeat on English issues (i.e. by having a less disproportionate number of MPs from Scottish seats in the British Government). However, his fundamental riposte was to argue that the Hague proposal reflected 'a complete misunderstanding of reality' in that 'England can, if it chooses, outvote Scotland, Ireland [sic] and Wales at any point'.

The Prime Minister's final point was either naive or disingenuous in that it would be valid only if a majority of English MPs acted together *as an English party* in the House of Commons and if their votes were permitted under revised Westminster procedures to trump the votes of MPs from all parts of the United Kingdom on legislation affecting only England. The truth is that there is not, nor is there likely to be in the foreseeable future, an English nationalist party at Westminster and that, while the present Parliamentary arrangements persist alongside the devolution of primary legislative powers to the Scottish Parliament, there will continue to be a structural unfairness to English MPs and their constituents – what Tam Dalyell had dubbed 'the West Lothian Question', namely that Scottish MPs retain the right to speak and vote on exclusively English or Welsh business in the House of Commons, whereas English and Welsh MPs (indeed *all* Westminster MPs) no longer have equivalent rights over areas of policy devolved to the Scottish Parliament.

To pretend, as the Prime Minister did, that this old chestnut of unfairness to the English does not really matter is deliberately to ignore a bigger and more important point: that under the well-established electoral system for elections to the Westminster Parliament 'the winner takes all' and, in certain political circumstances, a United Kingdom Government *could* get its way by a narrow majority in the House of Commons which did *not* include a majority of English MPs, even when the legislation under consideration dealt with an important issue (e.g. the future of English grammar schools or the settlement of the Rate Support Grant for English local authorities) which ostensibly affected only English interests. For Mr Blair and his colleagues in the Labour Party, this situation may be regarded as just an anomaly of asymmetrical devolution which either should be quietly accepted by predominantly English Tories or *could* be resolved (a most unlikely scenario) by introducing a truly balanced federal system of government in the United Kingdom. For Mr Hague and his colleagues in the Conservative Party, it was very much *not* a matter of indifference that asymmetrical devolution to Scotland, Wales and Northern Ireland had gone ahead and they had absolutely no intention of solving the problem by deliberately moving to a federal system of government for the entire United Kingdom.

Orthodox regionalism on request

There is no long-established tradition of democratic regional government in England or, indeed, in other parts of the United Kingdom. The same is true for regional administration by central Government in that the establishment of nine Government Offices for the Regions by the Conservatives soon after their re-election at the 1992 General Election had few historical precedents in times of peace.[18]

Admittedly, if you go back to the seventeenth century, you find that Oliver Cromwell divided England into eleven different territorial components during his 'rule of the Major-Generals' in the 1650s, but this regional structure of government did not survive the Restoration and no one tried to replicate it for centuries thereafter. A unitary approach to government under the jurisdiction of one supreme Parliament for England (and by extension the United Kingdom) became the dominant political model and this left little or no scope for convincing regionalism to emerge.

It was not until the 1960s that the Ministry of Housing and Local Government began to advocate the concept of *extended city regions*. This conventional wisdom of the time was reflected in Derek Senior's Memorandum of Dissent from the 1969 Report of the Redcliffe-Maud Commission on Local Government Reform, when he advocated essentially a two-tier structure of local government in England based upon 'the facts of social geography', in which the upper tier (outside London) would have been constituted of 35 directly elected regional authorities.[19] Four years later, in 1973, when Lord Crowther-Hunt and Professor Alan Peacock produced their Memorandum of Dissent from the Kilbrandon Commission Report on the Constitution, an equally serious case was made for the division of England into five administrative Regions.[20] This idea was more in line with the main Redcliffe-Maud Report which had proposed that the top tier of English local government (outside London) should be eight Provinces and it was based upon the then prevalent view that since central Government was seriously overloaded, a layer of regional government would improve both administrative efficiency and democratic accountability, while also reflecting the diversity of English social geography. Two years later, in 1975, the drive to regenerate the outlying parts of the United Kingdom resulted in the

establishment of the Scottish and Welsh Development Agencies. Once these public bodies began to demonstrate their worth for Scotland and Wales, it was only a matter of time before certain Labour-controlled regions of England (notably the north-east and the north-west) began pressing for similar Agencies of their own.

Before coming to power in 1997, the Labour Party, which had been in Opposition since 1979 and whose strongest political support was concentrated in the outlying English regions, became more warmly disposed towards the idea of boosting regional capabilities *vis-à-vis* central Government. There were, however, two rather different sets of reasons for this more favourable disposition. Those in the party represented by John Prescott and Richard Caborn, who had been impressed by the success of the Scottish and Welsh Development Agencies in attracting new investment and creating new jobs in those parts of the United Kingdom, wanted to see similar agencies established for similar purposes in each of the standard English regions. Those in the party represented by Jack Straw and others closely in touch with *Charter 88* and similar pressure groups (including the Liberal Democrats, then working with Labour in a joint committee on constitutional reform) who were critical of the growth of unaccountable public bodies under the Tories, and concerned about the democratic deficit which had been created by the establishment of the nine largely unaccountable Government Offices for the Regions in England, wanted to make this layer of regional administration in some way more accountable to institutions based in and elected by the people of each region.

There were, therefore, conflicting priorities between the *economic* and the *constitutional* interests of the English regions, which were reflected in different parts of the 1997 Labour Manifesto.[21] The business chapter said: 'we will establish one-stop Regional Development Agencies to coordinate regional economic development, help small business and encourage inward investment'. The chapter on politics and Government pointed out that 'local authorities have come together to create a more coordinated regional voice' and promised that 'Labour will build on these developments through the establishment of Regional Chambers to coordinate transport, planning, economic development, and bids for European funding and land-use planning'. The first commitment represented a straightforward contribution to an active supply-side policy and had little to do with conscious constitutional change; the second was part of Labour's overall constitutional agenda, but represented the cautious tendency led by Jack Straw and Tony Blair (sensitive to the concerns of local government) rather than the ambitious tendency led by the party's Scottish heavyweights, such as Gordon Brown, Robin Cook and the late Donald Dewar.

Once in office, the Labour Government moved swiftly to introduce legislation to create eight English Regional Development Agencies (nine including London) and the new bodies eventually came into existence in April 1999. They are business-led, appointed bodies which are accountable to Ministers who in their turn are answerable to Parliament: with the exception of the London Development Agency, they are not democratically accountable at the regional or local level, other than in a rather tenuous way to the various non-statutory Regional Chambers which have been set up largely on the initiative of their constituent local authorities. This rather wishy-washy attempt to provide English RDAs with a modicum of democratic oversight and accountability inside the territorial boundaries within which they operate reflected the varying degrees of enthusiasm for real devolution in England that exist within the Labour leadership. John Prescott seemed to carry the banner for orthodox regional government in England, but even he was careful to add the *caveat* that the Government would proceed with this policy only 'where there is a demand for it' and to emphasise that 'we are not in the business of imposing it'.[22] Jack Straw, as Home Secretary from 1997 to 2001, reflected Whitehall caution towards such a constitutional experiment which, while it pleased the Campaign for a Northern Assembly and the Campaign for the English Regions, incurred fierce resistance from Conservative-controlled Shire Counties and was not favoured by a number of urban politicians and regional policy

experts who preferred a 'city region' model of sub-national government in England.

The case *for* English regionalism in any of its various forms is likely to be based upon the desirability of emulating the perceived success of the Scots and the Welsh in boosting their 'regional' economies and their 'national' pride, and upon the appeal of achieving better democratic control of the upper level of sub-national government. On the other hand, the case *against* is likely to be based upon the extra cost and disruption of introducing a regional tier of democratic government, coupled with a frank recognition of the relative weakness of territorial consciousness in the regions of England.

At the time of writing it is unclear which of these two points of view will carry the day. Indeed, even among those who advocate a dose of democratic regionalism for England, there is genuine disagreement about which would be the best model. For example, some academic experts, such as Professor Gerry Stoker, argue that the London model of regional governance, with democratic control over a Development Agency, a police service, public transport undertakings and a range of other functions all answerable to a directly elected Mayor who is accountable to a proportionally elected Assembly, would be preferable to either of the orthodox models of regionalism – especially in those parts of England where the lives of people in the large conurbations are integrally connected with what happens in their suburban and rural hinterland.[23]

The main reason for caution in regional policy is that senior Ministers are all too aware that public demand for real devolution to the English regions is only patchy and far from overwhelming. Admittedly, many of the regional *notables* in the North-East, the North-West and the West Midlands have been pushing hard for it and these political figures are allied with some prominent leaders of manufacturing industry who feel ill-served by economic decision making in London and resentful of the relatively privileged status of their counterparts in Scotland and Wales. Yet these stirrings do *not* amount to an irresistible surge of public demand for a fully fledged structure of devolved regional government in England and there must be some doubt as to whether the orthodox regionalists would win the day in many future regional referenda.

Another reason for caution is that the Labour Party, even if it suffers a set-back at a General Election in 2005 or 2006, is likely to remain a formidable *national* political force in which the interests of 'middle England' – i.e. everything south of a line from the Humber to the Severn, together with the more prosperous parts of some northern Counties – will prevail over those of constituencies further removed from the centres of economic and political power. Moreover, it is not as if Labour MPs re-elected from constituencies in Scotland and Wales are likely to campaign hard for an English regionalist policy which might dilute the *relative* economic and social advantages which their constituents derive from having the extra clout of the Scottish Parliament or the Welsh Assembly. So if and when legislation is brought forward for implementing what might be called the strong version of Labour's regionalist policy, it seems likely that the Parliamentary Labour Party will be divided on the issue and some Labour back-benchers could be opposed to it. The Labour Manifesto of 2001 essentially reiterated the commitments on local government which were made in the 1997 Manifesto, so there is still much to play for and no certainty about how things will work out in the end.[24]

Another rather powerful reason for caution is that many Councillors and officials in local government are distinctly wary of – not to say opposed to – any further structural reform of local government such as would be required to create uniformly unitary local government beneath the putative regional level. The fact that by April 1998 there were 46 unitary local authorities in England, created as a consequence of the 'local option' approach offered by the previous Conservative Government in the 1992–97 Parliament, does not invalidate the point that most English local Councillors feel more threatened than attracted by an ambitious prospectus for regional government. This is because it would probably entail redistributing some functions upwards to the Regions from the County and District Authorities and others downwards to the Regions from central Government. Coming after a long period of centralisation under the last Conservative Government, a policy of determined regionalisation might be equally unwelcome and strongly resisted by many in local government.

The final reason for caution is that experience has demonstrated that it is usually impossible to make any significant structural changes to local or sub-national government without spending more public money on the new arrangements than was spent on the old. This may be seen as a sort of 'Parkinson's law' which can be applied to all changes of this kind. Thus when a passage in the 1997 Labour Manifesto clearly stipulated the requirement that independent auditors (probably the National Audit Office) would have to certify that 'no additional public expenditure overall would be involved' before Labour's plans for directly elected regional government in England could proceed, the cautious tendency in the Labour leadership was in the ascendant. However, this obstacle seems to have been removed from the 2001 Labour Manifesto which only mentioned two prerequisites for directly elected regional government: the existence of predominantly unitary local government and majority support from local people in a referendum.[25]

Viewed in the round, Labour's policy in favour of orthodox regionalism in England remains a bit of a muddle. Its earlier insistence upon unitary local government beneath the regional level as a *prior* condition of further progress seems no longer to be a decisive feature of the policy, presumably because it accords ill with the fact that 34 of the 39 English Shires retain two tiers of local government (not counting Parish Councils).[26] A uniform system of regional government should logically entail the elimination of the Counties and the redistribution of their functions either upwards to the Regions or downwards to the Districts or more likely a bit of both. On the other hand, one could foresee the absorption of much County territory into the larger conurbations and, indeed, this option would remove the rationale for many Shire Districts altogether, notably those which fall within the economic and social orbit of the large conurbations.

In any of these eventualities one can foresee political problems emerging for the Labour Government, especially now that there is a Department of Environment, Food and Rural Affairs to propitiate the powerful countryside lobby.

The truth is that the introduction of real democratic government at the regional level in England ought to imply not only the exercise of coherent political will by Ministers and their Parliamentary supporters, but also a thorough-going reform of local government. Moreover, it would be highly desirable for such structural changes to be preceded, or at least accompanied, by the growth of a genuine sense of regional identity in all the English regions. In the absence of such popular support, there would not be a culture of consent and the newly created political structures would lack vital democratic legitimacy. Doubtless, the advocates of regional government will rely on the results of regional referenda to demonstrate public support and legitimacy for their policy. Yet the low turn-out of 35 per cent in the referendum on London government in May 1998 bodes ill for similar exercises in the English regions either before or after the legislation has been approved by Parliament.

In view of all these difficulties, the second Blair Administration is proceeding cautiously with its policy for regional government in England. It seems that we can expect the Government to produce a Green Paper or a White Paper with green edges on the options for regional governance, to be followed by widespread consultations with all the regional stakeholders and other interested parties. At the same time the existing Regional Chambers and other regional lobby groups will be working out detailed proposals for elected Assemblies in their regions, and doing so in such a way that they maximise their chances of achieving both local government consensus and public support. This suggests that the necessary legislation will not appear until the second session of the Parliament at the earliest and that the new Regional Assemblies in the parts of the country which want them will not be in existence before 2004 – a year too late for the first elections to such bodies to be combined with the next elections to the devolved Assemblies in Scotland and Wales which are due to be held in 2003.

Throughout the twentieth century English politics were essentially class-based rather than territorially based, while in this new century it looks as though England is now too small and too economically and socially integrated to become very fertile ground for territorial politics at the regional level. It is possible, however, that the situation in England may change in future if genuine regional consciousness grows further in the light of Scottish and Welsh devolution and in response to encouragement from the European institutions and a growing desire to emulate the self-conscious regionalism in other parts of the European Union.

The London model of governance

'Regional government is not the answer to the English question': so said Professor Gerry Stoker, one of the leading academic experts on sub-national government in the United Kingdom.[27] If this is true – and recent surveys of British public opinion have tended to suggest that the alternative model of 'city regions', run by directly elected Mayors who may or may not be accountable to city-wide Assemblies, are a more attractive option in the eyes of the general public – then it would be sensible for the Government and Parliament to reflect carefully upon the relative merits and demerits of *all* realistic answers to the English question before acceding to the demands of some English regions for the implementation of orthodox regionalism.

Perhaps the main point to be made about this is that in England there has been no strong tradition of mayoral government. On the continent of Europe, by contrast, most notably in the national capitals but also in other major cities, Mayors have often been important and popular political figures, while in the largest cities of the United States Mayors have wielded real political power and have often used their positions as a springboard from which to run for higher office, such as a state Governorship, a US Senate seat or even the Presidency. In the special case of London, there is an anomalous division between the City of London and the rest of the capital which has not been overcome in any of the various attempts to reform English local government over several centuries. Since the 1830s the English tradition in municipal government has tended to favour a committee structure of Councillors advised by professionally qualified officials, with the position of Mayor being largely ceremonial and filled by senior Councillors in agreeable rotation. In these circumstances the idea of a powerful Mayor with significant executive powers, directly elected by and accountable to the people of his city, is foreign to the traditions of English local government.

More generally, the national politicians of note who first rose to political prominence in municipal local government are distinguished by their rarity. One thinks of Joseph Chamberlain as Liberal leader of Birmingham City Council in the 1870s, his son Neville Chamberlain as Conservative Mayor of Birmingham during the First World War, and Herbert Morrison as Labour leader of London County Council in the 1930s. After that it is hard to think of other prominent examples until David Blunkett was Labour leader of Sheffield City Council in the 1980s. The principal explanation for this relative paucity of memorable figures is the enduring supremacy of Parliament, which has tended to reduce the attractions of service in municipal local government for those who aspire to influence in national politics.

From about the 1960s onwards there were some rather feeble and desultory attempts to challenge this general trend towards Parliamentary hegemony, but these helped to bring nemesis to local government during the three successive Thatcher Administrations from 1979 to 1990. The 1968 Redcliffe-Maud Report recommended the creation of 58 unitary local authorities in England in place of the veritable mosaic of more than 1,300 local authorities of different shapes and sizes which then existed; the *Memorandum of Dissent* by Derek Senior, on the other hand, advocated an alternative two-tier structure of 35 regional authorities and 148 district authorities. Both these blueprints recognised the growing interdependence of town and country which had long been substantiated by 'the patterns of settlement, activity and community

structure in which a motor age society organises itself'.[28] Yet they may also have underestimated the political gulf between town and country, even in a polity as small as England. Neither report was so radical as to propose directly elected Mayors and both assumed a continuation of the traditional committee-based structure of English local government.

A more recent landmark in what continued to be only a low-key debate about different models for 'regional' governance in England was arguably the publication of Michael Heseltine's self-serving book *Where There's a Will* in 1987.[29] In what was essentially a manifesto for his future leadership campaign against Margaret Thatcher and a work which was also informed by his fondness for all things 'European', this dashing Tory contender for ultimate political fame and fortune strongly advocated the creation of an English Development Agency. His arguments for this were partly influenced by the obvious success of the Scottish and Welsh Development Agencies and partly by his own formative experience as Environment Secretary in the early 1980s when he had tried hard to bring about the regeneration of Liverpool and other disadvantaged English cities during the deep economic recession of that period. It was also apparent from his speeches at the time and subsequently that he thought that large urban communities would benefit from a reformed local government structure in which a single dynamic personality (i.e. a directly elected Mayor with extensive executive powers) could give a decisive lead to his city and get to grips with the multiple problems of urban decay and social demoralisation which beset so many of them.

Nothing really came of these ideas for the rest of the Conservative period in office, since Margaret Thatcher was obsessed with her campaign to emasculate Labour-controlled local government and John Major (assisted by Michael Heseltine who was reinstalled as Environment Secretary) had to devote much of his energy to scrapping the Thatcherite poll tax and replacing it with the more publicly acceptable council tax. Thus an attractive idea for revitalising urban local government in England was ignored for about a decade until the arrival in power of the first Blair Administration in 1997. Even then the Labour Government was wary of adopting this 'foreign' approach to the reform of local government and has not really encouraged great cities, such as Birmingham, Manchester, Liverpool, Leeds, Sheffield and Newcastle, to follow London's example by opting for a directly elected Mayor who has to answer to a proportionally elected Assembly.

When in Opposition, Tony Blair had made no secret of his enthusiasm for the principle of a directly elected Mayor for London. On coming into Government, he maintained this attitude, but qualified it with the prudent stipulation that such an innovation would go ahead only if the people of London voted in favour of the idea in a *prior* referendum. In May 1998 the referendum was duly held and the result was that the people of London voted by 72 per cent to 28 per cent (in a turn-out of only 35 per cent) in favour of the Government's proposals.

The policy amounted to giving the people of London the chance to vote directly for mayoral candidates in an electoral system known as the supplementary vote (SV). This system meant that electors were asked to cast two votes on a single ballot paper – first a vote for their favourite candidate and then a vote for their second preference. If a candidate won more than half of the first-choice votes, he or she would be elected. If no candidate achieved this, then all but the top two candidates would be eliminated and the second-choice votes of the eliminated candidates would be allocated to the two remaining candidates in line with the voters' preferences until one of them achieved an overall majority and hence was elected.

Simultaneously, each elector would have two votes for a 25-member Greater London Assembly in an electoral system known as the additional member system (AMS). Fourteen of the members would be elected by the familiar British system of first-past-the-post as constituency members, each representing a constituency of two or three London Boroughs. The remaining eleven Additional Members would be elected from closed party lists (i.e. their position on the list would be determined by their own party rather than by the electorate) to

represent the public on a London-wide basis in proportion to the votes cast for their respective parties right across the capital. There was also to be a threshold set at 5 per cent of the entire London vote which would have to be achieved for a party to qualify for any Additional Members. The system was designed specifically to exclude small extremist parties, such as the British National Party, but it also threatened the prospects of more worthy small parties such as the Greens. Parliament passed the necessary legislation in the 1998–99 session, which enabled the elections to be held in May 2000 and the new Greater London Authority to be established a month later in June 2000.

The legislation stipulated that the Mayor, who would be elected for a four-year term of office, would have political responsibility for transport, planning, economic development and regeneration, the environment, policing, fire services and emergency planning, public health, culture, media and sport throughout the area covered by the 32 London Boroughs and the City of London. In the process he would need to answer to the Assembly and to the people of London for an annual budget of more than £3 billion. The new Assembly was empowered to approve the Mayor's annual budget and strategic priorities, monitor his behaviour in office and review the performance of the various Agencies to which he would make senior appointments and over which he would exercise political control. The package involved transferring to the Mayor and the Assembly – collectively known as the Greater London Authority – powers of political oversight over a wide range of policy areas and politically sensitive organisations, such as a London Transport Authority, a London Development Agency and the Metropolitan Police. Perhaps most significant, however, was the degree of publicity which would inevitably surround the winning candidate, who would be not only the first directly elected Mayor for the whole of London in its history but also a national political figure of major proportions, since he would be able to claim to speak for about 7 million Londoners – by far the largest single constituency in the United Kingdom.

Having indicated his enthusiasm for the mayoral model of regional governance – at any rate its suitability for London – Tony Blair then made the terrible mistake of trying to ensure that the London Labour Party (LLP) chose as its candidate for the mayoral election in May 2000 essentially anyone but Ken Livingstone, the maverick 'old Labour' MP for Brent East who as Leader of the Greater London Council in the early 1980s had also been a thorn in Margaret Thatcher's flesh and had so exasperated her with his provocative gesture politics that she eventually decided to put through Parliament legislation which abolished the GLC and the other Metropolitan Counties. In his obstinate determination to stop Ken Livingstone Mr Blair cast around for anyone plausible – whether politician or businessman – who could carry the flag for New Labour. His people in the London Labour Party were left with the clear impression that they simply *had* to select anyone but Livingstone. In the end, after much media speculation and political skulduggery, the LLP chose the hapless Frank Dobson, a bearded northerner who at the time was MP for Camden and Secretary of State for Health. This manipulation of the selection process had the predictable effects of discrediting Frank Dobson, who came to be seen by the media and the public as Tony Blair's poodle, and subsequently provoking an angry Ken Livingstone to stand as an independent candidate for the office.

As things developed, this first London-wide mayoral election process began as tragedy and ended as farce. The Conservatives had their own embarrassments in the shape of Lord (Jeffrey) Archer, who was forced by the media to withdraw as the Conservative candidate after having been branded as a congenital liar, and in the shape of Steve Norris, who eventually became the Conservative standard-bearer in the contest in spite of his notorious and colourful past both as a serial philanderer and as an effective Minister for London Transport. When the election finally took place in May 2000, there was a disappointingly low turn-out (35 per cent), but Ken Livingstone won a moral and political victory as an independent candidate who should really have been the official Labour candidate and would have been, indeed, if the control freaks around Tony Blair had not advised him that he could both introduce a new structure of mayoral governance in London and painlessly impose upon the capital city a candidate of his own choice. In general, it was most unfortunate for the overall cause of constitutional reform that the idea of mayoral governance for London should have been damaged at the outset by Mr Blair's gratuitous interference in the Labour selection process – just as devolution for Wales was initially damaged by similar interference when the Prime Minister succeeded (if only temporarily) in imposing his placeman, the hapless Alun Michael, as First Minister of the new Welsh Executive responsible to the Welsh Assembly.

Notwithstanding this sequence of misfortunes in London, the fact remains that there are some good arguments to be advanced in favour of the mayoral model of local governance in England – arguments which can equally be applied to the circumstances in other parts of the country where there are large conurbations which dominate their natural hinterland. *Firstly*, there are the arguments based upon economic and social geography. All great cities, such as London, Birmingham or Newcastle, effectively dominate their regions and act as industrial, commercial, political and cultural magnets for the people who live and work for miles around. In the case of London with all its commuters, it could be said that decisions made in the capital by responsible London-based decision makers can affect millions of people within a radius of at least 50 miles of Charing Cross and often much further afield. These points serve to emphasise the fundamental interdependence of town and country in a relatively small territory such as England. They also call to mind the points which were made so persuasively in the Redcliffe-Maud Report of the late 1960s to support its case for the introduction of a uniform pattern of 58 unitary local authorities in England, thus highlighting the ever-increasing integration of cities, suburbs and countryside, especially in densely populated English territory.

Secondly, there are the arguments based upon executive efficiency and democratic accountability.

It is no coincidence that many of the sectors of functional responsibility allocated to the Mayor of London – e.g. transport, environment, planning and economic regeneration – are most efficiently tackled on a London-wide basis and arguably an even wider basis than that. If this observation is correct, then it makes good sense in terms of policy coherence and executive efficiency to concentrate the decision making in one place upon the shoulders of one person – albeit someone who is professionally advised by competent experts. The alternatives of leaving these matters to warring factions in smaller units of local government or to the vagaries of market forces have been shown to be much worse – e.g. in the push and pull between different local authorities and vested interests in efforts to solve London's traffic problems by introducing red routes or congestion charges.

The argument *for* mayoral governance on the ground of democratic accountability is that it is better to have a single person with the clear political responsibility for all the major decisions taken in a given city region than a range of committees where the lines of political responsibility can be blurred and the Councillors involved may find it easy to pass the buck to others. If a comparison is made with the alternative of directly elected regional assemblies, these have the disadvantage of creating larger territorial units which are likely to make the centres of regional decision making seem more remote than they would have been in city regions. Moreover, in an age of growing media coverage of sub-national politics, it is possible for articulate mayoral candidates to dramatise and personify policy choices in ways which may promote higher election turn-outs in due course.

The arguments *against* a mayoral model of local governance are based very largely upon the familiar antipathy between people in rural and urban areas, with the former determined not to have their priorities and principles compromised by possible submersion in a new form of local government which would have to combine rural and urban interests in a single representative structure; and upon the strong misgivings felt towards potentially autocratic, even demagogic,

directly elected Mayors by most local Councillors whether at District or County level. In traditionalist quarters there is felt to be something 'un-English' about the idea of directly elected Mayors with substantial executive powers, since these are more often associated with patterns of local governance on the continent of Europe or in the United States. With conservative instincts persistent in much of English local government, the onus is really upon the advocates of the directly elected mayoral model to demonstrate that it is the best way forward.

It is too soon to tell whether the new mayoral model of local governance will be able to coexist easily with other developments at regional level which are already under way or whether in the end there will be scope for only a single model of regional governance to take root and thrive. In the opinion of Robert Hazell and Brendan O'Leary, the winning model 'may depend upon who occupies the [regional] political space first' and in 1999 they put their money somewhat tentatively upon directly elected executive Mayors.[30]

General reflections

It is evident that the English have usually had a rather easy-going attitude towards the constitutional arrangements under which they are governed. In the first place the Glorious Revolution of 1688–89 and its political consequences over the ensuing two or three decades enabled the English ruling class to feel confident that they had firmly established Parliamentary government under a constitutional Monarchy and that the Protestant (later the Hanoverian) succession was secure. Second, it was during this period of English history that it became obvious that England was the dominant entity within the United Kingdom. This was not just because the Scottish Parliament agreed to the Acts of Union in 1707, but also because English territory was no longer seriously challenged by any threats emanating from within the British Isles. It was increasingly noticeable as the eighteenth century unfolded that the English people were establishing their self-confident identity, particularly in the course of frequent overseas wars on behalf of the expanding British Empire. There was therefore no recognisable 'English question', since the great issues of identity and territory had to all intents and purposes been resolved in England's favour and since the land-owning ruling class felt confident about the durability of the constitutional arrangements which had been established.

In many ways it has been this sublime self-confidence of the English ruling class down the centuries which has not only kept the 'English question' off the political agenda for so long, but also caused intense annoyance and resentment among the other nationalities with whom we have shared these islands. Indeed, the complacent constitutional assumptions and the legendary insensitivity of the English ruling class towards the needs and aspirations of the non-English peoples in the British Isles were probably responsible for provoking initially the Irish and later the Scots and the Welsh to rebel against English political tutelage. It can be said that the English have been insular in their attitudes and behaviour *within* the United Kingdom as well as without: indeed, this national characteristic led us to project our power naturally from the empire within the British Isles to the Empire overseas. It must have been even more galling for patriotic Irish, Scots and Welsh whenever we exhibited our familiar tendency to elide our English and British identities.

The evidence of history shows that the English identity has had at least as much to do with poetic ideas, social mores, customary attitudes and even climate as the more orthodox components of national identity in other countries, such as territory, language or religion. 'English' has usually been more of an adjective than a collective noun, and there has been no explicit or self-conscious English state since the Tudor period. Only now, at the beginning of the twenty-first century, is there once again some serious consideration of the 'English question' and this has been brought about almost entirely because many of those who are politically aware of the possible constitutional consequences of devolution to Scotland, Wales and Northern Ireland have begun to wonder whether, and if so in what way, the English should respond

to the challenge of revived nationalism in each of the non-English parts of the United Kingdom.

In the emerging constitutional circumstances of a *quasi-federal United Kingdom*, England seems to have been largely left out of the nationalist equation, since the English themselves have tended, perhaps complacently, to assume that they did not need to recognise their own sensitivities in ways even remotely comparable with the concessions that have been made to the Scots, the Welsh and the nationalists in Northern Ireland. Yet there is a respectable case for saying that asymmetrical devolution may cause political problems for the United Kingdom which will only be resolved by making radical changes to governance in England.

One balancing factor against English dominance of the institutional arrangements in the United Kingdom has been the extent to which non-English politicians and other professionals have often risen to the top of the various career ladders in the British state, including the political parties, the law, the churches and the armed services. Another balancing factor has been the deliberate over-representation in the House of Commons of the Scottish and Welsh as compared with other parts of the United Kingdom. This particular imbalance is due to be rectified in Scotland by 2007, but not in Wales as long as the members of the Welsh Assembly have no primary legislative powers.

There remain some elusive and paradoxical aspects of the English question which mean that it does not lend itself to easy or simple answers. This chapter has reviewed the four main options for tackling the problems of English governance and the institutional relationships between England and the other component parts of the United Kingdom. They are:

1   preservation of the present constitutional position, i.e. asymmetric devolution to some but not all the parts of the union state;
2   institutional differentiation for England symbolised by the creation of an English Parliament or new arrangements within the Westminster Parliament to ensure only 'English votes on English laws';
3   orthodox regionalism in England delivered by

a programme of voluntary rolling devolution to those regions that want to have such structures of sub-national government;

4   replication of the London model of local governance in other English conurbations, once again via a voluntary rolling programme but subject to some fairly demanding conditions set by central Government.

It remains to be seen which of these options will contain the most suitable answers to the contemporary English question.

Questions for discussion

1   Has the disproportionate weight and size of England always blighted the prospects for good government of the United Kingdom?

2   Which is the most appropriate constitutional model for the governance of England in the early years of the twenty-first century?

3   Which structure of governance at the regional level is most likely to fit the varied needs and conflicting loyalties of the localities in England?

Notes

1   J. Paxman, *The English*; Michael Joseph, London, 1998; p. 23.
2   *Ibid*; p. 144.
3   Quoted in *ibid*; p. 143.
4   Linda Colley, *Britons – Forging the Nation – 1707–1837*; Pimlico, London, 1992; p. 111.
5   Ann Dummett, 'Citizenship and national identity', in R. Hazell (ed.) *Constitutional Futures*; Oxford University Press, Oxford, 1999; p. 229.
6   Roger Scruton, *England, an Elegy*; Chatto & Windus, London, 2000; p. ix.
7   See IFS, 'Financing regional government in Britain', in R. Hazell (ed). *op. cit.*; p. 202.
8   See David Smith, 'Brown's spending goes north', *Sunday Times*, 18th June 2000.
9   See 'Industry and unions may get role in regions', *Financial Times*, 11th November 2001.
10   Report of the Urban Task Force, *Towards an Urban Renaissance*; DETR, London, 1999.
11   R. Hazell, 'Three policies in search of a strategy', in S. Chen and T. Wright (eds) *The English Question*; Fabian Society, London, 2000; p. 35.
12   This idea is closely associated with the proposals put forward by William Hague in two speeches on constitutional issues post-devolution, both delivered to audiences at the Centre for Policy Studies in London, one on 24th February 1998 and the other on 15th July 1999.
13   See Consultative Document, *Devolution: the English Dimension*; HMSO, London, December 1976.
14   *Ibid*; para 19.
15   See William Hague, Speech to Centre for Policy Studies, 24th February 1998.
16   See William Hague, Speech to Centre for Policy Studies, 15th July 1999.
17   See Tony Blair, Speech to regional newspaper editors, London, 28th March 2000.
18   In the twentieth century the exceptions to this rule were the regional organisation of the United Kingdom for national defence purposes during the Second World War and the introduction of a structure of economic regions by the Labour Government's new Department of Economic Affairs in 1964.
19   See D. Senior, *The Regional City*; Longman, London, 1966; and his *Memorandum of Dissent from the Royal Commission Report on Local Government Reform*, Cmnd 4040-I; HMSO, London, 1969.
20   See N. Crowther-Hunt and A. Peacock, *Memorandum of Dissent from the Royal Commission Report on the Constitution*, Cmnd 5460-I; HMSO, London, 1973.
21   Both quoted in R. Hazell (ed.) *op. cit.*; p. 37.
22   See John Prescott's Introduction to the White Paper *'Building Partnerships for Prosperity – Sustainable Growth, Competitiveness and Employment in the English Regions*, Cm 3814; HMSO, London, 1997.
23   See Gerry Stoker, 'Is regional government the answer to the English question?', in S. Chen and T. Wright (eds) *op. cit.*; pp. 63–79.
24   This uncertainty has been reflected in press comment on the subject – see *Financial Times*, 11th November 2001.
25   Labour Party Manifesto, *Ambitions for Britain*; London, 2001; p. 35.
26   See Hilary Armstrong in *Hansard*, 16th January 2001, Vol. 361, Col. 182W.
27   G. Stoker, *op. cit.*; p. 75.
28   See Cmnd 4040-I; para 558.
29   M. Heseltine, *Where There's a Will*; Hutchinson, London, 1987; p. 326.
30   R. Hazell and B. O'Leary, 'A rolling programme of devolution', in R. Hazel (ed.) *op. cit.*; p. 41.

Further reading

Vernon Bogdanor, *Devolution in the United Kingdom*; Oxford University Press, Oxford, 1999.

S. Chen and T. Wright (eds) *The English Question*; Fabian Society, London, 2000.

Linda Colley, *Britons – Forging the Nation – 1707–1837*; Pimlico, London, 1992.

Teresa Gorman, *A Parliament for England*; This England Books, Cheltenham, 1999.

Robert Hazell (ed.) *The State and the Nations: the First Year of Devolution in the U.K.*; Imprint Academic, London, 2000.

Simon Heffer, *Nor Shall my Sword: the Reinvention of England*; Phoenix, London, 1999.

Christopher Hibbert, *The English – a Social History, 1066–1945*; Guild Publishing, London, 1987.

Jeremy Paxman, *The English*; Michael Joseph, London, 1998.

Reaching out: the Role of Central Government at Regional and Local Level; Performance and Innovation Unit, London, 2000.

M. Sandford and P. McQuail, *Unexplored Territory – Regional Assemblies in England*; Constitution Unit, London, July 2001.

Roger Scruton, *England – an Elegy*; Chatto & Windus, London, 2000.

J. Tomaney and M. Mitchell, *Empowering the English Regions*; Charter 88, London, 1999.

website for Campaign for the English Regions: www.cfer.org.uk

Part III

MODERNISING GOVERNMENT

Modernising central Government

The theme of 'modernisation' has been integral to the New Labour project ever since Tony Blair became Leader of the party in 1994. Each of the two leaders of the party before that – Neil Kinnock (1983–92) and John Smith (1992–94) – were political modernisers in their different ways, but as Leaders of the Opposition who never became Prime Minister, they could only contribute to the modernisation of the Labour Party, not of the Labour Government. Tony Blair has been a moderniser from conviction rather than political convenience and has been prepared to accept and carry forward large parts of the Thatcherite legacy in ways which neither of his predecessors would have been inclined to do. For what began with his determination to modernise the Labour Party – e.g. the introduction of One Member One Vote and the deliberate downgrading of the role of the affiliated trade unions in the party policy-making process – has continued since the party has been in office with his determination to introduce a wide range of reforms to modernise the institutions which make up the executive, legislative and judicial branches of government in the United Kingdom.

At the superficial level of political rhetoric, the cry of 'modernisation' has proved to be a good one and, after eighteen years of Conservative rule as the end of the century approached, there was at least presentational logic behind the Labour Party's 1997 General Election slogan: 'New Labour, New Britain'. It was also fairly persuasive for Tony Blair and his senior colleagues to suggest during the 1997 General Election campaign that if the general public were prepared to give them credit for modernising the Labour Party in order to make themselves electable, then once in Government they would deserve equal credit and support for their policies to modernise Britain.

There is the added attraction that the concept of 'modernisation' is a conveniently elastic term which can be presented to the public as simply a matter of reforming *the machinery* of government or can be used as a political euphemism to mask much more radical and socially interventionist policies. In a country with an inherently conservative (small c) political culture, the general public usually finds it much more palatable if an incoming Government presents its reforms as a matter of bringing established arrangements 'up to date' rather than taking a scythe to the old order so that it can be replaced with something radically new. This political consideration was particularly important to Tony Blair and his senior colleagues, since their Labour predecessors had succeeded in 'frightening the horses' in 1992 and they considered it vital to their electoral chances not to do the same in 1997. Moreover, Tony Blair was smart enough to understand that what 'middle England' really wanted in 1997 was a continuation of conservatism without the Conservatives, which made him even more determined to be reassuring on taxation and public expenditure and to present most of his initial agenda of constitutional reforms as examples of 'modernisation'.

Whether presented in a flamboyant or a reticent way by the so-called spin doctors of New Labour, there is no denying the comprehensive scope and potential longer-term significance of the Labour Government's constitutional reform agenda. At the Labour Party Conference of 1994 Tony Blair had described it as 'the biggest programme of change to democracy ever proposed'. Yet this apparently hyperbolic claim was substantiated by the spate of constitutional reform legislation introduced in the 1997–2001 Parliament.[1]

In different ways the various elements in Labour's constitutional reform agenda could be seen as responses to the lessons which the party had learned during its long years in Opposition, at any rate until John Major's second Administration fell into terminal disarray in September 1992 when Sterling had to leave the European Exchange Rate Mechanism. For thirteen years before that time the country had been subjected to a long succession of radical, centralising measures and the power of the Prime Minister (and, by extension, all the officials and political advisers working at and connected with 10 Downing Street) had significantly increased over Government and Parliament alike, while most, if not all, of the countervailing power centres in the British polity had been neutered or smashed. In many ways these developments substantiated the persuasive force of the arguments which had been put forward by Charter 88 and other constitutionalist pressure groups that were quite close to many leading New Labour figures when the party was in Opposition. Yet there were other important elements in what Tony Blair and Gordon Brown resolved to do at the outset of the Parliament – e.g. making the Bank of England operationally independent via the 1998 Bank of England Act – which owed little or nothing to constitutionalist influence but nearly everything to their desire to build market credibility for the new Labour Government.

Of the twelve constitutional Bills introduced during the first long session of the 1997–2001 Parliament, seven (if you include the Bill to provide for a referendum on the future governance arrangements for London) were to do with devolution in its various aspects, two were to do with elections and electoral reform, two reflected Labour's more favourable attitudes towards political obligations and constitutional safeguards stemming from EU treaties or European conventions, and there remained the legislation on operational independence for the Bank of England which has already been mentioned. It can therefore be demonstrated that right from the outset the Labour Government has been determined to introduce more 'modern' constitutional arrangements in the United Kingdom.

Modernising policy and administration

The key text on government modernisation under the first Blair Administration was undoubtedly the March 1999 White Paper entitled *Modernising Government*.[2] This followed an internal review in 1998 which Tony Blair had asked the Cabinet Secretary, Sir Richard Wilson, to conduct into the workings of policy and administration in central government.

'The Government has a mission to modernise', declared Tony Blair in his Foreword to the White Paper, 'renewing our country for the new millennium'. After referring briefly to the modernisation of schools, hospitals, the economy and the criminal justice system, he trumpeted the modernisation of 'our democratic framework with new arrangements for Scotland, Wales, Northern Ireland, the English regions, Parliament and local authorities'. Then came the punchline of this particular message: 'but modernisation must go further; it must engage with how government itself works – modernising government is a vital part of our programme of renewal for Britain'. Later in the Executive Summary was the reassurance that 'in line with the Government's overall programme of modernisation, modernising government is modernisation for a purpose – to make life better for people and businesses'.[3]

In the six chapters which followed, the civil service authors of the document (doubtless closely supervised by Sir Richard Wilson, the Cabinet Secretary who was also Head of the Civil Service) faithfully explained in greater detail firstly the 'vision', then how policy making would be modernised, then what would be entailed in responsive and high-quality public services, then the implications of 'information age government', and finally a chapter of studied reassurance which began with the sonorous words that 'the Government is committed to public service and public servants'.[4] We shall shortly explore the more interesting and significant points which arise under each of these headings. However, before doing so, it is worth taking a somewhat cynical look at the philosophical and linguistic pedigree of Tony Blair's entire 'modernisation project', since in this way we may discover the true meaning of institutional modernisation in the United Kingdom today. See *Box 6* for a summary of the key points in the 1999 White Paper.

The growth of power and capacity at the centre of government was a key characteristic of British political development throughout the twentieth century. Such a long-term development was in many ways a logical response to the imperatives of total national mobilisation in two world wars and political acceptance of increased state responsibility both for protective action of last resort in the Depression of the 1930s and for national reconstruction in the late 1940s. It has also been fostered in less perilous times by the influence of certain strong personalities, such as Margaret Thatcher and Tony Blair, both of whom have been strong

Box 6 Key points in the 1999 White Paper *Modernising Government*

- Emphasis upon tackling cross-cutting issues, e.g. social exclusion, problems of small businesses
- Emphasis upon evidence-based policy making which draws upon the expertise of expert and interested outsiders
- Improvements to public service delivery with pragmatic reforms and contractual Public Service Agreements
- Widespread use of task forces and review groups as ways of involving or co-opting senior business figures into central Government
- A new Civil Service Management Committee to take forward a more corporate approach to the management of central government and a programme to turn the Civil Service into a 'learning organisation'
- Emphasis upon new information technology for the delivery of public services and ambitious targets for the achievement of electronic government on-line
- Systematic use of partnerships between central Government and a wide range of national and local service providers, including those in the private and voluntary sectors

centralisers for different purposes in their different ways. The cumulative effect of all these various influences over nearly a century has been to generate a long-term secular trend towards the growth of power and responsibility at the centre of British government; and a variant of modernisation has often provoked or accompanied each new burst of centralisation, even when (as in the case of New Labour's commitment to devolution) another thrust of public policy has been in the contrary direction of decentralisation.

Of course, certain *caveats* have to be entered if such a generalisation is to remain broadly defensible – for example, centralisation has not been a linear development in the United Kingdom in the twentieth century, by no means all Prime Ministers have appeared to be megalomaniac, some wanted to assert themselves but did not really succeed, while others did not even try very seriously. Moreover, in spite of the secular trend, the real world context within which British politics are conducted has changed significantly in various ways which have led real power to *escape* from the central institutions of nation states and to be accumulated or expropriated by other centres of decision making in the corporate and private sectors.

Intelligent political leaders and their advisers have been aware of these trends, along with the related qualifying factors, and they have sought, not unnaturally, to influence outcomes in directions which favour the interests of their parties or which accord with their personal priorities in governing the country. In the case of New Labour, Tony Blair's modernisation goals have *necessarily* involved giving further impetus to centralisation in the United Kingdom for at least three simple reasons. *Firstly*, the modernisation project has required a revolution from the top – a *coup de tête* – within the ranks of the Labour Party. *Secondly*, it has been personally symbolised by and is ultimately dependent upon the particular characteristics of Tony Blair's crusade for 'New Labour – New Britain'. *Thirdly*, it has had to be implemented – as far as the machinery of government is concerned – via a reshaped and more muscular Cabinet Office, which has taken on the role of corporate head-quarters for the civil service as a whole, but also via a more assertive and fully staffed 'Prime Minister's Office' at 10 Downing Street.

In order to give political substance and momentum to this centralisation of government, Tony Blair has appointed a series of Ministers to take charge of the Cabinet Office and its wider agenda of modernisation in government. During the first Blair Administration this involved merging the former Office of Public Services into the Cabinet Office and creating two new units at the heart of Whitehall – the Performance and Innovation Unit to monitor and improve the delivery of policy and the Centre for Management and Policy Studies (which incorporates the Civil Service College) to promote Tony Blair's brand of managerialism throughout the public administration. The Cabinet Office was strengthened and enlarged with a complement of three Ministers (one in the Lords and two in the Commons – not counting the Prime Minister himself) and became one of the institutional power-houses of the first Blair Administration.

In the immediate aftermath of Labour's re-election in June 2001, Tony Blair gave further impetus to the thrust of centralisation by making his Deputy, John Prescott, responsible for over-seeing *the delivery* of Labour's Manifesto pledges, especially those which related to investment in and reform of the public services. He also sought to tie in the Labour Party more closely to the Blairite New Labour project by appointing Charles Clarke to the chairmanship of the party with a seat in Cabinet as Minister without Portfolio and he appointed Lord Macdonald as a senior Minister in the Cabinet Office to act as the main progress-chaser for the delivery of Government policy in the second term.

At the same time the Prime Minister made a significant reorganisation of structures and person-nel at 10 Downing Street. The 'non-political' Private Office and the political Policy Unit have been merged under the Chief of Staff, Jonathan Powell, and the Principal Private Secretary, Jeremy Heywood. The Press Office has been ostensibly depoliticised and two senior civil servants from the Government's Information and Communications Service have been put jointly in charge, so that the once notorious Alastair Campbell could switch from being the Prime Minister's Official Spokes-man to taking charge of a new lower-profile Communications and Strategy Unit working on strategic political issues behind the scenes. Another communications structure (called 'Political and Government Relations') was established under Anji Hunter, one of the Prime Minister's longest-standing personal friends, but is now headed by Baroness Morgan, a former Labour Party official who was Tony Blair's Political Secretary in Opposition. As for the administrative implemen-tation of Government policies in the second term, this is being coordinated by the so-called Delivery Unit headed by Professor Michael Barber.

The Performance and Innovation Unit is contin-uing its work, but it seems to have been merged with a new Forward Strategy Unit under Geoff Mulgan and physically located in the Cabinet Office. The Women's Unit, the Social Exclusion Unit and the Regional Coordination Unit are continuing as before, although the latter two are now answer-able to the Deputy Prime Minister, John Prescott. There is a new Office of Public Services Reform headed by Wendy Thomson, formerly of the Audit Commission, which will advise the Prime Minister on the Government's radical reform of the civil service. Lord Birt, a former Director-General of the BBC, has also been brought into 10 Downing Street to advise the Prime Minister on modernisation and efficiency in government. As the Prime Minister declared the day after his General Election victory in June 2001, the British people had given him a mandate with 'an instruction to deliver' and he intended to heed their wishes.

It seems clear that the net effect of all these developments is further centralisation within the Blair Administration in particular and the political system in general, notwithstanding the counter-vailing effects of asymmetrical devolution. Some aspects of *policy delivery* in the United Kingdom may have been diffused and localised, but *political responsibility* for the results of policy has been further focused upon the Prime Minister himself since June 2001. This fundamental tension within the Blair Project could store up big political problems for the Labour Party in future if and when the British economy turns down and there are greater pressures to contain public expenditure.

The 1999 White Paper, in its first chapter entitled 'Vision', included fourteen references to modernisation in just 20 paragraphs, applying it to central government, devolved government and local government. Clearly the authors regarded frequent repetition of the 'm word' as essential to the success of the policy (and no doubt their own promotion prospects as well). 'Partnership' came a poor second in the buzz-word stakes, although partnership with the devolved governments, local authorities, other bodies (often voluntary organisations) and other countries was put forward as the best solution to the problems or failings identified in parts of the public service.[5]

With regard to *the policy-making process*, it was recognised that there was a good deal of room for improvement in efforts to create 'policies that really deal with problems', that are 'forward looking and shaped by the evidence rather than a response to short term pressures', that 'tackle causes not symptoms', that 'are measured by results rather than activity', that 'are flexible and innovative rather than closed and bureaucratic', that 'promote compliance rather than avoidance or fraud', and that involve 'a process of continuous learning and improvement'.[6] It also rehearsed two familiar complaints, often heard in the past from academics and idealists, that 'policies too often take the form of incremental change to existing systems rather than new ideas that take the long term view and cut across organisational boundaries to get to the root of a problem' and that the system is too risk averse in so far as 'the cultures of Parliament, Ministers and the civil service create a situation in which the rewards for success are limited and penalties for failure can be severe'.[7]

Against the background of these heavy indictments, the call was for 'a new and more creative approach to policy making' based upon a number of key principles which included: policy based upon shared goals and defined results; policy that was fair and inclusive; policy which avoided imposing unnecessary burdens upon business, policy that involved developing new relationships with others in the wider community; policy which improved the way in which risk was managed, policy which was more forward- and outward-looking notably in relation to the European Union, and evidence-based policy making which involved a continuous learning process and which was systematically evaluated.

It soon became apparent that the two most prominent objectives for the new policy-making process were, firstly, to find better institutional ways for *tackling the so-called cross-cutting issues*, such as social exclusion, drug abuse and the needs of small businesses; and, secondly, to find appropriate ways of *involving a wider range of expert and interested outsiders* who had a stake in the implementation of policy or who were directly affected by it. The first of these requirements has increasingly been met by the work of special units attached to 10 Downing Street and reporting ultimately to the Prime Minister or Deputy Prime Minister, such as the Performance and Innovation Unit or the Social Exclusion Unit. Indeed, it was a Report of the Performance and Innovation Unit (PIU) in January 2000 which laid out the basis for improving the formulation and management of cross-cutting policies and services.[8]

The central message of the PIU report was that simply removing barriers to inter-departmental cooperation was not enough and that more needed to be done if cross-cutting initiatives were to hold their own against purely departmental objectives. Some of the solutions would be financial and contractual – as in Public Service Agreements – and some would be methodological and all to do with stronger leadership from Ministers and senior civil servants, modernising the skills and capacities of civil servants and giving more emphasis to the views and interests of those outside central Government who deliver or use public services. A common refrain was that the centre of Government (defined as 10 Downing Street, the Cabinet Office and the Treasury) had an important role to play in promoting the cross-cutting approach to problem solving and public service delivery. Significantly, the authors of the Report also warned that 'the centre should only intervene where cross-cutting working is difficult to initiate or sustain without central intervention and the activity is crucial to the organisation's [the Government's] overall objectives'.

Although having consciously tried to learn from private sector experience that direct intervention from the centre should only happen as a last resort, Tony Blair and Gordon Brown have often shown impatience not only with the perceived short-comings of their Ministerial colleagues – e.g. Nick Brown at the Ministry of Agriculture at the time of the foot and mouth crisis in the summer of 2001 – but also with the institutional inertia in the whole Whitehall system of government. Tony Blair's attitude has been encapsulated in the mantra 'what matters is what works' and it is clear that he carries no Socialist or statist baggage on his long and arduous journey to reform the public services. Gordon Brown, by contrast, has sometimes seemed to be more ideological and he was keen to use the *Spending Review 2000* to give progress reports on no fewer than fifteen cross-cutting reviews of such diverse policy areas as Sure Start for the Under Fives, Rural and Countryside Programmes, and Nuclear Safety in the Former Soviet Union.[9]

The second objective has been addressed by setting up a plethora of task forces and review groups led by or heavily composed of senior business figures who are well disposed to New Labour, some of whom were significant financial contributors to the party in Opposition. At one time during the first Blair Administration there were estimated to be 148 of these various bodies in existence, some of them with a narrow focus and of short duration and some of them seemingly permanent advisory or executive bodies with no obvious chain of public accountability other than to the Ministers who set them up.[10] It was people such as Professor Peter Hennessy who drew these matters to the attention of the Neill Committee when it was conducting its review of progress made in reinforcing standards in public life and both the Commissioner for Public Appointments, Sir Leonard Peach, and the House of Commons Select Committee on Public Administration expressed concerns about the lack of openness and account-ability in such practices.[11]

Tony Blair and other New Labour Ministers have been convinced ever since their time in Opposition that central Government can benefit from attracting into its sphere of activities senior business people who bring an extra dimension of private sector experience to public policy making. There was also a less explicit, but nonetheless vital,

agenda for Tony Blair who desperately wanted to create a more business-friendly image for New Labour both in Opposition and in Government. In one respect we can now see that he succeeded beyond his wildest dreams in doing this, but in the process he laid his party in Government open to the charge that the intimate dialogue with business people was deliberately excluding other legitimate partners in the process of government – e.g. Labour backbenchers. Even worse was the suspicion fanned by the media and often shared by the unreconstructed parts of the Labour Party that the mere possession of personal wealth and corporate power could put someone in line for an influential public appointment – e.g. Lord Haskins who was asked to advise the Prime Minister on the future of rural policy, or Lord Sainsbury and Lord Macdonald who were invited to join the Government as Ministers.

While it has to be admitted that many previous Governments of various parties have also had what appeared to be a similar fascination with business people, many thoughtful commentators considered that this growth of personal advisers, task forces and review groups had got out of hand and was not necessarily doing anything positive for the Government or its public reputation. In January 2000 the Neill Committee recommended that an agreed definition of a task force should be established and adhered to, a review should be conducted to establish the number of such bodies in existence and their status and longevity, and if any of them had been in existence for longer than two years, a decision should be made by the Cabinet Office in conjunction with the relevant sponsoring Department as to whether a given task force should be disbanded or reclassified as an advisory (permanent) non-departmental public body with duties to account formally and clearly to its sponsoring Department. In its *Response to the Sixth Report* in July 2000 the Government accepted the Committee's recommendations, so it is expected that things will change in this respect when a civil service statute is brought forward later in Tony Blair's second Administration.[12]

As for the continuing process of *civil service reform*, among the bolder or more controversial suggestions for future action contained in the modernisation White Paper were the undertaking to develop in a newly formed Civil Service Management Committee a more corporate approach which would ensure that the above-mentioned principles were translated into decisions on staff selection, appraisal, promotion, posting and pay; and the rather more diffident suggestion that via the auspices of the newly formed Centre for Management and Policy Studies there should be *joint* policy training and a programme of peer reviews for Ministers and officials 'to ensure Departments implement the principles of *Modernising Government*'.

In the past the modernisation of public administration has been a continuing task to which successive Governments have often paid little more than lip-service, because most Ministers regarded it as none of their business and many senior civil servants were bored by it. However, at the outset of the new century Tony Blair and his colleagues saw very clearly both the propaganda advantages of preaching the gospel of modernised government and the practical arguments for 'achieving joined up working between different parts of government and providing new, efficient and convenient ways for citizens and businesses to communicate with government and to receive [public] services'.[13]

Essentially, since 1997 this has boiled down to the development of a corporate Information Technology (IT) strategy for government which encourages all Departments and Agencies of government to see that their IT systems converge and interconnect, so that central Government itself can act as a credible champion of electronic commerce throughout the economy and so that the needs of citizens and businesses can be met by public services delivered 24 hours a day, seven days a week. Examples given in the 1999 White Paper were NHS Direct for telephone access to health advice, dedicated call centres for the Inland Revenue to provide improved services to taxpayers, and the National Grid for Learning which is destined to connect all schools to the Internet by 2002. The aim is to ensure that by 2002 more citizens will be able to interact electronically with Government for a number of useful purposes, such

as looking for work, getting information about benefits and submitting self-assessed tax returns, while within the same timescale businesses will be able electronically to make VAT returns, file required information at Companies House and receive payment (in good time) from government for goods and services supplied.

Ministers have acknowledged public concerns about the shortcomings which can arise in data protection and about the probability that many of these technological developments will exclude a considerable number of poor or elderly people who may find it difficult or impossible to connect directly with government. In general, there is a need to balance the case for more open and accessible government with the need for levels of personal data security sufficient to sustain public confidence that we are not moving irreversibly into the sort of dystopian society so ominously predicted by George Orwell and Aldous Huxley many years ago.[14]

There is no doubt that the prospect of electronic government, like electronic commerce, is widely regarded by nearly everyone from Tony Blair downwards as the wave of the future. Certainly this area of governmental modernisation has provided many opportunities for Ministers to indulge their fondness for official targetry: for example, the Prime Minister announced in 1997 that by 2002 25 per cent of dealings with Government should be capable of being done by the public electronically and this target has been included in the Public Service Agreements of individual Departments. After that, with exceptions allowed for 'processes that for operational or policy reasons are incapable of delivery electronically or for which it is genuinely unlikely that there will be demand', it is intended that the equivalent targets should be raised to 50 per cent by 2005 and 100 per cent by 2008.[15]

This is yet another area of modernisation policy under New Labour in which we are told in ringing terms that 'vision must be turned into reality'.[16] Yet Ministers and civil servants admit that there are certain organisational implications which are likely to have significant effects upon the ways in which government is delivered and perceived. On the delivery side, nearly everything involves the clustering of related government functions, stronger central coordination, and progress against targets set and monitored by key people at the centre of government, such as Andrew Pinder, the current e-envoy. On the perception side, the assumption is that the general public will be consulted and asked for its views on the process much more frequently and systematically than in the past when we had more traditional government procedures. This raises important political questions about *who* will be consulted, *how* they will be consulted and *what* the whole procedure may actually mean if conducted by a Government which often seems more interested in its own managerial and promotional objectives than in genuine public participation in the policy and decision-making process.

Two critiques of modernisation

On one level it is hard for anyone seriously to object to the idea of modernisation in a rapidly changing world and it would be equally hard to maintain that the process of modernisation should stop short of the sphere of central Government when it is unavoidably affecting the rest of the public sector, the private sector and the voluntary sector. Thus the *stated objectives* of New Labour modernisation in the sphere of central Government cannot really be criticised; but the *techniques* can and have been the subject of criticism predictably from Opposition politicians and, less predictably, from dispassionate commentators and academic experts who are not motivated by party political considerations. For example, there has been considerable media criticism of the so-called Strategic Communications Unit in 10 Downing Street which for a time was run in a very aggressive way by the Prime Minister's influential Press Secretary Alastair Campbell.

To summarise and deal with the party political criticism first, we can say that the Conservative Opposition resents (but secretly may well admire) the professionalism and ruthlessness shown by New Labour in its ability seemingly to exploit for its own party political advantage every opportunity provided by being in office – whether via the extensive use of 'spin doctors', the more than doubling in the number of 'special advisers', or the cynical and repeated announcements of the same extra public spending by the simple device of repackaging the extra money each time. Conservatives and others (including the former Speaker, Betty Boothroyd) have also deplored the growing tendency for New Labour – and Tony Blair in particular – to by-pass and downgrade the House of Commons by making public announcements of policy at other gatherings or leaking policy initiatives to selected media journalists. It was for this reason that in opening a full-scale debate on Parliament and the Executive in the House of Commons on 13th July 2000, William Hague, then Leader of the Opposition, argued that 'Parliament's powers in relation to the Executive have been declining for a century and have done so under Governments of all political persuasions, *but this Labour Government has rapidly accelerated that process*'.[17]

This was, in fact, a measured criticism of the Government's 'modernisation' policy, because while implicitly recognising that the present Labour Government has not behaved in an unprecedented way when compared with its Conservative predecessors, Mr Hague nevertheless drew attention to the *extent* to which the Blair Administration (largely under the guise of modernisation) has gone further and faster than any of its predecessors towards the centralisation and the manipulation of executive power for party political advantage. For example, the Thatcher and Major Administrations may have instructed Treasury civil servants to cost Labour spending commitments in the run-up to the 1987 and 1992 General Elections, but the first Blair Administration took the blurring of governmental and party political interests a significant stage further by publishing a series of *Annual Reports* on the Government's progress towards its stated objectives – documents which were drafted by civil servants, promoted by Alastair Campbell and other 'spin doctors' and produced at the tax-payers' expense.[18] It was pointed out by some journalists and others that this markedly *corporate* approach to government, in which Tony Blair and his Ministers consciously mimicked the practices of large firms in the corporate sector, did not even have the saving grace of being subjected to a genuinely independent audit – e.g. by the National Audit Office – in order to certify whether or not the claims made in the documents were 'fair and true'. The only assurance of impartiality offered to the public was that senior civil servants rather than party officials were said to have drafted and checked the documents. Yet in an age when many worry about the politicisation of the senior civil service (under Governments of different parties), this was no great comfort and the elasticity of the modernisation policy made it suspect in the eyes of those who believe that the spirit of Britain's uncodified constitution was under threat.

Turning to some of the academic criticism of New Labour's 'modernisation' strategy, it is worth noting the observations of Professor Norman Fairclough who has made some cogent points about the *language* of the Blair Administration and what it signifies, whether in transparent or coded terms.[19] Drawing upon the work of Anthony Barnett and others, Professor Fairclough characterised Tony Blair's modernisation policy as 'corporate populism' and he used quotations of the Prime Minister's own words (notably in the first Government Annual Report in 1998) to substantiate his argument. He traced the influence upon Government policy of New Labour-sympathising think tanks, such as Demos and the Institute for Public Policy Research (IPPR), and showed how the dominant notions of 'modernisation', 'partnership' and 'governance' all had a similar pedigree and might have been imported into the language and the practice of the Government via a network of sympathetic advisers, many of whom worked in the Policy Unit at 10 Downing Street. His key point was that 'despite a discourse and rhetoric of government, which often represents the processes of government as political and dialogical [*sic*], the processes are in fact overwhelmingly managerial and promotional'.[20] In other words, an Administration which has claimed to be open, inclusive and responsive to public preferences (via electronic interaction, focus groups, private polling, etc.) has actually been very managerial in its approach to government and manipulative in its treatment of interest groups, the media and public opinion.

For there to be genuine dialogue between the Government and the people in New Labour's New Britain, Professor Fairclough suggested that five conditions needed to be met: (1) the people, rather than the Government's focus group coordinators, should decide when to exert themselves in the political process and when not to; (2) there should be equality of access and opportunity for those who wish to participate; (3) open disagreement should be allowed and differences of view frankly recognised; (4) there should be space for consensus to be reached and alliances to be formed; and (5) the various forms of public consultation and public participation should make a difference by leading to the adjustment of policy where that is desired by those consulted. These are, of course, pretty high hurdles for Philip Gould (the Prime Minister's private pollster) or anyone else working at the heart of the New Labour project to surmount; and it is perhaps ironic that if this were to be how things habitually worked out, Tony Blair and his closest colleagues would almost certainly encounter strongly matching criticism from all those who believe that government by focus group is a contradiction in terms to be avoided at nearly all costs. Taking the vivid example of the Government's campaign for welfare reform but applying the observation more generally, Professor Fairclough caustically concluded that 'it is very difficult [for the public] to engage in real dialogue with someone [Tony Blair] whose every word is strategically calculated'.[21]

As for the separate but related issue of excessive centralisation within what is already described as 'central Government' and in what has traditionally been the most centralised polity in the advanced world, the true picture is one of dynamic and fluctuating change, which means that the full constitutional implications cannot be finally determined. Yet we can still make a few unexceptionable comments. Firstly, since the British nation state began to accept increased responsibility for the conditions of life of all its citizens in the early years of the twentieth century, the role of the Treasury as a force for *economic centralisation* has grown and, though suffering occasional set-backs, has not been significantly diminished. Secondly, since the time of Sir Maurice Hankey as Cabinet Secretary in Lloyd George's Coalition Administration in the First World War, the role of the Cabinet Office has grown as a force for *bureaucratic centralisation* within Whitehall in its continuing efforts to impose coherence and efficiency upon the process of inter-departmental government in the United Kingdom. Thirdly, since the mid-1970s when Harold Wilson first established a Policy Unit at 10 Downing Street, the role of the Prime Minister's political staff has grown as a force for *political centralisation*, aided and abetted in recent times by the pervasive influence of the media which seem to insist upon treating politics in highly personalised terms with the result that politicians have become almost a branch of the entertainment industry. Thus there have been several different types of centralisation in the British political system, each developing on a different time-scale but all broadly moving in the same direction.

Under the first Blair Administration in the late 1990s, even with the advent of devolution which appeared to be a significant move in the direction of diffusing state power, it seemed that political responsibility for the key public services remained essentially with the party in Government at Westminster. Moreover, the second Blair Administration has gone out of its way to link its political fate with the successful delivery of improved public services and the British people still expect these services to be equally available to all at a comparable standard, regardless of where people live or the effect of particular initiatives at a more local level. Briefly stated, whatever the champions of devolution and the empowerment of local government may say, the centralisation of political responsibility for the key public services inevitably contributes to the further centralisation of political power. This has reinforced not only a long-term secular trend in British government, but also the natural inclinations of Tony Blair and his closest political colleagues who had adopted a centralising approach to create a new Labour Party and have since adopted a similar approach to create a New Britain.

Creating improved and inclusive public services

The goal of improving public services and making them equally available to all UK citizens on a comparable basis has been an important theme in the New Labour agenda to modernise Britain and one which has been sustained and intensified under two Blair Administrations since 1997. In principle, it is not particularly new or original, since all previous Governments since the Second World War have sought to achieve it in their own ways. Margaret Thatcher's second and third Administrations (but not her first) believed that privatisation was the route to improved public services. As things turned out, this Thatcherite belief always owed more to dogma than empirical research and before long it proved necessary to protect the interests of citizens and consumers by establishing new regulatory bodies, such as Oftel, Ofgas and the Rail Regulator. Moreover, experience in the United Kingdom since the mid-1980s seems to confirm that while the *provision* of public goods and services may best be effected by private sector organisations, the *responsibility* for seeing that they are provided, financed and regulated is best undertaken by Government, whether central or local, and by regulatory institutions created by Parliament.

John Major as Prime Minister threw his weight behind the so-called *Citizen's Charter* which he launched in July 1991 as the 'big idea' of his first Administration. This was intended to be a ten-year programme to improve standards and efficiency in all the public services and notably the core services, such as education, health, transport and policing, which it seemed difficult to imbue with the private sector values of competition and choice. To some extent the campaign was a misnomer, since it was more concerned to empower the 'consumers' of public services and hence encourage better public service management than to establish genuine citizen's rights. The Citizen's Charter soon spawned 40 other national charters – e.g. for patients or for parents – and subsequently over 10,000 local charters in the sphere of local government.

In the name of increased efficiency and improved public services, the second Major Administration pressed ahead with the ideas of contracting out, market testing and even privatising certain core public services – e.g. the administration of some low security prisons or support services in NHS hospitals – which understandably encountered strong resistance from public sector trade unions and, to a lesser extent, from the general public. In overall terms this slightly quixotic combination of central Government initiatives under John Major at least laid some longer-term foundations upon which the Blair Administration has chosen to build, albeit without strong commitment to further privatisation and giving little or no credit to its predecessor in office.

By the time that the new Labour Government produced its first Annual Report in July 1998, it was pretty clear that improving the public services was intended to be a large element in the Government's modernisation programme. At a superficial level this could be measured in the fourteen references to the 'm word' in the nine-page text of Tony Blair's introduction. In general terms, Mr Blair wrote that 'modernisation and fairness are the guiding aims of our strategy in the key policy areas', but more specifically he made it clear that 'our aim is to put more money into our public services in return for modernisation and reforms to improve the efficiency of public services and root out waste'.[22] This was a statement which neatly encapsulated the essence of New Labour's approach to improving the public services – with extra public expenditure as the investment and modernisation as the dividend.

As for the more detailed prescriptions contained in the Government's modernisation White Paper in March 1999, there were two chapters on public services, one which focused upon the need for the Government to be *responsive* and the other which put the emphasis upon *quality*. In the first case, the authors of the document conjured up 'a genuine partnership between those providing services and those using them' and stated flatly that 'we want public services that respond to users' needs and are not arranged for the provider's convenience'.[23] To begin with, this implied taking greater pains to listen to people's concerns, to involve the public more closely in decisions on how services are provided, to organise the services in ways which reflect the conditions and constraints of people's lives, and to make it easier to secure representation and redress when things go wrong. It involved catering more appropriately for the needs of different user groups – e.g. the elderly, the disabled and ethnic minorities – and generally setting more rigorous service standards for central Government which were supposed to take effect from 1st October 1999. It also involved the establishment of a new Small Business Service designed to assist this sector of the economy in a coherent and joined-up way right across the spectrum of government. It catalogued a number of examples of best practice in public service delivery and identified the principles common to all of them: partnership with other sectors, user participation, improved access to services for citizens and businesses, an accent upon experiment and innovation, the spread of best practice, and measurable outcomes in terms of, for example, improved health, better education and enhanced value for money overall.

The chapter on *'responsive public services'* contained some firm statements of intent about future action which included launching a second round of bids for money from the Invest to Save Budget, extending the Ombudsman's jurisdiction to cover an additional 158 public bodies, improving the management of the Government estate, and working to align the immensely varied and conflicting territorial boundaries of different public bodies. The chapter concluded with a list of targets for Government action to be achieved, in most cases, by a specified date – e.g. by the end of 2000 everyone should be able to telephone NHS Direct 24 hours a day, by the end of 2000 elderly people should benefit from joined up services and integrated planning in at least half of all local authorities, and by 2002 students of all ages should have access to the National Grid for Learning.

As for the Government's objective of achieving *high-quality public services*, the authors of the White Paper began with some self-criticism which included the recognition that 'the incentives to modernise have been weak' and cautioned that 'we must not assume that everything Government does has to be delivered by the public sector'.[24] It identified a number of levers for raising the standards of public services, notably the introduction of cross-cutting *Public Service Agreements* (PSAs) which set out in detail the improvements in quality which can be expected in return for the extra public expenditure made available to the Government's priority services under the periodic Comprehensive Spending Reviews. The undertaking was given that the priorities set out in the PSAs would be 'cascaded through the targets and measures which will be set for all public bodies in consultation with those who receive services' and that in setting targets and carrying out inspections, an appropriate balance would be struck 'between intervening where services were failing and giving successful organisations the freedom to manage'.[25]

These management mantras were all very worthy stuff, but it is hard to believe that they genuinely enthused more than a relatively small number of senior civil servants for whom the use and application of such language may be a perverse form of pleasure. Obviously, it is important for the sake of the eventual beneficiaries of the public services and the tax-payers who finance them that all effective means should be employed to improve the performance of the system, which is why the second Blair Administration has been keen to work closely with the Public Audit Forum comprising all the national audit agencies in order to encourage innovation and spread best practice. In the latter context, much emphasis has rightly been put upon public sector benchmarking and specifically a 'business excellence model' which by the spring of 1999 had been achieved by 65 per cent of central Government Agencies and 30 per cent of local authorities.

Under the heading of future action, the authors of the document insisted that the Government was committed to achieving 'continuous improvement in central government policy making *and service delivery*'.[26] These goals were to be achieved by taking appropriate action under five exhortatory headings all beginning with c: *'challenge'* to establish whether the policy was being delivered in the right way by the right people; *'compare'* to see whether actual performance matched the original

promises made and the best standards achieved elsewhere; *'consult'* in order to be responsive to the various needs of users, staff and other stakeholders; *'compete'* to remind all the contenders that only the best suppliers would be awarded the contracts to deliver public services; and *'collaborate'* to encourage everyone involved to 'work across organisational boundaries to deliver services that are shaped around user needs and policies and that take an holistic approach to cross-cutting problems'. It is hard to resist quoting these last words in full since, worthy and sincere as they undoubtedly are, one is inescapably reminded of lines which could have been flawlessly delivered by the fictional Permanent Secretary, Sir Humphrey Appleby, to the Minister for Administrative Affairs, James Hacker, in the TV satire *Yes Minister*.

Having offered this almost Maoist-style incantation on the principles of New Labour's approach to public sector management, the authors of the document under Sir Richard Wilson's tireless tutelage still had the energy and commitment to insist that 'improving the quality and efficiency of public services requires a new approach to the question of who should supply services', with the emphasis upon finding the 'best supplier' who might as easily come from the private sector or a public–private partnership as from the traditional public sector. While not prepared to go as far as the Conservatives had done with crude versions of competitive tendering, Labour Ministers averred that 'competition [to supply public services] will be considered seriously as an option in every case'.[27]

Other ways of raising the quality of public services which got a favourable mention before the authors of the document must have collapsed in a mood of moral exhaustion were the adoption by Government and its agencies of the various private sector quality management schemes – such as Charter Mark, Investors in People, ISO 9000 and the so-called Business Excellence Model – and the establishment of a Best Value Inspectorate Forum which would encourage closer cooperation between the various public sector Inspectorates.

If we briefly review the essential elements or stages in the present Government's policy for improvement of the public services, we can discern a pattern of linear development with various mutually supportive aspects which strengthen the chances of success. *Firstly*, there is the Government's determination to make appropriate enquiries at the outset of a policy-making process in an effort to ensure that any initiative is based upon empirical evidence – i.e. what the situation really is, what the people want or need, rather than simply an extension of what has previously been provided. *Secondly*, there is the willingness to assemble and allocate the necessary resources (financial and otherwise) to the policy objectives, but only if the Government is in some sense 'repaid' with a healthy dose of 'modernisation' by all those involved in providing the public services in the priority areas concerned.

Thirdly, there is the Government's strong commitment to higher standards and improved performance in all the public services, whether this is achieved by responding to what users and beneficiaries say they have a right to expect (as expressed by focus groups or in opinion poll findings) or by insisting upon political objectives set by Ministers themselves in party Manifestos or Ministerial speeches – e.g. single-focus gateways to work, one-stop shops for small businesses, or special action zones to improve failing schools. *Fourthly*, Ministers have realised that such performance standards will not be credible unless they insist upon the introduction of transparent and reasonably objective measurements of the progress made year by year and often over a longer period than a full Parliament. This explains much of the fashionable emphasis upon 'benchmarking'; it also explains Ministerial efforts to focus the attention of lobby groups, media and the general public on outcomes rather than simply resource inputs. *Fifthly*, there is considerable stress upon the importance of public audit and accountability – audit which is carried out, wherever possible, by independent institutions, such as the National Audit Office or the Public Audit Forum, and accountability which is either contractual, as with the Public Service Agreements binding upon Departments and Agencies, or political, as with the need to honour Manifesto pledges and answer questions in Parliament.

Finally, the Government has strongly pursued the important cross-cutting theme of *social inclusion*, which is primarily designed to ensure that the whole range of public services in the United Kingdom energetically tackle the problems of social exclusion. The latter is defined in official Cabinet Office terms as 'a short-hand term for what can happen when people of [geographical] areas suffer from a combination of linked problems, such as unemployment, poor skills, low incomes, poor housing, high crime, polluted environments, bad health and family breakdown'.[28] In order to give institutional momentum to this initiative, the Prime Minister set up the *Social Exclusion Unit* in December 1997 with a remit to produce 'joined up solutions to joined up problems'. The Unit, which is staffed by a mixture of high-flying civil servants and secondees from other Departments and Agencies, business and the voluntary sector, is part of the Cabinet Office, works closely with Ministers and the No. 10 Policy Unit and now reports directly to the Deputy Prime Minister. It draws extensively upon the best research, external expertise and practice in order to help the public sector bodies and other Agencies delivering public services to solve a wide range of intractable problems. During its first two years of operation it focused on five key challenges: truancy and school exclusion; rough sleeping; neighbourhood renewal; teenage pregnancy; and new opportunities for 16–18-year-olds not in education, training or employment. The Unit's remit covers only England, but it cooperates closely with Ministers and officials in the devolved Administrations in other parts of the United Kingdom who are represented in its network.

Tony Blair and his closest advisers have attached great importance to the catalytic work of the Social Exclusion Unit and have regarded such work as a vital part of policy modernisation and the improvement of public services. After a review of the Unit's activity in 1999, it was decided that its success in influencing Government policy and the delivery of public services for previously excluded groups justified an extension of its remit to the end of 2002 when it would be reviewed again. The Prime Minister set new priorities for the Unit as a result of the 1999 review. These were to develop and complete the National Strategy for Neighbourhood Renewal, to work closely with the Treasury and other Departments to ensure that the year 2000 Spending Review reflected the Government's high priority for tackling poverty and social exclusion, and enhanced the arrangements for monitoring the implementation of its earlier reports. Moreover, the need for full Ministerial involvement in this exercise was underlined by the Prime Minister's appointment of a network of Departmental Ministers, chaired by the Minister for the Cabinet Office (then Mo Mowlam), to chase progress across government and to act as a sounding board for the determination of future priorities.

In all these various ways the Labour Government has made considerable efforts to demonstrate its modernising credentials and to ride as long as possible the wave of media and public support on which it came to office in 1997. However, it became clear at the 2001 General Election that public enthusiasm for the 'Blair project' had become distinctly muted and that the re-elected Government was effectively put on notice to deliver in its second term of office many of the improvements which it had failed to deliver during its first term. Once again Tony Blair and his Ministerial colleagues were fortunate in having to face only a demoralised and discredited Conservative Opposition, a factor which contributed significantly to the electorate's willingness to give Labour a second chance. Yet in general terms the drive to modernise policy and administration in central Government has been entirely worthwhile, especially when it has delivered better outcomes than before; the commitment to reform and modernise the public services, which is an explicitly big idea for the second Blair Administration, may also bear fruit in the longer term, provided it can be adequately financed in the later years of the present Parliament and assuming that it does not raise public expectations to levels which cannot be satisfied.

Embedding human rights in all public functions

Senior members of the Blair Administration (and the late John Smith before them) long wanted to put more emphasis upon human rights as an integral part of Labour's programme to modernise the United Kingdom. Under the auspices of the *1998 Human Rights Act*, which has been in operation since October 2000, they have ensured that human rights considerations are reflected in the work of all organisations performing public functions. In adopting this approach, Ministers have been influenced by a number of political factors.

Firstly, their experience of Conservative Government from 1979 to 1997 made them distinctly wary of human rights abuses being perpetrated by what they saw as a dogmatic Government (especially under Margaret Thatcher) which often had a populist agenda that stigmatised and discriminated against unpopular minority groups – e.g. immigrants, homosexuals, asylum seekers, terrorists, criminals and certain trade unions. *Secondly*, during their long period in Opposition they fell under the influence of certain persuasive campaigning groups, such as the National Association for the Care and Resettlement of Offenders, Liberty and Charter 88, which had argued for a long time that Parliament and the judiciary seemed incapable of adequately protecting individual or group liberties and rights from interference or even elimination by a secretive and over-mighty Executive – exemplified by the Government's ban on trade union representation at GCHQ in 1984 or its ruthless use of so-called public interest immunity certificates in the arms to Iraq affair during the early 1990s.

Thirdly, they had been subjected to the cumulative influence of powerful intellectual arguments in favour of more explicit statutory protection for human rights in our own jurisdiction – arguments put forward by Lord Lester ever since the publication of his well-argued Fabian Society pamphlet in 1968, by Lord Scarman in the first of his Hamlyn Lectures in 1974, and by the Society of Labour Lawyers in 1996. *Fourthly*, they had observed the ways in which their Conservative predecessors in office had seemed to be opposed to the very idea of democracy and they were therefore all the more resolved to 'govern for the many and not the few'.[29] All of this explains why for New Labour in office it has not been a question of *whether* the Government should put more emphasis on human rights, but rather *how* this should best be done.

The 1997 Labour Manifesto, in a section entitled 'Real rights for citizens', was clear about the overall objective and the means which a Labour Government would adopt, at least in the first phase. It said: 'citizens should have statutory rights to enforce their human rights in the U.K. courts' and promised that 'we will by statute incorporate the European Convention on Human Rights (ECHR) into UK law to bring these rights home and allow our people access to them in their national courts'.[30] It was careful to add, however, that 'the incorporation of the European Convention will establish a floor, not a ceiling, for human rights', with the implication that Parliament would remain free to enhance those rights in areas where the Convention was silent or where human rights campaigners could persuade Ministers that it did not go far enough – e.g. on public rights of access to official information. This left open the big question as to whether the incorporation of the ECHR into UK statute law represents sufficient progress on human rights or whether the matter should be taken further (as the Liberal Democrats and many in the constitutionalist lobby would like) by establishing an independent Human Rights Commission and legislating for an entrenched Bill of Rights as part of a wider constitutional reform which might also involve the creation of an independent Supreme Court and perhaps even moves towards real separation of powers in a federal system of government.

The problems caused for successive British Governments by the fact that the United Kingdom has been a party to the ECHR have been mitigated by the fact that almost every Article is qualified to a greater or lesser extent by the case law which has developed over the years and by the specific derogations which are allowed under the Convention itself. For example, Article 11, which guarantees rights of peaceful assembly and trade union membership, allows restrictions for reasons of national security or public safety and puts members of the armed forces, the police and the civil service in special categories beyond

the reach of the Article. Even more salient for successive United Kingdom Governments has been the effect of Article 15 which allows member states, in cases of war or public emergency deemed threatening to the life of the nation, to derogate from some obligations of the Convention as long as the Council of Europe is kept fully informed of the exceptional measures taken. This led the Labour Government in 1974 to seek a derogation in respect of the maximum period of detention for suspected (IRA) terrorists under the Prevention of Terrorism legislation which had to be rushed through Parliament at that time and which a few years later in 1978 was accepted by the European Court of Human Rights.

On the other hand, in 1995 the Conservative Government was found by the Court to be in breach of Article 2 (the right to life, liberty and security of the person) after members of the SAS had been revealed by the media some years earlier to have killed suspected IRA terrorists in Gibraltar before the latter had been able to commit their intended terrorist outrage. In this case no derogation was available to the United Kingdom, because Article 15 only allows derogations from Article 2 for lawful acts of war and the action of the SAS was considered by the Court not to have satisfied that criterion. In the event, the United Kingdom Government was ordered by the Court to pay the applicants' costs, but not any damages. This decision was embarrassing for British Ministers at the time, but they resisted calls from backbenchers in Parliament to withdraw the United Kingdom from the ECHR jurisdiction. However, in the light of these events the Foreign Office did put forward some British proposals for further reform of the ECHR system, notably that the Court should take more account of the so-called 'margin of appreciation' which allows it to recognise and defer to the judgement of national authorities within a certain area of tolerance and therefore refrain from interfering with national actions which it concedes are within such a margin.[31]

Successive United Kingdom Governments have been affected in their policy and administration, and in the legislation which they put through both Houses of Parliament at Westminster, by opinions of the European Commission on Human Rights and rulings of the European Court on Human Rights. Whenever this has happened and the United Kingdom authorities have been found to be in breach of the European Convention, they have had to give effect to such opinions and rulings, often by changing the law in this country. Indeed, there has been to date a total of at least 50 occasions on which areas of British law have had to be changed for such reasons, including the closed shop in 1981, corporal punishment in 1982, telephone tapping in 1984, immigration rules in 1985 and discretionary life sentences in 1990. In other cases the British courts have chosen to take the ECHR into account in order to clarify ambiguities or fill in gaps in our common law – e.g. with reference to Article 7 of the Convention in *Waddington v. Miah* of 1974 which involved following those principles of the Convention which prohibit retroactive criminal law (in this case in relation to an aspect of UK immigration policy), or with reference to Article 10 in the notorious *Spycatcher* case of 1987 which raised issues on the extent to which it was proper for the British Government to limit freedom of expression.

In an interesting speech to a legal conference in Cambridge on 17th January 1998, Lord Irvine, the Lord Chancellor, explained that the Human Rights Bill (as it then was) had two particularly important and distinctive features. The first was in essence that 'it maximises the protection of human rights without trespassing upon Parliamentary sovereignty' and the second was that 'the Act should apply to *any* organisation charged with functions of a public nature'.[32] So far as government in the United Kingdom is concerned, this second point is undoubtedly one of the most distinctive and 'modernising' features of the legislation in that the need to take full account of the ECHR and the case law which has flowed from it has been extended not just to what Lord Irvine described as 'the obvious bodies' – such as the civil service, local authorities and the police, all of whose functions are of a public nature – but also to other bodies because *some* of their functions are of a public nature – e.g. the privatised Railtrack in respect of its safety responsibilities but not its commercial property

dealings. This reflected the fact that in the United Kingdom today there is a complex patchwork of bodies which carry out what are still recognisably public functions and this patchwork is not made up solely of traditional public sector bodies.

Thus under the 1998 Human Rights Act not only must every Government Bill and Statutory Instrument be 'ECHR proof' before the relevant Minister can sign it off and send it to either House of Parliament for scrutiny, but *all* bodies exercising executive functions of a public nature must exercise their powers in a way which is compatible with the Convention.[33] Provided they are directly affected, people or organisations who are aggrieved by any executive actions or acts of omission by bodies performing functions of a public nature are able to take such matters to court at any level and argue that their Convention rights have been infringed. This enables Convention rights to be applied from the outset in relation to the facts and background of a particular case and makes legal remedies available at a much earlier stage in the proceedings than was the case before the Act was passed, when plaintiffs had to exhaust all possibilities of a domestic legal remedy before taking their cases to Strasburg. In hearing such cases, British courts have to take account of relevant opinions of the European Commission on Human Rights and rulings of the Strasburg Court. However, under Article 10 they will also have to balance the protection of individual rights with a whole raft of limitations designed to safeguard the ability of national Governments to defend 'the interests of national security, territorial integrity or public safety' among a long list of other precautionary considerations. The appropriate remedy in such cases, as the authors of the 1997 White Paper put it, will depend 'both on the facts of the case and on a proper balance between the rights of the individual and the public interest'.[34]

Even allowing for the full range of 'public interest' tests which the British judiciary may well apply to cases brought before them under the 1998 Human Rights Act, it seems pretty certain that this new form of human rights jurisprudence will give everyone exercising 'public authority' cause to check very carefully that they are following correct procedures and taking executive decisions of substance which are compatible with the human rights that have been 'brought home' under the Act. The longer-term effect of the legislation upon the sphere of government and governance in general is also likely to be significant in that it may foster what has been described as 'a positive human rights culture' which has hitherto been largely absent from English public administration and legal traditions.

Through a careful combination of the duty placed upon Ministers to ensure that legislation which they introduce and administrative decisions which they make (or are made in their name by civil servants) are compatible with the terms of the Convention, and the opportunity for the higher courts to make a declaration of incompatibility where they believe that a legislative provision or an executive decision is incompatible with the Convention, Lord Irvine argued that the Human Rights Bill would make 'a significant contribution towards the creation of a culture of respect for human rights at the heart of our democracy'.[35]

Finally, it is worth noting that these effects are not confined to England, since under the devolution arrangements the Scottish Executive will have no right to make subordinate legislation or to take executive action which is incompatible with the Convention. If it did, its actions could be overridden by the Scottish courts invoking European Convention rights. Indeed, the Act will bite harder in Scotland and Northern Ireland than in England and Wales, since the Scottish and Northern Irish Executives are responsible to subordinate legislatures in the United Kingdom, whereas the Government of England and Wales (essentially the UK Government for all practical purposes) cannot have its executive actions or its primary legislation struck out by the courts on human rights or any other grounds, because the hallowed principle of Parliamentary supremacy will only permit a 'declaration of incompatibility' by the Law Lords if an aspect of legislation or a Ministerial decision is held to be inconsistent with the European Convention.

It seems likely that the 1998 Human Rights Act will make one of its greatest contributions to the emerging positive rights culture in the United Kingdom by injecting respect for European Convention rights into the very bloodstream of public administration and public functions in this country. However, its success will also have to be measured by the number of occasions on which it proves *unnecessary* for anyone to feel so aggrieved about a threat to his human rights as to initiate legal action based upon the statutorily guaranteed opportunities now available to everyone in the United Kingdom. Yet this is always a difficult evaluation to make, because it is impossible to prove a counter-factual proposition.

Inter-governmental relations in the United Kingdom

The policy of devolution has been regarded by successive Blair Administrations as a 'modernising' response to the issues of nationalism and national identity within the United Kingdom. It can also be applied to the English regions if there is sufficient demand for it and the hurdles placed in its path can be overcome. Whatever may be the longer-term consequences of 'devolution all round', the asymmetrical devolution already achieved has given rise to potential problems of inter-governmental relations between the UK Government and each of the Executives in Scotland, Wales and Northern Ireland.

The general effect of the devolution arrangements is gradually to transform the United Kingdom from a unitary to a union state. This means, in the words of Richard Cornes, that 'much of what is currently internalised within Whitehall consultative processes will be externalised in inter-governmental processes post-devolution'.[36] However, in making this shift to inter-governmentalism, Ministers and officials in London are embarking upon new arrangements which are in many ways typically British in that the mechanisms proposed are intended to be essentially informal, *ad hoc*, cooperative and conciliatory. To borrow another phrase from Richard Cornes, they are 'for the most part sub-constitutional'.[37]

The definitive document, which set the tone for

this whole exercise in inter-governmentalism within the United Kingdom, was the *Memorandum of Understanding* between the UK Government and the variously named 'governments' of Scotland, Wales and Northern Ireland.[38] This Memorandum represented the keystone of the new structure, which includes a range of supplementary agreements and concordats and provides for further subordinate concordats between the relevant Whitehall Departments and the various Executive Administrations. Right at the outset, the authors of the document made clear their approach towards this potentially difficult range of relationships. 'This memorandum is a statement of political intent', it said, 'and should not be interpreted as a binding agreement; it does not create legal obligations between the parties; and it is intended to be binding in honour only'.[39] The legal framework for all aspects and consequences of devolution has been provided in the primary legislation. Any legal disputes between the UK Government and any of the devolved Administrations will ultimately have to be resolved by the Judicial Committee of the Privy Council, but the clear intention has been to keep these matters out of court.

On one interpretation, the policy of informal cooperation between the four different Administrations could be characterised as Whitehall and Westminster keeping their iron fists sheathed in velvet gloves, since under the devolution legislation the UK Parliament retains the authority to legislate on any issue, whether devolved or not, and since the three Administrations in Edinburgh, Cardiff and Belfast are all in their various ways *subordinate* partners in their relations with Whitehall. On another interpretation, the political logic and dynamics of the devolution process may be moving towards *more equal* inter-governmental relationships within what could become a *quasi-federal* United Kingdom in which the Government at the Union level and the 'Governments' at the sub-Union level exercise coordinate and concurrent powers.

The intended arrangements for inter-governmental relations will be subjected to conflicting pressures – on the one hand, for the exercise of greater autonomy by the Administrations in Edinburgh, Cardiff and Belfast and, on the other,

for broad conformity of administrative action induced by unitary traditions, financial arrangements, national media influences and persistent public expectations of fair treatment for all citizens in all parts of the United Kingdom. Only time will tell in which direction the pressure of events will push inter-governmental relations within a devolved United Kingdom. The single certainty seems to be that there will be no going back to the *status quo ante* when this country was a completely unitary state.

Essentially, Lord Irvine and the other prime movers of devolution policy within the first Blair Administration sought to create some new and very British *conventions* which would strongly influence the ways in which devolution worked in practice and, more particularly, the ways in which the four Administrations in the United Kingdom would relate to one another. Firstly, it was assumed that the UK Government would 'proceed in accordance with the convention that the U.K. Parliament would not *normally* legislate with regard to devolved matters, except with the agreement of the devolved legislature'.[40] This was a powerful example of the principle of *self-denying ordinance* which underlay much of the devolution settlement and which was supposed to be observed by both the UK Government and its devolved counterparts. The parity of obligation was not exact, however, in that the devolved legislatures were entitled to debate non-devolved matters, but the devolved Executives would *encourage* their respective Legislatures to bear in mind the responsibility of the UK Parliament in these matters.

Secondly, it was confidently declared in the *Memorandum of Understanding* that 'all four Administrations are committed to the principle of good communication with each other and especially where one Administration's work may have some bearing upon the responsibilities of another Administration'.[41] In this context it was strongly suggested that any of the four separate Administrations should warn the others as soon as practicable of any forthcoming issues which might prove significant; that each should give appropriate consideration to the views of the others; and that, where appropriate, provision should be made for developing joint policies where responsibility is shared under the terms of the primary legislation.

Thirdly, it was clearly established that 'all four Administrations want to work together, where appropriate, on matters of mutual interest' and that 'the Administrations recognise the importance of *cooperation* across a range of areas'.[42] In fact, this convention is likely to prove difficult to maintain over the longer term, because inter-governmental cooperation has not been exactly the hallmark of British governance over the years, notably in the relations between central and local government and especially when each of the main levels of government has been controlled by a different political party. Things may run fairly smoothly in the early stages of the devolution adventure, because the Labour Party forms the Government (or is at least the dominant Coalition partner) in three of the four Administrations. But one is bound to wonder whether all will be sweetness and light if the nationalist parties are elected into government in Edinburgh or the Conservatives are returned to power at Westminster.

Fourthly, the framers of the devolution settlement made it clear that they intended to establish a convention of *mutual consultation* which would allow each level of government in the United Kingdom to consult the others in a timely manner. Provided this was done, it would oblige the UK Government in particular to take fully into account the interests of the devolved Administrations on non-devolved matters – e.g. anything to do with Britain's international relations or negotiations within the European Union which are matters reserved exclusively to Whitehall and Westminster.

Fifthly, there was a strong will to establish methods of day-to-day working between the four Administrations which are based upon the full *participation* of each of them in the business of government. Thus it was declared that 'the U.K. Government and the devolved Administrations commit themselves, wherever possible, to conduct business through normal administrative channels, either at official or Ministerial level'.[43] However, there was also an understanding that this might not always be possible, which explains why the *Joint Ministerial Committee* (JMC) and its equivalent at official level were established to iron out any difficulties which might not be capable of solution at a more quotidian level.

Finally, there was the ticklish issue of the reserve powers available to the Secretaries of State for Scotland, Wales and Northern Ireland to intervene in devolved matters and to the UK Law Officers to refer questions of *vires* to the Judicial Committee of the Privy Council for final adjudication. Although Ministers are prepared to use such reserve powers if necessary, they see them very much as a matter of last resort. The preferred approach is one based upon *discussion* so as to avoid any action or omission by the devolved Administration having an adverse impact on non-devolved matters.

The reader should note that this is yet another asymmetrical proposition in that it postulates the alternatives of cooperative discussion or draconian intervention by the UK Government to remedy any abuse of power by one of the devolved Administrations, but is silent about the corollary that a devolved Government *should* have constitutional rights which it can invoke against any abuse of power by the UK Government in London. This makes it clear that, *at the outset at least*, there is nothing federal, or even quasi-federal, about the devolution arrangements as they are intended to work between the four parts of the United Kingdom. Such a constitutional re-balancing would only happen in due course, if at all, and then only as a result of shifting political relationships in what could become a dynamic and unstable constitutional settlement.

It is because of the widespread concerns that the process of devolution could lead to the disintegration of the United Kingdom that the first Blair Administration left nothing to chance in the sphere of inter-governmental relations. It did this by creating a cascade of administrative arrangements throughout Whitehall and linking central Government with each of the devolved Administrations in order to bind all four 'national' Administrations into the network of agreements and conventions which, it was hoped, would effectively constrain all varieties of nationalists and keep the 'four nations' together in perpetuity. The more idealistic proponents of devolution have claimed that the implementation of the policy has actually *strengthened* the integration of the United Kingdom against the centrifugal forces of Celtic nationalism. The more realistic proponents claim only that the policy was an expedient necessity to contain the forces of nationalism which might otherwise have come to rule the hearts and minds of the non-English minorities in the United Kingdom.

Civil servants working for the devolved Administrations remain part of a *unified* UK civil service under the Crown, and the management of the civil service is a reserved matter under the primary legislation on devolution. This means that all fundamental aspects of civil service management, such as recruitment, pay and conditions, senior appointments, ethical standards, etc., remain the responsibility of central Government and specifically of Sir Richard Wilson, as Head of the Home Civil Service, and the Cabinet Office which in May 1997 took over the responsibilities of the Office of Public Services. Admittedly, the First Ministers of the different devolved Executives have delegated responsibilities for managing their own civil servants, but only within the terms of the Civil Service Management Code and financially in a manner consistent with the UK Government's policies on public sector pay. Indeed, it is assumed that both the training and development needs of all civil servants and the goal of inter-administration mobility will be steered centrally by the Centre for Management and Policy Studies and by the Cabinet Office as additional ways of maintaining a cohesive and unified civil service.

Not only do these objectives link into the Labour Government's modernisation agenda, they also constitute some of the administrative ligatures intended to keep the United Kingdom bound together following devolution. Well-meaning and even pious reassurances may have been given to the effect that 'where the Cabinet Office proposes major changes to the framework for the management of the Home Civil Service . . . this will be done, wherever possible, by mutual agreement' (with the devolved Administrations) and that 'all informal dispute resolution procedures will be exhausted in seeking to reach agreement' –

presumably before the big guys in Whitehall get heavy with their lesser counterparts in Edinburgh, Cardiff and Belfast.[44] Yet the real power and control in this vital administrative area is supposed to remain with the mandarins in Whitehall and notably in the Cabinet Office, so this is simply one more example of New Labour's tendency to let go with one hand and hold on with the other. The logic of devolution is to let go of at least some centralised governmental power, but the logic of central Government modernisation is to hold onto it in order to achieve the main policy objectives.

Keeping the fiscal strings attached

Regardless of whether or not these elaborate inter-governmental arrangements will ensure high levels of well-intentioned cooperation between the UK Government and the three devolved Administrations, we can definitely agree with the view of Robert Hazell and Richard Cornes that 'what is different about the British model of devolution [as compared with other countries] is the extent to which the centre will retain financial control'.[45] Even a cursory look at the UK financial arrangements for Scotland, Wales and Northern Ireland reveals the extent to which each of these parts of the country depends upon British (largely English) tax-payers for the public expenditure which is disproportionately allocated to them to take account of their *traditional* relative economic deprivation *vis-à-vis* England as a whole.

The fact that recent figures suggest that Scotland is the third richest 'region' in the United Kingdom in terms of GDP per head (after London and the South-East, followed by East Anglia) adds an ironic twist to the uncomfortable reality that it continues to enjoy the most favourable differential between the share of UK public expenditure which it receives and its traditionally calculated 'needs', while Wales is probably still the poorest 'region' in the UK and Northern Ireland is the most economically dependent upon external sources of financial support. As Hazell and Cornes have pointed out, fiscal transfers and economic dependency on this scale raise serious questions about the degree of autonomy which the devolved Administrations will be able to exercise and real concerns about their lack of fiscal accountability to their own electors. Certainly such marked financial imbalances between a largely 'donor' UK Government and largely 'recipient' devolved Administrations are bound to make for unequal relationships and to cause continuing difficulties and resentments between the various centres of political power within the United Kingdom.

It is almost certainly not a good basis for healthy relations between the UK Government and the devolved Administrations to have a situation in which such a significant part of GDP in Scotland, Wales and Northern Ireland is accounted for by fiscal transfers from London.[46] It is not good for self-respecting emergent 'nations' because it locks them into an anachronistic dependency culture; and it is not good for evolving attitudes in England where there is simmering resentment especially towards the Scots who seem to be milking the English financially and benefiting from disproportionate representation in the House of Commons.

The authors of the *Spending Review 2000* may have trumpeted the fact that 'the devolved Administrations have freedom to make their own spending decisions within the overall totals [allowed by the Treasury] on functions under their control in response to local priorities',[47] yet this 'freedom' amounts to less scope for fiscal autonomy than is currently available to any level of English local government, even after a long period of emasculation at the hands of the Thatcher and Major Administrations from 1979 to 1997. The reasons for this are, firstly, that any changes in the budgets of devolved Administrations have long been linked (by the 1974 Barnett formula) to changes in the spending plans of UK government Departments, thus giving Scotland, Wales and Northern Ireland a population-based share of planned changes in comparable spending in England, and, secondly, that the devolved Administrations have scarcely any tax-raising powers, hypothecated revenues or pre-emptively allocated customs duties – as was the case with English local government before 1928. The sole exception is the power of the Scottish Parliament to vary the standard rate of income tax paid by people in Scotland by up to 3 pence in the pound either way, this it has been estimated, could raise up to about £500 million extra for Scottish public services – hardly a shining example of serious fiscal autonomy.

The truth is that neither the Treasury at the heart of the UK Government nor the English-dominated House of Commons at the heart of our Parliamentary system is keen to share serious amounts of real financial power with any sub-ordinate institutions in the United Kingdom. Indeed, they find it hard enough to share power with the supra-national institutions in Brussels, to which portions of this country's much vaunted fiscal sovereignty have been transferred under the aegis of the 1972 European Communities Act and subsequent European legislation, without having to contemplate doing the same with sub-national institutions in the United Kingdom.

Since the Labour Government has chosen to retain the traditional, highly centralised fiscal mechanisms in a post-devolutionary United Kingdom, the political pressures are likely to increase for a long overdue reform of the Barnett formula. On the one hand, the devolved Administrations and the locally elected politicians to whom they are answerable will press for a larger measure of real autonomy in relation to both taxation and expenditure (witness the dispute between Labour and the Liberal Democrats in the Scottish Parliament on the sensitive issue of student tuition fees in Scotland). On the other hand, representatives of the English regions, both those which feel themselves to be relatively disadvantaged in terms of public expenditure to meet their social needs and those which resent having to pay high levels of taxation to support Scotland, Wales and Northern Ireland, will press for an up-to-date and transparent needs assessment covering the whole country on fair and equal terms *and* probably for the claimant regions/nations to pay more towards the cost of their own support. Yet the logic of granting a larger degree of fiscal autonomy to the devolved Executives and Assemblies was almost entirely ruled out by those who determined the 'devolution settlement', just as the sensible proposal for local income tax was ruled out by the Labour Government in the 1970s in the wake of the Layfield Report into local government finance.

One suspects that these issues will claim a good deal of the time and attention of both officials and Ministers within the mechanisms of inter-governmental relations already described. They are likely to become more acute as time goes by, especially if the nationalist parties are elected into government at future elections to the devolved Assemblies, and the situation might also become harder to handle if the Conservatives were returned to power at Westminster on a Manifesto which gave greater prominence to English national interests. We are all familiar with the American revolutionary cry: 'no taxation without representation'. In a post-devolution United Kingdom we should pay equal heed to the corollary: 'no representation without adequate power to tax'. In these circumstances it seems that inter-governmental relations within the United Kingdom are not going to be plain sailing, no matter what smooth reassurances have emanated from Whitehall.

General reflections

We have seen in this chapter that the theme of *modernisation* can be stretched to cover a huge agenda of constitutional and institutional reform. Under the first Blair Administration this included everything from modernising the process of policy and administration in the sphere of central Government, to improving the delivery and quality of public services, to raising the levels of participation in politics and public life especially by previously under-represented groups. It has also been necessary to include other aspects of modernisation in government, such as the application of the *Human Rights Act 1998* to the whole range of public functions performed by central government agencies and others, and the emerging procedures and conventions involved in inter-governmental relations within the United Kingdom post-devolution.

This still leaves us with a genuinely sceptical question which needs to be answered: is New Labour's fondness for *modernisation* just a matter of 'spin' or is it a matter of substance? The most plausible and sensible answer must surely be that it is both. We also need to establish the balance between the two interpretations of modernisation and to understand the compelling *presentational* reasons why the concept has been stretched by Tony Blair and his closest colleagues almost to the point of absurdity.

One reason is that the concept of modernisation has been conveniently millenarian and has been relatively easy to link in the public mind with the matching ideas of New Labour, New Britain and New Millennium. This type of symbolic word association has been very evident in Tony Blair's speeches and his language in interviews both before and since New Labour came to power. It was supposed to reach its architectural apotheosis in the Millennium Dome at Greenwich, but the less said about that punctured symbol of political aspiration the better.

A second reason is that the political goal of modernisation is obviously less threatening – on the surface at any rate – than other more honest terminology for radical reform which might have been used by Ministers and spin doctors to describe the New Labour project. After all, in a world in which most people prefer to have modern gadgets which work than old gadgets which frequently break down, it is not surprising that Ministers and others have cloaked their institutional and other changes in the language of modernity in order not to disturb or alarm the great mass of 'middle England' upon whose votes the Blair Government depends for its re-election. The alternative might have been to speak in more traditionally radical and exhilarating terms – as Gladstone, Lloyd George and Margaret Thatcher all did at different times of institutional upheaval over the past 150 years – and in the process act as a recruiting officer for the Opposition.

A third reason is that the 'm word' can always be used in Ministerial speeches and other political announcements in neat contrast to 'the forces of conservatism' which is the phrase that has been used by Tony Blair (with mixed success, it must be said) in his efforts to discredit all the attitudes and institutional practices which the Government's institutional reforms are designed to address. The presentational logic in this case is quite simply that New Labour policies can be presented as being directed towards progressive goals with attractive connotations of novelty and modernity, while the Conservative alternatives can mostly be dismissed as old-fashioned and discredited. It must be added, however, that in a society as deeply conservative (small c) as Britain, this presentational task has proved to be quite challenging and has occasionally come unstuck, as when Tony Blair was 'given the bird' at the Women's Institute National Conference in the summer of 2000.

A fourth reason is that the clarion call of modernisation is perhaps a clever way of presenting the need for constitutional and institutional reform in a country, such as the United Kingdom, in which the institutions of representative government are characterised by their longevity and their reassuring familiarity in the minds of the public. Moreover, it provides an approach to institutional reform which does not fall into the familiar trap of the traditional Left–Right dichotomy in British politics – something which Tony Blair has striven particularly hard to avoid by speaking and writing repeatedly in terms of 'the Third Way' which, he asserts, is not simply a matter of triangulation between Old Labour and discredited Conservatism.

A final reason might be that the idea of modernisation seems very compatible with the spirit of the times at the dawn of the twenty-first century. We are very conscious, at least in the advanced post-industrial world, of living in an age which has become non-ideological in the traditional Left–Right sense of the term and which is becoming increasingly apolitical because of a diminishing public interest in the process of politics and everything party political. This is not to say that our age is devoid of political issues – far from it – but it is to say that these issues are now increasingly addressed and resolved by dialogue between the authorities and an ever growing network of pressure groups, media and non-governmental organisations. In such circumstances most of us (with the likely exceptions of the poorest and the oldest members of society) are positively influenced

by modernity and the apparent opportunities which it brings in its wake – and the political class seems to be as infected with this virus as many other sections of society. The 'm word' is therefore an important piece in the constitutional jigsaw of our times.

Questions for discussion

1   Is it legitimate to argue that the modernisation of either central or local government is tantamount to constitutional change in the United Kingdom?

2   How is it possible to reconcile the centralisation of central government with devolution to the nations and regions of the United Kingdom under successive Blair Administrations?

3   Describe the changing role(s) of the civil service at a time when partnership with the private and voluntary sectors is growing and high standards of efficiency, equity and probity need to be achieved.

Notes

1   See 'Reforming the constitution', *Political Quarterly*, Vol. 72, No. 1, January–March 2001, pp. 39–49, for a convenient summary of Labour's programme of constitutional reform in the 1997–2001 Parliament.

2   See *Modernising Government*, Cm 4310; HMSO, London, March 1999.

3   *Ibid*; p. 6.

4   *Ibid*; Chapter 6, para 1.

5   Briefly stated, these problems were that public services can be dominated by providers rather than users, parts of the public service can be left to fail for too long, too much priority can be given to levels of funding rather than actual outcomes, the system is too often risk averse, too little attention is paid to the best ways of meeting people's needs and especially to working across institutional boundaries, and public servants have been wrongly denigrated and demoralised by those who presume that the private sector is always best.

6   *Modernising Government*; Chapter 2, para 2.

7   *Ibid*; para 5.

8   *Wiring It up – Whitehall's Management of Cross-*

cutting Policies and Services, Report of the Performance and Innovation Unit; London, January 2000.

9 See *Spending Review 2000*, Cm 4807; HM Treasury, London, July 2000; Section V.

10 House of Lords *Hansard*, 22nd April 1999, Vol. 599, Col 174.

11 See *Sixth Report of the Committee on Standards in Public Life*, Cm 4557-I; London, January 2000; Chapter 10.

12 See *The Government Response to the Sixth Report of the Committe on Standards in Public Life*, Cm 4817; HMSO, London, July 2000; pp. 18–19.

13 *Modernising Government*; Chapter 5, para 5.

14 See George Orwell, *Nineteen Eighty-Four*; Penguin, London, 1954; and Aldous Huxley, *Brave New World*; Chatto & Windus, London, 1932.

15 *Modernising Government*; Chapter 5, para 16.

16 *Ibid*; para 20.

17 *Hansard*; 13th July 2000, Vol. 353, Col. 1088.

18 It is interesting that Tony Blair quietly announced an end to the practice of producing Annual Reports on the Government's activities immediately after his party's re-election in June 2001.

19 See N. Fairclough, *New Labour, New Language?*; Routledge, London, 2000; pp. 119–41.

20 *Ibid*; p. 124.

21 *Ibid*; p. 132.

22 See *1998 Government Annual Report*, Cm 3969; London, 1999; pp. 10–11.

23 *Modernising Government*; Chapter 3, para 1.

24 *Ibid*; Chapter 4, paras 2, 5.

25 *Ibid*; para 6.

26 *Ibid*; para 9; my italics.

27 *Ibid*; para 12.

28 See leaflet, *Social Exclusion*; Cabinet Office, London, July 2000.

29 See Labour Party Manifesto, *Britain Will Be Better with New Labour*; London, May 1997.

30 *Ibid*.

31 See DEP/3 3297, *European Court & Commission of Human Rights: Note on the Position of the British Government*; FCO, London, April 1996.

32 Speech to a conference on constitutional reform in the United Kingdom given at the Centre for Public Law, Cambridge University, 17th January 1998; my italics.

33 See *Rights Brought Home: the Human Rights Bill*, Cm 3782; HMSO, London, October 1997; para 2.2.

34 *Ibid*; para 2.6.

35 See the first Annual Constitution Unit Lecture given by Lord Irvine at Church House, Westminster, 8th December 1998.

36 See R. Hazell (ed.) *Constitutional Futures*; Oxford University Press, Oxford, 1999; p. 157.

37 *Ibid*; p. 158.

38 See *Memorandum of Understanding & Supplementary Agreements*, Cm 4806; HMSO, London, July 2000.

39 *Ibid*; para 2.

40 *Ibid*; para 13; my italics.

41 *Ibid*; para 4.

42 *Ibid*; para 7; my italics.

43 *Ibid*; para 24.

44 *Ibid*; para 15.

45 R. Hazell (ed.) *op. cit.*; p. 196.

46 Figures provided in the *Spending Review 2000* show that in 2000–1 the total financial transfer to Scotland was £15,047 million, to Wales £7,758 million and to Northern Ireland £5,306 million.

47 *Ibid*; para 21.1.

Further reading

Amy Baker, *Prime Ministers – the Rule Book*; Politico's, London, 2000.

Tony Blair, *New Britain: My Vision of a Young Century*; Fourth Estate, London, 1996.

Tony Blair, *The Third Way: New Politics for a New Century*; Fabian Society, London, 1998.

Jeremy Croft, *Whitehall and the Human Rights Act 1998*; Constitution Unit, London, 2000.

Mark Evans, 'Studying the new constitutionalism: bringing political science back in', *British Journal of Politics and International Relations*, Vol. 3, No. 3, October 2001.

Norman Fairclough, *New Labour, New Language?*; Routledge, London, 2000.

Robert Hazell (ed.) *Constitutional Futures*; Oxford University Press, Oxford, 1999.

Peter Hennessy, *The Hidden Wiring: Unearthing the British Constitution*; Indigo, London, 1996.

D. Kavanagh and A. Seldon, *The Powers behind the Prime Minister: the Hidden Influence of Number Ten*; HarperCollins, London, 1999.

Modernising Government, Cm 4310; HMSO, London, March 1999.

Johanne Poirier, *The Functions of Inter-governmental Agreements: Post-devolution Concordats in a Comparative Perspective*; Constitution Unit, London, 2001.

Reaching out: the Role of Central Government at Regional and Local Level, Performance and Innovation Unit, London, 2000.

F.F. Ridley and M. Rush (eds) 'U.K. 2000: modernisation in progress?', *Parliamentary Affairs*, Vol. 54, No. 2, April 2001.

Wiring It up – Whitehall's Management of Cross-cutting Policies and Services; Performance and Innovation Unit, London, 2000.

website for the Cabient Office: www.Cabinet-office.gov.uk

website for 10 Downing Street: www.number-10.gov.uk

Modernising local government

It is difficult to make a serious claim to institutional modernisation in this country without seeking to modernise local government, as successive national Governments of different political persuasions have sought to do. Indeed, the second Labour Administration led by Tony Blair seems to have given equal and parallel importance to the modernisation of government at both central and local level – with the principal difference between the two being that in a unitary state such as the United Kingdom, national Government can always ultimately impose reform upon local government via the constitutional mechanism of primary legislation at Westminster, whereas Ministers can often find it more difficult to impose reform upon their own Administration.

There is also an interesting link to the English question which we discussed in Chapter 6 in that it is difficult to modernise local government in this country without influencing the answer to the English question, while it is equally difficult to answer the English question without reforming the structures of local government in England. This connection underlines the high degree of interdependence between national and local government in the United Kingdom which has long been reflected in a *subordinate* rather than a coordinate role for the lower tiers.

The traditional constitutional position of local authorities in the United Kingdom was made clear in the Explanatory Note on the 1999 Local Government Bill in which it was pointed out that 'local authorities are statutory corporations and operate within a framework laid down by [Parliamentary] statute: they have no powers to act other than when they are expressly authorised by law to do so'.[1] Admittedly, this contingent and dependent role for local authorities has been modified by the introduction of a greater measure of executive autonomy under Section 2 of the *Local Government Act 2000* which empowers local authorities to act for the economic, social or environmental well-being of their communities, except where there are specific prohibitions, restrictions or conditions in other primary legislation – thus largely reversing the traditional position whereby they might only take initiatives in

those matters for which statute law had given them express statutory duties or permissive statutory powers. Whereas both the type and the balance of powers exercised by local authorities have recently been changed in meaningful ways, the structure of local government (especially in England) has not changed very much since the mid-1980s and still resembles a fragile mosaic.[2]

The mosaic of English local government

There are two structural issues for English local government which would be consequential upon the adoption of either model of regional government already discussed in Chapter 6. *The first* is whether anything should be done to restore the six former Metropolitan Counties (West Midlands, Merseyside, Greater Manchester, South Yorkshire, West Yorkshire, and Tyne and Wear) which were abolished by Parliament under the Thatcher Administration in 1984–85 and which, unlike Greater London, have not been resurrected by the Blair Administration. The effect of the Conservative reforms in the mid-1980s was to leave cities as large as Birmingham and Manchester as Metropolitan District Authorities theoretically on a par within their Metropolitan Counties with much smaller towns such as Sandwell and Salford. This situation has created some structural anomalies, yet there are few signs that anyone in authority wants to do anything about it.

What we have described in Chapter 6 as the orthodox model of regionalism may well not appeal to the political leaders of the great English cities who will probably feel resentful towards the elected leaders of new Regional Assemblies as and when such bodies begin to function as serious political entities – unless they can devise ways of ensuring that they themselves lead the Regional Assemblies. On the other hand, the London model of regional governance may appeal to them more, since civic pride and competitive instincts may well be stirred by the prospect of establishing directly elected mayoral authorities in Birmingham, Liverpool,

Manchester, Sheffield, Leeds and Newcastle along similar lines to the mayoral authority in London.

The second key structural issue is what to do about the 34 English Shire Counties. The reason for focusing upon this question is that while these proud and historic units of local government, traditionally connected with famous regiments and still associated with inspiring cathedrals and less inspiring county cricket clubs, were not actually abolished by the Major Administration when it sought to encourage the spread of unitary local government from 1992 to 1997, they were in many cases mutilated by the successful efforts of proud and growing towns and cities – such as Bristol, Plymouth, Hull, Swindon and Luton – to break free from the Counties in which they had felt 'imprisoned' and thus re-establish themselves as born-again County Boroughs or free-standing Cities untrammelled by the alien and interfering influence of artificial constructs such as Avon or Humberside.

As we noted in Chapter 6, the current prospects for the English Counties look rather bleak, since they are under pressure from above and below. Any systematic attempt to create a uniform layer of regional government in England – whether based upon orthodox regionalism, city regions or the London model – would tend to leave no distinctive role for the Counties and so they would probably lose most, if not all, their strategic functions to the new regional authorities; while any further move towards completely unitary local government at the sub-regional level (as has already taken place in Scotland and Wales) would probably see the 'people-focused' functions of the Counties taken completely on board by enlarged and more powerful District Authorities. On the other hand, the fate of the Shire Counties might not be so grim if the London model of regional governance were adopted by most, if not all, the largest provincial cities, since the boundaries of such new local government units would probably be co-terminous with the major English conurbations and this change could leave some Counties with a viable, albeit geographically truncated, role involving the delivery of strategic services, such as education, social services or structure planning, in the truly rural areas of England.

Many academics who have specialised in the study of local government have been justifiably critical of the centralising tendencies of the previous Conservative Administrations (1979–97) and indeed of the Labour Administration since 1997. For example, Professors George Jones and John Stewart promoted the term 'the new magistracy' to describe the growth of so many powerful quasi-autonomous non-governmental organisations (quangos) in the 1980s which did so much to emasculate and supplant the traditional role of local government.[3] Equally, Professor Ian Loveland is one of those who in the late 1990s mounted a powerful critique of Labour's initial failure in office to distribute real power to the people at local level (notwithstanding the significance of the devolution policy for Scotland and Wales) by failing to show its acceptance of the proposition that 'the government of England is a task that can appropriately be carried out at the sub-central level'.[4] In many ways such arguments serve to remind us that when we address the English question we should seek to answer it with ideas based upon a coherent and logical scheme for the modernisation *and up-grading* of English local government.

Reforming local authority practices

Chapters 2 to 5 dealt with the far-reaching changes involving asymmetrical devolution to the various non-English parts of the United Kingdom and Chapter 6 with some of the structural changes in English local government which are on the way to being realised. It is now appropriate to focus attention upon the reform of local authority practices which has been pursued since 1997 and has been presented by Ministers to the public as essential to Labour's modernisation agenda.

This section considers what has been happening to local authority governance *in England*, because in both Scotland and Wales the structure of governance is simpler as a result of the introduction of unitary local government by the Major Administration; Northern Ireland already had unitary local government as an inheritance from the earlier period of direct rule. Any future reform of local government in Scotland has been entrusted under the 1998 Scotland Act to the devolved Executive and Parliament in Edinburgh. However, changes to local authority governance in Wales will continue to be determined in the first instance by primary legislation passed at Westminster, although it will be for the Executive and National Assembly of Wales to *implement* the changes laid down by Westminster.

Within England, we have already described the arrangements inherited by the New Labour Government in 1997 as a fragile mosaic, but it could just as well have been dismissed as a dog's breakfast. Since English local authorities vary in population and resources from Kent, a County Council responsible for 1.3 million people and a budget of more than £1 billion in 2001–2 to Teesdale, a District Council in County Durham responsible for 24,000 people and gross expenditure of just under £7 million in 2001–2, it is little wonder that one of the main themes of Labour's local government reform has been the need to offer to local authorities and the people whom they serve a range of different options for local governance – albeit within an overall framework of prescriptive principles on which Ministers have insisted.[5]

The most senior Labour politicians have been convinced for some time that far-reaching reforms were needed to modernise local government. For Tony Blair the motivation stemmed from his impatience with some 'Old Labour practices' in local government, notably in those Labour-controlled Councils, such as Monklands in Scotland, where serious corruption had been exposed by the media in the early 1990s. When Labour was in Opposition at Westminster, this experience led Mr Blair to favour a new mayoral model of local governance backed by an elaborate structure of disciplinary arrangements inspired very largely by the stated views of the Nolan Committee on Standards in Public Life.[6] Once John Prescott got the bit between his teeth as Secretary of State for the Environment, Transport and the Regions (a huge Ministerial portfolio which he held from 1997 to 2001 and which included Ministerial responsibility for local government), you could not apparently get a cigarette paper between him and the Prime Minister over their respective personal commitments to the 'modernisation' of local government. For example, there were eight mentions of the 'm word' or one of its linguistic derivatives in the fifteen paragraphs of Mr Prescott's personal foreword to the 1998 White Paper on Local Government.

When the White Paper on *Modern Local Government* was published in 1998 it advanced some simple but powerful arguments in favour of extensive change. The main objectives were defined as follows: 'to achieve its potential, local government needs the right framework which encourages Councils themselves to reform and modernise' and 'such a framework should promote openness and accountability, provide incentives to Councils for improvement and innovation and produce effective community leadership'.[7] The authors of the document went on to indict all those aspects of local authority governance which stood in the way of achieving modern, efficient and responsive local government: e.g. the old-fashioned paternalism of too many Councillors and officials, the inward-looking culture which could open the door to corruption, and the failure of Councillors to reflect the full spectrum of the community they represented. All these things together have contributed to the lowest average turn-out in sub-national elections anywhere in the European Union. See *Box 7* for the key points in the 1998 White Paper.

These aspects of Labour's inheritance in local government were partly consequences of what was described as 'the old culture', but it was argued that the situation had been made worse by 'the old framework' within which local government still had to operate. These features were instanced as the nineteenth-century legal principles which still governed the ways in which Councils were supposed to work according to which too many decisions were still the responsibility of large and unwieldy committees and there was too much duplication of effort between such committees and the full Council; the distortion of Councillors' priorities, which meant they spent too much time at fruitless committee meetings and too little on representative work on behalf of their communities;

Box 7 Key points in the 1998 White Paper on *Modern Local Government*

- The introduction of Beacon Councils, when a local authority achieves validated excellence in the delivery of one or all of its public services, offering increased freedom and flexibility for such Councils
- The abolition of Compulsory Competitive Tendering and its replacement with a statutory duty on all local authorities to achieve Best Value in the delivery of public services
- The introduction of an obligation upon all local authorities (except Parish Councils) to reform their local governance by drawing a clearer distinction between executive Councillors involved in local government and representative Councillors involved in local representation
- The offer of three different models of local governance from which local authorities can choose: (1) directly elected executive Mayor with his Cabinet appointed from among local Councillors; (2) directly elected non-executive Mayor with a Chief Executive having delegated responsibility for strategic and administrative decisions; and (3) a Council Leader at the head of a local authority Cabinet composed of senior local Councillors
- The establishment of a new ethical framework for local government with new statutory Codes of Conduct for local Councillors and the establishment of the Standards Board for England to investigate allegations of unethical conduct
- The introduction of new discretionary powers for local authorities to promote the economic, social and environmental well-being of their localities for the benefit of the people who live and work in them

---

the weaknesses and anachronisms of the procedures for registration and voting at local elections and the almost total absence of adequate formal arrangements to test public opinion on issues of local importance between periodic local elections. Moreover, Ministers and officials were well aware of, but did not publicly admit, the fact that the shortcomings in public accountability had been exacerbated by local government's high dependence upon national Government for most of its funding and equally of the damage to public confidence caused by the disreputable personal conduct of certain Councillors and officials.

Although this diagnosis of local government's problems was long and serious, it studiously avoided addressing perhaps the two most important reasons for the parlous condition of local authority governance in the United Kingdom. *Firstly*, there was no explicit discussion of the problems of *legitimacy* in local government which, it could be argued, are caused by the lack of real autonomy for local government within the British political system – especially the absence of any real constitutional entrenchment for local government in a system based upon Parliamentary supremacy. *Secondly*, there was no proper discussion of the lack of *financial autonomy* for local government in England – something which, in recent decades at any rate, has been principally attributable to the low proportion (about 20 per cent on average) of total local government expenditure that is financed from sources of revenue over which local authorities have any significant political control.

When the first Thatcher Administration came to power in 1979, local authorities in England were able to finance on average more than half of their expenditure commitments from taxation raised locally which was broadly under their political control. The contrast with the position more than two decades later is most marked, since the council tax can still be capped by central Government (in spite of Labour's alleviation of the regime by ending 'crude and universal capping') and since local authorities are still denied control over the level of business rates in their areas. These facts are living proof, if such were needed, of continuing Treasury dominance in the relations between central and local government.

Having diagnosed the ills of local government, the authors of the White Paper were honest enough to recognise that the prescription – modernisation – was an immense task for everyone involved. Ministers have been strongly committed to the 'm word', but only on the understanding that the role of national Government is 'to support and motivate change, through legislation where necessary, working in partnership with local government and others including business and professional bodies'.[8] It must also be said that to a considerable extent Labour Ministers have been working with the grain of managerial changes already under way in local government and changes in opinion led by the Local Government Association (LGA) and other representative bodies. For example, Lord Hunt of Tanworth (a former Cabinet Secretary and more recently Chairman of the LGA) chaired a committee which produced a report in 1996 advocating, among other things, a new law to allow local Councils to reform their internal management – a proposal which the then Conservative Government accepted in principle but did not implement before it left office.[9]

The incoming Labour Government welcomed the willingness of those in local government to participate in the process of reform and at an early stage Ministers initiated regular so-called Central–Local Partnership Meetings chaired by the Deputy Prime Minister, John Prescott, at which good ideas and best practice could be shared. For symbolic reasons of solidarity with local government, they were also quick to sign the European Charter of Local Self-Government in 1997 and to secure its ratification by Parliament in 1998. This move was intended to be another signal of the value which Labour Ministers attached to healthy local government and a deliberate contrast with the perceived attitude of contempt for local government which had been attributed to many of their Conservative predecessors. In early 1998 the Government published a series of consultation papers on various aspects of its proposals for the modernisation of local government and these gave rise to an impressive number of formal responses to the DETR and 'hits' upon its website.[10] This evidence enabled Ministers to claim there was strong support for the Government's analysis of local government problems and the need for local government modernisation.

Thus there appeared to be broad agreement upon the goals of local government modernisation and Labour's apparently consensual approach went a long way towards allaying the suspicions of nearly everyone in local government, except perhaps the most recalcitrant Tories in some English County Councils. It was clear from the outset that progress with some of the reforms (e.g. the identification of so-called Beacon Councils) could be made without new legislation; some required pretty straightforward legislation to fulfil clear Labour Manifesto commitments (e.g. the abolition of Compulsory Competitive Tendering and the introduction of so-called Best Value in its place); and some would involve hastening slowly on a basis of broad consensus towards the constitutional reform of local government – an approach clearly visible in the arrangements made by Ministers in May 1999 to subject a *draft* Local Government (Organisation and Standards) Bill to detailed pre-legislative scrutiny at the hands of a Joint Select Committee drawn from the Lords and Commons.

Ministers made it clear that the role of national Government was to renew the overall framework within which local government had to operate and that the guiding principles of the new framework would be: (1) 'to give Councils all the opportunities they need to modernise, to promote the well-being of their communities and to guarantee quality local services'; and (2) 'to provide effective incentives for Councils to embrace the modernisation agenda'.[11] In fact, notwithstanding all the warm rhetoric about 'partnership', 'best practice' and 'modernisation', the Government's policy for reforming local authority practices has relied upon a familiar Whitehall combination of carrots and sticks. The carrots are in the form of tangible rewards for successful modernisation: for example, a rather vague promise of additional statutory powers for out-performing Councils and another of greater fiscal and financial benefits for those which achieve Beacon Council status or enter Local Public Service Agreements. The sticks, on the other hand, are in the shape of penalties for those which fail to modernise: notably, the penalty of direct central Government intervention when Local Education Authorities fail by a mile to achieve national education targets or when Social Services Departments are shown to have failed in their duties of care for vulnerable people.

The first reforming idea, which did not require new legislation, was the establishment of a scheme and a methodology for identifying so-called *Beacon Councils* in which either a particular service or the entire gamut of a local Council's activities set it apart as a centre of excellence and hence a shining example to all its counterparts. Such Beacon status, which would be awarded only after a rigorous assessment of performance by officials, auditors and an independent advisory panel, would be for a fixed period (perhaps three or five years) at the end of which the Council would have to re-apply if it wished to retain its privileged position. A Council with Beacon status for a particular service might be given, as a reward, more freedom to make extra capital investment in that service or enjoy eased controls in secondary legislation upon its methods of service delivery. A Council with overall Beacon status might be given not only greater discretion in its delivery of all public services, but also additional statutory powers and freedom from existing restrictions in order to give it greater scope to act for the benefit of the people in its locality.

The Beacon scheme was to be taken forward in two phases: the first non-statutory phase would focus upon identifying the best-performing Councils and then spreading such best practice gradually among the rest; the second statutory phase would allow Beacon Councils to test new freedoms and flexibilities prior to applying such procedures to local government more widely. The scheme was intended to apply to England only and any Welsh equivalent would be a matter for the Welsh Executive and Assembly. Officials at the DETR were careful to stress, however, that the scheme was only one item on the menu of ways in which Ministers intended to raise the game in local authorities. Other methods and incentives would include active partnerships with the Local Government Association and the newly established Local Government Improvement and Development Agency in order

to manage, motivate and facilitate change; the introduction of Best Value pilot schemes; and the application of the Local Government Improvement Model.[12]

The second stage in the first Blair Administration's policy of local government reform was embodied in the *1999 Local Government Act*. Looking back on it, we can already see that this legislation achieved two strategic purposes. Firstly, it abolished Compulsory Competitive Tendering (CCT), which had been a central plank of previous Conservative policy, and replaced it with a statutory duty on all local authorities to make arrangements for the achievement of *Best Value* in the performance of all their functions.[13] Secondly, it repealed the 'crude and universal' council tax capping procedures inherited from the Conservatives; it introduced instead what were described by Ministers as 'sophisticated and specific' reserve powers designed to be more flexible and less onerous upon local authorities. In particular, this part of the statute made provision for payments between different tiers of local government, so that any shortfall in council tax benefit due to one level of local government but arising from excessive increases in council tax levied by another level of local government would have to be made up by whichever one was originally responsible for the shortfall.

It seems that one of the factors which assisted the process of local government reform under the first Blair Administration is that during the second half of the Parliament the Chancellor, Gordon Brown, felt able to accede to the strong desire of John Prescott and other DETR Ministers for a generous public expenditure settlement for local government in England over the three-year period from 2001–2 to 2003–4.[14] It is not so much that these Treasury decisions were destined to affect the actual financial circumstances of local authorities during Labour's first term of office, but rather that they promised to serve as a lubricant for the implementation of Labour's legislative reforms of local government during the early years of the next Parliament. As well as this planned increase in revenue funding, there will also be a substantial boost in capital investment for local authorities, including a doubling of the contribution from private sector financial sources over the same three-year period.

Labour's argument has been that stability and predictability of funding can improve the planning and performance of statutory functions by local government. This policy has encouraged Ministers to work in partnership with the leaders of local authorities by extending the operation of Public Service Agreements (PSAs) to the provision of local services by local government. Pilot projects are being run in about 20 local authorities in 2001–2, before much wider application of local PSAs in subsequent years. The specific objectives set for local Councils in the Government's *Spending Review 2000* included overall improvements in cost effectiveness of at least 2 per cent per year and the achievement of 100 per cent capability in electronic service delivery by 2005. Significantly these objectives were linked to another target that by December 2002 every Council should have adopted and put into practice a new internal constitution which was transparent, accountable and efficient.[15]

The 1998 White Paper *Modern Local Government* had taken a studiously agnostic attitude towards the reform of political structures and boundaries for local government in England. The only objectives of this kind on which Ministers seemed to be agreed were, first, that Parish Councils should not really be affected by the drive for reformed local governance and, second, that local authorities should continue to make special provisions for a coordinated approach to the delivery of social services and to the representation of both church and parental interests on all local education committees. In general, the authors of the policy seemed content with the considerable diversity which characterised the political structures of local Councils and they even ventured a forecast that there would be greater diversity in future 'as Councils innovate and introduce new structures to meet the challenges they face'.[16] It was intended that Ministers would only use the power of statute to persuade Councillors to pursue structural reforms according to local preferences after meaningful consultations with local electorates, but the pages of detailed regulations and guidance from Whitehall rather belied those stated intentions.

New models of local governance

Ministers and others have for some time clearly recognised the shortcomings in what may be described as the traditional committee system of English local government. The weaknesses were pithily summarised in a White Paper entitled *Local Leadership, Local Choice*, in which it was said that the traditional committee system 'is inefficient, opaque and weakens local accountability'.[17] Despite the time and resources devoted to running the traditional committee system, the most important local decisions were invariably taken elsewhere by a few key individuals in the leadership of the ruling political group, often in a caucus meeting before the formal meetings of the statutory committees or the full Council. The result was that 'people lose confidence in their Council's decisions, individual Councillors become disillusioned with their ability to influence local decisions, and people are discouraged from standing for [local] election'.[18]

In the light of these views, which apparently reflected the result of extensive consultations, Ministers decided that the new models of local governance should be designed to achieve greater efficiency, transparency and public accountability, together with higher standards of personal conduct. The organising principles of the new structures of political management in local authorities would be essentially two: first, a clear separation of the executive and representative roles of local Councillors, with a small number of leading Councillors focusing upon the former and all the rest focusing upon the latter; and second, improved mechanisms of consultation and choice for people in the localities, no matter which of the different models of governance was chosen by a given local authority. These principles were embodied in the Bill which later became the *Local Government Act 2000* and now forms the current statutory framework for modernised local governance in England and Wales.

The establishment of a clearly separate Executive in each local authority (excluding Parish

Councils for *de minimis* reasons) was intended to ensure that decisions could be taken more quickly and efficiently than in the traditional committee system, the individuals responsible for decision making could be more readily identified by the local media and local electorate, and the decision makers could be held more satisfactorily to account by newly established overview and scrutiny committees of backbench Councillors acting more clearly on behalf of their local constituents.

This principle was a significant departure in English local governance which had been based upon the traditional committee system (part executive, part representative and generally all-party) since the local government reforms of the 1830s. Formal separation of the members of the political Executive (which governs the locality) and the other elected Councillors (who are left with exclusively representative functions) had not previously been recognised in statutes concerned with local government or, to any great extent, in the political conventions which had grown up in local government. There had been an important distinction in practice between the two faces of local authorities – the executive face and the representative face – but for a long time previously the former had been associated with local government *officials* and some leading Councillors and the latter with largely *non-executive Councillors*.

The menu of choice in the primary legislation offered three models of local governance, although Ministers were careful to point out that the Bill would provide them and their successors with statutory powers to propose *other* forms of local Executive at a later date if that was deemed appropriate in different political circumstances – for example, the special arrangements permitted for Councils with populations of under 85,000. However, this could happen only after approval for a change in local governance had been given by the general public in a particular locality in a local referendum triggered by the Secretary of State. It therefore suggested only a remote possibility of future institutional uncertainty once definitive choices had been made as a consequence of the *Local Government Act 2000*.

The *first model* proposed was that of a directly elected Mayor with a Cabinet selected from among the Councillors in the local authority concerned. Under this model the chief executive officer and the top echelon of senior officials would still be appointed by the Council as a whole in line with current practice. Yet before this model could be chosen, the public within the local authority area concerned would have to vote for it in a local referendum, which could be triggered by a petition of 5 per cent or more of the local electorate. This model of local governance resembles a corporate model of an executive Chairman of a public company in whom ultimate power and responsibility are concentrated, but flanked and supported by senior colleagues each with executive responsibility for a particular portfolio held at the Mayor's behest. In effect, this offered the most radical departure from traditional custom and practice in British local government and had been inspired in the minds of some Ministers by the model of directly elected Mayors in the United States.

The *second model* was that of a directly elected Mayor backed by a Chief Executive or Manager appointed by the full Council, with the Chief Executive having delegated responsibility for strategic policy and administrative decisions. Once again this model would require the prior approval of local people in a local referendum before it could be introduced. This model resembles a corporate model of a non-executive Chairman of a public company who guides and supervises a professional Chief Executive and senior executive officers. It is also analogous to the usual pattern of corporate governance in non-departmental public bodies. It may therefore be regarded as neither fish nor fowl and it may be hard for people to see the point of going through an organisational upheaval in a given locality simply to produce this model of local governance. It is also hard to see how awkward conflicts could be avoided between the political authority of the elected Mayor and the professional authority of the appointed Chief Executive, although arrangements along fairly similar lines are said to work all right in New Zealand.

The *third model* was that of a Council Leader at the head of a local authority Cabinet made up of other senior Councillors either appointed to their executive positions by the Leader or elected by the full Council (which in practice would probably mean the ruling political group). In this model the Leader would depend upon other members of the Council rather than the local electorate for his authority and between local elections such a Leader could always be replaced by his Council colleagues. The members of the Cabinet would take delegated executive decisions either as individual portfolio holders or collectively as a ruling group, while the professional Chief Executive of the Council and his most senior official colleagues would be appointed by the full Council as under the traditional system. This model offered the least radical departure from the traditional committee model of local governance and at the time of writing there is growing evidence that it is the preferred model in most local authorities.

In so far as Ministers expressed any preference for one of these three models at the outset of the policy, probably the clearest indication was given by the statement in the July 1998 White Paper that 'the benefits of these new structures are greater the more the executive role is separated [from the representative role] and the more direct the link between the Executive and the community it serves'.[19] The document suggested a Ministerial preference for the first model, although the civil service authors of the document were also careful to note a few lines later that 'such a figure may not be the right form of political leadership for every Council'.[20] This studied ambiguity in the drafting could perhaps be explained by the fact that Tony Blair was known to favour the somewhat 'presidential' model of a directly elected Mayor, whereas John Prescott and senior officials in his Department leaned towards the Leader and Cabinet model.

Realising that the greatest misgivings, even perhaps opposition, to any of the three models set out in the legislation were likely to come from Councillors themselves (and perhaps from Old Labour Councillors in particular), Ministers have been careful to argue all along that their reforms of local governance will provide new opportunities for all Councillors, whether or not they are able to play a prominent executive role in one of the new arrangements. The compensating idea is that every

reformed Council will also need to establish Overview and Scrutiny Committees made up of active backbench Councillors whose principal role will be 'to represent the people to the Council rather than to defend the Council to the people'.[21] Such committees could perhaps be seen as analogous to Select Committees in Parliament and thus provide an alternative career path for the majority of Councillors in all parties who either do not seek or are unsuitable for executive responsibilities.

The second main objective of the *Local Government Act 2000* was to establish a new ethical framework for local government. This exercise involved the introduction of statutory codes of conduct for Councillors, the principles of which were much influenced by the recommendations of the Nolan Committee, but which Ministers decided to surpass by insisting upon methods of investigation and discipline which were external to and independent of local government.[22] Thus the Act made it a requirement for every local authority to adopt a statutory code of behaviour covering its elected members and its officials and to create a permanent Standards Committee. Beyond that, provision was also made for the establishment of a new non-departmental public body, the Standards Board for England, which is to provide an independent process for investigating allegations of unethical conduct by Councillors, including any allegations that the code of conduct has been breached. These arrangements are more rigorous and elaborate than those which they replaced (derived from Section 83 of the Local Government Act 1972), although they removed the threat of a criminal offence under Section 94(2) of the same Act for failure by any Councillor to declare a pecuniary interest (if one exists) in a matter under discussion in Council.

The third main objective of this important piece of primary legislation was to give local authorities new discretionary powers to promote the economic, social and environmental well-being of their localities for the benefit of the people who live or work in them. These opportunities included statutory powers to develop community strategies *in partnership* with other bodies and interested parties, such as local businesses or voluntary groups. The effect of this part of the legislation has been to move from the traditional rule according to which local authorities had no power to act other than in those areas of activity in which Parliament had expressly authorised them to do so to a new rule according to which the scope for legitimate local authority action is broadened and the scope for legal challenge to what they do is narrowed. Ministers hope and believe that this change will serve the cause of modernisation by making all local authorities seem more relevant and attractive in the eyes of the public.

The emasculating effects of modernisation

In seeking to modernise local government, Ministers in the first Blair Administration were confident that the medicine of modernisation would prove equally restorative to local and central government alike. Specifically, they hoped that modernised local government would become revived local government in the sense that a wider range of better-quality people would seek election as Councillors and that the general public would show more interest in and commitment to the processes of local government by voting in greater numbers at local elections and taking advantage of the enhanced opportunities for public participation. It is too soon to tell whether or not Labour's reforms of local government have had such beneficial effects. We shall be able to form a fair and reliable judgement only after a decade or so of the new dispensation.

Certainly no dispassionate observer could deny that by the end of the Conservatives' eighteen years in office local government had fallen into an embattled and demoralised condition. This predicament could most obviously be measured in the haemorrhage of able people, both Councillors and officials, leaving local government; but it could also be measured in the dearth of able people coming into local government, especially at the elected level among younger or female or ethnic or disabled candidates.[23] Another indicator of deep malaise and apathy about local government was the low and still declining level of voter turn-out at local elections, which suggested that the electorate either did not like what they saw in local politics or had become completely indifferent to the ways and means of the politicians and officials involved or, conceivably, were largely satisfied.

While incoming Labour Ministers in May 1997 may well have thought that the causes of this unsatisfactory situation were varied and complicated, they were soon convinced that a more representative spread of candidates standing at local elections held more frequently would assist the cause of democratic legitimacy in local government and create a better chance that their modernising reforms would be successful. Or perhaps the proposition could be turned on its head by the argument that any of the new forms of governance in local authorities, which involved pinning power and responsibility more clearly upon a single politician or such a person and his chosen executive team, should improve the chances of raising levels of public interest and participation in local government.[24] Either way, it seemed that the path of modernisation was worth trying in local government, especially if it might have the effect of enhancing the vitality of local democracy in this country, which has been one of the principal stated aims of the Government's overall policy of constitutional reform.

Labour Ministers made clear their strong belief that the time had come to consider some innovations in electoral procedures designed to refurbish the democratic legitimacy of local authorities. To this end provisions were included in the *Local Government Act 2000* which gave the Secretary of State the power, by Order, to alter the frequency of elections to local authorities and the years in which such elections are held. The Act defined three different schemes of local elections which might be applied to principal Councils: (1) all-out elections with the whole Council being elected once every four years; (2) elections by halves with half the Councillors being elected every other year; and (3) elections by thirds with one-third of the Councillors being elected each year in three years out of four. The Government's preference was for the third option, not least because it was compatible with the previous habits of unitary Councils throughout England and all Metropolitan District Councils – but there was no specific commitment to this effect in the 2001 Labour Manifesto.

Looking further into the future, Ministers believe that the time has come to consider some more radical innovations in electoral procedures designed to encourage more people to register as local electors and then to vote in local elections, especially among the younger generation and the ethnic minorities. They therefore intend to put legislation before Parliament to enable local Councils to experiment in the ways in which local elections are conducted – e.g. via electronic voting, more extensive postal voting or voting between different hours and on different days (perhaps on Sundays, as happens on the Continent). It was also considered that so-called rolling registration, rather than registration of voters during one limited period at one time of year, would be worth taking forward and this is now beginning to happen.[25]

When it comes to the possible impact of the voting system upon election turn-out and political participation, Tony Blair's first Administration was cautious, preferring initially to hide behind the Jenkins Report on the Voting System published in October 1998 and later to say that it was 'unpersuaded' of the case for change, at any rate for elections to the House of Commons.[26] The Government's line on local government elections in England – apart from allowing a change to the supplementary vote for the mayoral election in London – has been to say that it does not regard changes to the system of local voting as a panacea for the weaknesses of local government and to add, rather defensively, that 'local government modernisation is more fundamental than simply changing how people cast their vote'.[27] In relation to the more general goal of increased public participation in the processes of local politics and decision making, Ministers have made it clear that they prefer to encourage Councils to practise what most of them now preach about the virtues of public consultation, if necessary by placing upon all public authorities a new statutory duty to consult and engage with their local communities and by providing legislative backing for the power available to Councils to hold local referenda.

The Jenkins Commission on the Voting System which reported in November 1998 had been confined by its terms of reference to elections for the Westminster Parliament. However, the Modern Local Government White Paper of July 1998 had made it clear that once the Commission had reported and the people had decided in a referendum which voting system they preferred, 'the Government will wish to assess the implications for local government'.[28] This was hardly a ringing endorsement of electoral reform for local government, still less for the introduction of the single transferable vote or any other form of proportional representation.

There is, in fact, a strong theoretical case for introducing some form of proportional representation into elections for local government and, indeed, this was put into practice in 1973 in the special circumstances of Northern Ireland once power sharing was recognised as a priority. Yet this case had not been recognised as a priority in the Consultation Paper *Modernising Local Government: Local Democracy and Community Leadership* published in February 1998 which downplayed the potential of PR as a means of revitalising local democracy and made it clear that 'reforms to the electoral, political and consultation arrangements . . . are of greater importance and urgency'.[29] So far the introduction of the supplementary vote (similar to the alternative vote) for the direct election of the Mayor of London in May 2000 has constituted the only gesture towards electoral reform in English local government, although it is possible that the extension of mayoral government to other metropolitan areas might lead to a similar electoral system being used in other parts of the country.

Two academic experts, Colin Rallings and Michael Thrasher, have documented what is already widely known, namely that many local Councils are demonstrably unrepresentative of their local electorate and this has had a debilitating and alienating effect upon public attitudes towards local democracy.[30] Parties know that they can never win local government seats in certain parts of the country under the existing first-past-the-post electoral system and the multiplier effects between the percentage of votes cast and the percentage of Council seats won by a particular party can be dramatic in both directions – i.e. disproportionately benefiting the locally dominant party and disproportionately penalising the locally weaker parties.[31]

Because local government is less obviously a matter of 'government' than central Government in our quasi-unitary state, the case for introducing a measure of proportional representation at the local level is all the stronger. It would certainly make a difference to the pattern of political control in many local authorities and might well produce many more 'hung Councils' or local Administrations based upon inter-party coalitions. The influential Local Government Association has begun to indicate cautious support for PR as a means of reviving political participation and possibly increasing voter turn-out at local elections. Yet any variant of electoral reform in local government will need to be made compatible with other changes in electoral arrangements, such as any extension of cascaded annual elections in local authorities, and any further use of the supplementary vote in mayoral elections could complicate the situation even more.

This chapter has shown the clear intention of Ministers in the second Blair Administration to revive English local government and public interest in it. Implementing this intention has involved creating a new legislative framework for local government, but one which takes full account of the Conservative legacy of 'tight financial control, legally constrained discretion and the recognition of the need for local Councils to work in partnership with a variety of locally based agencies'.[32] Thus in many cases local authorities have found themselves strongly nudged under successive Governments of different parties towards a reduced enabling role in their localities with a growing amount of the financing, regulation and provision of public services being done by other bodies. Labour Ministers may have given local Councils enhanced incentives to embrace the modernisation agenda – e.g. in the ideas of Beacon Councils and Local Public Service Agreements – and they may have persuaded local Councils to measure their delivery

of public services against demanding benchmarks, such as Best Value; but at the end of the day all these good intentions – and the warm Ministerial rhetoric about central Government's role being to monitor, motivate and manage the process of change 'in partnership' with local government – have scarcely transformed the realities of life in most local authorities.

Whether the occupant of 10 Downing Street is New Conservative (Margaret Thatcher) or New Labour (Tony Blair), the reality for local government has been emasculation, or something akin to it. The effects of the liberalisation and privatisation of public services under Margaret Thatcher were seriously to reduce the power and independence of all local authorities. Yet paradoxically the effects of modernisation under Tony Blair have been equally emasculating for local government, only in different ways. For example, Labour Ministers in Whitehall have frequently intervened to rescue failing schools or vulnerable children and elderly people in care from the negligence or depradations of weak or shambolic local authorities. The methodology of incentives for good performance and penalties for bad performance, as monitored and measured by a bewildering and increasing array of independent audit bodies and inspectorates, has seriously reduced the room for manoeuvre and the margin for discretionary action by all classes of local authority, so that they have become increasingly conformist agencies for the delivery of standard public services rather than the multi-functional representative bodies that they used to be. Above all, the second Blair Administration – like its Conservative predecessors – has steadfastly refused to give local authorities any significant degree of financial autonomy (in contradistinction to the token tax-varying powers given to the Scottish Parliament) and has even more steadfastly set its face against the enlightened idea of real guarantees for the constitutional position of local government in England and Wales (in marked contrast with the satisfactorily entrenched position of the *Länder* in Germany).

Moreover, it is not as if the spheres of local authority competence have been secure from central Government-inspired attack from other agencies of various kinds. Special purpose non-departmental public bodies (NDPBs), such as housing action trusts or education action zones, have been established or developed by the second Blair Administration to take over large slabs of previous local authority responsibilities. More than 300 review bodies or task forces have been established since May 1997 principally to allow ambitious and often naive business people to meddle in policy areas about which they know very little and for which local authorities often previously had entire or partial responsibility.[33] However, most controversially of all, private sector service companies have continued under the Blair Administration to enjoy the benefits of competing successfully against 'in-house' local government providers for lucrative contracts which previously would have been awarded without a moment's second thought to the relevant branch or directorate of the local authority.

In all these different ways the policy of 'modernisation' under New Labour has proved to be as emasculating for local government as liberalisation and privatisation were under Margaret Thatcher's regime. Truly it can be said that in this respect, as in many others, Blairism has been a continuation of Thatcherism by other means.

General reflections

The brief discussion in this chapter about the modernisation of local government and some of its more obvious implications still leaves us to wrestle with some important and interesting questions about the most appropriate balance to strike between local and national interests in the United Kingdom in the early twenty-first century. Those who champion the cause of local government in this country must begin by recognising the awkwardness of its predicament in what is probably one of the most unitary states in the European Union – notwithstanding the recent loosening of national ties both reflected in and caused by the recent developments of devolution to Scotland and Wales.

In the first place, after centuries of being treated merely as subjects, people in these islands (with the obvious exception of those in the Republic of Ireland) are now established as citizens of the United Kingdom and as such can enjoy the legal and constitutional rights which go with that citizenship. This degree of empowerment has led national political parties competing for office at every General Election to offer competing, and often escalating, programmes of public goods and services which they promise in their Manifestos to deliver if elected into power. This familiar political process creates and reinforces a drive for improved national standards, or at any rate the nearest practicable approximations, which produces a secular trend towards national uniformity rather than local diversity in what is provided for ordinary people. This tendency then fans public expectations or aspirations which encourages vote-maximising politicians to compete even harder with each other to offer quantitatively or qualitatively the best 'products' to the electorate both at election times and between elections as well.

In the working out of this dynamic political process there is a natural tendency for policy-induced differences between different localities to be reduced over time as people in relatively disadvantaged parts of the country succeed in their lobbying for measures to close the gaps. Thus if one local authority decides to give extra financial support to students via discretionary awards or to provide free or heavily subsidised care for its elderly residents in nursing homes, this disparity soon creates pressures upon other local authorities to do likewise until eventually there is a general public clamour for the relative advantage of one locality to be turned into an absolute entitlement for the entire country. Indeed, the process can sometimes be taken even further at the instigation of particularly determined and uncompromising lobby groups who may well campaign not just for equality of opportunities but for equality of outcomes.

The important point is that as a consequence of such developments local autonomy and local diversity are gradually squeezed out and may soon be on the way to complete elimination via the familiar mechanisms of policy convergence and financial redistribution leading eventually to national standardisation. The consequence of this is that local government, as the institutional expression of a given locality, is also squeezed and sooner or later is effectively downgraded into merely another agency for the delivery of standard national services.

The alternative thesis might be that people can be strongly committed to a real sense of local interest and identity and to the ideal of attractive diversity within a single polity. The leading examples of this point of view might be the citizens of the United States, Germany and Switzerland. Yet it is apparent that those who hold this position must eschew any idea of giving their top civic priority to the achievement of nation-wide individual rights and uniform national standards. Such people must accept with good grace real diversity both in the methods of delivery and in the distribution of public goods and services, or at the very least in the order of priorities established by different communities in different localities.

Two significant questions are raised in this scenario. *Firstly*, can or will the population of a given nation state accept differences of this kind for long or even at all, especially if politicians, interest groups and the media all make the general public aware of them? One suspects that the answer will be No unless the true facts remain shrouded in mystery and official obscurity, as has been largely the case with the operation of the Rate Support Grant as between different local authorities in England or indeed the so-called Barnett formula as between England as a whole and Scotland, Wales and Northern Ireland respectively.

Secondly and more fundamentally, is there any significant natural support in our British political culture for the degree of real diversity which would accompany or result from genuine local government in this country or would the only acceptable degree of diversity amount to little more than inessential window-dressing with second-order policies (e.g. policies on hunting, abortion or manifestations of local culture) that do not really affect fundamental distributional issues between different economic or social interests? Once again, one suspects that in the British context the answer is No, because of our long and relatively stable

history of national solidarity which was so notably exemplified during the Second World War.

In the end this line of argument leaves us with the ultimate question about local government in this or any other advanced society. To take England as our case in point, is local government really all about organising the optimum delivery of broadly uniform public goods and services? If this were so, then we could comfortably dispense with our aspirations to build local democracy and concentrate instead simply upon the efficiency of provision, the take-up of entitlements and the responsiveness of the system to its 'consumers'. Alternatively, is it really all about self-sufficiency and self-government at the level of recognisable local communities? If this were so, then it would be logical to repeal most of the Westminster legislation which guarantees national entitlements in each local government area and indeed the *Human Rights Act 1998* as well, so that we could concentrate instead upon enjoying our freedom to look after ourselves and to govern ourselves mainly, if not solely, within defined local communities with no obvious or excessive inter-ference from any outsiders.

Logically, this second broad option would imply not simply moves towards greater local autonomy within an essentially unitary state (as might be expected with further rolling devolution to different parts of England), but in due course the political determination to create meaningful local states within a new monarchical federation. And just in case any reader is feeling sanguine or relaxed about such a prospect, even the unlikely achieve-ment of this option would still leave big questions about the appropriate allocation of responsibilities between the different levels of governance and would almost certainly engender fierce debate about the extent of the rights and responsibilities to be accorded to the federal and state levels of the polity.

Questions for discussion

1   What is the likely constitutional significance of the various models of governance being promoted in English local government?

2 Does the process of local government reform in the various parts of the United Kingdom necessarily and invariably involve further centralisation in Whitehall and at Westminster?

3 In the context of this country's membership of the European Union is there a more rational model for sub-national government in the United Kingdom?

Notes

1 See Explanatory Note for the 1999 Local Government Bill, para 6.
2 In 1984 and 1985 the Thatcher Administration, when frustrated by Labour-led political resistance to its local government policies for the large conurbations, legislated to abolish the Greater London Council and the other Metropolitan County Councils in England.
3 See G. Jones and J. Stewart, *The Case for Local Government*; Allen & Unwin, London, 1983.
4 Ian Loveland, 'Local authorities', in R. Blackburn and R. Plant (eds) *Constitutional Reform*; Longman, London, 1999; p. 325.
5 See *Modern Local Government – in Touch with the People*, Cm 4014; HMSO, London, July 1998.
6 See in particular the Third Report of the Committee on Standards in Public Life, *Standards of Conduct in Local Government in England, Scotland & Wales*; Cm 3702, HMSO, London, July 1997.
7 *Modern Local Government*; para 1.3.
8 *Ibid*; para 2.2.
9 See the *Local Government Chronicle*, 8th November 1996.
10 The six consultation papers listed in para 2.8 of the White Paper were on: local democracy and community leadership; improving local services through best value; business rates; improving local financial accountability; capital finance; and a new ethical framework.
11 *Modern Local Government*; para 2.15.
12 The DETR Prospectus on the Beacon Council Scheme (available on the Internet) makes it clear that the main functions of the *Local Government Improvement and Development Agency* are: (1) to assist local authorities in England and Wales to improve their performance through mechanisms which support and promote innovation and modernisation; (2) to develop and encourage arrangements among local authorities for supporting peer group review, self-regulation and continuous improvement programmes; (3) to encourage and promote capacity building arrangements among local authorities which link training and development needs, exchange of good practice and access to assistance in improving service areas in general and particularly those at risk of difficulty or failure; (4) to stimulate the provision of appropriate training and development opportunities for Council members and all staff and to help ensure that the whole workforce can make a contribution to the achievement of improved performance; and (5) to commission and ensure the collection, validation and effective dissemination of best practice information in specific policy areas relevant to local government. The DETR website also made clear the four elements in the so-called *Local Government Improvement Model*, which is supposed to provide a framework for assessment of the achievements of a Council and its ability to change: (1) a specially developed benchmark of a fully effective and continuously improving Council; (2) an analysis of a Council's strengths and weaknesses to determine the gap; (3) help in formulating an improvement plan in order to address areas of concern and to begin to bridge the gap; and (4) practical support and advice on carrying through the improvements identified.
13 The official definition of *Best Value* is: 'securing continuous improvement in the exercise of all functions undertaken by the [local] authority, whether statutory or not, having regard to a combination of economy, efficiency and effectiveness'.
14 The *Spending Review 2000* actually allowed for an average real increase of 3.1 per cent a year (allowing for changes in responsibility for various services) in the Standard Spending Assessments for 2001–2, 2002–3 and 2003–4.
15 *Spending Review 2000*; Box 33.1.
16 *Modern Local Government*, para 3.3.
17 *Local Leadership, Local Choice*; HMSO, London, 1998; para 1.10.
18 *Ibid*; para 1.14.
19 *Modern Local Government*; para 3.26.
20 *Ibid*.
21 *Ibid*; para 3.42.
22 See *Standards of Conduct in Local Government*.
23 Figures provided in *Local Leadership, Local Choice* showed that, according to the 1997 Local Government Management Board national census of Councillors in England & Wales, only 3 per cent of Councillors were from ethnic minorities and only 11 per cent were disabled. As for turn-out at local elections, Great Britain came bottom in a league of European Union nations for average turn-out in sub-national elections with a figure of 40 per cent; in the May 1998 local elections in England the average

level of turn-out was even lower at about 33 per cent in London and lower still in other parts of the country where in certain wards it was only 10 per cent.

24 Disappointingly for those who have argued this case, the turn-out in London's mayoral election in May 2000 was lower than at the previous London Borough elections.

25 These issues are covered in more detail in Chapters 13 and 14 below.

26 See *Report of the Independent Commission on the Voting System*, Cm 4090–1; HMSO, London, October 1998.

27 *Modern Local Government*; para 4.26.

28 *Ibid*; para 4.27.

29 See *Modernising Local Government: Local Democracy and Community Leadership*; HMSO, London, February 1998; para 3.47.

30 See Colin Rallings and Michael Thrasher, *Local Elections in Britain*; Routledge, London, 1997.

31 Examples of this phenomenon were Labour dominance in Knowsley, the Conservatives in Bracknell Forest, and the Liberal Democrats in Richmond-upon-Thames.

32 Martin Loughlin, 'The restructuring of central–local government relations', in J. Jowell and D. Oliver (eds) *The Changing Constitution*; Oxford University Press, Oxford, 2000; p. 160.

33 See A. Barker, *Government by Task Force*; Politico's, London, 1999, for more on this subject.

Further reading

A. Barker, *Government by Task Force*; Politico's, London, 1999.

Robin Hambleton, *Directly Elected Mayors: Reinvigorating the Debate*; LGA, London, 1999.

George Jones and John Stewart, *The Case for Local Government*; Allen & Unwin, London, 1983.

Local Leadership, Local Choice; HMSO, London, 1998.

Modern Local Government – in Touch with the People, Cm 4014; HMSO, London, 1998.

Modernising Local Government – Local Democracy and Community Leadership; HMSO, London, 1998.

Colin Rallings and Michael Thrasher, *Local Elections in Britain*; Routledge, London, 1997.

R.A.W. Rhodes, *Beyond Westminster and Whitehall*; Routledge, London, 1992.

J. Stewart and G. Stoker (eds) *Local Government in the 1990s*; Fabian Society, London, 1995.

J. Tomaney and M. Mitchell, *Empowering the English Regions*; Charter 88, London, 1999.

website for the Local Government Association: www.lga.org.uk

Part IV

OTHER FORMS OF INSTITUTIONAL MODERNISATION

Redefining the Monarchy and the Crown

In studying constitutional change in the United Kingdom, we can in many cases only understand the present against the background of the past. The constitutional Monarchy under which we now live was delineated in its essentials by the Glorious Revolution of 1688–89 and still functions today under the influence of the Parliamentary statutes and political conventions which were established at that time and during the years immediately thereafter.

The contemporary project of redefining the Monarchy has had three main objectives. The first is to ensure the efficacy and the credibility of constitutional Monarchy as the best available form of government for the United Kingdom (and for those members of the Commonwealth where the Queen is accepted as the Head of State). The second is to maintain media and public respect for the House of Windsor as the extended family group from which the Monarch and her successors on the throne are drawn. The third is to demystify, without destroying, the idea of the Crown as the most familiar symbol of political, judicial and even ecclesiastical authority – the last because the Monarch is still 'Supreme Governor of the Church of England' and 'Defender of the Faith'.

The dilemma for those in the Palace and in politics who have wished to revive the Monarchy and permanently raise it onto a higher plane of public support and affection stems essentially from the paradoxical fact that it is an old and long-established institution which inevitably symbolises national continuity and tradition but nevertheless has been under recurrent pressure to change, modernise and reform. Ever since Queen Elizabeth II came to the throne in 1952, she and her family have been under growing media and public pressure to let more light into the institution of Monarchy; to present themselves as a model, modern family; to become more demotic in their speech, dress and general style of life; and, most recently, to appear more politically correct in an age when this seems to be an increasingly important passport to public approval, at any rate among some influential people. If one looks at old newsreels and reads the newspapers of the 1950s and 1960s, it is clear that these problems for the Royal Family

were not as acute 40 or 50 years ago as they have become more recently. This is partly because of the marked decline in public deference since that time, but it is also because several members of the Royal Family have brought embarrassment and even opprobrium upon themselves in ways which have served occasionally to weaken the institution of Monarchy.

The Queen spoke in a speech at the Guildhall in November 1992 of an *annus horribilis* during which Prince Charles and Princess Diana had announced their separation and the Palace had shown a marked reluctance to pay anything towards the costs of restoring Windsor Castle, part of which had been destroyed in a fierce fire. Yet a nadir in the fortunes of the Royal Family was undoubtedly reached in September 1997 when, for several weeks following the tragic and untimely death of Princess Diana, the Monarch and her advisers were castigated by the media and vociferous sections of the public for being aloof, insensitive and out of touch with the national mood. For a time at least it seemed that people might storm Buckingham Palace in disgust at the Royal Family's apparently cold and indifferent response to the tragedy, and thousands seemed determined to sanctify Princess Diana by laying a carpet of flowers outside her home at Kensington Palace.

It is fair to say that since that time the fortunes of the Monarchy have revived considerably. This is in part thanks to expert and timely advice to the Palace from the Prime Minister's Press Secretary, Alastair Campbell, on how to handle the media aspects of the crisis; in part thanks to Tony Blair's intuitive flair for catching and leading the public mood at the time; but mainly a function of the passage of time which proved to be the greatest healer of these particular psychological scars in public opinion. Nevertheless, the fundamental problem for the British Monarchy has remained: which aspects of the institution and its practices should be conserved, and which should be jettisoned – or at any rate seriously reformed – in the interests of institutional modernisation?

Ensuring the efficacy of constitutional Monarchy

The concept of constitutional Monarchy, as it is understood in the United Kingdom today, was first authoritatively explained in an English context by the great historian Thomas Babington Macaulay in his *History of England* published in 1855. Since this coincided with the second phase of Queen Victoria's reign, when she was effectively joint Sovereign with her husband Prince Albert, it is clear that a recognisably modern constitutional Monarchy was already in existence by the time the term entered into literary usage. In modern times Professor Vernon Bogdanor has supplied a pithy definition of constitutional Monarchy, namely 'a state which is headed by a Sovereign who reigns but does not rule'; but he has also offered a more subtle formulation which captures the very *British* political context within which our constitutional Monarchy operates, namely 'a set of conventions which limit the discretion of the Sovereign, so that his or her public acts are in reality those of Ministers'.[1]

Of course, this is only the beginning of the story and it is evident from the trajectory of British history since the time of Queen Victoria that there have been times when both she and some of her successors have had to work hard (with the help of wise advisers) to restore the efficacy and credibility of constitutional Monarchy in this country, just as there have been other times when the principal need was simply to maintain the system in good order. For example, when Victoria came to the throne in 1837 after nearly two decades of licentiousness under George IV and then buffoonery under William IV, the young Queen had to try to rebuild the constitutional Monarchy as she then understood it under the tutelage of her first Prime Minister Lord Melbourne. She had to engage in a similar repair effort in the late 1870s under the persuasive influence of Benjamin Disraeli, only this time the damage to the Monarchy had been done by herself during her long period of mourning for the death of Prince Albert in 1861 when she effectively withdrew from public life and left the field open to republicans and other critics of the Monarchy.

In the twentieth century, George V and Queen Mary had to restore the reputation of the Monarchy after the colourful but brief reign of Edward VII; George VI and Queen Elizabeth had to do the same after the even briefer and (to some) scandalous reign of Edward VIII which had ended in abdication when the young King had chosen marriage to an American divorcée, Mrs Simpson, in preference to a life on the throne which she could not have shared as Queen; and the present Queen Elizabeth II has occasionally been faced with a comparable, uphill task in the wake of the embarrassments and difficulties surrounding the divorces of three of her four children and the controversial business practices of her youngest son, Prince Edward, and his wife, the Countess of Wessex. The main thing which sets the present Queen apart from all the other Monarchs already mentioned is that she has been an exemplary constitutional Monarch who has performed her constitutional duties during her long reign with consummate skill and assiduity; unfortunately the same cannot be said for a number of her predecessors who fell short of the high standards expected of those who occupy the British throne.

Against this background, the objective of restoring the efficacy and credibility of constitutional Monarchy was probably the least difficult of the tasks before the Queen and her advisers. After all, the system of constitutional Monarchy still works rather well and the familiar conventions which govern its practices are well established and understood by the people that matter. For example, the convention that every Government is 'Her Majesty's Government' is predicated upon the understanding that this is true in name only, since the political responsibility for the decisions and acts of Government rests with the Prime Minister and his Ministerial colleagues in the governing party who, while they owe allegiance to the Sovereign (like all other subjects of the Queen), are constitutionally answerable to Parliament between elections and to the electorate at periodic General Elections. Equally, the convention that the Government of the day is opposed by 'Her Majesty's Loyal Opposition' conveys the idea that in opposing the policies of the Government and in criticising the personalities in the Government, the principal Opposition party does *not* oppose the state itself and, like the Government, owes a patriotic allegiance to the Monarch who personally symbolises the state.

All the many constitutional duties which the Monarch performs – such as the State Opening of Parliament or laying a wreath on behalf of the whole nation at the Cenotaph on Remembrance Sunday – are meant to reinforce the principal convention of constitutional Monarchy in the United Kingdom, namely that the Monarch reigns but does not rule. As Lord Palmerston put it in a letter to Queen Victoria in 1859, 'if wrong be done, the public servant [politician] who advised the act and not the Sovereign must be held answerable for the wrong-doing'.[2] The Monarchy acts, therefore, as a dignified and often convenient veil for the actions of Ministers in government, but few people any longer believe that the Monarch actually governs or takes any active part in the often partisan business of government.

This is the essence of the Queen's formal role in our system of constitutional Monarchy, although informally she retains her historic rights (in the famous formulation of Walter Bagehot) to be consulted, to encourage and to warn.[3] We can never know with any certainty what the exercise of these rights by the Sovereign really amounts to, since her audiences with ten successive Prime Ministers who between them have led nineteen different Administrations are entirely confidential and the contents of the exchanges are not recorded for the benefit of scholars or the general public.

A long-standing argument claims that a Republic would be a better, and certainly more modern, form of government for this country in the early twenty-first century than our constitutional Monarchy which, arguably, has not changed in its essentials since the Glorious Revolution in 1688–89. Republicanism enjoyed a brief political currency under the radical influence of Sir Charles Dilke MP in the early 1870s, but it did not capture mainstream political support in this country at that time or subsequently. Although Keir Hardie, the first Leader of the Labour Party, was a self-confessed republican, the idea of creating a Republic in this country was heavily defeated both at the Labour Party Conference in 1923 and in the House of Commons in the wake of the Abdication crisis in 1936. In more recent times one or two maverick or relatively marginal figures, such as Willie Hamilton, Tony Benn and Tom Nairn, have raised the standard of republicanism in one form or another; and a wider range of politicians and others have seriously questioned aspects of royalty in this country – especially when dramatic events such as the death of Princess Diana caused many people to doubt both the good sense and the public utility of the Royal Family and its courtiers. Moreover, the influence of the foreign-owned national press has been significant, since the Australian media tycoon Rupert Murdoch is a self-confessed republican and his Canadian counterpart Conrad Black is believed to have some sympathy with the republican cause.[4]

Bearing in mind that six of the other member states of the European Union (Belgium, the Netherlands, Luxembourg, Denmark, Sweden and Spain) are modern constitutional monarchies, Vernon Bogdanor has argued that 'there is ... no correlation whatever between republicanism and modernisation'.[5] From a conventional viewpoint, this verdict is hard to challenge. Certainly anyone who is part of or connected with the present Labour Administration and who may wish to flirt with this particular form of institutional 'modernisation' (as Mo Mowlam did) would do well to think twice before giving voice to this view in the United Kingdom because the general public has clung to the conviction that constitutional Monarchy is a form of government which is authentically British and unimpeachable, whereas republicanism in all its forms is generally seen as alien and eccentric. Moreover, the creation of a Republic in this country would entail giving more power and status to party politicians, an idea which would hardly be popular with the general public. In the case of Australia, which in 1999 held a much publicised national referendum upon whether to continue with the Queen as Head of State or replace her with an Australian President, there was enough of a public backlash to defeat the republican campaign which really foundered on public hostility (especially in rural Australia) to the idea that a republican President would be chosen by the Australian

REDEFINING THE MONARCHY AND THE CROWN 189

political parties rather than directly by the Australian people.

Although an outside observer of New Labour's constitutional reform programme might be tempted to think that reform of the Monarchy ought logically to follow reform of the House of Lords as part of a common attack upon the hereditary principle, and although the institution of Monarchy in this country has undoubtedly been through a very rocky phase since the early 1990s in particular, it seems likely that any radical tampering with the principles or even some of the practices of constitutional Monarchy would still be political dynamite for any Government which tried it. There are much better causes of constitutional reform than this upon which any political party could spend its political capital.[6] For all the manifest faults and human failings of the British Royal Family, very few politicians who have held high office in this country seriously question the continuing value of our system of constitutional Monarchy, because it has proved to be such a convenient and effective veil for the exercise of real power by any Government. Moreover, the Queen herself remains generally popular and respected (even if several members of her family do not) and she plays her constitutional role with admirable assiduity and skill. This is not to say that there is no need for running repairs to the Monarchy, but rather that one of the merits of the institution is that it can be 'modernised' and adjusted at any time without terminal damage necessarily being done to the underlying structure and assumptions of British constitutional arrangements.

On the other side of the argument, it needs to be noted that *constitutional monarchy* is really a misnomer for the current form of government in the United Kingdom. It is not a Monarchy in the pure sense of the word (meaning rule by a single person), but rather rule by a committee of the largest party in the House of Commons (the Cabinet) *in the name* of the Queen who is referred to as the Monarch or the Sovereign. Equally, such a system is not really constitutional in the sense of being conducted in accordance with a justiciable constitution which is superior to every statute or convention in the land. Rather it provides a symbolic facade for the various manifestations of

Executive power which are defined by a set of *constitutional conventions* that have evolved over more than three centuries, free of any real limitation by the courts.[7] Indeed, it could perhaps be argued that the Prime Minister of the day has equally become a kind of constitutional Monarch, especially when he or she commands an impressive majority in the House of Commons and enjoys a high level of public popularity. This reflects the 'presidential' nature of Prime Ministerial power in the British political system and it has been widely recognised by politicians, pollsters and political scientists alike. All such manifestations of 'monarchy' are, of course, transient and precarious, depending upon the vagaries of changing political circumstances and volatile public opinion. Nevertheless, the media profile of a modern British Prime Minister has something in common with that of a Monarch, since the occupation of each public office can raise its holder head and shoulders above all challengers and both are largely unconstrained by *formal* constitutional rules.

Maintaining media and public respect for the Royal Family

Another objective for the Palace and 10 Downing Street alike has been to maintain media and public respect and, if possible, affection for the Royal Family. This is obviously connected with the first objective which we have just discussed in that if the public is reassured that the Queen is performing the duties of constitutional Monarchy in an effective and exemplary way, then it is likely that this positive impression created by the Monarch herself will rub off on the House of Windsor as a whole. The Royal Family has been in the doldrums before and may well be again; so what matters is that all the members of the Royal Family should show themselves capable of learning the lessons of experience.

One of the inherent problems faced by the Queen and her advisers in pursuit of this goal is that the media and the public tend to want two contradictory forms of behaviour from the Royal Family. They seem to want *both* a magical and mystical Monarchy, full of pageantry and cultivated anachronism, which harks back to the traditions and practices of former times, *and* a thoroughly modern Monarchy with which everyone (who wants to) can identify in their personal emotions and daily lives – in other words, an institution which is simultaneously extraordinary and very ordinary. Needless to say, this double act has proved difficult to perform, notably since the fateful decision was taken by the Queen and her advisers in the late 1960s to portray the British Monarchy as 'just another family' by inviting Richard Cawston and the BBC to make the famous TV documentary entitled *Royal Family* in 1969 – the very year in which Prince Charles was invested as Prince of Wales in an archaic ceremony which can be traced back to the reign of Edward I in the early thirteenth century.

In seeking to restore public respect and affection for the House of Windsor, the Queen and her advisers have been faced with some problems which seem to have recurred over the centuries, at least since the time when the family name was Saxe-Coburg-Gotha. These have included: the alleged remoteness and aloofness of the Royal Family, the long-standing criticism that the lifestyle and paraphernalia of royalty in this country are profligate and ought to be curbed, the widely held view that its members have exhibited many of the hallmarks of a dysfunctional family, and the latent belief that a Monarchy of this kind is an expensive anachronism in the twenty-first century.

The first rule of symbolic leadership or symbolic representation, which is one of the prime functions that the Queen and other members of the Royal Family perform, is for the royal persons concerned to show themselves frequently and majestically to the people. It is therefore not understood or appreciated by the people (and certainly not by the tabloid media who need visible Royalty to sell newspapers and magazines and to boost TV ratings) if key members of the Royal Family retreat into privacy, as Queen Victoria did for a decade in the 1860s following Prince Albert's death from typhoid in 1861 or as the core members of the Royal Family appeared to do in the days following the death of Princess Diana in 1997.

Fortunately for the monarchy, mistakes of this kind have not been made very often over the centuries and for the most part successive Monarchs and their advisers have been well aware that the members of the Royal Family have both a need and a duty to demonstrate that they are visibly connected with and sympathetic towards the hopes and fears of the British people. This is why in normal times they act as patrons of so many charities and good causes, why they become colonels-in-chief of regiments or visitors at universities. It is also why they pay highly publicised visits to hospitals and schools, mingle visibly with disadvantaged communities, and personally represent the United Kingdom in public ceremonies both at home and abroad. In the extreme circumstances of war-time, there was no doubt that the very visible courage of King George VI and Queen Elizabeth in staying in this country throughout the Second World War and thus sharing the fate of their people (unlike some Continental monarchs and their families who cooperated with the Nazis or fled from their countries) served to cement bonds of loyalty and affection between the Monarchy and the people which have served the Royal Family in good stead ever since.

On the whole, the 'modern' Monarchy in this country (i.e. since the reign of George V) has grasped the need and the duty to perform its symbolically representative functions and done so with exemplary professionalism. Even Tom Nairn, a self-confessed republican, has written that 'people do feel the Queen stands for them or for something about them; and what this feeling denotes is another, deeper mode of representation – something like the way a work of art represents its subject'.[8] In the light of this acknowledgement, it is perhaps strange that the members of the core Royal Family are sometimes criticised for being *too* visible or for lending themselves too much to the cult of celebrity in our society. The Queen and members of her immediate family are seen by thousands on ceremonial occasions, such as summer garden parties and investitures at Buckingham Palace, and by even larger numbers on television when opening Parliament, welcoming other Heads of State to this country or attending important national ceremonies, such as Remembrance Sunday or Trooping the Colour. The accusation that the British Monarchy is too remote and aloof from the people therefore seems to be both inaccurate and unfair.

The criticism of the profligate life-style and extravagant paraphernalia of royalty in this country is long-standing. It can be traced back at least to the 1860s and 1870s and arguably long before that. It seems possible, therefore, that one way of restoring the reputation of the House of Windsor would be to reform or modernise the complicated and somewhat opaque financial arrangements for the Monarchy and Royal Family. This has proved to be easier said than done in view of the ways in which the private and public income of the Royal Family have been interwoven and the difficulties in separating the private and public expenditure of the Monarchy.

Like nearly everything else to do with the British Monarchy, there are complicated historical reasons for this state of affairs. For centuries before the constitutional settlement of 1688–89, there was no meaningful distinction between the Monarch's income and expenditure and that of the state: indeed, the Civil War really broke out over this issue which had become unacceptable in the eyes of many Parliamentarians. After the great constitutional watershed of 1688–89, the issue was gradually regularised by Parliament, although the 'modern' dispensation, which involves a mixed economy for the royal finances in the United Kingdom, was not established until 1830 when for the first time the Sovereign's personal expenditure was separated from general government expenditure, and the Civil List (a sum of public money which had first been voted by Parliament in the *Civil List Act* of 1697 and was voted thereafter at the beginning of every reign) was made available for 'the dignity and state of the Crown and the personal comfort of their Majesties'.[9] In constructing this framework, successive Monarchs and generations of Parliamentarians have sought to balance the Sovereign's need for constitutional independence with Parliament's need for financial control. Yet this has been difficult to achieve when individual Monarchs or members of their extended family have offended political and public sensibilities and in such circumstances the siren song of republican reform can become more alluring.

It is striking how the contemporary criticism of the House of Windsor on this score has remarkable echoes of criticism in the past. Sir Charles Dilke in the early 1870s and *Reynolds Newspaper* in the 1880s were vociferous and persistent in their criticism of the unacceptable burden upon the taxpayer of supporting the extended Royal Family and its hangers-on in the manner to which they had become accustomed.[10] There were, for example, strong complaints about the cost of the royal train and successive royal yachts. In the 1880s and 1890s such criticism was not confined to complaints about the financial burdens imposed by Royalty upon taxpayers, but encompassed disparagement of the Prince of Wales for his love of the chase – both of wild beasts and of other men's wives. In general, the radical critique of the British Monarchy in the latter part of the nineteenth century made great play of the extravagance, immorality and militarism of the extended Royal Family – e.g. the Duke of Cambridge (Queen Victoria's cousin), who was Chief of Staff of the British Army from 1856 to 1895. Since that time political and public attitudes towards the House of Windsor (formerly Saxe-Coburg-Gotha) have become generally more favourable, especially when certain Monarchs obviously discharged their duties in exemplary fashion – e.g. George V, George VI and Elizabeth II. Nevertheless, some themes of public criticism have endured, notably the cost and extravagance of the whole institution of Monarchy and the fact that from the early 1950s to the early 1990s the Monarch and her close family enjoyed immunity from taxation upon their private income.

It may well be that Elizabeth II and her immediate family are now through the worst of such financial criticism from some MPs and the media and that the concessions made by the Queen in 1992 have largely defused previous misgivings. The deal which the then Prime Minister, John Major, announced to the House of Commons was that from 1993–94 onwards the Queen would pay tax upon the Privy Purse and the rest of her personal income.[11] The Prince of Wales made a similar concession which meant that from 1993–94 he too has paid tax upon the income which he receives from the Duchy of Cornwall in addition to the tax which he has paid on his other income. Other members of the Royal Family have continued to pay their taxes like other British citizens. On the other hand, royal incomes from the Civil List, Government Departments and various grants-in-aid continue to be tax-free, as are the inalienable assets of the Queen which attach to her position as Monarch – e.g. Buckingham Palace, Windsor Castle, the Crown Jewels and the Royal Collections.

In the cause of greater economy, the Royal Yacht *Britannia* was decommissioned in 1998, but the Royal trains and the Royal flight are still operational and paid for out of public funds. Balmoral Castle and Sandringham House are 'grey areas' in that the Queen performs royal duties while she is in residence, but they remain her private houses. Financial support for individual members of the Royal Family (with the exception of the Queen herself, the Queen Mother and the Duke of Edinburgh) has been reimbursed by the Queen to the Government of the day under the terms of the 1992 agreement. This means that only these three members of the Royal Family have been personally in receipt of public money which is not reimbursed to the Exchequer by the Queen out of her private income. Complicated though these arrangements may be, Vernon Bogdanor was surely right to conclude that their essential purpose is 'to distinguish between the public and the private income of the Sovereign and to tax the Sovereign only on his or her private income'.[12]

The disparaging and disdainful charge that the Royals are a dysfunctional family has obviously done considerable damage to the image of the House of Windsor, not least because conscious decisions were taken years ago by Queen Victoria and many of her successors to portray the Royal Family as a model family for the rest of the nation to emulate and admire. Bearing in mind some of the personalities involved in the Royal Family down the generations and the recurrent tendency of the press and other media to build them up and then take obvious delight in knocking them down, we can see that it has been a dangerous strategy

to project each new generation of Royals as individual paragons. Yet one must also ask whether there was ever any real alternative to this dynamic and destructive course of action in view of the impossibility of such privileged people leading truly private lives and the unhealthy mixture of adulation and denigration which has often been implanted in the public mind by the media. Perhaps all we can really say is that membership of the core Royal Family is bound to be a high wire act, even when everything seems to be running smoothly, and that it is likely to become an even more difficult assignment for the Royals as the media become more ruthless and the public less deferential.

Against this background, it has been necessary for Prime Ministers and other influential figures to attempt to save the Windsors from themselves. This was very evident when Stanley Baldwin tried to steer Edward VIII through his personal crisis in 1936 towards an outcome (abdication) which, although shocking and divisive for the country, did not do terminal damage to the institution of constitutional Monarchy in this country, mainly because of the subsequent devotion to duty of King George VI and Queen Elizabeth.[13]

The need for Prime Ministerial intervention was evident again during the days immediately following the death of Princess Diana in 1997 when Tony Blair had to use all his presentational skills to shepherd the Monarchy through the crisis of public confidence which the Queen and her advisers seemed to create for themselves by the initially rigid way in which they responded (or failed to respond) to the public mood. No one who lived through and in some way experienced those highly charged events at the beginning of September 1997 is likely to forget the way in which the public in its thousands seemed to set the agenda, the way in which the media initially followed, then led the public mood, the almost seditious terms in which Earl Spencer expressed his indictment of the Windsors at Princess Diana's funeral, and the strong feelings that swept through the country leaving the emotional landscape upon which the Royal Family performs its public duties deeply scarred and perhaps permanently damaged.

The crises of 1936 and 1997 may indeed have been defining moments for the House of Windsor, yet in the longer run these memorable events do not seem to have had any lasting *constitutional* effects. This suggests that the institution of Monarchy in this country is still more robust and durable than any forces which may seek to challenge it.

On the other hand, it is hard to rebut the alternative argument that the *cumulative* effect of the various personal crises in the family history of the House of Windsor has been to lower the reputation of the Monarchy in the eyes of some British people and thus make it less certain than it would otherwise have been that the institution will survive intact and essentially unchanged following the demise of the present Queen. While the political conventions which govern the behaviour of constitutional Monarchy in this country have been determined by political custom and practice over the years, the continued existence of this institution is ultimately dependent upon public tolerance and public support. If this were ever to be dissipated – for example, in the event of Prince Charles deciding to marry Camilla Parker-Bowles, a divorcée and 'the other woman' in the eyes of all the supporters of the late Princess Diana – then it is not certain that even someone as popular as his elder son, Prince William, would be able to save the Monarchy in anything like its traditional form.[14] In such circumstances there would be a real possibility that a non-deferential and highly diverse British public would conclude that the institution of Monarchy was an expensive and unsatisfactory anachronism which should be dispensed with in favour of some other institutional device for providing our Head of State.

Demystifying and redefining the concept of the Crown

The greatest constitutional challenge in any attempts to modernise and reform the Monarchy is to demystify and redefine the concept of the Crown. Roger Scruton has usefully reminded us that, strictly speaking, the Crown is

> not a person or a state or a government, but a corporation sole, a collective with at most one member – an

entity recognised only by the common law of England, an ancient product of the English imagination interred like some adamantine relic in the subsoil of our culture.[15]

In order to get to grips with this arcane subject, we shall explore the various manifestations and meanings of the Crown in the contemporary political context, mindful of the fact that nearly all of them derive from age-old traditions and understandings. (See *Box 8* for a summary list.)

Box 8 Manifestations and meanings of the Crown

- A symbol of national unity throughout the United Kingdom
- A symbol of kingship and sovereignty
- A symbol of the power of the state and its civil servants
- A dignified emblem for the Government of the day and its agencies
- A dignified emblem for the judicial system and its judges
- A reminder that the Sovereign remains 'Supreme Governor' of the Church of England
- A reminder that the Monarch is Head of the Commonwealth
- A reminder that the Sovereign remains Commander-in-Chief of the armed forces
- A symbol of the nation on postage stamps, coins and medals
- A symbol exploited for sporting, charitable and commercial purposes

Originally, the Crown was essentially a symbol of kingship and sovereignty. From those beginnings in Saxon times it metamorphosed over the centuries into feudal Monarchy under the Normans and Plantagenets through absolute Monarchy under the Tudors and Stuarts to constitutional Monarchy in 1688–89 and thereafter. The result of this long historical evolution is that the Crown is now the pre-eminent symbol of constitutional Monarchy, but more associated in the public mind with jewellery in the Tower of London and periodic ceremonies of Coronation than with any theory of the constitution.

In the British context the Crown became a symbol or even a substitute for the public power of the state. Yet the English common law tradition never fully recognised the concept of the state, in contrast with the French-inspired absolutist tradition on the Continent in which it seemed perfectly natural for Louis XIV to declare: 'l'état, c'est moi'. Manifestations of the English tradition are to be seen in the crowned head of the Queen on postage stamps or the Crown atop the Royal coat of arms on British passports (even though these have been reduced in size, are now burgundy in colour and carry the words 'European Community' on the front cover). Some academic lawyers have regretted the relative weakness of the 'state tradition' in our public law, but most politicians who have been Ministers and senior civil servants still feel comfortable with a constitutional convention that has tended to present the Crown as a symbol of the state. This situation has had real attractions for the governing class in the United Kingdom, not least because it has enabled them to operate in what Martin Loughlin has called 'the dead ground of the constitution': namely, 'a sphere of immunity from legal process or at least a domain of decision-making in which the appropriate constitutional checks were Parliamentary rather than judicial'.[16]

The Crown has become very largely a dignified emblem for the Government of the day and its agencies. It seems natural, therefore, that in formal terms we should refer to 'Her Majesty's Government' and that it is the Monarch who reads the Speech from the Throne at every State Opening of Parliament. For those who may feel uneasy about this conflation of the Government and the Crown, reassurance has long been provided by the very English idea of 'His (or Her) Majesty's Opposition', which can be traced back to 1826, and by the office of 'Leader of the Opposition', which first achieved formal statutory recognition in the *1937 Ministers of the Crown Act*. However, we should not allow ourselves to be lulled into a false sense of security by this typically English constitutional device, since what it has really achieved is the co-option of the principal Opposition party into our front-bench constitution – something which has often served to inhibit truly effective Parliamentary scrutiny or control of the Executive. In short, the Crown has come to be associated with the dominant form of governance in this country – namely Executive power and discretion – and in the process it has developed additional dimensions of symbolism along the way, starting with sovereignty, later becoming emblematic of the state and since the nineteenth century a dignified veil for the Government of the day in all its manifestations.[17]

The Crown is very much the sponsor of the judicial system in this country. Since the reign of Henry II in the twelfth century, justice has been dispensed in the name of the Monarch with the result that we refer to the *Royal* Courts of Justice and speak of the need 'to keep the *Queen's* peace'. Equally, when the responsibility for criminal prosecutions was taken away from the police in the 1980s, it was entrusted to a newly formed *Crown* Prosecution Service; and when villains are sentenced to a term in jail, they serve their time in one of *Her Majesty's* Prisons. All this symbolism is supposed to convey what has been described as 'the majesty of the law'. Although the fact that justice is still dispensed in the name of the Crown may have contributed to the maintenance of law and order in this realm down the centuries (especially when social deference was a marked characteristic of public attitudes), it has also contributed to the failure of constitutional reformers to bring the Crown and its agents *completely* under the rule of law.

The Crown serves as a symbol and reminder of the fact that the Sovereign remains 'Supreme Governor' of the Church of England in a tradition which can be traced back to Henry VIII's break from Rome in 1534, but which was really defined by the *Act of Supremacy* in 1559 at the beginning of Elizabeth I's reign and later confirmed by the *Bill of Rights* in 1689 as part of the Whig constitutional settlement. Subsequently, the *1707 Acts of Union* placed the Sovereign under a statutory duty 'to maintain and preserve inviolably' the Presbyterian Church of Scotland, although the latter institution became self-governing under the terms of a 1921 statute and now every new British Monarch has only to swear an oath to preserve the Church of Scotland at a meeting of the Privy Council which immediately follows the Sovereign's accession to the throne. Among the consequences of these traditions (and specifically those created by the *1701 Act of Settlement*) are that the Monarch is still prohibited from being a Catholic or marrying a Catholic and is placed under a declaratory duty to be 'Defender of the (Protestant) Faith'. These things can still cause some embarrassment to the Palace – for example, in the year 2000 there was an outcry among the evangelical element in the Church of England when it was reported that the Queen intended to pray with the Pope for a brief period during her state visit to Italy.[18]

The Monarch, who wears the crown of the United Kingdom, is also Head of the Commonwealth and in that capacity she is still recognised as Head of State in fifteen of the 54 member states of this large multi-national and multi-racial organisation.[19] This contemporary situation is a legacy of Empire and notably the period from the Durham Report in 1839 to the Statute of Westminster in 1931 when the dominions (Canada, Australia, New Zealand and South Africa) and the growing number of colonies were regarded by the British political class at any rate as bound together by a common allegiance to the British Crown and subservient, at least in respect of their external relations, to the *Imperial Parliament* at Westminster.

With the passage of time and the subsequent British retreat from Empire, this constitutional arrangement became increasingly hard to justify, especially after 1949 when India insisted upon its new status as a Republic within the Commonwealth and Ireland left the organisation altogether. A compromise was found at the Commonwealth Prime Ministers' Conference in 1952 when it was decided that each of the member states should decide upon its own relationship with the British Crown rather than have such matters decided for it by Parliament at Westminster. Thus under the *Royal Titles Act 1953* the Queen became officially: 'Elizabeth II, by the grace of God of the United Kingdom of Great Britain and Northern Ireland and of her other Realms and Territories, Queen, Head

of the Commonwealth, Defender of the Faith'. This cumbersome description aptly summed up the eclectic nature of the Monarch's formal connections with the various territories and states of a shrinking British Empire and a growing Commonwealth. It also showed how the Monarch's overseas role has become something of a constitutional muddle – albeit one to which the present Queen is strongly attached.

The Crown has long been a powerful symbol of national community – first within England, then England and Wales, then England, Wales and Scotland, and later still, for the period of Union between Ireland and the rest of the United Kingdom (1800–1921), throughout the British Isles. Yet scarcely had this long process of national aggregation been completed under the symbol of the Crown and the banner of the Union Jack than it began to unravel under 'nationalist' pressures first in Ireland and later in Scotland and Wales. For a considerable period the archaic symbol of the Crown acted as a kind of psychological cement for the United Kingdom and, to a certain extent, the wider Empire and Commonwealth. This form of multi-national allegiance to the British Sovereign reached its apogee in the First World War, when men from all parts of the Empire and Commonwealth flocked to the colours to fight and die for 'King and Country', even though the King was an Imperial Monarch and the mother country a distant land far across the seas. In modern times it has become more difficult for people in what is now a multi-cultural and ethnically diverse United Kingdom to identify with the British Crown and regard it as a symbolic pole of attraction for their loyalty and allegiance, although both the Queen in her role as Head of the Commonwealth and the Prince of Wales with his own brand of 'socially inclusive royalty' have done a good deal to enhance the credibility of the Monarchy in the eyes of other races and religions.

It is clear that the wide scope and considerable elasticity of the concept of the Crown in British constitutional arrangements have caused real problems in at least two important quarters: Parliament and the courts. However, it is equally clear that considerable advantages have been derived from the concept of the Crown, which has been notably convenient for all members of the Executive from the Prime Minister down to the humblest civil servant in an obscure Department or Agency of government. It can also be argued that there have been wider benefits for the body politic in terms of institutional continuity and social cohesion.

Problems for Parliament with the Royal Prerogative

The Monarchy may now be only a 'dignified' rather than an 'efficient' part of our constitutional arrangements, to use Walter Bagehot's nineteenth-century terminology. Its prerogative powers may be only the residue of discretionary or arbitrary Royal authority which has been left with the Monarchy because the modern Monarch no longer has any real political power in our system of government. Yet Parliament still has problems with the Royal Prerogative because some of the powers available under this archaic heading are still exploited by Ministers and officials for the convenience of the Executive and to minimise the extent of Parliamentary control over some of the most sensitive areas of Executive action.

Over the years authoritative definitions of the Royal Prerogative have varied with the temper and priorities of the times, but have tended to reflect the prevailing political attitudes towards the proper scope of central Government. In the 1760s, when the apparatus of the central state was unusually small and relatively weak, Sir William Blackstone in his famous *Commentaries on the Laws of England* offered the following fairly narrow definition:

> that special pre-eminence which the King hath over and above all other persons and out of the ordinary course of the common law in right of his regal dignity . . . and . . . in its nature singular and eccentrical; that . . . can only be applied to those rights and capacities which the King enjoys alone.[20]

In the 1880s, when the scope of government and the state was larger and stronger, A.V. Dicey in his *Introduction to the Study of the Law of the Constitution* offered a broader and more permissive definition: 'nothing less than the residue of

discretionary or arbitrary authority which at any given time is legally left in the hands of the Crown'.[21]

A century later, in the 1980s – by which time the scope and influence of central Government had expanded a great deal further – Lord Diplock in what became known as *the GCHQ case* and reflecting the more interventionist attitude that had been adopted by some senior judges since the 1960s, offered this definition: 'a residue of miscellaneous fields of law in which the executive Government retains decision-making powers that are not dependent upon any statutory authority, but nevertheless have consequences for the private rights or legitimate expectations of other persons'.[22] This dictum emphasised the extent to which the Law Lords have been increasingly willing to make the Royal Prerogative justiciable as an antidote to Parliament's apparent unwillingness or inability to hold Ministers and officials fully to account when they exercise residual prerogative powers in the name of the Monarch.

There are several reasons why most members of the House of Commons appear to be relaxed or even apathetic about the use by Ministers and officials of the residual prerogative powers of the Crown. *Firstly*, the exercise of some prerogative powers which once posed a real threat to the authority of Parliament – such as the withholding of Royal Assent to legislation – has fallen into disuse and nowadays it would be unthinkable for the Monarch to exercise such a veto. *Secondly*, the personal prerogative powers which Monarchs used to exercise on their own initiative, such as the appointment of Prime Ministers or the dissolution of Parliament, now merely endorse the decisions of the ruling party and the electorate or the advice of the Prime Minister of the day. *Thirdly*, the creation of Peers, the granting of public honours and the making of all sorts of public appointments do not usually cause controversy or embarrassment – at any rate for the Monarch – because most people know that the Monarch is merely the formal conduit for such state patronage which is actually determined by Ministers and Opposition party leaders. *Fourthly*, the Royal Prerogatives of mercy or pardon for convicted criminals are acts of grace exercised on the advice of the Home Secretary and are now so rare as to cause no fuss in Parliament on procedural grounds, although they may sometimes stir opposition on substantial grounds related to an individual case.

Some members of the House of Commons, however, have expressed concerns about certain powers of the Royal Prerogative which still serve as convenient instruments for the Government of the day. These powers include most notably the power of Ministers acting in the name of the Crown to negotiate and sign treaties on behalf of the United Kingdom; the power to declare war and hence to commit the Armed Forces (of which the Monarch is formally the Commander-in-Chief) to battle or participation in UN sponsored peace-keeping operations; and the power to promulgate new constitutions for British colonies and to grant them independence. Such powers reflect the Crown's traditionally exclusive rights in the field of foreign policy and the conduct of military affairs. They have something in common with the so-called 'war powers' of the American President, whose office, in this respect at least, was modelled upon that of the British Monarch.[23]

There are other powers of the Royal Prerogative which are useful to all modern Governments for domestic purposes, notably for reorganising the structures of central Government. For example, Government Departments can be created, merged or abolished with the use of prerogative power; public corporations, universities and even cities can be created or designated in the same way – all on the grounds that these are acts or prerogatives of the 'Royal' Executive which owe their original justification to the idea that the Crown is entitled 'to set its own house in order' without seeking (formal or prior) permission from Parliament. Significantly, the normal instruments used to implement such acts of government are *Orders in Council* which have only to be approved by the Privy Council – a body which consists of senior Ministers and former Ministers, as well as the Leaders of the main Opposition parties, but whose active membership is usually confined to senior members of the party in office.

The pragmatic justification for the continued use of these prerogative powers is that it makes good sense to allow any Government to exploit the flexibility of such instruments, so that Ministers do not get unnecessarily bogged down by Parliamentary scrutiny or judicial review of the acts of government and so that the business of government can be conducted with efficiency and dispatch. Such a view will normally commend itself to civil servants and to those politicians who have held office as Ministers of the Crown. On the other hand, there is an alternative view which was originally put forward in the seventeenth century by the leaders of the Parliamentary Opposition to the Stuart Monarchs and which has been voiced in modern times by Tony Benn and others who share his republican sympathies. This view holds that such uses of the Royal Prerogative are undesirable manifestations of arcane and archaic power which ought to have no place in our contemporary constitutional arrangements. The effect of using such powers is to exclude all Members of Parliament who are *not* Privy Councillors from fulfilling their democratic functions of *prior scrutiny* of some of the most significant acts of government and to make it much more difficult for MPs to *stop* the Government of the day from embarking upon a potentially disastrous course of action – e.g. the conclusion of an unpopular treaty or the declaration of an unjustifiable war.[24]

In recent times there has been some overlap between the concerns of Tony Benn and those of Margaret Thatcher, at any rate when it comes to their common hostility to British Governments (of which they are no longer members) using residual powers under the Royal Prerogative to sign treaties with our partners in the European Union without first securing the consent of Parliament *and* the British people in a national referendum. Tony Benn has tended to emphasise the right of all MPs not in the Government to exercise their function as 'tribunes of the people' in order to prevent successive British Governments from signing away the democratic rights for which many people have fought and died ever since the seventeenth century. Margaret Thatcher asserted the right of the British people to accept or reject the 1992 Treaty of Maastricht in a national referendum held *before* rather than after the process of Parliamentary ratification. It seems that the arguments of these two great political figures have been accepted *de facto* in that it is now agreed on all sides that the United Kingdom will only abolish the Pound and adopt the Euro if the British people approve such a step in a national referendum and it is likely that other future European developments of constitutional significance for this country will be submitted to a similar referendum process.

As with so many other aspects of Britain's living constitution, the extent to which the residual prerogative powers of the Crown are used by Ministers and officials on their behalf is governed very largely *by convention*, in other words well-established custom and practice. For example, successive Speaker's rulings have precluded the House of Commons from interrogating the Prime Minister of the day upon the exercise of certain acts of the Royal Prerogative which are deemed too politically sensitive to permit Parliamentary interference – e.g. Ministerial advice on the Honours List and ecclesiastical appointments, the dissolution of Parliament, and the exercise of the prerogative of mercy. However, reliance upon the convention can be problematic, as when John Major as Prime Minister answered a Parliamentary Question which had asked for a list of the occasions on which Ministers had exercised prerogative powers during his Administration by saying: 'it is for individual Ministers to decide on a particular occasion whether and how to report to Parliament on the exercise of prerogative powers'.[25] Nor does Parliament necessarily benefit when the domain of the Royal Prerogative is prescribed by statute, since the terms in which the *Parliamentary Commissioner Act 1967* was drafted and approved by Parliament deliberately precluded the Ombudsman from investigating public complaints about the ways in which prerogative powers are used by Ministers and other Crown servants. In this sense Parliament itself has long been complicit in supporting rather than challenging the use of prerogative powers by successive Governments, while successive British Monarchs since the reign of George V have not sought to disturb established custom and practice.

There can be a good deal of self-serving and disingenuous talk from Ministers in any Government about how it would be for Parliament and not the Courts to hold them to account if they or their ilk were ever to abuse the prerogative powers available to them as servants of the Crown. Yet this line of argument blithely ignores the fact that Parliament (especially the House of Commons) is largely unable to exert proper Parliamentary control because of the degree of Executive and party political dominance of the Lower House by the governing party. While a robust and temporarily lethal separation of powers between the King and the Commons was brought about during the seventeenth century, and had the effect of making it difficult for future Monarchs and Ministers to abuse prerogative powers, constitutional developments since that time involved increasing penetration of the Legislature by the Executive to a point at which in the late nineteenth century these two branches of government became effectively fused under the influence of disciplined political parties striving to honour their commitments to an expanding electorate. Against this background it is not surprising that many people now give a hollow laugh whenever Ministers or senior civil servants attempt to reassure them about the effectiveness of Parliamentary control in the United Kingdom.

The meaning and effect of Crown immunities

The idea of Crown privileges or immunities stems originally from the medieval notion that 'the King can do no wrong'. This was closely connected with the principle that the King could not be sued in his own courts. Manifestly, this idea was severely challenged by the trial and execution of Charles I in 1649 following the defeat of the Royalists in the Civil War. However, the principle was restored with Charles II in 1660 and later confirmed by the architects of the Glorious Revolution in 1688–89, although essentially on Parliamentary terms. Since that time the idea has been gradually transformed into the concept of Crown immunity and it has been defined in a wide variety of ways.[26]

According to one rather archaic interpretation, it can mean that the Sovereign is *incapable of wrong-doing*. Yet this sounds anachronistic and incredible today in our modern constitutional Monarchy, since Crown servants (whether Ministers or others) *are* capable of unlawful behaviour, as the courts have found from time to time. According to another interpretation, it can mean that the Sovereign *has no legal right or power to do wrong*. Yet this too must be considered incredible unless it is applied narrowly and exclusively to the person of the Monarch rather than to Ministers and other servants of the Crown. In another sense it can mean that the Sovereign *is immune from legal process, except where a statute expressly provides otherwise*. This is a formulation which seems to accord more closely with contemporary realities, although since the leading case of *M. v. the Home Office* in 1994 it has become clear that Crown immunity (unless concerned with matters of 'high policy' which is Parliament's preserve) does *not* extend to Ministers of the Crown whose administrative decisions are justiciable and who can be found in contempt of court.[27]

The concept of Crown immunities has had a significant impact upon both Parliament and the courts, which bears out the general point made earlier in the chapter that developments in one institution of Parliament inevitably have effects upon the others – and indeed upon the judiciary as well. The principal effect on Parliament has been to demonstrate the inapplicability in the British context of Thomas Paine's maxim that 'a constitution is a thing antecedent to a government', essentially because in this country we had functioning monarchical government (powerfully symbolised by a meaningful Crown) before we had anything resembling a constitution and because even our current constitutional arrangements still permit the anomaly of residual Royal Prerogatives which can be exploited by any Government.

In English law the idea of Crown immunity was mitigated somewhat by the subject's right to petition the Crown against its effects where these could be shown to damage individual rights and by the possibility of securing declaratory relief in the superior courts. Gradually throughout the eighteenth century the legal doctrine developed that the Monarch could not be sued *in person*, but the Crown's servants could be sued and were not beyond the reach of the law. To cite a rather well-known example of this legal liability, Warren Hastings, the first Governor-General of India, was famously impeached (and eventually acquitted) in London on charges of cruelty and corruption in the service of the Crown in a trial which was held intermittently for 145 days from 1788 to 1795. His defence rested essentially upon the doctrine of Crown immunity, but this did not protect him from being subjected to a harrowing legal process at the behest of his Parliamentary opponents. The Monarch (then George III) may have been secure from impeachment; but not his servants, however eminent.

This aspect of constitutional law remained broadly unchanged throughout the nineteenth century and the first half of the twentieth century, although considerable concern did emerge in the 1920s and 1930s about the apparently inexorable growth of largely unaccountable public administration carried on in the name of the Crown but not, of course, by the Monarch in person.[28] The effect of two world wars was greatly to increase the power and scope of Executive action and to reinforce the British tradition of official secrecy in defence of the realm. Indeed, the record in war-time and for several decades thereafter showed that the notion of Crown immunity could be surreptitiously expanded behind a veil of official secrecy and with the connivance of an accommodating judiciary. Thus it was possible in 1942 for Lord Chancellor Simon to apply a doctrine of 'public interest immunity' in the leading case of *Duncan v. Cammell Laird & Co.* and later for that doctrine to be developed by the superior courts after the war (albeit with some adjustments) in *Conway v. Rimmer* in 1968 and then in what became known as the *NSPCC Case* in 1978.[29] On the other hand, judicial sympathy with the doctrine had begun to evaporate by the time the prosecution collapsed in the *Matrix Churchill* case in 1993 when the Major Administration was reeling from a series of political scandals. In such changed circumstances a more self-confident judiciary was evidently prepared to challenge the Government of the day if the latter was considered to have abused Crown immunities or other forms of Executive privilege.

Over the years the movement of influential opinion about Crown immunity has not been all in one direction. When peace returned in 1945, the argument for a statutory clarification of the concept became very persuasive and consequently the post-war Labour Government secured Parliamentary approval for the *1947 Crown Proceedings Act* which provided a statutory framework for this area of public law and administrative practice that was to last nearly half a century. The Act put the Crown (i.e. officers of the Crown) on the same footing as subjects of the Crown in disputes of contract or tort, but stopped short of providing for injunctive relief for plaintiffs or Court Orders for specific performance of prerogative remedies or the payment of damages to plaintiffs. It drew a distinction between the ability of plaintiffs to sue officers of the Crown (in their personal capacity) and the customary prohibition upon any litigation against the Crown itself, with the rider that the former could not be used as a way of circumventing the latter. In place of injunctive relief or Court Orders for the specific performance of prerogative remedies, it provided for declaratory judgements which would define the legal position in any given case, but leave the Crown free subsequently to respond to the plaintiff as it saw fit. This idea of having the Courts *declare* the law in favour of the plaintiff rather than enforce it with a coercive Order against the Crown was at the heart of the statute and influenced the development of case law on Crown immunity for several decades to come.[30]

One of the main explanations for the moves towards judicial activism in Britain since the 1960s has been the degree of frustration felt by senior judges at the apparent inability of Members of Parliament to control the Executive and to limit the effects of Crown immunity. This mood was captured in the enigmatic observation by Adam Tomkins that 'the sovereignty of Parliament does not extend to the Sovereign perhaps'.[31] Until 1992 a vivid example of this point was the Monarch's immunity from income tax and the tax privileges accorded to other members of the Royal Family. The general point, however, has always been broader and more abstract. Since there has been so little explicit recognition of any concept of the state in English law, the concept of the Crown (as a mystical symbol of the state) has enabled certain aspects of state activity to remain above and beyond the law. Furthermore, Parliament – which means in this context the prevailing majority in the House of Commons – has been discouraged from asserting itself and rectifying any anomalies caused by Crown immunity for three persuasive reasons: *firstly*, because the Monarchy is still formally one of the institutions of Parliament; *secondly*, because the Crown remains such a convenient facade for the actions of Government and its agencies; and *thirdly*, because with single-party Parliamentary government the majority in the Commons at any time usually regards its first duty as being to support rather than defy the Government of the day.

Crown privileges and immunities have tended to fall into two broad categories: those that are archaic and attached to the Sovereign in person, such as her freedom from arrest, the inviolability of the Royal palaces and the fact that she is not obliged to give evidence in her own cause; and those that have been more broadly construed and hence have tended to be inimical to the ultimate supremacy of constitutional law, such as the immunity of the Crown from interim injunctions or Court Orders for specific performance of prerogative powers, and the medieval principle of *bona vacantia* whereby all unowned or unclaimed property reverts to the Crown. Some elements in the latter category have been used by successive Governments for their own convenience as a way of evading effective scrutiny by Parliament or review by the courts. On the other hand, the Court of Appeal and the Law Lords have found the courage and determination to tackle some of the abuses of Crown immunity through the process of judicial review and have thus partly remedied the shortcomings in Parliamentary control. However, it took quite a while for the Courts to arrive at their modern view that the degree of justiciability should be determined by the subject matter of a particular case and the nature of the immunity in question rather than archaic and abstract legal principles.

In the 1984 *GCHQ case*, for example, Lord

Diplock found that the action of the second Thatcher Administration in banning trade union membership at the security-sensitive Government Communications Headquarters in Cheltenham *was* reviewable by the courts on the grounds that such Executive action had consequences for the private rights and legitimate expectations of the Government employees involved. Thus with the singular exception of issues of 'high policy', which the courts tend to regard as the preserve of Government and Parliament, the Law Lords are much more prepared than they used to be to see that all manifestations of public power (whether expressed in the name of the Crown or otherwise) do *not* escape from judicial scrutiny, but are subjected to what has been well described as 'a constitutional imperative of redressing Parliamentary inactivity and Executive dominance'.[32]

The current state of the law on Crown immunity was clarified by Lord Woolf in *M. v. Home Office* in 1994.[33] M. was a citizen of Zaïre (as it then was) whose application for political asylum in the United Kingdom had been refused by the Home Secretary, Kenneth Baker, and who was deported before his application for judicial review of the decision had been finally determined. His counsel argued that the Home Secretary had breached an undertaking given to the court and disobeyed an injunction made by a High Court judge, so the plaintiff asked the Law Lords to commit the Minister (acting on behalf of the Crown) for contempt of court.

Although Mr Baker was found not guilty of contempt since he had taken the decision to deport M. after full advice from and in consultation with his officials, in delivering the judgement of the court Lord Woolf took the opportunity presented by the case to make some important points of general application to the doctrine of Crown immunity. Firstly, he found that an interim injunction *could* be made against a Minister of the Crown acting in an official capacity. Secondly, he found that the Minister *could* be held to be in contempt of court. However, the third limb of his judgement went slightly in the opposite direction by holding that even if the Minister had been in contempt of court, it would not have been open to the court to make a coercive Order against the respondent to punish him for the contempt, but only to make a declaration of the legal position and then, by implication, invite the Minister to rectify the situation in the light of the court's finding. This ground-breaking judgement, which stopped just short of a direct constitutional challenge to the Government of the day, can be seen as something of a forerunner for the Declaration of Incompatibility which was the key idea adopted in the *1998 Human Rights Act* in order to avoid situations in which the Law Lords would otherwise have to strike down aspects of Ministerial decision making or Parliamentary legislation which they deemed incompatible with the articles of the 1951 European Convention. Lord Woolf's judgement was, therefore, part of a coherent judicial view which has sought to draw defensible boundaries between the rights of Government (as exercised by Ministers in the name of the Crown) and the duties of the judiciary to act as guardians of the judicial process and the constitutional rights of British citizens.

Even the most senior and adventurous members of the judiciary are rightly wary of challenging Ministers who claim Crown immunity or argue that they are using prerogative powers. This is because too bold a judicial advance into this territory might be construed as an attack upon the rights of Parliament and, as H.W.R. Wade has pointed out, 'if they [the judges] fly too high, Parliament may clip their wings'.[34] Notwithstanding the development of constructive judge-made law in this country, it is still unwise for the judiciary to mount a direct attack upon 'the High Court of Parliament', not only because the Law Lords themselves are part of Parliament, but also because Ministers, using their majority in the House of Commons, can overturn any legal judgement.[35] This should serve to remind us that in spite of the measures of constitutional reform that were put through Parliament by the first Blair Administration, nowhere in the United Kingdom is there a domestic jurisdiction based upon a codified constitution which would provide constitutional cover for senior judges who might wish to be bold in their restraint of the Executive. Indeed, Lord Woolf and his colleagues are well aware of the danger of a political backlash in the event of their acting too adventurously. In this sense there may be an instructive parallel between the need for constitutional caution on the part of the judiciary and the matching need for political caution on the part of the Monarchy.

General reflections

The first task of those in this country who wish the Monarchy well has been to save the Royal Family from itself. In spite of all the soap opera and scandals which have been so vividly portrayed in the tabloid media since the early 1990s, it is widely accepted that the Queen has performed her duties in an exemplary fashion and that as long as she lives the British form of constitutional Monarchy is secure from radical reform. The evidence shows that both the old-fashioned notion of absolute Monarchy and the alternative of a crowned Republic can be discounted as descriptions of our constitutional arrangements and do not accord with popular preferences or traditions in this country. Broadly speaking, the British people seem comfortable with the present constitutional arrangements which could accurately be described as a *Parliamentary democracy with a monarchical facade* rather than a 'constitutional Monarchy' as in the standard textbooks.

If this is the right view, it would not be timely or appropriate for members of a reforming Labour Government or anyone else to propose serious reforms of the Monarchy or significant adjustments to its place in our constitutional arrangements, at least until the Queen's Golden Jubilee in 2002 is over and probably until her eventual demise, well in the future. Only then might it make sense to begin a new constitutional era with a radical reform of the Monarchy and its role in our constitutional arrangements. It may, therefore, be worth concluding this chapter with a speculative sketch of what a reformed British Monarchy might look like in a reformed British polity which had been significantly altered by the passage of time and the modernising influence of the constitutional reforms carried through by successive Labour Administrations.

In the first place, a reformed Monarchy would need to be a scaled-down Monarchy with a smaller court and domestic establishment. This would probably entail some rationalisation of the Royal estate – perhaps with a sale and lease back of Buckingham Palace – and an end to expensive infrastructure such as the Royal train and the Royal flight. Sir Michael Peat, when Keeper of the Privy Purse, managed to reduce the cost of the Monarchy across the board by over 50 per cent in real terms over ten years and the annual cost of some £39 million in the year 2000 was little more than the cost of running the British Museum.[36] If economies on this scale have been possible, there is reason to believe that with a more restricted definition of the Royal establishment and with a more restrained Royal life-style, the Queen's successor could perform his essential duties at even lower public cost.

Secondly, a reformed Monarchy could be a secular Monarchy without the historic burden of having to be 'Defender of the Faith' and Supreme Governor of the Church of England. Such a constitutional change would require primary legislation to repeal the *1559 Act of Supremacy* and to amend the *1707 Acts of Union*, with procedural consequences for the Coronation ceremony and liturgical consequences for the Church of England. It might also call into question the right of even sixteen Church of England bishops to sit in a reformed House of Lords and it should end the Prime Minister's powers of ecclesiastical patronage. In the view of many people both inside and outside the Church of England, such changes might even have a liberating and revivifying effect upon the small and dwindling proportion of the adult population who worship regularly in the Church of England. At present the Anglican Communion is divided on this idea, but it has gained some support within the church itself and it was assumed that Prince Charles might be sympathetic to some changes along these lines.[37]

Thirdly, since one of the prime rationales for the British Monarchy is to act as a symbol for the United Kingdom, a more explicit role for the members of a reformed Royal Family might require each of the Monarch's closest relatives to identify publicly with one of the constituent 'nations' of the United Kingdom, rather in the way that the Queen has already assigned to the Princess Royal a particularly prominent representative role in and on behalf of Scotland. If this idea worked well within all parts of the United Kingdom (although there would be real reservations about the political feasibility of applying it to the divided Province of Northern Ireland where the loyalty of the Unionist community to the Crown has been a significant bone of contention for nationalist republicans), it could even be extended by agreement to some members of the Commonwealth which still recognise the British Monarch as their Head of State.

A fourth limb of policy reform might involve a deliberate move towards a slimmed-down and more narrowly focused Monarchy in which the duties of the Monarch as a non-political Head of State took precedence over all other aspects of the job. The adoption of such a proposal would produce a situation broadly similar to the more limited role performed by other constitutional Monarchs in Europe, notably in Scandinavia and the Netherlands. If it were to be adopted, it would demystify people who may still be dazzled by the totemic symbolism of the Crown and might thereby deprive future Governments of the convenient advantages which their predecessors have enjoyed of being able to act under the cloak of the Royal Prerogative or to minimise their public accountability by pleading Crown immunity. Essentially, it would mean separating the office and duties of the Monarch from the constitutional symbolism of the Crown, so that the rather stilted and archaic references to 'Her Majesty's Government' would be dropped and instead all Ministers and officials would simply be expected to act lawfully and accountably on the basis of statutory or common law authority. Such a reform need not detract from the dignity of our Head of State, but it would have the virtuous effect of ending a historic pretence which does the Monarch no particular favours and exposes the institution of Monarchy to reputational risks in the event that it has to deal with constitutional crises triggered by self-serving party politicians.

These are just the outlines of how the role of the Monarchy might be redefined in our constitutional arrangements. As long as the present Queen lives, most British people are unlikely to press for radical changes to the monarchical elements in our constitution. Indeed, they will almost certainly wish to retain their Monarchy as it is, because for them it has been 'not a form of political power, but a work of the imagination, an attempt to represent in the here and now all those mysterious ideas of authority and historical right without which no place on earth could be settled as a home'.[38] With its continuity and pageantry, the Monarchy lends some additional glamour and legitimacy to our political system. With its studied neutrality, it keeps our Head of State clear of party politics. In its human embodiment, it fosters a sense of national unity and belonging, especially on ceremonial occasions or at times of national grief. Yet if it did not exist, it would not necessarily have to be invented.

Questions for discussion

1   Would the people of the United Kingdom be better off in a Republic?

2   Is the Royal Prerogative either meaningful or justifiable in contemporary circumstances?

3   When we look back upon 50 years of Queen Elizabeth II's reign, what have been the lasting achievements of the Monarchy during that time?

Notes

1   Vernon Bogdanor, *The Monarchy and the Constitution*; Clarendon Press, Oxford, 1997; pp. 1, 65.
2   *Ibid*; p. 14.
3   See Walter Bagehot, *The English Constitution*; Cambridge University Press, Cambridge, 2001; p. 60.
4   Mr Murdoch's newspaper the *Sun* raised doubts about the long-term value of the Monarchy in an editorial on 4th April 2001, whereas Mr Black's republican leanings are believed to find expression only on more restricted occasions.
5   V. Bogdanor, *op. cit.*; p. 300.
6   For example, legislation to guarantee freedom of information (which was passed by Parliament in the form of the *Freedom of Information Act 2000*) or

purposeful initiatives for reform of the House of Commons.

7 See R.W.K. Hinton, 'The Prime Minister as an elected Monarch', *Parliamentary Affairs*, Vol. XIII, 1959–60.

8 Tom Nairn, *The Enchanted Glass, Britain and its Monarchy*; Radius, London, 1988; p. 353.

9 Quoted in V. Bogdanor, *op. cit.*; p. 184.

10 For an interesting account of this particular period of political and press criticism of the Victorian monarchy, see Antony Taylor, *Down with the Crown, British Anti-Monarchism and debates about Royalty since 1790*; Reaktion Books, London, 1999; pp. 80–143.

11 See Report of the Royal Trustees, HC 464, 11th February 1993, on the arrangements made, including a Memorandum of Understanding between the Palace and 10 Downing Street.

12 V. Bogdanor, *op. cit.*; p. 193.

13 For a good account of Stanley Baldwin's role in the 1936 Abdication crisis, see Keith Middlemass and John Barnes, *Baldwin, a Biography*; Weidenfeld & Nicolson, London, 1969.

14 Until he becomes King, Prince Charles could only marry again with the consent of the Queen who would be advised by the Prime Minister of the day. When he becomes King, Charles might find it difficult to marry a divorcée against the wishes of the Prime Minister and Cabinet, although he would not be *formally* constrained from doing so and the leading figures in a future Government might be less censorious about such an idea than their predecessors have been in the distant past. Such a development would require the passage of primary legislation in the United Kingdom and of constitutional amendments in the other Commonwealth countries in which the British Monarch is recognised as Head of State and the same conditions would apply before the historic prohibition in the 1701 Act of Settlement against a British Monarch marrying a Catholic could be removed.

15 Roger Scruton, *England, an Elegy*; Chatto & Windus, London, 2000; p. 3.

16 Martin Loughlin, 'The State, the Crown and the law', in M. Sunkin and S. Payne (eds) *The Nature of the Crown*; Oxford University Press, Oxford, 1999; p. 74.

17 See Lord Diplock's judgment in *Town Investments Ltd v. Department of the Environment* (1978) AC 359 for a clear statement of this position.

18 See John Humphrys, 'Why the Anglican Church monopoly should be broken', *Sunday Times*, 15th October 2000.

19 Those which still accept the Queen as their Head of State are: Antigua and Barbuda, Australia, Bahamas, Barbados, Belize, Canada, Grenada, Jamaica, New Zealand, Papua New Guinea, St Kitts and Nevis, St Lucia, St Vincent and Grenadines, Solomon Islands, and Tuvalu.

20 Quoted by Brigid Hadfield, 'Judicial review and the perogative powers of the Crown', in M. Sunkin and S. Payne (eds) *op. cit.*; pp. 197–8.

21 *Ibid*; p. 200.

22 *Ibid*; p. 216.

23 In relation to the armed forces, however, it is now clear that the Crown 'can no longer assert that those who serve in its armed forces are subject to its *sole* judgement, underpinned by notions of national security and defence of the realm, as to their rights at least during peace-time' (Peter Rowe, 'The Crown and accountability for the Armed Forces', in M. Sunkin and S. Payne (eds) *op. cit.*; p. 281). This change in the traditional dispensation came about mainly as a result of appeals to European human rights jurisdiction by armed forces personnel dissatisfied with the results of military jurisdiction in the United Kingdom – see for example *Alexander Finlay v. the United Kingdom*, Application No. 22107/93 on which the European Commission on Human Rights gave an Opinion against the UK on 5th September 1995 which was subsequently confirmed by the European Court of Human Rights on 25th February 1997.

24 It should be noted in this context that although a determined Government can plough ahead with its policy to declare war or conclude a treaty under the Royal Prerogative, it still needs to retain adequate Parliamentary support for its actions, otherwise it can be seriously damaged or even defeated by a vote of no confidence.

25 Quoted by B. Hadfield, *op. cit.*; p. 204.

26 For these definitions I have drawn heavily upon the work of Adam Tomkins, 'Crown privileges', in M. Sunkin and S. Payne (eds) *op. cit.*; pp. 171–95.

27 See Tom Cornford, 'Legal remedies against the Crown and its officers', in M. Sunkin and S. Payne (eds) *op. cit.*; pp. 257–62.

28 See Lord Hewart, *The New Despotism*; 2nd edn, Greenwood, West Point, 1945, and W. Robson, *Justice and Administrative Law*; 3rd edn, Stevens, London, 1951, for some of the original arguments against the growth of unaccountable public administration since the First World War.

29 See A. Tomkins, *op. cit.*; pp. 171–95.

30 In this deft approach to squaring judicial power with Parliamentary supremacy there seems to have been a clear parallel between the 1947 Crown Proceedings Act and the 1998 Human Rights Act in that each piece of influential legislation relied upon

the Law Lords making a *declaration* of the law and then left Parliament free to remedy any contradiction with an existing statute *if it chose to do so.*

31 See A. Tomkins, *op. cit.*; p. 171.
32 See B. Hadfield, *op. cit.*; p. 230.
33 *M. v. Home Office* (1994) 1 AC 377.
34 H.W.R. Wade, *Administrative Law*; 6th edn, Clarendon Press, Oxford, 1988; p. 30.
35 A much quoted example of this is the 1965 War Damage Act which swiftly overturned the House of Lords judgment given in the case of *Burmah Oil* earlier in the same year.
36 Michael Cassell, 'On Her Majesty's Service', *Financial Times*, 17th June 2000.
37 Articles in *The Times*, 24th October 2000, recalled the previously stated view of the Prince of Wales that the Monarchy should represent British people of all faiths and of none, which meant that he personally saw merit in declaring himself to be 'Defender of Faith' rather than 'Defender of the Faith' when he becomes King.
38 R. Scruton, *op. cit.*; p. 12.

Further reading

Walter Bagehot, *The English Constitution*; Cambridge University Press, Cambridge, 2001.

Anthony Barnett (ed.) *Power and the Throne*; Vintage, London, 1994.

A. Benn and A. Hood, *Common Sense: a New Constitution for Britain*; Hutchinson, London, 1993.

Vernon Bogdanor, *The Monarchy and the Constitution*; Clarendon Press, Oxford, 1997.

Jonathan Freedland, *Bring Home the Revolution: the Case for a British Republic*; Fourth Estate, London, 1999.

Tim Hames and Mark Leonard, *Modernising the Monarchy*; Demos, London, 1998.

Joseph M. Jacob, *The Republican Crown*; Dartmouth, Aldershot, 1996.

Tom Nairn, *The Enchanted Glass, Britain and its Monarchy*; Radius, London, 1988.

Ben Pimlott, *The Queen: a Biography of Elizabeth II*; HarperCollins, London, 1996.

M. Sunkin and S. Payne (eds) *The Nature of the Crown*; Oxford University Press, Oxford, 1999.

Antony Taylor, *Down with the Crown, British Anti-Monarchism and Debates about Royalty since 1790*; Reaktion Books, London, 1999.

website for the Monarchy or Buckingham Palace: www.royal.gov.uk

Reforming the House of Lords

Reforming the House of Lords was presented as one of the central elements of Labour's programme of constitutional reform when it came to power in 1997. Yet the fact that at the time of writing the process of reforming this august and ancient institution of Parliament has only reached a rather unconvincing Stage Two and senior Ministers seem determined to resist radical changes in its role and composition suggests a rather half-hearted commitment on the part of Tony Blair, Lord Irvine and their senior colleagues to the idea of producing a transformed Second Chamber within a trans-formed system of Parliamentary government. As Lord Reay, one of the hereditary peers elected by his colleagues to membership of the interim House in 1999 but now facing extinction in Stage Two of Lords reform, observed in the Lords debate on the Wakeham Report: 'from my reading of British history, we have only rarely proceeded by adopting blueprints or proceeded to constitutional reform at all, except in conditions of great, or even dire, necessity'.[1]

Settling old scores against hereditary peers

As with the Monarchy, so with the House of Lords, there is a good deal of history which bears upon the current attempts to reform the Second Chamber within our Parliamentary system of government. Without going back into the mists of time, it is reasonable to begin a brief historical summary by recalling that the *1911 Parliament Act* was, in the words of its Preamble, a provision 'for regulating the relations between the two Houses of Parliament' at a time of real constitutional crisis (thus satisfying Lord Reay's requirement). The crisis had been caused by the fact that the House of Lords, dominated at the time by Conservative and Unionist peers, had voted to defeat Lloyd George's radical Budget of 1909 and had threat-ened to defeat (as they had done before under previous Liberal Administrations) any legislative measure for Irish Home Rule. To begin with, this aristocratic recalcitrance had precipitated two appeals to the electorate in April and November

1910, but the results of both elections had been inconclusive and had not settled the constitutional dispute between the two Houses of Parliament or, more precisely, between the Liberal Government and the Tory Opposition. After the second General Election in 1910, the huge Tory majority in the House of Lords eventually gave way with ill grace to the Liberal Government in the Commons, which in its turn was dependent upon Irish Nationalist and Labour support in the Lower House, by narrowly agreeing not to insist upon its amendments. Thus, with some 300 Tory peers abstaining, the Bill was finally approved by the Upper House.

The upshot of the 1911 Act was threefold: the Lords' power to reject Money Bills was removed; their veto power over ordinary Public Bills was replaced with the power to delay such legislation for a maximum of two years; and as something of a concession to the Lords (although really an acknowledgement of the growing importance of the electorate as the final arbiter of constitu-tional disputes) the two Houses agreed that the maximum permitted span of a Parliament should be reduced from seven to five years. The Preamble to the Act made it quite clear that there was still a good deal of unfinished constitutional business between the two Houses and gave notice of the Commons' intention 'to substitute for the House of Lords as it at present exists a Second Chamber constituted on a popular instead of hereditary basis . . . in a measure . . . for limiting and defining the powers of the new Second Chamber'. However, the Preamble also made it clear that 'such substitution cannot immediately be brought into operation' – a pragmatic warning to future constitutional reformers who were, in any case, knocked off course by the outbreak of the First World War and all the momentous political developments which followed in its wake.

The device of a constitutional conference, chaired by Lord Bryce, on the reform of the House of Lords was attempted in 1917. However, it was held at an unpropitious time and was unable to command anything like the attention which was then focused upon the fierce fighting on the Western Front or the Communist Revolution in Russia.[2]

A similar device was used in 1948 when another attempt was made to grapple with the reform of the House of Lords by an inter-party conference established at the behest of the post-war Labour Government which was preparing legislation to limit still further the delaying power of the Upper House.[3] This conference also came to nothing and effectively broke down in the face of the mutually incompatible positions of the two main parties – notwithstanding the more restrained approach towards wielding the remaining power of the Lords which had been adopted since the war by Lord Salisbury and the leading Tory peers. The only tangible result of this flurry of governmental concern with the House of Lords was the *1949 Parliament Act* which was passed under the unilateral powers of the House of Commons provided in the 1911 Parliament Act. This was the legislative expression of the then Labour Government's rather modest intention to reduce the delaying power of the Upper House from two years to one year, which had been triggered by the Tory peers' resistance to the nationalisation of the iron and steel industries via a Bill which had not been foreshadowed in the 1945 Labour Manifesto and which Lord Salisbury therefore felt justified in asking his fellow Tory peers to oppose. However, as with the 1911 Parliament Act, no legislative attempt was made by the Government of the day to alter the composition of the House of Lords or to redefine its role.

With Conservative Administrations in office from 1951 to 1964, one might assume that there would have been no legislative or other political action affecting the composition or any other aspect of the House of Lords. One might expect Conservative Ministers to have left these things well alone, but not a bit of it.[4] In 1957 the Macmillan Administration introduced daily allowances for peers' attendance at the House of Lords and for defraying the costs of their travel to and from their homes – a measure which could charitably have been interpreted as a small move towards recognising the increased professionalism of some 'working peers'. In 1958 the *Life Peerages Act* made possible the creation of Life Peers, including peerages for women in their own right – a measure which could justifiably have

been described as a blow for 'modernisation' in a House which until that time had been completely hereditary – with the notable exceptions of 26 Bishops and 28 Law Lords who were appointed by the Monarch on the advice of the Prime Minister of the day. On the other hand, it should be noted that this Act provided a wonderful opportunity for Harold Macmillan, then Prime Minister, to expand the powers of patronage which he exercised in the name of the Crown, but actually to the political advantage of his own party.

In 1963 the *Peerage Act* enabled hereditary peers to renounce their titles (while not prejudicing the rights of their heirs and successors) in order to make themselves eligible for membership of the Commons. It also provided for female hereditary peers to sit in the Lords on the same basis as their male counterparts.[5]

Once again, no aspect of these reforms affected the right of hereditary peers to sit in the House of Lords or the right of the House as a whole to reject subordinate legislation, Private Bills and Bills to confirm provisional Orders. Moreover, the residual delaying power which the Upper House still possessed meant that it could dislocate any Government's legislative programme and, in the final year of a Parliament, defeat a Government Bill altogether.

The only other serious and Government-inspired attempt to reform the House of Lords prior to the arrival in office of 'New Labour' in 1997 was the ill-fated *Parliament (No. 2) Bill* which was introduced by the second Wilson Administration in 1968. This provided for the creation of a smaller Second Chamber and a two-tier membership consisting of those peers with the right to vote (about 200–250 active Life Peers plus the Bishops and serving Law Lords) and those non-voting peers who would only be entitled to sit and speak (made up of irregularly attending Life Peers and hereditary peers). With the planned creation of about 80 more Labour Life Peers, the idea was that no single party would have a permanent overall majority, but the Government of the day would have a 10 per cent majority over the combined Opposition parties with cross-bench peers holding the balance. It was an ingenious package addressed to the two principal problems of an unreformed House of Lords in Labour eyes: the preponderance of hereditary peers and the preponderance of peers willing to take the Conservative and Unionist whip. The voting peers were to be paid a salary and have a retiring age of 75 (like the Bishops). In the future, inheritance of a peerage would not qualify someone for membership of the House of Lords, so the link between accidents of birth and participation in Parliament would finally be broken. The proposals would have reduced the delaying power of the Upper House to six months and would have removed the Lords' power to reject secondary legislation. For the rest, Ministers seemed intent upon ensuring that there would be no fundamental distinctions between the activities of the Lords and of the Commons, but no constructive complementarity between the two Houses of Parliament either.

The Bill was effectively defeated in Committee on the floor of the House of Commons by a sustained filibuster by backbenchers on both sides led by Michael Foot (Labour) and Enoch Powell (then Conservative). These Parliamentary traditionalists in the House of Commons opposed any such reform of the House of Lords which, by making the Second Chamber more legitimate, was thought likely to strengthen its position in our constitutional arrangements at the expense of the Commons. In the face of such implacable opposition from both sides, the Wilson Administration decided to abandon the Bill in April 1969.[6] In the process the Labour Ministers of that time sent a clear message to their successors that any future attempt to reform the Upper House would have to include credible assurances that it posed no threat to the predominance of the House of Commons.

To understand how we have arrived at the present juncture in House of Lords reform, it is also necessary to review briefly the trajectory of Labour Party commitment to this goal. In 1934 the Labour Conference committed the party to total abolition of the House of Lords as an institution. This was still the formal position of the party at the 1977 Party Conference when a similar resolution was passed in favour of a unicameral Parliament. Of course, in the meantime two majoritarian Labour Governments had had chances to implement Conference policy, but had carefully refrained from doing so. By the 1992 Labour Conference the party was content with a bi-cameral Parliament, but committed itself to an elected Second Chamber with further reduced delaying powers.

In the 1997 Labour Manifesto the party became more cautious about fundamental reform of the House of Lords – especially the idea of making it completely elected – and concentrated instead upon its commitment to settle old scores with the Tory-dominated hereditary peers. Thus the first and only clear commitment – described as 'an initial self-contained reform not dependent upon further reform in the future' – was to end the right of hereditary peers to sit and vote in the House of Lords, while leaving the legislative powers of the Second Chamber unaltered. This was presented, however, as 'the first stage in a process of reform to make the House of Lords more democratic and representative' – words which were repeated in the Queen's Speech on 24th November 1998. Labour Ministers sought to ensure that 'over time party appointees as life peers more accurately reflect the proportion of votes cast at the previous General Election', but added that 'no one political party should seek a majority in the House of Lords'. They also declared a commitment 'to maintaining an independent cross-bench presence of life peers'. Finally, they promised to appoint a committee of both Houses 'to undertake a wide-ranging review of possible further change and then to bring forward proposals for reform'.

Once Labour was in Government, the procedural steps which it envisaged along the path of a two-stage reform seemed to be adjusted. The 1998 Queen's Speech referred to a simple Bill to end the right of the hereditaries to sit and vote in the House of Lords, a White Paper to set out the Government's approach to reform, including the arrangements for a new system of appointing Life Peers, and the establishment of a Royal Commission 'to review further changes and speedily to bring forward proposals for reform'. The promised White Paper was published in January 1999 and the Royal Commission was established in February 1999 under the chairmanship of Lord Wakeham, a former Tory Chief Whip in the Commons.

The legislative process to remove the hereditary peers from the Second Chamber proved to be somewhat messier than some might have expected. In the summer of 1999 a deal was worked out behind closed doors in considerable secrecy between the Prime Minister and Lord Cranborne (then Leader of the Opposition in the Lords), but it was immediately disowned by the Conservative Leader, William Hague, who promptly sacked Lord Cranborne for his unauthorised initiative. The idea of the deal was to enable a modest number of hereditary peers (92 out of a total of 759) to remain in the House at least until Stage Two of Labour's Lords reform policy was implemented.[7] Thus in the interim Second Chamber, which came into existence in November 1999, there has been an anomalous collection of peers with varying status and credentials. Thanks to the buccaneering instincts of Lord Cranborne, to the willingness of the Prime Minister to agree a temporary and face-saving stay of execution for a few of the hereditaries, and to the consensus-seeking efforts of Lord Weatherill and a number of other cross-benchers, it proved possible to carry an amendment to the Bill which gave legislative effect to the coincident intentions of these very different political interests.

The interim Second Chamber

As prescribed in the 1997 Labour Manifesto, Stage One of House of Lords reform was carried out broadly according to plan. The interim Second Chamber, which was brought into existence by the passage of the 1999 House of Lords Act, has had a markedly different *composition* to the Upper House that preceded it in that it is substantially smaller in total membership and the balance between the various categories of membership has been significantly altered.[8] The total potential membership (including peers without writs of summons and those on indefinite leave of absence) was reduced by nearly half from 1,295 in January 1999 to 695 in June 2000. The number of hereditary peers was reduced by nearly nine-tenths from 759 (59 per cent

of all peers) who had been in the House by right of succession to 92 (13 per cent of all peers) who were there as 'transitional' hereditaries following their election by an electorate of all their colleagues. The number of Life Peers was increased from 482 (37 per cent of all peers) to 533 (77 per cent of all peers) and, if you count the seventeen former hereditary peers who were appointed as Life Peers, as well as the 26 Bishops who still sit in the House *ex officio* and the 28 Law Lords who do likewise, it can be seen that the overall proportion of non-hereditary peers rose from 41 per cent to 87 per cent of the total membership from January 1999 to June 2000 as a result of the legislation.

On the other hand, no change was made in either the powers or the functions of the House, since Ministers had not intended to address this task until Stage Two of the reform process. This was supposed to follow a report from a committee of both Houses of Parliament which would be appointed 'to undertake a wide-ranging review of possible further change and then to bring forward proposals for reform', according to the 1997 Labour Manifesto. In the event, Ministers preferred to rely upon the Royal Commission which they established under the chairmanship of Lord Wakeham in February 1999 rather than upon what would probably have been a more party political committee of both Houses over which Ministers might have had less control.

Yet for those who imagined that Stage One of Lords reform would have little or no effect upon the *attitudes and behaviour* of the interim Second Chamber, there was something of a surprise in store. The evidence drawn from votes in the House of Lords over a 30-year period shows that the Parliamentary sessions since 1997–98 have clocked up a higher rate of Government defeats in the Lords than any session since 1978–79; and if one focuses only upon the 1999–2000 session (after the interim House had been established), one discovers that there were fifteen Government defeats in the Lords to the end of May 2000 (29 per cent of all divisions held during that period).[9] What this suggests is an interim Second Chamber which was more self-confident and arguably more independent-minded than any of its predecessors over about a 20-year period, and that the peers within it were quite prepared to use their *existing powers* with self-confidence and independence of spirit.

It seems that the principal explanations for this discernible shift in the attitudes and behaviour of the interim Second Chamber as compared with its institutional predecessor were to be found in the dialectical relations between the two Houses of Parliament. In the first place, as the membership of the House of Lords became more evenly balanced between Conservative peers (33 per cent of the total compared with 41 per cent of the total before) and Labour peers (28 per cent compared with 15 per cent previously), opportunities increased for Liberal Democrat peers (9 per cent compared with 6 per cent before) and Cross-Bench life peers (27 per cent compared with 10 per cent before) to exercise more political clout with their swing votes in what became effectively a 'hung' Second Chamber. Secondly, if conditions are ever finely balanced in the House of Commons – as they were between 1974 and 1979 when the Tories in both Houses of Parliament were able to frustrate the purposes of a vulnerable Labour Government, and as they could be again if a future General Election were to produce a 'hung' House of Commons – then the Upper House can come into its own and punch above its true political weight even as a largely appointed Second Chamber.

Since on many occasions in British constitutional history it has been true to say that *rien ne dure comme le provisoire*, it is worth analysing the interim Second Chamber to see whether it has been more democratic, more representative, more authoritative and more legitimate than the traditional House of Lords which it replaced. After all, these are some of the most important criteria by which the political class and other opinion formers in the constitutional debate are likely to judge any reform of the Second Chamber, so it seems both worthwhile and interesting to apply them to this institution, however provisional its existence may turn out to be.

Firstly, it is hard to argue that the interim Second Chamber has been more democratic than the one it replaced, unless one takes the election in 1999 of the 92 hereditary peers who continued as members of the Upper House as a valid indicator of democracy in this context.[10] A more democratic Second Chamber, whether interim or permanent, can only mean an institution in which a significant proportion of the members (conceivably all of them) acquire their rights to sit and vote by dint of having been elected under some system of universal adult suffrage. This need not imply a first-past-the-post election, as for members of the House of Commons, nor need it imply that such elections are held at the same time as General Elections. Whatever the method and timing of elections to the Second Chamber, the British public seems to prefer election to appointment and, indeed, direct election to indirect election or nomination from representative economic and social groups or distinctive territorial units.

On the other hand, it is possible to argue that the interim Second Chamber has been more representative than its predecessor, since the previous preponderance of hereditary peers has been largely removed and in the smaller interim House there has been more gender, social and ethnic diversity among the membership. However, the proportion of women has only increased from 8 per cent before the change to 16 per cent after it, the proportion of peers from a 'working-class' background remains small and has probably got smaller, while the proportion of peers from an ethnic background has risen only slightly and still remains below the proportion which such people account for in the population at large.[11] Moreover, the proportion of peers under the age of 50 has dropped significantly from 13 per cent of the former House to 7 per cent of the interim House as a direct result of the culling of the hereditaries, at least some of whom had inherited their titles and taken their seats in the Lords at a relatively young age. It is principally in *party political* terms that the interim Second Chamber has become more representative of the party balance in the Commons and in the country at large.

When it comes to assessing the criteria of authority and legitimacy of the interim House, comparisons are inevitably more subjective and difficult to make, since so much depends upon what the observer may mean by such elusive terms.

There is some evidence that the interim Second Chamber is *regarded* as more authoritative than the House of Lords it replaced in the sense that it seems to have become a more self-confident Assembly which is more frequently swayed by influential Cross-Benchers and expert and independent Law Lords than was the case before. This view was given credence by Baroness Jay, then Leader of the Lords, when she forecast that 'a decision by the [interim] House not to support a proposal from the Government will carry more weight, because it will have to include supporters from a range of political and independent opinions'.[12]

As for the intangible question of whether or not the interim Second Chamber has been regarded as more legitimate than its institutional predecessor, this invites an ambivalent answer. If one takes the Labour point of view that membership of any representative Assembly by dint of inheritance is inherently illegitimate, then the interim arrangements have been more legitimate than those they replaced. Yet if that is the case, what are we to make of the Monarchy, which is formally a part of Parliament? Are we to conclude that there is also no place for a hereditary Monarchy in our system of Parliamentary government? The 1997 Labour Manifesto merely stated cryptically: 'we have no plans to replace the Monarchy'. It seems, therefore, that the Monarchy is safe for the time being, although those of the Queen's close relatives who were peers of first creation were swept out of the Second Chamber in Stage One of Lords reform during the first Blair Administration.

From the Conservative point of view, the argument has been heard that the interim Second Chamber has been in some ways less legitimate than the institution which it replaced. Conservatives have maintained that the former House of Lords was made venerable and legitimate, at least in the eyes of those of a traditional disposition, by the very fact that it originally took precedence over the House of Commons and that many of its members came from families which had served this country over many generations. By contrast, they regarded the interim House as essentially an Assembly of political appointees and thus an example of the 'patronage state' which is thought to be excessively populated with Tony Blair's political cronies and various other figures who are known to have been substantial contributors to Labour Party funds.[13]

Of course, both main parties have engaged in some special pleading on these issues, so it is hard to reach an objective conclusion about the overall adequacy of the interim Second Chamber. Probably all that can be said at this stage is that there was bound to be a significant rebalancing of the membership with the departure of nearly all the hereditaries and for historical reasons this was bound to disadvantage the Tory cause. Yet close observation of the *political behaviour* of the interim Chamber suggests that no political appointee is ever a puppet of his or her patron for very long and the influence of the independent Appointments Commission chaired by Lord Stevenson may gradually offset the influence of party political patronage in a reformed Second Chamber once the next round of reform has come into effect.

The Wakeham Report – *A House for the Future*

It is clear that Ministers regard the Wakeham Report of January 2000, entitled *A House for the Future*, as the basis for the next stage of House of Lords reform. The Report defined the challenge as one of 'building on the strengths of the existing House of Lords, while creating a new Second Chamber better adapted to modern circumstances'.[14] It sought change 'in a direction and at a pace which goes with the grain of the traditional British evolutionary approach to constitutional reform, while taking this once-in-a-lifetime opportunity to produce a coherent blue-print for the Second Chamber of Parliament'.

On *the role* of the House of Lords, the Wakeham Commission said that a reformed Second Chamber should have four main roles: it should bring a range of perspectives to bear upon the development of public policy, be broadly representative of British society, play a vital role as one of the main checks and balances within the British constitution, and provide a voice for the nations and regions of the United Kingdom at the centre of national politics.

On powers, it argued that 'no radical change is needed in the balance of power between the two Houses of Parliament' and indeed that the Upper House should 'be cautious about challenging the clearly expressed views of the House of Commons on major issues of public policy'.[15] It did, however, concede that a reformed Second Chamber should retain the suspensory veto set out in the Parliament Acts, but suggested that the power to veto Statutory Instruments (which had fallen very largely into abeyance) should be abolished and replaced with an amending and delaying power. The only small sign of bravado by the Commission in relation to the powers of the Upper House was the suggestion that the Commons should no longer be able unilaterally to amend the Parliament Acts by using Parliament Act procedures, as had happened in the case of the 1949 Parliament Act.

On *functions*, the Commission was rather more bold and expansive in its recommendations for a reformed Second Chamber. It opined that there should be more pre-legislative scrutiny of draft Bills and more consideration given to promoting Bills drawn up by the Law Commission. It recommended the establishment of a new Constitutional Committee to scrutinise the constitutional implications of all legislation and to keep the operation of the constitution under review; and a new Human Rights Committee to scrutinise all Bills and Statutory Instruments with human rights implications – both of which Committees have now been established. It suggested that the reformed Second Chamber should give a voice at the centre of the political system to the non-English nations and English regions, but not by drawing such representatives from the devolved Administrations or the devolved Parliaments because – one suspects – this might have smelled a little of federalism. It advocated extended Second Chamber scrutiny of secondary legislation and strengthened arrangements for the scrutiny of European legislation. For good measure, it also recommended a new Committee to scrutinise treaties before ratification takes place, thus making a cautious Parliamentary incursion into one aspect of the Royal Prerogative.

On the *judicial role* of the Second Chamber and the internationally anomalous position of having the Lord Chancellor and the most senior judges in England and Wales as members of the Legislature, the members of the Commission obligingly funked a recommendation (having been told in the White Paper that this was not a matter for them) and contented themselves with the complacent observation that there was 'insufficient reason to change the present arrangements'. All in all, it was obvious that in most aspects of their remit the Commissioners saw themselves as builders or renovators, instructed to do no more than tinker with the existing structure and functions of the Lords with the express aim of 'broadening the Second Chamber's role rather than constituting a radical departure from what has gone before'.[16]

Having made rather minimal, even timid recommendations on the role, powers and functions of a reformed Second Chamber, the Commission devoted the bulk of its report to one of the favourite pastimes of the British Establishment – thinking of ways to select other people whom they might deign to include among their number. They approached this task not with any enthusiasm for extending the principles of democracy to the Second Chamber, but rather by listing some general *desiderata* for the reformed House as a whole and for the selection of people to join it. They expressed the view that the reformed institution should be 'authoritative, confident and broadly representative of the whole of British society'. They sought to achieve these goals by identifying the most desirable characteristics of the people who might be chosen to serve (whether by appointment or some form of election), such as breadth of experience, expertise, specialist knowledge, moral qualities and personal distinction – in other words, a rehearsal of the traditional criteria for choosing new peers to be included in the Honours List. Those members of the Commission who were themselves peers (or aspired to be) apparently succeeded in persuading their colleagues to support the further injunction that such admirable members of a reformed Second Chamber should be free from party domination, non-polemical and courteous in their manners, and able to take a long-term view of issues and events. They then managed to persuade themselves that 'a new Second Chamber with these characteristics should remedy the deficiencies of the old House of Lords, which lacked the political legitimacy and confidence to do its job properly, while preserving some of its best features'.[17]

So there was no suggestion here that the deficiencies of the old House were caused by the preponderance of its hereditary membership or by the fact that none of their Lordships was elected by the British people; no suggestion that the deficiencies might have been caused by the old House having too little power rather than too much; and no suggestion that its role as a Parliamentary Chamber, which (since 1911 at least) has been constitutionally subordinate to rather than coordinate with the House of Commons, might have had something to do with the problem. One can exonerate the Commissioners for their apparent inability or unwillingness to give credence to such alternative explanations only on the pragmatic grounds that Labour Ministers had not permitted them to think such heretical thoughts – at any rate out loud in their Report.

Thus the central, and confusing, recommendation of the Wakeham Commission was that there should be a reformed Second Chamber of about 550 members whose qualification for membership should no longer be the award of a peerage, but other more complicated and varied criteria. The preponderance of newly appointed Cross-Benchers should be nominated by a statutorily based and genuinely independent Appointments Commission. This body should have the statutory duty to maintain the proportion of Cross-Benchers in the reformed Chamber at about 20 per cent of the total, and to keep an eye upon the nominations of the politically affiliated members in an attempt to maintain an overall political balance among this portion of the membership which matched the balance of political opinion in the country as a whole, as expressed in the votes cast for each of the parties at the most recent General Election.

What the Commission described as 'a significant minority' of the members of a reformed Second Chamber should, it believed, be elected from the regions and nations of the United Kingdom in ways which reflected the balance of political opinion within each of those geographical areas. Yet to complicate matters still further, the Commission presented three different models for what it insisted upon describing as 'the selection' of these regional members – suggesting that at least some members of the Commission found it very difficult to use the 'e word' (election) in relation to the composition of the Second Chamber. See *Box 9* for summaries of the different models proposed in the Wakeham Report.

To promote continuity of membership and a longer-term perspective, all such regionally elected members (under all three models) should serve in the Second Chamber for a term of three electoral cycles or fifteen years (the maximum tenure for newly appointed members of the reformed Second Chamber), but with the possibility of being *reappointed* for a further period of up to fifteen years at the discretion of the statutory Appointments Commission. As if this was not enough, the Wakeham Commission threw in the added concession that 'to facilitate a smooth transition to the new arrangements, the *existing* Life Peers should become members of the new Second Chamber' – although somewhere deep in the detail of the Report it was diffidently suggested that such members might be encouraged to retire in order to limit the overall numbers and reduce the average age in the Chamber as a whole.[18]

It may be hard for a serious reader to keep a straight face here, since by this stage in the Report the Commission's contorted recommendations had become simply risible. Its members may sincerely have intended to produce recommendations which were (in the words of the Report) 'not only persuasive and intellectually coherent, but also workable, durable and politically realistic'. Yet in the event any objective observer could see that they had tied themselves in Establishment knots essentially because, although they had faithfully tried to follow Tony Blair's instructions, they could not entirely resist the logic of recommending that at least a proportion of the reformed Second Chamber should be elected, if only as a sop to the widely acknowledged need to endow the new institution with at least a measure of democratic

Box 9 Wakeham Report models for a reformed Second Chamber

- *Model A* implied a total of 65 regional members chosen at the time of each General Election by a system of 'complementary' election, which would mean that the votes cast for party candidates in each constituency at a General Election would be accumulated at regional level. The number of regional members which each party secured in each region would be proportional to each party's share of the vote in that region and the identity of the successful candidates would be determined by their respective places on closed party lists. One-third of the regions would hold 'elections' for such members at each General Election.
- *Model B* implied a total of 87 regional members elected at the time of each European Parliament election, with one-third of the regions participating in the electoral process each time. The relative strength of the parties at that election would determine how many candidates were returned to the Second Chamber to represent a given region. The success of individual candidates would depend upon their position in their own party list which (in the view of a majority on the Commission) would be a partially open list implying scope for the voters to indicate their preferences as between individual candidates on each party's list.
- *Model C* implied a total of 195 regional members elected by thirds at the time of each European Parliament election using the same partially open list system of proportional representation as in Model B.

legitimacy. On the other hand, while trying to work through these problems, the Commissioners must have seen the absurdity of recommending a mixed Chamber, part appointed and part elected, when their arguments for the elected part could so easily be dismissed as intellectually confused and the mechanisms proposed could so easily be represented as a token form of democracy.

In some ways one can feel quite sorry for Lord Wakeham and his fellow Commissioners, faced as they were with the unenviable task of producing a Report within rather limiting terms of reference and a very short period of time for an inquiry of this complexity. It could be said that the most important of the 132 recommendations were subject to the tyranny of the terms of reference which had insisted upon 'the need to maintain the position of the House of Commons as the *pre-eminent* Chamber of Parliament' and to take 'particular account of the *present* nature of the constitutional settlement'.[19] Put simply, this meant that the Commission would be out of bounds if its Report did not expressly prescribe a *subordinate* role in the Parliamentary firmament for a reformed Second

Chamber and if it sought to make wider constitutional recommendations which went beyond the confines of the *established conventions* which limit the powers and aspirations of the so-called Upper House. Within such a tight curtilage it was no surprise that the Report was somewhat mocked by the quality press, and the much respected Constitution Unit at University College London described it as merely an interim report.[20]

Debate on Lords reform in the Lords

The Lords debate on the Wakeham Report was held on 7th March 2000 and, predictably perhaps, those who spoke gave a mixed and sometimes complacent response to the main recommendations.[21] *Baroness Jay*, then Leader of the Lords, opened for the Government and began by making it clear that the Cabinet favoured a bi-cameral Parliament in which the House of Commons was the supreme institution and in which the reformed Second Chamber concentrated principally upon the scrutiny of legislation and detailed examination of certain appropriate aspects of Executive action, such as Statutory Instruments, constitutional matters, human rights and European legislation. She argued for no more than a small elected element – to represent the regions and the 'nations' of the United Kingdom – with the vast bulk of members there by appointment on the nomination of the Appointments Commission. She wanted to see matters arranged (or was it manipulated?) so that no single party commanded a majority in the Second Chamber, although she considered that the governing party might legitimately be expected to form the largest single contingent. Her only radical observation was to say that 'it is clearly relevant to explore de-coupling membership of the Second Chamber from the peerage'.

Lord Strathclyde for the Conservatives made it clear that his party favoured a larger elected element in a reformed Second Chamber and assured the House that 'a stronger Parliament is and will remain a central objective of my party's policy'. In terms of process, he urged upon the Government the early establishment of a Joint Committee of both Houses to look at how to take things forward from the Wakeham Report and to make further, perhaps more detailed recommendations. In terms of substance, he made what he described as four short-term proposals: (1) no reductions in the powers of the Lords *vis-à-vis* the Commons; (2) the introduction of a new power for the Lords to amend as well as reject secondary legislation; (3) the establishment of a Constitutional Committee to look at constitutional issues and legislative implications on the model of the successful Delegated Powers and Deregulation Committee; and (4) the establishment of the then non-statutory Appointments Commission on a statutory basis.

Lord Rodgers for the Liberal Democrats was more critical of the Wakeham Report which he described as 'cosy, comfortable and not unattractive to most of us here, including myself', but then went on to warn that 'many outside Parliament will see this as a sadly missed opportunity to reach a new constitutional settlement which would enable this Chamber to strengthen Parliament in its role

as a check on the abuse of executive power'. In this he was absolutely right and his remark was revealing in that it emphasised the clubbable and complacent atmosphere in the House of Lords which (for the Liberal Democrats at least) had apparently been unaffected by the culling of nearly all the Conservative hereditary peers. His other main point was to argue that 'only a predominantly elected Second Chamber will be acknowledged as the wholly legitimate half of a bicameral system that carries the authority that the Government cannot diminish'. Like Lord Strathclyde for the Conservatives, Lord Rodgers favoured 'cherry-picking' and getting on with anything recommended in the Wakeham Report which could reasonably be implemented without delay, such as the establishment of the Appointments Commission on an independent and statutory basis or the early formation of the Joint Committee of both Houses to discuss an agenda to be settled by agreement between the parties.

Lord Wakeham, when he spoke in the debate, unsurprisingly defended his Report and cautioned against 'cherry-picking' from among its many recommendations. As a former Conservative Government Chief Whip in the Lower House, he was robust in defence of the political supremacy of the Commons over the Lords and maintained that 'when the reformed Second Chamber challenges the Government and the other place [the majority in the Commons] . . . it should do so by strength of argument rather than relying upon an electoral mandate'. He based this dubious proposition on the argument contained in para 10.6 of his Report which claimed that it was an error to suppose that the authority of the Second Chamber could only stem from direct election of its members and that other factors – such as the 'representative' character of the peers, their expertise and breadth of experience, their personal distinction, the quality of their arguments and their relative freedom from partisan politics – all contributed substantially to the institution's overall authority and ability to make itself heard.

There was, by contrast, a whiff of aristocratic sulphur when *Viscount Cranborne* spoke. He began with the trenchant proposition that 'it would have been more sensible for any reform of Parliament to have begun with another place [the House of Commons] rather than here and to have set reform in that context'; he then expressed his preference for a reformed Second Chamber that was half elected and half appointed. *Lord Dahrendorf* (a Liberal Democrat), on the other hand, argued that there should be no directly elected element, no indirect election, no random appointments and no co-option of members. Instead he preferred a new House 'wholly appointed by a plausible and transparent process'.

Lord Norton of Louth (a Conservative academic) was also opposed to direct election of all or some of the members of a reformed Second Chamber on the classic grounds that what was most appropriate for the United Kingdom was 'a Second Chamber which is complementary to the first, fulfilling functions which are specific to or usefully performed by a Second Chamber without challenging fundamentally the democratic legitimacy of the first'. On the whole, his speech seemed to be a paean of praise to the characteristics of the *existing* House of Lords. Another distinguished academic, *Lord Smith of Clifton* (a Cross-Bencher) reminded the House that the Wakeham Report had been largely panned in the broadsheets; he characterised the debate as 'very much one of the Club talking to itself'. He was also pointed in his criticism of the Wakeham Commission which, he argued, had been 'handicapped from the outset by failing to reflect in its membership the broad spectrum of opinion on constitutional reform' and which had therefore produced 'an oligarch's charter'. Instead he strongly favoured a directly elected Second Chamber – as did the great majority of public opinion in a poll conducted in August 1999 for Democratic Audit which, although communicated to the Commission, had not been cited in its Report.

The Wakeham Report came under further heavy but civilised criticism from *Lord Richard*, the former Labour Leader of the Lords, who first posed and then answered his own fundamental question – namely, what are we trying to create in Lords reform? His simple answer was 'an effective Second Chamber'. For the attainment of this objective he recommended three preconditions: a Chamber

differently composed to the Commons; one with sufficient power to require the Government to think again; and one with sufficient legitimacy in the eyes of the public. His own proposal was for the creation of a reformed Second Chamber in which two-thirds of the members would be directly elected and one-third would be appointed – the latter consisting entirely of Cross-Benchers.

Lord Goodhart for the Liberal Democrats was really quite complimentary about the Wakeham Report and he accepted the argument that 'a wholly elected House would create a danger of confrontation with the other place [the House of Commons] and would lead to the risk that the Second Chamber would stop doing well what it now does well'. What worried him was that within the framework of mixed membership in a reformed Second Chamber not enough of the party political members would be elected. Moreover, in a reformed Chamber in which the preponderance of all the members were appointees, he was also worried about giving too much power and responsibility to the Appointments Commission.

The debate was closed by *Lord Williams of Mostyn*, then Attorney General, who kept his cards close to his chest and took care not to say anything which might have gone beyond or contradicted what Baroness Jay had said at the beginning of the debate. However, he did express a preference for the achievement of all-party consensus as a basis for the next stage of Lords reform and for constitutional change on a comprehensive basis 'if at all possible'.

In short, anyone listening to or reading the debate could not help being struck by the complacent self-congratulation on all sides of the House of Lords when peers endorsed the idea that most members of a reformed Second Chamber should continue to be appointed (by appropriate means) rather than elected; and by the disdainful hostility expressed towards anything as vulgar as party politics, especially as practised in the so-called elective dictatorship of the House of Commons. To this extent the main themes of the Wakeham Report were music to the ears of most peers in the interim House, although, as we shall see, that did not guarantee a favourable reception for it in the House of Commons nor did it necessarily commend the conclusions to interested public opinion beyond the confines of the Palace of Westminster.

Debate on Lords reform in the Commons

The significance of the debate in the House of Commons about three months later on 19th June 2000 lay not in the originality of what was said from either front bench nor in any sign from Margaret Beckett, then Leader of the House of Commons, that Government policy on Lords reform had evolved during the intervening period, but rather in the scorn and ridicule that was poured upon the Wakeham proposals by influential backbenchers in all three main parties.[22]

It was quite obvious from what *Margaret Beckett* said in opening the debate that she and other Cabinet sceptics about Lords reform must have needed some persuasion that a Second Chamber was necessary at all. However, even if the case for a reformed Second Chamber had been demonstrated to her satisfaction, she nevertheless advanced the view that the main purpose of the Upper House should be to make a distinctive contribution to the legislative process, but *not* to hold the Government of the day to account – a strange and dogmatic distinction which she sought to justify by saying that 'to have two Chambers, each with an identical role in that respect, would be bound to lead to conflict and confusion'. She regarded it as axiomatic, therefore, that the distinctive contribution which could be made by the Second Chamber required it to be distinctively constituted; this in her mind ruled out the possibility of an elected or largely elected body. The furthest she would go towards acknowledging the argument that a reformed Second Chamber would need a degree of democratic legitimacy was to repeat the Government's acceptance of the basic judgement of the Wakeham Commission that 'a largely appointed House with an elected element within it provides the range of expertise and experience that a reformed Second Chamber would need to add value to the legislative process'. In other words, the Second Chamber could continue to be a sort of institutional helpmate to the House of Commons, but within a carefully defined constitutional context and performing an explicitly subordinate role.

Sir George Young, who spoke for the Conservatives, began by making four brief general points. His first was that although most people represented the debate as a one-dimensional contest between the Lords and the Commons, the real contest was between Parliament and the Executive and 'in that battle the Houses are not rivals but partners'. His second was that it was difficult and perhaps undesirable to ring-fence Lords reform from Commons reform and that there was a case for tackling Commons reform first. His third was that the current position in the interim House of Lords was unsatisfactory in that although Ministers had asserted that it already spoke with more legitimacy and authority after disposing of most of the hereditary peers, there had been no sign of the Government respecting the Upper House, especially when the latter had defeated it on controversial legislative issues. His last general point was that the alleged unanimity of the Wakeham Commission had disguised a disagreement on the most contentious issue of the composition of the Second Chamber and had prevented the Committee from reaching conclusions on some other issues.

On the issues of policy, Sir George commended the Wakeham Report's formulation of what a reformed Second Chamber should aim to do – namely, 'to enhance the overall ability of Parliament as a whole to hold the Government to account . . . by using its particular strengths to develop arrangements which complement and reinforce those of the House of Commons'. On the composition of a reformed Second Chamber Sir George indicated that his party was likely to favour a higher proportion of elected members than in Model C of the Wakeham Report – i.e. more than 195 elected members in a House of about 600 members.

Sir George identified two principal arguments which had been put forward against elections to the Upper House: *firstly*, that elections would produce the wrong sort of politician; and *secondly*, that it would be intolerable if *two* Houses of Parliament claimed rival mandates from the British people. In answer to the first objection he argued that the behaviour of even the most domineering and abrasive politicians changed and mellowed when they reached the Upper House. His reply to the second objection was that 'the powers [of the House of Lords] are the powers given to it by this House, which is pre-eminent, and they cannot be unilaterally changed'. Essentially, what this meant was that the majority in the House of Commons would have a legislative veto over any unacceptable plans that a majority in the Upper House might hatch with a view to aggrandising their institution in a way deemed by the Lower House to be prejudicial to the sound working of our constitutional arrangements. Thus even if the reformed Second Chamber managed to attract much greater legitimacy in the eyes of the public, any deliberate increase in its *powers* would require the explicit approval of a majority in the Commons – so Members of Parliament who held these concerns should relax and stop feeling threatened by the prospect of a further reformed House of Lords.

Perhaps the main common theme of some of the more powerful backbench speeches from all parts of the House later in the debate was scorn and ridicule for the pusillanimity of the Wakeham Commission in running away from the powerful arguments for a largely or wholly elected Second Chamber and in taking refuge in a risible range of contrived recommendations on composition, none of which was coherent or persuasive. For example, *Robert Maclennan*, for the Liberal Democrats, argued that 'the absence of a commitment to democracy in the document is self-serving and oligarchic in its thrust rather than democratic as it ought to be'. He considered that the pre-eminence of the House of Commons was guaranteed by virtue of the fact that it provided and supported the members of the Government – indeed two of his own recommendations were that in future no Ministers should be drawn from the Upper House and that the link between the peerage and the Second Chamber should be broken – and he argued very forcefully that 'this Chamber's pre-eminence is not threatened by the creation of an effective Second Chamber of Parliament that does

what this Chamber has not done, cannot do or would prefer to be done elsewhere'.

Somewhat similar points were made by *Kenneth Clarke*, the former Conservative Chancellor of the Exchequer, who argued that 'it is obvious that a directly elected Upper House is the only one that will have full political legitimacy and the necessary clout properly to hold the modern Executive to account'. He then proceeded to demolish the arguments of the Wakeham Report for rejecting anything but a token elected element in a reformed Second Chamber on the grounds that (1) the British people would prefer an elected institution; (2) the relations between the two Houses of Parliament need not be a zero sum game and that giving the Upper House more legitimacy through elections need not diminish the authority of the Lower House; and (3) the constitutional role of the reformed Second Chamber could be reinforced and guaranteed by 'constitutional' legislation in the tradition of the 1911 and 1949 Parliament Acts which had produced *de facto* entrenchment of the previous dispensation.

Gordon Prentice, the Labour MP for Pendle and a member of Labour's National Executive Committee, described the Wakeham proposals as 'half-baked and risible'. He recalled that in his John Smith Memorial Lecture in 1996 Tony Blair had said: 'we have always favoured an elected Second Chamber', but he now foresaw the danger that his party would be democratically outflanked on the issue of Lords reform by both the Liberal Democrats and the Tories. He thought it would be indefensible for the Labour Government to adopt the Wakeham proposals. Indeed, he maintained that a predominantly appointed Second Chamber would be corrupting to Parliament. He mocked the criteria suggested by head-hunters at Pricewaterhouse-Coopers for selecting independent members of the proposed Appointments Commission.[23] He forecast that if the recommendations in the Wakeham Report were followed 'we shall be left with a bloated, elephantine Upper Chamber', since every year there would be further new appointees and the existing Life Peers would not be obliged to retire.

During the two wind-up speeches at the end of the debate, *Sir Patrick Cormack* for the

Conservatives felt obliged to concede that 'there is no consensus either in the House or in either party', and *Paddy Tipping* for the Government made a similar point when he said: 'there is unanimity neither between the parties nor within them'. If these comments from the two front benches meant that a worthwhile Parliamentary consensus on Stage Two of Lords reform would have been hard to achieve in the last Parliament, it seems equally clear that progress in the 2001–6 Parliament will depend upon the extent to which Ministers are prepared to use Labour's huge majority to force through further Lords reform against likely opposition from disaffected Labour backbenchers and a diminished Tory Party, which will probably support a larger elected element in a reformed Second Chamber.

Stage Two of reform and beyond

Having got as far as the elimination from the House of Lords of all but 92 of the hereditary peers and having considered the Report of the Wakeham Commission, the re-elected Labour Government and its Parliamentary supporters had to decide what to do about moving beyond the interim Second Chamber towards what Wakeham had called 'a

House for the future'. Labour's 2001 Manifesto stated that the party was 'committed to completing House of Lords reform, including removal of the remaining hereditary peers, to make it more representative and democratic, while maintaining the House of Commons' traditional primacy'.[24] It is now clear from the White Paper published in November 2001 that Stage Two of Lords reform will broadly follow the lines suggested in the Wakeham Report, but will also take account of the views expressed during a period of public consultation ending on 31st January 2002.[25]

The most controversial issues are likely to involve the *composition* of a reformed Second Chamber. The role and powers of a reformed Second Chamber are intended to remain broadly unchanged. As the Prime Minister put it in his Foreword to the White Paper, 'the imperative is for a reformed Second Chamber performing broadly the same functions as in the existing House of Lords, but in a more effective manner'.[26] (See *Box 10*.)

Although the Government is committed to put the independent Appointments Commission on a statutory footing, it seems clear that Tony Blair is unwilling to desist from exercising the traditional Prime Ministerial right to recommend individuals as party political members of the reformed Second

---

Box 10 Government proposals for Stage Two of Lords reform

- The reformed House of Lords to remain subject to the pre-eminence of the House of Commons
- No group in society to have privileged hereditary access to the House
- Its principal functions to continue to be the consideration and revision of legislation, scrutiny of the Executive, debates and reports on public issues
- Membership to be separated from the peerage which would continue to be an honour
- Its political membership should broadly reflect the relative voting strengths of the main parties as recorded at the previous General Election
- Its composition to be largely nominated, including a significant minority of independent members and some elected members to represent the nations and regions in the United Kingdom
- Increased representation of women and people from ethnic minorities
- Establishment of a statutory Appointments Commission to manage the balance and size of the House, to appoint the independent members and to assure the integrity of those nominated by the political parties

Chamber – just as it is customary for the other party leaders to do the same in respect of those whom they recommend. The role of the statutory Appointments Commission in this respect will be confined to ensuring that the proportions of appointed party members broadly match the distribution of votes between the parties at the most recent General Election. However, because the award of a peerage will no longer be a prerequisite for membership of the reformed Second Chamber, the extent of Prime Ministerial political patronage will be significantly reduced as compared with the traditional dispensation. Thus, if Ministers get their way when the second stage of reform is complete, the composition of the reformed Chamber of about 600 members will consist of: (1) 120 independent members appointed by the independent Appoint-ments Commission; (2) a maximum of 332 political members appointed on the recommendation of the party leaders; (3) 120 directly elected members representing the various nations and regions within the United Kingdom; and (4) 16 Bishops and at least 12 Law Lords appointed *ex officio*.[27]

On the equally important question of the *powers* of the reformed Second Chamber, Labour's 2001 Manifesto stated its support simply for 'moderni-sation of the House of Lords procedures to improve its effectiveness'.[28] Yet this begged the question of what is meant by 'effectiveness'. If it means something similar to what Margaret Beckett (when Leader of the Commons) meant when she applied it to the functioning of the Commons, then it would mean finding more efficient ways to process and approve Government legislation and generally to dispatch Government business. This would not, of course, be the way in which Conservatives, Liberal Democrats or Cross-Benchers would view the role of the Upper House, since they would wish to continue exercising their own (often independent) judgement upon the proposals and decisions of the Labour Government. On the other hand, if 'effectiveness' is to mean a Second Chamber which exercises its best judgement upon all the issues which come before it and which can do so with an enhanced degree of legitimacy because at least a proportion of its members have been elected by the people, then Labour Ministers may find that they

have created a reformed Second Chamber which gradually asserts a greater degree of legitimate authority in the eyes of the public.[29]

General reflections

We have seen in this chapter how the main obstacles to reforming the House of Lords have been the inability of any Government to put to Parliament a plan of reform starting from first principles and, as long as that approach is not available, the matching inability of the political parties in both Houses to achieve a binding all-party consensus on any plan which has been seriously put forward. Since it would probably require a constitutional crisis or at any rate a significant constitutional discontinuity to trigger these pre-requisites for substantial reform, the proponents of such reform should not hold their breath while waiting for it. The apparent impasse in the last Parliament was caused mainly by a lack of Ministerial enthusiasm for extensive Lords reform and an inherent conservatism in relation to reform of both Houses of Parliament on the part of key Ministers, notably the Prime Minister himself and Margaret Beckett when she was Leader of the Commons and Baroness Jay during her time as Leader of the Lords.

While waiting to see how things work out in the present Parliament, it is possible for interested observers of the political scene to sketch the out-lines of a sensible scheme for Lords reform based upon a combination of *ex ante* rationality and *ex post* rationalisation of what has happened so far. *Firstly*, the role of a reformed Second Chamber should be that of a coordinate rather than a subordinate House in a bi-cameral Parliament. *Secondly*, this means that it should be endowed with separate but equal constitutional powers and functions carefully delineated by statute in 'constitutional' legislation which would be effectively entrenched until such time as *both* Houses of Parliament agreed to amend or change it. *Thirdly*, the alleged problem of com-peting forms of legitimacy between the two Houses of Parliament could be alleviated, if not perhaps finally resolved, by ensuring that each Chamber was elected under a different electoral system – that is to say, first-past-the-post for members of the House of Commons who have to sustain or oppose the Government of the day and proportional representation based upon open party lists for the members of the reformed Second Chamber who need to be more representative of our diverse national community and more disposed towards statesman-like deliberation than partisan conflict.

Fourthly, the award of peerages as an elevated form of honour should be completely disconnected from membership of the Second Chamber which, as we have already suggested, should stem from elections under a PR system. *Finally*, the notion of special categories of membership in the Second Chamber reserved for certain prestigious groups – such as the Bishops or the Law Lords – should be ended, with the Church of England Bishops concentrating upon their Synod and the Law Lords being hived off into a separate judicial body which would effectively become a Supreme Court with the ability to give influential opinions on constitutional issues as well as matters of statute and common law.

In current political circumstances, however, any schemes of this kind may seem rather fanciful, because Ministers have firmly decided that 'the House of Lords should remain subject to the pre-eminence of the House of Commons in discharging its functions'.[30] Thus it seems that yet another opportunity for enlightened Parliamentary reform may be missed and the ideal of a reformed Second Chamber exercising enhanced and legitimate power in specific areas determined by 'constitutional' statutes may be rejected.

Questions for discussion

1 Why did it take nearly a century to reform the House of Lords?

2 Assess the pros and cons of a largely appointed or a largely elected Second Chamber.

3 'The anachronisms of both Houses should be tackled simultaneously'. Discuss this view of the process of Parliamentary reform in the United Kingdom.

Notes

1 House of Lords, *Official Report*, 7th March 2000, Vol. 610, Col. 1012.

2 *The Bryce Report* clearly defined four main functions for the Upper House: the examination and revision of Bills which had been considered by the Commons; the initiation of non-controversial Bills which would later be considered by the Commons; the ability to delay legislation of which it disapproves, especially legislation with constitutional implications, long enough to give the electorate a chance to pronounce upon it at a General Election before it becomes law; and the deliberative function involving full and free discussion of important matters in the Upper House, but in ways which do not directly threaten the Government's position. On composition, the Report proposed that three-quarters of the members of the Upper House should be indirectly elected by the Lower House on a proportional basis from the various regions of the country, while one-quarter should be chosen by the large complement of hereditary peers from among their own ranks.

3 At the 1948 Inter-Party Conference on the future of the House of Lords, the main ideas which were discussed but not finally agreed were: (1) inheritance and indirect election as equally valid bases for membership of the Upper House; (2) the role of the House of Lords to be essentially complementary to rather than in competition with the House of Commons; and (3) no single party to have a permanent majority in the Upper House.

4 This remark is a reference to Lloyd George's description of the House of Lords in 1909–10 as 'Mr Balfour's poodle', a famous comment which also provided the title of a book by Roy Jenkins on the constitutional crisis of those years.

5 The 1963 Peerage Act was a tribute to the sustained campaign of Tony Benn who had inherited the title of Viscount Stansgate and whose budding political career as a Labour MP had been stymied by the law as it then stood which prevented him from retaining his seat in the Commons following the death of his father. He was then able to use the new legislation to open the way for his re-election to the Commons, as were Lord Home and Lord Hailsham when they were both contestants for the Conservative Party leadership in 1963.

6 For a full account of this episode in British constitutional history see Janet Morgan, *The House of Lords and the Labour Government, 1964–70*; Clarendon Press, Oxford, 1975.

7 The hereditary element which survived in the interim Second Chamber consisted of 75 peers elected by their respective party or cross-bench groups (42 Conservatives, 28 Cross-Benchers, three Liberal Democrats and two Labour), fifteen peers elected by the whole House to act as Deputy Speakers or Committee Chairmen, and two largely ceremonial Royal appointments – the Earl Marshal and the Lord Great Chamberlain.

8 See House of Commons Research Paper 00/61, 15th June 2000, entitled *The Interim House, Background Statistics*.

9 The list of Bills on which the first Blair Administration suffered defeat at the hands of a more independent-minded and self-confident Upper House included: the Local Government Bill, the Financial Services and Markets Bill, the Immigration and Asylum Bill, the Sexual Offences (Amendment) Bill, the Representation of the People Bill, the Political Parties, Elections and Referendums Bill, the Freedom of Information Bill, the Learning and Skills Bill, the Teaching and Higher Education Bill, the Welfare Reform and Pensions Bill, and the Criminal Justice (Mode of Trial) Bill. All except the last mentioned eventually reached the Statute Book, but usually in amended form and in a few cases only after Ministers had invoked the reserve powers of the Commons under the 1949 Parliament Act.

10 There was nothing particularly democratic about the notorious 92, since none of them was elected by the people and all except two of them were chosen by ballot either of the whole House (the fifteen Deputy Speakers or Committee Chairmen) or of their respective party and cross-bench groups (the remaining 75).

11 Reliable figures for the proportions of peers from 'working-class' backgrounds are hard to define and even harder to find, as are the equivalent figures for those from ethnic minority backgrounds in the interim Second Chamber as compared with the previous House of Lords. Superficial and anecdotal evidence would suggest, however, that there are now fewer peers in the first category and more in the second category than there were before Stage One of Lords reform.

12 Baroness Jay's interview with *Parliamentary Monitor*, November 1999.

13 Of the 202 peerages announced between the 1997 General Election and June 2000, it is estimated that 50 per cent gave their allegiance to Labour, 18 per cent to the Conservatives and 15 per cent to the Liberal Democrats, while 16 per cent regarded themselves as cross-benchers and 1 per cent as 'other'. Among the new Labour peers who are known to have made financial donations to the party were Lord Sainsbury, Lord Haskins and Lord Levy.

14 Report of the Royal Commission on the Reform of the House of Lords, *A House for the Future*, Cm 4534; HMSO, London, 2000; Executive Summary, para 6.

15 *Ibid*; paras 13, 14.

16 *Ibid*; para 27.

17 *Ibid*; para 29.

18 *Ibid*; para 34, my italics.

19 The full terms of reference which had been written by Ministers were:

> having regard to the need to maintain the position of the House of Commons as the pre-eminent Chamber of Parliament and taking particular account of the present nature of the constitutional settlement, including the newly devolved institutions, the impact of the Human Rights Act 1998 and developing relations with the European Union; to consider and make recommendations on the role and functions of a Second Chamber, to make recommendations on the method or combination of methods of composition required to constitute a Second Chamber fit for that role and those functions, and to report by 31st December 1999.

20 See Meg Russell and Robert Hazell, *Commentary upon the Wakeham Report on Reform of the House of Lords*; Constitution Unit, London, February 2000; p. 1.

21 See House of Lords, *Official Report*, 7th March 2000, Vol. 610, Cols 910–1036.

22 See House of Commons, *Hansard*, 19th June 2000, Vol. 352, Cols 50–122.

23 The criteria guiding the assessment of nominations for non-party political Life Peers which are now used by the House of Lords Appointments Commission have become anodyne and wholly unexceptionable. Candidates are expected to be able to demonstrate: outstanding personal qualities of integrity and independence; strong personal commitment to the principles and highest standards of public life; a record of significant achievement within their chosen way of life; an ability to make an effective and significant contribution to the work of the House of Lords; some understanding of the constitutional framework within which the House of Lords is situated; sufficient availability to spend the time necessary to become familiar and comfortable with the workings of the House and to participate in its business; and independence of any political party.

24 Labour Party Manifesto, *Ambitions for Britain*; London, 2001; p. 35.

25 *The House of Lords – Completing the Reform*, Cm 5291; HMSO, London, 2001.

26 *Ibid*.

27 *Ibid*, para 64.

28 *Ambitions for Britain*; p. 35.

29 On the whole, representative samples of British public opinion have consistently preferred the option of replacing the traditional House of Lords with a new Second Chamber entirely elected by the people to either a partly elected and partly appointed body or keeping things as they were. See *British Public Opinion*; MORI, London, November 1998.

30 *The House of Lords – Completing the Reform*, Cm 5291; para 11.

Further reading

Lord Alexander, *Wakeham in the Long Grass: Can the Lords Guard democracy?*; Constitution Unit, London, 2000.

Robert Cranborne, *The End of Representative Democracy?*; Politeia, London, 1998.

A House for the Future, Royal Commission Report on the Reform of the House of Lords, Cm 4534; HMSO, London, 2000.

The House of Lords – Completing the Reform, Cm 5291; HMSO, London, November 2001.

Lord Longford, *A History of the House of Lords*; Sutton Publishing, Stroud, 1999.

Austin Mitchell, *Farewell my Lords*; Politicos, London, 1999.

Janet Morgan, *The House of Lords and the Labour Government, 1964–70*; Clarendon Press, Oxford, 1975.

I. Richard and D. Welfare, *Unfinished Business: Reforming the House of Lords*; Vintage, London, 1999.

Meg Russell, *Reforming the House of Lords, Lessons from Overseas*; Oxford University Press, Oxford, 2000.

Donald Shell, 'The future of the Second Chamber', *Political Quarterly*, Vol. 70, No. 4, 1999.

Andrew Tyrie, *Mr Blair's Poodle*; Centre for Policy Studies, London, 2000.

John Wells, *The House of Lords, from Saxon War Gods to a Modern Senate*; Sceptre, London, 1998.

website for *House of Lords*: www.parliament.uk

Modernising the House of Commons

The principal dilemma facing all those who have sought to 'modernise' or reform the House of Commons, at least since the arrival in power of the post-war Labour Administration in 1945, has been that incoming Governments with large and decisive majorities usually want to get on with putting their legislation through Parliament so that they can honour the pledges made to the electorate in their Manifestos, whereas parties which find themselves heavily outnumbered in the House of Commons and destined to remain in Opposition for a long time may become receptive to procedural and other reform proposals designed to limit the scope for 'elective dictatorship' available to any British Government with a commanding majority in the House of Commons. Thus powerful Governments have tended to have the power but not the inclination to reform the Commons in ways which would favour the Opposition and all backbenchers, whereas demoralised Oppositions have often had the inclination for Parliamentary reform but not the power immediately to do anything about it.

Earlier attempts at Commons reform

In spite of this rather bleak premise, there have been several exceptions to what may be accepted as the general rule applying to the behaviour of each of the main parties when in office. In 1966 Richard Crossman, a former academic who had written a well-known introduction to Walter Bagehot's *The English Constitution*, became Leader of the House of Commons in the second Wilson Administration and introduced experiments with morning sittings in the Chamber and the establishment of Select Committees on Agriculture and on Science and Technology. Notwithstanding strong intellectual backing from Professor Bernard Crick and other members of the *Hansard Society* who had long been campaigning for more effective mechanisms of Parliamentary control, this experiment was not considered to be a success and the momentum behind such Parliamentary reform soon diminished. In the mid-1970s under the fourth Wilson Administration, a singular but quite

influential Select Committee was established to examine the idea of a wealth tax in an analytical and relatively non-partisan way. Under the subsequent Callaghan Administration, a Select Committee on Procedure was established and a Select Committee on Expenditure with several sub-committees which achieved considerable Parliamentary influence at the time, because the then Labour Government first had only a slender majority and then no Parliamentary majority at all.

The next phase of Parliamentary reform was introduced at the outset of Margaret Thatcher's first Administration by Norman St John Stevas, a biographer of Bagehot and the Leader of the House of Commons from 1979 to 1981. He himself had served on the Procedure Committee when his party was in Opposition and his reforms, which entailed the establishment of a new structure of twelve Departmental Select Committees to monitor the Executive in twelve areas of Departmental activity (as well as the continuation of some cross-cutting committees such as the Public Accounts Committee), were a bold initiative which gave MPs in all parties new opportunities to exert a greater measure of Parliamentary control over the Executive.

Once Margaret Thatcher got into her political stride in the mid-1980s, one of the main thrusts of the Conservative Administration was to marginalise and weaken intermediate institutions which might otherwise have provided an effective opposition to her policies. This entailed a sustained assault upon the power and influence of the trade unions, the Church of England, the BBC and local government. It also entailed using all the powers at the disposal of central Government to disable, nullify or buy off with patronage any manifestations of opposition to her political project which stemmed from inside or outside the Conservative Party in Parliament. In such a Manichaean climate no Minister who valued his survival chances showed any interest in anything as 'subversive' as Parliamentary reform, especially if it might have had the effect of *strengthening* Parliament against the Executive. Thus Margaret Thatcher's political opponents were driven into recrimination and conspiracy, while serious constitutional reformers outside the House of Commons, such as the members of *Charter 88*, concentrated upon laying longer-term plans which, they hoped, would point the way towards replacing an elective dictatorship with a new political system subject to effective constitutional checks and balances in future. To this end, they made sustained and successful attempts to get alongside and then convince senior members of the Labour Party in Opposition – the Liberal Democrats already being enthusiastic supporters of the cause – that there was merit in a comprehensive agenda of constitutional reform, with the result that by the time there was a change of Government in 1997, most new Labour Ministers could be counted as friends rather than adversaries of the cause.[1]

Apart from the reform of Select Committees in 1979, just about the only initiative of Parliamentary reform which got through during the period of Thatcherite hegemony was the decision of the whole House on a free vote for the proceedings in the Commons to be televised. This was accepted by Members of Parliament on an experimental basis in November 1989 and made permanent in a free vote in July 1990 only a few months before Mrs Thatcher fell from office. It was a reform of some symbolic significance, not least for broadcasters like Sir Robin Day who had campaigned for it continuously since the 1960s. On the other hand, the conduct of Parliamentary proceedings since that time suggests that the insertion of the cameras into the Chamber has made little difference to the behaviour of MPs or the conventions of the House. It has merely emphasised the extent to which party politics have become almost a branch of the entertainment industry, with the general public both in this country and abroad watching Prime Minister's Question Time as if it were a blood sport rather than a method of Parliamentary control.

John Major, who had a markedly less dictatorial style of leadership than Margaret Thatcher and whose 'big idea' was the Citizen's Charter, seemed more of a friend to Parliamentary reform than his predecessor would ever have been. Yet the main thrust of the procedural reforms which were allowed through during his Administration had more to do with assisting the efficient processing of Government legislative business and meeting the human needs of MPs for more orthodox and sensible working hours than with strengthening the House of Commons as a check upon the Executive.

In February 1992 a Select Committee chaired by Michael Jopling, a former Conservative Chief Whip, recommended a package of modest procedural reforms which, after some prevarication on both sides of the House, was eventually debated and approved in December 1994.[2] The main components in the package of reforms were as follows.

1   The House would no longer sit on eight Fridays during each annual session so that MPs could be sure of honouring constituency engagements on such days.
2   The House would meet in plenary session every Wednesday between 10:00 a.m. and 2:30 p.m. to conduct short debates on subjects applied for by backbenchers and chosen by Speaker's ballot which would not lead to votes.
3   Debates on the Ways and Means Resolutions of Money Bills, which normally followed the end of a Second Reading debate after 10:00 p.m., would be limited to a maximum of 45 minutes in the interest of reducing some late sittings.
4   Most Statutory Instruments and European legislative proposals would be referred to a Standing Committee with any debates on the floor of the House being limited to 90 minutes.

These proposals represented a move towards more civilised Parliamentary hours and more reliable diary planning. Yet subsequent developments have shown that it can occasionally be as difficult as ever for the House of Commons to operate only during 'normal' working hours and that all Opposition parties will have recourse to the weapons of delay and obstruction from time to time.

Labour's agenda for modernisation

Labour's agenda for modernisation of the Commons was first revealed in a speech by Ann Taylor, then shadow Leader of the House, to a Charter 88 seminar on 14th May 1996.[3] Starting from the conventional position that the goal of Parliamentary reform in the Lower House was to make the Commons 'a more effective and efficient legislature', she went on to make a more idealistic case for stronger Parliamentary scrutiny and control of the Executive. She argued that 'a more accountable Government is a better Government and ultimately a more re-electable Government' and she was careful to add that 'Parliament must own the process . . . Parliament must change itself'. The rider was important, because it indicated either an overestimate of the scope for backbenchers to seize control of any reform agenda in the House of Commons or an underestimate of the harsh political reality that – except when there is a minority Government – nearly everything which happens, or fails to happen, in the conduct of House of Commons business is the result of political agreement through 'the usual channels' between the Government and the Opposition front benches.

When Labour came to power in May 1997, it was on the basis of a Manifesto which contained a passage committing the incoming Government to a *modest* package of Commons reform under the all-purpose rubric of 'modernisation'. The principal ingredients were:

1   establishment of an all-party Modernisation Select Committee chaired by the Leader of the House to review Commons procedures and make recommendations;
2   changes to the rules governing Prime Minister's Questions in order to make that particular highlight of the Parliamentary week 'more effective';
3   overhaul of the procedures for the timely scrutiny of European legislation;
4   a review of Ministerial accountability 'so as to remove recent abuses' – a reference to various scandals which had obliged John Major to establish judicial inquiries under Sir Richard Scott and Lord Nolan to investigate alleged malpractices and personal misbehaviour by some Conservative Ministers and MPs.[4]

It was significant that the Labour Party showed more interest in rooting out all forms of sleaze,

rectifying the under-representation of women in the House of Commons and promising a referendum on the voting system for Westminster elections than in any schemes of procedural reform. This was in keeping with the spirit of the times and the perennial fact that no political party is ever likely to increase its popular vote at a General Election by highlighting its commitment to Parliamentary reform.

By contrast, the Conservatives in their 1997 Manifesto were much clearer about what they *opposed* by way of Parliamentary and constitutional reform than about any measures for which they wished to take credit at the end of their term of office. They were opposed to any moves towards a codified constitution, electoral reform for Westminster elections and the elimination of hereditary peers from the House of Lords. Their single proposal for procedural reform in the House of Commons was to envisage the possibility that a given Queen's Speech might cover both the legislation for the year immediately ahead and the legislation planned for the year after that.

Characteristically, it was the Liberal Democrats whose 1997 Manifesto had included the most ambitious plans for Parliamentary and constitutional reform and who seemed perfectly happy to use the 'm word' in relation to the House of Commons. Their radical proposals bore a strong resemblance to the Charter 88 programme and included such elements as proportional representation for Westminster elections, fixed-term Parliaments of four years, and a House of Commons reduced in number by 200 or nearly a third of its total membership.

Liberal Democrat influence on these matters was not confined to the formal positions which the party took in its Manifesto, but had already been projected via a Joint Consultative Committee on Constitutional Reform with the Labour Party when both parties were in Opposition and via a Joint Cabinet Committee with senior Ministers once Labour was in Government. The Report of the Consultative Committee published in March 1997 maintained that 'renewing Parliament is the key to the wider modernisation of our country's system of government' and that it was precisely because of Parliament's importance in British national life that improvements should be made which would 'enable it to become a more effective legislature'.[5] The two parties agreed that the priorities for modernising the House of Commons were: to programme Parliamentary business in order to achieve fuller consultation, more effective scrutiny and better use of MPs' time; to improve the quality of legislation with more pre-legislative consultation and greater use of the Special Standing Committee procedure (when evidence could be taken from expert witnesses); to change Prime Minister's Question Time 'to make it a more genuine and serious means of holding the Government to account'; to overhaul the process of scrutinising European legislation in the interests of greater transparency and achieving a more clearly defined role for Parliament at Westminster; to strengthen the ability of MPs to make the Government answerable for its actions; and to enhance the role of Select Committees in order to ensure greater accountability in public adminis-tration. This agenda of reform was noticeably more ambitious than the list of commitments which found their way into the Labour Manifesto and it set benchmarks which have subsequently proved to be well in advance of what the Labour Government has been prepared to do in office. Once again, we can see evidence of the disparity between the way these things look to a party resigned to Opposition and the way they look to a party confident of forming the Government for which the political priority is usually to focus its Manifesto pledges on 'bread and butter' issues of policy.

Although Labour's agenda for the 'moderni-sation' of the House of Commons was initially modest in scope and certainly not very radical in intent, Ministers got off to quite a good start by setting up the new Modernisation Select Committee under the chairmanship of Ann Taylor, then Leader of the House, with a remit 'to consider how the practices and procedures of the House should be modernised'. The Committee produced a First Report on the Legislative Process in July 1997. This recommended the publication of Government Bills in draft to facilitate wider and less

hurried consultation; the timetabling or program-ming of all public legislation to ensure that all parts of a Government Bill were adequately scrutinised by the House of Commons; the greater use of Special Standing Committees during the early stages of a Bill's passage 'upstairs' in Committee; the carrying over of Bills from one annual session to another if they are at risk for lack of Parlia-mentary time in either or both Houses; and the introduction of Second Reading Committees for some Government Bills in place of Second Reading debates on the floor of the House.[6] See *Box 11* for a list of the key commitments in House of Commons modernisation.

The list of proposals from the Modernisation Committee seemed quite sensible, attracted the support of the Conservative and Liberal Democrat parties and was approved by the House in a vote on 13th November 1997. However, it did not seem to be so well received in the Government Whips Office when Nick Brown was Chief Whip or in some corners of 10 Downing Street where less indulgent views of the rights of backbenchers seemed to prevail. Evidence for this reticence was that the proposed reforms were not swiftly incorporated into the Standing Orders of the House and thus had only a marginal effect upon the passage of Government legislation, depending upon the willingness or otherwise of individual senior Ministers to treat the Commons as a whole with more courtesy and respect.[7]

Generally speaking, the progress of House of Commons modernisation from May 1997 to June 2001 was patchy, low-key and largely designed to make life easier for Ministers and Government backbenchers. This conclusion should not be all that surprising in view of the fact that Nick Brown as Chief Whip exercised a restraining influence on Commons reform during the first half of the Parliament and Margaret Beckett as Leader of the House exercised a similar influence during the second half of the Parliament.

In October 1999 the Modernisation Select Committee produced a *Second Progress Report* on its work during the first half of the Parliament which summarised in an Annex the recommen-dations which it had made thus far and the extent

---

Box 11 Key elements in House of Commons modernisation

- Key theme of enabling the House to carry out its functions more effectively, while enabling individual members to make better use of their time
- More pre-legislative scrutiny of draft Bills
- The programming in advance of all Government legislation to facilitate the passage of Government Bills
- The postponement of some votes previously taken after 10:00 p.m. to the next Wednesday afternoon when the House is sitting
- The carrying over of some Bills by agreement from one session to the next, leading to a more flexible rolling two-year programme of Government legislation to improve pre-legislative scrutiny
- The introduction of full and clear Explanatory Notes on Government Bills
- Improvements in the timely scrutiny of European legislation and secondary legislation
- The introduction of a 'parallel Chamber' off Westminster Hall for additional debates of local interest to backbenchers
- Revised sitting hours to provide more time for debate on Tuesdays, Wednesdays and Thursdays, while releasing more Fridays for constituency activity
- More frequent debates in the Chamber upon Select Committee reports
- More administrative support and status for those who chair Select Committees
- Less overt interference by the party Whips in selecting the members of Select Committees

---

to which each one had been implemented.[8] It pointed out that 47 of its 56 recommendations had been approved by the House and implemented either in full or in part. It described a consistent theme running through all its proposals which had been

> that of enabling the whole House more effectively to carry out its functions of legislating, debating major issues and holding the Executive to account, while at the same time seeking to ensure that individual members are able to make better use of their time.

The Report went on to provide brief summaries of the modernisation progress made under a variety of different headings. On *European legislation*, the European Legislation Committee had been replaced by the European Scrutiny Committee with enlarged terms of reference, including both pre- and post-Council of Ministers evidence sessions, and the number of European Standing Committees had also been increased. The scrutiny of *United Kingdom secondary legislation* would be reviewed by the Procedure Committee. As far as the Commons *debating process* was concerned, some of the

outdated and archaic practices had been done away with and more flexibility introduced into limitations on the length of Members' speeches. The House would experiment by organising a *'parallel Chamber'* for debates in the Grand Committee room off Westminster Hall to provide more opportunities for backbenchers to raise matters of public concern for which there was not enough time on the floor of the House, and to stage more regular debates upon Select Committee reports.

On *revised sitting hours*, a net addition of six hours per week had been achieved by adding to debating time on Tuesday and Wednesday mornings and Thursday afternoons, while releasing valuable time on Fridays for Members to spend the full day in their constituencies if they wished. On *Parliamentary documentation*, a new style of Order Paper had been introduced and agreement had been reached with the Procedure Committee of the House of Lords on a revised format for Bills and Acts of Parliament which took account of new printing technology. Finally, the idea of *electronic voting* had been considered informally but not resolved, although news of the experience of electronic and timed voting in the Scottish Parliament had been of some interest to members of the Committee.

Nearly all the Committee's recommendations which had not been implemented were technical and relatively insignificant, and arose from the Committee's First Report on the legislative process. Perhaps the only real disappointment was that more use had not been made of Second Reading Committees (with the exception of two Bills promoted by the Law Commission which had been referred automatically), since this procedural reform might have contained the germ of an idea which could have a much wider and more beneficial application.[9] The Committee said it was conscious that its recommendations had produced a mixed response in the House, with some Members of the opinion that it had gone much too far and others of the opinion that it had not gone nearly far enough. In such circumstances it had opted for 'experimental and evolutionary change rather than an enforced revolution'. For example, it proposed to conduct a systematic review of the legislative reforms already introduced, in particular of the relationship between Standing and Select Committees and the ways in which their work might be better integrated. It also eagerly awaited the Report of the Procedure Committee on the scrutiny of delegated legislation.[10] It indicated its awareness of concerns about 'the full range of relationships between Select Committees and the Executive' – a delphic reference to the simmering dispute between the backbench champions of the Legislature and leading members of the Executive which was later to erupt following a hard-hitting report from the Liaison Committee of Select Committee Chairmen who had the temerity to suggest, among other things, that the party Whips should not control the nominations of backbench MPs to Select Committees.[11]

The Committee undertook carefully to monitor the experiment with the parallel Chamber off Westminster Hall to see whether it would be sensible to extend its operations – a step which might reopen a useful discussion of the structure of the Parliamentary week and the Parliamentary year to see whether better use could be made of the time available by introducing more orthodox working hours and possibly more frequent sittings balanced by shorter recesses, especially in the summer. It also highlighted the dynamic effects which could be expected to flow from further reform of the House of Lords, the development of the devolved institutions in Scotland, Wales and Northern Ireland, and institutional developments in the European Union.

Reflecting the incremental nature of procedural and legislative reforms in the House of Commons, the Modernisation Select Committee returned to the issue of programming legislation in a Report published in July 2000 and it took the opportunity to float some proposals for the detachment of some votes from the debates to which they related and the deferral of such votes to a more convenient time on the Wednesday afternoon of the following week – assuming the House would be sitting.[12] On the first point, the Committee argued that real benefits could flow from more programming of legislation: it would give the Government a greater measure of certainty about when it would secure Parliamentary approval for each piece of its legislative programme; it offered the Opposition the opportunity to determine the structure and focus of legislative debates; it would give all backbenchers more certainty about when votes would be held and therefore enable them to make more efficient use of their time; and in the longer term it could reduce the need to table Government amendments late in the proceedings on a Bill and so mean better drafted legislation for the benefit of Parliament, the courts and the general public.

As for the more 'sensible' timing of votes and particularly the desirability of allowing some MPs to debate business after 10:00 p.m. without requiring all other MPs to hang around into the early hours of the morning for free-standing votes (i.e. those without tabled amendments) which might not be called, the Committee drew attention to at least one valid precedent for its proposal – the postponement until 10:00 p.m. of votes on financial Estimates even though the debate may have been concluded several hours earlier – and it foresaw that voting procedures could be made even simpler and swifter if MPs ever decided to adopt electronic voting.

These two recommendations were controversial both within the Modernisation Committee itself, which divided on these issues on party lines, and in the House as a whole, where some Labour backbenchers joined the Conservatives in the lobbies to vote against such measures. Notwithstanding these flickers of resistance, on 7th November 2000 the House eventually voted by a majority of 159 for the programming of Government legislation and by a majority of 119 for deferred divisions on unamended business taken after 10:00 p.m. The first motion represented a victory for the convenience of the Government; the second motion represented a victory for the personal convenience of individual MPs, most of whom have never enjoyed staying up late into the night on the off-chance that they might be called upon to vote at the end of a debate in which they themselves may not have participated and towards the outcome of which they are often indifferent.

As for what is likely to happen in future, the Labour Government re-elected in 2001 initially had few specific proposals for further House of Commons reform. Apart from a commitment to legislate to allow each party to make positive moves to increase its number of women MPs via positive discrimination in the selection of Parliamentary candidates, the only pledge under the heading of *Parliamentary reform* in the 2001 Labour Manifesto which related to the Lower House was that 'Labour will continue to modernise the procedures of the House of Commons, so that it can effectively fulfil its functions of representation and scrutiny'.[13] These cautious words could be interpreted as a coded indication that Tony Blair and his senior colleagues no longer felt that they had much to gain from further Commons reform, which might well benefit the Opposition and all backbenchers rather than the Government of the day. On the other hand, the new Leader of the House, Robin Cook, indicated in a speech to the Hansard Society and in an interview with *The Times* in July 2001 that he was interested in further reform, including (apparently) more frequent debates on Select Committee reports, more support and status for those who chair Select Committees and a more

flexible rolling two-year programme for Government Bills which would make systematic both pre-legislative and legislative scrutiny.[14] It is obviously sensible to wait and see how things turn out, although there have been indications that Robin Cook as Leader of the House intends to strengthen the ability of the Commons to act as a powerful check upon Ministers.[15]

The view from different angles

Reform or 'modernisation' of the Commons can stem from different motives and take different forms; it can be viewed from different angles. This is fundamentally because in the British system of Parliamentary government there is nearly always an underlying tension, if not conflict, between the interests of the *Executive* (i.e. Ministers, Whips, Parliamentary Private Secretaries and civil servants) and the interests of the *Legislature* or Parliament as a whole – in so far as such a distinction is actually meaningful in a political system in which the political members of the Executive are drawn from the two Houses of the Legislature and the Legislature is effectively controlled by the Executive using the reins of the Government Whips Office and employing a mixture of patronage and coercion.

The Executive is interested principally in the *efficiency* of the Parliamentary process in turning Ministerial decisions into legislation or administrative action. For this purpose, it puts a high value upon loyalty and discipline within the governing party in the House of Commons, thus placing Government backbenchers in a quandary when they feel torn between sycophancy and rebellion, as Kenneth (now Lord) Baker once memorably put it in an elegant speech from the backbenches. The Legislature (i.e. the Opposition parties and the more independent-minded Government backbenchers) is interested mainly in scrutinising legislation and the other actions of Government, delivering a measure of public accountability via Question Time in the Chamber and forensic inquiries in Select Committees, and safeguarding the integrity and status of Parliament in the eyes of the public. For these purposes the emphasis is put upon instruments designed to achieve Parliamentary control of the Executive and procedures designed to preserve at least the appearance of the representative principle.

During Tony Blair's first Administration, and formerly under Margaret Thatcher's three Administrations, such tensions and conflict persisted and perhaps got worse than they had been before. This is because both party leaders enjoyed positions of preponderance within their own parties and Government backbenchers are always torn between their urge to support the party and obey the Whips and their own ideological principles which may well bring them into conflict with Ministers. The irony is that the existence of huge Government majorities in the Commons does not always assist the cause of party discipline, while the growing professionalisation of politics has meant that many of the 1997 intake of Labour MPs were at first exhilarated and then frustrated by the experience of being lost in the crowd.

It has been well said that Government backbenchers can hold in their hands the power to redress the unequal balance between the Executive and the Legislature in British politics. The fact that the scales are usually tipped so heavily in favour of Ministers and the Executive merely raises the stakes for both the Government and its Parliamentary supporters in the event of the latter becoming so alienated from aspects of Government policy that they feel driven to rebel.

There are really two underlying problems. The first is that there is a fundamental clash between two different *theories* of the role of Parliament (really the House of Commons) in the British political system. Those who see the world through the prism of Executive interests tend to argue that both Houses of Parliament are there primarily to process Government legislation and to ratify, after due discussion and debate, the decisions of the Government of the day. Those who see the world from a backbench or oppositional perspective (but not, be it noted, the Opposition front bench) tend to argue that both Houses of Parliament are there to scrutinise and control the legislation and the administrative decisions of the Executive and to give Ministers and civil servants a hard time whenever it appears that their actions should be criticised or censured.

The second problem is the contradiction between *the theory of Parliamentary supremacy*, which insists that Parliament is the highest constitutional authority in the land and that the House of Commons ought to be able to control, censure and occasionally defeat the Government of the day, and *the practice of Executive control of Parliament*, which means that on most issues most of the time Ministers get their way on the strength of their democratic 'mandate' from the people and with the support of well-established Standing Orders faithfully recorded in Erskine May.[16]

These two fundamental problems have ensured continuing rivalry not only between the Government of the day and the Opposition, but also between the champions of the Executive and of the Legislature. Such rivalry came to a head in the year 2000 when *the Liaison Committee* of 33 'senior backbenchers', each of whom chaired a Select Committee or Sub-Committee in the Commons, issued an ambitious Report which advocated a shift in the balance of Parliamentary power in favour of Select Committees and against the Executive.[17] The Report began by noting that as successive Governments had become more powerful, the work of Select Committees in controlling the Executive had become more vital; yet in practice governmental power had always outstripped Parliamentary control. It recorded the success of the departmental structure of Select Committees which had been set up in 1979, but noted that this success had been patchy and on occasions the Government of the day had found it too easy to thwart the main role of Select Committees which was to provide independent scrutiny of Government. It emphasised that the prime concern was for the effectiveness of the system and observed that 'after two decades, and especially in the present climate of constitutional change, we think it is time for some further reform and modernisation'.[18]

The Committee's proposals for reform were bold and far-reaching. *Firstly*, it argued that it was wrong in principle that party managers (i.e. the Whips) should exercise effective control of Select

Committee membership and it proposed a new method of selection by a Panel consisting of a Chairman of (Select) Committees and two Deputy Chairmen appointed by the House as a whole at the very beginning of a Parliament and consisting of 'senior and respected Members of the House prepared to work in a wholly non-partisan way'. The Whips and others would still be free to suggest the names of suitable Select Committee Members, but final decisions on nominations would be made by the Panel. The nominations would then be put to the House as a whole in amendable, debatable motions, as was already the case under the existing system. The Panel would also take on the powers and duties of the Liaison Committee – e.g. choosing subjects for debate on Estimates Days and Select Committee Reports for debate in Westminster Hall – and it would be given general responsibility for all matters affecting Select Committees, such as the format and presentation of Reports.

Secondly, the Committee voiced a clear wish to create 'a better balance between the attractions of Government office and service on Select Committees' and expressed the belief that if all the recommendations in its Report were implemented, there would be 'a significant shift in that balance'.[19] However, it did not make many proposals for turning this aspiration into a reality, other than to canvass the idea of a pay supplement for the Chairmen of certain Select Committees and the possibility of making them eligible for a higher Office Costs Allowance to pay for additional secretarial and research support.

Thirdly, the Committee made a strong case for more debates in the House on Select Committee reports in order to give a higher profile to their recommendations. At that time the debating opportunities reserved for Select Committees comprised three days each session on financial Estimates, one day per session on reports from the Public Accounts Committee, and debates on Select Committee reports in the Grand Committee Room off Westminster Hall once every two weeks on a Thursday afternoon and on three Wednesday mornings each session. On other occasions Select Committee reports have been the subject of debates on substantive motions or on the Adjournment

and they are frequently 'tagged' (i.e. mentioned on the Order Paper) as relevant to other debates in the Chamber. Essentially, the Committee was looking for more opportunities for Select Committees to have a timely and effective influence upon proceedings in the House and to this end it came up with the idea that once a week after Questions on Tuesday there should be a brisk half an hour devoted to a brief debate on a Select Committee report chosen by the Chairman of the Select Committee Panel. This would be one way of ensuring that the work of Select Committees got more 'prime time' in the Commons and there would be some similarities with the brief debates on Starred Parliamentary Questions in the Lords.

The Committee urged that Government replies to Select Committee Reports should be produced more swiftly and certainly within the conventional period of two months. It also suggested that the quality of Government replies should be improved and urged all Select Committees to monitor and, if necessary, comment publicly upon this aspect of the iterative process between the Executive and the Legislature whenever the need arose. It saw some advantage in Select Committees issuing Annual Reports in which regular assessments could be made of the extent to which Ministers had accepted and implemented their recommendations and of any recurrent problems which had afflicted them in the course of their work – e.g. access to official documents or attendance of witnesses. In general, it expressed the hope that the work of Select Committees would be seen by Government as an opportunity for constructive cooperation rather than a threat to traditional Executive rights.

Fourthly, the Committee was very keen to take the bait which had been offered by the Select Committee on Modernisation by promoting the role that Select Committees could play in the pre-legislative scrutiny of draft Bills. It identified no fewer than seven areas for improvement under this heading and foresaw a prominent role for Select Committees and their members in all of them.[20] It also paid obeisance to Ministers' stated preference for 'joined-up government' by arguing that there should be more cooperation between Select Committees to complement the work of the existing 'cross-cutting' Committees, such as Environmental Audit or Public Administration.

Fifthly, the Committee argued that 'we cannot urge Committees into more extensive activity without ensuring that staff workloads are manageable and that additional Committee business can be properly supported'.[21] It therefore pursued the suggestion of the Procedure Committee in July 1999 that a new Committee Office, a modest Central Staff Unit specialising in issues of pre-legislative scrutiny and public expenditure, should be established to serve the needs of all Select Committees.

The Committee put down some markers for future dimensions of Select Committee work, each of which seemed ambitious within the conventions of British Parliamentary culture. The *first* was that Select Committees should seek to establish a new role for themselves by holding 'confirmation hearings' for important public appointments in their respective spheres of policy interest – somewhat along the lines of the 'advise and consent' procedure used by committees of the United States Senate. The *second* was that certain Select Committees (presumably the Foreign Affairs Committee in particular) should establish for themselves a formal role in the examination of treaties negotiated by the British Government under the Royal Prerogative. The *third* was that a closer look should be taken at the case for new mechanisms to ensure that the Intelligence and Security Services were made accountable to a *bona fide* Select Committee rather than to the informal committee of Parliamentarians appointed by and responsible to the Prime Minister which then provided a degree of Parliamentary oversight of this murky area of state-sponsored activity.[22]

The Report indicated the Committee's future intention to examine the powers of Select Committees to send for persons, papers and records, since over the years these had occasionally been defied by the Executive and many members doubted whether they were sufficient as they stood – notably in connection with the restrictions imposed by Crown privilege and the Royal Prerogative. The Committee concluded that in spite of the achievements of Select Committees over the years, their full potential had yet to be realised.

The Government's Response to the Liaison Committee Report constituted something of an iron fist in a velvet glove in that, although formally polite to the congeries of Select Committee chairmen, it gave no real ground on the recommendations which mattered.[23] Indeed, the respected columnist and political commentator Peter Riddell described it as 'arrogant, contemptible and mendacious'.[24] Ministers devoted nine paragraphs near the beginning of their document to refuting the idea that a Panel of senior backbenchers would be the appropriate mechanism for choosing the members of Select Committees and other tasks which the Liaison Committee had identified. The Response contained almost any argument which Ministers thought would serve their purpose of rebutting this threat to Executive dominance of the Commons. For example, it was recalled that the system of selection had been introduced in response to a 1978 Report from the Select Committee on Procedure in which the influence of political parties (read the Whips) was implicitly acknowledged. On the other hand, it refuted the idea that any Government would wish to see a docile set of Select Committees and even attempted to make the fatuous argument that 'the result of the Liaison Committee's proposals could well be that the House spent longer in debating membership of Select Committees than it did on substantive business'.[25]

The Ministerial response rejected the idea that Select Committees should have a formal role in scrutinising public appointments, that timely debates on Select Committee reports should take precedence over Government business on the floor of the House, and that those who had been members of a Select Committee previously involved in scrutinising a draft Bill should be allowed to speak but not vote during the Standing Committee stage of proceedings on the actual Bill. In response to other recommendations – e.g. the early publication of draft Bills, two-month deadlines for Government responses to Select Committee Reports and extra payments or other recognition for Select Committee chairmen – Ministers were prepared only to offer their best endeavours. Thus, if awards were given for Executive obduracy and hypocrisy towards any proposals for House of Commons reform intended to enhance the role of back-benchers, especially those on Select Committees, this document would be a leading contender for any such prize. Moreover, it must have been hard for the civil service authors of the document to keep a straight face when drafting the final sentence which read: 'the Government expect that in future [Select] Committees will continue as a valued, effective and independent part of the House'.[26]

Since the Labour Party was returned to power in June 2001 with another landslide majority in Parliament (although by no means in the country), it might seem unnecessary to sketch the publicly expressed views of the Conservative Party on these issues. Yet when William Hague was leader of the party (1997–2001), he did commission the Norton Report on *Strengthening Parliament* and he did make two well-publicised speeches on relations between Parliament and the Executive, and the arguments used on those occasions are worth mentioning.[27]

The first of these speeches was made in July 2000 when Mr Hague launched a major debate on this subject in the House of Commons to which the Prime Minister replied.[28] After opening with a scathing indictment of what he described as the dismissive and arrogant way in which, he claimed, Tony Blair and his fellow Ministers had treated the House of Commons and indeed Parliament as a whole, Mr Hague advocated four points of Parliamentary reform designed to improve the quality of legislation and to strengthen the hand of the Commons in relation to the Government of the day. *Firstly*, all parties in the Commons should accept the recommendation of the Liaison Committee that the appointment of backbench MPs to Select Committees should be taken out of the hands of the party Whips. *Secondly*, Departmental Select Committees should be given powers comparable to those of the Public Accounts Committee and in the process steps should be taken to establish a separate career path for those who became Select Committee Chairmen. *Thirdly*, much more extensive use should be made of two recent reforms – namely, the publication of more

Bills in draft and more frequent recourse to Special Standing Committees for the scrutiny of legislation. *Fourthly*, ways should be found of increasing the topicality of Parliamentary business – for example, by reducing the amount of notice required for the tabling of oral questions and by restoring Prime Minister's Question Time to two slots a week on Tuesdays and Thursdays for fifteen minutes on each occasion.

Mr Hague's other significant contribution to the public discussion about Parliamentary reform was made in a speech at Magdalen College, Oxford, in November 2000 when he argued in favour of 'giving the people of Britain control, through Parliament, over the decisions that affect their lives'.[29] In his view, this meant rebalancing the constitution in the wake of devolution by: reducing Scottish over-representation at Westminster and guaranteeing that only English MPs were able to vote on English laws; 'watching very closely and with considerable suspicion' the interpretation and application by the courts of the *Human Rights Act 1998*; entrenching certain statutory powers in order to preserve the supremacy of the Westminster Parliament in some reserved policy areas, so that European law could not override the will of the British Parliament in those areas of legal competence currently excluded from the European treaties; and taking steps to strengthen both Houses of Parliament as institutional counter-balances to the power of the Executive.

Mr Hague characterised the contemporary House of Commons as 'diminished, marginalised and side-lined' and equally he bemoaned the fact that the House of Lords had been turned into 'an over-sized Quango based upon little more than Prime Ministerial patronage'. However, he was prepared at that time to make only two firm pledges on behalf of his party: *firstly*, restoration of Prime Minister's Question Time to two slots a week on Tuesday and Thursday afternoons; and *secondly*, bolstering the independence of Select Committees by enabling them to choose their own members, free from the influence of the party Whips. It was hard to interpret this speech as a decisive endorsement of a renewed and strengthened House of Commons, yet it is understood that

Mr Hague really did want to see further procedural reform of the Commons even though he himself was not prepared at that time to be prescriptive about the precise form it should take.[30]

Lessons from other Parliaments

For centuries Members of Parliament at Westminster have tended to feel that they had nothing to learn from other Parliaments and other political traditions, because they regarded their institution as 'the Mother of Parliaments'. Indeed, in the nineteenth and most of the twentieth centuries they and their academic acolytes were in the habit of tutoring many of the former British colonies and newly independent nations within the Commonwealth in the virtues of Westminster-style democracy. Since the collapse of Communism, similar attempts have been made to apply these lessons in Parliamentary democracy to the 'nations in transition' which have emerged from the corpse of the former Soviet Union and its satellites in central and eastern Europe. Yet it could be argued that in the early years of the twenty-first century it is now the proponents of the Westminster model of Parliamentary democracy who ought to be rather humble and pay more attention to the procedures and practices of other Parliaments.

The new *Scottish Parliament*, which was elected on 6th May 1999 and officially opened by the Queen on 1st July 1999, benefited from the preparatory work carried out by a Consultative Group established by the late Donald Dewar under the chairmanship of Henry McLeish. This body included representatives of the four main parties in Scotland as well as civic groups and it made proposals for the procedural rules and Standing Orders of the new institution. The establishment of the first Scottish Parliament for almost 300 years provided a golden opportunity to create a new form of Parliamentary democracy that would be fit for the needs of contemporary Scotland. However, it has occurred to some people that the new model established for Scotland may have some lessons for Westminster as well.

At the outset it was readily agreed by the Steering Group, and subsequently confirmed by the entire Scottish political Establishment, that the new Scottish Parliament should operate on four key principles:

1　the sharing of power between the people of Scotland, the legislators (MSPs) and the Scottish Executive;

2　a clear chain of accountability from the Scottish Executive to the Scottish Parliament and from both of these to the Scottish people;

3　the achievement of maximum accessibility, openness and responsiveness in the Parliament in order to encourage a participative approach to the development and scrutiny of policy and legislation;

4　a recognition of the need to promote equal opportunities for all, especially in public appointments and in day-to-day operations.[31]

At the time of writing it is evident that the first principle provides the most striking contrast with the Parliamentary culture at Westminster and it was significantly reinforced by the outcome of the May 1999 election held under a partly proportional electoral system which produced a Labour–Liberal Democrat Coalition Government.

The practical effects of this power-sharing upon the political culture of the Scottish Parliament are cumulatively very significant and one can only presume that the same would be true in a reformed House of Commons if similar reforms were implemented. To give a few examples: the Presiding Officer (Speaker) of the Scottish Parliament is strong, independent of party and elected by ballot of all the MSPs; Parliamentary business is managed not by representatives of the Executive, but by an all-party Business Committee chaired by the Presiding Officer; in each main area of devolved policy the Parliament has powerful all-purpose subject Committees which combine the roles of Select and Standing Committees at Westminster, and have the power to initiate legislation as well as to scrutinise and investigate the legislative proposals of the Executive; legislation introduced by the Executive is subjected to a substantial period of pre-legislative consultation and scrutiny during which the Parliament's relevant subject Committee, interest groups (often organised within civic or youth forums) and the general Scottish public have opportunities to influence the outcome; and the general public has been given a substantial right of Petition (not a mere formal ritual as at Westminster) and there is a Public Petitions Committee with a wide range of procedural options for dealing with such matters.

The application of the principle of enhanced public accountability is less novel or revolutionary compared with the situation at Westminster, since the latter had to act decisively to cope with the consequences of 'Tory sleaze' in the last Parliament by setting up an external Committee on Standards in Public Life and subsequently by strengthening the remit of its own Standards and Privileges Committee. Nevertheless, in the name of greater accountability, the Scottish Parliament has the right to approve or reject Ministerial appointments both individually and collectively, while the right to table motions of no confidence in individual Ministers or in the entire Scottish Executive is not confined to the Opposition front bench (as at Westminster), but can be exercised by individual MSPs or groups of MSPs subject to certain procedural safeguards.

The commitment to greater public access and participation is genuine and stands in vivid contrast to the still rather defensive and archaic atmosphere and practices at Westminster. Admittedly, 'Blair's babes' and other members of the huge Labour intake of 1997 put pressure upon the House of Commons authorities to modernise the procedures to make them more family-friendly and this trend has continued in the present Parliament. Yet the new spirit and objectives of the Scottish Parliament are still in marked contrast to the more hide-bound state of affairs at Westminster where the conservatives (with a small c) in all parties can still deploy significant resistance to any proposed changes. Among the recommendations of the Consultative Group which have been adopted in Edinburgh are the introduction of normal working hours and Parliamentary recesses to coincide with Scottish school holidays; an emphasis upon committees meeting *outside* Edinburgh as much

as possible in order to provide additional public access to MSPs; more extensive use of electronic information technology by the institution itself and the MSPs within it, including public e-mail addresses for all MSPs and virtual tours of Parliament on the Internet; and the development of new initiatives in education for citizenship in order to encourage a better understanding of the Scottish political process and more widespread public participation.

The commitment to social inclusion and equal opportunities for all reflects one of the main priorities of New Labour throughout the United Kingdom and is not peculiar to the Scottish Parliament or to Scotland. However, it seems that the new procedures in Edinburgh are actually something of a test-bed for reforms which may well be carried forward at Westminster and elsewhere, since the Scottish Parliament has deliberately established an Equal Opportunities Committee to monitor the Parliament's performance on these issues and to promote what is described as the 'mainstreaming' of equal opportunities in all the work of the Parliament and the Executive. The authorities in Edinburgh have gone out of their way to adopt 'family-friendly' working hours and sitting patterns which are designed to assist MSPs of both genders to combine their work in Parliament more easily with their responsibilities for child-care and other aspects of family life; and they have also provided information about the Parliament's role and activities in ethnic minority languages, Gaelic, Braille, audio and, of course, English. Once again these developments seem to put the Scottish Parliament ahead of the House of Commons at Westminster, although not necessarily ahead of the estimable practices of the Information Office in the House of Lords.

The *European Parliament*, too, is way ahead of the House of Commons in certain respects, notably those which bear upon its powers of pre-legislative scrutiny (even legislative veto under the co-decision procedure), its ability to give or withhold assent to important international agreements entered into by the European Union, the budgetary powers which it shares with the Council of Ministers, its role every five years in appointing (and occasionally sacking) the President and members of the European Commission, and its autonomous multi-party control over its own agenda of Parliamentary business.[32] For too long MPs at Westminster have told themselves that they are superior in every way to the European Parliament and there is nothing they can usefully learn from its practices and procedures. Yet even a cursory examination demonstrates that this is clearly not the case.

Firstly, the European Parliament enjoys established powers of *pre-legislative* scrutiny under the so-called consultation and cooperation procedures for which there are no real equivalents at Westminster. Under the consultation procedure, the opinion of the Parliament has to be sought *before* a legislative proposal from the Commission can be adopted by the Council of Ministers – e.g. in relation to the annual agricultural price review. Under the cooperation procedure, the Parliament can improve draft legislation by amending it in two separate readings which give MEPs ample opportunities to review and amend both Commission proposals and the preliminary position of the Council – e.g. in relation to European regional policy, research policy, environmental policy or overseas cooperation and development. Under the co-decision procedure, the Parliament shares the decision-making power over legislation *equally* with the Council of Ministers; the Conciliation Committee – made up of equal numbers of MEPs and Ministers (with the Commission present) – is there to hammer out compromises which both sides can endorse. In the event of there being no agreement, the Parliament can use its power of veto and reject the proposal outright. This procedure has been applied to a wide range of policy issues, such as the free movement of workers, employment matters, consumer protection and trans-European infrastructure projects. Unlike Parliament at Westminster, the European Parliament has the right to give or withhold its consent to international agreements and treaties entered into by the European Union *before* these documents become part of Community law. For example, the accession of new member states, association agreements with third countries and the powers

and tasks of the European Central Bank have all been covered by this procedure.

Secondly, in relation to budgetary powers, the European Parliament – and especially its Budgetary Committee – can propose modifications and amendments to the Commission's initial budgetary proposals and to the position taken by the Council of Ministers at an early stage of the interinstitutional discussions. The Council of Ministers has the last word on important matters such as the expenditure authorised for the Common Agricultural Policy, but the Parliament has joint responsibility with the Council on a wide range of expenditure programmes, such as education, social policy, regional funds and environmental projects. In exceptional circumstances the Parliament has even voted to reject the entire European Budget when its views have not been taken sufficiently into account by the Commission and the Council of Ministers.

Thirdly, the European Parliament's power to supervise and control the Executive – the power to enforce public accountability between elections every five years – is admittedly less impressive and less well entrenched than the equivalent power which is available to national Parliaments. The Strasburg Parliament has not much more than a formal role in appointing (and on one occasion dismissing) the President and members of the European Commission at the beginning of their term of office every five years. It cannot really indulge in motions of no confidence at times of its own choosing (as national Parliaments can), essentially because there is as yet no 'European Government' and because effective political power is still widely distributed between the national Governments of the member states and, to a lesser and varied extent, the national Parliaments. However, the MEPs do have opportunities to question Ministers and to interact politically with the Heads of Government both before and after meetings of the European Council, although these Parliamentary occasions are undoubtedly less awe-inspiring for Ministers than the grillings to which they can be subjected in their own national Parliaments.

Finally, and again unlike the House of Commons, the day-to-day management of the European

Parliament's activities is the responsibility of the so-called Bureau (consisting of the President of the Parliament and fourteen Vice-Presidents drawn from different party groups) and the agenda of the plenary sessions is drawn up by the President in cooperation with the leaders of the various political groups (currently eight) in what is called the Conference of Presidents. Thus *all* party groups – and not just the Government front bench and the Opposition front bench, as at Westminster – have an effective and proportionate say in running the institution.

Perhaps the most distinctive characteristic of procedure and practice in the European Parliament which sets it apart from the House of Commons at Westminster (but not necessarily from other national Parliaments on the Continent) is the way in which the really effective and timely work is done by the *20 subject committees* rather than by the Parliament in plenary session. This reflects a more consensual and less confrontational style of politics than we have been used to at Westminster and it gives even backbenchers rights of legislative initiative and opportunities for real political influence which are normally only available to Ministers in London. Indeed, the European Parliament's practice of referring legislative proposals first to the relevant Parliamentary Committee *before* there can be any question of Parliament giving its approval to the measure as a whole at the equivalent of Second Reading is perhaps the most significant difference with the procedure at Westminster and the most important lesson which our national Parliament could learn from its multi-national counterpart.

If one pauses to consider what are the most significant features that the Scottish Parliament and the European Parliament have in common and from which the House of Commons might learn some lessons to its advantage, one is bound to conclude that their style of politics is less partisan and theatrical; their approach to legislative scrutiny and Parliamentary control of the Executive is more timely, constructive and even forensic; and their democratic legitimacy is based upon various forms of proportional representation which tend to encourage a spirit of inter-party compromise and the pursuit of social inclusion. Clearly these factors help to produce different political cultures in the Parliaments at Edinburgh and Strasburg as compared with the Lower House at Westminster. Yet it seems desirable that any substantial reforms of the House of Commons should induce its Members to emulate their counterparts in Edinburgh and Strasburg rather than the other way around.

General reflections

We have seen in this chapter how one of the problems of discussing the modernisation of the House of Commons has been caused by the fact that the term 'modernisation', when applied to the Lower House, has different meanings and connotations for different people. It is easy to think of at least five different perspectives upon this elastic and elusive term and it is clear that some of them are mutually exclusive. For example, modernisation for the convenience of the Government of the day and its loyal backbench supporters is unlikely to amount to the same thing as modernisation designed to strengthen Parliament as a whole in its continuing contest with the Executive. Equally, deliberate and self-conscious modernisation of the House of Commons at the behest of leading advocates of Parliamentary reform is unlikely to resemble the scatter of unrelated, and sometimes contradictory, changes which can result from the unintended consequences of other measures of constitutional reform.

To begin with the most trivial meaning of 'modernisation' as applied to the House of Commons, the term can be used to describe a policy of *sprucing up the image* of the old institution by blowing away some of the cobwebs and disposing of some of the more archaic customs and practices. Thus the Speaker elected in 2000, Michael Martin MP, decided to dispense with the wig, frock coat, silk stockings and buckled shoes traditionally worn by the Speaker when on duty in the Chamber and on other ceremonial occasions, and content himself with a simple dark suit and ordinary black shoes. If such informality catches on, it may not be long before MPs cease referring to each other as 'Honourable Members' and the forms of address during the course of debate become much more colloquial and demotic. One might have expected that the arrival of the TV cameras in the House in 1989–90 would have served to modernise the image and the practices of the House. Admittedly, it has had some effect in improving the behaviour of the most uncouth and loutish MPs, although the arrival in Parliament of a much larger contingent of women MPs after the 1997 General Election was probably more influential in calming down the wilder men and modernising the atmosphere.

Secondly, modernisation can be taken to mean the introduction of financial or procedural reforms designed *for the support and convenience of all MPs* by boosting the financial, human and material resources available to even the humblest back-bencher; and by altering the daily, weekly and annual sitting times in ways designed to reduce or alleviate the adverse effects of long Parliamentary hours and so make it easier for all MPs to lead a more normal life, whether with their families or otherwise. Of course, in the minds of most members of the public, there is a strong desire to see all MPs behaving as responsible public figures who can oversee the delivery of a range of useful public services, and there is a strong tendency for the public to regard the activity of MPs as a serious full-time job. To that extent, modernisation of this kind is generally favoured by the public. Yet at the same time many members of the public resent the substantial, and escalating, cost of improving the finance and the facilities available to modern MPs in a modern House of Commons, since they can easily be persuaded by the media or by their own experience that some MPs do not pull their weight or provide good value for money.

Thirdly, modernisation of the House of Commons can be pursued *for the convenience of Ministers* and in the interests of the Government of the day. This was exemplified at the beginning of the first Blair Administration when the decision was made to switch Prime Minister's Question Time from twice a week to once a week; and by the Government's decision in November 2000 to put before the Commons a range of procedural motions designed to initiate an experiment with the 'programming' of debates on all

Government legislation and to make possible deferred votes on so-called stand-alone business (i.e. motions without amendments) taken after 10:00 p.m.[33]

The desire to enhance the convenience of Governments has been the most frequent and powerful motive of previous attempts to 'modernise' House of Commons procedures ever since Arthur Balfour's procedural reforms in the 1880s which were designed to bring an end to the incessant disruption of Parliamentary proceedings caused by the Irish Nationalists under Charles Parnell. However, reforming Ministers have seldom explained their purposes in these terms and have usually spoken in terms which might lead the innocent bystander to believe that they have only the interests of Parliament at heart. Thus Margaret Beckett, in opening a debate on Parliamentary modernisation on 7th November 2000, argued that 'the purpose of the proposals is to improve the workings of the House of Commons, *to make it more efficient and effective*'.[34] In making this apparently reasonable point, she was predictably coy about the fact that the extra efficiency and effectiveness would principally be of benefit to the Government of the day by providing it with much greater certainty about its legislative timetable and enabling Ministers to organise their lives more reliably. By contrast, the best argument she could find to seduce Opposition MPs into approving of her plan was that they would have 'the power to choose to focus debate on the parts of legislation that . . . deserve most scrutiny and to expose the weaknesses of the Government's arguments – if they can'.[35] It was pretty clear that the advantages of this particular instalment of procedural reform would be unevenly distributed and that a 'more efficient and effective' House of Commons was really code for a more pliant Assembly disposed to deliver more predictable legislative outcomes.

A fourth meaning of modernisation can be a programme of reform designed *to strengthen Parliament as a counterweight to the Government of the day* by making all backbenchers more formidable as scrutineers and controllers of the Executive and by increasing the opportunities for many long-serving MPs to pursue meaningful political careers not as

Ministers or shadow Ministers but as Parliamentary watchdogs guarding the public interest. Although this connotation may be regarded by many as idealistic and even naive in view of the fusion of the Executive and Legislature in this country, it has gained ground in recent times not only among expert pundits and commentators, but also among senior backbenchers in all parties – notably those who are members of the Liaison Committee. Moreover, those members of the public who take an informed interest in our democratic institutions usually have little sympathy with the idea that MPs owe their principal loyalty to their party and are motivated principally by the self-serving ambition to serve on the front bench, preferably in Government as a Minister of the Crown. MPs would undoubtedly be more popular with the public if they acted mainly as tribunes of the people, representing their constituents and the wider public interest rather than simply the interests of their respective parties.

This form of 'modernisation' may well be doomed in the British political system because of the dominance of the two main parties and the inherent conservatism of nearly all the political class at Westminster – as personified by certain notorious figures such as Dennis Skinner or Eric Forth. It is therefore tempting to assume that the implementation of electoral reform for elections to Westminster is the only step which could change the situation for the better from the point of view of those who favour this interpretation of 'modernisation'. Yet one suspects that a switch to a more proportional system for Westminster elections based upon party lists in one form or another would actually tighten the grip of party managers and make life harder for genuine individualists on the backbenches in what would probably become an even more careerist political system.

Finally, there is a form of 'modernisation' which may come about through *force majeure*, almost as an *unintended consequence* of other constitutional and procedural reforms which have been carried through since May 1997. This point serves to underline the extent to which it is effectively impossible to do only one thing by way of constitutional reform in Britain's delicately connected web of political institutions. For example, further reform of the House of Lords is likely to have an effect upon the House of Commons; the operation of devolved Assemblies in Scotland, Wales and Northern Ireland has already had significant effects upon the work of the House of Commons and may well have further effects in future (e.g. on the number of Scottish MPs, the handling of purely English or English and Welsh legislative business, etc.); and all national Parliaments are likely to see their roles changed (if not weakened) by the growing role of the European Parliament and the changing balance between the various EU institutions. As Lord Norton of Louth observed in his report to William Hague, 'there has been little attempt to anticipate the consequences of one [constitutional] change for another and little attempt to think through the consequences for Parliament'.[36] Until this is done more systematically, the House of Commons will continue to experience serendipitous modernisation which may do as much harm as good.

Some well-informed observers and critics, such as Peter Riddell and Simon Jenkins, have been fairly scathing both about Ministers' motives and about their meagre achievements under the heading of House of Commons reform.[37] This is an understandable line of argument for anyone motivated by an idealistic or radical commitment to Parliamentary reform. However, anyone who takes a more world-weary view of the British political process is likely to conclude that leading politicians, who aspire to become senior Ministers, are unlikely to give up what Simon Jenkins has called 'their licence to professional autonomy'. In our front-bench constitution this is used by Ministers and their Opposition front-bench counterparts for their own party political purposes, but sadly it does not really advance the cause of Parliamentary reform.

Questions for discussion

1   Of all the various interpretations of House of Commons 'modernisation', which do you find the most convincing and why?

2 What are the most useful and relevant lessons that Westminster Parliamentary reformers could learn from other Parliaments?

3 It is commonly said that Parliamentary reform should encompass both Houses of Parliament at the same time. How far do you agree with this and to what extent should reform also encompass the behaviour of the Executive?

Notes

1 An examination of the 1997 Labour Manifesto and, even more, of the legislative output of the long first session of Parliament (1997–98) reveals how successful the advocates of constitutional reform had been in 'capturing' the Labour Party in Opposition.

2 See *Select Committee Report on the Sittings of the House (1991–92)*, HC 20; HMSO, London, 1992.

3 Quoted in House of Commons Library Research Paper 97/64, 'Aspects of Parliamentary Reform', 21st May 1997.

4 See the Scott Report, *The Export of Defence Equipment and Dual-use Goods to Iraq and Related Prosecutions*, Vols 1–5, HC 115, 1996; HMSO, London, 1996; and the first Nolan Report, *Standards in Public Life*, Cm 2850-I; HMSO, London, 1995.

5 Quoted in House of Commons Library Research Paper 97/64, p. 16.

6 First Report of the Modernisation Select Committee (1997–98), HC 190; 29th July 1997.

7 Jack Straw, then Home Secretary, seemed to be the only senior Minister to carry his views in Opposition with him into Government when he submitted the Asylum and Immigration Bill to a Special Standing Committee procedure.

8 See the First Special Report of the Modernisation Select Committee (1998–99), *Work of the Committee, Second Progress Report*, HC 865; 27th October 1999.

9 See the section below entitled 'The view from different angles' for more on this idea.

10 House of Commons Procedure Committee Report, *The Scrutiny of Delegated Legislation (1999–2000)*, HC 48; March 2000.

11 See First Report of the Liaison Committee (1999–2000), *Shifting the Balance, Select Committees and the Executive*, HC 300; 2nd March 2000.

12 See Second Report of the Modernisation Committee (1999–2000), *Programming of Legislation and the Timing of Votes*, HC 589; 5th July 2000.

13 See Labour Party Manifesto, *Ambitions for Britain*; London, 2001; p. 35.

14 See interview with Robin Cook in *The Times*, 12th July 2001, and his speech to the Hansard Society on the same day entitled 'The challenge for Parliament – making Government accountable'.

15 See the interview with Robin Cook in the *Sunday Times*, 4th November 2001, in which he indicated his intention to introduce further reform of the Commons. See also Appendix 3 below for the main points of the 'modernisation' proposed by Robin Cook on 12th December 2001.

16 For example, Standing Order 14 (1) lays down that 'save as provided in this Order, Government business shall have precedence at every sitting'.

17 See *Shifting the balance, Select Committees and the Executive*, HC 300.

18 *Ibid*; para 8.

19 *Ibid*; para 30.

20 Briefly stated, the seven recommendations were that there should be: (1) adequate notice given by the Leader of the House to Select Committees of the expected timing of draft Bills; (2) adequate time for Select Committees to discharge their pre-legislative scrutiny; (3) a presumption in favour of the most relevant Select Committee doing the scrutiny required and maintaining liaison with the sponsoring Department; (4) a formal referral motion in the House usually accompanied by a deadline for the Select Committee's Report; (5) freedom for a Select Committee to decline such a task if its own programme of work is already over-committed; (6) the ability for members of the most relevant Select Committee to be well represented on any Ad Hoc Committee; and (7) freedom for any member of the relevant Select Committee to attend and speak (but not vote) when legislation is dealt with at Standing Committee stage.

21 *Ibid*; para 73.

22 The *Intelligence Services Act 1994* had provided for the creation of the Intelligence and Security Committee (ISC) under the chairmanship of a senior Privy Councillor to supervise the work of the Security Service (MI5), the Secret Intelligence Service (MI6) and the Government Communications Headquarters at Cheltenham (GCHQ).

23 See *Government's Response to the First Report of the Liaison Committee (1999–2000)*, Cm 4737; HMSO, London, May 2000.

24 *The Times*, 22nd May 2000.

25 See *Government's Response*, Cm 4737; paras 8–10.

26 *Ibid*; para 58.

27 See *Strengthening Parliament*, Report of the Norton Commission written by Lord Norton of Louth, commissioned by William Hague and published in July 2000.

28 *Hansard*, 13th July 2000, Vol 353, Cols 1084–96.
29 See 'A Conservative view of constitutional change', speech given at Magdalen College, Oxford, 13th November 2000.
30 This was a point made in conversation with the author by Sir George Young Bt MP who was Shadow Leader of the House for a period in the 1997–2001 Parliament.
31 See *Shaping Scotland's Parliament*, Report of the Consultative Steering Group; Scottish Office, Edinburgh, January 1999.
32 See *Serving the European Union, a Citizen's Guide to the Institutions of the European Union*; 2nd edn, Office for Official Publications, European Communities, Luxembourg, 1999; pp. 5–8.
33 On 7th November 2000 these motions were carried by comfortable majorities. There were free votes on the Government side and a small number of Labour backbenchers opposed these reforms.
34 *Hansard*, 7th November 2000, Vol. 356, Col. 214.
35 *Ibid*; Col. 218.
36 *Strengthening Parliament*, p. 16.
37 See Simon Jenkins in *The Times*, 6th December 2000; and Peter Riddell, *Parliament under Blair*; Politico's, London, 2000.

Further reading

Tony Benn, *The Speaker, the Commons and Democracy*; Spokesman Books, Nottingham, 2000.

John Biffen, *Inside the House of Commons*; Grafton Books, London, 1989.

The Challenge for Parliament, Making Government Accountable, Report of the Hansard Society Commission on Parliamentary Scrutiny; Vacher Dod Publishing, London, 2001.

Making the Law, Report of the Commission on the Legislative Process; Vacher Dod Publishing, London, 1993.

Greg Power, *Parliamentary Scrutiny of Draft Legislation, 1997–99*; Constitution Unit, London, 2000.

Greg Power (ed.) *Under Pressure: Are We Getting the Most from Our M.P.s?*; Hansard Society, London, 2000.

Giles Radice, *Member of Parliament*; Macmillan, London, 1987.

Peter Riddell, *Parliament under Pressure*; Gollancz, London, 1998.

Michael Rush, *The Role of the M.P. since 1868*; Oxford University Press, Oxford, 2001.

Shifting the Balance, Select Committees and the Executive, First Report of the Liaison Committee (1999–2000), HC 300; London, March 2000.

S.A. Walkland (ed.) *The House of Commons in the Twentieth Century*; Clarendon Press, Oxford, 1979.

website for the House of Commons: www.parliament.uk

Transforming the legal system

From a political perspective, most observers would cite devolution to Scotland, Wales and Northern Ireland, the reform of the House of Lords and the growing influence of Britain's membership of the European Union as the most significant aspects of constitutional change in the United Kingdom since Labour came to power in 1997. Yet the transformation of the English (and Welsh) legal system will probably be acknowledged as of equal or even greater significance once all the dust has settled and it seems likely that Lord Irvine, the architect of Labour's legal reforms, will go down in British history as one of the great reformers in the historic office of Lord Chancellor.

Modernising judicial and court procedures

The overall aim of the Lord Chancellor's Department in transforming the legal system has been 'to provide a modern, fair and efficient system of justice which operates in the public interest and ensures value for money for the taxpayer'.[1] In order to do this Lord Irvine and his Ministerial colleagues set themselves six strategic objectives in 1998–99, at least two of which have had the effect of modernising judicial procedures. The first of these was 'to facilitate the fair, speedy and effective resolution of disputes, ensuring that costs and procedures are proportionate to the issues at stake'. The second was 'to enable criminal justice to be dispensed fairly, effectively and without undue delay, promoting confidence in the rule of law and contributing to the Government's aim of reducing crime and the fear of crime'.[2] Allowing for the rhetorical flourish about crime, this has involved building upon the tireless work of Lord Woolf who, as Master of the Rolls, completely rewrote the *Civil Procedure Rules* which came into effect on 26th April 1999. These now place greater emphasis upon active judicial case management in order to ensure that cases are dealt with in ways which are proportionate to the value of the claim and the issues at stake.

The modernisation of *civil justice procedures* was really a long overdue task for which the relevant

Ministers in the first Blair Administration inherited responsibility from their Conservative predecessors. Lord Woolf had been given *carte blanche* to review and suggest fundamental reforms to the whole compass of civil justice procedure. He duly did this in a magisterial Report which made more than 300 separate recommendations to improve and streamline the process of civil litigation.[3] His refreshing approach to the whole exercise was based upon the principle that 'disputes should, wherever possible, be resolved without litigation'; but where litigation was unavoidable, 'it should be conducted with a view to encouraging settlement at the earliest possible stage'.[4] In order to achieve these commendable objectives, Lord Woolf proposed that there should be a new unified code of procedural rules for civil litigation in both the High Court and the County Courts; a set of pre-action protocols to set standards and timetables for the initial stages of civil litigation; and a new three-track system for dealing with civil cases according to the value and complexity of each case.[5]

Within the overall framework of reform, the most significant changes in the Civil Procedure Rules which came into force in April 1999 are the statement of the 'overriding objective' in Part I and the case management powers for judges in Part III. *The overriding objective* is designed to enable the courts to deal with cases justly and more expeditiously than in the past. Specifically, judges are under a duty to ensure that the parties are on an equal footing both before trial and at trial; cases are handled in a way which is proportionate to the amounts of money at stake and which does not incur excessive costs; wherever possible, legal expenses are saved by the encouragement of pre-trial settlements or so-called Alternative Dispute Resolution procedures; and no more than an appropriate share of the court's resources (and hence of judicial and official time) is devoted to each case. Moreover, the Court of Appeal has emphasised that the parties in any civil litigation are under an obligation to help the court to achieve the overriding objective and this should take priority over any existing case law in the interpretation of the rules. The result has been to facilitate a greater throughput of litigation within a given period of time and to serve the interests of natural justice. It is also worth noting that the concepts of 'equality of arms' between the two sides in any court case and of 'proportionality' between the sums in dispute and the legal means employed to pursue a claim reveal the influence of continental European jurisprudence as developed by the European Court of Human Rights.[6]

The case management powers for judges constitute a deliberate attempt to shift the initiative from litigants and their lawyers to the presiding judge in each case. This is supposed to result in fewer delays, more weeding out of unjustified actions at an early stage in the court proceedings and even the penalisation of vexatious or incompetent lawyers via so-called 'wasted costs orders' by which the presiding judge can significantly reduce the fees paid to troublesome lawyers who do not abide by the new rules. Judges therefore have more power to take a timely grip on cases before them, to dispose of more cases via summary judgement and to prevent lawyers from using the least acceptable techniques of their trade, such as gratuitous obfuscation, repetition and time wasting for the sake of clocking up larger fees. This concept of more rigorous case management places responsibility for the nature and extent of civil litigation clearly in the hands of the judges rather than the parties to a dispute and it is fundamental to the implementation of the new rules.

At the time of writing it is too soon to make a final evaluation of what have come to be known as the Woolf reforms. However, as the Lord Chancellor's Department noted in its April 2000 Annual Report, 'there seems to have been a real shift in litigation culture towards a more collaborative and less combative approach'.[7] Work in the same vein has continued with a review of enforcement proceedings, new rules governing civil appeals and group litigation, and changes in court procedures for housing and land disputes which were scheduled for implementation by April 2002. To the layman all these changes to modernise the procedures of civil justice may seem rather dull, but they are certainly relevant to the wider constitutional debate since they have a direct bearing upon the quality and the accessibility of justice. Not only is it true that justice delayed can be justice denied; it is also true that obscure and costly judicial procedures have often deterred people from securing their human or property rights in court and thus prejudiced the principle of equality before the law.

The modernisation of *criminal justice procedures* has also formed part of Lord Irvine's agenda and some of the issues raised have certainly attracted more media and public interest than the Woolf reforms of civil justice. Once again, one of the principal objectives of the modernisation programme has been to eliminate unnecessary delays, while ensuring that the system as a whole is managed more efficiently. The 1998 Crime and Disorder Act and the Magistrates' Courts (Procedure) Act 1998 contained statutory provisions to reduce delays in criminal proceedings, and schemes to this end were piloted by Magistrates' Courts in six areas of England and Wales during 1998 and 1999. In Magistrates' Courts emphasis has been put upon promoting the early hearing of cases, usually a day or two after a defendant has been charged, and there has been a stated intention to introduce a streamlined procedure for sending certain cases for trial in the Crown Court. However, the Government's attempts to remove a defendant's right to opt for trial by jury in a Crown Court in so-called 'each way cases' was twice defeated by lawyer-led opposition in the House of Lords.[8] These setbacks for the Government should remind the reader that not all the 'modernisation' of criminal justice procedure has been greeted with acclamation and that it is possible for Ministers who seek to curry favour with the law-abiding public to alienate both legal practitioners and the civil rights lobby if they try to tip the scales of justice too far against the interests of defendants.

Predictably, there has been Treasury-led concern about the rising financial cost of criminal legal aid, which rose by 44 per cent from £507 million in 1992–93 to £733 million in 1997–98, while the number of such cases dealt with rose by only 10 per cent over the same period. Ministers have recognised that the idea of defraying this cost by means-testing defendants has been a failure in view of the fact that only 6 per cent of all defendants in the Crown Court have made any financial contribution. The decision was taken to replace the traditional criminal legal aid scheme with a new Criminal Defence Service (CDS) – established by the Access to Justice Act 1999 – which would negotiate contracts for different types of legal service with contract prices fixed in advance whenever possible. This way forward was designed to permit the CDS to negotiate overall contracts with firms of solicitors which would then be responsible for organising the full range of services for defendants from initial advice in the police station through to acquittal or conviction at the end of the trial process. The key decision on whether or not to grant a criminal defendant legal representation at public expense remains in the lap of the trial judge. In view of the abandonment of any attempt to means-test defendants at the outset, it is now for a Crown Court judge at the end of the case to order that a convicted defendant should pay some or all of his legal costs, depending upon the true level of his means which may well come to light during the course of proceedings in court.

Greater use is being made of modern technology not only to enable defendants remanded into custody to participate in preliminary hearings via video links from prison, but also to enable vulnerable or intimidated witnesses to give evidence remotely via TV links to court rooms. Furthermore, it is intended to provide better IT support for staff working in Crown Courts, and over a period to February 2004 to install a network of electronic links between all the main criminal justice organisations as a key component of the Government's inter-departmental strategy to deliver what is, characteristically, described as 'a joined-up criminal justice system'.

Since it is well established that the vast bulk of criminal offences are committed by young males between the ages of 15 and 25 and since it is in the Magistrates' Courts that nearly all these cases are dealt with (at least at first instance), it is not surprising that the main focus of the Government's reforms has been on introducing a fast track for dealing with persistent young offenders and on undertaking a thorough modernisation of the Magistrates' Courts. On the first point, Ministers

have declared that dealing with youth crime and improving youth justice are high priorities in their law and order policies, as demonstrated by the Government's pledges to halve the time from arrest to sentence for persistent young offenders and to assist the courts in managing cases more effectively. Through pilot and demonstration projects Ministers are deliberately trying to change the culture in youth courts by introducing a new style of operation which is more open, more direct and less adversarial.

On the second point, the Government has pursued an elaborate programme of reforms to modernise the ways in which the Magistrates' Courts operate. This has involved the amalgamation of Magistrates' Courts' Committees (MCCs) into fewer, larger areas (including the establishment of a new Magistrates' Courts' Authority for Greater London as a whole); clearer separation of the legal and administrative functions within MCCs; the implementation of a ten-year programme designed to ensure that all new court clerks are professionally qualified as barristers or solicitors; and improving the performance and accountability of Magistrates' Courts by ensuring that all MCCs are subject to annual Public Service Agreements, that a new grant allocation formula is in operation by 2001–2 to coincide with the final amalgamations, and that relevant training is delivered to equip all magistrates to deal with the judicial consequences of the *Human Rights Act 1998*. Magistrates' Courts will also be affected by the changes in the structure and operation of the criminal justice system which flow from the recommendations of the Auld Report.[9]

Because 97 per cent of all criminal cases begin and end in the Magistrates' Courts, Lord Irvine has gone out of his way to express the Government's confidence in the role played by magistrates in a modernised criminal justice system.[10] The *1999 Access to Justice Act* contained important provisions to unify the metropolitan and provincial stipendiary benches into one national bench under a single judicial office holder, known as the Chief Magistrate. Within this new structure all stipendiary magistrates are known as District Judges (Magistrates' Courts) and can exercise national jurisdiction for the first time. This reform is designed to facilitate 'the speedy and efficient execution of justice', which the Lord Chancellor's Department partially measures in terms of improved national consistency in sentencing. Yet it raises issues of perennial sensitivity for the large number of lay magistrates who may see their independence and local discretion under threat from such developments and who may need constant reassurance from Ministers on this sensitive point.

Broadly speaking, the constitutional significance of these and other measures to modernise judicial procedures has been twofold. In the sphere of civil justice, the principal effects have been to make the law more comprehensible and accessible to ordinary citizens while discouraging frivolous or vexatious litigation. Lord Woolf's excellent reforms have punctured the pretensions of lawyers and should reduce the expense of going to law for ordinary individuals (although probably not for companies). However, there has been some controversy over the introduction of American-style 'no win, no fee' agreements between civil lawyers and their clients and some commentators have criticised the absence of legal aid for personal injury cases. In general, though, the Woolf reforms have struck a blow for clarity and simplicity in what has traditionally been one of the most opaque and mystifying sectors of the English professions and have contributed to more modern and sensible procedures in a large area of legal practice.

In the sphere of criminal justice, the effects of 'modernisation' are likely to seem somewhat threatening, at least from the standpoint of those who are principally concerned with civil and constitutional liberties. For example, the rights of defendants to 'play the system' by insisting upon a jury trial in so-called 'each way cases' and by choosing not to disclose previous criminal offences which a jury might find influential in reaching its verdict are to be removed in the name of modernisation. Many traditionalists in both Houses of Parliament, as well as spokesmen for Liberty and similar libertarian pressure groups, are distinctly unhappy about such threats to the rights of individuals and it could well be that these aspects of the Government's law and order policies will be challenged in the English courts as contrary to Article 6(1) of the European Convention on Human Rights.

The Labour Government's modernisation agenda is also being applied to the sphere of *administrative law* and the operation of Tribunals. As a category of judicial instruments, administrative tribunals, ombudsmen and a range of other quasi-judicial regulatory bodies have expanded from about 30 in number at the time of the Franks Report in 1957 to about 100 tribunals and still more ombudsmen and regulatory bodies. One result is that the administrative justice system now handles more cases every year than the civil courts.

Ministers in the first Blair Administration decided to take stock of this varied and disparate area of justice and in May 2000 the Lord Chancellor announced that Sir Andrew Leggatt, a retired Appeal Court judge, had been appointed to conduct an independent and wide-ranging review of all tribunals and to submit a report by the end of March 2001.[11] The hope was that Sir Andrew would make suitable proposals for the modernisation of the administrative justice system to improve its coherence, accessibility and organisation in much the same way that Lord Chief Justice Woolf had done for the civil justice system and Lord Justice Auld would do for the criminal justice system. Lord Irvine indicated that Sir Andrew would be asked to pay close attention to six key areas in particular: fair, timely, proportionate and effective arrangements for handling disputes; administrative arrangements which meet European Convention requirements for independence and impartiality; arrangements for improving public knowledge and understanding of the system; efficient, effective and economical arrangements for funding and management; national performance standards; and the extent to which there is a coherent overall structure of institutions for the delivery of administrative justice. At the time of writing, Ministers are considering the Report with a view to introducing suitable reforms in the 2001–6 Parliament.

Democratising the judiciary and legal profession

For well over a century, first the trade union movement and then the Labour Party and its intellectual apologists have harboured deep suspicions, often extending to outright hostility, towards judges, magistrates and the entire legal profession, because of what the judiciary have seemed to represent and the class interests which its members have been seen to advance in their court judgments.[12] Indeed, for nearly all the twentieth century only the continued existence of the Tory-inclined hereditary peers as members of the House of Lords seemed to inspire a comparable sense of enmity in the breasts of those on the Left of British politics.

One of the six stated objectives of the Lord Chancellor's Department (LCD) during the 1997–2001 Parliament was related specifically to judicial appointments and was formulated in the following deceptively bland terms: 'to enable the Lord Chancellor to appoint or recommend sufficient numbers of judges, magistrates and other judicial post-holders of the right quality and to safeguard their constitutional independence'.[13] From this unexceptionable statement no innocent reader could easily divine the real intentions of Labour Ministers to reform, even perhaps transform, the character of the judiciary over a period of years. Certainly the formal methods for achieving this objective, as explained by the Lord Chancellor in several speeches and in other public information clearly posted on his Department's website, should cause no concern among critics of the Government's modernisation policies.

For example, in a section designed to explain the Lord Chancellor's policies and procedures in respect of judicial appointments it was made clear on the LCD website that the guiding principles are: (1) appointments should be made strictly on merit from among those who appear to be best qualified; (2) part-time service in a relevant judicial office should normally be a prerequisite for appointment on a full-time basis; and (3) significant weight should be attached to the independent (and confidential) views of existing judges and other senior members of the legal profession as to the suitability of candidates for judicial appointments. In this post-Nolan era, however, the formalities of the appointments process have become more punctilious in that most posts are advertised so as to encourage the widest possible competition, due process is followed with the maximum of transparency, and at the end of a three-stage process of application, consultation and interview, there is even the possibility for unsuccessful applicants to receive confidential feed-back from LCD officials about how they performed at interview and how they might do better in any application for a similar post in future.

As for appointments to the lay magistracy, fairly early in its first term of office the Government issued a Consultation Paper seeking views on whether it was still relevant to attempt to achieve a political balance on benches of lay magistrates and on the various Advisory Committees which recommend candidates for appointment to the magistracy.[14] Having reviewed the history of the matter and the salient contemporary considerations, Ministers and officials suggested that political balance was no longer an adequate proxy for the desirable social balance among magistrates and, indeed, might even be an impediment to such an objective. However, the result of the consultation process was that while most respondents favoured removing political affiliation as one of the criteria for the selection of magistrates, no suitable alternative emerged and the Lord Chancellor reluctantly decided to leave things as they were until a better and more modern measure of social balance in the magistracy could be found. In the meantime noticeable progress was made in appointing almost as many women as men to the bench, while appointments coming from the ethnic minorities were broadly in line with the proportion of such people in the population as a whole.[15]

Notwithstanding the cautious and correct approach to the process of judicial appointments visible in the public face of the Lord Chancellor's Department, the man himself has been unashamedly proactive in his determination to make the judiciary more socially inclusive and more representative of society as a whole. He has done this principally by constant exhortation in several well-publicised speeches to gatherings such as the Association of Women Barristers and the Minority Lawyers' Conference, and there are signs that his campaigning approach has made a positive difference.

For example, although it is more than 70 years since women were first called to the Bar, it is only recently that there have emerged enough women with over fifteen years' experience at the Bar to make their presence felt in the competition for judicial appointments. The proportion of women holding appointments in the main tiers of the judiciary increased from 7 per cent in 1994 to 9 per cent in 1998, still inadequately reflecting the fact that women account for 14 per cent of all barristers with at least fifteen years' experience at the Bar. At the highest levels of the judiciary women are woefully under-represented, since they account for none of the Law Lords, only one Head of Division (Dame Elizabeth Butler-Sloss, President of the Family Division), two Appeal Court Judges (6 per cent of the total) and eight High Court Judges (8 per cent of the total). Yet the proportion of women gets noticeably larger as you move down the judicial tree, with women accounting for 7 per cent of Circuit Judges, 9 per cent of Recorders, 16 per cent of Assistant Recorders, 13 per cent of District Judges, 15 per cent of Deputy District Judges, 15 per cent of Stipendiary Magistrates and 17 per cent of Acting Stipendiary Magistrates.[16] Meanwhile, women account for more than 43 per cent of all new recruits to the profession, which bodes well for the upward progress of women barristers to the higher levels of the judiciary in future.[17]

For Lord Irvine it has not been a matter of sitting back and waiting for this natural progression to take effect; he has also made a number of rhetorical appeals to suitably qualified women lawyers to apply for positions in the judiciary (repeating his mantra: 'Don't be shy, apply') and a number of deliberate changes designed to assist women's progress to the highest levels of the judiciary in future. *Firstly*, he has ended the traditional habit of making appointments to the High Court by invitation only in order to encourage more women to come forward via open and advertised competition. *Secondly*, he has experimented with ways of making part-time sitting arrangements more flexible (e.g. by opening up the possibility of judges sitting for more concentrated blocks of time) which might well suit the convenience of women who want to combine their judicial and family responsibilities. *Thirdly*, he has increased the upper age limit for appointment as an Assistant Recorder from 50 to 53 in order to help both women and men who may have entered the legal profession somewhat later in life than the average or who may have lost a few years of their career when devoting themselves to their family responsibilities. In all these ways Lord Irvine has proved himself to be a champion of women's judicial potential and in the longer run this seems likely to have some significant consequences.

For those who seek to apply the Government's doctrine of social inclusion to the ethnic composition of the judiciary, the reality is so far very disappointing. For example, only 1 per cent of all barristers who have been qualified for fifteen years or more, and who might therefore apply for or obtain judicial appointments, are of ethnic minority origin and there are currently no black or Asian High Court Judges. From New Labour's point of view this is an unacceptable situation and one which the present Lord Chancellor has said he is determined to rectify by supporting Codes of Equal Opportunities for both branches of the legal profession and by encouraging more ethnic minority candidates to apply for judicial appointments. In a well-publicised speech to the Minority Lawyers' Conference Lord Irvine declared: 'I am determined to preside over a judicial appointments process in which every lawyer – regardless of sex, race, colour or creed – has a fair and equal chance to show that they are the stuff of which a judge is made.'[18] These admirable intentions ought to have some virtuous effect over a period of time as non-white candidates climb the legal ladder and become both more qualified for judicial office and more confident about achieving it.

As with the upward mobility of potential women aspirants to the judiciary, so with ethnic minority lawyers, there are already some signs that at the more junior levels the younger cohorts are beginning to make their mark and this is likely to produce healthier figures in future.[19] In March 1999 the Lord Chancellor returned to the same conference and was able to report that at least 7 per cent of the applications for Assistant Recorder and at least 3 per cent of the applications for Silk were from candidates of ethnic minority origin, both figures representing signs of modest progress in the right direction.[20] The situation in the magistracy has become more promising in that 4 per cent of all magistrates are from ethnic minorities, compared with the 6 per cent that such people represent in the population as a whole; and in 1998 the Lord Chancellor appointed a few blind or partially blind magistrates for the first time, thus setting an encouraging precedent for people with disabilities who might be thinking of applying for a judicial appointment.

None of these advances provides any grounds for official complacency, but progress has clearly been made by extending more equal opportunities for women, ethnic minorities and people with disabilities to join the ranks of the judiciary – in the case of women increasingly at the higher levels in the hierarchy. However, one notable obstacle to the democratisation of the judiciary remains difficult to shift and that is the continuing failure sufficiently to open this powerful corner of the Establishment to the sons and daughters of ordinary working people. Obviously, with the rapid growth of higher education, a larger proportion of young people with such social origins is working its way, on merit, into prestigious professions. Yet it is still the case that the Bar functions with middle-class assumptions in a middle-class atmosphere. For as long as this remains true, so long will there be something of a psychological (and financial) barrier to the emergence of more judges with working-class backgrounds in this country.

The Lord Chancellor solidly and frequently avers that he is opposed to both negative and positive discrimination in the judicial appointments process. Yet there is a strongly held view among the 'forces of conservatism' that Ministerial exhortations to women, ethnic minorities and those with disabilities to apply for judicial appointments in

larger numbers have been egregious examples of Ministerial preoccupation with 'political correctness' at the expense of best practice. The real concern, which is felt but not often expressed in some quarters of the legal profession and beyond, is that positive discrimination is being practised and that the results, at least in some instances, may be to produce judges of a lower quality than would otherwise have been the case.

On the other hand, it would be fair to point out that intelligence, drive and ability are pretty evenly dispersed throughout the population and by now virtually every other branch of the power structure in this country has been opened up to people of talent from every conceivable background. There is therefore no earthly reason why the judiciary should be an exception to this general trend and Ministers have every justification for pursuing a policy of democratising the judiciary. Moreover, the policy will almost certainly succeed over a period of years as new cohorts of previously disadvantaged people build their qualifications and their self-confidence to such a point that the situation is permanently transformed for the better.

Improving legal services and access to justice

When Labour came to power in 1997, it made a Manifesto commitment to develop a new Community Legal Service which would largely replace what had become an unfair, ineffective and increasingly expensive system of Legal Aid. Senior Labour figures were determined, in the Lord Chancellor's words, 'to create structures which ensure that our most disadvantaged citizens have the ability to protect their interest in the areas that matter most to them' – areas such as housing, welfare benefits, employment rights, advice about debt or family problems, advice when in trouble with the police and consumer problems.[21] The main justification for improving legal services has therefore been a social one which dovetails with two of the leading themes of 'modernisation' – namely, joined-up public services and social inclusion.

Broadly speaking, the arrangements for legal services which Labour inherited were characterised by three main weaknesses, in addition to the ballooning cost of Legal Aid which had concerned the Treasury for many years in previous public expenditure settlements. *Firstly*, there was no satisfactory or systematic assessment of who needed what sort of legal help or advice. *Secondly*, there was a fragmentation of sources of legal help or advice for ordinary people. *Thirdly*, there was no assurance of consistent quality in the legal services available across the country.

To rectify this situation, Lord Irvine proposed to create a network of quality providers of legal services, supported by coordinated public funding and delivering appropriate services to local communities in the light of effective assessments of local needs. This required legislation in the *Access to Justice Act 1999* which provided, among other things, for the establishment of a new Legal Services Commission responsible for the Community Legal Service and the Criminal Defence Service. It also required considerable political commitment from Ministers and officials in central Government, and from newly formed partnerships consisting of the legal profession, voluntary agencies, local authorites, various task forces and even a cluster of celebrities in the so-called 'Panel of Champions'. By the time that the new Community Legal Service was officially opened by Cherie Booth QC, the Prime Minister's wife, on 3rd April 2000, 70 Community Legal Service Partnerships were in operation, involving 109 local authorities covering over one-third of the population of England and Wales. The Government's aim was that by April 2002 at least 90 per cent of the people of England and Wales should be covered by such arrangements.[22]

The new dispensation has not only been based upon a trail-blazing policy which holds that locally useful legal services do not necessarily have to be delivered by lawyers (or at any rate lawyers on their own), but has also created a new structure of non-departmental public bodies, funding arrangements and public–private partnerships at arm's length from government. The Legal Services Commission, which has replaced the Legal Aid Board, is responsible for maintaining and developing the Community Legal Service (CLS) and for managing the Fund which has replaced civil legal aid. The service itself involves both the provision of information (notably via the dedicated website *Just Ask!*) and the provision of legal help via a network of dedicated local offices. It is subject to a CLS Quality Mark in order to guarantee high standards and it is free for those who qualify, depending upon their financial circumstances and the nature of the case.

The money available to the CLS Fund is fixed by the Lord Chancellor (after negotiation with Treasury Ministers) and the Commission is under a duty to spend it in ways which secure the best possible value for money. The legislation allows the Commission to contract for legal services with quality-assured suppliers, including law centres and advice agencies as well as private sector lawyers, according to priorities set at national and local level. All applications for funding must satisfy the tests set out in the Funding Code approved by Parliament which sets *less* stringent tests for high-priority cases, such as immigration, mental health and family law cases; and *more* stringent tests for low-priority cases, such as personal money claims and business cases. The Commission can also refuse public funding altogether when alternative ways of resolving a dispute or funding litigation are available to an applicant. Most personal injury cases are removed from the scheme, since the Government believes that these are better funded via conditional fee agreements.

Overall, the scope of the new CLS Fund was narrower than that of civil Legal Aid which it replaced, which is why the Lord Chancellor provisionally allocated a smaller sum of public money in 2001–2 (£624 million) than in 2000–1 (£748 million). This was because it had been assumed that the lower number of cases approved under the new rules in 2000–1 would lead to lower spending by the Fund in 2001–2 and thereafter. It is fair to say that the new policy has been driven at least as much by a Treasury-led desire to reverse the previous spiralling growth of the legal aid bill as by the more idealistic terms of Labour's 1997 Manifesto commitment to introduce a Community Legal Service.

As the chairman of several Cabinet Committees on constitutional issues and the political head of what is now the leading Department in Whitehall dealing with constitutional reform, Lord Irvine has spoken for years with a special authority across the piece. In his speech on establishing a Community Legal Service, he argued that the promise to redefine the relationship between the individual and the state had been a central theme of Labour's 1997 Manifesto.[23] In this argument he instanced the human rights legislation; devolution to Scotland, Wales and London; what were then only proposals for freedom of information; the salience of electoral reform; and reform of the Second Chamber. He proceeded to bracket with all of the above the idea of creating a Community Legal Service as a new structure to ensure that the most disadvantaged citizens have the ability to protect their interests in the day-to-day areas of life that matter most to them. In his mind, therefore, there was an important unifying theme based upon making government more accessible, more modern and more responsive to the people in order to secure 'the levels of commitment, interest and trust needed to develop and maintain real, practising democracy in this country'.[24]

It can be seen from the record that the Labour Government has managed to improve legal services for those who really need them and found it difficult or impossible to get them under the old system. It is also clear that the Treasury should be pleased by the 'improvements' made by the Lord Chancellor's Department in this area of public administration, since eligibility for legal aid has been redefined (more narrowly) and hence there has been a saving in public funds compared with what would otherwise have been the case. Of these twin objectives, however, only the first could be said to widen the access to justice. Other improvements will depend upon the statutory provisions which Labour has introduced or has inherited for conditional fee agreements and legal costs insurance.

The law relating to this area has been reformed by the *Access to Justice Act 1999* which made conditional fees and after-the-event legal expenses insurance more attractive to defendants and those seeking non-financial redress, while further discouraging weak cases and encouraging out-of-court settlements. At the same time the Government has taken advantage of statutory authority which it inherited from the previous Conservative Administration by making Orders under the *Courts and Legal Services Act 1990* which specify the proceedings to which conditional fee agreements must relate and which set out the detailed requirements with which agreements must comply if they are to be enforceable.

Such changes have been designed to make access to justice easier and more affordable for those members of the public who were previously denied a real chance to exercise their legal rights either by the prohibitive cost of engaging lawyers or because they were too 'well off' to qualify for state-funded legal aid. The measures go some way towards redressing what the Lord Chancellor's Department has described as 'the fundamental problem of the British legal system' which is that most people are too 'well off' to qualify for legal aid but too poor to finance their own litigation. It is worth noting that this severe social problem was first highlighted by Ministers in the previous Conservative Government and this aspect of Labour's policy draws upon Conservative ideas for using market mechanisms largely copied from practice in the American legal system. The policy appears to have been more expedient than altruistic and it seems to have had little or no constitutional dimension. Yet it has been consistent with Labour's mission to modernise which has been encapsulated by Ministers in the slogan: 'What matters is what works'.

The other significant consequences which have flowed from the *Access to Justice Act 1999* are the extension of rights of audience in court to employed advocates (e.g. Crown Prosecutors) so that they are on equal terms with lawyers in private practice; the introduction of portable rights of audience for advocates who change their status (e.g. from barrister to solicitor); and the enablement of barristers employed by firms of solicitors to provide legal services directly to the public. What all of these changes really amount to is a further erosion of traditional restrictive practices in the legal profession – another policy which carries forward work begun by the previous Administration.

Incorporating human rights into statute law

For centuries British subjects had no positive rights, whether human or otherwise, but rather duties to their Sovereign and under him to their feudal Lords. In so far as people enjoyed freedoms, these were based upon negative rights – i.e. the right to do or say anything which was not proscribed by statute law promulgated in Parliament or by common law promulgated in the courts. When this situation began to change – notably in the wake of the so-called Glorious Revolution in 1688–89 – it was the people's representatives in Parliament rather than the people themselves who acquired positive rights, such as the right to take charge of their own destiny via the mechanisms of Parliamentary government and specifically the right to withhold public finance from the Monarch and the Monarch's Government unless and until the Executive paid heed to popular concerns and grievances.

Admittedly, there had been a precarious common law tradition, spasmodically upheld by the courts, of protecting the civil liberties of the subject against abuses of power by either the Monarch or Parliament. For example, Lord Chief Justice Coke in *Bonham's Case of 1603* famously declared that 'when an Act of Parliament is against common right and reason or repugnant . . . the common law will control it and adjudge such an act to be void'. However, the taking of such positions by the judiciary in defence of the rights of ordinary people was unusual, to say the least, both during the period of Divine Right when the Courts were more often an instrument of, rather than a bulwark against, Royal power and during the period of Parliamentary government after 1688–89 when the theory was that it was to Parliament that ordinary people should look for the redress of their grievances and the protection of their liberties.

It could perhaps be argued that this position of inherent dependency for most British subjects (there being no question at that time of citizenship) was mitigated by the fact that central Government was weak and often ineffective, something which could be explained by the fact that only a very small proportion of the people were enfranchised with a vote at Parliamentary elections. Thus the cynical and circular argument put by all conservatives, at least until the 1832 Great Reform Bill, was that ordinary people with virtually no positive rights (and often no literacy or education either) did not merit the vote, and because they could not make a legitimate claim to be full participants in the system of Parliamentary democracy, they could not expect to enjoy any positive rights.

This traditional elitist view of human rights gradually became less acceptable during the nineteenth and twentieth centuries in Britain, although it should be added that the inherent paternalism of our legal system persisted into what might be described as nearly modern times. This was plainly apparent in the notorious case of *Liversidge v. Anderson* in 1941 when a majority of the Law Lords held that since the Home Secretary had acted in good faith in detaining a person who he had reasonable cause to believe was in some way a threat to public safety or national security, they could inquire no further into the propriety of his action and could not determine whether the detention order (which obviously abridged one of the plaintiff's human rights) was in fact justified on objective grounds. At that time only Lord Atkin, in a memorable dissenting opinion which foreshadowed what was to become conventional wisdom in the senior judiciary 40 or 50 years later, had the courage and the character to declare that the protection of individual liberty was a vital task for the judiciary, no matter what the exigencies of state seemed to require even in war-time.[25]

In terms of governmental attitudes to human rights, the awful atrocities committed by the Axis Powers and others during the Second World War had a decisive effect upon the politicians in office in the post-war period, at any rate those in North America and the Western part of Europe. Thus the then fairly limited membership of the United Nations agreed in 1948 to the Universal Declaration of Human Rights. This was followed two years later by the European Convention on Human Rights which was swiftly ratified by the United Kingdom in 1951, although the dismissive attitude of Lord Chancellor Jowitt led the then Labour Government to insist upon excluding British subjects from the right directly and individually to petition the European Commission and Court of Human Rights. In November 1952 the United Kingdom ratified the First Protocol to the Convention which added rights to the possession of property, to education and to free elections; and much later, in January 1999, the United Kingdom ratified the Sixth Protocol which precluded the death penalty.

From about the 1960s onwards, judicial opinion in this country began to become more purposive and interventionist on behalf of the subject and against an increasingly powerful and all-pervasive Executive. One should not exaggerate the extent or the significance of this shift in judicial opinion at that time, but it was one of the factors which had a bearing upon the softening of attitudes in the first Wilson Administration towards the European Convention. One practical result was that in December 1965 Ministers accepted the right of direct individual petition to, and the jurisdiction of, the European Court of Human Rights in relation to cases brought by British citizens against public authorities in the United Kingdom. This was effected in January 1966 after an exchange of correspondence between the relevant Ministers (the Law Officers and Ministers in the Foreign and Commonwealth Office), and it is noteworthy that Parliament was not required to legislate to give effect to the decision nor was there any public consultation.[26]

Although virtually all the other European nations which were signatories to the European Convention treated it as if it were part of their constitutional patrimony, successive British Governments still felt inhibited from giving it full effect in domestic law. The first reason for this was to be found in the dualist tradition of English law whereby international treaties become part of our domestic law only through legislative incorporation (i.e. by passing a Westminster statute for the purpose); and the second reason was to be found in the traditional reluctance of the British political class to confer what were regarded as excessive powers upon the judiciary at the expense of our elected Parliament. In spite of these blocking realities, there were mounting pressures from the late 1960s onwards for the incorporation by statute of the European Convention into British law. This pressure began in 1968 with a Fabian pamphlet by Anthony Lester (now Lord Lester of Herne Hill), and was given extra force by the magisterial Hamlyn Lectures of Lord Scarman in 1974 and added urgency in the late 1980s by influential pressure groups, such as Charter 88, which formed an increasingly close alliance with Labour and Liberal Democrat politicians in Opposition.[27]

The turning point in favour of incorporation came in March 1993 when John Smith as Labour Leader committed his party to statutory incorporation of the Convention and the establishment of an independent Human Rights Commission to act as an institutional monitor for the cause.[28] With John Smith's untimely death in 1994, this became an important part of his political legacy to Tony Blair and a clear commitment to incorporation (although not to a Human Rights Commission) was duly included in Labour's 1997 Manifesto. When the Human Rights Bill was published in October 1997, along with a White Paper entitled *Rights Brought Home*, neither document included the promise of a Commission and in each case the issue was left open for consideration at a later date.[29] This was a major disappointment to what might be described as 'the human rights lobby', especially since an equivalent body *was* established in Northern Ireland. In general, however, there was no doubting the Labour Government's firm commitment to legislation for incorporation and the 1997 Human Rights Bill duly became the *1998 Human Rights Act*, with the widespread approval of both Houses of Parliament and senior members of the judiciary.

The case for incorporating the rights contained in the European Convention into British statute law was made very succinctly in the 1997 Government White Paper.[30] *Firstly*, it was argued that incorporation would give the British people more of a direct sense of ownership of the rights concerned.

Secondly, it would greatly reduce the delays and the costs associated with the previous procedures which had required plaintiffs in this country to exhaust all their domestic legal remedies *before* they were allowed to petition the European Court and which thus involved average costs of £30,000 per case. *Thirdly*, it meant that the catalogue of human rights contained in the European Convention would be brought much more fully into the jurisprudence of Courts throughout the United Kingdom and thus be more completely woven into the tapestry of our domestic law. *Fourthly*, it would correct the unfortunate and false impression that the authorities in this country did not attach sufficient importance to the protection of positive human rights – an impression which seemed to be corroborated by more than 50 cases in which the United Kingdom had been found in violation of Convention rights since 1951. *Fifthly*, it would lead to closer and more timely scrutiny of the human rights implications of new policies and new legislation. And *finally*, it would enable British judges to make their distinctively British contribution to the gradual development of human rights jurisprudence throughout Europe. For all these reasons the new Labour Government argued that the time had come for a Human Rights Act, even though all its predecessors had reached a more cautious conclusion whenever the possibility of introducing such a statute had arisen. See *Box 12* for the key features of the legislation.

When the *Human Rights Act 1998* (HRA 1998) eventually became law, it contained a number of important and memorable features. *Firstly*, it enables British citizens to defend and enforce European Convention rights with less delay and less cost within British courts. *Secondly*, it requires Ministers and civil servants to do their utmost to see that their administrative procedures and legislative proposals are 'action-proof' against the possibility of human rights litigation in the British courts. In the case of Government Bills, every Minister responsible for piloting legislation through Parliament is obliged to certify the Bill as compatible with the terms of the European Convention and if this cannot be done, then Parliament must expressly legislate for a derogation and this alerts the Courts to a conscious departure from the HRA 1998.

Box 12 Key features of the Human Rights Act 1998

- It enables British citizens to defend and enforce their rights under the European Convention with less delay and less cost within British courts.
- It requires Ministers and civil servants to see that their administrative procedures and legislative proposals are 'action-proof' against human rights litigation in the British courts.
- It prohibits a 'public authority' from acting in a way incompatible with the Convention and covers misuse of power by the state or any agency (public, voluntary or private) which performs a public function on behalf of the state.
- The British courts are obliged to interpret legislation as compatible with the Convention to the fullest possible extent in all cases which are brought before them.
- By providing the possibility of a Declaration of Incompatibility, it would be for the Government and Parliament – not any level of the High Court – to amend an aspect of legislation or public administration which had been found by the courts to be incompatible with the Convention, thus preserving at least the facade of Parliamentary supremacy.
- It remains possible for the Government of the day with the support of Parliament to introduce legislation which would contravene the Convention in cases of 'national emergency' by negotiating a temporary derogation from the Convention – e.g. in Sections 21–23 of the Anti-Terrorism, Crime and Security Act 2001.

Thirdly, under Section 6 of the Act, it is unlawful for a public authority to act in a way which is incompatible with one or more of the Convention rights and in this context a wide definition of 'public authority' is matched by a correspondingly wide definition of legal liability in order to provide as much protection as possible for the rights of individuals against the misuse of power by the state or any agency (public, voluntary or private) performing a public function on behalf of the state.[31] *Fourthly*, under Section 3 of the Act, the Courts are obliged to interpret legislation as compatible with Convention rights to the fullest possible extent in all cases coming before them. This was intended to be a strong form of incorporation which, while stopping short of permitting the Courts to strike down primary legislation, enables the Courts to set aside any inconsistent provisions in secondary legislation to the extent necessary to allow Convention rights to take full effect in this country.

The most remarkable feature of the Act and, in the opinion of Lord Irvine the greatest constitutional challenge to the Government in seeking to incorporate the European Convention into British statute law, was

> to find a way to do so which respected Parliamentary sovereignty and gave further effect to Convention rights directly in our domestic courts without interfering with the balance of powers between the legislative, executive and judicial arms of the state, and with the way in which our common law has developed over the centuries to protect the rights of our citizens and to provide appropriate remedies.[32]

This tricky balance in Section 4 of the Act was achieved by introducing the device of a *Declaration of Incompatibility*, which is available to the superior Courts in those rare cases in which a Minister is unable to certify a Bill as compatible with Convention rights and the even rarer cases in which Ministers and civil servants together fail to recognise incompatibility between a Government Bill and the Convention. It was envisaged that such a declaration would only be made if the Courts had exhausted all possibilities of construing the Bill in question as compatible with the Convention and there remained a significant stumbling block which could not be overcome without amending or

repealing the legislation. In that eventuality the responsibility for rectifying the situation would be returned to Parliament, where it belonged, and it would be open to the appropriate Minister to introduce an Order in Council (subject to the Affirmative Resolution procedure and approval of both Houses) to amend the primary legislation in such a way as to make it compatible with the Convention.

Lord Irvine was careful to stress the protocols applying to such ticklish procedures on numerous occasions in Parliament and outside. For example, just as the higher Courts are free to decide whether or not to make a Declaration of Incompatibility when they find an incompatibility, so Parliament (which really means Ministers in both Houses and their supporters) is free to decide whether or not to amend legislation to bring it into compliance with the Convention in the event that the Courts declare it to be non-compliant or incompatible. The higher Courts have not been given 'a power to create a whole new piece of primary legislation', but rather 'a power to remove an incompatibility in response to a clear finding from a United Kingdom court or from the Strasbourg court'.[33] Indeed, on a strict interpretation of Section 4 of the Act, the Government of the day may decide *not* to use the fast-track procedure for rectification which has been provided, because it believes the matter requires further and fuller consideration by Parliament in other ways; or conceivably, Parliament itself might decline to approve the remedial Order because there was a revolt on the Government backbenches. In either of these unlikely cases, Ministers could claim that the integrity of Parliamentary supremacy had been preserved.

In the great majority of what is likely to be a rather small number of cases where a Government is faced with having to respond to a Declaration of Incompatibility made by a higher Court, the expectation must be that Ministers would move swiftly to remove the offending provisions. This is not only because they would realise that if they did not, they would leave themselves exposed to legal action by private citizens or other litigants in this country who felt aggrieved that their enforceable human rights under the Convention had not been respected in some piece of Westminster legislation; it is also because the Labour Government can be considered to have been completely sincere in its desire to uphold Convention rights in this country and Ministers do not wish to have their policy or their legislation stigmatised by being in contravention of European human rights which they themselves were instrumental in 'bringing home' to the United Kingdom. So while it is possible to take a cynical view of this whole discussion and to argue that the device of a Declaration of Incompatibility is really little more than a clever way of paying obeisance to Parliamentary supremacy while masking the reality of inexorably growing judicial power, this author prefers to see it as a well-calculated balance between the interests of the senior judiciary and the interests of Parliament – always allowing for the very British anomaly of having the Lord Chancellor and twelve Law Lords sitting as legislators in the Upper House of Parliament while performing their judicial duties as members of the highest Court in the land.

It is widely agreed that the implications of the *Human Rights Act 1998* are likely to be very significant both for the British legal system and for the changing balance in the constitutional arrangements of the United Kingdom. On the first aspect, Lord Steyn (the senior Law Lord in terms of his age) forecast in 1999 that 'a new legal order will come into existence when the Human Rights Act comes into effect'.[34] The Act duly came into force in October 2000 and at the time of writing it seems a fair bet that Lord Steyn will be proved right in a number of important respects.

On the second aspect, Lord Irvine has been prepared to trumpet the constitutional significance of the Act on a considerable number of occasions. For example, in his Tom Sargant Memorial Lecture in December 1997 he spoke about the implications of shifting to a system of positive rights.[35] The Act would give the Courts the tools they need to uphold Convention rights at the very time when infringement is threatened – i.e. in the course of judicial proceedings in this country – and to do so by granting relief against an unlawful act by a public authority. If there were to be departures from the principles of the Convention in the political

and administrative decisions of Ministers or civil servants, these would have to be conscious and reasoned departures, not simply the product of rashness, muddle or ignorance. As the Lord Chancellor put it, 'human rights will not be a matter of fudge': the process should produce 'better thought-out, clearer and more transparent administration' and an 'improvement in both the efficiency and the openness of our legislative process'.[36]

The third implication was that statutory incorporation would enable the Courts in cases brought before them to reach conclusions which give full effect to the substantive rights guaranteed by the Convention. Although Articles 8 to 11 of the Convention lay down principled rights or freedoms which may be subject to limitation on other grounds – e.g. the preservation of national security, territorial integrity or public safety – the prime focus of the Courts will be on the positive rights in the Convention and only secondarily will the judges focus upon the justifiability of an exception. It will not be necessary for the Courts to find an ambiguity in our domestic law before they can intervene to uphold Convention rights; on the contrary, they will have a duty to interpret UK legislation in a way consistent with Convention rights unless the legislation is so demonstrably incompatible with the Convention that it is judicially impossible to do so. Thus the judicial presumption will be in favour of construing our law in accordance with the European Convention and the onus will be upon those who disagree with this to prove their case on the balance of probabilities. However, the legislative fall-out in this country from the terrorist atrocities in the United States on 11th September 2001 made it necessary for the Government to introduce the *Anti-Terrorism, Crime and Security Bill* which provided for explicit derogations from certain aspects of the HRA 1998 in relation to the detention without trial of suspected international terrorists in this country who are not British citizens.[37]

The final implication in the mind of Lord Irvine was that decisions of the Courts would henceforth be made on a more overtly principled, even moral, basis than before. By this he meant that our Courts will get into the habit in human rights cases of considering both the spirit and the letter of the matters on which they adjudicate and of looking at the merits as well as the procedures of the governmental or 'public' decisions which have given rise to litigation in the first place. In short, in Lord Irvine's words, the Act will produce 'decisions on the morality of the conduct and not simply its compliance with the bare letter of the law'.[38]

As for the effects of the *Human Rights Act 1998* upon the changing balance in the constitutional arrangements of the United Kingdom, Lord Irvine and other Ministers have been markedly more cautious about extolling its virtues, let alone claiming any decisive constitutional innovations. This is because, while justifiably celebrating the fulfilment of their 1997 Manifesto commitment, they have been keen to reassure the British political class in general (and Labour backbenchers in particular) that the traditional position of Parliament and hence the rights of any democratically elected Government have not been fatally compromised by the passage of the Act. Indeed, it would have been hard to imagine that the Lord Chancellor, acting as a pillar of both the Executive and the Legislature as well as head of the Judiciary, would have taken a different line on these sensitive issues.

In another lecture, delivered in memory of the well-known human rights lawyer Paul Sieghart, Lord Irvine described the Act in what seemed like a self-conscious *jeu de mots* as 'a constitutional balancing act' which required 'Courts to recognise that they have a fundamental contribution to make in this area, while appreciating that the other elements of the constitution also have important roles to play in securing the effective protection of the Convention rights in domestic law'.[39] One might almost have expected him to go on to speak in New Labour vocabulary of 'a partnership' between Parliament and the Courts to deliver the desirable objectives of the Act; yet he was drawn instead to commend the interpretative role of the Courts within what he claimed to be 'the doctrine of the separation of powers on which the constitution is founded'.

This was actually a rather monocular view of traditional British constitutional arrangements which only partially accords with the political facts. For centuries in the United Kingdom only the Judiciary and the Executive have been constitutionally separate and independent of one another to any marked degree, whereas the Legislature has been fused with the Executive and partly fused with the Judiciary in the persons of the Lord Chancellor and the twelve Law Lords. It was therefore not very helpful or enlightening for Lord Irvine to present the constitutional issues in this way and one can only assume that, for his own reasons, he was trying to obscure the political realities of the situation. Full and formal separation of powers has *not* been a defining characteristic of British constitutional arrangements for centuries past and there is no convincing evidence that the situation today is any different, even with the *Human Rights Act 1998* on the statute book. What is true, however, is that the relationships between the Judiciary, the Executive and the Legislature are likely to change as a result of the Act. While Parliament at Westminster will doubtless retain its claim to ultimate legal authority in the United Kingdom, it will be less able to exercise its supremacy in a manner that goes against the principles of the European Convention.[40]

European and other influences upon public law

European influences have been working cumulatively upon our public law ever since 1973 when the United Kingdom joined the European Communities (in the nomenclature of the time) and notably since the three *Factortame* cases in 1990–91.[41] The result has been that the growing importance of superior European Community law has led at various times to UK legislation being suspended, disapplied or declared unlawful.[42] This is a powerful illustration of the fact that by no means all the transformation of the British legal system has been attributable to political decisions taken by the Blair Administration and much of it can be traced back to the cumulative effect of this country's membership of the European Union. For example, the influence of European Community law has spilled over into the fields of judicial procedure and judicial decision making in this country. This could be seen most famously in the leading case of *Pepper v. Hart* in 1993 in which the Law Lords chose to follow the continental European practice of referring to the purposive context of legislation (in this case the *Hansard* record of what was said by Ministers at the time) in order to arrive at a better construction of legislation under dispute. It could also be seen in the growing tendency for British courts to apply the doctrine of *proportionality* to cases brought before them – a doctrine originally derived from German administrative law.

It can be anticipated that the effects of the European Convention on Human Rights upon our public law in the United Kingdom will be similarly influential, albeit via a weaker judicial route of constructive interpretation and declaratory incompatibility. Three examples may be given of the inevitable incremental effects of introducing this system of law to be applied alongside our traditional common law principles. Firstly, there is likely to be a more purposive and normative approach to statutory interpretation which over a period of time may lead British courts away from the literal and procedural approach which they have traditionally adopted. This Continental approach is sometimes known as the *teleological approach* to judicial construction, since it involves judges in putting themselves to some degree in the shoes of the legislators by asking what ends or purposes Parliament had in mind when passing a given statute.

Secondly, the *doctrine of proportionality* – already applied by the European Court of Human Rights in its jurisprudence – which holds that the action taken by a public authority to abridge Convention rights on grounds of national policy must be commensurate with the objective needs of the situation, is very likely to loom larger in the thinking of our National courts when they are dealing with human rights cases. Since this criterion applies a more demanding judicial test to the actions of public authorities than the so-called *Wednesbury Test* traditionally used in this country (i.e. whether in all the circumstances an action

seems reasonable to a reasonable man), it would imply more frequent and fundamental intervention by the Courts in the substance of policy issues.

Thirdly, the concept of the *margin of appreciation* is likely to gain ground at any rate in relation to the qualified Convention rights in Articles 8 to 11 rather than the absolute rights in Articles 2 to 4. This will have the effect of giving discretion to our national Courts when applying Convention rights on the reasonable grounds that they, rather than the European Court, are likely to be *au fait* with indigenous requirements and with the 'necessity' for a restriction or derogation in order to take such factors fully into account. Once again this would imply a more rigorous form of judicial scrutiny of Executive actions by our national courts than has been the case under our traditionally more constrained procedures of judicial review and hence more scope for judicial intervention on policy grounds.

Judges in this country will increasingly have to weigh whether the application of the doctrine of 'necessity' justifies the limitation of a positive human right and whether the degree of limitation is proportionate to the objective need for it in such areas as tax law, housing law and the interpretation of contracts. Even in non-Convention cases coming before the British courts, Lord Irvine has stated his belief that such 'European' judicial habits may grow in our soil and that 'some blurring of the line may be inevitable'.[43] In short, the *Human Rights Act 1998* and the considerable body of European Convention jurisprudence that comes with it is likely to encourage in our judiciary a significant shift of judicial preoccupation from matters of form and procedure to matters of substance and policy.

As regards the cross-fertilisation of legal norms, Lord Irvine and other Law Lords have been clear that different national and supra-national jurisdictions have been learning from each other and will continue to do so. Quite apart from the burgeoning body of European law stemming from both the European Community and the European Convention, there are the examples of the *Canadian Charter of Rights and Freedoms* which eventually achieved a broad measure of political and public acceptability in 1982, more than 20 years after the failure of a premature initiative in 1960, and the *New Zealand Bill of Rights Act 1990* which caught a high tide of judicial enthusiasm for the enforcement of fundamental human rights and the control of governmental power. In Lord Irvine's opinion, these two examples drawn from jurisdictions in other parts of the English-speaking world emphasised 'the importance of achieving a synthesis between political and legal culture and the measures by which the constitution is reformed'.[44]

In yet another magisterial lecture, delivered this time at the Inner Temple in March 2000, the Lord Chancellor expatiated at length upon the common origins of English and American law.[45] However, in his conclusion he observed that localising influences upon the law in all countries were diminishing, in view of the need to respond judicially to modern issues such as human cloning, regulation of the Internet and the war against global terrorism. With the progressive convergence of cultural and scientific influences across the world, the senior judiciary in every jurisdiction was likely to devote more attention to the evolving jurisprudence in other jurisdictions as a possible guide to its own decisions. In this context, he argued that the *Human Rights Act 1998* provided 'a fine example' of the ways in which English law could benefit from American experience which showed that 'a written declaration provides a more certain safeguard of individual rights than procedural democracy through a sovereign Parliament, indispensable though that is'. To the attentive student of the swirling debate surrounding the enforcement of human rights in the United Kingdom, this was a very interesting comment on two grounds: *firstly*, it gave equal or greater credit to *American law* rather than continental European law for influencing the decisive move to the statutory incorporation of human rights in this country; and *secondly*, it conceded that in the modern world a written declaration interpreted and enforced by an independent judiciary provided a better safeguard for individual rights than our traditional form of Parliamentary democracy in the United Kingdom.

While it should be clear that the drive for incorporation of European Convention rights in our statute law has depended upon achieving a credible balance between the roles of Parliament and the Courts, this development has also highlighted the need for achieving another balance between the competing imperatives of activism and restraint in the administration of public law in the United Kingdom. *Firstly*, this has involved the need to preserve the distinction between judicial review and judicial appeal – the former being relatively safe and familiar in the British legal system, whereas the latter has undoubtedly been regarded as more challenging to the status quo. *Secondly*, there are signs that the judiciary does not wish to trespass too far into the realm of common law constitutional rights, as was evident in the case of *Lightfoot* which concerned whether access to affordable justice under delegated legislation was or was not anything more than a matter for administrative decision.[46] *Thirdly*, it appears that the judiciary is not yet convinced that it is safe or wise to invoke the European Convention as a direct limit upon the decision-making powers of the Executive, at any rate as long as *Brind* and *Smith* are the leading cases in this evolving area of the law.[47] As Lord Irvine commented, 'to take such a step unilaterally would substantially affront the separation of powers . . . reducing Agency autonomy and usurping Parliament's constitutional responsibility for the domestication of international Treaties'.[48]

It is significant that even before the *Human Rights Act 1998* became fully operational in October 2000, the usual dialectics of judge-made public law within a constitutional setting of Parliamentary supremacy were clear for all to behold. On the one hand, the most senior British judges have been emboldened by the statutory incorporation of the European Convention and by the new judicial climate, both in this country and abroad, which seems increasingly well disposed towards the enforcement of positive human rights. On the other hand, several authoritative reminders have been given to the judiciary that activism must be tempered with restraint, especially in the light of the democratic imperative of Parliamentary supremacy and the need to respect the Executive's area of legitimate autonomy in decision making.

As Lord Irvine concluded in his Paul Sieghart Memorial Lecture of 1999, 'the typology of change in English public law is one of evolution, not revolution'.[49]

General reflections

It should be apparent from the account given in this chapter that it is not an exaggeration to say that the legal system has been transformed at the instigation of the Labour Government and that Lord Irvine, in particular, regards this transformation as an integral part of the Government's wider programme of constitutional reform. The main elements of the 1997 Labour Manifesto have been followed through. However, some constitutional proposals which were actively canvassed by the Labour and Liberal Democrat parties when they were in Opposition have not yet been acted upon by Labour in Government – e.g. the establishment of a Human Rights Commission. It remains to be seen whether such ideas will be implemented during the 2001–6 Parliament.

We saw in the previous section that by no means the whole transformation of the legal system is attributable to initiatives taken by the present Government and much of it reflects the interchange of ideas within the judiciary and the legal academic community both nationally and internationally. This can be explained by the fact that the law in any civilised society is a living thing and the state of the law at any given time tends to reflect the balance or dialectic between the received ideas of the past, the political realities of the present, and the perhaps more idealistic aspirations of lawyers and constitutional reformers for the future. Since Labour was returned to office in 2001 with another huge overall majority in Parliament which rendered any policy deals with the Liberal Democrats unnecessary, it seems unlikely that the Government's agenda for legal reform will be particularly ambitious, although aspects of the promised 'modernisation' of the criminal justice system are likely to be both controversial and constitutionally significant.

It will be interesting to see whether Ministers lose patience with the Law Society as the self-regulatory body for solicitors who constitute the greater part of the legal profession. If there is no further progress made by the Law Society in putting its own house in order, then it is possible that Ministers will act to end this form of self-regulation and introduce instead a statutory scheme for complaints against solicitors in England and Wales designed to ensure that the huge backlog of public complaints is more swiftly and satisfactorily dealt with.[50]

Equally, it is possible that the second Blair Administration may relent on its previous opposition to establishing an independent statutory Human Rights Commission to act as a permanent advocate and watch-dog for the cause of human rights within all corners of British society. After all there are the well-established precedents of the Commission for Racial Equality and the Equal Opportunities Commission which act as catalysts for better race and gender relations respectively, and more recently it has been decided to create a Children's Commissioner for Wales. So Labour Ministers may decide that the Joint Human Rights Committee of both Houses of Parliament is not a satisfactory substitute for an independent Human Rights Commission, but only time will tell.

A truly radical decision, which could have been taken by Tony Blair in the immediate aftermath of his second General Election triumph in June 2001, would have been to abolish the historic office of Lord Chancellor, which dates back to early medieval times, and then distribute the Lord Chancellor's many and varied duties between other more appropriate office holders. In fact, the Prime Minister moved in the opposite direction when he announced that the Lord Chancellor's Department would take over the wider constitutional responsibilities of the Home Office (including freedom of information, data protection and human rights), thus even more emphatically becoming the leading Department in Whitehall on constitutional issues.

As for the need to justify the office of Lord Chancellor, it is interesting to note that this task has been thought to merit a page and a half of explanation on the website of the Lord Chancellor's Department. The briefing begins by informing us that 'over the past thousand years or so the office of Lord Chancellor has evolved to become the answer to the problem of maintaining judicial independence in a constitution which concentrates supreme power in a democratically elected Legislature dominated by party politics'. Successive Lords Chancellor, we are told, have played various important roles in British Government over the centuries, but 'today the appointment has become in effect that of a Minister of Justice' – in other words, a senior member of the *Executive* as would be the case in most other European countries. What is thought to be a 'killer argument' is then boldly delivered in the following statement: 'by taking part in all three branches of Government, the Lord Chancellor appears to challenge the concept of the separation of powers; however, his effective purpose is actually to *maintain* the separation of powers'.

In response to this, it ought to be said that the office of Lord Chancellor is not *the* answer to the problem of maintaining judicial independence in our informal constitution, but rather one of several possible answers and arguably one of the least credible in the modern world. Judicial independence has long been entrenched by statute (specifically the *1701 Act of Settlement*) which still guarantees that judges serve *quam diu se bene gesserint* (as long as they behave themselves properly) and that a High Court judge can only be dismissed following a petition to and a formal vote in both Houses of Parliament. This position has also been heavily reinforced by long-established custom and practice over the centuries. It really has nothing very much to do with the Lord Chancellor or his venerable office, although this is the self-serving claim which Lord Irvine has made on several occasions.[51]

If it is true that the Lord Chancellor is effectively Minister of Justice, then it would be timely to tidy up the anomaly of his having to share the duties normally associated with a Ministry of Justice with two other senior Ministers. The Attorney General, as well as being the chief legal adviser to the Government of the day, is also nominally the leader of the English Bar and has Ministerial responsibility for the Crown Prosecution Service and the Government Legal Service which is distributed throughout the various Departments. The Home Secretary is Ministerially responsible for the criminal justice system, the police, the prison and probation services and penal policy generally. Such functional divisions could be largely overcome by the creation of a fully fledged Ministry of Justice led by a senior Minister answerable to the House of Commons, but it seems that the Prime Minister does not want this.

As for the discussion about the alleged separation of powers in the United Kingdom and Lord Irvine's confident assertion that his historic office actually serves to maintain such a principle, it is perhaps worth recalling what he had to say on this matter at an international common law conference in Edinburgh in July 1999.[52] *Firstly*, he argued that because of the significant authority of his office in all three branches of British government, its holder is uniquely well qualified to protect the independence of the judiciary by dint of his legal experience and political authority as a senior member of the Cabinet. *Secondly*, he maintained that the office of Lord Chancellor enables a senior Minister to be responsible to the public, through Parliament, for the overall efficiency and cost-effectiveness of the judicial system – in a way that the senior judges themselves cannot because of their need to remain outside party politics. *Thirdly*, he argued that the holder of his office can bring his weight to bear as the head of the judiciary by sitting and presiding over certain important cases, always provided that in his political role he abstains from expressing concluded views on issues which may come before him in his judicial capacity and that he does not sit as a judge in any case in which the interests of the Executive are directly engaged. This was a particularly controversial argument for him to use, since it depended critically upon the meaning of the words 'concluded' and 'directly'. On the whole it is simply incredible that any Lord Chancellor worth his salt will not have well-formed views upon the sort of issues which are likely to come before him when he is acting in a judicial capacity and it is equally incredible that the interests of the Executive will not be involved in many of the politico-legal cases which have to be dealt with by the Law Lords.[53]

Finally, Lord Irvine had the temerity also to argue exactly the opposite point, namely that the role of the Lord Chancellor is to compensate for the fusion of powers elsewhere. This was a breathtaking assertion from someone whose office itself is the very epitome of the fusion of powers in the British political system. It strains all credulity to argue that an acknowledged problem in the British system – namely, the deep fusion of powers – can be dealt with by a very senior political and judicial figure whose historic office is the institutional embodiment of the problem in the first place. Only in the British constitutional context would such a serious senior figure attempt with a straight face to make the case that his office was 'more valuable and necessary than ever as a buffer between the Executive and the Judiciary and a bulwark of our constitution'.[54]

In summary, the measures initiated or pursued by the Labour Government since 1997 to transform the legal system are likely to have significant and far-reaching constitutional consequences. The modernisation of judicial procedures in the civil courts represents a once-in-a-generation attempt to demystify and make more user-friendly legal customs and practices which were rooted in the past and often seemed to defy the needs of justice in the contemporary world. The deliberate democratisation of the judiciary and the whole legal profession is undoubtedly a long-term project of great social value, but one which is only likely to bear full fruit over several decades as new cohorts of younger lawyers rise up the professional ladder to replace their less representative predecessors. The improvement of the access to and the quality of legal services ought to be one of the beneficial consequences of Labour's decision to establish a new and comprehensive Community Legal Service. The modernisation of procedures in the criminal courts, however, is likely to be much more controversial and to raise issues of natural justice – e.g. the traditional right of defendants not to reveal previous convictions and to be protected from double jeopardy – which are considered constitutionally significant by many and which could lead to political defeats for Government legislation in the House of Lords.

Of all the various developments discussed in this chapter, it seems likely that the incorporation of the European Convention on Human Rights into United Kingdom statute law and the related impact of European and other jurisprudence upon our public law will prove to be of the greatest constitutional significance in the long run. The shift from negative freedoms to positive rights and from literal construction to purposive interpretation of the law in the higher courts is likely to modify our jurisprudence and to shift the balances within it for many years to come. Yet for all that, the *Human Rights Act 1998* may not have as great an effect upon our constitutional arrangements in this country as the *European Communities Act 1972* and all the Community law which has flowed from it over subsequent years. All we can say in conclusion is that the law today is in a state of flux and that Labour's policy to transform the legal system is likely to have significant constitutional consequences.

Questions for discussion

1   Assess the overall constitutional significance of Lord Irvine's transformation of the legal system in England and Wales.

2   Are the Human Rights Act 1998 and the doctrine of Parliamentary supremacy likely to be compatible in the long run and how should the Law Lords try to square the circle?

3   In what ways and to what extent is English public law being changed by European and other influences?

Notes

1   See *Annual Report*, Lord Chancellor's Department, Cm 4606; London, April 2000; para 1.
2   *Ibid*; para 2.
3   See Lord Woolf, *Access to Justice, Final Report*; HMSO, London, July 1996.
4   *Ibid*; Section III, Chapter 10, para 2.
5   See White Paper, *Modernising Justice*, Cm 4155; HMSO, London, December 1998.
6   See pp. 262–5 below for more on this aspect.

7 *Annual Report*, Cm 4606; para 38.
8 The Criminal Justice (Mode of Trial) Bill, which attempted to cut back upon the rights of defendants in 'each way cases', was savaged and effectively defeated in the House of Lords in November 1999. When similar legislative proposals were introduced in the Mode of Trial (No. 2) Bill of February 2000 they stirred up another hornet's nest of legal opposition and the Bill was defeated on Second Reading in the Lords on 28th September 2000. This was because a number of influential peers and some Law Lords considered that such proposals posed an unacceptable threat to one of the most basic liberties of the subject in this country, namely the right to opt for trial by jury in cases where the reputation and good name of the defendant is at stake. For a clear account of all the issues involved in this area of controversy see Lord Justice Auld, *Review of the Criminal Courts*; HMSO, London, October 2001; paras 141–9.
9 See Chapter 17, pp. 381–2 below, for details of the Auld Report published in October 2001.
10 See Lord Irvine at the Council of the Magistrates' Association on 25th March 1999.
11 See Lord Irvine's speech to the Council on Tribunals at Millbank Tower in London on 18th May 1999.
12 See J.A.G. Griffith, *The Politics of the Judiciary*; Fontana, London, 1997.
13 See *Annual Report*, Cm 4606.
14 *Political Balance in the Judiciary*, Consultation Paper, Lord Chancellor's Department; London, October 1998.
15 Official figures showed that in 1998 1,414 Magistrates were appointed (710 men and 704 women) and 6 per cent of all appointments were from the ethnic minorities.
16 Figures derived from the Lord Chancellor's Department website which were correct on 1st January 2000.
17 Figures taken from Lord Irvine's speech to the Association of Women Barristers at the Barbican, London, on 11th February 1998.
18 Speech by Lord Irvine to the Minority Lawyers Conference at the Law Society in London on 29th November 1997.
19 According to Lord Irvine's speech to the Asian Business Network in London on 22nd May 1998, ethnic minority candidates accounted for only 1 per cent of Circuit Judges and 1.5 per cent of Recorders. However, they made up 3.4 per cent of Assistant Recorders, 8.3 per cent of all barristers with between five and ten years of service and nearly 15 per cent of new entrants to the solicitors' branch of the legal profession; so things were likely to improve with the passage of time.
20 See speech by Lord Irvine to the Minority Lawyers Conference on 20th March 1999.
21 Speech by Lord Irvine to the Holborn Law Society in London on 2nd November 1998.
22 See Press Release No. 107/00 from the Lord Chancellor's Department on 3rd April 2000.
23 Speech to the Holborn Law Society, 2nd November 1998.
24 *Ibid*.
25 A portion of Lord Atkin's memorable speech deserves to be quoted in full:

> In this country, amid the clash of arms, the laws are not silent. They may be changed, but they speak the same language in war as in peace. It has always been one of the pillars of freedom, one of the principles of liberty for which on recent authority we are now fighting [a reference to the 1941 Atlantic Charter signed by Churchill and Roosevelt on behalf of Britain and the United States] that the judges are no respecters of persons and stand between the subject and any attempted encroachments on his liberty by the Executive, alert to see that any coercive action is justified in law.

26 These points are made by Lord Lester of Herne Hill QC in 'Human rights and the British constitution', in J. Jowell and D. Oliver (eds) *The Changing Constitution*; 4th edn, Oxford University Press, Oxford, 2000; p. 94.
27 See A. Lester, *Democracy and Individual Rights*, Fabian Tract No. 390; London November 1968; and Lord Scarman, *English Law, the New Dimension*; Hamlyn, London, 1974.
28 Lecture entitled 'A citizen's democracy' given to a Charter 88 meeting in London on 1st March 1993.
29 See *Rights Brought Home, the Human Rights Bill*, Cm 3782; HMSO, London, October 1997.
30 *Ibid*; paras 1.14–1.19.
31 For example, *Railtrack* provides and maintains the permanent way, signalling and stations which make safe and reliable rail travel possible. It is therefore a private undertaking performing public functions and it is covered by the Act.
32 See Lord Irvine's speech to a Clifford Chance conference on 'The impact of a Bill of Rights on English law' at 200 Aldersgate, London, on 28th November 1997.
33 *Ibid*.
34 See Lord Steyn, 'The role of the Bar, the Judge and the Jury – winds of change', *Public Law*, 1999; pp. 51–5.
35 See Lord Irvine's lecture on 'The development of human rights in Britain under an incorporated

Convention on Human Rights' given at the Law Society in London on 16th December 1997.

36 *Ibid.*

37 Clauses 21 to 23 of the Anti-Terrorism, Crime and Security Bill enable suspected international terrorists to be detained in circumstances where either a legal impediment derived from an international obligation or a practical consideration prevents removal to another country. In parallel with these provisions, the United Kingdom intends to make a derogation from Article 5 of the European Convention on Human Rights (ECHR) which deals with rights to personal liberty and security to the extent necessary to ensure that the measures contained in these clauses are not in breach of our obligations under the ECHR. Article 15 of the ECHR permits a derogation from Article 5 in a time of public emergency to the extent strictly required by that emergency (the doctrine of proportionality).

38 See Lord Irvine's lecture at the Law Society in London on 16th December 1997.

39 See Lord Irvine's Paul Sieghart Memorial Lecture entitled 'Activism and restraint – human rights and the interpretative process', delivered in London on 20th April 1999.

40 This point was made by Lord Irvine in a speech entitled 'Parliamentary culture in a time of change' given to a conference held in the Reichstag, Berlin, on 28th February 2000.

41 See *R. v. Secretary of State for Transport, ex parte Factortame Ltd* (1990); *R. v. Secretary of State for Transport, ex parte Factortame Ltd* (No. 2) (1991); and *R. v. Secretary of State for Transport, ex parte Factortame Ltd* (No. 3) (1991).

42 On this point, see the second Factortame case; *Marshall v. Southampton & South West Area Health Authority (Teaching)* (1993); and *R. v. Secretary of State for Employment, ex parte Equal Opportunities Commission* (1995).

43 See Lord Irvine's Tom Sargant Memorial Lecture, 16th December 1997.

44 See Lord Irvine's National Heritage Lecture at the US Supreme Court on 11th May 1998.

45 See Lord Irvine's lecture on 'The common origins of English and American law' at the Inner Temple, London, on 22nd March 2000.

46 See *R. v. Lord Chancellor, ex parte Lightfoot* (1998) 4 All ER 764.

47 See *R. v. Secretary of State for the Home Department, ex parte Brind* (1991) 1 AC 696 and *R. v. Ministry of Defence, ex parte Smith* (1996) QB 517.

48 See Lord Irvine's Paul Sieghart Memorial Lecture, 20th April 1999.

49 *Ibid.*

50 *Financial Times*, 6th January 2001.

51 For example, in his speech to the world-wide common law conference at the University of Edinburgh on 5th July 1999.

52 *Ibid.*

53 The much publicised Scottish case of Margaret Brown in the year 2000 involved the defendant citing the 1998 Human Rights Act in an initially successful argument to the effect that she had been denied a fair trial in a Scottish Magistrates' Court because the Deputy Sheriff (the Magistrate) who heard the case at first instance had executive as well as judicial responsibilities and because on grounds of privacy she did not have to incriminate herself by declaring whether or not she had been the driver of a car which the police had stopped on suspicion that the driver had been drinking. The claimant won her argument at the High Court, but subsequently lost her case on appeal.

54 Lord Irvine at the world-wide common law conference at the University of Edinburgh on 5th July 1999.

Further reading

Lord Justice Auld, *Review of the Criminal Courts*; HMSO, London, October 2001.

Jeremy Croft, *Whitehall and the Human Rights Act 1998*; Constitution Unit, London, 2000.

J.A.G. Griffith, *The Politics of the Judiciary*; Fontana, London, 1997.

Carol Harlow (ed.) *Public Law and Politics*; Sweet & Maxwell, London, 1986.

Sir Andrew Leggatt, *Review of Administrative Tribunals*; HMSO, London, 2001.

A. Lester, *Democracy and Individual Rights*, Fabian Tract No. 390; London, November 1968.

A. Le Sueur and R. Cornes, *What Do the Top Courts Do?*; Constitution Unit, London, 2000.

Modernising Justice, Cm 4155; HMSO, London, December 1998.

Onora O'Neill, *Bounds of Justice*; Cambridge University Press, 2000.

Rights Brought Home: the Human Rights Bill, Cm 3782; HMSO, London, 1997.

Lord Scarman, *English Law, the New Dimension*; Hamlyn, London, 1974.

A.S. Sweet, *Governing with Judges: Constitutional Politics in Europe*; Oxford University Press, Oxford, 2000.

Lord Woolf, *Access to Justice, Final Report*; HMSO, London, 1996.

website for the Lord Chancellor's Department: www.lcd.gov.uk.

Part V

NEW RULES, METHODS AND POLITICAL RELATIONSHIPS

Changing the rules
of the political game

So far the principal focus of this book has been upon the nature and extent of constitutional change in the *institutional* arrangements of this country both in the distant past (when that is necessary for an understanding of the present) and since the arrival in power of the Labour Government in May 1997. Yet the definition of constitutional change needs in all conscience to be broader than that if the reader is to get a complete understanding of what is implied by the word 'constitutional' in the British context. It needs to include some discussion of changes in the rules of the political game, which have been extensive under Labour since 1997, and in the methods of democratic decision making which are likely to have considerable longer-term significance for this country.

As we can clearly see from the four years of the first Blair Administration, Labour Ministers set out in 1997 to improve at least the public perception of standards in public life from the low point reached at the end of eighteen years of Conservative rule. They themselves have sometimes fallen short of the new standards – e.g. in the way they handled political donations from Bernie Ecclestone of Formula 1 or sponsorship of the Faith Zone in the Dome by the Hinduja brothers – but it would not be right to doubt the sincerity of Tony Blair's wish to renew democracy and civic engagement in this country.

Public concern about political behaviour

In modern times the need to raise standards of conduct in public life only became glaringly obvious and politically unavoidable towards the end of the long period of Conservative rule from 1979 to 1997. Prior to that time, the traditional assumption had been that Parliamentary supremacy meant that Parliament itself (i.e. each House of Parliament) was entitled to regulate its own affairs without any interference from the Courts or other outside bodies. In so far as there were any causes for public concern about the behaviour and practices of national politicians, these were dealt with for the most part as self-disciplinary matters within each House of Parliament or, if necessary, in statutes such as the *1872 Ballot Act*, which introduced the principle of secret voting at contested elections, and the *1883 Corrupt and Illegal Practices Act*, which made bribery and other forms of electoral corruption into criminal offences.

Under a self-regulatory regime of this kind it is notable how little and how seldom Parliament had to take action to deal with any dishonourable practices by its own members *between* elections. Yet whenever the House of Commons did act in this way, it relied upon Resolutions of the House for the exercise of internal discipline. For example, in a seminal case dealt with by the Committee of Privileges in the 1946–47 session of Parliament, the House as a whole passed a Resolution which declared that

> it is inconsistent with the dignity of the House, with the duty of a Member to his constituency, and with the maintenance of the privilege of freedom of speech for any Member of the House to enter into any contractual agreement with an outside body controlling or limiting the Member's complete independence and freedom of action in Parliament or stipulating that he shall act in any way as the representative of such an outside body in regard to any matters to be transacted in Parliament, the duty of a Member being to his constituency and to the country as a whole rather than to any particular section thereof.

In this instance the outside pressure complained of came from a trade union which was deemed unacceptably to have issued instructions to a Labour backbencher, W.J. Brown MP, whom it sponsored and with whom it had a contractual agreement.[1] However, the Resolution as worded did not prevent an MP from giving advice to an outside body as part of a contractual arrangement nor did it prohibit an MP from *voluntarily* speaking, lobbying or voting in support of an outside interest if he thought it right to do so and consistent with his duties to his constituents and the general public. Thus the traditional view very much depended upon what was later described in 1971 by Willie Whitelaw, then Leader of the House, as 'the general good sense of Members', and the Parliamentary consensus was that intrusive regulation by the House as a whole or, still more, by some outside body was unnecessary.[2]

As the years went by and the inter-penetration of economic and political interests became more significant, it became more common for a sizeable minority of MPs to hold paid consultancies of one kind or another and more difficult to take a sanguine and detached view of the determination of Members of Parliament to keep their own house in order, free from any external oversight or intervention.[3] Although formally one MP still referred to another as 'the Honourable Lady' or 'the Honourable Gentleman', it became apparent in the early 1990s that a few MPs were succumbing to the temptations of dishonourable conduct and even financial corruption; the House as a whole was unable to downplay or dismiss the damage which was being done to our system of Parliamentary government.

The issues were really brought to a head in July 1994 when the *Sunday Times* claimed that two Conservative MPs (Graham Riddick and David Tredinnick) had agreed in a journalistic 'sting' to table certain Parliamentary Questions in return for payments of cash in brown envelopes.[4] This led the Speaker, Betty Boothroyd, to allow a motion, which was carried unanimously by the House, to refer to the Committee of Privileges both the allegations against the two MPs and the conduct of the national newspaper. In a growing climate of so-called 'Tory sleaze' which was increasingly exposed by the media, three Conservative Ministers (Jonathan Aitken, Neil Hamilton and Tim Smith) were accused of dishonourable conduct of various kinds, notably failure to record certain financial benefits in the House of Commons Register of Members' Interests. This led all three Ministers to resign from the Government and two of them, Jonathan Aitken and Neil Hamilton, to initiate legal actions against the *Guardian* in separate attempts to clear their names and restore their personal reputations.

The scandal caused by these events spread rapidly and escalated as an issue throughout the body politic. Following extensive allegations of Ministerial impropriety made by Mohammed al Fayed, the Egyptian owner of Harrods who had been keen to secure a British passport, and subsequent investigations by the Cabinet Secretary, Sir Robin Butler, the Prime Minister, John Major, announced his decision on 27th October 1994 to set up a wholly new Committee on Standards in Public Life under the chairmanship of an Appeal Court Judge, Lord Justice Nolan, consisting of five other reputable people from *outside* Parliament as well as two senior MPs, one peer and a former Clerk of the House of Commons.[5] This Executive action was a ground-breaking departure in British national politics, since it was the first occasion in modern times when distinguished outsiders had been called upon to investigate and make *systemic* recommendations about 'any changes in present arrangements which might be required to ensure the highest standards of propriety in public life', notably, of course, in relation to Ministers and Members of Parliament. What is more, Mr Major made it clear in his statement to the House that he had decided to establish *standing machinery* to examine the conduct of public life and to make recommendations on how best to ensure that standards of propriety are upheld', even though he was careful to add the significant words that 'the purpose of the body is not to replace the House's own machinery which is the proper way to consider issues affecting individual members of the House'.

There was really no going back to the traditional ways of Parliament or any unalloyed claim to Parliament's previously exclusive right to regulate the conduct of its own members. It was immediately seen by the media and others as a significant constitutional innovation and the public standing of what became known as 'the Nolan Committee' was further enhanced when it proceeded to take evidence in public and produced its first authoritative report within seven months of its establishment.[6] The Committee's terms of reference had been broadly defined as being

> to examine current concerns about standards of conduct of all holders of public office, including arrangements relating to financial and commercial activities, and to make recommendations as to any changes in the present arrangements which might be required to ensure the highest standards of propriety in public life.

The unusual circumstances in which it had been established and the tide of media denigration of the Conservative Party which heralded the

Committee's deliberations effectively made its recommendations unchallengeable for the remainder of the Parliament. No one was fooled by the breadth of the definition of 'public life' into forgetting that it had been 'Tory sleaze' which had triggered the need for new procedures. Yet the significance of what happened outlasted the Conservative period in office in that it not only made a permanent change in the rules of the political game, but also had an influential effect by further increasing the proportion of professional politicians with little or no outside employment or experience.

The first Nolan Committee report

The First Report of the Nolan Committee (entitled *Standards in Public Life*) had powerful effects upon the conduct of Members of Parliament, Ministers and civil servants, and non-departmental public bodies with executive functions. It spelled out seven principles of public life 'for the benefit of all who serve the public in any way'.[7] (See *Box 13* for details.)

The Report recommended that there should be a non-statutory Code of Conduct for Members of Parliament which should be restated at the beginning of every Parliament. It did *not* recommend that Members of Parliament should no longer be allowed to have any paid outside interests, but it did recommend a reaffirmation of the 1947 House Resolution on the subject and the publication of clearer guidance on MPs' declarations of interest. Reflecting what seems to have been a division in the Committee between the Parliamentarians and those drawn from outside Parliament, it made a compromise proposal to ban MPs from working as general multi-client Parliamentary

---

Box 13 The seven Nolan principles of public life

- *Selflessness.* Holders of public office should take decisions solely in terms of the public interest. They should not do so in order to gain financial or other material benefits for themselves, their family or their friends.
- *Integrity.* Holders of public office should not place themselves under any financial or other obligation to outside individuals or organisations that might influence them in the performance of their official duties.
- *Objectivity.* In carrying out public business, including making public appointments, awarding contracts or recommending individuals for rewards and benefits, holders of public office should make choices on merit.
- *Accountability.* Holders of public office are accountable for their decisions and actions to the public and must submit themselves to whatever scrutiny is appropriate to their office.
- *Openness.* Holders of public office should be as open as possible about all the decisions and actions that they take. They should give reasons for their decisions and restrict information only when the wider public interest clearly demands.
- *Honesty.* Holders of public office have a duty to declare any private interests relating to their public duties and to take steps to resolve any conflicts arising in a way that protects the public interest.
- *Leadership.* Holders of public office should promote and support these principles by leadership and example.

These principles apply to all aspects of public life. The Committee has set them out here for the benefit of all who serve the public in any way.

Source: *Standards in Public Life*, First Report of the Committee on Standards in Public Life, Cm 2850-I; HMSO, London, May 1995; Vol I.

consultants, but not as advisers to or advocates for specific outside interests. It recommended full disclosure of consultancies and sponsorship arrangements in the Register of Members' Interests, policed by an independent Parliamentary Commissioner reporting to the Committee on Standards and Privileges.

Notwithstanding the scandal surrounding the alleged wrong-doing of the three Tory Ministers already mentioned (Jonathan Aitken, Neil Hamilton and Tim Smith), the Nolan Committee was not as censorious or radical in its chapter on Ministers and civil servants as it was in its assessment of the conduct of MPs. In the case of Ministers this was because, in the words of the Report, 'the evidence we have heard and received does not indicate that the public believes that Ministers are implicated in widespread wrong-doing', although 'it does ... suggest that people would welcome a greater clarity about the standards of conduct to be expected of Ministers and how these are enforced'.[8]

The starting point in this discussion was undoubtedly the document known as *Questions of Procedure for Ministers* (QPM) which is required reading for every Minister at the beginning of an Administration and for every new Minister joining the Government thereafter. It remained confidential within Whitehall Departments from 1945, when it was first drawn up in consolidated form, to 1992 when John Major as Prime Minister took the decision to put it in the public domain. It has no special constitutional status, but it is binding upon all Ministerial members of a Government. Over the years the title of the document has become something of a misnomer, because increasingly the substance has been concerned with giving guidance on appropriate and inappropriate Ministerial *conduct*, thus adding ethical criteria which responded to specific incidents and which also reflected 'a general trend, not confined to Government, towards codification of what might once have been assumed to be common ground'.[9]

Since individual responsibility to Parliament and the general public remained a hallmark of the British system of government, but since to remain in office every Minister had also to retain the personal confidence of the Prime Minister, the best

way forward in the eyes of the Nolan Committee was to amend the opening paragraph of the QPM to say: 'it will be for individual Ministers to judge how best to act in order to uphold the highest standards and it will be for the Prime Minister to determine whether or not they have done so in any particular circumstance'.[10] This suggested the need for a coherent series of principles and rules for ministers which could either be extracted from the QPM to form a free-standing Code of Conduct for Ministers or be incorporated within a new version of the QPM which might usefully be retitled 'Conduct and procedure for Ministers'. While allowing that the precise wording of this new guidance would be a matter for the Prime Minister of the day, the Committee went on to list six essential principles of Ministerial conduct which should be spelt out and supported where necessary by detailed rules.[11]

The Committee was quite unrepentant about the need for an explicit Ministerial Code of Conduct, even if some might have thought that it would state the obvious. It recalled that Ministers in the then Conservative Government had accepted the idea of a Code of Conduct for civil servants and saw no reason why the same approach should not apply to Ministers. However, it counselled against any codification of express sanctions and suggested that public and media scrutiny of Ministerial conduct in the light of a new Code was likely to be far more effective in deterring wrong-doing.

There remained the question of how Ministerial misconduct might best be dealt with if and when it did occur. On this the Committee briefly surveyed the options, ranging from criminal sanctions to be pursued by the police and imposed by the Courts to lesser instances of personal or financial impropriety which might best be dealt with by the Chief Whip and might lead to a Ministerial apology or resignation. It also addressed the ticklish question of whether and, if so, how far the Cabinet Secretary should be involved in investigating cases of alleged Ministerial misconduct and then advising the Prime Minister on what to do about the situation. It was rather delphic and diffident about tendering advice on this highly sensitive topic, but it did suggest two useful distinctions.

Firstly, if the allegations against a Minister concerned apparent breaches of the Ministerial Code, then the involvement and advice of the Cabinet Secretary might quite properly be sought; but if the allegations concerned an MP's behaviour before he became a Minister or in an area of his life quite unconnected with Ministerial duties, then it would not be proper to involve the Prime Minister's senior civil service adviser. *Secondly*, in the event of the Cabinet Secretary being called in to help the Prime Minister by investigating allegations of Ministerial misconduct and then advising on the most appropriate course of action, a clear distinction should be drawn between the report on his investigation which it might be appropriate to publish in the public interest and his advice to the Prime Minister which ought invariably to remain confidential in the interests of civil service impartiality. It is worth noting that these rather delicate observations had probably been influenced by the way in which Sir Robin Butler had been embarrassed when he was drawn into the Aitken affair and then represented (unfairly) as having cleared the alleged wrong-doer in a preliminary investigation.

Another aspect of 'Tory sleaze', which became fixed in the minds of the media and the public, was the apparent ease and speed with which Ministers retiring from Government managed to secure prestigious and well-paid jobs in the private sector, sometimes even with firms or business sectors which a few weeks or months previously they had been responsible for regulating. Such practices might not have been illegal, but they did create a rather tacky impression and definitely served to lower the already low esteem in which nearly all politicians were held. The Nolan Committee therefore recommended that there should be a new advisory system regulating employment taken up by ex-Ministers and that this should be based upon the existing rules for senior civil servants. These rules required that such a change of jobs should secure the approval of the Prime Minister (advised by the independent Committee on Business Appointments) and involve waiting periods of between three months and two years, as well as insistence upon so-called behavioural conditions

before such people might take up new positions in the private sector. Moreover, the Committee also recommended that the civil service business appointments system should be made more transparent, be actively monitored to ensure that the rules were being observed, and be extended to cover the growing band of so-called Special Advisers brought into Whitehall by Ministers to work personally for them on party political assignments in government.

The final area of investigation covered in the first report of the Committee was that of quangos, an awkward acronym standing for quasi-autonomous non-governmental organisations, which included executive non-departmental public bodies (NDPBs) and National Health Service bodies. Here the public concerns prevalent at the time were to do with allegations that Ministers had used their powers of appointment to such bodies to dispense excessive party political patronage and that the interests of propriety and public accountability were not sufficiently prominent in the administration of such bodies. The Committee did not concern itself with the rights or wrongs of the wider policy issue about whether or not there was too much 'government by quango', since that was not really within its remit of 'standards in public life'. Its principal concern was really with what might be described as the workings of the patronage state and in the evidence which it heard there had been a predictable clash of opinion between leading figures associated with the Conservative Party, who argued that public appointments had not been politicised, and those experts in the academic world and other quarters more sympathetic to the Labour and Liberal Democrat parties, who argued that such appointments had been too party political and hence detrimental to good governance.[12]

Having reviewed the situation on quangos to the best of their ability within the time available, the members of the Nolan Committee wisely concluded that 'taken as a whole, we find the available research and other evidence insufficient to support a conclusion [one way or the other]'.[13] The members of the Nolan Committee contented themselves with making a number of recommendations designed to improve the probity and transparency of the public appointments process and to improve the propriety and accountability of the bodies to which public appointments were made. They recommended that all such appointments should be made on the basis of merit in order to form Boards with an appropriate balance of skills and experience; and that the process should be open and positions should be advertised to attract a wide range of candidates whose claims should be assessed by advisory committees which should include independent members. Final responsibility for all such appointments should remain with Ministers, but an independent Public Appointments Commissioner should be appointed to regulate, monitor and report on the entire public appointments process.

If there was one Nolan-style device to which the Committee on Standards in Public Life clung from the beginning, it was the *Codes of Conduct* which were to be applied to Members of Parliament, Ministers, civil servants and all board and staff members of quangos. Equally, if there was one Nolan-inspired principle which was applied across the piece in an attempt to raise the standards of public life, it was the principle of *full disclosure*, making it easier for independent watch-dogs, the media and the general public to keep an eye on their political masters and thus discourage them from slipping back into any bad old ways. Indeed, the concerted attempt to generalise best practice in the governance of all parts of the public sector brought a new term into use, namely, to 'Nolanise' procedures or to make public sector practices 'Nolan-proof' against accusations of misconduct.[14]

The four general and 55 specific recommendations contained in the Nolan Committee's First Report were implemented over the ensuing years either in amended form or sometimes verbatim, with varying degrees of enthusiasm or cynicism.[15] No one who looks dispassionately at the effects of the Nolan Committee can deny that its work has had a significant *constitutional* impact in a political system where changing the rules of the game can be tantamount to introducing constitutional reform.

The House of Commons endorsed the principle of a Code of Conduct for MPs in a Resolution on 19th July 1995 and the newly established Select Committee on Standards and Privileges then drafted a Code which was broadly similar to the Nolan blueprint, although different in a number of respects including its rejection of the proposed ban on MPs working for multi-client lobbying firms and involving themselves in paid advocacy in Parliament on behalf of outside interests. The amended Code was subsequently approved by the House as a whole in a Resolution on 24th July 1996 and from then until the end of the 1997–2001 Parliament it was not subject to serious revision.

The idea of a refined and clarified Code for Ministers was accepted by the Major Administration in July 1995; yet no Executive action was taken to implement suitable revisions to the 'Questions of Procedure for Ministers' until after the election of the Labour Government when the document was reissued in July 1997 under its new title of *The Ministerial Code*.[16] The Blair Administration came up with its own formulation for the vital last words of Section 1 of the Code which now reads:

> it will be for individual Ministers to judge how best to act in order to uphold the highest standards; they are responsible for justifying their conduct to Parliament; and they can remain in office only for so long as they retain the Prime Minister's confidence.

However, it also raised the ethical stakes because the Prime Minister himself wrote a Foreword which reaffirmed his 'strong personal commitment to restoring the bond of trust between the British people and their Government' and to that end he specifically stated his expectation that all Ministers would work 'within the letter and spirit of the Code'.

Tony Blair was soon to find that the realities of exercising political power could challenge even the noblest ethical sentiments. For example, it was revealed in the press that Bernie Ecclestone, the multi-millionaire boss of Formula One Motor Racing, had made a financial donation of £1 million to the Labour Party before the May 1997 General Election and was considering another £1 million donation in the autumn of 1997 at about the time when the new Government agreed to postpone the application of its ban on tobacco advertising in sport, at least as far as snooker and motor racing were concerned. The Prime Minister was deeply and publicly embarrassed by the widespread suspicion that Government policy had been influenced by such large financial donations to the governing party and he was quick to consult Lord Neill, then Chairman of the Committee on Standards in Public Life, who advised him to instruct the Labour Party to return the money – advice which he took after having made a public apology to the British people on television. The wider fallout from this rather grubby episode was that on 12th November 1997 Tony Blair expanded the terms of reference of what had become 'the Neill Committee' by giving it the additional task 'to review issues in relation to the funding of political parties and to make recommendations as to any changes in present arrangements'.[17] Thus was conceived, if not born, the policy of regulating by statute both the organisation and the financing of political activity.

Interim assessment by the Neill Committee

If we are to make a brief and objective assessment of the extent to which standards of conduct in public life have been raised, first by the response under duress of the Major Administration to the financial and other scandals of 'Tory sleaze', and then by the more self-righteous efforts of the first Blair Administration to create a new and more ethical kind of politics, we cannot do better than refer to some of the observations and recommendations of the Neill Committee when it chose to review the progress made since May 1995.[18]

The Committee began by recognising that the First Nolan Report had created what appeared to be an unstoppable momentum for change in many political practices, together with a whole range of new benchmarks for standards of conduct in public life. The evidence so far suggested that standards of conduct in public life had improved, but it was important to keep up the pressure for further improvement.

With regard to Members of Parliament, the Committee was always diplomatic but firm in its view that *both* Houses of Parliament should be encouraged to raise their standards of conduct by

adopting Codes of Conduct incorporating the famous seven principles of public life. Indeed, in a subsequent Report on the House of Lords, the Committee advised the Second Chamber to establish a mandatory Register of Interests and to call upon the assistance of an *ad hoc* Investigator whenever the Sub-Committee on Lords' Interests (the relevant self-disciplinary body) had to consider the investigation and possible punishment of any wrong-doers. However, the accused individuals, who would have a right of appeal to the House of Lords Committee for Privileges, would face no more than 'naming and shaming' by their peers if they were found to have been in breach of the Code.[19]

In the case of the House of Commons, the Committee was more prepared to play the part of Inquisitor-General, but it drew a distinction between its willingness to investigate overall systems for maintaining the probity of public life and its refusal to investigate allegations about individual MPs or peers, which remained a matter principally for the relevant disciplinary committees in each House of Parliament. In July 1997 the Nolan Committee had recommended the introduction of a new statutory offence of 'misuse of public office' to cover a gap in the existing statutes, to achieve consistency across all public bodies (including notably local government) and to signal clearly the special terms on which all public offices are held; then, in January 2000, the Neill Committee urged the Government to introduce its proposed new legislation on the criminal law of bribery as soon as possible and to apply it to members of both Houses.[20]

Under each of its successive Chairmen the Committee has been very mindful of the requirements of natural justice in any quasi-judicial proceedings against Members of Parliament in either House and has obviously been influenced by the powerful views expressed by, among others, Lord Nicholls of Birkenhead, the Chairman of the Joint Committee on Parliamentary Privilege.[21] Indeed, the emphasis placed upon these aspects in its Sixth Report (entitled *Reinforcing Standards*) served to underline the growing juridification of all procedures to uphold standards and investigate and punish misconduct in a political system in which such an approach was traditionally regarded as quite alien.

With regard to Ministers of the Crown, there is a general impression among the academics and journalists who follow these matters closely that standards of conduct have risen during the period since the publication of the first Nolan Report. This is because the importance of striving for ethical behaviour in public life has been reinforced by all the 'Nolan procedures' and, frankly, the chances of getting away with the former lower standards have been reduced by the heightened media and public interest even in rumours of misconduct.

The Committee did not have very much to say about standards of conduct in the civil service, because objectively there was not very much to be concerned about. This feeling of complacent satisfaction about the normal incorruptibility of the British civil service was only marred by the realisation that the growth in the numbers of those appointed to influential positions in the civil service on secondments or short-term contracts from the private or voluntary sectors might mean that the hallowed public service values and ethos would be degraded, and also by the parallel risk that permanent heads of departments or agencies might have their performance assessed too politically when their contracts came up for renewal, a possibility which led the Committee to suggest that some element of independent validation should be introduced to preserve the tradition of political impartiality at the highest levels in the civil service.

In an effort to address the constant possibility that the civil service may be vulnerable to politicisation by the party in office at any time, the Committee recognised that one answer widely advocated since the early 1990s had been that there should be a Civil Service Act to give the role of civil servants a degree of constitutional entrenchment and to provide useful statutory backing for the Civil Service Code which was brought into force by Order in Council in 1996. The Neill Committee put its weight behind this idea, which had been recommended by the Treasury and Civil Service Select Committee in 1994 and accepted by the Joint Labour–Liberal Democrat Consultative Committee on Constitutional Reform in 1997, but omitted from the 1997 Labour Manifesto and the 1998 White Paper, *Modernising Government*. It seems likely that a Civil Service Bill will be introduced in the 2001–6 Parliament to give statutory backing to the Civil Service Code and other disciplinary procedures.

On the whole the Neill Committee was able to report that a fairly clear consensus had emerged from the evidence to the effect that informed concerns about the conduct of those engaged in national public life had shifted since 1995 'from allegations of direct financial reward for dubious ethical practice [i.e. corruption] to allegations of *privileged access*, the exercise of undue influence through political, social or business contacts or the donation of money or any other means of gaining preferential treatment'.[22] In defining its worries about privileged and unfair access to the policy and decision-making process of central Government, the Committee identified two areas of concern which were either new or which presented old problems in new forms.

The first was the concern about the growth in the number of so-called *Special Advisers* serving individual Ministers in Whitehall Departments and especially the Prime Minister in 10 Downing Street. Particular concern was expressed about the two very influential special advisers (Alastair Campbell, then Press Secretary, and Jonathan Powell, then Chief of Staff at 10 Downing Street) who had been given executive powers under an amended Order in Council in 1997 which empowered them to instruct civil servants on the Prime Minister's behalf. This was a development which was viewed with alarm by Sir Michael Bett, the First Civil Service Commissioner, who warned that if it were taken any further, it would represent 'a creeping change in the nature of the civil service in this country'.[23] While similar people have found their way into Whitehall under successive Governments ever since the time of Lloyd George in the First World War, the nature and scale of the phenomenon has grown over the years and markedly since New Labour came to power. At the beginning of 1997 there were 38 Special Advisers in Whitehall, but by December 1999 the number had increased to 74, of whom no fewer than 25 worked for the Prime Minister at 10 Downing Street. Essentially, these people represent a significant and growing species of unaccountable power within central Government. They are often resented by junior Ministers and backbench MPs who see such political *apparatchiks* as usurpers of the power and influence which should rightly be theirs. Moreover, in view of their disproportionate employment at 10 Downing Street, they represent a further concentration of political power in a system which is already far too centralised.

The Neill Committee addressed this problem with three main recommendations. *Firstly*, it suggested that the total number of Special Advisers in any Government should be capped by a provision in the proposed Civil Service Act and that any increase beyond that figure should be made subject to affirmative Resolution in both Houses of Parliament and that the same restraints should apply to any proposed increase in the number of Special Advisers with executive powers. *Secondly*, there should be a separate Code of Conduct for Special Advisers (analogous to the one for Ministers) and this should be included as a Schedule to the proposed Civil Service Act. Such a Code should try to ensure that Special Advisers (like Ministers under their Code) did not deliberately compromise the political impartiality of civil servants, it should include a section on their contacts with the media, and it should be enforced by Permanent Secretaries. In general, the Committee was keen to see the role of Special Advisers clarified for the benefit of the entire political process, so that there would be less danger of excessive politicisation of sensitive parts of the civil service, such as might happen if Ministerial Private Offices were turned into Ministerial *Cabinets* on the Continental pattern.

The Committee's second main cause for concern derived from the more general problems posed for the maintenance of high standards in public life by the growth of *private sponsorship of Government activities* and by the seemingly uncontrolled spread of so-called Task Forces and other inadequately monitored advisory bodies which act principally as institutional devices for co-opting leading business figures into the process of government. Underlying these concerns was a general sense of unease about what the Tory academic and peer Lord Norton

described as 'the current fad for the commercialisation of Government where the boundaries between commercial interests and good governance are being blurred'.[24] Such coarsening of the public interest had been quite prevalent during the Thatcher and Major Administrations, but in May 1997 one did not really expect it to continue and even become more marked under a Labour Government.

The Neill Committee saw the possibility that corporate sponsorship of Government activities might compromise some of its cardinal principles of public life, notably those of integrity, accountability and openness. It was particularly concerned that such sponsorship might breed a sense of financial or other obligation to outside individuals or organisations in the minds of Ministers or officials and that this would not be conducive to the propriety of public policy. Nor has this proved to be simply an abstract or theoretical concern, since some of the sums of private money involved have been large and some of the political consequences – as in the case of the so-called Hinduja Passport Affair in 1998 which led to the Ministerial resignation of Peter Mandelson in January 2001 – have been very embarrassing for the Blair Administration.[25] The Committee was not persuaded to recommend the banning of corporate sponsorship of Government activities, as had been suggested in evidence by the Association of First Division Civil Servants; but it did propose that the Cabinet Office should produce suitable guidance in the form of a set of principles which should be adhered to by all Government Departments. It also suggested that each Department should appoint the equivalent of a Compliance Officer to watch over the situation and that if the value to the Government of such sponsorship (whether in cash or in kind) was £5,000 or more, then this should be publicly disclosed in departmental Annual Reports.

As for the remarkable growth of Task Forces, Review Groups and other institutional devices for co-opting leading business people into the advisory web of government, this was a related issue of concern to the Committee which had arisen without much warning since New Labour arrived in power determined to demonstrate its respect for business opinion in a very tangible way. Thus the *Daily Mail* on 19th August 1999 reported that there were 110 Task Forces attached to Government Departments and a leading academic analysis of the phenomenon published in November 1999 suggested that there were 295 such bodies, yet the Cabinet Secretary in his evidence to the Committee had maintained in July 1999 that there were 'around 30'.[26] Furthermore, it is perhaps significant that some of the most prominent individual businessmen chosen to head such task forces and review groups, for example Lord Sainsbury and Lord Macdonald, subsequently joined the Blair Administration as Ministers, while others, such as Lord Haskins and Lord Stevenson, became pillars of the new Establishment and now head important and permanent quangos. The initial inclination of the Neill Committee was to suggest that the Cabinet Office should get a grip upon this burgeoning area of quasi-public administration by developing an agreed definition of these bodies and then deciding which should be wound up and which should be reclassified as advisory non-departmental public bodies. There was no suggestion that any decisive step had been taken towards a sleazy or disreputable state of affairs, but the Committee did observe that 'the proximity of business interests to the governmental process' raised suspicions of a similar kind to those raised by the growth of corporate sponsorship. It concluded by saying that this was an 'emerging issue' to which it would wish to return at a later date.

In conclusion, we can see that standards of conduct in public life have been raised and restored to a considerable degree since reaching a low point in 1994–95 towards the end of eighteen years of Conservative Administration. Paradoxically, a good deal of the credit for this must go to John Major for taking the radical step of establishing the Nolan Committee on a permanent basis in the first place. However, since 1995 the process of 'Nolanry' has taken on a momentum of its own and Tony Blair, who was so fulsome in his advocacy of exemplary standards of conduct in public life when his party was in Opposition, has clearly had an occasionally torrid time in Government in spite of his efforts to impose consistently high standards upon all members of his party and his Administration. It

remains to be seen whether a new equilibrium will be achieved between purposefulness and propriety in public life or whether in due course there will be something of a backlash against at least some of the manifestations of 'political correctness' which now characterise these aspects of public life in this country.

Regulating and funding political activity

Until the *Political Parties, Elections and Referendums Act* (henceforth PPERA 2000) became law in the year 2000, one of the strangest anomalies of British constitutional arrangements was that there was no explicit, statutory recognition of political parties and their central role at elections in this country. Political parties were voluntary bodies which were not subject to statutory regulation. Historically, this was not altogether surprising in view of the fact that for all of the nineteenth and much of the twentieth centuries their existence was seen by many influential people (including some politicians) as little more than a regrettable necessity or a necessary evil. The notion of 'party' was regularly conflated with that of 'faction', and more often than not both terms had unfavourable connotations.

In so far as the activities of political parties were regulated before PPERA 2000, the emphasis was upon limiting local campaign expenditure and defining fairly precisely which practices were lawful and which unlawful at election time. This was the justification for the *1883 Corrupt and Illegal Practices Act*, while the *1983 Representation of the People Act* a century later was really not much more than a consolidation of all the relevant legislation dating back to that time. As with the rules and conventions governing Parliamentary procedure, a pattern had been set in the 1880s which was not seriously challenged or broken until New Labour came to power in 1997.

The real anomaly inherited from the past was that the legislative provisions set fairly tight limits to the expenditure which might lawfully be incurred by or on behalf of candidates at Parliamentary elections, required detailed accounts to be submitted to the Returning Officer for each constituency by the candidates' agents and set tight limits on expenditure by 'third parties' (i.e. people or organisations other than candidates) who might wish to issue campaigning material which bears upon a particular person's candidature; but there was no legislation or legal requirement relating to the financing of political parties generally, whether at a regional or a national level, nor was there any limit on the expenditure which political parties might lawfully incur in connection with Parliamentary elections other than on behalf of particular candidates in particular constituencies. Yet the reality is that over the past 50 years or so we have seen the emergence of organised modern political parties which assume co-responsibility with their local counterparts for getting candidates elected and which massively out-spend all their local candidates put together in their efforts to win General Elections. Thus legislative restrictions which operate at constituency level no longer serve as an effective control on the much larger sums which are raised and spent by the parties nationally on fighting elections to gain or retain political power at the national level.

It was against this background that Labour came to power in May 1997 in a mood more conducive to changing these traditional arrangements than had been the case with any previous incoming Government for a long time. *Firstly*, Labour Ministers had to address media and public concerns about political 'sleaze', most of which had been generated by the behaviour in office of their Tory predecessors, but some of which were fanned by the Labour Party's reliance upon lavish benefactors such as Bernie Ecclestone and David Sainsbury. *Secondly*, in view of the incoming Government's plans to introduce different, more proportional elections to the European Parliament and to the devolved Assemblies in Scotland and Wales, there was a cogent argument that new legislative rules would be needed for new electoral systems. *Thirdly*, the Labour Party, which had always resented the ability of its Conservative opponent to raise and spend more money on General Elections, was inclined to seize its opportunity by setting statutory limits on election spending by the political parties.

Before embarking upon what was bound to be rather controversial legislation governing this financial aspect of politics, Tony Blair asked the Neill Committee 'to review issues in relation to the funding of political parties and to make recommendations as to any changes in present arrangements'.[27] This expedient move by the Prime Minister was not unexpected in view of the fact that the 1997 Labour Manifesto had declared that it would ask the Nolan Committee to consider how the funding of political parties should be regulated and reformed, and the fact that Labour's intentions had been flagged by Tony Blair at the 1997 Labour Party Conference when he promised delegates that 'at the next election all political parties will at last compete on a level playing field'.[28]

The *Registration of Political Parties Act 1998*, an interim measure, was confined to two limited purposes in order to leave the field open to the Neill Committee to review the whole subject and make comprehensive recommendations which were conceived as part of an overall scheme of reform. *Firstly*, it gave formal status to political parties which chose to register with the new Electoral Commission and so enabled them to field lists of candidates for elections under the new voting systems for the Scottish Parliament, the Welsh Assembly and the European Parliament. *Secondly*, it prevented the use of misleading party descriptions by requiring a registered party to authorise the use of its name and emblem on a ballot paper. The Act was therefore a tantalising trailer for the main feature.

At the outset Lord Neill and his colleagues made clear their view that 'political parties are essential to democracy' in order to remove any doubts that they were anti-party in their motivation. However, they went on to argue that, while there was no overt corruption in the constituencies and no overt trade in honours as there had been in earlier times, the public was concerned about 'the inscrutability of the sources from which the parties derive their money' and the general escalation or 'arms race' in the total expenditure by each of the main political parties on national campaigns.[29] The Committee also asserted that at least three of the original seven Nolan principles – namely, the importance in public life of integrity, accountability and openness – were relevant to the funding of political parties and it set out to make recommendations which would entrench these principles within the funding process.

The Committee recognised that its Fifth Report was concerned with broad issues of public policy as well the standards of conduct in public life which had been its remit in earlier work. This persuaded the Committee to rehearse the principal questions raised by its inquiry, all of which were highly controversial. Firstly, there was what the Committee described as *the misconduct question*: did the current methods of party political funding lead politicians to behave (or even appear to behave) in ways in which they ought not to behave according to the various Nolan codes of public life? Secondly, there was *the fairness question*: was it inherently unfair if one party consistently managed to raise more money than its opponents and so derived a decisive advantage at General Elections? Thirdly, there was *the over-spending question*: were all the parties simply spending too much money on electioneering and in the process alienating the voters from the entire political process?

Fourthly, there was *the civic engagement or public participation question*: was the existing system of party political funding conducive to encouraging large numbers of people to partici-pate as campaigners, activists, fund raisers and spokesmen for political parties or did it simply turn them off, to the detriment of the democratic process? Fifthly, there was *the political effectiveness question*: did the current system enhance or reduce the ability of the Opposition parties to perform their principal functions, such as monitoring the Government of the day and developing new policies for the future? Finally, there was *the question of freedom*: to what extent was the state entitled to intervene (via the law) to curtail freedoms and rights of privacy in relation to party political donations? In many ways this was the fundamental question in the inquiry and the Neill Committee stated very clearly that its *presumption* was in favour of such a freedom, 'save where we identify an overriding public interest calling for some limitation'.[30]

The Political Parties, Elections and Referendums Act 2000

The main elements of PPERA 2000, dealing with the regulation and funding of political parties, faith-fully followed the recommendations of the Neill Committee in all but about three respects.[31] Part I of the Act established the Electoral Commission and a Parliamentary body, the Speaker's Committee, to oversee the work of the Commission, which would include reporting on the conduct of elections and referenda, allocating policy development grants to parties and promoting public understanding and participation in our democratic processes. Part II provided for the registration of political parties by re-enacting, with modifications, the Registration of Political Parties Act 1998.[32] Part III set out the accounting requirements for registered parties, which were modified in Schedule 4 to fit the circumstances of parties with separate 'accounting units'. This meant that in the case of a national party with a network of constitutency associations and ward branches, each component (provided it had income or expenditure exceeding £25,000 a year) would maintain its own accounting records and produce its own annual statement of accounts, thus absolving the central organisation from having to produce omnibus accounts for the whole party.

Part IV of the Act was concerned with the control of donations to political parties, including the definition of donations, the prohibition of foreign donations, and the requirements for reporting donations to the Electoral Commission. It also dealt with donations to individual members of a political party, groups composed of party members and holders of elective office in various Parliaments, Assemblies and local authorities. In line with the 1997 Labour Manifesto and the recommendations of the Neill Committee, all foreign donations to political parties were banned, as were all anony-mous donations above £50. Legislative provision was made for full disclosure of all donations in cash of £5,000 or more to a party nationally and £1,000 or more to a party in a single constituency in any one financial year from any one person or single source, and all donations in kind when the market value or the value to the party was more than £100. In general, donations to political parties were allowed only from a 'permissible donor' and were banned from so-called blind trusts of the kind which had contributed to Tony Blair's Private Office when Labour had been in Opposition.[33] In principle, the Act imposed no criminal liability on donors or would-be donors, unless they conspired with party political recipients to evade the restrictions imposed.

Part V placed limits on the campaign expenditure which could be incurred by registered political parties and introduced a new regime for the authorisation and payment of campaign expenditure, the settlement of claims, and the submission and auditing of party returns for inspection by the Electoral Commission and the public. The most important point under this heading was undoubtedly the statutory definition of 'campaign expenditure', 'election campaign' and 'election purposes'. These terms had to be watertight if the statutory limits were to be effective. Essentially, 'campaign expenditure' was defined as any expenditure incurred for election purposes during the relevant period (normally defined as up to 365 days before a General Election). The definition of the term 'election purposes' was cast in broad terms in order to capture all national expenditure incurred by a party with a view to enhancing its electoral prospects, but not expenditure in support of any particular candidate as this was covered in other legislation.

The Neill Committee had recommended a limit of £20 million (index-linked) for each party on national campaign expenditure towards a General Election and this included the value of benefits in kind. The legislative draftsmen carefully followed this guidance by setting arithmetical formulae for financial limits on expenditure by any party for General Election purposes which, when aggregated across the entire United Kingdom, came to a maximum expenditure limit of £19,770,000 if a party contested all 659 seats in the House of Commons.[34] However, since not even the two main parties contest every constituency in the United Kingdom, the actual maximum figure at the 2001 General Election was smaller, and appreciably smaller for the minor parties or those which chose to contest

seats only in limited geographical areas. For example, the maximum permitted expenditure for a party which contested only the 72 Parliamentary constituencies in Scotland (e.g. the SNP) was £2,160,000 and the equivalent figure for a party which contested only the 40 seats in Wales (e.g. Plaid Cymru) was £1,200,000, whereas the comparable figure in England (perhaps for a future English National Party) would be £15,870,000.

Recent changes in the electoral system for the Scottish Parliament, Welsh Assembly and for the election of British MEPs to the European Parliament, all of which entailed the adoption of list-based elections either in whole or in part, mean that expenses incurred for the benefit of one or more candidates on a party's list have to be treated as campaign expenditure incurred by the party as a whole. On the other hand, expenditure incurred by candidates in a party's list for elected members of the Greater London Assembly continues to be accounted for under Section 81 of the *Representation of the People Act 1983*, like other party expenditure on local government elections.

Part VI limited expenditure by 'third parties' (already defined above) to promote or oppose the election of a political party or any of its candidates. These provisions were introduced in the light of the 1998 *Bowman* case in which the ECHR held that the limit of £5, which then applied to 'third party' expenditure under Section 75 of the 1983 Representation of the People Act, had essentially prevented Mrs Bowman and her organisation (the Society for the Protection of the Unborn Child) from publishing information intended to influence the electorate in Halifax at the 1997 General Election to vote in favour of an anti-abortion candidate and against the Labour candidate who had been a pro-abortion Member of Parliament.

The main purpose of this part of the Act was to ensure that politically motivated organisations or single-issue pressure groups, which are in effect *virtual* political parties campaigning strongly for or against certain registered parties on certain issues, should be caught within the provisions of the legislation every bit as securely as regular political parties registered with the Electoral Commission. Thus, for example, if some wealthy industrialist who dislikes the European Union decides to spend some of his fortune urging the British public not to support official Conservative candidates who are known to be pro-European but rather to support those who declare that they share his anti-European views, he and his collaborators would be caught by the Act once he had notified the Electoral Commission of his intention to incur 'controlled expenditure' in excess of £10,000 in England or £5,000 in either Scotland or Wales or Northern Ireland during the regulated period before an election.

The financial limits on the controlled expenditure of such bodies (known as 'recognised third parties') would be 5 per cent of the limit which would apply to a registered party if it contested all the seats in the election in question. This formula would produce a permitted maximum expenditure of £988,500 for a General Election in the United Kingdom as a whole, £195,759 for a European Parliamentary election; and £75,800, £30,000 and £15,300 for elections to the Scottish Parliament, the Welsh Assembly and the Northern Ireland Assembly respectively. Controls on donations to such bodies and requirements for them to account to the Electoral Commission and the general public are equivalent to those for registered parties, including the requirement to disclose donations of £5,000 or more and the ban on foreign donations. Likewise, it is a criminal offence for the designated representative of such an organisation either to make a false declaration to the Electoral Commission or to fail to provide a declaration. Finally, documentary material published by or on behalf of such a body has to carry the name and address of both the printer and the publisher in the same way that party literature has to have such an imprint at a General Election or a by-election.

Of the remaining four Parts of the Act, only one (Part IX) was of significance in the context of this chapter in that it amended the *Companies Act 1985* to require companies to obtain prior shareholder consent for donations to registered parties and other political expenditure. This had the desirable, but belated, effect of putting companies on all fours with trade unions as far as donations to political parties were concerned.

Although PPERA 2000 was a compendium statute of striking breadth and although the Neill Committee had tried to address every significant aspect of party political funding, not a great deal of *legislative* progress has been made towards addressing the issues on which the interests of the media and the political parties intersect. For the sake of containing *the costs of political campaigning*, the Committee had strongly recommended maintaining the regime of free access to radio and television for party political broadcasts (PPBs) and party election broadcasts (PEBs), as well as the long-standing ban on political advertisements on radio and television, although *not* (be it noted) in the press or on advertising hoardings.[35] However, the chapter on media and advertising was strangely *piano* and it ended with the rather mild injunction that the proposed Electoral Commission (among its many other duties) 'should be specifically charged with monitoring the working of the current arrangements for the provision of party political and election broadcasts and the effect on political advertising generally of developing communications technologies'.[36]

Under the present Labour Government and, indeed, its Conservative predecessors, there seems to have been a strong inclination on the part of politicians and the media alike to leave the current informal arrangements for political broadcasts well alone and to allow them to be handled informally according to understandings reached between the industry and its regulators and reported in a Consultation Paper in January 1998. Furthermore, there is neither any sense of crisis nor any constructive consensus to drive radical change in this area of political competition. Only in relation to the arrangements for referendum broadcasts has any significant party political controversy emerged.[37] Certainly the draftsmen of PPERA 2000 were diffident about making legislative changes in this area and really in only two instances were media issues addressed. Section 11 provided that the Electoral Commission's broad oversight of the way elections are conducted should extend to providing impartial guidance on the allocation and scheduling of party political broadcasts. However, the explanatory notes on the legislation were careful to add that it is *not* the purpose of these provisions to give the Commission a prescriptive role in relation to editorial and broadcasting decisions which are properly a matter for the broadcasters themselves, nor is it intended that broadcasters should be required to seek the views of the Commission before deciding whether to transmit each and every party political broadcast.[38]

Sections 37 to 40 were even less ambitious and more technical in that they merely re-enacted Sections 14 and 19 of the *Registration of Political Parties Act 1998* and prevented broadcasters from transmitting a PPB on behalf of a party which is not registered.

On all matters to do with the regulation and funding of political parties, the Labour Government has been keen to take its lead from the Neill Committee recommendations. On the whole both the Committee and the Government have been primarily concerned to do what is *right* on the merits of the issues and both have seemed to be largely unmindful of the *political consequences*. Yet there was one notable paragraph in the opening pages of the Fifth Report in which the Committee acknowledged that some of its recommendations might have an adverse effect upon the *ability* of the political parties to raise money; but it added the balancing belief that some of its other proposals would have a significant dampening effect on the *need* for parties to raise so much money in the first place.[39] It was possible to detect some sensitivity on the Committee's part to possible outcomes flowing from the proposed system, especially if the Government and Parliament were to follow its advice on party funding to the letter. In fact, the experience of the 2001 General Election was pretty satisfactory in this regard in that none of the main parties overspent the nationally prescribed limits, mainly because there seemed little point in spending a fortune on a campaign the result of which seemed a foregone conclusion from the outset. If things are different at a future General Election, then the era of fully fledged state funding of political parties according to an agreed formula (which the Neill Committee carefully considered but eventually rejected in its report) may not be long delayed.

From a culture of official secrecy

Whereas the conduct of all those in public life has been significantly influenced by the First Report of the Nolan Committee and everything which has flowed from it, and whereas the governance of political parties is likely to be transformed by PPERA 2000, it is more uncertain whether the causes of open government and participatory democracy will be well served by the *Freedom of Information Act 2000* (FOI Act 2000) which marked the culmination of a pressure group and media campaign to these ends dating at least from the late 1970s.[40]

The fundamental reason for the uncertainty about the effects of the FOI Act 2000 is that there has long been a culture of secrecy, or at any rate excessive confidentiality, in British central Government which has appeared to suit the interests of Ministers and policy-advising civil servants, but also to deprive the British people and their elected representatives of certain rights to information which for several decades have been regarded as taken for granted in countries like Sweden and the United States. This culture of official secrecy has proved very difficult or impossible to extirpate from the world of Whitehall and there remain institutional bastions of 'national security', such as the Ministry of Defence, the Home Office and the Intelligence Services (MI5 and MI6), which are never likely to be genuinely sympathetic to the interests of 'open government'. It is therefore accurate in the United Kingdom to refer to a very long and halting transition from official secrecy to freedom of information, albeit one which is by no means complete, as we shall see in the rest of this section.

Our story must begin with the notorious *Official Secrets Act 1911* which, in a blunderbuss legislative response to a wave of panic about German espionage, outlawed in Section 2 any disclosure, retention or receipt of official information which had not been authorised by a responsible Minister. The Act provided those charged with no obvious defence, other than the required Ministerial authorisation. For example, neither the fact of prior disclosure by someone else nor a claim that the disclosure was in the public interest nor an obligation on the prosecution to show a defendant's intent to disclose was permitted as a legitimate defence for anyone charged with breaching this draconian Section of the Act. When the original crisis had passed, successive Governments were content to leave this legislation on the Statute Book as a massive deterrent to anyone who might be tempted to transgress. The Act remained symbolic of the secrecy culture in Whitehall, a culture which was later reinforced by the imperatives of the Second World War and the espionage threats of the Cold War after that.

After several highly publicised but failed criminal prosecutions under the Act in the 1970s and 1980s – notably the prosecution in 1985 of Clive Ponting, a senior MOD official, which failed when the jury acquitted him after accepting his defence that he had acted in the public interest by disclosing to Parliament the true facts about the sinking of the Argentinian cruiser *Belgrano* during the Falklands conflict of 1982 – Margaret Thatcher and her senior colleagues reluctantly came to the conclusion that Section 2 of the Act could no longer be sustained and would have to be replaced with a more targeted and effective piece of legislation. The then Conservative Government was also influenced in coming to this conclusion by an equally bruising experience in 1987–88 when it tried but failed to enforce the principles of the Act by applying for injunctions in the civil courts to restrain publication in the United Kingdom and other jurisdictions of *Spycatcher*, a book of memoirs produced by Peter Wright, a former MI5 official then living in Australia.[41] Initially, the High Court in London granted the Government a temporary injunction against further publication and disclosure, but the Law Lords refused to grant a permanent injunction against the newspapers and publishers involved in serialising the memoirs, mainly on the grounds that the information had already been disclosed at an earlier date in the United States and other jurisdictions.

The White Paper of June 1988 and the legislation which flowed from it – the *Official Secrets Act 1989* – purported to be an enlightened reform of Section 2 of the original 1911 Act, but actually resembled the replacement of a blunderbuss with a high-powered rifle. The scope of criminal offences was reduced to five main areas of government activity: (1) defence, security and intelligence; (2) international relations; (3) confidential information supplied by other Governments or international organisations; (4) official information which could be misused by criminals; and (5) intercepted post, telephone calls and other communications. However, the range of people who might be caught by these offences was widened to include not only all officials, military personnel and contractors to the state, but also third parties, such as people working for the media or non-governmental organisations, who might reasonably be expected to appreciate the harm to national security which could result from disclosing unauthorised official information. Once again, there was no public interest defence available to those charged under the Act and even the prior publication of information disclosed without authorisation would only be admissible as a defence where it could be shown to have mitigated the harm done by disclosure. Even the *mens rea* test was not significantly alleviated in that a defendant would still have to demonstrate that his unauthorised disclosure had been unintentional – something which would be very hard to prove to the satisfaction of a court in such a case. This was really no relaxation of the previous law and constituted no decisive attenuation of the secrecy culture in British central Government.

The Major Administration tinkered with the legislative framework for the security services (MI5 and MI6) and expanded the role of MI5. The *Security Service Act 1996* (which was a refinement of the *Security Service Act 1989*), as well as reiterating the earlier definition of national security as protecting the state from espionage, terrorism and what were described as 'actions intended to overthrow or undermine Parliamentary democracy by political, industrial or violent means', empowered MI5 to deal with any threat which 'involves the use of violence, results in substantial financial gain, or is conducted by a large number of persons in pursuit of a common purpose'. In conjunction with the powers which had been provided in the *Interception of Communications Act 1985*, permitting telephone tapping and mail opening, this legislation effectively gave MI5 *carte blanche* to develop a new role for itself in the post-Cold War world against every conceivable type of activity, whether criminal, terrorist or plain loony, which could be construed in any way as subversive of the interests of the state. In spite of the rather half-hearted efforts to move away from the old traditions of official secrecy towards the new ideal of open government, successive Conservative Administrations were remarkably cautious when it came to reforming the arrangements for our national security which have long been beyond effective political control even by the Prime Minister of the day.

It is worth noting at this point that little of significance really changed in respect of political control over the security services after Labour came to power in May 1997. The only small achievement for those who had long sought reassurance that the security services were not completely out of control in this country was the *Regulation of Investigatory Powers Act 2000* (henceforth RIPA 2000). This provided for the Prime Minister to appoint an Interception of Communications Commissioner with a duty to keep under review the exercise and performance of the powers granted under the Act to the Home Secretary of the day and those of his officials (mostly in MI5) involved in the interception of communications, the carrying out of surveillance and the use of decryption technology to have access to data otherwise protected by encryption or electronic passwords. In parallel it provided for the Prime Minister to appoint an Intelligence Services Commissioner to keep under review all those aspects of the secret intelligence services not covered by the other arrangements in the legislation – i.e. the external activities of MI6 and military intelligence 'in places other than Northern Ireland'. This exception for Northern Ireland took account of the fact that the provisions of the Act created a separate Investigatory Powers Commissioner for Northern Ireland and a Chief Surveillance Commissioner (with additional functions under the *1997 Police Act*) who might be supported in his activities by a number of Assistant Surveillance Commissioners. In short, if the quantity of oversight were the most important criterion for assessing the adequacy of these elaborate statutory arrangements, then the people of the United Kingdom and their elected representatives could feel reassured that the security and intelligence services would not be able to get up to any mischief which threatened the public interest. Yet quantity may not be the most important consideration, especially when all these various Commissioners are political appointments by the Prime Minister of the day and are not directly accountable to Parliament.

Labour Ministers were obviously aware, however, that a new dimension to the situation had been created by the passage of the *Human Rights Act 1998* (HRA 1998), which in Section 7 gave a person claiming that a public authority had acted or was proposing to act in a way which was unlawful under the Human Rights Convention the right to bring proceedings in the appropriate court or tribunal and to rely on the Convention rights concerned in any legal proceedings, provided that he was or would be a victim of the unlawful act. To meet their legal obligations under HRA 1998, Ministers made provision in Sections 65 to 70 of RIPA 2000 for the creation of a new Tribunal to hear and determine any public complaints about allegedly unlawful conduct carried out by or on behalf of the security and intelligence services, the armed forces, the police and officials of the Customs and Excise. On hearing such public complaints – excluding those which were frivolous or vexatious and those which were made more than one year after the event – the Tribunal may require the relevant Commissioner to appear before it and use its statutory power to make an interim Order and later an award of compensation or some other form of redress as it sees fit. At the end of the proceedings the Tribunal is under a duty to the complainant to issue a statement either that a determination has been made in his favour or that no such determination has been made. However, if the circumstances of the case reveal officially authorised wrong-doing, then the Tribunal is under a duty to report its findings to the Prime Minister. So at the end of this long and elaborate process, the matter returns to the Prime Minister and the Government in whose name and at whose behest the security and intelligence services conduct their murky operations in the first place.

Towards freedom of information

It is clear that there has been no linear progression in the United Kingdom from official secrecy to freedom of information. The fact that the principles of secrecy and disclosure still coexist rather uneasily in the British political system does not in any way remove the tensions which can arise between different vested interests in government and protagonists holding different views of government. Freedom of information is a means to an end – namely, a genuinely open and participatory process of government – not necessarily an end in itself, notwithstanding the fact that the long-running Freedom of Information Campaign treated it as such. The real conflict of interest has been between the protective, sometimes punitive role of the state in its efforts to safeguard 'national security' and the legitimate expectations of its subjects/citizens that they can or should be allowed to share in a more open and participatory form of politics. There is also a parallel conflict between the privacy interests of private individuals, who want confidential access to and safeguards for the security of official information about themselves, and the public interest of society as a whole which may occasionally require the sharing or disclosure of sensitive personal information at least on a 'need to know' basis within and sometimes beyond the institutions of government. Even if the *general* case for a Freedom of Information Act has been conceded by the most reluctant Ministers and officials, there have been vigorous internal arguments within Whitehall and Westminster about the *particular* application of this principle to particular categories of official information and about the pace of implementation.

When the Major Administration produced a White Paper on open government in 1993, it proposed three reforms to the then existing disclosure regime which went beyond the measures it had already introduced for greater openness – e.g. information on hospital waiting lists and school league tables. *Firstly*, there was to be a statutory right of access to personal information held on individuals by the institutions of government and public authorities, including information held in non-automated form, thus widening the scope of the 1984 Data Protection Act. *Secondly*, there was to be a statutory right of access to the official information held by the Health and Safety Executive and other similar regulatory bodies, which was intended to be particularly helpful to employees and their trade union representatives. *Thirdly*, there was to be an administrative Code of Practice requiring government Departments and other public authorities to grant public access on request to all official information, save certain exempt categories, with a mechanism for formal complaints to the Parliamentary Commissioner for Administration (the Ombudsman) if such information were wrongly withheld.

This package of measures constituted a significant step forward, but it did not satisfy the campaigners for fully fledged freedom of information largely because the Code of Practice, which came into effect in 1994, allowed for too many exceptions and exemptions.[42] Other serious shortcomings in the eyes of the campaigners included the subtle fact that the Code required public access to *information* rather than *documents*, which offered civil servants wide opportunities to provide sanitised extracts or *précis* of documents rather than documents in their entirety; the fact that the Code applied only to the government Departments and public bodies subject to the jurisdiction of the Ombudsman under the 1967 Act; and the fact that Departments and Agencies were allowed to charge full-cost fees for responding to public requests for information which might deter many ordinary people from exercising their rights under the Code. A revised edition of the Code was subsequently produced in January 1997, but this did not represent any further substantial progress towards open government and, by definition, it did not constitute the step-change to a statutory right of access to all official information (with minimum exceptions) for which the all-party and non-party Freedom of Information Campaign had been pressing for so many years.

The Labour Party came into power in May 1997 with a clear Manifesto commitment to a Freedom of Information Bill which would introduce a statutory right of access to official information on request and make certain information publicly available without request. By December 1997 the Chancellor of the Duchy of Lancaster, Dr David Clark, who was then Minister in charge of the policy, introduced a White Paper entitled *Your Right to Know* which contained a wide-ranging set of proposals more radical and liberal than many campaigners had expected.[43]

On the positive side for the campaigners, the Government's proposals were set to apply to a very wide range of bodies, including about 1,200 non-departmental public bodies and, notably, some private sector organisations performing public tasks. Applicants were free to apply for official information in any form and would not have to make do with information extracted from official documents, as had been the case with the 1994 Administrative Code. Fees for access were to be confined to no more than £10 per request, with the possibility of higher charges for commercial undertakings. The criteria for refusing disclosure would include a test of 'substantial harm' and a 'public interest' test which could be judicially interpreted either way, with the emphasis for these decisions governed more by the contents of a given document than by its Whitehall classification. Above all, an independent Information Commissioner would be appointed who would be answerable to the Courts and not to Parliament and who would not be subject in her decisions to any Ministerial override. Indeed, the Commissioner was to have the power to require disclosure of all but the statutorily excluded categories of information and to make final decisions, subject only to the possibility of judicial review if she could be shown to have gone *ultra vires* or to have acted unreasonably. She was also encouraged to work in close cooperation with the Data Protection Registrar established by the *1984 Data Protection Act.*

Those unpersuaded of the overwhelming merits of such legislation could feel some relief that the Cabinet was not rushing forward to legislate in this tricky area for Government. After a Ministerial reshuffle in July 1998, there was even greater relief when responsibility for the Bill was transferred to the Home Office which had always been among the most cautious Departments on these issues.

It was not until May 1999 that the Government published a Consultation Paper which included a draft Bill and this latter document disappointed many of the campaigners for freedom of information because it was seen as a retreat from many of the positions taken in the 1997 White Paper.[44] In June 1999 the Public Administration Select Committee began its pre-legislative scrutiny of the draft Bill which was soon criticised for the class or category exemptions to which no test of harm applied and for the fact that the Information Commissioner would only be able to require public authorities *to consider* the public interest when exercising their discretion about disclosure rather than herself enforce release of official information on that ground. However, the idea of making the freedom of information legislation compatible with the updated data protection legislation (the *Data Protection Act 1998*), which had been necessitated by the need to comply with an earlier European directive, was widely welcomed on practical grounds, as was the decision to have a single independent Commissioner to oversee the operation of both pieces of legislation.

Following this unusually long period of consultation and reconsideration within Whitehall, the Freedom of Information Bill was eventually published in November 1999 and received its Second Reading in the Commons on 7th December 1999. The legislation did not resile from the main principles of the White Paper, but it did reflect a number of important pre-legislative adjustments which had been insisted upon by Jack Straw, then Home Secretary, and others in the Government. The statutory right for anyone to request access to official information remained unchallenged, but the defined exemptions constituted a formidably long list in Part II of the Act.[45] Furthermore, there was an additional public interest test which public authorities were obliged to apply in considering whether to release information, even if it fell within one of the defined exemptions. However, it was hard for uncommitted observers to see these provisions as more than a rather empty gesture, since the discretion remained with the public authority concerned which was not obliged to give its reasons for a refusal if these would involve the disclosure of exempt information.[46] Official information containing personal details or involving personal records held by public authorities was dealt with in Part VII of the Act which served to amend sections of the *Data Protection Act 1998* in order to bring procedures into line with the latest consolidated position.

A new office of Information Commissioner was created which was to absorb the functions of the Data Protection Registrar. The Commissioner would be able to examine complaints that public authorities had not carried out their duties under the Act, examine decisions on the extent of exemptions and enforce disclosure where appropriate by means of a decision or enforcement notice, and recommend that a public authority should reconsider its duty in relation to the public interest, but without any final power of enforcement. Any appeals against decisions of the Commissioner were to be heard by an Information Tribunal (absorbing the Data Protection Tribunal) and appeals on points of law could be heard by the Courts.

During the period of pre-legislative scrutiny and throughout the subsequent consideration of the Bill by both Houses of Parliament, further pressures were exerted in continuing efforts to turn it into a genuine Freedom of Information Act rather than leave it as something not much more than a statement of good intentions by the Government of the day. The main areas of Parliamentary concern were highlighted in Select Committee reports from both the Commons and the Lords.

Firstly, there was the criticism that the Government did not seem to appreciate the important distinction between a genuine Freedom of Information Act creating statutory rights with the minimum of closely defined exemptions and a paternalistic measure to promote open government with Ministers deciding what the public need to know. The Government responded to this by proposing some cosmetic changes in the long title of the Bill and by changing the order of some of the Clauses.

Secondly, on the public interest test to be followed by public authorities when deciding on each-way cases for possible disclosure, Ministers made some important concessions – e.g. that unless there was a compelling reason to the contrary, the public interest should be construed in favour of disclosure – but they were not prepared to abdicate from *their own* responsibilities to balance the public interest in disclosure against the public interest in non-disclosure, a formula which used the term 'public interest' in two contradictory ways. This meant that Ministers gave no ground to the argument that the Information Commissioner should have the statutory power to order disclosure (the so-called 'public interest override') in exceptional cases where *she* concluded that disclosure would be in the public interest. In the final analysis, all she would be able to do was require the public authority concerned to make its decision on disclosure in accordance with criteria set out in the Act and specify matters to which it must have regard.[47] Yet the role of the Commissioner in this respect would still be essentially advisory and the exercise of discretion would still be a matter for Ministers – unlike the situation in Scotland and in Ireland where the balance in the equivalent legislation is tipped in favour of the Commissioner. Fundamentally, the Labour Government (like all its predecessors) was not prepared to accept the idea that official information should be regarded as public property, a fact which led the House of Lords Select Committee in its Report on the Bill to comment that 'the law may be regarded as a statement of good intentions, but it is not a Freedom of Information Act as that term is internationally understood'.[48]

Thirdly, there was the criticism that the exemptions in the Bill, which were both class-based and contents-based (i.e. dependent upon the classification of the document and the material contents of the document), were either undesirable (e.g. in relation to the formulation and development of Government policy) or too broad (e.g. in relation to the interests of commercial confidentiality). Once again Ministers stood their ground against these criticisms by arguing that the limited number of class-based exemptions was justified and that the test of 'harm' or 'prejudice' involved in assessing a potential disclosure should be kept consistent with other related legislation, such as the 1972 Local Government Act and the 1998 Data Protection Act. Any higher hurdle in the way of a decision not to disclose, which might be achieved by adding the adjectives 'significant' or 'substantial', remained undesirable and potentially confusing in the Government's view. However, it did make a concession to the House of Lords Select Committee on Delegated Powers by agreeing to amend Clause 36 of the Bill (Section 75 of the Act), which gave the Home Secretary power to add new exemptions by Order, so that the power should be limited to contents-based exemptions subject to a prejudice test.

Fourthly, both Select Committees examining the Bill were discontented about the breadth of the class-based exemption for information on Government decision making and policy formulation as it included all public authorities covered by the Bill. In many ways this was the last ditch for the entrenched Whitehall interests and, realistically, there was no way in which *any* British Government was likely to concede on these points. The essential argument put by Ministers was that freedom of information must allow for 'the efficient and effective conduct of public affairs' and especially the provision (by civil servants) of free and frank advice and the free and frank exchange of views for the purposes of policy deliberation. Initially, Ministers and the civil servants who advise them were resolutely set against any attempt to draw a statutory distinction between factual and background information on the one hand and naked policy advice on the other, as had been urged upon them by the FOI campaigners who argued that the former should be disclosed, while accepting that the non-disclosure of the latter might just be defensible. In the end Ministers did concede on this point by placing a new duty on public authorities in Section 35(4) of the Act to have regard to the public interest in disclosing factual information used to provide an informed background to decision making. It was only a limited concession, because official and Ministerial discretion was preserved and actual policy advice, whether from civil servants to Ministers or from Clerks to officers of either House of Parliament, was excluded as 'exempt information'.

Finally, with regard to the relationship between freedom of information and Parliamentary privilege, the Act made due obeisance to Parliament's historic claims to absolute privilege in relation to freedom of speech and exclusive jurisdiction over its own procedures and regulatory affairs. In such sensitive areas Section 34 made it quite clear that either the Speaker in the Commons or the Clerk of the Parliaments in the House of Lords had power to issue a certificate exempting certain Parliamentary information from the provisions of the Act. Only the Joint Committee on Parliamentary Privilege in its report of April 1999 had previously had the temerity to enter this secret garden and suggest some clarifying amendments.[49]

One of the morals of this interesting tale is that the time-consuming move from official secrecy towards freedom of information in the United Kingdom is not yet complete and indeed may never be, because there are always likely to be compelling interests of state which will require official secrecy, or at least scrupulous confidentiality, in much of the private domain of public government. It is still worth drawing attention to the powerful principles which stand arrayed on each side of this argument, and worth emphasising that these principles raise constitutional issues of considerably wider significance. For example, there is the cardinal principle of *freedom of expression* which is celebrated and safeguarded in all civilised societies, but which has to be tempered by requirements of truth or at least fair comment; otherwise the law of libel comes into play. There is the principle of *freedom of information* enshrined in the legislation we have been discussing in this section and sometimes formulated as 'the public's right to know'. Yet it is obvious that this right is relative not absolute, as indeed is the case with virtually all other human rights, and perhaps this partly explains why there have been such fierce arguments about these issues over the years. There is equally the principle of *the public interest*, yet it must be noted that this can be invoked by both sides of the argument – i.e. by those who assert a public interest in full disclosure and those who defend non-disclosure in certain cases also on grounds of public interest.

On the other side of the constitutional (almost philosophical) fence are certain equally compelling principles, some of which may be going out of fashion but are no less important for that. There is the principle of *personal privacy*, which is increasingly recognised as a human right by many people, but cannot always be upheld in all contemporary circumstances and sometimes conflicts with notions of the public good – e.g. in the case of the 'right' of parents to know of the whereabouts of paedophiles in their local community or the 'right' of insurance companies to insist upon full disclosure of all relevant personal details before consenting to insure someone who may have Aids. The dilemmas become more acute perhaps when the media discover instances of double standards being practised by leading figures in public life and decide to infringe any right to privacy which may be claimed by a politician or a celebrity or simply someone unfortunate enough to be in the news, with intrusive door-step interviews or invasive photography using telephoto lenses and other modern technical means. There is the principle of *executive confidentiality* (or is it convenience?) which has long been claimed by Governments through the centuries going back at least to Tudor times, but which can, and often does, tip the scales unfairly against all those not in the Government at any time – a large army of people which includes back-benchers in the governing party, Opposition parties, non-governmental organisations, the media and the general public. Finally, there is the principle of *national security* which is often used as a portmanteau term to justify hushing up any facts or opinions which may be embarrassing to the Government of the day, but which may also be used for the sake of those national interests – such as the defence of the realm at times of clear and present danger – which nearly everyone in their right mind is prepared to concede to the legitimate national authorities.

Whatever may be the most appropriate synthesis of these often deeply conflicting principles, it is heart-warming to note the small steps which have been taken in the wake of the *Freedom of Information Act 2000* to advance the cause of open government. One aspect of the legacy is visible on the Internet where the websites of the Home Office and other public authorities now provide copious amounts of (not always useful) information to anyone with access to a terminal, including new codes of practice for implementing the legislation and details of the Advisory Group on Openness in the Public Sector. However, the Act will not be fully implemented by all Government Departments until 2005.

General reflections

Each of the previous sections of this chapter has served to exemplify certain common themes in the changes to the rules of the political game which have been made since Labour came to power in 1997. The first theme worth noting is the way in which Members of Parliament in both Houses have been obliged by their own failings and by the moving spirit of the times to submit themselves to a degree of *external regulation* which would have been unthinkable to their predecessors even a generation ago. This has applied both to the conduct of individual politicians and to political parties (the principal corporate bodies in this sphere) and as a result has given a further, perhaps unintended boost to the professionalism of politics and to the longer-term argument for funding political parties at tax-payers' expense.

The second theme worth noting, which is in part a consequence of the first, has been the trend towards the *codification of conventions* and the *juridification of regulatory procedures* which spread from the civil service in 1996 to Ministers and MPs in 1997 and to political parties, elections and referenda in the year 2000. It may or may not have run its course, but it seems likely that the special category of Political Advisers will also be regulated as a result of the next round of legislation covering these matters, as was recommended in the Sixth Report of the Committee on Standards in Public Life.[50]

This trend has also spawned a much larger category of independent institutions and high officials (the so-called Commissions or independent Commissioners), created by statute to monitor and police various branches of political or administrative activity – whether the Parliamentary Commissioner for Standards to keep an eye on MPs, the Electoral Commission to keep an eye on party political activity, the Intelligence Services Commissioner to keep an eye on MI6, or the Information Commissioner to keep an eye on the openness of Whitehall and all public authorities. Such worthy institutions and impeccable individual regulators have joined what was already a significantly large category of public institutions – represented by the Parliamentary Commissioner for Administration, the Public Appointments Commissioner, and the Comptroller and Auditor General, to mention just a few examples of the species. This can be taken as another indication of the break-down of trust between the governors and the governed.

The third common theme worth noting has been the growing emphasis upon the virtues of *full disclosure* in virtually every sphere of the nation's political life. Of course, this is one of the main answers to the suspicions and the realities of political sleaze which reached a critical point towards the end of the previous Conservative Administration, but which have not been completely allayed during successive Blair Administrations with all their self-righteous talk about a new style of cleaner politics. Full disclosure is a necessary but not a sufficient condition for developing a new kind of more open and participatory politics – one in which many more people than simply those in the limited cadres of the traditional political and bureaucratic elites can have genuine opportunities to influence the development of public policy.

In all these ways it has been possible to demonstrate that in the United Kingdom changing the rules of the political game is tantamount to engaging in constitutional reform. We shall see in the next chapter that the same is true when politicians adjust the methods of democratic decision making. Yet in that case it is not so much an agenda which has been forced upon them as one which they adopted because they believed it would be for the good of the entire political system.

Questions for discussion

1   Were the elaborate Nolan arrangements the most appropriate response to the problems of political sleaze and to what problems has 'Nolanry' given rise?

2   To what extent has the Political Parties, Elections and Referendums Act 2000 fundamentally changed British constitutional assumptions?

3   Explain the critical differences between open government, a public right to know, and freedom of information.

Notes

1   During the 1945–50 Parliament there were two egregious and notorious cases which shaped Parliamentary attitudes on these matters. W.J. Brown MP, who had continued as the General Secretary of the Civil Service Clerical Association after his re-election to Parliament in 1945, complained to the Committee of Privileges about unacceptable pressures being put upon him as an MP by his employers in the trade union, and the House of Commons sustained him in the position he took. John Belcher MP, on the other hand, was found guilty by his Parliamentary colleagues of accepting presents and benefits in kind from an outside organisation which were considered to have compromised his independence as an MP and by extension to have brought the House of Commons into disrepute. Accordingly, he was censured and forced to resign his seat in Parliament. However, such cases were comparatively rare and many people at the time thought that Belcher had been victimised by his colleagues, presumably *pour encourager les autres*.

2   Quoted in *Standards in Public Life*, First Report of the Committee on Standards in Public Life, Cm 2850; HMSO, London, May 1995; para 28.

3   Analysis of the 1995 Register of Members' Interests suggested that almost 30 per cent of eligible MPs (i.e. those not holding Government posts) held registered consultancies with outside interests.

4   See *Sunday Times*, 10th July 1994.

5   See *Hansard*, 27th October 1994, Cols 758–9.

6   *Standards in Public Life*, Cm 2850.

7   The seven principles of public life were set out in full in *ibid*; p. 14. They were elaborated under the following headings: (1) Selflessness; (2) Integrity; (3) Objectivity; (4) Accountability; (5) Openness; (6) Honesty; and (7) Leadership.

8   *Ibid*; Chapter 3, para 7.

9   *Ibid*; para 10.

10 *Ibid*; para 13.

11 The six principles of ministerial conduct were set out in *ibid*; Chapter 3, paragraph 16. They were as follows:
    1   Ministers must ensure that no conflict arises or appears to arise between their public duties and their private interests.

2 Ministers must not mislead Parliament and they must be as open as possible with Parliament and the public.

3 Ministers are accountable to Parliament for the policies and operations of their Departments and Agencies.

4 Ministers should avoid accepting any gift or hospitality which might, or might appear to, compromise their judgement or place them under an improper obligation.

5 Ministers in the House of Commons must keep separate their roles as Minister and constituency Member.

6 Ministers must keep their party and Ministerial roles separate, and they must not ask civil servants to carry out party political duties or to act in any other way that would conflict with the Civil Service Code.

12 Those in the former camp included Sir Norman Fowler MP, Chairman of the Conservative Party; David Hunt MP, a former Conservative Cabinet Minister; Lord Armstrong, a former Cabinet Secretary; and Alan Langlands, a Conservative-appointed CEO of the NHS. Those in the latter camp included several academics from Democratic Audit at the University of Essex and the Institute of Local Government at the University of Birmingham.

13 *Ibid*; Chapter 4, para 24.

14 See the Draft Code of Practice for Public Appointments Procedures which was set out in *ibid*; p. 81. This covered the following aspects: (1) defining the task (job description) and the qualities sought (person specification); (2) identifying a field of candidates; (3) selecting a shortlist and recommending candidates to Ministers; (4) choosing the preferred candidate(s); (5) confirming the appointment.

15 The four general recommendations were: (1) The general principles of conduct which underpin public life need to be restated. (2) All public bodies should draw up Codes of Conduct incorporating these principles. (3) Internal systems for maintaining standards should be supported by independent scrutiny. (4) More needs to be done to promote and reinforce standards of conduct in public bodies, in particular through guidance and training including induction training.

16 See *The Ministerial Code*; HMSO, London, July 1997.

17 *Hansard*, 12th November 1997, Cols 899–900.

18 See *Reinforcing Standards*, Sixth Report of the Committee on Standards in Public Life, Cm 4557; HMSO, London, January 2000.

19 See *Standards of Conduct in the House of Lords*, Seventh Report of the Committee on Standards in Public Life, Cm 4903; HMSO, London, November 2000.

20 More recently, the Government has indicated its intention to legislate on both these matters by creating a single offence of corruption which will form part of a Criminal Justice Bill introduced in the 2001–2 Session of Parliament.

21 Lord Nicholls identified the minimum requirement of fairness for an accused Member in serious cases as being: (1) a prompt and clear statement of the precise allegations; (2) adequate opportunities to take legal advice; (3) the opportunity to be heard in person; (4) the opportunity to call relevant witnesses at the appropriate time; (5) the opportunity to examine other witnesses; and (6) the opportunity to attend meetings at which evidence is given.

22 *Reinforcing Standards*, Cm 4557; para 2.20.

23 *Ibid*; para 6.56.

24 Quoted in *ibid*; para 8.16.

25 The so-called Hinduja Passport Affair concerned three Indian brothers who had offered in 1998 to sponsor 'the faith zone' in the Greenwich Dome to the tune of millions of pounds and who subsequently tried to use their contacts with Peter Mandelson, then Minister with responsibility for the Dome, in their efforts to secure British passports. The matter surfaced again in the media in early 2001 when Peter Mandelson initially denied having spoken on the telephone about the Hinduja passport applications to Mike O'Brien, the Home Office Minister for Immigration. However, he then admitted having had such a telephone call, but claimed he had done nothing improper. Nevertheless, he caused such political embarrassment for Alastair Campbell, the Prime Minister's Press Secretary, and for the Government as a whole, largely by changing his story from one day to the next, that Tony Blair felt bound to insist upon his resignation in January 2001.

26 See A. Barker *et al.*, *Ruling by Task Force*; Politico's, London, 1999.

27 *Hansard*, 12th November 1997, Col. 899.

28 Quoted in the *The Funding of Political Parties in the United Kingdom*, Fifth Report of the Committee on Standards in Public Life, Cm 4057; HMSO, London, 1998; para 1.5.

29 *Ibid*; para 2.6.

30 *Ibid*; para 2.27, my italics.

31 The Government did *not* follow the recommendations of the Neill Committee on some matters – e.g. tax relief for individual donations to political parties, defining election expenditure according to its purpose, or rules for the financing and conduct of referenda.

32 Under Section 70 of the Registration of Political

Parties Act 1998 any political party's entry in the Register kept by the Electoral Commission must now contain the following information: (1) the registered name of the party; (2) the address of the party's headquarters; (3) the name of the party's registered leader, registered nominating officer, registered treasurer and, if applicable, registered campaigns officer; (4) where a party has accounting units, the name and headquarters address of each accounting unit and the name of the treasurer and one other officer of each such unit; (5) the registered emblems of the party; (6) the name and office address of up to twelve deputy treasurers; (7) the date of registration; (8) any other information prescribed by the Electoral Commission in accordance with paragraph 6 of Schedule 4 of the Act.

33 The principal purpose of the concept of the 'permissible donor' was to require political parties to reject donations which are anonymous or which do not appear to be from a person registered to vote in the United Kingdom or from a company incorporated in the European Union and carrying on business in the United Kingdom or from an unincorporated association having its main office and its principal sphere of operation in the United Kingdom.

34 The arithmetical formula for calculating the maximum amount that a party may spend is determined by multiplying the sum allowed per constituency (£30,000) by the number of the constituencies contested. Thus the maximum total amount of campaign expenditure which a party could incur if it contested all the constituencies in each part of the United Kingdom would be £19,770,000.

35 A position which may be subject to legal challenge before long on the grounds of free speech under Article 10 of the European Convention on Human Rights now incorporated into UK statute law by the Human Rights Act 1998.

36 See *The Funding of Political Parties in the United Kingdom*, Cm 4057; Chapter 13 and Recommendation 97.

37 For more on the controversy over referendum campaign funding and broadcasting see pp. 316–18 below.

38 See Explanatory Notes on the Political Parties, Elections and Referendums Bill, para 51.

39 *The Funding of Political Parties in the United Kingdom*, Cm 4057; para S.8.

40 The British Section of the International Commission of Jurists recommended a Code of Practice for the disclosure of official information by all Government Departments and other public bodies to be supervised by the Parliamentary Commissioner for Administration (the Ombudsman). See ICJ, *Freedom of Information*; Justice, London, 1978.

41 See *Attorney-General v. Guardian Newspapers* (1987) 3 All ER 316; *Attorney-General v. Newspaper Publishing plc* (1987) 3 All ER 276; *Attorney-General v. Observer Ltd* (1988) 1 All ER 385; *Attorney-General v. Guardian Newspapers (No. 2)* (1988) 2 WLR 805; and *Attorney-General v. Times Newspapers, Guardian Newspapers and the Observer* (1988) 3 WLR 776 (HL).

42 The White Paper listed 200 statutory secrecy requirements and a further 80 matters which could not be probed by Parliamentary Questions.

43 *Your Right to Know: the Government's Proposals for a Freedom of Information Act*, Cm 3818; HMSO, London, December 1997.

44 See *Freedom of Information: Consultation on Draft Legislation*, Cm 4355; HMSO, London, May 1999.

45 The long list of defined exemptions included information intended for future publication, disclosure of information likely to prejudice relations between any two Administrations within the United Kingdom, disclosure of information likely to prejudice UK economic interests, disclosure of information likely to prejudice audit functions, formulation of Government policy including the operation of a Ministerial Private Office, disclosure of information likely to prejudice the effective conduct of public affairs in the reasonable opinion of a qualified person, communications with Her Majesty and honours, information provided in confidence, and disclosure of information likely to prejudice the commercial interests of any person. In addition, under Clause 43 the Home Secretary was given the power to create further exemptions by Order if they related to information whose disclosure would have particular effects 'adverse to the public interest'.

46 Clause 13(4) of the Bill imposed a duty upon a public authority, when exercising its discretion, to have regard to all the circumstances and to the desirability of informing the applicant 'whenever the public interest in disclosure outweighs the public interest in maintaining the exemption in question'.

47 The Government's revisions to Clause 13(4) included the removal of the right to request reasons from the applicant for disclosure of official information, the removal of the right to impose conditions upon the release of the information, and a new duty on a public authority to consider the desirability of communicating factual information used, or to be used, to provide an informed background to decision making.

48 House of Lords Paper 97 (1998–99), para 21.

49 See House of Lords Paper 43 and House of Commons Paper 214 (1998–99).
50 See *Reinforcing Standards*, Cm 4557; Chapter 6.

Further reading

Jim Amos *et al.*, *A Practical Guide to the Freedom of Information Act 2000*; Constitution Unit, London, 2001.

A. Barker *et al.*, *Ruling by Task Force*; Politico's, London, 1999.

The Funding of Political Parties in the United Kingdom, Fifth Report of the Committee on Standards in Public Life, Cm 4057; HMSO, London, 1998.

Clive Ponting, *The Right to Know*; Sphere Books, London, 1985.

Reinforcing Standards, Sixth Report of the Committee on Standards in Public Life, Cm 4557; HMSO, London, 2000.

Standards of Conduct in the House of Lords, Seventh Report of the Committee on Standards in Public Life, Cm 4903; HMSO, London, 2000.

Standards in Public Life, First Report of the Committee on Standards in Public Life, Cm 2850; HMSO, London, 1995.

S. Weir and D. Beetham, *Political Power and Democratic Control in Britain*; Routledge, London, 1999.

Your Right to Know: the Government's Proposals for a Freedom of Information Act, Cm 3818; HMSO, London, 1997.

website for the Freedom of Information Campaign: www.cfoi.org.uk

Chapter 14

Adjusting the methods of democratic decision making

By the time that the Labour Party came into office in May 1997 there was a demonstrable need to modernise the electoral arrangements of this country which, in many respects, had been little altered since the end of the nineteenth century. Since May 1997 this form of modernisation has duly happened. Electoral reform, on the other hand (i.e. changing the voting system by which politicians are elected), has long been a more controversial cause, especially in relation to elections to the Westminster Parliament. However, with Labour's 1997 Manifesto commitment to establish devolved Assemblies in Scotland and Wales, it did not seem so outlandish even to the self-selected guardians of our familiar first-past-the-post electoral system to contemplate the introduction of a mixed system (part plurality and part proportional) for the proposed Parliament in Edinburgh and Assembly in Cardiff – just as many years before in 1973 the British political class had acquiesced in the introduction of a system of proportional representation for elections to the power-sharing Assembly in Northern Ireland and for local government elections in the Province.

As for the gradually growing use of the referendum as a method of democratic decision making in the United Kingdom, this was a constitutional trend which in modern times could be traced back to the 1973 border poll in Northern Ireland. Little more than two years later this was followed by the 1975 UK Referendum on whether or not this country should remain in the European Communities. Nearly four years later, in March 1979, two referenda were held simultaneously in Scotland and Wales to approve or disapprove of the then Labour Government's legislation for devolution in those two parts of the United Kingdom. Thus by 1979 it had become implausible to argue that referenda did not belong in our constitutional arrangements in this country.[1]

Since 1997 it has become even more unsustainable to argue the case that referenda have no place in our constitutional arrangements, since they have been used on four important occasions and Labour Ministers have acknowledged that this procedure will be the appropriate way to decide the vexed issues of whether or not the United Kingdom should abolish the pound and join the Economic and Monetary Union in Europe, and whether or not we should adopt some form of proportional representation for elections to Parliament at Westminster.[2] Moreover, the political effect of referenda is effectively *to entrench* decisions on some of the most controversial issues in such a way that it becomes politically impossible for a subsequent Government and Parliament to overturn them. Thus, for example, it would be unthinkable for the Mayor of London and the Greater London Assembly to be abolished by a simple Act of Parliament in the way that Parliament at the behest of the second Thatcher Administration agreed to abolish the Greater London Council and the other Metropolitan County Councils by a simple Act of Parliament in 1985. It seems clear that the use of referenda to decide big political and institutional questions, which are difficult to resolve in Parliament or at a General Election, is now an established feature of our constitutional arrangements in the United Kingdom.

Modernising electoral arrangements

The law governing free elections is a vital part of any democratic nation's constitutional arrangements. It provides some of the most essential 'rules of the game' under which political parties compete for power. It can affect electoral outcomes, because different electoral systems can produce very different electoral results in a single polity, as we have seen since Italy and New Zealand changed their electoral systems in the early 1990s. It can also influence the nature of politics in a given democracy. For example, a plurality or first-past-the-post electoral system will tend to encourage adversarial politics and relatively accountable Government, whereas a proportional system will tend to encourage consensual politics and less readily accountable coalition Government.

Moreover, election law and the electoral system can have significant effects upon public attitudes towards voting at elections and participation between elections. For example, voluntary voting combined with a winner-takes-all electoral system, as in the United Kingdom, may contribute to voter apathy and relatively low levels of participation in the institutions and processes of politics (especially when the result of an election seems to be a foregone conclusion); but compulsory voting combined with an electoral system which is at least partly proportional, as in Belgium, may contribute to stronger voter identification with the political parties, but a degree of resentment or cynicism about the inherent compromises of coalition politics.

In the case of the United Kingdom, our electoral arrangements have long been arcane, anomalous and somewhat anachronistic. In spite of the important changes made to these arrangements in parts of the *Political Parties, Elections and Referendums Act 2000* (henceforth PPERA 2000), our electoral law is still in need of modernisation and this could help our Parliamentary democracy to attract greater public respect than at present.

This was fully recognised by the Labour and Liberal Democrat parties when they were in Opposition to the Conservative Government before 1997. For example, issues to do with the mechanics of electoral registration and the conduct of Parliamentary elections in general were seriously addressed by the Labour Party in a 1993 policy report entitled *A New Agenda for Democracy* and in the Plant Report on electoral systems which was published at about the same time.[3] Both these influential documents advocated the creation of an independent Electoral Commission which would be 'directly and solely responsible for all aspects of electoral administration and for ensuring freedom and fairness in all aspects of our electoral system'.[4]

Even without giving huge prominence to issues of election law and administration in its 1997 Manifesto, the Labour Party was clearly in favour of substantial modernisation and reform in this area when it arrived in power. Jack Straw, then Home Secretary, set up a Ministerial Working Party in January 1998 under his junior Home Office colleague, George Howarth, to look into the more technical aspects of the subject and it soon became clear that the Government would put suitable legislation to Parliament once it had explored all the issues. The Home Affairs Select Committee of the Commons made a number of recommendations which pushed Government policy in the same direction.[5]

At the same time the Neill Committee was inquiring into the funding of political parties and the Jenkins Commission was investigating alternatives to the present electoral system for Westminster elections.[6] Whether by accident or design, both of these august bodies reported in October 1998 and both recommended the establishment of an independent Electoral Commission. This weighty and influential combination of forces seemed to have had its effect upon public policy, since a White Paper published in July 1999 described the role envisaged for the proposed Electoral Commission and included for wider consultation a draft Bill which eventually became the Political Parties, Elections and Referendums Act 2000.[7]

The Electoral Commission and its tasks

PPERA 2000 established the Electoral Commission, which is a body corporate independent of any Government Department and which reports directly to Parliament. The six Commissioners enjoy considerable security of tenure, are appointed for up to ten years (with the possibility of reappointment) and can only be removed from office by the House of Commons as a whole if the Speaker's Committee produces a report saying that one or more of the grounds for removal has been established. The Speaker's Committee – which includes two Government Ministers, the Chairman of the Home Affairs Select Committee and six other MPs appointed by the Speaker – is there to exercise general Parliamentary oversight of the Commission and, in particular, take responsibility for approving its budget and five-year corporate plan. The legislation seeks to balance the need to ensure the Commission's financial independence with appropriate safeguards to ensure proper financial control.

The Act allots to the Commission such a strikingly broad range of functions that there must be some doubt as to whether it will be able to discharge all of them with equal success. Under Section 4 the Commission, acting as an election monitor, is required to prepare and publish reports on the administration of elections to the Westminster, European and Scottish Parliaments and to the Welsh and Northern Ireland Assemblies. It is also required to do the same in relation to referenda held on 'reserved matters' throughout the United Kingdom or in one or more of its constituent parts (including the nine English regions). Under Section 5 the Commission has an equally wide-ranging duty to keep under review and report upon all matters relating to elections and referenda, the redrawing of Parliamentary and local government boundaries, the regulation and funding of political parties, political advertising and the law relating to *all* such matters.

The Government of the day remains responsible for the law on the conduct of elections and referenda. Nevertheless, changes in electoral law or changes in the regulations governing campaign expenditure can only be introduced after consulting the Electoral Commission. In general, the Commission is empowered to take over from the Home Office the tasks of promoting best practice in electoral administration. In this capacity it can be expected to offer advice and assistance to Returning Officers, registered political parties, recognised 'third parties' and permitted participants in referendum campaigns. For example, the Commission has looked at the unusually high level of postal votes cast at the 2001 General Election to see if there were any abuses of the newly extended system which might require tighter regulation in future.

There is even provision in the Act for the Commission to exercise broad oversight of party political broadcasts and to offer guidance to the various broadcasting authorities on the discharge of their statutory duties under other legislation covering these matters. Thus Section 9 places a duty upon the broadcasting authorities to have regard to the views of the Electoral Commission when determining, for example, the scheduling of party political broadcasts.

In what might prove to be a portent of wider state funding of political parties, the Commission has a duty to develop and, if it is approved by the Home Secretary, administer a scheme for the payment of so-called policy development grants to registered political parties, the qualification for which is to have at least two sitting MPs in the House of Commons. The total sum available for such grants is restricted to £2 million in any financial year and the money is only payable for the development of policies designed to form part of the political platforms of individual parties.

More broadly, Section 11 imposes a duty upon the Commission to promote public awareness of 'electoral systems and matters', 'systems of local government and national government' and 'the institutions of the European Union'. This Section provides for the Commission to have a role in encouraging voter participation in the democratic process. It is expected to do this both by carrying out programmes of education and information on its own account and by supporting similar efforts mounted by other bodies, such as the Department for Education and Skills in its citizenship programme or the Hansard Society in its educational work about Parliament. It was deliberately drafted as a wide-ranging Section in order

> to ensure that such voter education is not restricted to addressing the mechanics of exercising the vote, but is also able to address – through attention to the role of Government and other elected bodies both at local, national and European level – the purpose and importance of exercising the vote.[8]

It will be recalled that the Neill Committee in its Report on the Funding of Political Parties and the Jenkins Commission on the Voting System did not agree about whether or not the Electoral Commission should assume the responsibilities of the Boundary Commissions which have determined the boundaries of Parliamentary constituencies in the four component parts of the United Kingdom since 1949. The Neill Committee observed that 'the existing system for the revision of Parliamentary boundaries seems to work reasonably well and . . . to transfer it to the Election (sic) Commission might seriously overload that body whose responsibilities . . . will be onerous enough as it is'.[9] On the other hand, the Jenkins Commission recommended that 'there should be greater coordination of the work of the separate Boundary Commissions for England, Scotland, Wales and Northern Ireland and ... this function should be entrusted to an Electoral Commission'.[10] In the event, Labour Ministers favoured the latter view and made provision in Sections 12 to 17 of the Act for the Electoral Commission to establish four Boundary Committees, one for each main part of the United Kingdom, which would take over the functions discharged until that time by the Parliamentary and Local Government Boundary Commissions. However, a relatively distant target date of 2005 was set for the transfer of these functions, so nothing will happen under this heading until the next review of constituency boundaries has been completed.

Now that the new Electoral Commission has begun to function as intended in the legislation, there is an extensive agenda of possible issues for it to address in the general sphere of electoral administration and, more significantly, the rules of political competition between the parties at election times.[11] All the items on this agenda to modernise election law in this country are responses to the historical anomalies which have characterised many of our constitutional arrangements for so long.

Firstly, there is the important question of *the timing of General Elections*. Under the Royal Prerogative, the Prime Minister of the day can call a General Election more or less whenever it suits him and his party within the five-year maximum span of a Parliament. The fact that the timing of modern General Elections is usually rather predictable does not detract from the significant advantage which this political convention can give to the party in office. The alternative, which was advocated in the 1992 Labour Manifesto and which is still Liberal Democrat policy, is to move to fixed-term Parliaments. This would require a provision for the dissolution of Parliament and the calling of an election if and when in mid-term the Government of the day loses the confidence of the House of Commons. The Electoral Commission has shown interest in doing work on fixed-term Parliaments; but at present neither of the two main parties has been prepared to give up this 'prerogative power' of calling for a dissolution when it suits the Prime Minister of the day.

A second significant question which might be put on the agenda of the Electoral Commission is whether to introduce *compulsory voting* in this country, as in Australia, Belgium and Italy. The Labour Party came close to adopting this policy in 1993 when it had just lost a fourth General Election in a row, and there are respectable arguments for it. For example, it can be presented as a way of enforcing the civic duty as well as the civic right to vote in a democratic society where these things should be cherished. Some people also maintain that it would give more legitimacy to the Government of the day because the voter turnout would, by definition, be close to 100 per cent. Yet there is something rather reminiscent of the old Soviet Union about these arguments and one cannot help feeling that such a change in election law would offend the voluntarist and largely apolitical spirit in which politics is approached by most people in this country.

Thirdly, there is a whole raft of possible measures for improving the administrative working of the electoral system for Westminster which involve the rules governing *Parliamentary candidatures* on the one side and *voters' rights* on the other. For example, the minimum age for a Parliamentary candidate could be lowered from 21 to 18, in line with Australia, Canada and Germany; and the size or even the existence of a financial deposit (now £500 per candidate at Parliamentary elections) could be changed and possibly replaced with a requirement for a certain number of signatures from electors resident in the constituency. With regard to voters' rights and obligations, the present system of numbered ballot papers with counterfoils could be replaced by a legal requirement for every voter to show some form of recognised identification to the polling clerk, as already happens in Northern Ireland; the idea of a rolling Electoral Register, which is continuously updated and therefore much more accurate, has been introduced in place of the traditional system which relied upon a 'snapshot' of all those living in a particular locality on a given qualifying date in October every year; and the tendency of people with two or more homes (or students) to register in two or more constituencies for the right to vote could be ended and replaced by a simple rule based upon their declaration of a 'principal residence'.

Finally, there are two miscellaneous matters. In relation to *overseas voters*, British citizens resident overseas lose the right to vote in British Parliamentary elections after they have completed ten years' residence overseas instead of the 20 years which applied under previous legislation. In relation to *Christian priests*, the *House of Commons (Removal of Clergy Disqualification) Act 2001* removed the small but symbolic legislative anomaly under which certain former and serving ministers of the Christian religion had been disqualified from becoming Members of Parliament.

The uncertain path to electoral reform

Electoral reform in the United Kingdom – in other words, changes to the system of voting under which politicians are elected – has not been off the constitutional agenda for nearly 200 years. It was often connected in one way or another with the successive extensions of the franchise in the nineteenth and twentieth centuries and over the years there have been a number of changes and many attempts at reform. All the political parties have taken a close interest in the subject – sometimes to defend an electoral system from which they benefited and sometimes to change one from which they did not benefit. The result is that there has been very little altruism in the continuing debate about electoral reform and virtually all the participants in it have had a self-serving agenda of one kind or another.

In 1917 an all-party Speaker's Conference unanimously recommended a switch to a system of single transferable votes in the cities and large towns, together with a system of alternative votes in the counties. In 1931 under the second Labour Government a Bill for the introduction of the alternative vote passed through the House of Commons, but was rejected by the House of Lords and was lost when the Labour Party split and a National Government under Ramsay Macdonald was formed later that year. The result was that

first-past-the-post remained almost by default the predominant method of election to the United Kingdom Parliament. Even so, it was not until the 1950 General Election that all MPs were elected by this method, since until that time various anomalies had persisted, such as the fact that in a number of Boroughs there were two Members of Parliament for a single constituency (often MPs of different parties) and four of the twelve university seats were multi-member constituencies elected under a proportional system of single transferable vote. This was a throw-back to the days when higher education was regarded as a superior qualification for the right to vote, in much the same way as property qualifications had been regarded for most of the nineteenth century.

As long as the Labour and Conservative parties succeeded in dominating British politics from 1945 to 1974, there was not much compelling pressure to change the electoral system and only the Liberals and a few idealists in the Electoral Reform Society upheld the banner of proportional representation as the leading alternative to first-past-the-post. On the other hand, the celebrated stability and familiarity of the plurality or first-past-the-post system of voting can be seen as yet another example of the British propensity to invent traditions when it suits them, whether in the constitutional arena or in other spheres of life, since we have not used this electoral system in unadulterated form for very long and the arguments in its favour have tended to come from those in the two main parties who have gained most from it.

The dam began to break in the early 1970s when the Heath Administration decided to introduce proportional representation (single transferable vote) for local elections in Northern Ireland as part of its conscious attempts to promote power sharing between Protestant Unionists and Catholic Nationalists in the Province. With the Labour Party narrowly returned to Government in the two General Elections of 1974 and then finding itself in a minority position in the House of Commons from 1977 to 1979 and dependent upon the so-called Lib-Lab Pact and the tacit support of other small parties, the climate for electoral reform improved and a significant all-party campaign (which was supported by about 100 Conservative MPs) was conducted for the adoption of proportional representation (PR) in some form. However, as the 1998 Jenkins Commission Report later observed when reviewing the successive attempts of electoral reformers over the years to change the system in a more proportional direction, 'their desire to improve the electoral system has tended to vary in inverse proportion to their ability to do anything about it'.[12]

In 1979 the elections to the European Parliament were held under a uniform electoral system of proportional representation in all the member states of the European Community *except* the United Kingdom. Throughout the long period of Conservative rule from then until 1997, political opinion in the other parties became increasingly well disposed towards a move to PR, although there was always a strong and determined group within the Labour Party that wanted to cling to first-past-the-post for their own party political reasons.[13]

The result of all these cumulative developments was that by the time of the 1997 General Election the Liberal Democrats were committed in their Manifesto 'to introduce proportional representation for all elections in order to put more power in the hands of voters and make government more representative'; meanwhile the Labour Party was careful in its Manifesto to avoid committing itself explicitly to PR for Westminster elections, but was prepared to commit itself to the creation of a devolved Scottish Parliament and a devolved Welsh Assembly, both of which would be elected by a semi-proportional additional member system.

The constitutional plot thickened, however, when in four paragraphs of the Report of the Joint Labour–Liberal Democrat Consultative Committee on Constitutional Reform, which was published only weeks before the 1997 General Election, it was made clear that 'both parties believe that a referendum on the system for elections to the House of Commons should be held within the first term of a new Parliament' and both parties agreed that 'the referendum should be a single question offering a straight choice between first-past-the-post and one specific proportional alternative'. The document went on to commit both parties to the

establishment of a Commission on Voting Systems early in the new Parliament (which would be asked to report within twelve months) 'to recommend the appropriate proportional alternative to the first-past-the-post system' in a way which would 'command broad consensus among proponents of proportional representation'.

The sub-text of this document was clear for all to see: the Liberal Democrats were trying to nail down the Labour Party to an unambiguous and actionable pledge 'to allow the crucial question of how our Government is elected to be decided by the people themselves' in a referendum to be held during the first term of a Labour Administration, whereas many leading figures in the Labour Party (although not all) were trying to leave themselves enough room for manoeuvre either to press ahead towards PR if Liberal Democrat support proved to be essential to their holding office or to wriggle out of the 'commitment' if the Labour majority was sufficient to enable them to do without any such deals with a junior partner. In retrospect we can clearly see that the cautious faction in the Labour leadership won the day and that the Liberal Democrats have not so far managed to get any closer to their supreme objective which is PR for elections to the UK Parliament at Westminster.

Proportional representation in practice

Following New Labour's resounding victory in the May 1997 General Election, the path to electoral reform was initially routed via the new voting systems for Scotland, Wales, Northern Ireland, Greater London and Europe – in fact, anywhere but Westminster and the mosaic of local government.

In Scotland, Labour came to power in 1997 with a commitment to implement the proposals of the Scottish Constitutional Convention, which had included a proportional voting system at the insistence of the Liberal Democrats. The system chosen was a mixed electoral system (known as the additional member system) under which 73 members of the Scottish Parliament were elected from single-member constituencies by first-past-the-post, but a further 56 members were elected from closed party lists in each of the eight Scottish regions which corresponded to the European Parliament constituencies.

In adopting this strategy, the Labour Party in Scotland was reconciling itself to a sub-optimal performance in the Scottish Parliament election, compared with the boost it would have received under first-past-the-post, but consoling itself with the thought that it had taken out a reliable insurance policy against an outright SNP victory which could be a prelude to moves for Scotland's secession from the United Kingdom. In the event, when the Scottish Parliament elections were held in May 1999, Labour achieved its strategic objective of seeing off the SNP. Yet the actual result was ironical in that Labour won 73 per cent of the first-past-the-post constituency seats with only 39 per cent of the constituency votes, whereas with an additional 34 per cent of the regional list votes it was only able to win 5 per cent of the regional list seats. On the other hand, the electoral multipliers worked in the opposite direction for the Scottish National Party in that with 29 per cent of the constituency votes it won only 10 per cent of the constituency seats, whereas with 27 per cent of the additional regional list votes it won fully 50 per cent of the regional list seats.

In Wales, Labour came to power in 1997 with formidable voting strength in the Principality, but with the Welsh Labour Party deeply divided over the merits of the devolution policy. In order not to frighten the anti-devolution faction, Ron Davies decided the Welsh Assembly should be as small as possible, with a total of just 60 members: 40 constituency members and 20 additional members to provide an element of proportionality. Whereas in Scotland the ratio between constituency and additional members had been 57 per cent to 43 per cent, in Wales it became 67 per cent to 33 per cent. Even with the benefit of this more limited proportionality, the Labour Party in Wales was able to win overall only 47 per cent of the seats in the Welsh Assembly, which translated into only 28 out of 60 Members and hence obliged Labour to form a minority Administration. Whereas the multipliers in this mixed electoral system had not worked

well in Labour's favour, it was interesting to note that Plaid Cymru's result in regional list votes across the Principality was close to strict proportionality in that the party won 28 per cent of the seats in the Assembly with 30 per cent of the regional list votes.

The real political story in both these elections for the devolved Assemblies in 1999 was that the Labour Party preferred *to share power* by forming Coalition Administrations with the Liberal Democrats rather than risk ceding power to either the Scottish National Party or Plaid Cymru. Thus it was that the late Donald Dewar, as Leader of the Labour Party in Scotland, formed a Coalition Administration with the Scottish Liberal Democrats led by Jim Wallace at the outset of the Edinburgh Parliament's existence, while in Wales it took a further year of precarious minority government and a change of Labour Party leader in the Principality to persuade the Wales Labour Party to form a Coalition Executive with the Welsh Liberal Democrats.

Power sharing has also been the *leitmotiv* of politics *in Northern Ireland*, at any rate since the Heath Administration abolished the first-past-the-post Stormont Parliament in 1972 and introduced in its place an ill-fated power-sharing Executive and Assembly in 1973. For this reason above all others and in view of the continuing attempts by successive British Governments to overcome the sectarian divide in Northern Ireland, the political imperative has been to use a non-majoritarian voting system both for local elections and for elections to any Northern Ireland Assembly.

The chosen system in Northern Ireland has been the single transferable vote (STV), to which the Irish both north and south of the border have become quite well accustomed. The results of the Northern Ireland Assembly elections held under STV in June 1998 revealed an almost exact correspondence between the proportion of first preference votes achieved by each of the four main parties in the Province and the proportion of seats which each won in the Assembly.[14] Once again, we have an example of how British politicians in Government in London have sought to tailor each electoral system to the priorities for each elected body in the different parts of the United Kingdom rather than pursue a more coherent vision of what all electoral systems are supposed to achieve.

In the case of the May 2000 elections for *London*, the new Mayor of London, Ken Livingstone, was elected by supplementary vote, while the members of the Greater London Assembly were elected by the additional member system. The rationale for this distinction was essentially that the Mayor of London has some real, but limited, executive powers – e.g. in relation to public transport, law and order and environmental management – and should therefore benefit from an electoral system which ensures that the winner can claim a popular mandate by emerging with at least 50 per cent of the votes cast. On the other hand, the Members of the Greater London Assembly have only the supervisory task of holding the Mayor to account between elections every four years and are therefore elected by a more proportional system.

In the case of the June 1999 elections to the *European Parliament*, there were two justifications for these to be held under a proportional list system according to which the people voted regionally for one party's list of candidates in preference to others and, depending upon the strength of public support, a party could get all or most or some or none of its candidates elected to the Parliament. The first justification was that the United Kingdom had a long-standing commitment to align the way European Parliament elections were conducted in the United Kingdom with the uniform electoral procedure adopted in all the other member states in accordance with Article 138(8) of the 1957 Rome Treaty. The second justification was that since the European Parliament does not supply or even directly support Ministers in Government (that being the principal role of the national Parliaments), it is appropriate for its Members to be elected according to a proportional system which places more weight upon trying to achieve fair representation than strong public accountability.

However, the regional list system for European Parliament elections has two peculiar characteristics. *Firstly*, because of variations in the population of the different regions of the UK, the voters are not able to elect the same number of MEPs in each region. In England in 1999, for example, the minimum threshold of voting support needed to secure at least one MEP varied from 8 per cent in the South East to 12 per cent in the South West. *Secondly*, the lists are 'closed lists' in which the party bosses, not the voters, decide the order of precedence on their own party lists, thus preventing the voters from being able to plump for one particularly favoured candidate in preference to all the others.

The Jenkins Commission and the future

The big prize which has so far eluded those who have been campaigning for some form of proportional or semi-proportional representation is any change in the basis for elections to the UK Parliament at Westminster. Tony Blair and his senior Ministerial colleagues were able to dodge having to make a time-specific commitment to a referendum on this subject during the 1997–2001 Parliament, and hit upon a suitably vague formula for the subsequent Parliament which was actually less bankable for the Liberal Democrats than the one they thought they had before.[15]

It is worth recalling the terms of reference given by Ministers to the Jenkins Commission on the Voting System in December 1997. These were that the Commission should feel free 'to consider and recommend any appropriate system or combination of systems in recommending an alternative to the present system for Parliamentary elections to be put before the people in the Government's referendum'; and that in doing its work the Commission should 'observe the requirement for broad proportionality, the need for stable Government, an extension of voter choice and the maintenance of a link between M.P.s and geographical constituencies'.[16]

From the outset of its swift inquiry the Jenkins Commission had to juggle with the four mutually incompatible requirements which were inserted into its terms of reference. The Commission was able to escape from these constraints only by exploring the full degree of elasticity inherent in the requirements. For example, it took the requirement for *broad proportionality* to mean limited rather than full-blown proportionality; it took the requirement for *stable government* to include coalition government as well as single-party government; it took the requirement for extended *voter choice* to mean choice between individual candidates rather than choice between parties to form a single-party government; and it exploited the loophole provided by the reference to *a link* between MPs and geographical constituencies (rather than *the* link) in order to make this requirement a less decisive obstacle than it would otherwise have been to any form of multi-member constituency representation. The Commission's method was to arrive at its conclusions and recommendations by a process of elimination which involved looking at virtually every conceivable form of proportional or semi-proportional representation in the world and then searching for the one which could be presented as the most compatible with the four requirements. It gave short shrift to the existing first-past-the-post system (FPTP) because the whole purpose of the exercise was to come forward with *a single alternative system*, so that this could be put to the British people as one of only two choices in a future referendum.

Towards the end of its elegant report, the Commission recognised that the essence of its task had been

> to use the flexibility of a Top-Up system to strike such a balance as best to reconcile the four requirements of our terms of reference with our view of fairness, both of representation and of proportionality of power . . . and to do so in a way which offers a reasonable chance of our work being fecund rather than sterile.[17]

In other words, Lord Jenkins and his colleagues were keen to make a clear recommendation which could be used as *the* alternative to the existing system in a national referendum on electoral reform rather than simply to write yet another learned and elegant report which would gather dust in a Home Office filing cabinet. Recognising that there was no such thing as a perfect electoral system, they were prepared to cut corners, chop logic and make compromises. Lord Jenkins himself understandably wanted to keep all five members of the Commission on board (something which he failed to do, since Lord Alexander felt impelled to write a strong *Note of Reservation*) and he made a genuine attempt to propitiate *all* the political parties whose future electoral prospects were bound to be at stake.

With these thoughts in mind, all five members of the Commission endorsed the idea of a mixed electoral system which would be made up of constituency MPs and list MPs drawn from open top-up lists, but only four of them endorsed the alternative vote as the way of electing the constituency MPs, since Lord Alexander strongly preferred to use the existing FPTP system for this purpose. Thus the central recommendation of the majority of the Commission was that the best alternative to the existing FPTP system would be a two-vote mixed system which could be described either as a limited additional member system (a dilute version of the German electoral system) or an alternative vote system (similar to the system for the Australian House of Representatives), but modified by additional MPs drawn from open top-up party lists in which the order of precedence of the candidates could be determined by the voters and not by the parties. The vast majority of MPs (80 to 85 per cent) would continue to be elected by individual constituencies which under AV (alternative vote) might produce more *disproportional* results than the present FPTP system. The remaining 15 to 20 per cent of MPs would be elected on a top-up basis which would significantly reduce this disproportionality and the geographical schisms which are inherent in FPTP. In other words, the majority of the Commission came up with a compromise which was close to the German electoral system, but nothing like so proportional and intended not to be so party-dominated.

The majority of the Commission strove mightily, and rather defensively, to explain the 'positive features' of this system as follows. *Firstly*, there would be fewer wasted votes than under FPTP, since the second preferences of voters who did not vote for the candidate who led on the first count could potentially influence the final result, thus perhaps encouraging a higher turn-out. *Secondly*, it would encourage serious candidates to pitch their appeal to the broad majority of their constituents rather than simply the hard core of their party faithful, which should result in more inclusive politics than under FPTP. *Thirdly*, and really another formulation of the same point, it would discourage all candidates from making intemperate attacks upon their rivals in other parties, and thereby forfeiting the possibility of attracting the second preferences of voters who had supported other candidates on the first count. The objective once again was to contribute to a more consensual and less confrontational style of politics.

Fourthly, it was claimed that the use of the additional vote would empower the *voters* before the election and disempower the *parties* after the election by making it less likely that the result of a General Election would be vitiated by party leaders doing deals after an election when they had campaigned fiercely against each other before the election. *Finally*, the use of AV would guarantee that constituency MPs were elected (perhaps after several counts) by a majority of the votes cast in their constituencies which, it was hoped, would give them more democratic legitimacy in the eyes of the electorate than they had derived from FPTP at the 1997 General Election, for example, when only about three-fifths of all MPs could claim this degree of support.

It is worth dwelling upon Lord Alexander's *Note of Reservation* about the use of the alternative vote for the election of constituency MPs, since it crystallised many of the weak or suspect points in the majority recommendation. His preference was to stick with FPTP for the election of the constituency MPs, because the system was sound in principle, easy to understand and capable of commanding the enduring respect of the electorate. He then took issue with the arguments put forward by his colleagues in favour of AV on the following grounds.[18]

Firstly, Lord Alexander argued that most votes in British General Elections are cast essentially for *a party* to form the Government rather than for an individual candidate to be an MP – indeed, in most voters' minds the latter is only a means to achieve the former. *Secondly*, he disputed the importance of his colleagues' preoccupation with trying to achieve a less confrontational style of politics and cited the example of Australia to cast doubt upon the assertion that AV necessarily produces a more consensual style. *Thirdly*, he challenged the key assertion of his colleagues that AV would give more power to the *voters* before a General Election and less to the *parties* after it by pointing out that tactical voting under AV 'could further heighten the tendency and lead to attempts by two parties to marshal their supporters so as to gang up on a third'. *Fourthly*, he detected no groundswell of enthusiasm for AV in the evidence submitted to the Commission in view of the fact that the Conservative Party preferred FPTP, the Liberal Democrats and the Electoral Reform Society preferred STV, the Labour Party had not explicitly endorsed AV, and the electoral systems introduced for the Scottish Parliament and the Welsh Assembly involved the use of FPTP, not AV, for the election of constituency MPs.

Lord Alexander's fundamental objection to AV, however, was that it could not be regarded as sound or fair in principle and its effects were likely to be more *disproportional* than proportional, as his colleagues on the Commission had conceded. Indeed, AV would have a tendency to punish unpopular parties *disproportionately*, no matter whether they had been in Opposition or in Government – e.g. the Labour Party in 1983 or the Conservative Party in 1997. In particular, he could not support a system such as AV, which gives weight to the second preferences of those voters who support the least attractive candidates on the first count, but ignores the second preferences of those voters who support the two candidates with the highest proportion of first preference votes. Moreover, he could not support the idea implicit in AV that the second preferences of the former group of voters should be given equal weight with the first preferences of the latter group. He also forecast an element of cruel hazard in the way that AV would probably work in constituencies where the issue was not decided at the first count. For example, in a seat where the Conservative candidate came first on the first count (but did not achieve an overall majority of first preferences) his or her fate would depend entirely upon whether the second preference votes of the third and subsequent candidates were given to the runner-up or to some other candidate lower down the pecking order on the first count. What this really demonstrated was that electoral outcomes would be as vulnerable to the perversity of tactical voting under AV as they have been under FPTP.

The method of voting unanimously proposed by the Commission for the additional *top-up members* was necessarily complicated in detail, but was aimed in general at correcting the acknowledged dispro-portionality of the results under an AV system for the preponderance of constituency members.[19] This second vote, which would be available to the electorate on the ballot paper, could be cast either for an individual candidate or for a party list, and the counting of such second votes should be done in such a way that the corrective leverage towards proportionality was maintained. This meant that account would have to be taken not only of how many second votes a party received, but also how many constituency seats within the top-up area it had already won.

The size of the top-up areas would be a key variable in that the larger they were, the more proportional the electoral outcomes were likely to be. The Commission opted for relatively small top-up areas – i.e. traditional Counties in most rural areas and Metropolitan Districts in most urban areas. This was consistent with the Commission's stated preference for no more than *limited propor-tionality* as a corrective to the disproportionality of the alternative vote. Furthermore, parties should not be eligible for top-up seats unless they had contested at least half of the constituencies in a top-up area, in order to preclude the possibility of a party simply becoming a top-up party. As to whether there should be a minimum of electoral support to be achieved by any party before it qualified for representation in Parliament, the Commission saw no need for such a threshold since on the basis of the 1997 General Election result the lowest percentage of the total vote which would have placed a party in likely contention for a top-up seat would have been the 11 per cent achieved by the Liberal Democrats in Nottinghamshire.

As the Commission saw things, the principal advantage of such a mixed, two-vote system was its *'flexibility'*. It retained the single-member constituencies which are so dear to most MPs at Westminster, while introducing a modest element of proportionality. The 80:20 split recommended by the Commission would produce only a semi-proportional outcome, but one which, the members hoped, might prove more acceptable to guardians of the status quo in each of the two main parties. Lord Jenkins and his colleagues hoped and assumed that their recommendations would be taken seriously and observed rather wryly that 'if this disposition persists, this Labour Government will have the unique distinction of having broken the spell under which parties when they want to reform do not have the power and when they have the power do not want to reform'.[20]

Although the Jenkins Report received a favourable media response on publication, the recommendations and conclusions put forward by the Commission proved fairly easy for Tony Blair and Jack Straw to pigeon-hole. This is essentially because the Labour Party has been divided about the need or desirability of introducing electoral reform for elections to Westminster and because there is no overriding reason why the Labour Government should concede to persistent Liberal Democrat pressure on this issue unless a future Blair Administration becomes convinced that this is the best way to engender a Labour–Liberal Democrat Coalition Government and hence lock the Conservatives out of national political office for a generation or more.

Of course, much of the discussion on this issue has been predicated upon the assumption that in a national referendum the British people would vote *for* electoral reform and, in particular, for the rather complicated variant recommended in the Jenkins Commission Report. Yet it is hard to argue that such an outcome would be a foregone conclusion, especially if the opponents of change were able to demonstrate convincingly that the real intention of the advocates of electoral reform was indefinitely to exclude one of the two main parties from participating in national Government. Indeed, the Jenkins Commission was careful in the final two paragraphs of its analysis to say that, even if a change in the electoral system for Westminster were made following a national referendum in which the people voted for it, a review should take place (advised and very probably conducted by the independent Electoral Commission) after perhaps two General Elections had been held under the new system.

The role and regulation of referenda

We noted at the beginning of this chapter that, with the single exception of the Northern Ireland Border Poll initiated by Edward Heath's Conservative Administration in March 1973, it has been successive Labour Governments which have had increasing recourse to referenda as expedient devices to resolve tricky political or constitutional problems which at the relevant times appeared insoluble by exclusively Parliamentary means. To some extent this has reflected the diminishing authority and legitimacy of Parliament, at any rate as it is habitually used and abused by the Government of the day. Yet there has also been a perfectly rational and respectable case for the increasing use of referenda in this country, essentially because, in the absence of a codified constitution, no other means of decision making can command such unanswerable authority, especially on those issues in which the very future of our Parliament is engaged. Indeed, the case for having more frequent recourse to referenda in this country was acknowledged by the Labour Party in one of its policy documents published in Opposition.[21]

In the early years of the twentieth century, A.V. Dicey advocated the use of a referendum as a 'democratic' device for defeating Liberal policy on Irish Home Rule at a time when the Asquith Administration had support for the policy from a sizeable majority in the Commons but the Tories were successfully resisting it in the House of Lords. Nothing came of his initiative at that time and for years thereafter referenda remained unused in the United Kingdom. Indeed, the idea became seriously discredited as a constitutional device for the United Kingdom as a result of its association with the manipulated plebiscites held by Hitler to endorse some of his policies in Nazi Germany.

What is more, Britain's heroic experience in the Second World War served to reinforce the nation's commitment to its own variant of Parliamentary government. Thus Clement Attlee gave the idea short shrift after the war, and many years later what became the conventional Parliamentarist point of view on this issue was endorsed by Margaret Thatcher soon after she became the Leader of the Opposition in 1975.[22]

However, by the mid-1970s many prominent members of the British political class felt much less sanguine about the authority of Government and Parliament, and there was much intellectual chatter about how this country had allegedly become ungovernable. In these circumstances the tide of political opinion began to turn and people began to look more favourably upon a referendum as a convenient and effective device for resolving big constitutional issues for which the authority of Government and Parliament combined was clearly insufficient. This was especially true in relation to Britain's contested membership of the European Communities which split both main parties and which had to be resolved by a national referendum in June 1975. That successful experience was undoubtedly influential in persuading the precariously based Callaghan Administration to agree to referenda with special conditions on the almost equally contentious issues of devolution for Scotland and Wales – an optimistic step which ended in tears for the Labour Government when the people of both Scotland and Wales failed to give the policy a sufficiently ringing endorsement to bring the legislation into effect.

Thus the experience of referenda in this country before May 1997 was not uniformly satisfactory.[23] Although the political elite discovered the utility and attractions of a referendum in some cases, it was obvious that the device had a boomerang quality which could come back to damage some of those who used it. Nevertheless in an age when political deference had declined almost to vanishing point and the traditional authority of Government and Parliament was seriously damaged if not totally discredited, politicians of Tony Blair's generation could see the attractions of referenda, especially as a way of inhibiting potential opposition to controversial policies from within the governing party or settling large constitutional issues on which each of the main parties was split and the usual forms of party discipline were likely to be ineffective in delivering the required political results. See *Box 14* for the results of referenda held in the United Kingdom to date.

For better or for worse, the use of referenda – whether at national, regional or local level – seems to have become an acknowledged part of our constitutional arrangements in the United Kingdom. It is therefore worth identifying the steps along the way which have influenced the present statutory rules and informal conventions which govern the use of these formerly alien constitutional instruments.

In April 1996 the Constitution Unit and the Electoral Reform Society set up a joint Commission under the chairmanship of Sir Patrick Nairne, a former Whitehall Permanent Secretary,

> to prepare for the possibility that referendums may, in the future, be invoked as an instrument of decision making in the United Kingdom by examining the problems involved in the conduct of referendums; and setting out organisational and administrative guidelines for the conduct of referendums.[24]

There were four main conclusions in the Nairne Report.

Firstly, the Commission recognised that referenda could significantly assist Governments in laying the ground for controversial legislation and provide extra legitimacy for controversial policy decisions after legislation had been enacted. *Secondly*, it argued that the holding of referenda need not pose any threat to Parliamentary sovereignty in so far as it remained open to the Government of the day and to Parliament to legislate for a referendum either on a one-off basis or as a generic Referendum Act which could later be amended or repealed. *Thirdly*, in his Foreword Sir Patrick observed that since previous referenda had been held on the hoof, it would be important in future to establish generally agreed guidelines which would 'ensure consistency of administration in their conduct and maximize confidence in the legitimacy of their results'.[25] The Report duly suggested 20 organisational and administrative guidelines which were deemed essential if future

referenda were to be conducted in a manner that could be regarded by everyone as efficient and fair. *Fourthly*, it argued that because the Government of the day was invariably *parti pris* in relation to the issues put to a referendum for decision, the conduct of such campaigns should be supervised and policed by an independent statutory Commission or by a new Electoral Commission if one were established.

When, nearly two years later, the Neill Committee on Standards in Public Life produced its report on *The Funding of Political Parties*, it took advantage of its broad remit to look at many of the political issues raised by referendum campaigns.[26] This undoubtedly created a further head of steam in the first Blair Administration to include new rules for the conduct of referenda in any legislation which it planned for the regulation of political parties and election campaigns.

The Neill Committee proposed a regime of statutory registration for individuals and organisations wishing to take part in any referendum campaign, a regime which would ensure full disclosure of both donations and support in kind for those taking part. It suggested entrusting to the proposed Electoral Commission responsibility for deciding which organisations, if any, should qualify for core funding from the tax-payers and strongly recommended that each side in a referendum campaign should be treated equally in this respect, as well as in respect of free mailing, free broadcasting and free use of premises for public meetings. The Committee's most controversial and least realistic recommendation was that the Government of the day should remain neutral in any referendum campaign and should not distribute even purportedly 'factual' material on the issues for public decision. This last stricture, along with some other recommendations in the Report, proved unacceptable to Labour Ministers and in a subsequent White Paper the Government rejected some of the Neill Committee's proposals.[27] For example, Ministers were only prepared to place a ban upon campaigning material produced by the Government of the day for a period of up to 28 days before the date set for a referendum and they favoured the imposition of overall spending limits upon

Box 14 Results of referenda held in the United Kingdom

Northern Ireland border poll, 8th March 1973
Do you want Northern Ireland to remain part of the United Kingdom? – 98.9 per cent
Do you want Northern Ireland to be joined with the Republic of Ireland outside the United Kingdom? – 1.1 per cent
Turn-out: 58.7 per cent

Referendum on UK membership of the EEC, 5th June 1975
Do you think that the United Kingdom should stay in the European Community (the Common Market)?
Yes 67.2 per cent No 32.8 per cent Turn-out: 64 per cent

Referendum on devolution for Scotland, 1st March 1979
Do you want the provisions of the Scotland Act 1978 to be put into effect?
Yes 51.6 per cent No 48.4 per cent Turn-out: 63.6 per cent
At least 40 per cent of the qualified electorate had to vote Yes for the legislation to take effect. In the event only 32.8 per cent voted Yes, so the result was inoperative.

Referendum on devolution for Wales, 1st March 1979
Do you want the provisions of the Wales Act 1978 to be put into effect?
Yes 20.3 per cent No 79.7 per cent Turn-out: 58.8 per cent
At least 40 per cent of the qualified electorate had to vote Yes for the legislation to take effect
In the event only 11.9 per cent voted Yes, so the result was inoperative

Referendum on Scottish devolution, 11th September 1997
I agree that there should be a Scottish Parliament – 74.3 per cent
I do not agree that there should be a Scottish Parliament – 25.7 per cent
I agree that a Scottish Parliament should have tax-raising powers – 63.5 per cent
I do not agree that a Scottish Parliament should have tax-raising powers – 36.5 per cent
Turn-out: 60.2 per cent

Referendum on Welsh devolution, 18th September 1997
I agree that there should be a Welsh Assembly – 50.3 per cent
I do not agree that there should be a Welsh Assembly – 49.7 per cent
Turn-out: 50.1 per cent

Referendum on the establishment of a Greater London Authority, 7th May 1998
Are you in favour of the Government's proposals for a Greater London Authority made up of an elected Mayor and a separately elected Assembly?
Yes 72 per cent No 28 per cent Turn-out: 34 per cent

Referendum on the Belfast Agreement, 22nd May 1998
Do you support the Agreement reached at the multi-party talks in Northern Ireland and set out in Command Paper 3883?
Yes 71.1 per cent No 28.9 per cent Turn-out: 81 per cent

campaigning groups rather than any particular permitted time period.

The statutory outcome of this lengthy iterative process to develop a suitable regulatory framework for the conduct of referenda was Part VII of the *Political Parties, Elections and Referendums Act 2000*. The purpose of the legislation was to make generic provision for the conduct of major referenda in the United Kingdom, but it was envisaged that dedicated primary legislation would normally be required to provide the legislative basis for any particular referendum. Under Section 96 an outer limit of six months was prescribed for the referendum period (i.e. from the introduction of the enabling legislation to the date of the poll) and under Section 97 a minimum of 28 days was set for a campaign period (from the time when the Electoral Commission designated the competing campaign organisations to the date of the poll). Section 98 gave a statutory definition of 'permitted participants' in any referendum campaign; these might be either a registered political party or an individual, company or unincorporated association which had made the necessary declaration.

Section 101 enabled the Electoral Commission to designate two or more umbrella organisations which would then qualify for the receipt of public funds. Section 103 enabled the Commission to award to each designated organisation, subject to certain conditions of financial accountability, a grant of up to £600,000. Benefits may also be conferred on designated organisations similar to those conferred on individual candidates and political parties in election campaigns – namely, one free postal delivery to every household or elector, the use of premises free of charge for public meetings and access to free broadcasting time, subject to the decisions of the broadcasting authorities.

Section 110 made it an offence for anyone to incur referendum expenses of more than £10,000 unless they were deemed by the Electoral Commission to be a 'permitted participant' and Section 111 together with Schedule 13 imposed precise limits upon the referendum expenses which might be incurred by permitted participants – i.e. £5 million for a designated umbrella organisation, various sums between £5 million and £500,000 for a registered

political party (arithmetically related to the percentage of the votes cast for each party at the previous General Election), and £500,000 for any other permitted participant.[28]

Section 118 was controversial in that it debarred the Government of the day or a local authority or any other publicly funded body (other than the Electoral Commission) from publishing, displaying or distributing promotional material relating to any aspect of a referendum only for a maximum of 28 days prior to the date of the poll – and then only material made available to the public at large, *not* material specifically *requested* by a member of the public. This provision looked set to drive a coach and horses through the restrictive regime that had been advocated by the Neill Committee in its wish to eliminate the disproportionate effects of Government information and propaganda upon the outcome of any referendum campaign. Yet realistically it would have been very surprising if any Government had reached any other conclusion on this point since, having the sole effective right to *initiate* referenda in this country, it is hardly likely to throw away its propaganda advantage completely; and as Jack Straw argued in defending the Government's position, a Government has a duty to inform the public.

Issues raised by the use of referenda

The most fundamental issue raised by any national referendum in this country is whether it is intended by the Government of the day to preserve or overcome the position taken by Parliament on the public policy issue concerned. A referendum held *after* Parliament has approved a certain decision taken by the Executive – sometimes referred to as a post-legislative or confirmatory referendum – is likely to be regarded by the Government of the day as welcome confirmation if it gets its own way or perhaps merely advisory if it does not. Thus when the result of the 1975 referendum was Yes to continued British membership of the European Communities, the Wilson Administration in office at the time felt able to regard the public's decision as a ratification of the decisions previously taken by the Government and endorsed by Parliament. However, if the result had been No, the same Ministers might well have tried to argue that the public's vote was merely advisory and need not affect the broadly pro-European direction of Government policy.

On the other hand, a referendum held *before* Parliament has been asked to approve a certain course of action – sometimes referred to as a pre-legislative or precautionary referendum – is likely to be regarded by the Government of the day as a convenient way of overcoming or at least minimising opposition to its preferred policy, whether from among its own political supporters or elsewhere, and in those circumstances the result is effectively binding upon Parliament and the nation at large. Thus the two sets of questions put to the Scottish people in the 1997 referendum on Scottish devolution were carefully designed to secure the *imprimatur* of the Scottish people soon enough in the game to leave any opponents of devolution, whether at Westminster or in Scotland, in no doubt about the political unwisdom of opposing the policy. Admittedly, in our representative democracy with its doctrine of Parliamentary supremacy, it may be argued that all referenda are *theoretically* no more than advisory. Yet in practice the results are usually *mandatory* in the sense that any British Government in modern circumstances is likely to abide by the people's decision, however awkward that may be for the continuation of established Government policy – at least until a suitable opportunity arises to put the question to the people again.[29]

Another issue which arises is who should be allowed *to initiate* a referendum and thus have the capacity to influence its timing. In the United Kingdom, although influential individuals and groups can campaign for a referendum to be held on a given issue at a given time, only the Government of the day supported by a working majority in the House of Commons has the power to initiate a referendum and to determine when it will be held. Thus the timing of a future referendum on whether or not this country should abolish the Pound and adopt the Euro as its currency is effectively a matter

of Executive privilege; Tony Blair and Gordon Brown will be careful to put the question to the people only if and when they believe that their recommended course of action will attract majority support from the general public. This is in marked contrast with the constitutional position in some other democracies, such as Italy or certain states of the United States, where the right to initiate a referendum (subject to certain minimum thresholds being crossed) can be exercised, in Italy, by a petition from at least 500,000 voters or five Regional Councils and has to be ratified by the Constitutional Court or, in California, by a write-in campaign by a sufficient number of qualified voters to put the 'Proposition' on the ballot at a state election.

There are other related issues too. Who should be able to formulate the question or questions to be answered in a referendum? Who should make up the appropriate electorate empowered to take the decision? (In the referenda on Scottish and Welsh devolution, for example, should it have been people throughout the UK rather than simply those living in Scotland and Wales?) Who should decide whether the result should be subject to the approval of a minimum proportion of those voting or the eligible electorate, as was the case with the 1979 referenda on devolution to Scotland and Wales? All these apparently small details connected with the conduct of a referendum can influence or even determine the result, so it is probably just as well that we now have the benefit of the independent Electoral Commission whose chairman, Sam Younger, has already made it clear that he and his fellow Commissioners will advise the Government on the intelligibility and the fairness of referendum questions. Indeed, there may be media and public pressure for the Electoral Commission to take responsibility for dealing with some of the other issues mentioned which are currently still in the hands of the Government of the day.

Finally, it is worth sketching what are likely to be the most significant effects of future referenda held within the United Kingdom. On the negative side, it seems likely that more frequent recourse to referenda will contribute to the further diminution of Parliament in the eyes of the people, as various forms of direct democracy come to rival or even surpass representative democracy as ways of taking at least some political decisions in this country. Moreover, the nature of debate during referendum campaigns can provide opportunities for demagogues and especially tabloid journalists to mislead the public with their sensationalism and so increase the danger of perverse decisions. On the positive side, any well-conducted referendum campaign will provide valuable opportunities for members of the public to pay more attention than usual to difficult political issues and to give constructive thought to important political questions before making up their collective mind. It will also offer a means of resolving (not necessarily for ever) difficult constitutional issues which, it seems, can no longer be settled by the political class on its own acting within our traditional political institutions.

General reflections

There are a number of important themes which run through the adjustments which the first Blair Administration made to the various methods of democratic decision making in this country. The first is undoubtedly *the deliberate move away from self-regulation* towards more independent and transparent arrangements for the policing of elections and referenda – now under the control of the newly established Electoral Commission. This was in marked contrast with the traditional approach in the United Kingdom which allowed the House of Commons to regulate not only its own procedures but also the ways in which its members were elected and re-elected.

The second theme is *the self-conscious drive to increase democratic participation* in our society by making our electoral and decision-making arrangements more voter-friendly in every conceivable way. This reflects the widespread concern about low and seemingly declining levels of turn-out at General Elections which have fallen from a peak of 84 per cent in 1950, when the two main parties together accounted for over 90 per cent of the votes cast, to a low point of just under 60 per cent in 2001 and what threaten to be still lower levels at future

General Elections unless the recent remedial measures have a positive effect. The situation has been even worse at European Parliament elections (in 1999 the turn-out across the UK was only 24 per cent) and in local government elections where the normal turn-out is typically about 30 to 40 per cent. Maybe there is some hope to be found in the pronouncements of senior Labour Ministers who have seemed determined to develop new ways of enhancing democratic participation for the benefit of society at large. For example, the Lord Chancellor, Lord Irvine, made an encouraging point to the Franco-British Lawyers' Association in Paris in February 1998 when he spoke of 'our determination to ensure that people have their say in major constitutional change – this is essential in restoring public confidence in government'.[30]

The third theme is *the movement towards more representative political institutions* which Labour Ministers and Labour Party officials evidently believe can be achieved, at least in part, by manipulating or tilting the processes of candidate selection in ways designed to favour previously under-represented categories. For example, in the 2001 Labour Manifesto a clear commitment was made to introduce legislation to allow each party to make positive moves to increase the representation of women at Westminster.[31] This may have been because the number of Labour women selected for winnable seats in June 2001 was actually *below* the number elected in May 1997 and the numbers of candidates from among people with disabilities and the ethnic minorities were also disappointingly low.

Those who oppose New Labour on this point, who are to be found within the ranks of the Labour Party as well as outside it, accuse Ministers of seeking to distort traditional democratic processes and limiting freedom of local choice. Yet this form of affirmative action, which is sometimes dismissed by its opponents as 'political correctness', has definitely taken hold of various institutions throughout our society (e.g. the police, the legal profession and the Church of England) to such an extent that even the formerly reactionary Conservative Party has felt obliged to alter its official rhetoric, and perhaps its practices, to take account of this contemporary social trend.

This theme is consistent with another stated goal of New Labour – namely *social inclusion* – which has been a cross-cutting objective in nearly all Labour policy where it can be sensibly applied. It has been advocated on the philosophical ground of fairness and the demagogic ground of anti-elitism. However, we should pay particular heed to the *constitutional* argument which is all to do with the worthy goal of enhancing the authority and legitimacy of democratic decision making in our society. The idea is that more representative political institutions will tend to produce more democratically acceptable decisions and so attract stronger public support and achieve greater political legitimacy.

The final theme in this chapter has been the search for a method of democratic decision making which will be able to produce *more legitimate and more durable political decisions* on some of the biggest and most controversial issues which face the country. Most, if not all, of these issues have a significant constitutional content, which is why we are gradually moving towards a dispensation which differentiates between 'ordinary' political decisions, which can continue to be made by elected and representative institutions, and 'constitutional' decisions, which require the extra legitimacy that can only be provided by a suitable mechanism of direct democracy – notably the referendum. This sort of distinction is accepted in nearly all the other member states of the European Union and it may only be a matter of time before it is accepted in the United Kingdom.

The main barrier to all such changes is to be found in the constitutional conservatism of influential Ministers, shadow Ministers and backbenchers in the House of Commons, supported by academic and legal apologists, who seem unwilling or unable to abandon the twin doctrines of Parliamentary supremacy and single-party rule. The former doctrine would suggest that it is theoretically impossible to entrench any constitutional change, no matter how significant or far reaching it may be. The latter severely discourages any form of coalition Government between the parties represented at Westminster, but not – be it noted – in the devolved Assemblies or local authorities elsewhere in the United Kingdom.

In practice these two problems are beginning to produce two familiar solutions. Decisive verdicts in referenda can go a long way towards creating an entrenched political position which cannot realistically be changed by Parliament, but can be altered by a subsequent referendum. Electoral reform, involving the introduction of various forms of proportional representation, has already modified the political culture and hence the nature of political decision making in the devolved Assemblies and the European Parliament. It is probably only a matter of time before it reaches Westminster – courtesy of a future referendum. In these respects it seems that we may be approaching a new constitutional settlement which effectively substitutes popular sovereignty for Parliamentary sovereignty and inter-party cooperation for intra-party compromise. Yet all this would be much easier to achieve if we confronted the fundamental and enduring problems caused by the absence of a codified constitution in the United Kingdom.

Questions for discussion

1 Now that the Electoral Commission regulates the conduct of elections and referendum campaigns, do the advantages outweigh the disadvantages?

2 Analyse the cases for and against electoral reform for elections to the Westminster Parliament.

3 Is it desirable that referenda should be used more often in deciding important political issues even if this weakens the authority of Parliament?

Notes

1 Since 1973 eight referenda have been held in the United Kingdom on the following subjects: the Northern Ireland border (to decide on Northern Ireland's status in or out of the UK) on 8th March 1973; UK membership of the European Community

on 5th June 1975; devolution for Scotland and for Wales both on 1st March 1979; Scottish devolution on 11th September 1997; Welsh devolution on 18th September 1997; the Government's proposals for a Greater London Authority on 7th May 1998; and the Belfast Agreement on 22nd May 1998.

2 The proposed referendum on whether or not Britain should join the single European currency (the Euro) will only be held if the Labour Government, backed by a majority in the House of Commons, decides that the so-called five economic conditions (first formulated by Gordon Brown in November 1997) have been met and that it is therefore timely and appropriate to put the issue to the British people for a final decision. The possibility of a referendum on the voting system for elections to the Westminster Parliament is more problematic and will depend upon a number of party political calculations, including the evolution of the somewhat volatile relationship between the Labour and Liberal Democrat parties.

3 See Labour Party, *A New Agenda for Democracy: Labour's Proposals for Constitutional Reform*; London, September 1993; and Labour Party, *A Report of the Working Party on Electoral Systems*, Plant Report; London, 1993.

4 *A New Agenda for Democracy*; p. 39.

5 See House of Commons Home Affairs Select Committee Report on Electoral Law and Administration, HC (1997–98), No. 768.

6 See the *Report of the Independent Commission on the Voting System*, Cm 4090; HMSO, London, October 1998; on the Neill Committee, see pp. 284–5 above.

7 See the Government Response to the Fifth Report, *The funding of Political Parties in the United Kingdom*, Cm 4413; HMSO, London, July 1999.

8 Explanatory Notes on the Political Parties, Elections and Referendums Bill, para 53.

9 See *The Funding of Political Parties in the United Kingdom*, Fifth Report of the Committee on Standards in Public Life, Cm 4057; HMSO London, 1998; para 11.27.

10 *Report of the Independent Commission on the Voting System*, Cm 4090; para 165.

11 See, for example, R. Blackburn, 'Electoral law and administration' in R. Blackburn and R. Plant (eds) *Constitutional Reform*; Longman, Harlow, 1999; pp. 82–108.

12 *Report of the Independent Commission on the Voting System*, Cm 4090; para 23.

13 This group was dramatically vindicated at the 1997 General Election when the Labour Party won 63 per cent of the seats in the House of Commons on the basis of only 44 per cent of the votes cast.

14 The figures for the Social Democratic and Labour Party were 22 and 22 per cent respectively, for the Ulster Unionists 21 and 26 per cent, for the Democratic Unionists 18 and 18 per cent, and for Sinn Fein 18 and 17 per cent. In so far as there were still discrepancies in these figures, these could be attributed to the long-term effects of deliberate manipulation of constituency boundaries over many years by the once dominant Protestant and Unionist majority.

15 The salient words in the 2001 Labour Manifesto were: 'we will review the experience of the new [electoral] systems and the Jenkins Report to assess whether changes might be made to the electoral system for the House of Commons – a referendum remains the right way to agree any change for Westminster'.

16 *Report of the Independent Commission on the Voting System*, Cm 4090; p. v. In Chapter 4 the Commission reviewed all the leading variants of proportional and semi-proportional representation to be found in other democratic countries. These included the single transferable vote in the Republic of Ireland, the additional member system in Germany, the two ballot system in France, the mixed member proportional system in New Zealand and the alternative vote system in Australia. The advantages of the first-past-the-post system used in the United Kingdom, Canada and the United States – not to speak of the mainly plurality system recently adopted in Italy in place of a proportional system – were largely discounted.

17 *Ibid*; para 113.

18 See *Note of Reservation* by Lord Alexander of Weedon in the *Report of the Independent Commission on the Voting System*, Cm 4090; pp. 53–5.

19 For an explanation of how the allocation of top-up seats would proceed see *Report of the Independent Commission on the Voting System*; para 110.

20 *Ibid*; para 26.

21 Labour Party, *New Politics, New Britain*; London, September 1996.

22 See *Hansard*, 11th March 1975, Cols 304–17.

23 For example, pressure from Tony Benn and a few other anti-Europeans in the early 1970s in favour of holding a referendum on Britain's entry into the European Community exacerbated the emerging splits in the Labour Party which did so much damage to Labour's electoral chances in the late 1970s and early 1980s. Pressure from the Thatcherite wing of the Conservative Party (the so-called Euro-sceptics) in the early 1990s for a referendum on the 1992 Maastricht Treaty undoubtedly contributed to damaging Conservative splits. However, the common denominator in both cases was the explosive nature of the European issue in British politics.

24 See *Report of the Commission on the Conduct of Referendums*; Constitution Unit and Electoral Reform Society, London, November 1996.

25 *Ibid*; foreword by the Chairman, Sir Patrick Nairne.

26 See especially Chapter 12 in the Fifth Report of the Committee on Standards in Public Life; HMSO, London, October 1998, for a discussion of referenda.

27 See the Government's proposals in *The Funding of Political Parties in the United Kingdom*, Cm 4413.

28 If such a referendum campaign had been held in the 1997–2001 Parliament, the Labour and Conservative parties would each have qualified for £5 million, the Liberal Democrats for £3 million, and each of the smaller parties for £500,000.

29 As happened when the Danish people were asked a second time to approve the 1992 Maastricht Treaty after they had rejected it on the first occasion.

30 Speech by Lord Irvine entitled 'Constitutional change and modernisation of the law in Britain' to the Franco-British Lawyers Association in Paris, 26th February 1998.

31 Labour Party Manifesto, *Ambitions for Britain*; London, 2001; p. 35.

Further reading

Raymond Blackburn, *The Electoral System in Britain*; Macmillan, London, 1995.

Vernon Bogdanor, *Power and the People: a Guide to Constitutional Reform*; Gollancz, London, 1997.

Candidate selection in the United Kingdom, Report of the independent Riddell Commission; Electoral Reform Society, London, 2002.

Philip Cowley *et al.*, *What We Already Know: Lessons on Voting Reform from Britain's First P.R. Elections*; Constitution Unit, London, 2001.

Elections in the Twenty First Century: from Paper Ballot to E-voting, Report of an independent Commission on Alternative Voting Methods; Electoral Reform Society, London, 2002.

Labour Party Manifesto, *Ambitions for Britain*; London, 2001.

Pippa Norris: 'The twilight of Westminster: electoral reform and its consequences', *Political Studies*, Vol. 49, No. 5, December 2001.

A. Ranney (ed.) *The Referendum Device*; American Enterprise Institute, Washington, DC, 1981.

Report of the Commission on the Conduct of Referendums; Constitution Unit and Electoral Reform Society, London, November 1996.

Report of the Independent Commission on the Voting System, Cm 4090; HMSO, London, 1998.

Report of the Working Party on Electoral Systems; Labour Party, London, 1993.

website for the Electoral Commission: www.electoral-commission.gov.uk

The people, society and the state

This chapter will provide a thematic discussion of the ways in which the British people have evolved in their political behaviour and their constitutional attitudes, and the consequences of this evolution for both society and the state in this country. It will equally examine the ways in which ideas of the state have changed – notably those aspects relating to its powers and responsibilities – and the consequences of such changes for the British people and for the society in which they live. In this interactive process, the people and the state have not evolved at strictly comparable rates, nor has the process always been equally beneficial to the two elements, notwithstanding the assumption, in modern times at any rate, that the state should be the servant of the people rather than the other way around. There are aspects of considerable tension, even opposition, between the interests of individual citizens and the interests of the state (which can be regarded as the principal instrument of all citizens collectively), not to mention the tension between individuals and society.

The intention of this chapter is to complement the discussion in the previous two chapters and to provide some theoretical underpinning for earlier parts of the book as well. For example, we noted in Chapter 3 that a preponderant section of the Irish people have for many years not accepted allegiance to the British Crown, the pre-eminent symbol of the British state, and equally that the British state found it ultimately impossible to enforce such an allegiance upon the unwilling majority in the 26 counties of the Irish Republic and indeed upon the unwilling minority of Irish nationalists in the six counties of Northern Ireland. Another example was provided in Chapter 9 by the evolving relationship between the Monarchy and the people, a relationship which has become more problematic since the former encountered public relations problems of a serious and repeated nature and the latter were able to become self-conscious *citizens* (as well as subjects) with the heightened expectations which such a status implies. Yet another example was provided in Chapter 12 in the discussion of our transformed legal system in that the incorporation of positive human rights into UK statute law via the *Human Rights Act 1998* is bound to shape the nature and quality of relations between the people and the state.

The people as subjects and citizens

For centuries the British people have been subjects of the Crown in what was a gradually consolidated United Kingdom. To begin with, it was a matter of consolidating the kingdom of England under Norman and Angevin rule; Wales was incorporated by medieval conquest under Edward I and by statute under Henry VIII in 1536; Scotland was incorporated by Royal succession in 1603, when James VI of Scotland also became James I of England, and by statute or (in the eyes of many Scots) what was in effect an international treaty approved by both Parliaments and became the *Acts of Union* in 1707, Ireland was treated as an English colony from the Middle Ages to the end of the eighteenth century when finally an *Act of Union* was agreed in 1800 between a corrupt Irish Parliament and a pre-reform British Parliament whose members were only too conscious of the need to secure Britain's strategic flank during a lull in the long war against revolutionary France. Thus it would be fair to say that until the beginning of the nineteenth century all varieties of the British people became British subjects as an incidental consequence of war, conquest, international treaty or the imperatives of overwhelming English power within the British Isles.

The status of British subject commanded general acceptance and grudging respect in all parts of the United Kingdom for perhaps a century until the forces of Irish nationalism began to challenge the assumption that Irish people should continue to be British subjects owing ultimate allegiance to a British Monarch. From the Easter Rebellion in Dublin in 1916 and certainly from the Anglo-Irish Treaty in 1921, the idea of being a British subject began to lose its lustre first for a growing proportion of the Irish people (with the notable exception, of course, of the Protestant Unionists in Ulster) and later for growing minorities of Scottish and Welsh nationalists who disputed the seemingly arrogant English assumption that all residents of the British Isles should consider themselves fortunate to be subjects of the British Monarch and part of the British Empire and Commonwealth.

All of this may seem rather dated, even unreal, to contemporary readers who are likely to have a much less deferential attitude than their forebears towards the British Monarchy and who probably feel the need to suspend their disbelief (and suppress a giggle) when reading the portentous words on the first inside page of their British passports.[1] Yet, on the other hand, it is undeniable that many people both within and outside the British Isles are only too keen to secure a British passport as a confirmation of British citizenship in a world in which this document still commands a relatively high degree of status and, alas, a substantial black market value. Such people are not particularly interested in the dignified aspects of British subjecthood, but they are undoubtedly interested in the utilitarian benefits of British citizenship which now come with possession of a *bona fide* British passport.[2] See *Box 15* for a pithy and up-to-date briefing note on the word 'citizenship' in the context of British nationality legislation and *Appendix 4* for the words of a proposed citizenship pledge for people becoming British citizens.

Even among the English, the inherent attractions of being a British subject seem to have suffered a long and remorseless decline beginning with the decline in social deference dating back to the permissive 1960s and gathering pace in the early 1990s when the Monarchy was in such public relations difficulties and John Major was introducing the Citizen's Charter. In more recent times since the election of a 'modernising' Labour Government in 1997, the idea of being a British subject has come to seem more and more feudal, anachronistic and patronising to any British people who give the situation more than a moment's thought or who listen to even a cursory explanation of how we have arrived at the present position. For example, Tony Wright, the distinguished Labour MP and academic, has argued very persuasively that 'a [political] culture and structure for subjects will not serve well the needs of citizens' and that 'in the case of Britain, what we find is a political culture in which democracy has been the uninvited guest rather than the active participant'.[3] So the British people are still lumbered with an ancient political culture built upon deferential principles for 'subjects' rather than a modern political culture built upon democratic principles for 'citizens'. This fact alone represents a serious obstacle to achieving a significant and fundamental transformation of British constitutional arrangements.

If one poses the question of why the constitutional status of the people in the United Kingdom

---

Box 15 The word 'citizenship' in British nationality legislation

The word 'citizenship' has been used in the context of our nationality legislation since the British Nationality Act 1948 first as 'British subject: citizen of the U.K. and Colonies' and then in the British Nationality Act 1981 as 'British citizenship'. Citizenship in this context already embraces allegiance to the Sovereign and applicants for naturalisation as British citizens swear or affirm loyalty to the Queen. Although we have historically used the term 'British subjects', this status is now quite narrowly defined in our legislation and is limited to small groups of people who have links with pre-1949 Ireland and the Indian sub-continent as well as informal reference to those living here. So, in promoting citizenship in the manner described in this White Paper, we are building on an existing legal definition in a way that is fully consistent with our position as subjects of a constitutional Sovereign. There is no contradiction in promoting citizenship so that people uphold common values and understand how they can play their part in our society while upholding our status as subjects of H.M. the Queen.

Source: *Secure Borders, Safe Haven: Integration with Diversity in Modern Britain*, Cm 5387; HMSO, London, February 2002; p. 29.

has remained so archaic when compared with the situation in almost every other advanced society in the world, one is inclined to answer with three main points. *Firstly*, there is the remarkable *continuity* of our institutional and constitutional arrangements over the centuries which has enabled our rulers to carry forward into the modern age what are essentially medieval relationships between the governors and the governed, at least in terms of the formal language, if not the daily realities, of politics.

Secondly, there is the historical fact that, having in the seventeenth century disposed of the Divine Right of Kings by executing Charles I and entrenched the principles of constitutional Monarchy by reaching a lasting accommodation between Parliament on the one hand and William and Mary on the other, our forebears became quite relaxed in the eighteenth century and subsequently about according *formal deference* to our Head of State and in the process describing themselves as subjects, because they knew all along that the *substance* of their relationship with their rulers (both the Monarch and the Monarch's Ministers) was much less deferential than at first sight it might seem to have been.

Thirdly, there is the historical fact that the *republican cause* has never been able to attract any large measure of sustained public support in this country, essentially because this point of view was regarded as eccentric, alien and unnecessary as long as the Monarchy remained a popular and dignified part of our constitutional arrangements. However, if that situation had changed – for example, in the nineteenth or early twentieth centuries when other Royal families were toppling like nine-pins following defeat in war or popular uprising – and if our Monarchy had become associated in the public mind with pernicious forces of reaction or tyranny, then the British people might well have been attracted to the creation of a Republic and the republican ideals of citizenship.[4]

Notwithstanding the rather docile attitude of the British people since the seventeenth century and the fact that our modern form of democracy had to be grafted onto a sturdy and much older constitutional tradition, certain political outsiders have seen the populist attractions of citizenship as an alternative, or at least a complement, to the traditional status of subjecthood. For example, Tony Benn, after a fairly orthodox political apprenticeship as the heir to a hereditary peerage, became a leading advocate for the virtues of citizenship in a Republic free from what he has often described as the mumbo-jumbo of the Crown and the doctrine of Royal Prerogative.

More significantly, John Major, when he was Prime Minister from 1990 to 1997, developed his own big idea which he called the *Citizen's Charter* and which really amounted to a way of empowering all those members of the public who use public services and giving them improved means of redress in the event of a given public service not coming up to the specified standard.[5] Acute observers, such as Tony Wright, noted that 'we have a citizen's charter, but not a citizens' charter, and the apostrophe matters'.[6] Cynical commentators claimed it was just another example of window-dressing to cover up the Tory Government's inability seriously to reform what remained of the public sector. Yet the fact remains that it did popularise the concept of *citizenship* (as opposed to subjecthood) and it did introduce an extra new dimension to public accountability in the public sector – namely, *direct accountability* of public servants to the *users* of public services, alongside the traditional form of indirect accountability via the familiar chain of responsibility running through Ministers and then Parliament to the general public.

At about the same time that John Major was involved in launching his Citizen's Charter, he and his most senior Ministerial colleagues were also involved in the long-running Inter-Governmental Conferences which led up to the 1992 Treaty of Maastricht. It is a fair assumption, therefore, that by the time Conservative Ministers had to consider and approve what was to become Article 8 of the Maastricht Treaty on 'Citizenship of the Union', they were reasonably well disposed towards the concept of citizenship for British subjects – even if it was established courtesy of the newly declared European Union by European law.

As things turned out, the twelve member states began rather cautiously in this domain by declaring quite simply that 'every person holding the nationality of a Member State shall be a citizen of the Union', thus making European citizenship conditional upon national citizenship (or subject-hood), not the other way around. The specific civil rights guaranteed elsewhere in Article 8 were rather modest – for example, the right for all citizens of the European Union to move and reside freely within the territory of the member states, the right to vote and to stand as candidates in municipal elections and in European Parliament elections in member states of which they are not nationals, the right when in the territory of a third country to protection by the diplomatic or consular authorities of a member state other than their own, the right to petition the European Parliament and to apply to a European Ombudsman, a new office. How-ever, the door was left open under Article 8(e) of the Treaty for the Council of Ministers (acting unanimously on a proposal from the Commission and after consulting the European Parliament) 'to adopt provisions to strengthen or to add to the rights laid down in this Part which it shall recommend to the Member States for adoption in accordance with their respective constitutional requirements'.[7]

The late John Smith, as Leader of the Labour Party, was a dedicated constitutional reformer who really wanted to create 'a Citizen's Democracy'.[8] He argued very powerfully for a new constitutional settlement – 'a new deal between the people and the state that puts the citizen centre stage'; and, in case there was any lingering doubt about what he meant by this, he added that he wanted to see

> a fundamental shift in the balance of power between the citizen and the state – a shift away from an overpowering state to a citizen's democracy where people have rights and powers and where they are served by accountable and responsive government.

In John Smith's mind what he described as 'our crumbling constitution' could no longer be dismissed as a sideshow – it was at the heart of what was wrong with the entire country. Such sentiments were so sincerely and deeply held by this talented man that one can safely assume that if he had lived to become Prime Minister, the commitment of the Labour Party in Government to all aspects of comprehensive constitutional reform (with the possible exception of electoral reform) would have been paramount and that in the process the concept of active and empowered citizenship would have been strongly promoted by the Prime Minister himself.

In the event, such determined and coherent leadership on constitutional issues has not been forthcoming from Tony Blair and the difference has been plain for all to see. For example, in his John Smith Memorial Lecture given in February 1996, Tony Blair was merely cryptic about the importance of citizenship when he declared that 'our ambition is to create a young Britain with a new politics which treats people as full citizens and gives them greater power over Government'; and later in the same speech he seemed to muddle up two very different concepts when he said that 'new politics is about a stakeholder democracy as well as a stakeholder economy' – not a formulation to inspire confidence in his audience that he was thinking seriously about anything other than the best sound-bites.[9]

All those who really knew and cared about making a decisive shift from subject to citizen in this country had to wait for a speech by Lord Chancellor Irvine to the Citizenship Foundation in January 1998 on the theme 'Creating a nation of real citizens – partnership between the people and the state'.[10] Lord Irvine called on the citizens of this country 'to participate fully in the life of the nation, so that the system is a democracy in practice as well as principle'. This appeal for 'practising citizens' was a constant refrain in the speech which sought to invoke the principle of reciprocity between a Government determined to give the British people 'real rights and powers' and a citizenry fully prepared 'to work together to strengthen their country'.

Lord Irvine drew attention to four different strands in the New Labour project: *firstly*, the promotion of a greater understanding of the rights and responsibilities that underpin a civilised demo-cratic society; *secondly*, education and training in the skills and knowledge needed by active citizens to participate effectively in their communities and in social and political debate; *thirdly*, genuine opportunities for citizens, and especially young people, to gain the experience needed to be real practising democrats; and *fourthly*, the modernisation of the political system so that power is returned to the people. In short, the goal was 'to create a nation of able, informed and empowered citizens who, on the one hand, know, understand and can claim their rights; and, on the other, recognise that one path to fulfilment lies through active involvement in strengthening their society'.[11]

Efforts to clarify people's rights and responsibilities as citizens were being taken forward by the Citizenship Foundation and by public-spirited lawyers working for Citizens' Advice Bureaux and Law Centres. Education for active citizenship was being taken forward both inside and outside the school curriculum by the Department for Education and Skills on the advice of a high-powered group chaired by Professor Bernard Crick. There was also a Labour Party Manifesto pledge to develop a national programme of citizens' public service for young people and this was being applied in the Millennium Volunteers programme covering tens of thousands of people between the ages of 16 and 25.

Notwithstanding all this progress in the right direction for making citizenship a living reality for many more people, Lord Irvine acknowledged that the greater problem – the alienation of ordinary people from politicians and political life – had not been solved and he reiterated Ministers' determination 'to clean up politics and rebuild the bond of trust between Government and citizens'.[12] However, he made a direct and positive link between the Labour Government's 'radical programme of constitutional and political renewal' and a style of politics which would be 'more accessible, more modern and more responsive to the aspirations of the people'. Indeed, he went further by warning that 'unless we modernise, we will never secure the levels of commitment, interest and trust among our citizens needed to develop and maintain real practising democracy in this country'.[13]

Ambivalent participation in an eroded society

It is clear from the empirical evidence that the British people are ambivalent about their participation in British society. In one sense it is, of course, obvious that if you live in the United Kingdom, you *have* to participate in British society – at least to a degree consistent with the legal and practical obligations which are imposed upon you. So, for example, you have to pay your taxes and do jury service when summoned to do so. In another sense, however, many forms of participation in civil society are *voluntary* – for example, voting in elections, joining a political party, giving time to charitable organisations, and lobbying Government via pressure and interest groups.

The solidarity of society has become somewhat eroded in the years since the Second World War. Many of the social bonds familiar to people of older generations have become attenuated or broken, while many of the newer bonds in society seem distinctly provisional, if not pathological in some cases. For example, the combination of the widespread fear of crime (especially in inner-city areas) and the nearly ubiquitous private ownership of television, video and other forms of home entertainment induces fewer people to go out to social gatherings – still less to public meetings – and persuades them to stay in the relative safety of their homes and gardens. Equally, the widespread and growing ownership and use of private motor vehicles, coupled with planning policies which have had the effect of separating residential areas from places of work and retail consumption, has meant that the natural camaraderie of the streets is increasingly rare for more and more people (apart from the socially active young generation) with the result that the 'privatisation' of society has taken on disturbing new connotations of loneliness and alienation for many. Of course, it would be a mistake to exaggerate these arguments or to make them carry constitutional implications which they cannot really bear. Yet a reasonable case can be made for the *ambivalence* which many people feel about participating in civil society today and for the gradual *erosion* of many of the social bonds and ligatures which used to hold our society together, whether as local 'tribes' or as a nation.[14]

It was ridiculous and (to some people) offensive when Margaret Thatcher declared in 1987 that there was 'no such thing as society'.[15] Yet apart from the fact that media reports of her remark were highly partial and selective – since the rest of her observation celebrated the role of individuals and families – there was more than a grain of truth in what she said, especially if it was understood as a description of certain defining characteristics of modern British society rather than a recommendation as to how we should all lead our lives. If we are honest, both our individual experience and many of the official statistics show that the *cohesive* society, which was so characteristic of the United Kingdom during the first two or three decades after the Second World War, has indeed been significantly eroded and it is by no means entirely clear whether, and if so how, other forms of social cement can be made to strengthen our enfeebled civil society.[16]

The argument can be buttressed with a few vivid indicators of social change.[17] The proportion of one-person households increased over the period from 1961 to 1998–99 from 4 per cent to 14 per cent among those under pensionable age and from 7 per cent to 15 per cent among those over pensionable age. Equally, the traditional nuclear family (mother, father and two children) declined from 52 per cent of the total in 1961 to 39 per cent of the total in 1998–99. Moreover, of all families with dependent children, lone mothers were the head of household in 7 per cent of cases in 1971, but this rose to 22 per cent of cases in 1998–99. Marriage or deliberate and loyal cohabitation may still be the actual or desired model for the majority of people, yet this form of social unit declined from 92 per cent of all families in 1971 to 75 per cent in 1998–99 and, within that overall trend, the incidence of first marriages (for both partners) in 1997 was less than half the number in 1970. So if conventional families are regarded as a training ground for participation in society, they are demonstrably less common in the early twenty-first century than they were in the 1960s or 1970s.

If one scales up these social observations from the level of households to that of intermediate institutions positioned between households and the institutions at national level, the picture is no more reasssuring for those who believe in the value of participation in civil society. Total active adult membership of Christian churches declined by about one-third from 1970 to 1990 and has almost certainly continued to fall since then. On the other hand, over the same period the equivalent figures for Muslims nearly quadrupled. Turning to another part of the voluntary sector, on the basis of a snapshot rather than a longitudinal trend, we find that about four out of ten adults in Great Britain in 1998 were involved at least once in the previous year in either charitable or voluntary activities (admittedly not a very demanding test of public participation), but fewer than one in twenty were involved in political parties, political movements or election campaigns. Equally, trade union membership, which suffered a catastrophic decline of nearly 50 per cent from 1979 to 1997, seems to have stabilised more recently since the unions themselves adopted the more 'modern' approach of providing individual services to their members – e.g. legal advice, medical insurance and financial planning for retirement.

So the general picture which seems to be emerging is that our levels of *committed membership participation* in the *traditional representative institutions* have declined over recent decades and have reached disturbingly low levels, whereas our participation in discretionary gatherings of like-minded people who come together either temporarily or permanently for a common purpose – whether it be gardening, socialising at the pub, working out in a health club or relaxing in front of the television – has remained steady or may even have grown beyond its already high levels. Moreover, since individuals can be alone in a crowd or even in their chosen discretionary community, the grounds for an optimistic interpretation of the new forms of social participation may have been overstated.[18]

It seems pretty obvious that the economic polarisation and social fragmentation of the Conservative years from 1979 to 1997 helped to produce a more heterogeneous society which, arguably, became more difficult to unite in common causes and hence more difficult to govern. This factor alone may have provided some persuasive arguments for the leading figures of New Labour to embark upon measures of constitutional reform as part of what can best be described as a 'cultural revolution'. *Firstly*, in a country in which three of the four traditional nationalities became discontented, to a greater or lesser extent, with English dominance of the United Kingdom, it was sensible to adjust the arrangements for territorial governance by introducing asymmetrical measures of devolution.

Secondly, in a society in which (in 1998–99) about 7 per cent of the population were from a non-white ethnic group, the age structure of the various ethnic groups differs considerably. The Bangladeshi British had the youngest age structure, with 43 per cent of their population in this country under the age of 16, compared with 20 per cent of white people. In contrast, 16 per cent of the white population were aged 65 or over, compared with only 3 per cent of Pakistanis and Bangladeshis. It is therefore obvious that multi-culturalism is here to stay as a defining characteristic of British society, and will become more important in future as the relatively young non-white ethnic minorities become a larger proportion of the whole population. Political and constitutional reforms designed to entrench our new culture of positive human rights and to promote social inclusion will need to be pursued as high priorities during the coming years.

Thirdly, the spread of new forms of consumer technology, coupled with the huge diversification of all the various media of communications, seems likely to give continuing impetus to the fragmentation of society which is already under way. For example, more than four out of five households in Great Britain have a video recorder, compared with just under one out of five in 1983, while the proportion of households with a home computer almost doubled from 18 per cent to 34 per cent between 1988 and 1998–99, with the most rapid growth of this phenomenon (49 per cent) in households with children and the least rapid growth (4 per cent) in households containing only people aged 60 and over. If these developments are set alongside the fact that people spent 25 hours per week on average watching television in 1998 (with

drama, soap operas and so-called 'reality television' the most popular programmes) and the fact that there are more than 30 million mobile telephones in private use in the United Kingdom (a growing proportion of which are connected to the Internet and capable of sending and receiving text messages), then it is clear that we are moving into an information-loaded society which will encourage a further increase in the volume of communications, but which is unlikely to be so effective at encouraging deliberative processes which create greater public understanding. The need for intelligent interpretation of all the data which are available on the Internet and elsewhere is one pressing problem, as is the need to include in our social and political networks all those who may still be too poor, too old or too demoralised to take part in the information age society.

One significant consequence of the marked shift in the *content* of all this new technology is that the media moguls and their expert advisers believe that their markets are becoming more differentiated and can therefore be profitably segmented by the producers of the blizzard of information, entertainment and education now on offer to the public. On broadcast television there will continue to be a wide range of free-to-air services catering for the average viewer and the same is likely to be true of broadcast radio. Yet the figures suggest that it may be an increasingly uphill struggle to hold the market share of quality output designed for serious viewers and listeners. For example, BBC 2 and Radio 4 already have ageing audiences, which implies that over the longer term they may not exert as much social influence as they do today. When this is set alongside the disproportionate influence of the tabloid newspapers upon both media and public opinion, it is hard to be optimistic about the chances of maintaining a high-quality public discourse on many of the issues which are likely to matter in our society over the years to come.

To caricature the prospects, most of the children will be playing computer games or sending text messages to each other on their mobile telephones, most of the men will be reading the *Sun* or watching endless football on Sky TV, and most of the women will be watching *Pride and Prejudice* on BBC

TV or reading *Hello!* magazine. At the same time media ownership will become increasingly polarised between a small number of global media conglomerates producing mainly moronic material for a largely mindless mass market and a large number of often precariously based niche companies. This is likely to reinforce the segmentation of British society into self-selecting fragments and make it harder for Governments to resist the temptation to be manipulative, demagogic or both.

When taken together, these developments seem likely to reinforce the existing tendency towards a society composed of 'sovereign individuals' – i.e. people who are treated by Governments, corporations, advertisers, media organisations and others as essentially *consumers* of goods and services or *spectators* of sport, drama and the political process. If this tendency goes unchallenged and unchecked, it could encourage a political culture which is essentially passive, reactive and punctuated with hysteria, complicated by a pattern of behaviour in the public authorities which is devious, manipulative and amoral. Such a situation could encourage the general public to adopt infantile attitudes and expectations about what any Government can deliver and so degrade any more healthy relationship which might have developed between the state and its citizens. The social forces which have traditionally held this country together could be weakened still further; and the fissiparous tendencies which have put our social cohesion under strain could be strengthened by a malign combination of materialism, individualism and short-termism that would make all forms of altruistic behaviour less common. In such circumstances the rules of the political game and the formal constitutional arrangements would become more important as frameworks to support the cohesion of British society and the efficacy of the British state.

Satisfactory and lasting constitutional arrangements need support from unifying institutions which can command widespread public respect, from unifying experiences which bind together people from all ethnic groups and walks of life, and from unifying policies pursued by the Government of the day in the interests of the people as a whole. Instead, we have to grapple with the constant problems posed for our society by multiple and often conflicting identities, moral relativism, political correctness and a decision-making elite which sometimes seems to have lost confidence in its own purposes and standards. It is little wonder that people feel socially ambivalent and that society is being eroded in ways which make both government and public participation more difficult.

The media and other voices of the people

The classic idea of representative democracy in Britain has tended to assume that the hopes and fears, instincts and prejudices of the people will be moderated or occasionally magnified by the people's elected representatives, whether within Parliament at Westminster, elected local government or most recently the 'national' Assemblies of Scotland, Wales and Northern Ireland. However, as political parties came to organise and channel political opinions and then to claim electoral mandates for the action which they took once elected into office, the balance of power between the people and their elected representatives began to shift in favour of the latter at a time when the respect enjoyed by MPs and Councillors was actually declining. This paradox has created a real dilemma for our system of representative democracy, but in an increasingly fragmented and pluralist society it has also created new temptations and opportunities for others to become self-appointed tribunes of the people.

While it is obviously true that people do not elect the *Sun* newspaper or Jeremy Paxman and John Humphrys to represent them in a classic and formal sense, in terms of ascribed or assumed representation such organs and leading figures in the media *can* claim to speak for their readers or their viewers and listeners and their claims have to be taken seriously in our modern media-influenced democracy. Equally, there is a wide range of other 'representative organisations' whose spokesmen or leaders may not have been elected even by their own membership and certainly not by the general public, but who nevertheless can make credible claims to represent significant sections of public opinion – sometimes, arguably, larger sections of public opinion than unrepresentative or eccentric political parties.

Indeed, in modern political conditions one could extend the list of those who can make a credible claim to be tribunes or representatives of the people to include pressure groups and non-governmental organisations (NGOs), e.g. the Consumers' Association or the National Trust; non-departmental public bodies (NDPBs), e.g. the Post Office Users' National Council or the Rail Passengers' Committee; independent regulatory bodies, e.g. the Office of Fair Trading or the Broadcasting Standards Commission; and even virtual organisations, e.g. the People's Fuel Lobby which was briefly so influential during the fuel crisis in the autumn of the year 2000. The fundamental point is that, whatever may be the conventions of our constitution, the advantages and burdens of representing the people are nowadays widely shared both by our traditional representative institutions and by other individuals or organisations which have made credible claims to do so.

This very disparate range of political 'representatives' share a number of common characteristics which set them apart from our traditional forms of political representation. The individuals concerned may be either self-appointed or appointed by Ministers and employers; they are not democratically elected by the people. They are irresponsible both in the constitutional sense of lacking any institutional accountability to the general public and in the colloquial sense of not necessarily caring about the consequences of their actions for the public at large. They tend to be predominantly self-interested in that they usually put their own narrow interests above the general good. They are capable of influencing, if not capturing, the public policy-making process in ways which are often opaque and usually unaccountable. The only restraints upon them are their own misjudgements if they press their case too far, the public complaints of their less successful rivals and the backlash of public opinion if there is manifest unfairness or injustice in what they do.

Moreover, we have been warned by these people themselves of their ability and their intention to complement, if not supplant, the activities of those involved in the traditional institutions of representative democracy. For example, Peter Oborne, a tabloid journalist, claimed that the lobby journalists in the early 1980s became 'an elite at Westminster' who, for the most part, 'were cleverer, more self-assured, far better paid and very much more influential than most of the people they were writing about'.[19] In a similarly self-confident vein, George Monbiot, a leading environmental activist, argued that 'activists in the media have often been able to reach parts of the public psyche that no one else can touch, as they articulate sentiments that have never been put into words before'.[20] Reputable political scientists who have no particular axe to grind, such as Professor Pippa Norris, have also drawn attention to the ways in which the media and other self-appointed representatives of public opinion can influence policy outcomes and successfully play the role of tribunes of the people by being the main sources of information for the public, setting the agenda for public debate, being the main allocators of credit or blame, and influencing or at least reinforcing public voting behaviour at General Elections.[21]

All the main political parties have made efforts to attract business people and others not traditionally very interested in political participation into their lists of Parliamentary candidates. For example, the Conservatives under William Hague (a former management consultant) went so far as to retain a leading firm of executive head-hunters to scout for leading business figures who might be persuaded into Parliamentary politics. For its part, the Labour Party under Tony Blair has adopted a deliberate policy of co-opting senior business people into a range of 'task forces' and other consultative bodies with the dual purpose of persuading the business community that New Labour is on their side and neutralising the possible threat of business opposition when economic conditions deteriorate. Life peerages have also provided Mr Blair with a useful form of political patronage in his campaign to reassure and co-opt the business community.

The disproportionate role of the media and other self-appointed 'representatives' of the people in modern British politics stems from several separate causes. One is obviously the long, secular decline of public respect for the political parties and the public distaste for their dominant role in Parliament. A second is the self-confidence, even arrogance, of some leading figures in the media and the business world who know that their power and income is much greater than all but a handful of the most senior politicians.[22] A third cause has been the conscious attempts made by Margaret Thatcher and more recently by Tony Blair to enlist the most influential sections of the media and the business community in their respective political causes. Thus Margaret Thatcher went out of her way to cultivate influential editors, such as Sir David English of the *Daily Mail* and Kelvin Mackenzie of the *Sun*, not to mention TV celebrities such as Sir David Frost and Sir Jimmy Young. Tony Blair, as Leader of the Opposition, flew half way around the world in 1995 to pay court to Rupert Murdoch, the boss of News International, and as Prime Minister he has gone to great lengths to curry favour with Paul Dacre, editor of the *Daily Mail*, and to give exclusive information to Trevor Kavanagh, the political editor of the *Sun*.[23]

It could be argued that leading politicians have been largely responsible for their own undignified subservience to the mass media which, unsurprisingly, have sought to exploit the political opportunities handed to them on a plate. The same argument applies to the corporate bosses who have been flattered by successive Prime Ministers into heading task forces or special commissions or non-departmental public bodies on the dubious grounds that their managerial experience in the corporate world is useful for solving the very different problems of the political world, when the reality is more likely to be quite the reverse: running J. Sainsbury plc is *not* the same as being a Cabinet Minister and 'the business of government' does not necessarily benefit from government by business people.

The fundamental problem with all these modern forms of 'representation' is that real democratic accountability is missing. Ordinary citizens *en masse* could not vote Piers Morgan, the editor of the *Daily Mirror*, out of office when he was accused of insider trading; only the shareholders of the huge media

company for which he worked could do that and predictably they failed to do so. Ordinary citizens have no realistic means of redress if they are libelled or defamed by a large national newspaper or by a leading TV programme because they are unlikely to qualify for legal aid in such cases and the regulatory bodies are often more likely to protect rather than punish the media organisations which they are supposed to regulate. Powerful multinational companies, often with a turnover larger than many member states of the United Nations, have only just begun to experience some of the disciplines of 'public accountability' as a result of the interventions of some non-governmental organisations such as Greenpeace or Jubilee 2000.

The institutions of representative government have declined in popular esteem as the power of the media and other (strictly) non-representative and unaccountable bodies has grown. This may mean that fully representative Parliamentary democracy, of the kind which is still appreciated by many in these islands and elsewhere, will become something of a historical aberration. It may well be that this particular model of representative democracy will be supplemented, modified or even replaced in the fullness of time by a modern version of direct democracy based upon much more frequent use of referenda at the various levels of government and the application of the latest interactive technology to the processes of democratic decision making in our society.[24]

Direct action and direct democracy

All forms of representation which have developed over the centuries have had acknowledged shortcomings of one kind or another. This fact of political life has contributed to repeated public dissatisfaction with both the processes and the outcomes of policy and decision making in this country and abroad. It has led in its turn to certain frustrated groups resorting to various forms of direct action: for example, trade unionists opposed to the public–private partnership proposed for London Underground, the People's Fuel Lobby opposed to the level of taxation on motor fuel, and environmentalists in Greenpeace and other NGOs opposed to aspects of global capitalism.

In the international sphere we have seen increasingly frequent coordinated action and protests against the member states of the World Trade Organisation, the Group of Seven largest industrial countries and several other international bodies regarded by protesters as symbolic of global capitalism. Such anti-capitalists have shown their impatience and their ideological opposition to multi-national companies and to the national Governments which they perceive to be merely apologists for the interests of global corporations. They have also shown their contempt for the mechanisms of representative democracy by preferring to use the various techniques of direct action. In some respects these techniques do not differ very much from those of terrorist groups, such as the Real IRA, the Animal Liberation Front or the Basque group ETA, since they are quite prepared to use targeted violence to gain global publicity for their political ends.

The response of the British and other Governments to such forms of direct action has been to explore and, where possible, make use of mechanisms of direct democracy to complement the traditional representative processes and revive a sense of true democracy in the minds of the general public. Thus the Labour Government and some Labour-controlled local authorities have made use of referenda in order to secure public confirmation for courses of action upon which they were already minded to embark and to secure extra legitimacy for controversial decisions in which the authority of Government and Parliament was insufficient to secure public acceptance. In this context there have been some interesting examples, such as the local referendum in Bristol in February 2001 in which on a 40 per cent turn-out the local electorate voted against any increase in council tax to pay for improved local services, although that was the declared policy of the ruling Labour group on the local authority and in line with the majority view as expressed in opinion polls. Referenda are also being held before the introduction of directly elected Mayors. By the end of 2001 voters in six local authorities in England had opted for elected Mayors, whereas in seven other cases the local referendum had gone against the idea.

The Labour Government has introduced a wide range of consultative mechanisms designed to inform the process of policy making. Examples of such mechanisms are the People's Panel to test policy ideas on a nationally representative sample of more than 600 people or the various Focus Groups which have been created to explore likely public reactions to potential or actual Government initiatives.

Quite apart from these and other forms of private opinion polling in which all political parties have engaged, Ministers and officials have made a virtue of this approach to more structured consultation of the British public. On the Cabinet Office website and through other channels efforts have been made to draw public attention to what has been described as 'two major developments in the way the Government consults people which will play an important part in improving the way new policies are developed or how new services are provided'.[25] *Firstly*, a new Code of Practice has been produced on how the Government will handle its written consultations with interested bodies on matters of policy. These consultations are designed to reach all groups that might be affected by a proposed decision, allowing enough time for the iterative process to work and for Ministers to provide substantial and comprehensible explanations as to why certain options were or were not pursued. *Secondly*, a new Register of Consultations has been established on the website of UK Government On Line which catalogues all the main written consultations taking place at any time, is constantly updated to take account of Government decisions as they occur and makes it possible for people to be notified by e-mail of new consultations in areas of policy that may interest them, as well as receiving new guidance on the time-scale for policy implementation.

These techniques for more comprehensive and continuous *consultation* of the general public fall short of real direct democracy, but can be said to empower many more people and to provide wider and more frequent opportunities for public participation in what has been traditionally one of the most elitist and opaque policy- and decision-making processes in the Western world. The fact that the people who take part in such structured consultations tend to be drawn disproportionately from the growing range of professional inter-mediaries and non-governmental organisations in the orbits of Whitehall Departments does not detract from the validity of the process from the Government's point of view. However, it should serve to remind us that not everyone has the time or the inclination or the means to participate in the policy-making community. The main reasons why such techniques fall short of real direct democracy are that there is no transfer of the power of *final decision* from the elected Government to the people and that there is no provision for the people to hold their elected representatives to account, if necessary by removing them from office, other than at periodic General Elections when so many other issues come into play.

It is difficult to see how we could ever arrive at real direct democracy in the United Kingdom, because the country is probably too large and probably too diverse both territorially and socially for such a thing to achieve general public consent. Yet there are a growing number of people who advocate the development of e-politics and e-democracy as ways of making it possible to connect *every* citizen to a single electronic network and so enable everyone to participate in virtually simultaneous public decision making on the great issues of the day. On the other hand, those with a more traditional view of democracy find the idea eerily reminiscent of the cautionary tales of George Orwell in *Nineteen Eighty-Four* and Aldous Huxley in *Brave New World*.

It is as well to recognise that electronic direct democracy could have serious disadvantages even if it turned out to be technologically possible and socially acceptable. It could also have significant political and constitutional implications. *Firstly*, instantaneous electronic politics would tend to blur the distinction between governing and political campaigning and so turn the process of government into a perpetual long-running electoral campaign. *Secondly*, in such an unmediated and unreflective form of politics, short-term, emotional and selfish responses from the public would tend to pre-dominate. *Thirdly*, with the influence of political parties already in decline, there could be a marked lack of consistency in political objectives, since parties have traditionally provided the organising principles of ideology or collective interest which are necessary for the formation of coherent and sustained public policy.

Fourthly, the general public seems ill-equipped to take calm and rigorous decisions, especially about complex issues of scientific and technological choice, without a great deal more useful information which the media are unlikely to provide. *Finally*, such government by instant plebiscite implies the constant danger that the issues would be dealt with in a trivial, cursory or sensational manner and hence the public would be wide open to manipulation by cynical mass media or sinister vested interests practising the murky arts of mass persuasion.

Direct democracy may have its place if it is used mainly to achieve wider and more frequent public consultation. Yet political leaders should think long and hard before pressing it into service as a replacement for the tried and tested procedures of representative democracy, since these still encourage due deliberation on difficult issues and leave scope for the exercise of principled leadership.

The changing character of the state

The state in the United Kingdom and many other countries has changed its character and its scope over the centuries, especially since the late 1980s when Socialism began to decline and Communism to collapse (with a few notable exceptions, such as the People's Republic of China). Nation states first emerged as institutional structures designed to enforce law and order at home and to project military power abroad. Over the centuries their character gradually changed from an essentially military and power-political role to encompass a wider function which included the essentially civil mission of building a welfare state which could much more readily serve the needs and retain the allegiance of all its citizens.

In peace-time the pioneers of this stage of development were Bismarck's Germany and the United Kingdom under Asquith and Lloyd George. Yet, ironically, it was the imperatives of total mobilisation during the darkest days of the First World War after 1916 which transformed the character and aspirations of all nation states for most of the rest of the twentieth century. Following the Treaty of Versailles in 1919, the map of Europe was littered with nation states created as territorial fall-out from the disintegrated Ottoman and Austro-Hungarian empires. These new members of the international community were keen to exercise their newly acquired rights of self-determination, but many of them were hopelessly ill-equipped to do so.

In the United Kingdom, as elsewhere, the political class in the 1920s sought briefly and un-realistically to return to the model of a smaller (civilian) state which had been prevalent for much of the nineteenth century. However, the course of economic events revealed this idea to be unsustainable, especially after the financial market crash of 1929–30 and during the ensuing Great Depression which persisted almost until the Second World War. With the outbreak of hostilities the British political class and the British people had a better understanding of the need for total mobilisation in such a war, while on the Home Front more and more people developed an appreciation of the arguments for building an enhanced welfare state when the war was over.

After the Second World War, the people of the United Kingdom moved to adopt a new definition of the role of the state which had never been more all-encompassing. It was to be a universal welfare state from cradle to grave, while the scope of state responsibilities was dramatically expanded by nationalisation of the means of production, distribution and exchange according to the goals laid down in the Labour Party's 1918 constitution. Notwithstanding this ideological drive from the Left, a mixed economy survived in the immediate post-war period and soon those in the political mainstream accepted the post-war consensus and the more ambitious definition of the state and its responsibilities which this implied.

It was not until the two world oil crises of the 1970s (1973–74 and 1979–80) that the United Kingdom and other advanced industrial countries were shaken out of their complacency about the viability of such an extended state. From the early 1980s onwards three successive Conservative Administrations under Margaret Thatcher demonstrated a determination to 'roll back the frontiers of the state' with an aggressive policy of privatisation. The post-war consensus on the role of the state was first punctured, then transformed and eventually established on a much more restricted basis derived from the theories of Friedrich Hayek and Milton Friedman. The Thatcherite consensus, which was so painfully established in the 1980s and 1990s, assumed a much more limited role for the state which largely confined it to enabling, regulating, purchasing and redistributing goods and services produced by the private sector – in short, a regulatory state with preoccupations which could be symbolised as those of partner and referee for the private sector.

The cumulative effect of these historical developments in the United Kingdom and elsewhere is that the present character of the state, which New Labour inherited in 1997 and which has operated unchanged in its essentials since then, reflects the conclusions reached by the political class as a whole in the light of the economic, social and political developments of recent times. Some of these conclusions have been embodied in initiatives taken by Labour Ministers, but many more have been responses to global trends which have affected the fortunes of this country and other countries around the world.

The first conclusion is that the United Kingdom and most other nation states have seen their claims to effective sovereignty within their borders pierced by the arrows of globalisation fired at them by multi-national corporations, globally integrated financial markets and mass media with a global reach. This diminished national sovereignty means that sensible Governments are careful not to promise their people too much by way of political protection against global economic forces, but are involved in the tricky business of managing public expectations in a more sustainable direction. In short, national authorities can now do less on their own to protect their perceived national interests, so they are learning that they should promise less and hold out to their people only a modest vision of the state and its capabilities.

The second conclusion is that a growing number of people are likely to seek local solutions to problems which are brought to their doorsteps by global forces outside the control of national authorities. Hence the resonance of the modern mantra of many of today's environmentalists: 'think globally, but act locally'. This being the case, national politicians have been increasingly persuaded by the arguments for decentralisation or devolution as partial institutional answers to the seemingly inevitable erosion of their jurisdictions and as ways of responding more effectively to local expectations. This partly explains why the incoming Labour Government in 1997 was quick to implement its Manifesto commitment to devolution for Scotland and Wales and power sharing for Northern Ireland. Indeed, the notion of power sharing is essential to any understanding of the political rationale for devolution, since it also implies the sharing of responsibility and hence the ability of the Labour Government in London to share any blame for things which go wrong with the devolved institutions and other sub-national authorities.

The third conclusion is that repeatedly disappointed public expectations of the state and its agencies have bred a degree of public cynicism towards the political process from which it will be hard to recover. In the United Kingdom since 1990 or so this public disillusionment has bordered upon alienation which was created as much by problems of 'sleaze' in both main political parties as by any rational assessment of the limited effectiveness of the nation state and national authorities. Whatever the explanation and however much a similar public mood is now to be found in many other advanced industrial societies, it has begun to change the conventional wisdom about the character and limits of the nation state.

The response of the first Blair Administration to this public mood was astute in that from the beginning of its term of office in 1997 New Labour was careful to limit the number and the scope of its election pledges (originally focused upon five key pledges printed upon a plastic card) and since then senior Labour Ministers have spent a good deal of their time trying to lower public expectations.

Of course, according to another point of view which has regained some ground since Labour was re-elected in June 2001, the state still holds certain irreducible responsibilities, notably the delivery of modern and universal public services, and it would be distinctly risky for any Government to shift those duties onto someone else. The second Blair Administration is discovering that there can still be genuine ideological disputes about the extent to which the state should take responsibility for *providing*, as well as regulating and paying for, public services, while practical disagreements can arise about how far regulatory authorities should intervene to compensate for market failures or to correct market distortions.

In the debate about the changing role of the state there are special characteristics attaching to the United Kingdom, because in our political tradition there has been scant recognition of *the idea of the state* as distinct from frequent rehearsals of the more familiar concepts of *the public interest* and *Parliamentary supremacy*. It becomes doubly difficult to steer the changing character of the state in a society in which the very ideas of the state and of public interest have been much less prominent than in the nations on the Continent of Europe. Such discrepancies, however, may be eased as the tide of European jurisprudence rises up our legal and constitutional shores and as the *Human Rights Act 1998* begins to influence our common law.

Some of the most tricky constitutional problems of the British state have been to determine who, if anyone, owns the state, who can authoritatively define the interests of the state and who is the legitimate spokesman for the state? In answer to the last question, it has long been accepted that Ministers in the Government of the day (and their official spokesmen) are the legitimate voice of the state and are entitled to define the interests of the state. Yet difficulties have arisen when Ministers (or judges reviewing their decisions in the courts) equate 'the interests of the state' with 'the public interest' as, for example, in the ban on trade union membership at GCHQ in Cheltenham and the prosecution of Clive Ponting under the 1911 Official Secrets Act.[26] These were not the only occasions in the last two decades when there was a serious clash in the courts about which party in such a legal dispute – whether the Government of the day or the people being prosecuted (typically Government employees or intrepid journalists) – could most plausibly invoke '*the public interest*' in support of its position.[27] More often than not, the senior judiciary has supported the classic position that it is for Ministers or their spokesmen to define 'the public interest' at any given time.

Nevertheless, this important and elusive term – '*the public interest*' – can have a wide range of meanings. For example, when it is used as a defence by journalists against libel actions, it is often defined to mean whatever the public may be *interested in* at a particular time on a particular issue. More generally, it has been regarded by the courts as an abstract and theoretical concept often recognised in public law as a synonym for 'the interests of the state', which are normally defined by Ministers. The term is only just beginning to be treated as a general value which can be identified with individuals or private bodies and can therefore be distinguished from the interests of the state in certain circumstances.

As for the abstract question of who, if anyone, owns the state, an answer should perhaps begin by pointing to the long British tradition whereby the Government of the day uses what might be described as 'the command machinery' of the state to act imperiously in the name of Parliament (as if Ministers owned the state), but not necessarily with the approval of the people who have not usually been consulted on the matter. This habit was exemplified in the sensitive sphere of 'national security' in the 1914 and 1939 *Defence of the Realm Acts*, the 1975 and subsequent *Prevention of Terrorism Acts*, the *Regulation of Investigatory Powers Act 2000* and most recently the *Anti-Terrorism Act* of 2001. In other spheres of the law one could cite the 1947 and subsequent *Town and Country Planning Acts* or the *1948 Mental Health Act* as examples of the potentially dictatorial powers that British Governments have taken upon themselves with the support of a majority in the House of Commons for what were presented at the time as compelling 'reasons of state', but which sometimes lacked a convincing rationale to justify such draconian powers.

In contemporary circumstances the balance of power between the representatives of the state and those of the people has been redressed to some extent, partly by influential media playing upon a volatile public opinion and partly by energetic and highly effective non-governmental organisations working in partnership with the media. The situation will also be affected by some of the Labour Government's constitutional reforms – notably the *Human Rights Act 1998* and the *Freedom of Information Act 2000* – which should make it easier in due course for intrepid citizens to assert their positive rights against the state and its agencies. The challenge is therefore to find effective ways of rebalancing the constitutional relationship between the people and the politicians in office, so that the former can assert their recently established positive rights and the latter can be held to account in more continuous and meaningful ways.

General reflections

It is possible to identify a number of significant shifts of emphasis which have taken place within the triangular nexus of the people, society and the state and which are likely to have extensive constitutional implications. The first is the shift for everyone from subjecthood to citizenship. This is as yet by no means complete and it certainly does not imply the end of popular allegiance to the Monarchy for most British people. Yet it is probably irreversible since the majority community in our society has become so much less deferential and many more people will come to appreciate the wide range of positive rights which have been made accessible to them by the passage of the *1998 Human Rights Act*. There is also the little matter of Article 8 of the 1992 Maastricht Treaty which created some open-ended possibilities for citizens of the European Union to campaign for further positive rights which may go beyond those enshrined in the 1951 European Convention.

The second shift of emphasis is from a cohesive society, with a high degree of social solidarity resulting from intensive public participation in a wide variety of voluntary institutions, to a new society where aspects of individualism seem to be more highly prized and social participation is expressed mainly in contingent networks of like-minded people who communicate for common purposes but then withdraw when their personal goals have been achieved. This is a loose-weave society in which it will be harder for politicians and others to organise people for overriding national purposes. It may also vitiate the development of effective consensus politics in which generally accepted policy positions can be maintained for a long time. It suggests the desirability of constitutional arrangements which may encourage more people to organise and act locally; if these are established, the spread of real devolution in England is probably unstoppable.

The third shift of emphasis is from our previous reliance upon party political representation through Members of Parliament or Councillors to more ill-defined forms of representation which may depend upon the active involvement of celebrities, non-governmental organisations and self-styled spokesmen for apparently spontaneous protest movements. Furthermore, the normally apathetic general public is apparently willing to follow the lead given by unelected people who have no democratic mandate but appear to be tuned into the *Zeitgeist* of various fashionable and popular causes.

The fourth shift of emphasis is from representative democracy to direct democracy. This has happened because the general public has become increasingly frustrated and disappointed with the apparent inability of elected politicians to solve many intractable problems. People then look for a lead from well-known figures in other walks of life who appear to carry no political baggage. However, when these unorthodox leaders also fail, they are likely to cause similar public disappointment and frustration which may well provoke sections of the general public in their exasperation to turn to various forms of direct action.

The final shift of emphasis is from a strong state with pretensions to omnicompetence to a weaker, more limited state led by a much less confident political elite. In these circumstances British national institutions seem set on a path of declining power and increasingly contested competences. This implies that within perhaps the next ten to 30 years the United Kingdom may become a quasi-federal and multi-national union state in which people feel comfortable about giving roughly equal weight to their local identity, their national identity, their European identity and their global identity. If that happens, the constitutional implications could indeed be far reaching.

Questions for discussion

1 What constitutional changes are needed for the British people to be able to experience the full rights and duties of citizenship?

2 Is representative democracy 'old hat' and bound to be replaced with new procedures of direct democracy and wider public participation?

3 In what ways are conceptions of the state changing in the United Kingdom and what are the likely constitutional implications?

Notes

1 The Declaration in the UK passport reads:

> Her Britannic Majesty's Secretary of State requests and requires in the name of Her Majesty all those to whom it may concern to allow the bearer to pass freely without let or hindrance and to afford the bearer such assistance and protection as may be necessary.

2 This seems to have been the main reason why both Mohammed al Fayed, the Egyptian tycoon who owns Harrods, and the Hinduja brothers, from the billionaire Indian business family who donated £1 million in sponsorship for the Faith Zone in the Millennium Dome, pressed so hard for so long to get British passports.

3 Tony Wright, *Citizens and Subjects*; Routledge, London, 1994; pp. 50, 52.

4 Some of the strongest appeals for fundamental reform, if not abolition, of the Monarchy have been

made by certain national newspapers. For example, on 6th December 2000 the *Guardian* devoted its entire front page and four further pages to the subject; an appeal on the front page was headlined 'A challenge to the Crown: now is the time for change'. The coverage included a monstrously long leading article calling upon the Monarchy to 'let in the daylight' and the results of a public opinion poll which suggested substantial public opposition to the 1701 Act of Settlement which still bans Catholics, bastards and adopted children from succeeding to the throne and which showed that 60 per cent of those polled wanted to be *citizens* compared with only 32 per cent who wanted to be *subjects*, while 8 per cent said they had no opinion on the matter. On 4th April 2001 the *Sun*, which is owned by Rupert Murdoch, a prominent republican, printed two opposing views on the future of the Monarchy one in favour by William Shawcross and the other against by Jonathan Freedland. It then argued strongly in its leading article against the idea that the hereditary principle should determine who became Head of State, commenting that it created 'a fundamentally wrong state of affairs which is, in the end, doomed'.

5   See the White Paper entitled *Citizen's Charter, Raising the Standard*, Cm 1599; HMSO, London, July 1991.

6   T. Wright, *op. cit.*; p. 91.

7   *Treaty on European Union*, Cm 1934; HMSO, London, May 1992.

8   See John Smith's keynote speech on this theme at a conference organised by Charter 88 in London on 1st March 1993.

9   See Tony Blair's John Smith Memorial Lecture at the Queen Elizabeth II Conference Centre in London on 7th February 1996.

10 See Lord Irvine's speech to the Citizenship Foundation given at the Law Society in London on 27th January 1998.

11 *Ibid.*

12 *Ibid.*

13 *Ibid.*

14 See Ralf Dahrendorf, *Life Chances – Approaches to Social and Political Theory*; Weidenfeld & Nicolson, London, 1979.

15 Margaret Thatcher said this during an interview with *Woman's Own*, 31st October 1987.

16 It is arguable that some national male obsessions – e.g. football, snooker and darts – can be seen as modern versions of primitive male pastimes which still have the capacity to bind men together.

17 All the figures in these paragraphs are taken from *Social Trends 30*, one of a series of well-known annual publications produced by the Office for National Statistics.

18 For an exposition of this argument in relation to the United States (but with application to the United Kingdom) see Robert Putnam, *Bowling Alone*; Simon & Schuster, New York, 2000.

19 In Keith Sutherland (ed.) *The Rape of the Constitution*; Academic Imprint, Thorverton, 2000; p. 314.

20 See George Monbiot, *An Activist's Guide to Exploiting the Media*; Bookmarks Publications, London, 2001.

21 Pippa Norris, *Electoral Change since 1945*; Blackwell, Oxford, 1997; p. 216.

22 The tendency for 'press barons' to throw their weight around politically has a long tradition in British politics which can be traced back at least to the early twentieth century when Lord Northcliffe's *Daily Mail* and Lord Beaverbrook's *Daily Express* seemed to have an ability to make or break political careers and to shape the political agenda.

23 For example, Alastair Campbell is reliably believed to have informed Trevor Kavanagh, the political editor of the *Sun* – before Tony Blair saw fit to inform his senior Cabinet colleagues – of the Prime Minister's decision to postpone the General Election from early May to early June 2001 because of the continuing bad publicity for the Government associated with the foot-and-mouth crisis.

24 This idea was seriously canvassed by Peter Mandelson in a speech at the British Embassy in Bonn when he speculated that one day we may be faced with a choice between hopelessly trying to revive a dying Parliamentary democracy and opting for a new kind of electronic direct democracy. See the *Guardian*, 16th March 1998.

25 See Cabinet Office Press Release in the name of Mo Mowlam, then Chancellor of the Duchy of Lancaster, posted on the world wide web on 27th November 2000.

26 See *Council of Civil Service Unions v. Minister for the Civil Service* (1984) 1 WLR 1174 for the view of the Law Lords that the judicial process was unsuitable for reaching decisions on national security and that decisions on whether the requirements of national security outweighed an employer's duty of fairness to his employees was a matter for the Government and not the Courts.

27 See Clive Ponting, *The Right to Know*; Sphere Books, London, 1985, for a clear exposition of the view that there is a superior concept of 'the public interest' which can occasionally be invoked by civil servants and others and which may be seen by a jury to override the wishes of the Government of the day.

Further reading

Anthony Barnett, *This Time: Our Constitutional Revolution*; Vintage, London, 1997.

Citizen's Charter: Raising the Standard, Cm 1599; HMSO, London, 1991.

Citizenship: Challenges for Councils; Local Government Information Unit, London, 2000.

Bernard Crick, *Essays on Citizenship*; Continuum, London, 2000.

Ralf Dahrendorf, *Life Chances – Approaches to Social and Political Theory*; Weidenfeld & Nicolson, London, 1979.

Anthony Giddens, *The Third Way: the Renewal of Social Democracy*; Polity Press, Cambridge, 1998.

David Held, *Political Theory and the Modern State*; Polity Press, London, 1989.

Anthony King, *Does the United Kingdom Still Have a Constitution?*, Hamlyn Lectures: Sweet & Maxwell, London, 2001.

George Monbiot, *An Activist's Guide to Exploiting the Media*; Bookmarks Publications, London, 2001.

Geoff Mulgan (ed.) *Life after Politics: New Thinking for the Twenty First Century*; Fontana, London, 1997.

Pippa Norris, *Electoral Change since 1945*; Blackwell, Oxford, 1997.

Keith Sutherland (ed.) *The Rape of the Constitution*; Academic Imprint, Thorverton, 2000.

S. Weir and D. Beetham, *Political Power and Democratic Control in Britain*; Routledge, London, 1999.

Tony Wright, *Citizens and Subjects*; Routledge, London, 1994.

Part VI

A REFORMED UNITED KINGDOM WITH A EUROPEAN FUTURE

The European Union and other challenges

Until relatively recently, the principal challenges to the United Kingdom or to any nation state came from other nation states acting and reacting in what Hans J. Morgenthau definitively described as 'an international society of sovereign nations'.[1] Of course, there were also internal challenges from secessionist or disaffected movements within the United Kingdom and elsewhere, but for several centuries the nation state existed mainly to protect its subjects or citizens from external threats and to promote social well-being within its borders. What is distinctive about contemporary circumstances at the beginning of the twenty-first century is that there are *multiple* challenges to nation states around the world.

For the United Kingdom today the first challenge is to come to terms with our European future. The European Union may currently be complementary to its member states, but it threatens eventually to become a replacement for them. There is no durable consensus among all the current member states – and even less likelihood of a consensus among a larger number of member states in future – about whether the European Union should remain essentially a Community of member states or move gradually to become a multi-national super-state. Without a convincing consensus about the ultimate goals, political structure and geographical scope of the European Union, it will be difficult for the United Kingdom and several other member states to come fully to terms with a European destiny.

Secondly, there is the challenge of political fragmentation within the United Kingdom and other nation states. This is driven within Europe by the siren song of renascent nationalism among such as the Scots, the Welsh, the Basques, the Corsicans, the Bretons and several other self-conscious 'nationalities' who believe that they have had a bad deal from the governing elites in the metropolitan centres of power.

Thirdly, there are the contemporary challenges of globalisation which are most obviously derived from the lightly regulated activities of global markets for goods and services, finance capital and information, and the emerging global markets for land and labour. However, globalisation is also manifested in terms of military security and foreign affairs, organised crime and terrorism, formal and informal networks of diplomacy, and social and cultural influences in the broadest sense. In all its forms globalisation is a highly potent force which is likely to prove increasingly corrosive of traditional national capabilities and even loyalties in all nation states.

What all this adds up to is that national authorities are under pressure from above and below, within and without. This is why we refer to *multiple* challenges to the nation state and why it is worth examining rather carefully the extent to which the United Kingdom seems likely to withstand such pressures. It is possible that this country will manage to do so, but likely that this will require further modifications to its traditional constitutional arrangements. After all we live in an age when local and private loyalties can be stronger than national and public loyalties and when global consciousness is rising among all except the most primitive and remote peoples in the world.

Coming to terms with the European Union

In the United Kingdom coming to terms with the European Union has been a long and painful process for politicians, constitutional lawyers and public alike. It has been made more difficult than it might have been both by the singular history and experience of the British people and by the dynamic, sometimes deceptive, character of the European Union which throughout the first half century of its existence has demonstrated many of the characteristics of a chameleon.

On the British side of the equation, we have been self-consciously an island people for more than a thousand years, as memorably evoked by John of Gaunt's famous speech in Shakespeare's *Richard II*, and we still feel ourselves to be fundamentally different from our partners and allies on the continent of Europe. For this and other reasons we were relatively late in joining the European Community and hence we denied ourselves the seminal influence which we would have enjoyed if the United Kingdom had been a founder member.

When we did eventually join in 1973, we did so with a divided political class, with all parties to a greater or lesser extent split on the issue and without the prior support of the British public in a referendum.[2] While some of the member states had looked to the United Kingdom to make a positive political contribution to the future development of the European Community, we actually brought as our constitutional dowry a set of well-established constitutional conventions that hinged upon the concept of Parliamentary supremacy and our dualist legal tradition, neither of which was very compatible with the codified constitutions and monist legal traditions of the six original member states.[3]

Furthermore, over the years all these problems have been compounded by a lack of frankness on the part of politicians and others in both the pro- and anti-European camps about the nature of the enterprise which we had joined. On the pro-European side of the argument, the dishonest tone was set by the bald statement in the 1971 White Paper of the then Conservative Government which said: 'there is no question of any erosion of essential national sovereignty; what is proposed is a sharing and enlargement of individual national sovereignties in the general interest'.[4] This dissembling approach has been maintained by the proponents of British membership ever since, whether by the Wilson Administration in 1974–75 which maintained that British membership was satisfactory but only 'on the right terms', or by the Major Administration which in 1996 referred misleadingly to what had by then become the European Union as 'a partnership of nations', or by the most senior Ministers in the first Blair Administration who consistently denied that there would be any significant constitutional implications in a possible future British decision to abolish the Pound and adopt the Euro as our currency.

On the anti-European side of the argument, the so-called 'Euro-sceptics' (which is itself a less than frank description of the views of those who are often paranoid or phobic about the European Union) have consistently exaggerated the dangers of further steps in European integration and have often adopted a hysterical attitude towards the European Union, which betrays an unattractive combination of instability and insincerity. For example, they have tended to argue that in a more deeply integrated Europe the British people will lose their distinctive national identity (as if the French were any less French or the Germans any less German by dint of each country's membership of the European Union), and the anti-European tabloids such as the *Sun* have pretended that before too long the peoples of the United Kingdom will be required to give up the British Monarchy for the sake of building a European super-state, notwithstanding the fact that as many as six other member states are constitutional Monarchies and show no signs of preparing to abandon this status in order to comply with the stipulations of membership of the European Union. In other words, the confused and largely agnostic British people have been poorly served by the opinion-forming elites on all issues to do with the European Union.

As for the European Union and its institutional prototypes, the first point to make is that the constitutional order with which the British people have been expected to come to terms has metamorphosed from a *Common Market* (which was generally thought to be a good thing by virtually everyone in the United Kingdom, except perhaps the Empire and Commonwealth loyalists) to a *European Economic Community* (note: no reference to politics) to the *European Communities* which comprehended all three separate Communities (ECSC, EEC and Euratom) to a *European Community* (in which the Single European Market was a vital driving force) to a *European Union*. Moreover, this last is the proud possessor of its own legal personality, anthem, flag and citizens. This has naturally been rather unsettling for the cautious majority in the United Kingdom. It has reminded all too many people of a game of grandmother's footsteps in which every time you look round, you find that the other players have managed to move stealthily closer to their ultimate destination, although you may never see them move. Even if one keeps firm control over one's incipient paranoia about this characteristic drive towards ever closer union (i.e. deeper integration) between the European peoples, it would still be much better if the European political elite had been more open about its nation-building ambitions instead of continuing with the policy advocated by Jean Monnet of pursuing the political unity of Europe by indirect and stealthy means.

The second major problem about the European Union for the British people and their political leaders is that it has been all along *a hybrid institution* (or set of institutions) which is neither entirely international nor entirely supra-national in its nature, but which has significant components of both types in its institutional make-up, not to speak of a growing emphasis upon sub-national institutions as well. This hybridity, which is sometimes celebrated as one of the constitutional secrets of the European Union, has tended to work against the chances of reassuring the British people about the nature of the project in which they are involved. It has also made it easier for the *communautaire* elite on the Continent and in this country (where they exist in much smaller numbers) to lie to themselves and to the general public about the ultimate purposes of the project and thus, when found out (as they were in several member states during the referendum campaigns prior to ratification of the Maastricht Treaty), to damage the credibility and the democratic legitimacy of the whole enterprise.

The third significant problem for British political and public opinion caused by the way in which the European Union has developed over many years is *psychological* in that from quite early on in the history of European integration a definite notion of historical inevitability, even manifest destiny, has attached itself to the European project. This led successive British Governments reluctantly to conclude that since Britain could not beat the members of the European Community at their own game, then it had better try to join them. This was actually rather a humbling experience for a once proud imperial nation, not least because its European neighbours, all of whom had been defeated or occupied during the war, seemed to have 'won the peace' more effectively than it had won the war. British participation in the European Community from 1973 onwards was therefore often rather grudging and unconvincing and, in any case, it was begun more than 20 years too late.

A fourth problem is the democratic deficit.

There is still no self-conscious European *demos* (the attentive public or electorate) to match, make demands upon and be represented by the central institutions that do exist. As long as this remains the case, the various peoples of the different member states may feel that the collective government of the European Union is not really *their* Government and in consequence the European Union institutions will continue to lack real democratic legitimacy.

Clearly neither the elite policy of building Europe by stealth, as conceived and advocated by Jean Monnet and the founding fathers, nor the high-minded and abstract ideal of 'European constitutional patriotism', as advocated by Jürgen Habermas and based upon the development of a participatory democracy of active European citizens, has proved sufficient to take the European project all the way to its ultimate destination.[5] For the pro-European purists the goal is usually a well-balanced and universal federal polity (a sort of Germany writ large), but for the realists it now seems to be the creation of a single European state out of however many member states are willing and able to form the political core of an enlarged European Union organised broadly in concentric circles within which the degree of economic and political integration increases the closer you move towards the centre. However, Jan Zielonka has argued that the most important ingredients which seem to be missing from the European Union in its current multi-layered form are 'the emotional sustenance, cultural affinity and historical symbolism that make [diverse] people invest their trust and loyalties for any serious collective endeavour'.[6]

United Kingdom membership of the European Union has had more influence upon the constitutional arrangements of this country than any other policy adopted by any British Government over the past quarter century. Two key characteristics of English law have shaped the constitutional position of the United Kingdom as its politicians, judges and academics have tried to come to terms with membership of the European Union. The first is the idea of *Parliamentary supremacy*, according to which there are no limits to the law-making capacity of Parliament; no Parliament can bind its successors; and, whenever there is a conflict between an earlier and a later Act of Parliament, the latter prevails (the doctrine of implied repeal). It may also be held that no Parliament can limit Parliamentary supremacy, whether its own or that of some future Parliament.

The second characteristic of English law is that it is *dualist* rather than monist in its treatment of international law. This means that Treaties, such as the 1957 Rome Treaty or the 1992 Maastricht Treaty, are regarded as being quite separate from national law and, if their provisions are to apply within United Kingdom jurisdiction, this can only happen as a result of their incorporation in national legislation. Thus all the various Treaties of the European Union to which the United Kingdom is a party are applicable and enforceable in this country only because an Act of Parliament (or a Statutory Instrument pursuant to such primary legislation) has been duly passed to give effect to their provisions. This means that all European law, whether directly effective Regulations or indirectly effective Directives, has a separate but contingent status in the United Kingdom – i.e. its validity and enforceability in the Courts is contingent upon national legislation, originally the *European Communities Act 1972*. See *Box 16* for the main characteristics of English law.

Box 16 Main characteristics of English law within the European Union

- The idea of *Parliamentary supremacy* which holds that there are no limits to the law-making capacity of Parliament within its jurisdiction; no Parliament can bind its successors; and whenever there is a conflict between an earlier and a later Act of Parliament, it is the later one which prevails.
- The idea that English law is *dualist* rather than monist in its treatment of international law – i.e. all the various European Treaties are only applicable and enforceable in this country because an Act of Parliament or a consequential Statutory Instrument has been passed to give effect to their provisions in this country.

On the other hand, there are three characteristics of European law and judicial practice which have had comparable significance in the civilised but titanic struggle between the forces of nationalism and supranationalism in the European Union. The first is the *legal supremacy of the European Treaties* (the current constitution of the European Union) which are the definitive texts in any constitutional or legal dispute within the European Union. The second is the *institutional supremacy of the European Court of Justice* (ECJ) as the final interpreter of the Treaties, arbiter of disputes and legal enforcer in the event of non-compliance with European law by any party whether public or private. The third is the fact that continental European judges, and hence the ECJ itself, take a *monist view of the law* which holds that international law and national law are qualitatively indistinguishable. This means that European law enshrined in the Treaties can take *direct effect* in the member states as a body of law with its own independent validity and there is no need for any prior approval by the national legislatures of the member states. It is not, therefore, in any way contingent upon national law, but rather superior to national law in those matters covered by the Treaties. See *Box 17* for the main influences of European law upon the United Kingdom.

However, the story of European law does not end there, characterised as it is by its dynamic quality which is especially evident in the ambitious claims that have been made over the years by the European Court of Justice. Two in particular stand out. *Firstly*, there is the controversial issue of the Court's role in relation to amendments of the founding Treaties, amendments which in substance have invariably taken the form of new Treaties of which there were thirteen between 1951 and 2001.[7] On the one hand, the ECJ conceded in its *Defrenne v. Sabena* ruling of 1976 and again in its judgment in the *ECHR case* of 1996 that modifications or amendments to the Treaties could only be made in accordance with the procedures of Article 236 of the Rome Treaty (now Article 309 of the Amsterdam Treaty) which require the unanimous agreement of all member states and subsequent ratification by all of them in accordance

---

Box 17 Main influences of European law upon the United Kingdom

- The *legal supremacy of the European Treaties* (sometimes referred to collectively as the *acquis communautaire*) over all national laws in the areas covered by the European Treaties.
- The *institutional supremacy of the European Court of Justice* (ECJ) as the final interpreter of the Treaties, arbiter of constitutional disputes within the European Union and legal enforcer of last resort for European law.
- The *doctrine of direct effect* for certain categories of European legal instruments – notably Regulations of the EEC institutions and Decisions of the ECSC High Authority – which means that such law does not have to be approved by national legislatures before it is applied to citizens in this or any other member state.
- Continental European judges, and the ECJ itself, take a *monist* view of the law, which means that for them international law and national law are qualitatively indistinguishable and the validity of the former is not dependent upon the validity of the latter.
- *Other features of European jurisprudence* have become increasingly influential in this country over the years since the UK joined the European Community – e.g. the doctrines of subsidiarity, proportionality, purposive judicial construction and positive human rights.

---

with their respective constitutional procedures. These rulings were apparently intended to reassure the member states that the ECJ would not attempt to make substantial new European law by a process of judicial *fiat*, thus usurping the exclusive rights of the member states in the sphere of European law making.[8]

On the other hand, in the German *Maastricht case*, the Federal Constitutional Court (*Bundesverfassungsgericht*), ruling on the compatibility of the 1992 Maastricht Treaty with the German constitution, declared that any attempt by the ECJ to increase the power of any European institution (including its own) or to confirm an act of any European institution that was *ultra vires* must be invalid, at any rate in Germany.[9] This suggested a genuine constitutional concern (which has been shared in the United Kingdom, France and Denmark) about possible 'judicial creep' by the ECJ into the European legislative sphere via either the doctrine of *implied powers* or the doctrine of *effet utile*.[10]

The second controversial issue arising from the ideological ambitions of the European Court concerns whether or not it is literally above the

(European) law, as well as being the ultimate authority on European law, in so far as it can demonstrate an unchallenged ability to determine the nature and extent of its own jurisdiction. Is there any balancing or even superior power – whether judicial or political – which can control or, if necessary, defeat the judges of the ECJ if they overstep the mark when they are in one of their creative and ambitious moods? In this country Parliament is there to play just such a balancing or trumping role against even the highest Court in the land (the Law Lords) when such a political response is considered necessary.

These questions of jurisdictional authority for the European Court of Justice have been put to the test in proceedings in the German Constitutional Court in 1993 (described above) and in the Danish Supreme Court in 1998 when each tribunal was asked to consider the compatibility of the 1992 Maastricht Treaty with its own national constitution.[11] In the former case, the Court declared that the system of European law was applicable in Germany only because the German national laws ratifying the Treaty of Maastricht had established that it was. Moreover, the European institutions had no authority to increase their powers or to extend their jurisdiction (*Kompetenz-Kompetenz*), because the European Union was a *Staatenverbund* (a union of states), which was constitutionally contingent upon unanimous agreement among the member states, and not a *Bundesstaat* (federation) or state with the right to increase its own powers conceivably without the consent of its constituent parts.

In the latter case, the Danish Supreme Court declared firmly that the European Union was essentially an *international* organisation and, as such, under Section 20 of the Danish constitution could neither be given powers contrary to the terms of the national constitution nor be permitted to exercise self-determination with regard to its own powers. It stressed that the European Union possesses only those powers conferred upon it by the European Treaties and insisted upon a restrictive definition of the Article 235 power in the 1957 Rome Treaty (subsequently Article 308 in the 1997 Amsterdam Treaty) which allows the Council of Ministers to take appropriate measures to attain the objectives set out in the European Treaties if the necessary powers have not already been provided in the existing texts. It found that the Article 177 power of Treaty interpretation available to the ECJ *was* compatible with the Danish constitution, provided this power was used within the terms of the Treaties; but it also ruled that the Danish national Courts retained the right to arrive at their own judgments on whether or not any actions of the European institutions went beyond the powers actually conferred upon them in the Treaties. Such robust reassertions of the inherent *limits* of European jurisdiction and of the subsisting *rights* of national courts acting in accordance with their own national constitutions should give reassurance to all those in the United Kingdom who have complained about the apparently ratchet effect of European law.

It is clear, therefore, that the United Kingdom is not the only member state in which some of the political and legal elite find it difficult to come to terms with the European Union. The constitutional goals of the European Union can be reconciled with the constitutional assumptions of the political class in the United Kingdom, but only with difficulty and usually by indulging in some almost metaphysical casuistry. The essence of the argument goes something like this. Within the scope of the European Treaties it is conceded that European law has priority over national law, which means that when the two conflict – as in the *Factortame* cases of 1990–91 – the provisions of the European Treaties must prevail over national legislation passed, whether before or after, by Parliament at Westminster.[12] Yet in recognition of the enduring doctrine of Parliamentary supremacy, the validity of European law in the United Kingdom is necessarily contingent upon national legislation – notably Sections 2(1) and 2(4) of the *European Communities Act 1972* – for its legitimacy and dependent upon our national Courts for its enforcement.

The United Kingdom has been increasingly influenced over the years since 1973 by European jurisprudence – e.g. the doctrines of subsidiarity, proportionality, purposive judicial construction and positive human rights. Yet we cannot ultimately be forced to adopt a codified European constitution if we do not wish to do so as long as we adhere to our own doctrine of Parliamentary supremacy, and as long as the European Court of Justice upholds Article 236 of the Rome Treaty which requires unanimity among the member states for each and every amendment to the original Treaties. Thus Government and Parliament in this country, and in all the other member states, *retain* an effective veto which can prevent our subordination to a new European constitution (e.g. in the form of a new Treaty of Berlin in 2004), provided we and our European partners stick by the letter and the spirit of the Treaties of the European Union.

In the real world of European politics further constitutional difficulties may arise if we in the United Kingdom continue to insist upon our undiluted national rights as a full member of the European Union by using them either for a British opt-out from further proposals for justiciable common European policy or for some form of 'renegotiation' of our existing European commitments which would involve picking away at the *acquis communautaire*. The exercise of either option would signify British politicians trying to have their European cake and eat it, and disappointment or failure would be very likely to follow.

Continued British use of the opt-out procedure (on the model of the opt-out from the Social Chapter at Maastricht in 1992) or the exercise of an agreed right for Britain to postpone its decision on participation in the Economic and Monetary Union are likely to have the political effect of stratifying the European Union into core and peripheral member states. We have already seen this with the emergence of 'the Euro-12' of Finance Ministers who meet regularly to deal with economic policy in the Euro Currency Zone in the absence of their colleagues from the United Kingdom, Sweden and Denmark. This emerging practice of acquiescing in *Europe à la carte* has already led the French and German Governments to promote the notion of 'enhanced cooperation' (a euphemism for deeper integration) between the so-called 'core' members of the European Union to the potential detriment and exclusion of those outside the core. This problem is likely to be further complicated and compounded as and when the European Union is enlarged to take in the next wave of new member states, some of which may be mustard-keen to be included in the 'Euro-core' even though geographically and developmentally they may be considered peripheral or second class.

The ultimate European response to repeated use of the opt-out tactic by the British could even be for many or most of the other member states to meet in separate conclave and then agree a new European Treaty among themselves for the dual purposes of ensuring much deeper political integration and deliberately excluding the United Kingdom and any other faint-hearted member states. If this were attempted, it would be a nightmare for the Commission, the Court and the other European institutions, not to speak of the damaging uncertainty and confusion that it would cause for all the economic and social interests that are woven into the existing European Union. It might even precipitate the disintegration of the political unity which has been so laboriously built up in Europe since 1950.

As for the alleged alternative of 'renegotiating' the terms and conditions of the United Kingdom's current membership of the European Union, this is simply dangerous and fanciful rhetoric which comes from a currently unelectable Conservative Opposition and would be shown up for the empty and counterproductive ploy that it is if ever a future Conservative Government were to attempt to put it into practice. On one level, of course, the operations of the European Union entail a process of continuous *negotiation* between all the institutions, interests and member states involved. But this reality should not be confused with the fiction of *renegotiation* by one member state which, in the minds of the other national Governments, would immediately raise the spectre of unravelling the *acquis communautaire*, something which would damage the credibility of the European Union and be unacceptable to all the other member states.

These various aspects of what might be called 'the Doomsday Scenario' for relations between the United Kingdom and the rest of the European Union need to be linked with the established constitutional position on both withdrawal and expulsion. *Firstly*, the possibility of a member state withdrawing from the European Union was implicitly recognised by the British Government and Parliament during the passage of the European Communities Bill in 1972, explicitly recognised by the German Constitutional Court in its October 1993 decision on the compatibility of the Maastricht Treaty with the German constitution, and put into practice by the 1982 referendum in Greenland which led to a successful negotiation between Denmark and its European partners resulting in the departure of Greenland from the Community in 1985. Thus if a future Government and Parliament in this country were to decide that the United Kingdom should leave the European Union, such a move could be implemented – although it might be thought politically expedient to get the decision ratified by a prior national referendum. Although under European law as a variant of international law our European partners would have the possibility of legal redress against the United Kingdom for a unilateral breach of the Treaties, it is likely that in the real world a political accommodation would be reached between the two sides during the course of amicable negotiations.

Secondly, there is no legal provision in the European Treaties for the expulsion of a member state, no matter how frustrating or troublesome it may have been to its European partners by obstructing or vetoing progress sought by all the other member states in the European Union. In the real world, however, if a future United Kingdom Government were to go out of its way consistently to thwart the political plans and ambitions of its partners in the European Union, their patience with us might run out and it is possible that political circumstances could be created which might have the effect of precipitating a decision by the United Kingdom Government and Parliament that the European game was no longer worth the candle. In those circumstances our departure from the European Union might be facilitated by persuading us to withdraw, although the distinction between that and expulsion might seem rather academic.

On the other hand, if one casts one's mind back to the so-called *French sheepmeat affair* in 1978–79, when the French Government openly and persistently banned the import of British lamb even in defiance of an adverse judgment by the European Court under Article 169 of the Rome Treaty, one can see that cases of open defiance by a single member state do occasionally lead to victory for the recalcitrant party.[13] In this instance the European Court did not finally pursue its action against France under Article 171 of the Rome Treaty (which provides for the enforcement of judgments of the ECJ) and France managed to secure Community backing for a new sheepmeat regime designed to support its own embattled sheep farmers. This example serves to emphasise that the most difficult future eventuality for a recalcitrant United Kingdom and its European Union partners would arise if our Government decided, ostensibly in the national interest and with the backing of Parliament, to pick and choose between those pieces of established European law which it accepted and those which it rejected. If such a practice were to become generalised, it would soon be a primrose path to the disintegration of the European Union. It is because the relevant national officials and politicians know this in their heart of hearts that sufficient self-restraint is

likely to be exercised to keep the European show on the road.

Unlike the doctrine of Parliamentary supremacy at Westminster, according to which no Parliament can bind its successors and a later statute is considered by the UK courts to trump an earlier one, in European law and practice there is a strong prejudice against the amendment or repeal of existing Community law and in the European Court of Justice there is a strong prejudice in favour of the Community interest in preference to any national interest in the interpretation and application of Community law. This underlines the fact that the constitutional preferences and practices of our European partners, with their accent upon codified constitutions and creative jurisprudence, have been far removed from our own in these islands – a difference which has not made it any easier to combine the two systems.

In these circumstances it may well be wondered why European supra-nationalists on the Continent (and their fewer counterparts in this country) have not felt able to declare victory in their long-running struggle with nationalists in the United Kingdom, Denmark and other member states. The main reason is because the European Union is still essentially a Community of member states rather than a supra-national democracy of the European people. Indeed, as we noted earlier, the basic Treaties of the European Union recognise only *European peoples* (in the plural) and once again the words used are indicative of important political intentions and political realities, at any rate at the time when the Treaties were drafted. It is possible that the combined member states of the European Union may one day metamorphose into a single European state not too dissimilar to other large member states of the United Nations, such as the United States, Australia or Canada. Such a momentous development would require the spiral process of European integration to progress a good deal further than it has done so far. It would also presuppose a much greater degree of democratic legitimacy than currently exists to support the European Union in its present form. This might only be derived from achieving a favourable majority verdict in each of the member states in a

European referendum on the new constitutional arrangements for the entire European Union.

Subsidiarity and sub-national politics

The doctrine of subsidiarity was introduced into European law in the shape of Article 3(b) of the 1992 Maastricht Treaty. It marked the first collective attempt by the twelve member states at that time to address the growth of sub-national politics in nearly all their national jurisdictions. For the Germans, it seemed a natural extension of the constitutional principles which underpin their *federal* Republic. For the French, it appeared to be a fairly harmless declaratory concession to the foibles of the Germans and other member states where sub-national government was well established. For the British Government, however, it was something of a lifeline to which Ministers clung when trying to explain to Parliament at Westminster how they had successfully begun to set a limit to creeping Community competence. However, the significance of all this for the constitutional debate in the United Kingdom is that the doctrine of subsidiarity has been a useful argument for the Scottish, the Welsh and the Northern Irish to use in support of their aspirations for greater political autonomy *vis-à-vis* Whitehall and Westminster.

Britain's membership of the European Union has thus contributed to the process of devolution in two ways. One is to do with the urge to imitate the apparent political success of the sub-national level of government in other member states. Thus nationalists in Scotland and Wales have been aware for several decades of the political strides towards autonomy and self-government which have been made by the Catalan movement in Spain, the Corsican movement in France and the proponents of the five 'Special Regions' in Italy, and they have been keen to emulate or even outdo them. In a paramilitary context, Irish terrorists in Northern Ireland have cooperated with and learned from their Basque counterparts in ETA.

The second factor is the impetus which has been provided by the European Commission and the federalist elements in the Council of Ministers in the form of political and economic initiatives designed to boost the viability and autonomy of the regions in the European Union in contradistinction or (some might say) opposition to the national authorities of the member states. Thus a Committee of the Regions was established in Brussels under the auspices of the 1992 Treaty of Maastricht and although it has not yet become an institutional power-house, it does provide a forum for representatives of the various regions to lobby and relate to the European Commission and the European Parliament. Wales has joined the partnership of the four so-called 'motor regions' of Baden-Württemberg, Rhône-Alpes, Lombardy and Catalonia. The Scottish Parliament and the Welsh Assembly have followed the example of other sub-national institutions by opening offices in Brussels to lobby the European institutions.

Linking the internal drive for devolution with the external need to resist the transfer of further powers from the member states to the European institutions is the doctrine of subsidiarity. Originally this was a doctrine advanced by Pope Pius XI in 1931 as part of Roman Catholic teaching on the characteristics of a well-ordered society.[14] It was also both familiar and reassuring to the German political class as a principle underlying their *Grundgesetz* or Basic Law of 1949. The doctrine, which has been used as a background consideration in some judgements of the European Court, essentially supports the principle that power should be exercised at as low a level of political organisation as possible (i.e. the national or sub-national level) unless certain criteria suggest the need to exercise it at the supra-national level of the European Union or, by extension, at the global level in certain cases. A declaratory formulation of this kind was insisted upon by the German, British and Danish Governments during the Inter-Governmental Conferences of 1990–91 and duly became Article 3(b) of the Maastricht Treaty in 1992.[15]

It soon became clear that such a formulation could not be relied upon to contain the *Kompetenz* ambitions of the European institutions, as had been hoped by the British and Danish Governments and the German *Länder*. Unlike the provisions in the

American constitution which carefully reserve all constitutional rights to the constituent states of the Union *except* those which are specifically allocated to the federal institutions, Article 3(b) cannot be relied upon to prevent the granting of new powers to the European institutions; it can only be applied to the actual exercise of power in those areas of policy where the central institutions share *concurrent* powers with the member states, *not* those which already fall under the *exclusive* competence of the central institutions; and it has already become apparent that the so-called 'necessity test' in Article 3(b) for determining whether or not 'the scale or effects of the proposed action [can] be better achieved by the Community' is open to widely differing interpretations among the Ministers from the various member states who are the first people required to apply the test.

In an attempt to clarify the situation and make subsidiarity more useful as an operational concept in the European Union, the fifteen member states agreed to add a 'Protocol on the application of the principles of subsidiarity and proportionality' to the 1997 Treaty of Amsterdam. This emphasised that *both* the preconditions in Article 3(b) had to be met before a proposed action by the European institutions could pass the subsidiarity test – i.e. that the objectives of the proposed action could *not* sufficiently be achieved by the member states and that they *could* be better achieved by the central institutions. Then on a belt-and-braces principle the member states agreed some *Guidelines* to assist them in deciding whether or not the preconditions had been met.[16] Even so the words used included a number of qualifying phrases which merely emphasised once again the arguable and essentially subjective nature of this supposedly helpful concept.

In order to assess the meaning of this debate for the evolution of constitutional thinking in the United Kingdom, it is worth noting several points. *Firstly*, the idea of political subsidiarity is evidently a much more compelling argument in a federal state like Germany than in a quasi-unitary state like the United Kingdom. This was underlined by the fact that in Germany it was from the German *Länder*, in their keenness to preserve their own constitutional space, rather than from the Federal Government

that the pressure came for a binding doctrine of subsidiarity. *Secondly*, while the Major Administration was in the habit of defining subsidiarity solely in terms of protecting *national* competences from what it saw as predatory and empire-building European institutions, the first Blair Administration, with its commitment to meaningful devolution, was somewhat more in sympathy with the simple point that the principle of subsidiarity should apply *pari passu* both between the European Union and the member states and between the member states and their sub-national political components. *Thirdly*, even though Germany, Denmark and the United Kingdom found themselves (with others) on the same side of the argument over subsidiarity, they were temporarily in the same camp for rather different reasons and the other member states did *not* share the British and Danish view that the onus of proof should be upon the advocates of more European competences rather than upon those who wish to preserve the rights of member states.

The very fact that there has been such an obvious sense of urgency and insecurity on the part of successive British Governments when dealing with the issue of subsidiarity suggests that Whitehall has never felt wholly reassured by the safeguard of unanimity contained in Article 236 of the Rome Treaty. Successive Governments in the United Kingdom have felt the constant need to buttress their minority position in the European Union with the doctrine of subsidiarity when attempting to counter the ratchet effect of European integration. Perhaps one consolation for the emerging sub-national authorities in Edinburgh, Cardiff, Belfast and even English metropolitan centres, such as London, is that the doctrine of subsidiarity may prove to be an effective argument with which to defend their role in government against the Jacobin tendencies in Whitehall and Westminster.

Overall, the close observer of contemporary British politics gets the impression that political fragmentation within the United Kingdom is unlikely to degenerate into real disintegration, partly because Labour Ministers have made real efforts to stay 'ahead of the curve' of popular expectations at the various sub-national levels of government and partly because it will take a while before any shortcomings in the devolution settlement become so serious as to threaten to destroy the good results of the policy so far. So while it looks as if political fragmentation is now a permanent condition, the process is unlikely to prove so damaging as to call into question the future integrity of the United Kingdom.

The current challenges of globalisation

At first sight it may appear contradictory that from the late 1960s to the present day many nation states have experienced a process of political fragmentation – in the United Kingdom this process had its origins in revived national consciousness at the sub-national level, i.e. in Scotland, Wales and Northern Ireland – yet from about the same time we have lived through a process of growing globalisation in which most nation states could be held to ransom by multi-national companies and non-governmental organisations, national markets have been increasingly penetrated by exports, direct investment, new technologies and social trends from other countries, and the locus of political regulation for a vastly expanded liberal market economy has shifted increasingly to supranational institutions. A moment's thought is enough to make one realise that these trends are complementary rather than contradictory.

The common threads in what has been happening to the political structures of the world are that all nation states have been losing any monopoly of real power that they may once have enjoyed within their own borders and that all established political authorities, which are still overwhelmingly national in their jurisdiction, have found it increasingly difficult to deal on equal, let alone superior, terms with the most powerful of the other actors in the global arena. As Susan Strange so clearly put it,

> the impersonal forces of world markets, integrated over the post-war period more by private enterprise in finance, industry and trade than by the cooperative decisions of [national] Governments, are now more powerful than the states to whom ultimate political authority over society and economy is supposed to belong.[17]

In other words, nation states have been challenged from above and below, within and without; but in recent times the challenge from without has probably been the most significant.

The process of globalisation has ebbed and flowed during the course of the nineteenth and twentieth centuries, occasionally with disastrous results for the peace and prosperity of the world. It seems clear from the historical record, however, that periods of retreat into national autarchy have been more damaging to people's basic interests than periods when the opportunities have been seized for regional or global integration *by peaceful means*. Globalisation in its current form is both a reality and a doctrine – in the latter case, a doctrine as determinist in its nature as the ideas of 'manifest destiny' or 'melting pot' in the consciousness of Americans. It is these almost hegemonic characteristics of globalisation which have obliged national political elites in the United Kingdom and nearly all other countries to adjust not only their national policies but in many cases their constitutional arrangements to fit the new economic and political realities.

The challenges which can arise for the United Kingdom and other nation states are very significant and, so far at least, have proved very difficult to counter. The most familiar challenge has come from trans-national companies which control huge amounts of foreign direct investment and corporate income flows that can influence levels of economic activity and employment in different national jurisdictions and hence the well-being of many people.[18] Such corporate monsters have been at least as involved in the struggles for political power in the world as any elected politicians and often much more. However, since the shocking attack on the World Trade Center on 11th September 2001, the threats to nearly all states and societies from nihilistic global terrorism have demonstrated a new kind of asymmetry which has exposed even the United States as seemingly incapable of defending its home population and retaliating effectively against the perpetrators of these foul deeds.

One of the most important constitutional effects of the exercise of power by trans-national corporations is that it is one of the factors which undermines the capacity of national authorities to exercise effective sovereignty within their own jurisdictions. Once the penny drops and the issues have been explained to the people by academics, media pundits and other commentators, the authority and the legitimacy of all national institutions, whether elected or otherwise, are reduced in the eyes of their subjects and citizens. It can therefore be more than a demystifying experience: it can be a demoralising experience which makes it harder for Governments at any level to govern and harder for ordinary people to accept the relative impotence of those institutions in which they have traditionally put their trust. Such dispiriting experiences can lead many people to question the validity of their traditional national identities and if this happens it tends to erode the essential feelings of citizen loyalty towards the state and hence the legitimacy of the state and its institutions in the eyes of many people.

The most familiar political responses to these problems for nation states and national authorities have been either for national Governments to combine, as they do in the European Union, to develop supra-national regulatory responses to global corporate threats or for local communities within nation states to mobilise with a view to establishing institutions of self-government which may give them a better chance of taking charge of their own local destinies, even if the results of their arm-wrestling with trans-national corporations invariably prove to be disappointing. In the former case, the remedy may be relatively more effective than leaving things to national authorities which can be divided and ruled by trans-national corporations, but the great disadvantage is usually the creation of a democratic deficit since the new mechanisms of supra-national regulation tend not to be particularly accountable in conventional democratic terms. In the latter case, the remedy may be relatively more democratic than leaving things to the national authorities and certainly there may be a greater sense of 'national' or community solidarity at the local level, but the disadvantage is normally that small economic and political units have less clout than large ones in dealing with any threats from globally organised entities.

We have seen examples of both these responses in the United Kingdom in recent years and notably since the Labour Government came to office in 1997. The willingness to participate in a supra-national response (albeit somewhat downplayed and disguised by British Government spin doctors for party political reasons) was visible in Tony Blair's decision at the very beginning of his first term of office in May 1997 when he went to the Amsterdam Inter-Governmental Conference and withdrew the previous British (Conservative) objections to most elements in the European Social Charter. He did this in the hope that he would not only win some credit with his new European partners, but also associate the United Kingdom with Community mechanisms designed to exert some countervailing power against trans-national corporations. The recourse to localism, on the other hand, was visible in the Labour Government's devolution policy.

Another severe challenge to nation states and national authorities comes these days from global financial markets which tend to be highly volatile and which seem to pay distressingly little regard to economic or political fundamentals in the United Kingdom or any other 'national' economy. One has to refer to 'national economies' in quotation marks, because in many ways this conventionally descriptive term is losing its traditional meaning as more and more economic and social activity becomes globally influenced or determined. Even the United States economy, which might seem to be in a category of its own with at least a measure of real autonomy, is increasingly influenced by global financial forces, such as dramatic movements in Latin American or Asian financial markets and rapid changes in the real price of crude oil and other commodities.

In institutional terms attempts are made to 'manage' financial markets, notably through the interest rate policies of the leading central banks in the United States, Japan, the Euro Zone of the European Union and the United Kingdom. These attempts usually constitute more of a response to or validation of financial market movements than anything more proactive, although it is undeniable that rapid cooperation between the main central banks in the past (e.g. in the wake of the 1987 stock markets crash or the Asian financial crisis in 1996) had some beneficial effect in steadying the nerves of panicky market operators. From the point of view of those who would like to inject some sort of constitutional order into this sector of economic activity in the world, the results so far have been very disappointing, largely because there is no single central bank or monetary authority for the entire globe and it does not look likely that one will emerge in the foreseeable future – even though the Chairman of the US Federal Reserve sometimes acts as if he were such a global authority. In short, it seems that such global institution building is for the time being beyond the collective will and capacity of the leading nations or groups of nations which would have to be involved if such an innovation were to be made. Thus, as far as financial markets are concerned, there is a dual deficit at the global level, both in effective monetary authority and in public accountability for such authorities as do exist, albeit only in embryonic form and based upon *ad hoc* cooperation between otherwise competing monetary institutions.

It might be argued that another real challenge posed by globalisation has come from the activities of the global media corporations and in one sense these are a sub-set of the general challenges posed by trans-national corporations which have already been discussed. Yet huge media conglomerates, such as Rupert Murdoch's News International, Ted Turner's CNN or Michael Eisner's Disney Corporation, do have some distinguishing characteristics which may pose a real threat to certain societies' cultural homogeneity, a feature which is often highly valued by the ruling elites because it is part of the essential social glue which holds their societies together as desirably distinctive social entities. Obviously, these challenges (which come from the liberal market and individualist political stable) can seem particularly threatening to undemocratic and authoritarian regimes, such as those in the People's Republic of China, Iraq or North Korea. But they are also felt to be culturally

threatening, to a greater or lesser extent, by Governments in France, Malaysia and Afghanistan – to name but three examples. The fact that successive Governments and opinion formers in the United Kingdom do not seem to have identified the globalisation (or rather the Americanisation) of our national culture as a particular problem against which strategies of resistance should be developed does not diminish the reality of these global influences.

As to what, if anything, the United Kingdom Government and Parliament could do (if it wished) to bring global media within the pale of our national constitutional arrangements, the simple answer seems to be not much. It is almost as if these great media corporations inhabit a supra-national space in which they can ignore traditional notions such as national sovereignty or cultural homogeneity within a single nation state or even a potential nation state such as the European Union. This reflects essentially an absence of *national capacity* in pluralist societies in the modern world to prevent citizens from being exposed to these global influences. For example, there are already many international agreements under the auspices of the World Trade Organisation, the International Broadcasting Union, the Council of Europe, UNESCO and other bodies – not to speak of the protection for free speech afforded by the First Amendment to the American constitution or by the European Convention on Human Rights – which effectively outlaw jamming, censorship and similar measures normally associated with the behaviour of authoritarian regimes such as the Baathist regime in Iraq or the military Junta in Myanmar. It also reflects an absence of *political will* in genuinely pluralist societies to impose legal inhibitions or restraints upon the media, whether locally or globally based, since this would be contrary to the letter and spirit of free speech under the law and contrary to established social traditions in free societies. If national regulation of global media in free societies is likely to be both ineffective and unpopular, any idea of global regulation would seem to be quite fanciful.

There are many other global challenges in the face of which national Governments and national

Parliaments often seem weak almost to the point of impotence and which have certainly not yet been tamed by national constitutional arrangements. It seems that the best that can be done is for legitimate national authorities to cooperate closely and to reach international agreements which they could then set about implementing in good faith. For example, the Rio Agreement in 1996 and the Kyoto Agreement in 1999 were commendable attempts to address the challenges of global warming, and similar agreements have been reached at regional level to combat water pollution and indeed water shortage, e.g. along the Mekong river in South-East Asia or the Tigris and Euphrates basin in the Middle East. These efforts have been all to the good, but they can founder upon the obduracy of one or two key participants – such as the present United States Administration with its apparent unwillingness and inability to persuade the US Congress to implement the Kyoto Agreement or the hostility between the Turkish and Iraqi Governments in their dispute over the vital rivers which irrigate and power both their countries.

Another category of intractable global challenges to nation states and national institutions is to be found in the sphere of globally organised crime and international terrorism. These too have been the subjects of many international meetings, some covert and some overt, and such matters are increasingly put on the agenda at meetings of the Group of Seven, the Group of 20, the Commonwealth and other such gatherings. All these international efforts are commendable, but all fall a long way short of the constitutional ideal which is to address global challenges within a recognised, legitimate and effective global framework.

It is painfully obvious, however, that the most glaring institutional weaknesses at the global level are to be found in the United Nations and all its various agencies which have never really lived up to their idealistic potential. The conclusion to be drawn from rather bitter experience over nearly 60 years in the United Nations is that the organisation is still more of a facade and a charade than an effective instrument for the resolution of international disputes and this will continue to be the case as long as some of the most powerful nations in the world, such as the United States and China, continue to be uncooperative or threatening when they believe their vital national interests to be at stake.

We can see from any examination of sensitive global issues, such as international arms sales, military intervention in Kuwait or the former Yugoslavia, and the protection of human rights, that the members of the Security Council and other leading member states often behave with hypocrisy and occasionally treat the United Nations with contempt. The UN Charter is often more honoured in the breach than the observance, and the organisation as a whole has been debilitated by the unwillingness of Congress to pay the full American subscription in a correct and timely way. United Nations sanctions have often been abused, circumvented or flouted; successive Secretaries-General have often not been given the political backing which they need from all the Great Powers; and many sections of the UN Charter have remained a dead letter ever since its promulgation in 1945.[19]

It seems that well-meaning people in the world are still waiting for the emergence of an effective and enforceable global jurisdiction to match most, if not all, the global challenges which have been mentioned in this section. The outcome so far has been decidedly patchy, with some relative success for global jurisdiction in areas such as trade and money under the auspices of the WTO and the IMF, but with disappointment and failure in other areas such as arms control, human rights and global terrorism. A recent, rather surprising ray of hope has been the moves towards the establishment of an International Criminal Court at the Hague, but in this instance too the world community knows that the prospects for this institution are to some extent dependent upon the political mood in Washington DC.

Common pressures and convergent responses

Nearly all nation states in the modern world are under common pressures from above and below, within and without. As we noted earlier in this chapter, however, the United States (as the only real superpower) and the People's Republic of China (as the most populous nation in the world and one whose regime seems disturbingly resistant to political pluralism) may be temporary exceptions to the general rule. Yet one cannot help observing that even the Great Powers are not immune from many global influences – e.g. financial markets, new technologies, WTO regulations and now (after 11th September 2001) international terrorism – so it is legitimate to generalise about common pressures at least in broad terms.

Susan Strange's analysis of the situation was based on three hypotheses:

1   that power has shifted upward from weak states to stronger ones with global or regional reach beyond their frontiers;

2   that power has shifted sideways from states to markets and thus to non-state authorities deriving power from their market shares;

3   that some power has evaporated so that no official bodies are exercising it.[20]

The first point took account of the *stratification* of state power which has resulted in the most powerful becoming relatively much stronger and the least powerful becoming relatively much weaker – developments which were traditionally attributed to the lead taken by the United States and, to a lesser extent, by the other leading nations, especially in new technology developments funded by risk capital institutions. The second point took account of the *privatisation* of much state power and the general diffusion of power away from public sector institutions to new partners or competitors in the private sector within or beyond their borders. This has happened largely as a consequence of deliberate governmental decisions to privatise great swathes of what had been rather bloated public sectors in many nation states ever since the Second World War – decisions which have been taken as much by left-of-centre Governments as by their right-of-centre counterparts. The third point took account of the *complexity* of power in the modern world which can sometimes make it

difficult for even trained observers to locate power and certainly makes it difficult for politicians and others to insist that power is used in publicly accountable ways. If the exercise of political power is often opaque and if the dispersion of power means that no one is clearly or unambiguously held responsible for its exercise, there is bound to be a democratic deficit of one kind or another.

This is precisely the point in the argument at which the particular constitutional arrangements of the various nation states become relevant to the discussion. Unless the exercise of political power in all its forms is subordinated to clearly delineated and independently enforced constitutional arrangements – whether at the national, sub-national or supra-national level of government – then problems of political authority and legitimacy can arise which may call into question the validity of governmental practices in many nation states.

If there has been a high degree of commonality in the various pressures outlined above, it should not be thought surprising that nation states – sometimes with very different political and constitutional traditions – have come forward with convergent and often similar policy responses. As Frank Vibert has pointed out, the changes that have taken place in British political style and constitutional habits of mind have set us on a convergent course with our European partners. For example, we in the United Kingdom have been getting used to more devolved structures of government, more consensual politics, a greater emphasis upon positive human rights, and greater reliance upon independent institutions such as the operationally independent Bank of England. At the same time, we have already experienced a move in this country from 'politics as an *ad hoc* activity to one which is better placed within more formal arrangements'.[21]

As for our European partners, the process of policy convergence seems to have been more noticeable in their gradual adoption of market-driven economic policies necessitated principally by the need to maintain European competitiveness in the global market. Whereas Labour Ministers in the United Kingdom since 1997 have been inclined to emulate some of the constitutional attitudes and practices which were already well established on the Continent, our European partners, in some cases rather grudgingly, have felt a need to emulate the liberal market economic policies pioneered by the American and British Governments in the early 1980s. Whatever the final balance in this equation may turn out to be, Frank Vibert is one of those who have been cautiously optimistic about the dividends which may be derived from constitutional renewal in this country which, he has forecast,

> will make it [the U.K.] a more confident and convincing advocate of institutional and procedural change in the [European] Union, better able to help form the winning coalitions on matters of principle and, as a result, a more comfortable member of the Union.[22]

General reflections

It seems clear that for practical, if not idealistic, reasons there is a European future for the United Kingdom and the cumulative effect of the various measures of constitutional reform which have been introduced since 1997 is to make this outcome more, rather than less, likely. The real question which follows from this is: on what basis will such a European future for the United Kingdom be built? It is worth concluding this chapter with some well-founded speculations about our European future.

The first key variable will be the evolution of the European Union over the next five to ten years. Fritz Scharpf, Director of the Max Planck Institute in Cologne, has highlighted one of the central dilemmas, namely that the process of European integration 'has greatly reduced the range of national policy options for the governing of capitalist economies without being able to recreate a commensurate governing capacity at the European level'.[23] This is an insight which is perhaps better appreciated in Germany and other Continental countries than it is (explicitly at any rate) in this country where most of the political class seems disinclined to face the fact that the European Union is unsustainable in its present hybrid form. The present German Chancellor, Gerhard Schröder, and other political leaders on the Continent have

been much more open than their British counterparts about the need for institutional reform at the European level, including the desirability of hammering out a proper European constitution by the time of the European Council meeting in Berlin in 2004 in order to settle in Treaty form the distribution of powers between the various levels of government in Europe.[24] In the continuing European constitutional debate, the key 'swing vote' will be that of France. Yet there will be real opportunities for the second Blair Administration to influence the outcome if it can summon up the political courage to tackle the constitutional issues head on.

The second key variable as far as the constitutional future of the United Kingdom is concerned will be the willingness, or otherwise, of the second Blair Administration to come off the fence in favour of the Euro, to campaign strongly for replacing the Pound with the Euro in a national referendum on the subject and – assuming victory for the pro-European cause – then to take a positive line in the inter-governmental discussions leading up to the projected Treaty of Berlin in 2004. If any link in this chain of events were to be broken or if there were to be a significant failure of nerve on the part of the Prime Minister and the Chancellor of the Exchequer, it is most unlikely that the United Kingdom would be able to enter the core zone of the European Union and so complete the long journey towards a fully European destiny which has been available to this country since 1950, but which so far the British political elite and most of the British people have not wished to embrace.

A third key variable will be the combined effect of the pressures upon the United Kingdom and other nation states from above and below the national level of governance and from within and without national jurisdictions. In the view of Professor Rod Rhodes and other experts in public administration, such pressures have resulted in 'the hollowing out of the nation state'.[25] If national authorities of all kinds continue to lose ground to the pressures from devolution and globalisation, then Rod Rhodes's rather bleak observation may well be borne out. If, on the other hand, those in charge of our representative national institutions manage to build structures and processes which are recognised as democratically legitimate and which prove constitutionally durable, then there will still be a leading role for national structures of governance.

A final important variable in the United Kingdom will be the mood and the aspirations of the British people. In our pluralist, fickle and sometimes alienated democracy no big constitutional changes will take root in our political culture if the preponderance of public opinion does not identify with them. Such a sense of identification may require the introduction of some form of proportional representation for elections to the House of Commons; further reform of the Monarchy, the Lords and the Commons; and the gradual transformation of the United Kingdom from a quasi-unitary into a quasi-federal state as the devolved institutions gain in self-confidence and authority. This last set of developments is more likely to occur if those outside Whitehall and Westminster decide to press ahead with their own contributions to constitutional renewal rather than wait passively for leading members of the national political class graciously to share more power with them.

Questions for discussion

1   How credible is it to maintain the doctrine of Parliamentary supremacy when the European Treaties to which the United Kingdom is a signatory legislate for the superiority of European law over national law?

2   Is the doctrine of subsidiarity a reliable way of containing the creeping supra-national competences of the European Community?

3   What evidence is there to suppose that the common pressures of globalisation will lead nation states to develop convergent policy responses?

Notes

1   Hans J. Morgenthau, *Politics among Nations*; Knopf, New York, 1960; p. 501.

2   However, public endorsement was given to British membership of the European Communities *ex post facto* as a result of the 1975 national referendum which approved continued membership on so-called 'renegotiated terms' by a majority of two to one.

3   According to *dualist* legal doctrine as applied in the United Kingdom, there is a clear distinction between international law and national law, with the former contingent upon the latter for its legal validity in this country. According to *monist* legal doctrine as applied in Continental European countries, an international treaty that is sufficiently clear and precise can apply directly within a national legal system and does not need to be incorporated in or provided for by national legislation before it can achieve legal validity in the country concerned.

4   See *The United Kingdom and the European Communities*, Cmnd 4715; HMSO, London, 1971; para 29.

5   See *Praxis International*, Vol. 12, No. 1, April 1992, for an exposition of the Habermas argument about European constitutional patriotism.

6   Jan Zielonka, *Explaining Euro-Paralysis*; Macmillan Press, Basingstoke, 1998; p. 79.

7   A list of the thirteen Treaties is as follows: 1951 Treaty of Paris (creating the European Coal and Steel Community), 1957 Treaty of Rome (creating the European Economic Community and Euratom), 1965 Merger Treaty (merging the three European institutions to form the European Community), 1970 first Budgetary Treaty (establishing the system of 'own resources' for the European Community), 1972 first Treaty of Accession (providing for the entry of United Kingdom, Ireland and Denmark), 1975 second Budgetary Treaty (refining the budgetary arrangements and introducing a scale of financial contributions linked to a percentage of national budgets), 1979 second Accession Treaty (providing for the entry of Greece), 1985 third Accession Treaty (providing for the entry of Spain and Portugal), 1986 Single European Act (providing for the gradual creation of a European Single Market), 1992 Treaty of Maastricht (providing for the creation of the European Union and within that an Economic and Monetary Union), 1994 fourth Accession Treaty (providing for the entry of Sweden, Finland and Austria), 1997 Treaty of Amsterdam (consolidating earlier Treaties and reinforcing the idea of European citizenship), and the 2001 Treaty of Nice (still to be ratified by all the member states, incorporating a Charter of Human Rights and paving the way for 'enhanced cooperation' between those member states which may wish to integrate more deeply than the rest).

8 Opinion of the European Court of Justice, 28th March 1996, in the *ECHR Case*, Opinion 2/94 (1996) ECR I-1759.

9 Decision of the Federal Constitutional Court, 12th October 1993, in *Brunner v. European Union Treaty* (1994) 1 CMLR 57.

10 The doctrine of *implied powers* is the theory that if a European Treaty gives a European institution a particular task or responsibility, it must have been the intention of the signatory states to confer upon it the necessary powers to carry out such a task or responsibility and so the ECJ 'discovers' such powers and declares that they exist, even if they are not explicitly written into the Treaty. The doctrine of *effet utile* is the theory that all European Treaties should be interpreted by the Courts in ways which enhance rather than reduce their effectiveness.

11 Notably in the decision of the German Constitutional Court on *Brunner v. European Union Treaty*, 12th October 1993 (1994) 1 CMLR 57 and the judgment of the Danish Supreme Court in *Carlsen v. Rasmussen*, 6th April 1998.

12 See *R. v. Secretary of State for Transport, ex parte Factortame* (1990) ECR I-2433 and *R. v. Secretary of State for Transport, ex parte Factortame* (1991) ECR I-3905 which effectively nullified Part II of the Merchant Shipping Act 1988 and the Merchant Shipping (Registration of Fishing Vessels) Regulations 1988 as contrary to European law.

13 Notably in *European Commission v. France*, Case 232/78 (1979) ECR 2729.

14 The doctrine of *subsidiarity*, which has its philosophical origins in Roman Catholic social teaching, can be traced back at least to the pronouncement by Pope Pius XI in 1931 in his *Rundschreiben über die gesellschaftliche Ordnung* (Encyclical on Social Order).

15 Article 3(b) of the 1992 Maastricht Treaty stated that

> in areas which do not fall within its exclusive competence, the Community shall take action, in accordance with the principle of subsidiarity, only if and in so far as the objectives of the proposed action cannot be sufficiently achieved by the Member States and can therefore, by reason of the scale or effects of the proposed action, be better achieved by the Community.

16 The agreed Guidelines in the *Protocol on the Application of the Principles of Subsidiarity and Proportionality* attached to the 1997 Treaty of Amsterdam stated that the necessary conditions were likely to be fulfilled if '(1) the issue under consideration has transnational aspects which cannot satisfactorily be regulated by action by Member States; (2) actions by Member States alone or lack of Community action would conflict with the requirements of the Treaty ... or would otherwise significantly damage Member States' interests; and (3) action at Community level would produce clear benefits by reason of its scale or effects compared with action at the level of the Member States'.

17 Susan Strange, *The Retreat of the State – the Diffusion of Power in the World Economy*, Cambridge University Press, Cambridge, 1996; p. 4.

18 Figures for 1992 quoted by Susan Strange on the trends for trans-national corporations (TNCs) suggested a total number of 35,000 TNCs with some 150,000 affiliates and a total book value of foreign direct investment world-wide of $1,700 billion. More recent estimates produced by Noreena Hertz in her book *The Silent Takeover*, Hutchinson, London, 2001; suggest that of the 100 largest economic units in the world (including nation states) 51 were transnational corporations and the imbalance between corporate and state power was continuing to shift in favour of the former at the expense of the latter.

19 See Rosalyn Higgins, *The United Nations – Appearance and Reality*, Hull University Press, Hull, 1993; and H.G. Nicholas: *The United Nations as a Political Institution*, 5th edn, Oxford University Press, Oxford, 1975.

20 S. Strange, *op. cit.*; p. 189.

21 Frank Vibert, 'British constitutional reform and Europe', in R. Hazell (ed.) *Constitutional Futures*, Oxford University Press, Oxford, 1999; pp. 61–2.

22 *Ibid*; pp. 65–6.

23 Fritz Scharpf, *Governing in Europe – Effective and Democratic?*; Oxford University Press, Oxford, 1999; p. 193.

24 For example, the German Social Democratic Party agreed a plan sponsored by Chancellor Schröder at its 2001 Party Congress which, if eventually implemented in the European Union, would transform the European Commission into an effective Government of the Union answerable to a strengthened European Parliament (Lower House) and to the Council of Ministers (Upper House) in a bi-cameral institutional framework modelled on the Federal Republic of Germany and designed, among other things, to help close the democratic deficit in the European Union.

25 See Rod Rhodes, 'The hollowing out of the state', *Political Quarterly*, Vol. 65, 1994, pp. 138–51.

Further reading

G. De Burca and J. Scott (eds) *Constitutional Change in the European Union – from Uniformity to Flexibility?*; Hart Publishing, Oxford, 2000.

Trevor C. Hartley, *Constitutional Problems of the European Union*; Hart Publishing, Oxford, 1999.

David Held, *Political Theory and the Modern State*; Polity Press, Cambridge, 1989.

Rosalyn Higgins, *The United Nations – Appearance and Reality*; Hull University Press, Hull, 1993.

L. Hooghe and G. Marks, *Multi-level Governance and European Integration*; Rowman & Littlefield, Oxford, 2001.

Jörg Monar and Wolfgang Wessels (eds) *The European Union after the Treaty of Amsterdam*; Continuum, London, 2001.

Hans J. Morgenthau, *Politics among Nations*; Knopf, New York, 1960.

H.G. Nicholas, *The United Nations as a Political Institution*; 5th edn, Oxford University Press, Oxford, 1975.

Fritz Scharpf, *Governing in Europe – Effective and Democratic?*; Oxford University Press, Oxford, 1999.

Susan Strange, *The Retreat of the State – the Diffusion of Power in the World Economy*; Cambridge University Press, Cambridge, 1996.

Hugo Young, *This Blessed Plot: Britain and Europe from Churchill to Blair*; Papermac, London, 1999.

Jan Zielonka, *Explaining Euro-paralysis*; Macmillan Press, Basingstoke, 1998.

website for the European Union www.europa.eu.int

Cumulative change and dynamic outlook

As we noted at the beginning of this book, there has been both continuity and change in the constitutional arrangements of the United Kingdom. During the first Blair Administration from 1997 to 2001 we witnessed an unusual amount of constitutional change by the standards of this country over a relatively short period of time. It is clear that the drive for constitutional change under New Labour is by no means over, although what we can expect under this heading during the second Blair Administration seems likely to be less ambitious than the programme of constitutional reform from 1997 to 2001.

Some have argued that the main reason for the relative incoherence in Labour's approach to constitutional change is that Tony Blair himself was never a true believer in what was essentially a policy which he inherited from John Smith. According to this school of thought, he was quite content to charge Lord Chancellor Irvine with the coordinating responsibility for steering the constitutional measures onto the Statute Book and the presentational responsibility for justifying the various parts of the policy on a basis described as 'principled pragmatism'.[1] Yet this is by no means the whole story, because the idea of *institutional modernisation* has also been an important cross-cutting theme in Tony Blair's whole approach to governing the country and it belongs fair and square under the overall heading of constitutional change in a polity which has few formalised constitutional arrangements and no codified constitution.

Another important explanation of why the process of constitutional change has taken the course which it has is that much of what would have been a matter of constitutional jurisprudence in other countries boils down in this country to being a matter of changing the rules of political competition, adjusting the methods of voting and responding to shifting political relationships within our unique polity. This is the school of thought which maintains that the correct mode of constitutional change in the United Kingdom is that of incremental and pragmatic adjustment to changing social and political circumstances and which is still loath to embrace a more holistic approach based upon building a *corpus* of constitutional law.

There may be much to be said for this traditional British approach, but it is likely to be increasingly challenged by what might be called European constitutionalism, embodied in successive European Treaties to which this country is a signatory and then elaborated in a growing body of case law derived from judgements of the European Court.

Creating new constitutional arrangements

It is not hard to substantiate the case that the Labour Government has already brought about a situation in which politicians and all other participants in the political process are now operating under new constitutional arrangements as a consequence of the wide raft of constitutional statutes and other measures which have been passed by Parliament since 1997. On the other hand, these new arrangements have not in all instances superseded the old arrangements and in many cases it has been a matter of grafting new shoots onto old plants or pouring new wine into old bottles. In other words, the evolutionary tradition is alive and well in Whitehall and Westminster.

To begin with, there have been constitutional changes which belong under the heading of *issues of identity and territory*. In Northern Ireland these have produced a fragile and precarious power-sharing Executive and Assembly which have been supported by the broad mass of the nationalist community, but much less by the Unionists. However, the development of the peace process following the 1998 Good Friday Agreement has become the object of growing suspicion and resentment among much of the Unionist community who feel that they have made nearly all the political concessions but have got little that is bankable in return from Sinn Fein and the Provisional IRA.[2] In Scotland a much more secure political structure has been created which, after a gap of nearly 300 years, has restored a Scottish Executive and a Scottish Parliament to the Scottish people. In Wales the Welsh Assembly and the Welsh Executive were at first very precariously based upon evenly divided Welsh public opinion and a split Welsh Labour

Party, but more recently these institutions too seem to have got into their stride and there is almost certainly no going back under any Government to the *status quo ante*. The thrust of political opinion in all parties in Wales (even in the Conservative Party) is that they should aim for parity of status and esteem with the Scottish Parliament. This means that in due course the Welsh Executive and Assembly are likely to press for primary legislative powers and the authority to vary the level of income tax.

In England, on the other hand, there was no significant groundswell of English nationalism before Labour came to power in 1997. Even in the relatively disadvantaged regions – e.g. the north-east and the south-west – while there may have been a degree of political resentment towards central Government in London because of the generosity which it had shown towards Scotland and Wales, there was no self-conscious nationalism. The main reason for this is that full integration has long seemed to be much more advantageous than disadvantageous for people in all parts of England – in Newcastle or Plymouth, Liverpool or Ipswich – because many of them have benefited from fiscal transfers and other forms of regional assistance and in the better-off parts of the country the question never really arose.

This rational self-interest in preserving the benefits and obligations of an integrated United Kingdom was sorely tested during nearly two decades of Conservative Government (1979–97) when the needs of the outlying regions of England, as well as those of the peripheral 'nations' of the United Kingdom, seemed to be neglected by the Thatcher and Major Administrations. The result was that Labour Party opinion in the regions of England began to take a stronger interest in active regionalism and thus the political foundations were laid for what has come to be called 'rolling devolution'. This will allow the English regions to opt into stronger arrangements for representative regional government once they secure the approval of Labour Ministers and the endorsement of their own people in regional referenda. The logic of this permissive policy points towards a much more regionalised United Kingdom by the end of the 2001–6 Westminster Parliament.

The second main theme to emerge from the constitutional changes which have taken place since Labour came to power in May 1997 has been that of *institutional modernisation*. This is an idea which was a consistent refrain in Ministerial speeches throughout the first Blair Administration and it chimed in well with the linked themes of 'New Labour – New Britain – New Century'. In presentational terms the 'm word' has been a convenient way of talking about institutional and constitutional reform without seeming too radical or threatening to most people who seem quite comfortable with our traditional institutions. It is a theme which has been juxtaposed and contrasted with 'the forces of conservatism' – notably in Tony Blair's speech to the 1999 Labour Party Conference – and in this way it has been possible for senior Ministers to associate their constitutional reforms with the future, while denigrating and dismissing their political opponents (both Conservative and Old Labour) as reactionary representatives of the past.

In this respect the idea of modernisation has had an intellectual link with the theme of 'the Third Way' which Tony Blair and his closest political advisers have refused to abandon in spite of being subjected to media and academic ridicule for the apparent vacuity of the concept. Indeed, in a self-consciously important article for *Prospect* magazine written only a few months before the 2001 General Election, Tony Blair argued that the ideas associated with the Third Way were still the wave of the future for progressive politics in this country and in a list of six new challenges for a second term of Labour Government he included institutional modernisation and democratic renewal.[3]

New Labour has had an ambitious agenda for modernising central Government, but it is still unclear how much of this programme is a matter of substance and how much a matter of presentational 'spin'. On the one hand, few would deny the significance for central Government of devolution, statutory incorporation of human rights and access to public services on-line; and in the past it has been relatively unusual for Ministers and civil servants to apply to themselves the reforms and changes which they were keen to impose upon others. On the other hand, there is some doubt and cynicism about whether all the brave talk and glossy documents that celebrate the modernisation of the policy- and decision-making processes in Whitehall really amount to much more than an expensive public relations exercise which senior civil servants of the old school may not fully believe in but feel obliged to promote for reasons of self-protection. Certainly it seems that all the 'Sir Humphreys' in Whitehall have mastered the new jargon of 'evidence-based policy making', 'cross-cutting issues' and 'social inclusion' and there is an impressive-sounding Centre for Management and Policy Studies which has been established to inculcate the new doctrines at every level in the civil service. Yet for all these efforts the well-informed observer is left with a nagging doubt about whether the hype may exceed the practical benefits in day-to-day public administration.

The modernisation of local government has had a more modest agenda since May 1997, perhaps partly because previous Conservative Administrations did much to discredit themselves by overdoing the 'reform' of local government structures and local government finance and because Labour Ministers had concluded when they were in Opposition that they should not repeat the mistakes of their political opponents. However, this did not prevent the first Blair Administration from introducing a wide-ranging White Paper, *Modern Local Government*, in July 1998 which contained some ambitious reforms to improve the efficiency and responsiveness of local authorities. Nor did it prevent Ministers from providing the option of directly elected Mayoral government for those urban localities which wished to take it up following public endorsement in a local referendum.

In the event Labour Ministers made at least two radical interventions in local government during the first Blair Administration. The first was to insist upon a new approach to local authority governance by drawing a clear distinction between executive and representative Councillors, but leaving the precise form of local executive to be chosen locally from three different models sketched out by Ministers. The second was to threaten local authorities with direct intervention from central Government if any Local Education Authority manifestly failed to deliver adequate standards of school education or if any Social Services Department betrayed the interests of vulnerable children or elderly people in its statutory care.[4]

The theme of institutional modernisation has also been applied by Labour Ministers to Parliament, although with markedly more enthusiasm to the House of Lords than to either the Monarchy or the House of Commons. Yet even in the case of the House of Lords one cannot help feeling that Tony Blair has been relatively content with the shape and composition of the so-called interim House and (along with some of his senior colleagues in the Commons) may have needed persuading that a further stage of Lords reform involving a significant component of elected peers would be worthwhile.

In relation to the Monarchy, the main task for the first Blair Administration was to help restore media and public respect for the Royal Family at a time when it had been through some very turbulent waters. When Tony Blair became the Queen's First Minister in May 1997, the Monarchy was still feeling the long-term effects of the events of 1992 – a year which the Queen herself had referred to as her *annus horribilis*. Yet within the space of only a few months the Prime Minister and his Press Secretary were urgently trying to steer the Queen and her Palace advisers through the immediate aftermath of Princess Diana's tragic and untimely death when for a few days it looked as though hysterical media and a grieving public might have wanted to send the whole Royal Family packing. Further embarrassment was undoubtedly caused to the Queen and her Palace advisers in early 2001 by the Countess of Wessex (the wife of Prince Edward) with her unguarded and insensitive remarks about the rest of the Royal Family to a tabloid journalist posing as an Arab sheik.[5]

A serious *constitutional* issue which will have to be addressed sooner or later is whether ways can be found to demystify without destroying the concept of the Crown. Certainly if the Prime Minister ever wishes to blunt the campaign that has been led by an unlikely alliance between the editors of the *Guardian* and the *Sun* and republican critics of the Monarchy such as Tony Benn and Tom Nairn, he and his advisers will need to think carefully during Labour's second term of office about whether there are any changes that should be made to the doctrines of Royal Prerogative and Crown immunity which still lie at the heart of our habits of 'monarchical' government.[6]

It took the Labour Party about 100 years to bring about the removal of the hereditary peers from the House of Lords. Now there is the slightly ironic situation that the only serving members of the House of Lords who have been elected, albeit on a very limited franchise consisting of all their colleagues, are the 92 hereditaries who retained their places in the so-called interim House thanks to the compromise reached between Lord Cranborne and Tony Blair in 1998 as background to Stage One of the reform process. All the other members of the interim House have been appointed at one time or another – most of them in the traditional manner on the advice of the Prime Minister, but some of them by the recently established Appointments Commission chaired by the cross-bench peer Lord Stevenson. A further irony is that the overwhelmingly appointed interim House has proved in its short life to be more independent-minded and less susceptible to Government pressure than the unreformed House stuffed with hereditary peers which it replaced. It seems that the discipline of patronage wears off pretty quickly once an individual has been appointed to the Upper House, assuming that he or she does not crave the treadmill of Ministerial office.

It became clear from the set-piece debates on the Wakeham Report and from other indications since then in the Labour Manifesto and the Queen's Speech of 2001 that following further consultation the Government would introduce legislation to implement the second phase of Lords reform.[7] Ministers have since published a White Paper setting out how they hope to complete the reform of the Second Chamber by abolishing the remaining hereditary peers, providing for at least one-fifth of the reformed House to be directly elected, and severing the historic link between the grant of a peerage and membership of the Upper House.

However, nothing much has changed in the inter-institutional politics of House of Lords reform, since some MPs on both sides of the Commons still feel threatened by a more powerful Second Chamber which would derive extra legitimacy from being even partially elected. On the other hand, the modernisers in all parties believe that the reputation of Parliament and the quality of legislation would benefit from the creation of a more democratically legitimate Second Chamber and a greater number of independently appointed independent members.[8]

Radical modernisation of the House of Commons has not taken place since Labour came to power in 1997, but with Robin Cook as Leader of the House in the second Blair Administration there may be more impetus for incremental reforms. Some evidence for this belief can be found in an interview and a speech which Robin Cook gave soon after taking up his new post and in the growing restiveness on the Labour backbenches.[9] On the other hand, most British Governments of all political persuasions are usually not in the habit of knowingly fashioning Parliamentary rods for their own back and a second Blair Administration with a more controversial policy agenda is unlikely to relish dealing with a reformed House of Commons which is better equipped to hold it to account.

The final subject which we dealt with under the heading of *institutional modernisation* was the reform of the legal system in England and Wales. After careful examination of the huge agenda of legal reform masterminded by Lord Irvine as Lord Chancellor, it is justifiable to argue that the legal system has been *transformed*. The two Woolf Reports have led to a streamlining of civil procedure and more active case management by the judges. Similar streamlining and rationalisation of a fragmented system should follow from the fundamental reforms recommended by Lord Justice Auld for the criminal courts and by Sir Andrew Leggatt for the tribunal system.

In general, the energetic Lord Irvine seems to have left no stone unturned in applying his reforming and modernising zeal to the legal system. He has sought to democratise the judiciary and the higher ranks of the legal profession by using his influence over judicial and legal appointments in favour of greater social inclusion. He has sought to improve public access to legal services by establishing a new Community Legal Service (CLS) and promoting a wider network of legal advice centres which can offer cheaper and more accessible legal services on issues such as housing and consumer credit, divorce and child abuse. He has even decided – God bless him – to end 'the anachronism' of judges and barristers wearing wigs in the civil courts.

Yet unquestionably the most significant and long-lasting changes in the legal system, which were made by the first Blair Administration with widespread support from the Labour and Liberal Democrat benches in both Houses of Parliament, are those which flow from the *Human Rights Act 1998*. By willingly taking this body of European jurisprudence into the bloodstream of English common law, Parliament took a giant step which may very well transform our legal system and change the balance of the constitutional arrangements in the United Kingdom. When the Act came into force in October 2000, it was greeted by Lord Steyn (the longest-serving Law Lord) as 'a new legal order' and it was arguably the most significant single measure of constitutional reform promoted by the first Blair Administration.

The main point in *Part V* of the book was to remind the reader that in the United Kingdom some constitutional changes are responses by the Government of the day and by Parliament to perceived political necessity – e.g. the urgent need to clean up British political life after the sleaze and scandals of the 1990s – and some are consequences of deliberate political initiatives – e.g. Labour's long-standing association with the campaign for freedom of information. There is also an important distinction between constitutional changes introduced by one Government which are intended to build upon or bring to fruition constitutional changes made by a previous Government – e.g. unfinished business such as Lords reform or devolution to Scotland and Wales – and those which deliberately break fresh constitutional ground, such as the *1972 European Communities Act* or any future decision by the British public in a national referendum in favour of some form of proportional representation for elections to the Westminster Parliament. Above all, in a political system very much shaped by the doctrine of Parliamentary supremacy, there are informal rules and conventions, procedural adjustments agreed by Parliament and attitudinal shifts experienced by the politically attentive public which can be as important as statutes and can contribute to significant constitutional change of one kind or another. These then influence the delicate skein of political customs, obligations and expectations which form the basis of our constitutional arrangements at any given time.

Thus the rules of the political game and of competition for power between the parties have been significantly changed, although the origins of the process are traceable back to the period before Labour came to power in 1997. In many respects these reforms were unavoidable because the Conservatives had done so much to discredit themselves and, by extension, the entire political class, with their antics, sleaze and bitter divisions during the 1992 to 1997 Parliament. These forms of political misbehaviour by certain Tories made it necessary in 1994 for John Major to puncture the hallowed principle of Parliamentary self-regulation in the House of Commons and set up a *permanent* Committee on Standards in Public Life as a device to investigate what had gone wrong and defuse what had become a political crisis for the Government of the day. Since that time the Committee under successive chairmen has issued a wide range of sometimes controversial reports with far-reaching implications for the conduct of politics under both Conservative and Labour Administrations.

The constitutional consequence of this spate of regulatory advice from the Committee was the legislation modernising the rules of the political game in the form of the *Political Parties, Elections and Referendums Act 2000* which came into effect in time to govern the conduct of the 2001 General Election. For the first time in British history this put the political parties and other political campaigning groups under the aegis of what might be called a 'constitutional' statute which in a sense was there to protect them from themselves, but which also obliged them to abandon their long tradition of self-regulation.

Another example of how the rules of the political game have changed is the apparent move from a culture of official secrecy towards statutorily guaranteed freedom of information (with certain important exemptions). This may affect the balance of power between the Government of the day and its critics and opponents more than the ritual competition for office between the governing party and the official Opposition. Labour Party advocates of the *Freedom of Information Act 2000* have sought to argue that this piece of legislation is a blow for open government and a significant extension of citizens' rights. Their critics in the all-party Freedom of Information Campaign and in other non-governmental organisations have been scathing about the legislative loopholes which remain.

In the last years of the twentieth century other considerations of fairness and participation came to the fore. We can find evidence of these trends in the adjustments made to electoral arrangements in the *Political Parties, Elections and Referendums Act 2000* and especially its statutory provisions for the conduct of referenda. Only the future of the electoral system for elections to the Westminster Parliament still seems to be in the hands of the political parties, no doubt because the rules of this particular political game influence, if not determine, who wins and who loses the one type of contest which really matters to them. The 'assurances' which the Liberal Democrats secured from Labour in 1997 that there would be a national referendum on electoral reform before the end of the 1997–2001 Parliament proved to be non-bankable and the formula that Labour offered in its June 2001 Manifesto was actually more vague and less binding than the previous one.[10]

Politicians and political commentators often worry about what they see as the deteriorating relationships between the people, society and the state. They measure their concerns in the apparently weak commitment of British subjects to the new-found concept of citizenship, in the disturbing shift from a willingness to participate in the processes of our democracy to a growing alienation from it, especially among the young, and in what increasingly appears to be the chronically unattractive condition of representative government. In these circumstances the political elite has turned its attention to our constitutional arrangements both for an explanation and for a possible solution to such social and political problems.

For example, at the outset of the 2001 General Election campaign Simon Jenkins, the well-known columnist, asked 'for what causes are non-voters not voting?' and the answer which he provided was that 'some blame must attach to a constitution which, in Britain, is so hostile to participation and which erects so many arcane barriers of ceremony and secrecy between voters and the government'.[11] In making this point he was really criticising what is left of our elitist and imperial constitutional arrangements which date back to the times when Britain was a self-confident Great Power and the ruling political elite tolerated but did not truly believe in genuine democracy. Some Left-wing critics, such as Tony Benn, would say that this is still an accurate description of our political culture and that real democracy will not be achieved until we remodel the role of the Monarchy, clip the wings of the senior judges and abolish the archaic aspects of the state, such as the Royal Prerogative and Crown immunity. Others, such as Stephen Coleman of the *Hansard Society*, believe in the value of making democracy more visible and prefer to put their faith in the potential of the new interactive media as participatory networks of public communication which could inform and invigorate our rather apathetic democracy.[12] Whatever the most appropriate answers may be, it seems clear that constitutional change will be at least one approach to solving the problem of how to engage the whole population in our liberal democracy.

The final dimension of constitutional change which has featured almost throughout this book is the cumulative impact of UK membership of the European Union, and indeed our general participation in the global community of nations, upon our constitutional arrangements in this country. To a greater extent than many people in this country may realise, our evolving constitutional arrangements are influenced by the *acquis communautaire* of the European Union; by the developing case law of the European Court of Justice and the European Court of Human Rights; and increasingly by the emerging legal norms which are being developed by various institutions with a global jurisdiction (e.g. the World Trade Organisation, the United Nations and the embryonic International Criminal Court at the Hague) as a counter-balance to the growing anarchy of the global economy and the emerging global society. Although an island people, we in the United Kingdom cannot isolate ourselves from such trends which have already had an influence upon our constitutional arrangements.[13]

With a significant degree of entrenchment

It is ultimately impossible to entrench any law in this country, however fundamental it may be thought to be, because of the doctrine of Parliamentary supremacy. This essentially *theoretical* proposition has a high-octane political content and it is repeated by Members of Parliament whenever they wish to assert their collective superiority over any other authority within the United Kingdom or to rebuff what they may see as insufferable challenges to British national sovereignty from European law or other jurisdictions. Yet *in practice* there are innumerable examples of statute law, common law and even political conventions which have achieved a significant degree of entrenchment in that the chances of a given measure being overturned, or even drastically altered, are very small. Hence the tendency to acquiesce in significant constitutional changes, which were originally only temporary or provisional measures, is greater than Parliamentary purists would have one believe.

A few well-known historical examples may serve to illustrate the argument. No one would seriously claim that the various Reform Bills and Representation of the People Acts of the nineteenth and twentieth centuries are now anything other than entrenched by the passage of time. No Government and no Parliament – short of a lapse into dictatorship – is going to legislate to restrict the franchise for Parliamentary elections. No one would seriously claim that the Parliament Acts of

1911 and 1949 are going to be overturned, because it is politically unrealistic to assume that the directly elected Lower House will permit the Upper House (even if partially elected) to be put back onto anything like an equal footing with the Commons.[14] Few people would seriously forecast that the 1972 European Communities Act will ever be repealed, because this constitutes the legislative foundation for the United Kingdom's membership of the European Union and it is considered politically and economically unrealistic by most people to contemplate British withdrawal.

The same broad argument applies to most of the constitutional changes made at the instigation of the first Blair Administration, especially those endorsed in specific referenda. For example, it is politically inconceivable that the devolution settlement in Scotland or Wales would be overturned by Parliament at Westminster, because the vast majority of English MPs would not presume to deprive the Scottish and Welsh people of their institutions of self-government and because all the main political parties realise that such action would be politically damaging to their prospects in those parts of the United Kingdom. It would require majority support in Scotland and Wales, registered in separate Scottish and Welsh referenda, to embolden a largely English House of Commons to overturn the devolution settlements. Even then, any further constitutional change would be more likely to go in the direction of national independence for Scotland and Wales than a return to the previous Unionist dispensation.

Thus it is necessary to distinguish between those examples of constitutional change which are effectively entrenched by the course of events and the passage of time and those which do not achieve such a status. It seems that the key differentiating factor is the will of the people, if clearly expressed at a General Election or a referendum. In the absence of a codified constitution, central Government with the support of the House of Commons can theoretically do what it likes within the United Kingdom, although in practice there will often be persuasive political reasons for caution and accepting the status quo.

By contrast, the measures of 'modernisation'

which have been applied since 1997 to the institutions of Government and Parliament are to a greater or lesser extent changeable, if not reversible, by a future Government and Parliament of a different political persuasion – perhaps one which defined 'modernity' in different terms to the present Government. It would, however, be difficult for the Conservatives (the only likely candidate for this role) to adopt the politics of reaction *and* achieve electoral success with such policies which would go against the *Zeitgeist* of the early twenty-first century. So although constitutional purists might argue that the Blairite drive to modernise the institutions of Government and Parliament does not really qualify as constitutional reform and is not entrenched, if most of its characteristics are accepted by the Conservatives when they eventually return to office, that will amount to *de facto* entrenchment.

The extent to which constitutional changes become entrenched in the United Kingdom often depends upon very practical factors. For example, the transformation of the legal system in England and Wales since 1997 has been so far reaching that any comparably ambitious agenda would only be seriously contemplated about once every 50 years. It is simply not sensible to rewrite legal procedures more often than that, which suggests that the comprehensive reforms flowing from the Woolf, Auld and Leggatt Reports are likely to be here for a long time to come.

The permanence of constitutional changes can also depend upon factors to do with the influence of media and public sentiment upon the rules of the political game. For example, the new rules of disclosure and forms of independent regulation which now govern the conduct of political parties, elections and referenda are almost certain to be entrenched, because it is hard to see how any politicians in future will be able to win enough trust to persuade the media and the public to let them run their own affairs once again on a basis of opaque self-regulation. The social trend towards greater transparency in public life, fuller public participation by those previously outside privileged circles and more genuine democratisation of the political process are all likely to have the effect of entrenching the arrangements which have been introduced since the establishment of the Committee on Standards in Public Life in 1994. In a modern democracy once you light up the scenery and invite the audience onto the stage, there is no realistic prospect of returning to a traditional performance of the play by an exclusive company of familiar political actors.

The same argument applies to the use of referenda to decide big political issues with constitutional implications. At the very least political expediency dictates that a national referendum will have to be held to give the people the final say on whether or not to abolish the Pound and adopt the Euro as our currency. Equally, it is generally agreed that any official proposal backed by the Government of the day to change the system for elections to Parliament at Westminster will have to be put to the people for their approval or rejection in a national referendum. In each case the authority of Government and Parliament is no longer sufficient to legitimise such momentous constitutional changes and it is accepted that only the result of a subsequent referendum would be able to trump an earlier decision of the people by the same method.

On the other hand, there must be some doubt about the permanence of the gradual shift from subjecthood to citizenship in this country. The concept of citizenship was broadened and deepened at the behest of the first Blair Administration when Parliament passed the 1998 Human Rights Act which provides direct access to positive rights. Yet there are reasons why the shift from subjecthood to citizenship seems rather problematic. *Firstly*, it runs counter to nearly 1,000 years of British history during which time the people of these islands have become used to being subjects of a Monarch and this enduring fact has left a mark upon the national psyche. *Secondly*, the modern concept of citizenship implies the performance of duties as well as the enjoyment of rights – a set of matching obligations upon citizens and the state which is unlikely to be universally appreciated in our self-centred social and political culture.

In short, it must be emphasised that in the British political system radical reform only becomes entrenched by the passage of time if the governing party retains power and follows consistent policies for two or three consecutive terms of office and if the principal Opposition party accepts the changes on its return to Government. Whenever these conditions have been satisfied in the past, effective entrenchment of the previous Government's reforms has tended to follow, even if the policy measures concerned were initially regarded as highly controversial. We saw an example of this phenomenon in the late 1980s and early 1990s when the Labour Opposition came to accept many of the policy reforms initiated by Margaret Thatcher – although significantly not the reforms with deleterious constitutional consequences, such as the emasculation of local government. It is possible that we shall see an analogous development as and when the Conservatives accept Labour's legacy of constitutional reforms.

Prospects of further change to come

Having reviewed the new constitutional arrangements which have been introduced by the Labour Government since 1997 and having offered grounds for thinking these new arrangements may well become entrenched, it is time to peer into the future to see whether this burst of constitutional reform has run its course or whether there is further change to come.[15] Following Labour's re-election in June 2001, some guidance can be found in the 2001 Labour Manifesto and the Queen's Speech of the same year.

Devolution in Scotland

Labour Ministers firmly believe that 'devolution has strengthened the United Kingdom, preserving the Union on the basis of a fairer partnership'.[16] In the case of *Scotland*, Ministers in London have absolutely no intention of developing the policy any further or devolving any more powers from Westminster to Edinburgh. Short of huge gains for the Scottish National Party in the 2003 Scottish

elections, it seems most unlikely that there will be any significant changes in the Scottish devolution settlement.

There are, however, some unexploded political mines in the *Scotland Act 1998*, notably in Section 86 which provides for the number of Scottish MPs at Westminster to be reduced in line with the electoral quota for England at the time of the next Parliamentary Boundary Commission review due to be completed between 2002 and 2006. Moreover, Schedule 1 of the Act provides for a parallel reduction in the number of constituency MSPs in the Scottish Parliament and a corresponding reduction in the number of additional MSPs elected by the proportional list system. The net effect of these changes in the third term of the Scottish Parliament will be to reduce the total number of MSPs from 129 as now to less than 110 after 2007. Such interference by the Westminster Parliament in the affairs and the careers of Edinburgh Parliament MSPs could be bitterly resented, but the catch is that only the Westminster Parliament is empowered to pass the amending legislation which would be necessary to break the link between the constituencies of Scottish MPs and those of Scottish MSPs. Such issues might be capable of amicable resolution as long as there is a Labour Government in London and a Labour–Liberal Democrat Coalition in Edinburgh. The outcome might be very different in the event of the SNP coming to power in Edinburgh or the Conservatives coming to power at Westminster. For the sake of the Scottish Boundary Commission, it will be necessary for Labour Ministers to decide upon their policy one way or another in 2001–2 and then bring forward the necessary Westminster legislation by 2004–5 at the latest if these tricky issues are to be resolved.

Devolution in Wales

In the case of *Wales*, Ministers in London seem disinclined to do more than 'build on the already successful legislative partnership with the [Welsh] Assembly and continue to enact specific legislation for Wales where appropriate'.[17] This is a reference to the intention of many in the Wales Labour Party and certainly all in Plaid Cymru to go on making a case for the Welsh Assembly to become a real devolved Parliament with primary legislative and tax-varying powers comparable with those of the Scottish Parliament. This situation led Rhodri Morgan to initiate two reviews of a constitutional nature: one which began in December 2000 under the chairmanship of the Presiding Officer, Lord Elis-Thomas, to look at the current working of the Assembly within its existing legislative framework; the other stemming from the October 2000 Partnership Agreement between Labour and the Liberal Democrats which would involve the establishment of an independent Commission to look at the overall adequacy of the devolution settlement for Wales. This second review would not commence until after the next election for the Welsh Assembly in 2003 and would be expected to put forward its conclusions some time during the following four years. It would, of course, be necessary to amend the *Government of Wales Act 1998* in order to implement any constitutional changes proposed in the second review. At this stage it looks rather doubtful whether the second Blair Administration will wish to disturb the 1998 constitutional settlement for Wales, but the outcome may well depend upon whether or not Plaid Cymru makes significant political gains in the 2003 election to the Welsh Assembly.

As for the over-representation of Wales at Westminster (but not in the Welsh Assembly), there would be natural justice in reducing this from the present 40 to perhaps 33 MPs if the English electoral quota were taken as the benchmark. However, there is no provision in the primary legislation to do this and there is a legitimate Welsh argument for saying that such over-representation at Westminster is justified as long as the UK Parliament retains its exclusive right to pass Welsh primary legislation. On the other hand, if the Labour Government in London relented and gave primary legislative powers to the Welsh Assembly to bring it into line with the Scottish Parliament, then the need to deal with Welsh over-representation at Westminster would probably be more widely recognised – although the opposite case could be made for the Welsh Assembly which

would then have too few members to cope with its extra legislative responsibilities. Once again, much will depend upon the changing balance of political fortunes in Wales and how these compare and contrast with the evolution of party politics at Westminster.

Devolution in Northern Ireland

In the case of *Northern Ireland*, Labour Ministers were pledged in the 2001 Manifesto 'to ensure that the Good Friday Agreement is implemented in full and the new institutions take root'. The political situation in Northern Ireland remains very precarious, especially since David Trimble and the Official Unionists have long believed that they have been strung along by Sinn Fein and the Provisional IRA on the intractable issue of terrorist arms decommissioning. For their part, Sinn Fein and other Irish nationalists have long been dissatisfied with the slow progress towards the transformation of the Royal Ulster Constabulary and the eventual goal of general demilitarisation in the Province.

What is more, the break-away terrorist group calling itself the Real IRA has resumed an intermittent bombing campaign on the mainland of Britain and thereby threatened to upstage the Provisional IRA which remains on ceasefire and broadly loyal to the Good Friday Agreement. This deteriorating situation led David Trimble to submit his own post-dated resignation as First Minister of the Northern Ireland Executive which, in the absence of progress on the vital issue of weapons decommissioning, became operative on 1st July 2001. The political forces on both sides of the historic divide in Northern Ireland were then caught up in another round of brinkmanship with the Unionists threatening to collapse the power-sharing Executive and Assembly and the Nationalists letting it be known that without any real progress in implementing the Patten Report on police reform in Ulster and British demilitarisation in the Province, the IRA would withdraw its offer to begin decommissioning its arms.

In the wake of the shocking events on 11th September 2001 in the United States when Islamic suicide terrorists succeeded in killing thousands of people in four coordinated terror attacks upon New York and Washington, DC, the IRA High Command felt constrained by the wave of American revulsion against all forms of terrorism to make an offer of at least partial arms decommissioning in October 2001. This striking initiative was subsequently endorsed by General John de Chastelain and the members of the independent decommissioning body set up under the 1998 Belfast Agreement. This endorsement then paved the way at the eleventh hour for the Ulster Unionists to permit their leader, David Trimble, to rescind his previous resignation and put himself forward once again as a candidate for the position of First Minister of the Northern Ireland Executive responsible to the devolved Northern Ireland Assembly.

However, because of the complex voting requirements laid down in the Belfast Agreement, it was necessary for David Trimble to get the support of at least 50 per cent of the Unionist members of the Northern Ireland Assembly and in the event two of his own party colleagues in the Assembly refused to support his candidature. The immediate consequence was that even though he got about 70 per cent support in the Assembly as a whole, he fell short of the required level of support from his own colleagues by just 1 per cent. Two members of the non-sectarian Alliance Party in the Assembly were persuaded to redesignate themselves as Unionists for the purposes of the leadership election and with that temporary manoeuvre it became possible for David Trimble to be re-elected as First Minister of Northern Ireland. The next Assembly elections will test whether there is still majority support in both communities for the power-sharing Executive which lies at the heart of the Belfast Agreement.

Devolution in England

In *England* there is a large agenda of unfinished constitutional business which relates to the development of regional government and the consequential effects for the sub-regional tiers of local government. In the 1997–2001 Parliament the Labour Government was undecided, if not divided, about how hard to press for devolution to the regions of England. The resulting initiatives were confined to the establishment of nine Regional Development Agencies (RDAs), including London, and the emergence of consultative Regional Chambers composed of nominated local Councillors and other stakeholders in local communities to supervise the work of the RDAs.

It was clear from the 2001 Labour Manifesto that re-elected Labour Ministers are likely to respond positively to the growing groundswell for greater political autonomy in the English regions. Yet primary legislation for directly elected regional government will only be introduced if a number of prior conditions are met. People in the regions themselves will have to demonstrate a clear demand for it – through regional referenda – and the regional elites will have to develop workable proposals with the relevant stakeholders. Ministers have decided to produce a White Paper on regional governance in 2002 and they will probably insist upon a unitary system of local government beneath the regional tier as a further precondition for any such reforms.

Although it was boldly stated in the 2001 Manifesto that 'some functions are best tackled at regional level', Labour Ministers are still not prepared to *impose* a uniform pattern of regional government in England. This means that in those parts of England where the traditional Counties are well established – e.g. Kent or Norfolk – there may be no regional layer of government or only minimal regional governance via Regional Chambers exercising scrutiny of the Regional Development Agencies. In other parts of England, however, where the drive for regionalism has been particularly strong – e.g. the North-East or the North-West – the County Councils may be at risk of eventual abolition or forced merger with the District Councils, especially if Ministers really do insist upon there being only one tier of local government between the Regions and the Parishes. All in all, it looks as if regional government will arrive in fits and starts and will not cover the whole of England until well into a possible third term of Labour Government – and maybe not even then.

The Labour Manifesto 2001 reiterated previous Blairite support for directly elected mayoral government in English urban areas, but once again with the *caveat* that this should only happen if the local citizens opted for it in a referendum – as happened with the introduction of mayoral government for London. This policy holds out the prospect of continuing political competition between would-be Mayors and the existing leaders of District or County Councils to fill the 'democratic space' between the Parishes and directly elected Regional Assemblies. In such circumstances the structures of English local government are likely to remain an illogical mess, largely because political caution continues to be the watchword for most Labour Ministers who apparently remain divided about the merits of any radical reforms of English local government. In any event, there are some hard choices to be made and it is very likely that, whichever way things go, some local government noses will be put out of joint. The degree to which any clarity emerges will depend upon how much political momentum builds up behind regional government in the various parts of England and whether a sufficient number of senior Ministers espouse the cause.[18]

Central Government

The second broad area of constitutional reform under the first Blair Administration covered *issues of institutional modernisation* and there are still pockets of unfinished business to be addressed by the second Blair Administration. In the sphere of central Government, one of Tony Blair's main priorities in his second term of office seems to be the deliberate strengthening of the political control and bureaucratic resources available to him *at the centre of Government* in support of his own 'presidential' objectives – notably the delivery of improved public services. He has tried to do this politically by appointing a trusted Ministerial colleague, Lord Macdonald, as Chancellor of the Duchy of Lancaster in the Cabinet Office to take political charge of a new *Delivery Unit* and report directly to him on the progress of all the Depart-

ments and Agencies of central Government involved in the improvement of public services. He has tried to do this by reorganising 10 Downing Street and the Cabinet Office to make both bureaucracies more sharply focused upon political and policy support for himself and to anticipate problems by steering policy in ways designed to strengthen the Government's ability to deliver its core political agenda.

Thus within the walls of 10 Downing Street or the Cabinet Office there are at least fifteen different Units or special offices, each of which is designed to pull together policy in one or more of the Government's priority areas and all of which are answerable to the Prime Minister or the Deputy Prime Minister or one of the other Ministers at the heart of Government.[19] On the assumption that all these different Units do not simply get in each other's way or indulge in futile battles for the Prime Minister's ear, they should provide a powerful capacity for Tony Blair to square up to the established power of the Treasury and to get his 'presidential' way with all the other branches of central Government. The Chancellor and senior Treasury officials wield the powerful weapon of *Public Service Agreements* and exert the traditional disciplines of *Public Expenditure Reviews* every three years, so they remain the other formidable power centre at the heart of British government. Even though these changes seem impressive and have undoubtedly enhanced the bureaucratic resources available to the Prime Minister at the centre of government, it is worth noting that his counterpart, the German Chancellor, has more than 400 officials working for him in the *Bundeskanzlersamt* in Berlin. Tony Blair has 27 special advisers (temporary civil servants) working directly for him on political and policy matters at 10 Downing Street and a further 244 civil servants working for him and the Government as a whole in the various Cabinet secretariats.[20]

There are nearly always temptations, which Prime Ministers find it difficult to resist, to adjust the institutional architecture of central Government to take account of constitutional changes in other areas of policy or to serve their own political objectives for the future. For example, in June 2001 the much criticised Ministry of Agriculture, Fisheries and Food was abolished and in its place a new Department of Environment, Food and Rural Affairs was created to address the wider brief of countryside issues which had given the Government so many headaches during its first term of office. Other examples were the refocusing of the Department of Social Security to become the Department for Work and Pensions, and the removal of certain functions from the Home Office to enable it to focus more closely upon tackling crime and international terrorism, asylum and immigration. Although the full reshuffle was more extensive, the main purpose was to improve the Government's chances of delivering its political agenda during its second term and to reinforce the Prime Minister's dominance of the Government and, to a lesser extent, of the Labour Party as well.[21]

The 2001 Labour Manifesto made it clear that Ministers do not believe they have completed the task of modernising the *civil service*. While being careful to stress that 'Labour is committed to maintaining the political impartiality of the civil service' – in answer to media and other accusations of civil service politicisation during the first Blair Administration – the authors of the document argued that further reform was needed to make the civil service more effective and more entrepreneurial and to improve the skills of all its employees. This will include more recruitment of senior civil servants through open competition with candidates from the private and voluntary sectors, as well as wider use of the latest information technology and the eventual delivery of all public services on-line. Neither in the Manifesto nor in the Queen's Speech was there any mention of a Civil Service Act to put civil servants and their Codes of Practice within a protective statutory framework, but it seems likely that such legislation will be introduced in the 2002–3 session of Parliament.

Local government

In the sphere of *local government*, Labour Ministers claimed in their Manifesto that their ambition was 'a partnership of mutual respect and mutual responsibility' between central and local government and they gave a strong plug for partnership between local government and the voluntary and private sectors. They set targets for electronic service delivery and emphasised the need for citizens to have a voice in all these matters and to be 'the driving force in the procurement and delivery of local services'. On the whole, their policy for local government during the current Parliament is likely to be a gentle development of their policy in the previous Parliament, notably by extending Local Public Service Agreements to all upper-tier Councils which could then be rewarded with extra public investment and a greater degree of financial autonomy.

In the sphere of our *Parliamentary institutions*, there is a good deal of potential reform which could be attempted if Ministers were to become seriously radical during the next phase of their constitutional reform agenda. However, experience in the last Parliament and the Manifesto agenda for this Parliament lead one to believe that any temptation to be radical will be kept tightly under control.

The Monarchy

In the case of *the Monarchy*, there is a deafening silence. This should come as no surprise, since it is conventional to keep party politics out of the Monarchy and the Monarchy out of party politics. All recent Prime Ministers have been very protective of the monarchy and one cannot really imagine Tony Blair, the champion of 'middle England', taking any overt political risks on this front. Yet there could be opportunities to make timely and sensible changes to the Monarchy as a national institution, to the rules of conduct for the Royal Family, and to the mystifying concept of the Crown.[22]

While no radical changes are likely to be made to the Monarchy during the life-time of the present Queen, and especially not in 2002, the year of celebrations for her Golden Jubilee, the tide of institutional modernisation could reach this higher ground once the hereditary principle has been finally washed away in Stage Two of Lords reform.

When the time eventually comes – and it may not be until Prince Charles succeeds to the throne – a number of radical possibilities for reforming the Monarchy could find their way onto the political agenda.

The constitutional straitjacket of the *1701 Act of Settlement* could finally be taken off, the anathema against a Roman Catholic succeeding to the throne or the heir to the throne marrying a Catholic could be ended, and female heirs to the throne (Heirs Presumptive) could be put on a basis of equality with their male counterparts (Heirs Apparent). Parliament and the Synod could finally agree to disestablish the Church of England, which would liberate the Monarch from having to be head of a declining national church and possibly reinvigorate the Anglican Communion. The new Monarch could recognise the logic of our increasingly multicultural society, in which the fastest-growing forms of religious observance are the Muslim and Sikh faiths, by declaring himself 'Defender of Faith' (without the usual definite article) as part of a modernised and more inclusive Coronation Oath. A Scandinavian-style Royal Family with fewer members supported by the tax-payer could emerge, so that only the Monarch and his immediate family would be included within a much tighter definition of the Royal Family, while the members of the extended family would be expected to fend for themselves.[23]

Such changes to the Royal Family would have considerable symbolic impact. Yet it is the formal identification of the Monarch with the Government of the day (captured in the traditional notion of 'Her Majesty's Government') which really needs to be redefined. Such a redefinition could prevent Ministers of all shades of political opinion from using the concept of the Crown as a dignified veil and potent symbol cloaking their political actions and it would mean that civil servants, military personnel and others in authority could no longer wrap themselves in the mystery, often secrecy, which still attaches to matters of Royal Prerogative or exploit the exemption from normal legal requirements (including even Parliamentary statutes) provided by Crown immunity.

The House of Lords

In the case of the *House of Lords*, it was announced in the June 2001 Queen's Speech that 'following consultation my Government will introduce legislation to implement the second phase of . . . reform'. The White Paper of November 2001 proposed that only 120 or one-fifth of the reformed Second Chamber of 600 members should be elected by proportional representation for a term of fifteen years or possibly less to represent the various nations and regions of the United Kingdom. The rest of the membership is to be split between 332 members appointed by the political parties and 120 appointed by the statutory Appointments Commission as independent members. As the 2001 Labour Manifesto made clear, the remaining hereditary peers are to be removed 'to make it [the House of Lords] more representative and democratic while maintaining the House of Commons' traditional primacy', although the large number of appointed peers in the existing House of Lords will be allowed to stay on until they die or choose to retire.

After Stage Two of Lords reform has been completed, there will be no members of the reformed Second Chamber who are there by hereditary right and the great majority of members will have been appointed under the system in operation since the Life Peerages Act of 1958. Only gradually will these members be supplanted by those appointed via the independent Appointments Commission which Ministers are committed to put on a statutory footing. Tony Blair appears to regard the two-stage process of reforming the House of Lords as complete when the ancient link between possession of a peerage and a seat in the Upper House has been severed. Thereafter, neither those who are newly appointed nor those who are elected to the Second Chamber will become peers, while those who are honoured with a peerage will not automatically become members of the reformed Second Chamber. Thus for the first time commoners will be able to sit as members of the Upper House and a peerage will be an honour which does not necessarily entail a seat in Parliament.

The House of Commons

In the case of the *House of Commons*, it seems unlikely that radical reform will be embarked upon by the second Blair Administration, since it has much higher political priorities in areas of substantive policy, such as the reform and improvement of the public services. However, the current Leader of the House, Robin Cook, is a strong 'House of Commons man' who is proving to be better disposed towards what he describes as 'incremental rather than revolutionary reform' than his predecessor, Margaret Beckett. He has signalled that he wants to see the House of Commons command more public respect, be better at Parliamentary scrutiny of the Executive and assist the Government in delivering the programme on which it was re-elected in June 2001.[24]

These comments underline the fact that 'modernisation' and reform of the House of Commons can be understood in at least two very different senses. As Tony Wright (the Chairman of the Select Committee on Public Administration) put it, 'modernisation is a weasel word: it means either that the Government get their business more efficiently or that we shift the balance between Parliament and the Executive'.[25] The latter interpretation might even imply parallel attention to the electoral system for Westminster elections, deliberate steps to separate the powers and functions of the three different branches of government (Executive, Legislature and Judiciary) and the elaboration of a codified constitution to create a body of constitutional law superior to ordinary Parliamentary statutes. Rather surprisingly, Lord Bingham of Cornhill, the senior Law Lord, has openly canvassed the idea of the Law Lords turning themselves into an independent Supreme Court.[26] It seems at least possible that this could be a portent of things to come, even if it is manifestly not on Ministers' agenda for the foreseeable future.

The predominant view of Parliamentary reform in the Parliamentary Labour Party – discounting a few traditionalist members of the awkward squad – is that the House of Commons should be made more family friendly to attract more women MPs; it should not be disrupted by anything resembling

the proposal from some Tories for a separate English Parliament or even special voting arrangements on devolved issues; and it should continue to be elected under the first-past-the-post electoral system which usually guarantees a dividend of extra seats for the winning party at every General Election.

All these objectives were subscribed to in the 2001 Labour Manifesto, albeit in slightly veiled language. The point about encouraging more women MPs was made in the commitment to legislate to prevent anti-discrimination legislation now on the Statute Book from nullifying any positive moves which the parties might otherwise wish to make in order to boost their female representation in public life – and this commitment was reiterated in the June 2001 Queen's Speech. The answer to Tory ideas for addressing the West Lothian Question was given in the straightforward assertion that because the Westminster Parliament makes the essential financial allocations to all devolved bodies and English MPs make up 85 per cent of the UK Parliament, 'there is no case for threatening the unity of the United Kingdom with an English Parliament or the denial of voting rights [on English issues] to Scottish, Welsh and Northern Ireland M.P.s at Westminster'.[27]

The point about possible electoral reform for Westminster elections was made in a passage which, in an exquisite put-down of the Liberal Democrats, declared that 'we will review the experience of the new [electoral] systems [for the other elected Assemblies in the UK] and the Jenkins Report to assess whether changes might be made to the electoral system for the House of Commons'.[28] With this sort of political undertaking to go on, Liberal Democrats should not hold their breath on the journey to their promised land.

Bearing in mind all these considerations, it seems likely that in practical terms any further modernisation of the House of Commons in the 2001–6 Parliament will be fairly modest and will not involve much more than tinkering with established procedures. Part of the tinkering will probably consist of making permanent two reforms introduced on an experimental basis towards the end of the 1997–2001 Parliament and renewed on a further experimental basis in votes on 28th June 2001. The first is the comprehensive programming of Government legislation at every stage of its progress through the House of Commons. The second is the deferral of some votes on free-standing and unamended propositions debated after 10:00 p.m. until a more convenient time the following Wednesday afternoon. Beyond these two modest measures there is a whole agenda of enhanced Parliamentary scrutiny waiting to be tackled if both Government and Opposition business managers are minded to do so.[29]

Other measures of Commons reform, which were not foreshadowed in the 2001 Labour Manifesto but which may well be carried forward by the second Blair Administration, are the more extensive use of legislative committees rather than the Chamber as a whole for the scrutiny of legislation and strict time limits on the various stages of such debate. Business in the Chamber may commence earlier in the day, with legislation and other contentious issues being concentrated in the first three days of the week and uncontentious issues being debated on Thursdays and Fridays, so that MPs can spend more time in their constituencies and perhaps with their families. All such changes would be motivated by a desire to make membership of the House of Commons more like a normal nine-to-five job and thus supposedly more appealing to candidates from a wider range of backgrounds. Yet the continuing desire of Labour Ministers to facilitate the passage of Government business through the House of Commons is always likely to be the most powerful motivating factor.

In the longer term, MPs should perhaps consider the radical idea of reversing the usual sequence in the legislative process, so that a public Bill is considered *first* by the relevant (Select) Committee, where any shortcomings could be dealt with on a relatively non-partisan basis, before it is reported, perhaps in slightly amended form, for a debate in the whole House at the end of which it could be accepted or rejected on party political lines. This would surmount the familiar obstacle to effective scrutiny of legislation in Standing Committee, which is that Ministers invariably say of even a sensible amendment that its adoption

would be contrary to the earlier approval of the Bill by the House at Second Reading and should therefore be rejected. Robin Cook has intimated that he would like to move to a situation in which as many Bills as possible are published in draft, so as to permit more consultation and give back-benchers earlier and more effective opportunities to influence legislation at a formative stage during what he has described as 'a more flexible two year rolling programme of legislation'.[30] This would have the benefit of bringing another aspect of Westminster procedures more into line with normal practice in national Parliaments on the Continent and in the European Parliament where specialist committees play a much more important and timely role than at Westminster.

Legal reform

Turning to the large agenda of *legal reform* which was pushed through by the Lord Chancellor, Lord Irvine, during the 1997–2001 Parliament, Labour's 2001 Manifesto made it clear that there is more to be done under this general heading in the current Parliament. Some of the items are a continuation (or repackaging) of what has gone before – for example, the extension of the Community Legal Service to cover 90 per cent of the population by April 2002 or the commitments to closer scrutiny of the legal profession for restrictive practices and to independent monitoring of judicial appointments by an independent Judicial Appointments Commissioner.

A large and important part of the current legal agenda stems from the Auld Report which has pointed the way to some far-reaching and highly controversial reforms of the criminal justice system in England and Wales.[31] In the Manifesto the stated purposes of such reforms were 'to promote public confidence and to speed up criminal proceedings'. For these reasons, the Labour Government has pledged an extra 300 prosecutors by 2004; the introduction of a unified three-tier system of criminal courts; the establishment of specialist courts and specialist judges for specialist cases, such as fraud or domestic violence; and greater flexibility of court sittings in high crime areas to ensure the minimum of delay in dealing with criminals. In an effort to make the processes of criminal justice less daunting to those who cooperate with the courts, Labour is introducing procedural changes to enable witnesses to refer to signed statements when giving evidence in court and to enable children to give evidence by video link from outside the court. There will be a new legal offence of corporate manslaughter to deal with company negligence which leads to the death of employees or members of the public. There will be a Victims' Charter to give the victims of crime a right to present their views in court after a verdict has been reached but before the defendant is sentenced; prosecutors will be allowed to challenge defence pleas in mitigation; and legislation for 'a Victims' Bill of Rights' may include financial compensation.

Where the second Blair Administration has entered much more controversial territory is in its attempts to tip the scales of justice slightly, but decisively, in favour of the prosecution. Ministers seem determined to return to the idea of removing what they described in the 2001 Manifesto as 'the widely abused right of defendants alone to dictate [in each way cases] whether or not they should be tried in Crown Court'. They have also aired the possibility of legislation to reinforce recent case law permitting the admissibility of evidence on the defendant's 'previous conduct' (i.e. previous offences) 'where relevant', thus placing upon the defence a duty of full and timely disclosure matching that already placed upon the prosecution. Furthermore, in the light of the Stephen Lawrence case and the subsequent recommendations of the Law Commission, Ministers plan legislation to end the 'double jeopardy' rule under which criminal suspects cannot be tried more than once for the same criminal offence.

The logic behind all these changes is that there should be a so-called 'equality of arms' between the prosecution and the defence. Yet English criminal justice has traditionally favoured the accused with a presumption of innocence, high standards of proof (beyond reasonable doubt), a duty upon the prosecution to prove guilt rather than the defendant

to prove his innocence, and the finality of a single trial process. All such hallowed principles are likely to be threatened by the measures proposed in Labour's 'modern criminal justice system' and many of the Government's critics will doubtless claim that constitutional issues are at stake.

On administrative law, Sir Andrew Leggatt delivered his Report on reforming the tribunal system at the end of March 2001.[32] Ministers have been studying the Report which lays the basis for future legislation to reform the tribunal system when Parliamentary time permits. After inviting extensive consultation, Sir Andrew examined both the strengths and the weaknesses of the existing system of administrative law in this country, noting in his initial Consultation Paper that there were three times as many tribunals in existence in 2000 as there had been in 1957 at the time of the Franks Report when the whole issue was last reviewed. Implementation of the Leggatt Report could help to rationalise the complexity, diversity and even anarchy within the system of tribunals; but it will require strong leadership from the Lord Chancellor's Department to guide reform of this increasingly incoherent sector of the judicial system.

An active enabling state

As for the rest of Labour's programme, there are three broad themes in the Labour Manifesto of 2001 which are likely to inform the ways in which Ministers seek to present themselves and their policies in the 2001–6 Parliament. *The first theme* is the idea of creating, in the words of Tony Blair's Foreword, 'an active enabling state' which puts 'power, wealth and opportunity in the hands of the many, not the few'. Yet it remains the case that after more than one term of Labour Government some core elements of the state are almost as secretive and exclusive as before. For example, the Freedom of Information Act 2000 will not be fully implemented until 2005, while invasions of privacy by the state and its agencies will enable personal data to be shared between different arms of the state and allow the police and security services access to private e-mail and telephone text messages in the name of fighting serious crime and terrorism. Thus there is clear evidence that even the so-called 'enabling state' under the second Blair Administration can be a powerful and invasive institution which – especially in its core activities of defence, national security, law and order, and the allocation of taxation and public expenditure – is unlikely to grant effective reciprocal rights of supervision and accountability to ordinary people or their elected representatives in Parliament.[33]

Empowered citizens and vital democracy

The second theme is that, when New Labour Ministers speak of empowered citizens and participatory democracy, these appear to be aspirations which will only be brought to fruition with a great deal of consistent encouragement and political inspiration over the years ahead. Much will depend upon the extent to which Labour's rather radical proposed reforms of the delivery mechanisms for essential public services will bear fruit in local communities up and down the country. Much will also depend upon how far the judges are prepared to develop a jurisprudence of positive rights under the rubric of the *Human Rights Act 1998* which can be of direct benefit to citizens who wish more easily to enforce these rights against Ministers, officials and all agencies of the state. The ruling in one of the leading cases on these matters (*R. v. Secretary of State for the D.E.T.R. ex parte Holding & Barnes plc*), which went all the way to the House of Lords, made it very clear that while the legality of a Ministerial decision (in this case on a planning application) and the procedural steps taken by Government had to be subject to sufficient judicial control, 'none of the judgements before the European Court of Human Rights required that the Court should have full jurisdiction (pursuant to Article 6(1) of the Convention) to review policy or the overall merits of a planning decision'.[34] As Lord Hoffmann put it sharply in his own speech, 'the Human Rights Act 1998 was no doubt intended to strengthen the rule of law, but not to inaugurate the rule of lawyers'.

As for the vitality of our democracy, at a time when the overall turn-out at the 2001 General Election was only 59 per cent (the lowest since 1918), the second Blair Administration will no doubt try to develop its existing policy of encouraging participation at local and national elections by the introduction of all sorts of modernised electoral arrangements designed to make the act of voting easier and more attractive to ordinary people. However, the omens for our traditional democratic rituals do not look very good, so deeper questions will have to be explored as to why so many people, and especially the younger cohorts, do not seem to value the democratic rights for which their forebears fought and in some cases died and which are cherished in emerging democracies around the world. It is true, of course, that in our modern polity democratic participation takes many different forms – such as single-issue pressure groups, spontaneous public demonstrations and virtual policy campaigns orchestrated on the Internet. We should not, therefore, fall into the trap of equating the long-run secular decline of political parties with general moribundity in the political system. Moreover, the growth of direct and interactive democracy in all its various forms may actually be a cause for hope and point the way forward in an age of increasingly presidential politics when there is less scope for polarisation between the parties and the power of global economic forces leaves decreasing room for manoeuvre for any politicians seeking office at the national level.

Constructive engagement in Europe

The third theme is all to do with what Tony Blair has described as constructive engagement in Europe and on this issue at least there *does* seem to be a significant contrast between the Labour Government and the Conservative Opposition. However, it is not quite as clear as it might be, because both parties have dissembled when speaking about their European policy. Labour's Manifesto in 2001 declared that 'we do believe a Europe made up of nation states and offering a unique blend of *intergovernmental cooperation where possible and integration where necessary* can be a major force for good for its own members and in the wider world'.[35] This suggested support for a hybrid European constitution which would be part international and part supra-national. While this may be a fairly accurate description of what the European Union is now, it is woefully inadequate as an informed projection of what the European Union may well become in just a few years' time as a result of the Berlin Inter-Governmental Conference in 2004.

Because the United Kingdom has survived for so long without the straitjacket of a codified constitution, its political leaders have tended to feel comfortable with the flexibility of evolving custom and practice made possible by the elastic doctrine of Parliamentary supremacy; but commensurately uncomfortable with the emerging prospect of participation in a codified constitution for the European Union. This was dramatised by Joschka Fischer, when Foreign Minister of Germany, who foresaw a federal future for the enlarged European Union in which national Governments would no longer have the predominant political power, because the central institutions of the EU would have more democratic legitimacy under the cover of a codified European constitution.[36] The dilemma for the United Kingdom was made more pointed when Jacques Chirac, the President of France, responded with an endorsement of 'enhanced cooperation' among the 'pioneer group' of member states and urged that the Charter of Fundamental Rights, for which he later pushed so hard at the European Council in Nice in December 2000, should be made justiciable in the European Court of Justice.[37]

Both these visions of the future of Europe – not to mention those of Romano Prodi, President of the European Commission, and the leaders of some smaller member states – have put the fear of God into most British politicians who, for reasons to do with their own timidity in the face of a mainly Europhobic press and a largely ignorant public opinion in the United Kingdom, can only contemplate a future constitutional determination based upon a statement of principles which would be 'a political, not a legal document', as Tony Blair put it in his own definitive speech about the future of Europe made in Warsaw in October 2000.[38] Unless the British Government were deliberately to opt for second-class political status in the European Union or perhaps the more radical option of UK withdrawal, this country will probably find itself endowed, sooner or later, with a codified constitution, courtesy of its continuing membership of the European Union.

Neither main party in this country is doing the British public or the European cause any real service by the way in which it has handled these enormous political and constitutional issues. It is only to be hoped that, if and when a national referendum is held on whether or not to abolish the Pound and adopt the Euro as our currency, the nature of the debate will be more honest, the level of the debate will be more sophisticated and the scope of the debate will encompass all the constitutional issues. If such a referendum is actually held and if the British people say Yes to the Euro, then we should be in no doubt that a permanent and probably irreversible decision will have been taken which will mean that in the long run the United Kingdom and its political component parts become much more deeply integrated into an emerging European nation.

Conclusion

The time has come to offer a brief summary of the essential thesis of this book. Such a summary must focus upon the most significant and enduring themes of constitutional change under Labour since 1997, but it also needs to remind the reader of how and why this period of change came about and whither it may be tending.

The process of constitutional change under the first Blair Administration was carried through using a route map inherited from the days when John Smith was Leader of the Labour Party in Opposition. It was therefore a legislative tribute to the ideals of John Smith and a tangible way of fulfilling his most enduring political legacy. In this context it is not without significance that the coordinating figure for the whole programme of constitutional change under New Labour has not been Tony Blair, but rather Lord Irvine, the Lord

CUMULATIVE CHANGE AND DYNAMIC OUTLOOK

Chancellor. The programme very much reflected the conclusions drawn by a dispirited Labour Opposition when it was under the spell of Charter 88 and other groups which had nearly despaired of placing effective restraints upon the Conservative Government in its most ideological phase.

The proximate political imperative for devolution, one of the most significant parts of the overall constitutional reform programme, was the felt need in the Labour Party to make timely concessions to the forces of nationalism in Scotland, Wales and Northern Ireland. In some ways this could be linked with a weaker political imperative which gathered momentum around John Smith and the growing band of pro-Europeans in the Labour Party, to the effect that greater weight should be given to Britain's European destiny and hence the claims of supra-nationalism at least in those sectors of policy where the Labour leadership believed this would be in our national interest. Thus, unlike most of their Conservative opponents, Ministers in the first Blair Administration were willing to acknowledge the *legitimacy* of the challenges from both above and below to the constitutional arrangements of the British nation state.

The pattern of constitutional change under Labour since 1997 has been characterised by a process of marked centralisation *within* the sphere of central Government which has run in parallel with a process of decentralisation and devolution within the whole of the United Kingdom. Paradoxically, as national institutions have become relatively weaker within the United Kingdom, the Prime Minister and the Chancellor have become relatively stronger within Whitehall and Westminster. This has led to the further downgrading of the Cabinet into not much more than a dignified part of our constitutional arrangements (in Bagehot's terminology in *The English Constitution*) and, as a corollary, to the relative marginalisation of Parliament. It should be emphasised that this centralisation within central Government is a continuation, after a hiatus under John Major, of a longer-term trend in the United Kingdom and many other Parliamentary democracies.

It has been possible to discern during the period of constitutional change under Labour, and even before they came to power in 1997, a gradual retreat of the state as provider – even in respect of the core public services of health, education, transport and law and order – balanced to some extent by the advance of national regulatory institutions established by Parliament and operating at arm's length from Government. The result is that we are now living in an age of independent regulation by quasi-judicial regulators or regulatory bodies which cannot easily be held to account for their decisions even when these are manifestly perverse. Thus we have been moving from a traditional model of regulation dependent upon political control exercised largely by elected Ministers who are democratically accountable to Parliament towards a model of regulation dependent upon largely unaccountable quasi-jurisprudence delivered by Ministerial appointees.

It has been significant that the Labour Government since 1997 has adopted deliberate policies of social inclusion and political co-option designed to make opportunities available to people traditionally disadvantaged in our competitive society and to provide shelter in Labour's 'big tent' for all but 'the forces of conservatism'. On one level this has been a party political project, but historians may perhaps come to regard it as a form of *democratisation* in our society which until quite recently was shaped by the traditional assumptions of our elitist political culture and our imperialist past. Just as the nineteenth and early twentieth centuries in Britain were constitutionally notable for successive extensions of the franchise, so it is likely that the early twenty-first century will be a period when Britain becomes more democratised and leadership positions in all sectors of society are opened up to the many and not the few.

The period of two Labour Administrations since 1997 has been characterised by moves towards a richer definition of citizenship in the United Kingdom, mainly as a result of the 1998 Human Rights Act which has made positive rights more accessible and more easily enforceable in our domestic courts. This legislation signified a decisive step towards a more European interpretation of the appropriate relationship between citizens and the state and it may eventually consign the British idea of subjecthood to the pages of history. Although the courts have so far been cautious in their interpretations of this Act, sooner or later the Law Lords will need to issue 'declarations of incompatibility' which will require Parliament to react and probably change aspects of certain statutes on the grounds that some provisions are incompatible with the European Convention on Human Rights. Provided people in Government and Parliament do not have rushes of blood to the head and retreat into an attitude of xenophobia, this period may be seen as an early but important stage in the long journey towards eventual codification of our constitutional arrangements.

Constitutional changes made at the behest of the first Blair Administration have amounted to a new constitutional settlement for the United Kingdom. Yet we should take note of Tony Blair's personal Foreword to the 2001 Labour Manifesto in which he declared that 'my passion is to continue the modernisation of Britain' – a statement which should serve to remind us that this Prime Minister has tended to regard 'modernisation' as one of the distinctive themes of his premiership and will continue to do so in Labour's second term. There are no signs that constitutional reform, if defined in this way, has run its course in the United Kingdom and there is a wide range of unfinished business still to be addressed. Constitutional change is always likely to be with us and a steady state is neither desirable nor attainable.

Questions for discussion

1   Does the wide range of constitutional legislation and other measures passed by the 1997–2001 Parliament amount to a new constitutional settlement in the United Kingdom?

2   Are there political and other grounds for believing that the constitutional measures introduced by successive Blair Administrations will be effectively entrenched against future repeal?

3   What are the most significant items of unfinished constitutional business in the United Kingdom and what are the chances of their being tackled successfully?

Notes

1   See Lord Irvine's lecture 'The Government's programme of constitutional reform' to the Constitution Unit at Church House, Westminster, on 8th December 1998.

2   Notably, on the decommissioning of IRA weapons which was a key element in the Good Friday Agreement promised again during the inter-party meetings in May 2000, but which did not begin to be implemented until October 2001.

3   See 'Third Way – Phase Two', *Prospect*, March 2001.

4   Such intervention from central Government has taken place from time to time following revelations of really poor performance by local authorities in managing local schools (e.g. in the London Borough of Hackney) or in protecting children in care (e.g. in Clywd in North Wales). The possibility of further intervention by central Government was flagged in the 2001 Labour Manifesto, notably in the section on education.

5   See 'Edward and Sophie glad to remain Royal workers', *Sunday Telegraph*, 8th July 2001, for information on the *News of the World* 'sting' in February 2001 and its consequences for the Royal Family.

6   The two most notable press campaigns for reform of the Monarchy were in the *Guardian* on 6th December 2000 and in the *Sun* on 4th April 2001.

7   At the time of writing the leading assumption is that the second Blair Administration will initiate another round of 'consultation' on Lords reform and then come forward with a Bill to implement most, if not all, of the Wakeham recommendations for Stage Two. As for the elected element in a reformed Second Chamber, it is widely expected that Ministers will try to limit this to no more than one-third of all the members who will probably be elected from regional constituencies under a closed (party) list form of proportional representation.

8   It now looks as though the 'modernisers' in both Houses of Parliament may get their way by persuading Ministers to allow for a much greater proportion of elected members in Stage Two of Lords reform than was at first proposed.

9   For Robin Cook's preliminary thinking about reform of the House of Commons see *The Times*, 12th July 2001, and the full text of his speech to the Hansard Society at Church House, Westminster, on the same day.

10 The precise formula in the 2001 Labour Manifesto was: 'we will review the experience of the new [electoral] systems and the Jenkins report to assess whether changes might be made to the electoral system for the House of Commons' and 'a referendum remains the right way to agree any change for Westminster'.

11 *The Times*, 9th May 2001.

12 See Stephen Coleman, *Electronic Media, Parliament and the People*; Hansard Society, London, 1999.

13 Since the shocking terrorist attacks in the United States on 11th September 2001, Ministers in this country have urgently reviewed our national defences against global terrorism and have brought to Parliament a number of legislative measures designed to make it easier to identify potential terrorists, to forestall their acts of terror and to extradite them to other jurisdictions where that is appropriate.

14 In order to restore parity of public esteem and legislative power to the two Houses of Parliament it would be necessary for Stage Two of Lords reform to create a new Second Chamber at least half of which was composed of directly elected members. This has been resisted by the champions of the status quo in the House of Commons in the past and there is no good reason to suppose that it would not be resisted in the future by Government and Opposition, Ministers and backbenchers alike.

15 See R. Hazell, *Unfinished Business: Implementing Labour's Constitutional Reform Agenda for the Second Term*; Constitution Unit, London, May 2001.

16 Labour Party Manifesto, *Ambitions for Britain*; London, 2001; p. 35.

17 *Ibid.*

18 For example, it may have been significant that the Chancellor of the Exchequer, Gordon Brown, spoke favourably of regional government in a speech at the University of Manchester Institute of Science and Technology on 29th January 2001.

19 See *Appendix 1* for details of all the Units at 10 Downing Street or in the Cabinet Office at the beginning of the second Blair Administration in June 2001.

20 See *Hansard*, 12th November 2001, Written Answer to John Maples MP.

21 Leading figures in 'Old Labour' have become increasingly disturbed by Tony Blair's centralising tendencies which they regard as a threat both to the well-being of the Labour Party and to British constitutional arrangements. For example, Lord Hattersley in an article entitled 'Tony's takeover' asserted that 'history will say the Prime Minister was more successful in usurping a party and changing it from a great reforming movement to the instrument of his own will than any politician in the twentieth century'; *Sunday Times*, 18th November 2001. For details of all the Departments which were renamed or refocused in the immediate aftermath of the June 2001 General Election see *Appendix 2*.

22 See Andrew Roberts, 'Charles is the only one standing in his way', *Sunday Telegraph*, 8th July 2001, on the radical ideas of the Prince of Wales for the future of the Monarchy.

23 One of the more eccentric ideas for reforming and modernising the Monarchy has been to privatise it by transferring all the Royal assets and properties into a new public corporation which would be owned by its Class A shareholders (the Monarch and possibly the heir to the throne), run by a professional board of management and financed (at least in part) by its Class B shareholders who could be ordinary members of the public who had paid cash for such shares not exceeding 40 per cent of the total equity capital of the corporation. The idea is that this would end the financial dependence of the Monarchy upon the state for the income and expenses of the Royal Family, yet generate enough revenue to ensure that the whole operation was properly funded, reserves were accumulated and dividends were paid to investors who would be voluntary supporters of the Monarchy rather than compulsory subscribers as tax-payers. See letter from Lord Poole in *The Times*, 15th May 2001.

24 See Robin Cook's speech to the Hansard Society at Church House, Westminster, on 12th July 2001. See also *Appendix 3* for Robin Cook's plans to modernise the House of Commons submitted to the Modernisation Select Committee on 12th December 2001.

25 *Hansard*, 21st June 2001; Vol. 370, Col. 161.

26 See the interview which Lord Bingham gave to *The Times* on 17th July 2001 in which he said there was 'a very strong case' for having a Supreme Court in the United Kingdom that is in 'the same position constitutionally as Supreme Courts in every other country in the world'. This implied eventual separation from the House of Lords both physically and constitutionally and the need to look at 'certain anomalies in our constitutional structure', which was a coded reference to the idiosyncratic position of every Lord Chancellor as a senior member of the Executive, a senior member of the Judiciary and 'the Speaker' of the Upper House in the legislature.

27 *Ambitions for Britain*; p. 35.

28 *Ibid.*

29 See, for example, 'The challenge for Parliament: making Government accountable', *Report of the*

Hansard Society Commission on Parliamentary Scrutiny (chaired by Lord Newton of Braintree); Vacher Dod, London, 2001 for a comprehensive analysis of this wider agenda.

30 *The Times*, 12th July 2001; see also Robin Cook's Memorandum to the Modernisation Select Committee, 12th December 2001.

31 See Lord Justice Auld, *Review of the Criminal Courts*; HMSO, London, October 2001.

32 See Sir Andrew Leggatt's Consultation Paper on *The Review of Tribunals*; HMSO, London, June 2000.

33 For example, the *Regulation of Investigatory Powers Act 2000* has created a pretty draconian framework for the interception of communications, the use of surveillance and access to encrypted data by various investigatory agencies. Labour Ministers have no declared plans to offset these developments with long overdue reform of the legislation on official secrecy.

34 See *R. v. Secretary of State for the Environment, Transport and the Regions, ex parte Holding & Barnes plc* and related cases reported in *The Times*, 10th May 2001.

35 *Ambitions for Britain*; p. 38; my italics.

36 See 'From Confederacy to Federation – thoughts on the finality of [European] integration', a speech by Joschka Fischer, Foreign Minister of Germany, at Humboldt University, Berlin, on 12th May 2000.

37 See 'Our Europe', a speech by Jacques Chirac, President of France, to the German *Bundestag* in Berlin on 27th June 2000.

38 See 'Superpower not superstate', a speech by Tony Blair, Prime Minister of the United Kingdom, at the Warsaw Stock Exchange on 6th October 2000. More recently, there seems to have been something of a *rapprochement* between the French and British positions on the future of Europe with both Governments apparently agreeing that the purpose of the European Union is in large part to enhance the authority of its member states. See *Financial Times*, 1st December 2001.

Further reading

The Challenge for Parliament: Making Government Accountable, Report of the Hansard Society Commission on Parliamentary Scrutiny; Vacher Dod, London, 2001.

Stephen Coleman, *Electronic Media, Parliament and the People*; Hansard Society, London, 1999.

M. Foley, *The Politics of the British Constitution*; Manchester University Press, Manchester, 1999.

Robert Hazell (ed.) *Constitutional Futures: a History of the Next Ten Years*; Oxford University Press, Oxford, 1999.

Robert Hazell, *Unfinished Business: Implementing Labour's Constitutional Reform Agenda for the Second Term*; Constitution Unit, London, 2001.

Anthony King, *Does the United Kingdom Still Have a Constitution?*, Hamlyn Lectures; Sweet & Maxwell, London, 2001.

Labour Party Manifesto, *Ambitions for Britain*; London, 2001.

John Morrison, *Reforming Britain: New Labour, New Constitution?*; Pearson Education, Harlow, 2001.

The Queen's Speech, 20th June 2001; HMSO, London, 2001.

F.F. Ridley and M. Rush (eds) 'UK 2000: modernisation in progress?', *Parliamentary Affairs*, Vol. 54, No. 2, April 2001.

K. Sutherland (ed.) *The Rape of the Constitution?*; Imprint Academic, Exeter, 2000.

Unlocking Democracy; Charter 88, London, 2000.

APPENDICES

Appendix 1

Political and official support for the Prime Minister and Deputy Prime Minister at 10 Downing Street and in the Cabinet Office

Chief of Staff: Jonathan Powell, a former Foreign and Commonwealth Office (FCO) diplomat in Washington, now a Special Adviser – i.e. a political appointee with temporary civil servant status.

Director of Communications and Strategy: Alastair Campbell, formerly Political Editor of the *Daily Mirror* and Press Secretary to Tony Blair in Opposition (1994–97) and then in Government (1997–2001), now a Special Adviser with temporary civil servant status in charge of press, strategic communications and research.

Head of Political and Government Relations: Baroness (Sally) Morgan, former Labour Party official and Political Secretary to Tony Blair, now responsible for relations across Government, with the devolved Administrations and some foreign Administrations.

Integrated Policy Directorate for domestic policy advice to the Prime Minister, formed by the merger of the Number 10 Private Office and the Policy Unit; headed by Jeremy Heywood, a former Treasury civil servant.

European Adviser's Office for European policy advice to the Prime Minister; headed by Sir Stephen Wall, an FCO official who also heads the European Secretariat in the Cabinet Office.

Foreign Policy Adviser's Office for foreign policy advice to the Prime Minister; headed by Sir David Manning, an FCO official who is also Head of the Overseas and Defence Secretariat in the Cabinet Office.

Delivery Unit, based in the Cabinet Office and headed by Michael Barber, a former Professor of Education at London University, there to help ensure the achievement of priority objectives in health, education, crime and transport under the political supervision of Lord Macdonald, now Minister for the Cabinet Office and formerly a Scottish media tycoon.

Office of Public Services Reform, based in the Cabinet Office and headed by Wendy Thomson, a former local authority Chief Executive, reporting to the Prime Minister through the Cabinet Secretary to explore ways of taking forward radical reform of the civil service and the public services.

Forward Strategy Unit, headed by Geoff Mulgan, formerly at the think tank *Demos* and then in the Policy Unit at 10 Downing Street (1997–2001), to undertake strategy projects at the Prime Minister's request and to work closely with the Performance and Innovation Unit in the Cabinet Office which is also headed by Geoff Mulgan.

Political Office, consisting of four political staff headed by Robert Hill and five administrative support staff, with its staff costs met by the Labour Party and its marginal costs met from the overall budget for 10 Downing Street.

Social Exclusion Unit, headed by Claire Tyler, a civil servant from the Department for Education and Skills, which reports to the Prime Minister on social exclusion issues through the Deputy Prime Minister, John Prescott.

Regional Coordination Unit, headed by Rob Smith, a former civil servant at the Department for Education and Employment, which reports on regional issues to the Deputy Prime Minister supported by the Minister of State at the Cabinet Office, Barbara Roche.

Women and Equality Unit, headed by Susan Atkins, a former Home Office civil servant, which reports on women's issues to the Ministers for Women, Patricia Hewitt, Secretary of State at the DTI, and Barbara Roche.

Business Coordination Unit, headed by Mark Savigar, which reports to Barbara Roche with a remit to increase Ministerial interaction with business.

Regulatory Impact Unit, headed by Philip Wynn Owen, a former Treasury civil servant, which reports to Lord Macdonald and which advises on ways to keep Government regulations within sensible bounds.

Office of the e-envoy, headed by Andrew Pinder and reporting to Patricia Hewitt and Douglas Alexander on e-commerce and to Lord Macdonald on e-government.

Joint Intelligence Organisation, chaired by John Scarlett and reporting to the Prime Minister via the Cabinet Secretary.

Performance and Innovation Unit, headed by Geoff Mulgan (see Forward Strategy Unit above), to examine ways of improving the efficiency and effectiveness of Government policy across the board and reporting to the Prime Minister through the Cabinet Secretary.

Honours Scrutiny Committee, chaired by Rt Hon. Lord Thomson of Monifieth and reporting directly to the Prime Minister.

Civil Service Management Board, chaired by the Cabinet Secretary, and reporting to the Prime Minister on civil service management issues, including those arising in the Government Information and Communication Service.

Sources: Information derived from *Hansard*, Written Answers, 11th July 2001, Cols 573W–575W, and 19th October 2001, Cols 1361W–1362W; and from the Cabinet Office in December 2001.

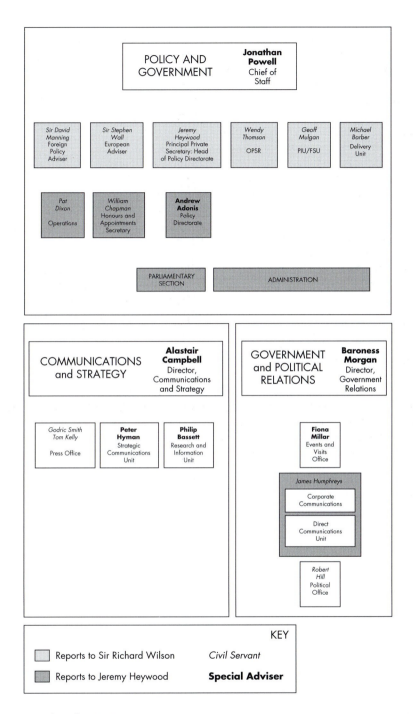

Figure 1 Organisation chart for 10 Downing Street
Source: Document provided by the Cabinet Secretary to the House of Commons Select Committee on Public Administration in December 2001

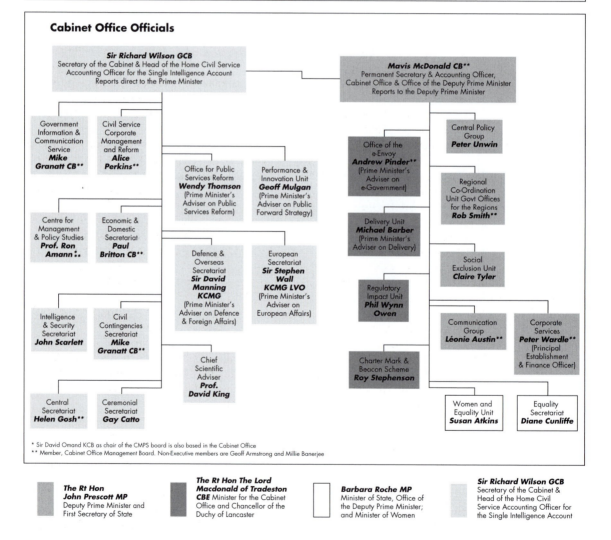

The Rt Hon Tony Blair MP
Prime Minister, First Lord of
the Treasury and Minister for
the Civil Service

Cabinet Office Ministers

The Rt Hon John Prescott MP
Deputy Prime Minister and First Secretsry of State

Also located in the Cabinet Office:

The Rt Hon Robin Cook MP
President of the Council
and Leader of the House of Commons

**The Rt Hon The Lord Macdonald
of Tradeston CBE**
Minister for the Cabinet Office and
Chancellor of the Duchy of Lancaster
Reports to the Prime Minister

Barbara Roche MP †
Minister of State,
Minister of Women

**The Rt Hon The Lord Williams
of Mostyn QC**
Leader of the House of Lords

Christopher Leslie MP
Parliamentary Secretary

Charles Clarke MP
Minister without Portfolio
and Party Chair

† Reports to the Secretary of State for Trade and Industry
and Minister for Women, Patricia Hewitt MP, on women's
issues.

Stephen Twigg MP
Parliamentary Secretary

Cabinet Office Officials

Sir Richard Wilson GCB
Secretary of the Cabinet & Head of the Home Civil Service
Accounting Officer for the Single Intelligence Account
Reports direct to the Prime Minister

Mavis McDonald CB**
Permanent Secretary & Accounting Officer,
Cabinet Office & Office of the Deputy Prime Minister
Reports to the Deputy Prime Minister

Government
Information &
Communication
Service
**Mike
Granatt CB****

Civil Service
Corporate
Management
and Reform
**Alice
Perkins****

Office for Public
Services Reform
Wendy Thomson
(Prime Minister's
Adviser on Public
Services Reform)

Performance &
Innovation Unit
Geoff Mulgan
(Prime Minister's
Adviser on Public
Forward Strategy)

Office of the
e-Envoy
Andrew Pinder**
(Prime Minister's
Adviser on
e-Government)

Central Policy
Group
Peter Unwin

Regional
Co-Ordination
Unit Govt Offices
for the Regions
Rob Smith**

Centre for
Management
& Policy Studies
**Prof. Ron
Amann**.

Economic &
Domestic
Secretariat
**Paul
Britton CB****

Defence &
Overseas
Secretariat
**Sir David
Manning
KCMG**
(Prime Minister's
Adviser on Defence
& Foreign Affairs)

European
Secretariat
**Sir Stephen
Wall
KCMG LVO**
(Prime Minister's
Adviser on
European Affairs)

Delivery Unit
Michael Barber
(Prime Minister's
Adviser on Delivery)

Social
Exclusion Unit
Claire Tyler

Intelligence
& Security
Secretariat
John Scarlett

Civil
Contingencies
Secretariat
**Mike
Granatt CB****

Regulatory
Impact Unit
**Phil Wynn
Owen**

Communication
Group
Léonie Austin**

Corporate
Services
Peter Wardle**
(Principal
Establishment
& Finance Officer)

Chief
Scientific
Adviser
**Prof.
David King**

Charter Mark &
Beacon Scheme
Roy Stephenson

Central
Secretariat
Helen Gosh**

Ceremonial
Secretariat
Gay Catto

Women and
Equality Unit
Susan Atkins

Equality
Secretariat
Diane Cunliffe

* Sir David Omand KCB as chair of the CMPS board is also based in the Cabinet Office
** Member, Cabinet Office Management Board. Non-Executive members are Geoff Armstrong and Millie Banerjee

**The Rt Hon
John Prescott MP**
Deputy Prime Minister and
First Secretary of State

**The Rt Hon The Lord
Macdonald of Tradeston
CBE** Minister for the Cabinet
Office and Chancellor of the
Duchy of Lancaster

Barbara Roche MP
Minister of State, Office of
the Deputy Prime Minister;
and Minister of Women

Sir Richard Wilson GCB
Secretary of the Cabinet &
Head of the Home Civil
Service Accounting Officer for
the Single Intelligence Account

Figure 2 Organisation chart for the Cabinet Office and Office of the Deputy Prime Minister
Source: www.cabinet-office.gov.uk

Appendix 2

Changes in Departmental structures and Ministerial responsibilities in June 2001

On 8th June 2001, the day after the General Election, the Prime Minister made a number of major changes to the machinery of central Government. Taken together, they were intended to ensure a much sharper focus upon the Government's priorities for its second term and the need to deliver better public services.

- An *Office of the Deputy Prime Minister* was established within the Cabinet Office. John Prescott was the chosen Minister and it was announced that, among other things, he would have responsibility for the Social Exclusion Unit, the Regional Coordination Unit and the Government Offices in the Regions. He would also chair Cabinet Committees on Domestic Affairs, the Nations and the Regions, and on the Environment.
- A new *Department for the Environment, Food and Rural Affairs* under Margaret Beckett was established to replace the Ministry of Agriculture, Fisheries and Food, and to take on responsibility for the environment, rural development, countryside and wildlife, and sustainable development from the huge Ministerial portfolio of the previous Department of the Environment, Transport and the Regions (DETR). It would also take on responsibility for animal welfare and hunting from the Home Office.
- A new *Department for Transport, Local Government and the Regions* under Stephen Byers would take on the responsibility of the previous DETR for these subjects, together with housing, planning and urban regeneration. It would also take over responsibility for the Fire Service and for electoral law from the Home Office.
- A new *Department for Work and Pensions* under Alastair Darling would bring together the previous Department of Social Security (DSS) and the Employment Service (formerly under the Department for Education and Employment) and be charged with continuing the reform of the welfare state. It would combine the employment and disability responsibilities of the former DfEE with the welfare and pensions responsibilities of the former DSS.
- A new *Department for Education and Skills* under Estelle Morris would focus upon the further raising of education standards, especially in secondary schools. It would also seek to get more students into higher education and to improve work-based training and lifelong learning.
- The *Department of Trade and Industry* (DTI) under Patricia Hewitt would take over responsibility for the Regional Development Agencies and for the construction industry from the former DETR, while a single Minister of State holding office in the DTI and the FCO would take responsibility for British Trade International. It would also take over the

previous responsibility of the Home Office for summertime and Sunday trading.

- The *Home Office* under David Blunkett would be streamlined, losing a number of secondary functions to allow it to focus upon tackling crime, reform of criminal justice and the asylum system. In this context it would take over responsibility for the Anti-Drugs Coordination Unit from the Cabinet Office.
- The *Lord Chancellor's Department* under Lord Irvine would take over from the Home Office responsibility for the constitutional issues of freedom of information, data protection and human rights.

- The *Department for Culture, Media and Sport* under Tessa Jowell would take over from the Home Office responsibility for gambling, licensing, censorship and video classification, horse racing and planning for the Queen's Golden Jubilee in 2002.
- The *Ministry of Defence* under Geoff Hoon would take over responsibility for the security services from the Cabinet Office and for the War Pensions Agency from the former Department of Social Security.

Source: Press Notice, *Delivering Effective Government*, 10 Downing Street, 8th June 2001.

Appendix 3

Modernisation of the House of Commons:
main points of a Memorandum submitted by
Robin Cook to the Modernisation Select Committee
of the House of Commons on 12th December 2001

The Leader of the House, Robin Cook, submitted his reform programme for consultation on 12th December 2001. It was expected that the main elements would be considered and later implemented by the House of Commons during the 2001–6 Parliament. Many of the changes are likely to be introduced first on a provisional basis and then subsequently confirmed by further votes of the House. The test of success is whether modernisation 'increases the esteem of the public for their Parliament' and it was asserted at the outset that 'Ministers and backbenchers alike have a common interest in an effective House of Commons'.

Work in hand

- It was noted that the Modernisation Select Committee has already begun an examination of how to give Select Committees more influence over their own destinies.

Scrutiny of the Executive

- Parliament could do more business if debates were generally shorter in length but greater in number – e.g. if the main debate of the day were occasionally limited to three hours instead of the traditional six hours – and MPs could make better use of their time if they knew in advance whether and when they would be called to speak.
- The notice period for Oral Questions to Ministers might be reduced to less than the current two weeks and there might be a separate entry on the Order Paper for Ministerial Statements and a separate entry for their publication in *Hansard*.

Scrutiny of Legislation

- More Government Bills should be made available in draft form for early scrutiny by the relevant Select Committees and sometimes by a devolved Assembly. Select Committees could also consider proposals for legislation on the basis of policy put forward by Government Departments.
- It should be possible for the scrutiny of a Bill to be carried over from one Session to the next, but on condition that all Bills complete all stages within a fixed period of months.
- Select Committees could also be involved in post-legislative scrutiny to see how new legislation has worked out in practice and to

propose remedies for any problems high-lighted by such evaluation.

- A Secondary Legislation Scrutiny Committee might be established for an experimental period to sift Statutory Instruments as the European Scrutiny Committee now sifts European legislation.

Modernising working practices

- The Commons should make better use of the earlier hours of the day in an age when 'the great majority of MPs are full-time Parliamentarians and only a minority have outside business interests'. For example, the House of Commons could meet on Wednesday mornings and Prime Minister's Questions could be moved forward to noon on that day.
- More 'constituency Fridays' could be introduced when the House does not sit and MPs can guarantee to be in their constituencies. Any Friday debating time lost could be switched to Wednesday after 7:00 p.m. when the House could also debate more Select Committee reports.
- Oral Statements by Ministers could be brought forward from the customary 3:30 p.m. to 1:30 p.m., thus allowing an hour for such statements immediately before Departmental Questions at 2:30 p.m. Notice of such Ministerial Statements should normally be given every Monday for the week ahead, but provision should also be made for 'Immediate Statements' in the event of an emergency.
- The Parliamentary calendar would be more sensible and predictable if the House rose for its summer recess in the first half of July and returned in early September, to be followed in late September with a three-week recess for the Party Conferences. The Christmas, Easter and Whit Recesses would remain unchanged.

Making use of modern technology

- The introduction of electronic voting by MPs, combined with a continuing requirement for MPs to attend divisions in person, would enable MPs to vote on multiple divisions at the same time and so provide more time for debate and scrutiny in the Chamber.
- Options should be examined for tabling Parliamentary Questions and amendments to legislation by e-mail, but this should not prevent other MPs doing these things in the traditional way.
- The Internet could be used more systematically by Select Committees (and individual MPs) for communication and consultation with the general public.

Making the Commons more accessible

- The Commons should examine how it could widen the media coverage of Parliament – e.g. by releasing Written Answers by noon rather than after 3:30 p.m. as at present.
- Select Committee reports could be produced and printed in a more attractive way – e.g. with computer graphics and colour printing.
- Select Committees could introduce web-streaming of their hearings and it should be routine for coverage of public committee sittings to be available on the Internet.
- Conditions could be improved for the visiting public with a Visitors' Cafe scheduled for February 2002 and the possibility of a dedicated Visitors' Centre with interactive technology being created thereafter.
- A proactive Education Service to promote Parliament could be established to educate and inform school children and on Fridays when the House was not sitting frequent and regular visiting days could be introduced for young and old alike to help counter public ignorance and even alienation from the Parliamentary process.

Author's note

The overall objective of this package of Parliamentary reforms is to restore public esteem for Parliament via more effective scrutiny procedures and more efficient use of MPs' time. If these reforms are implemented, they will sound the death-knell for part-time MPs and the diminishing number with paid outside interests. Such reforms will reinforce the rapid professionalisation of Parliament to match the professionalisation of politics.

Appendix 4

Proposed citizenship pledge for people becoming British citizens

'I [swear by Almighty God] [do solemnly and sincerely affirm] that from this time forward I will give my loyalty and allegiance to Her Majesty Queen Elizabeth the Second, her Heirs and Successors and to the United Kingdom. I will uphold its democratic values. I will observe its laws faithfully and fulfil my duties and obligations as a British citizen.'

Source: *Secure Borders, Safe Haven: Integration with Diversity in Modern Britain*, Cm 5387; HMSO, London, February 2002.

Index